CASES IN URBAN MANAGEMENT

The MIT Press
Cambridge, Massachusetts, and London, England

CASES IN URBAN MANAGEMENT

John R. Russell

This book was printed and bound in the United States of America.

Library of Congress Cataloging in Publication Data

Russell, John R
Cases in urban management.

1. Municipal government--United States--Case studies.
2. Municipal services--United States--Case studies.
I. Title.
JS356.R95 352'.008'0973 73-20228
ISBN 0-262-18066-9

PUBLISHER'S NOTE

This format is intended to reduce the cost of publishing certain works in book form and to shorten the gap between editorial preparation and final publication. The time and expense of detailed editing and composition in print have been avoided by photographing the text of this book directly from the author's typescript.

The MIT Press

CONTENTS

PREFACE

The cases in this book form the core material for my second-year elective at the Harvard Business School entitled "Management of Urban Operations." The course is taught to classes consisting mostly of MBA candidates with an interest in working in the public sector but also including smaller numbers of students from other graduate schools. My purpose in developing and presenting the course has been twofold: First, to respond to and to stimulate student interest in improving the management of America's cities; second, to test whether or not the case system is an effective way to equip young people for managerial positions in the public sector, particularly at the local level. The book has been compiled in the hope that it will be useful to teachers at other schools who also wish to offer courses in some aspect of urban management, who want to use cases in these courses, and who are faced with the same dearth of material that I encountered several years ago.

Most of the cases are drawn from New York City. This does not imply that New York's experiences are directly transferable to most, or even some, of the nation's cities. It does reflect the extraordinary interest of Mayor John Lindsay's administration in trying to improve the management of that city and the innovations--both successful and unsuccessful--that resulted from that interest. It also reflects my belief that the cases provide a sense of managerial opportunity and constraint and a set of insights into the urban management process that will be useful in urban contexts other than New York.

As with any case-writing effort, the cooperation and help of an enormous number of people were necessary to complete this one. Several cases are the work of others--specifically:

Emergency Ambulance Service (A) and (B)
Graeme A. Taylor and Richard J. Gill
Management Analysis Corporation, Inc.

The Boston Redevelopment Authority (A and B)
Professor Joseph L. Bower and
Assistant Professor John W. Rosenblum
Harvard Business School

Model Cities Sanitation Project (C)
New York City Housing Authority Incinerator Air Pollution Abatement Project
Assistant Professor Lawrence A. Bennigson
Harvard Business School and London School of Business

I appreciate their willingness to let me include the material. Subrata Chakravarty, who worked as a research assistant during the academic year 1971 to 1972, and Robert Svensk and Jerald Posman, who wrote cases during the summers of 1971 and 1972, respectively, are responsible collectively for the research and initial drafting of six more of the cases.

Numerous people were exceedingly helpful to me and my colleagues in providing us with the interviews and written data on which the cases are based. Within New York City government, Herbert Elish, Administrator of the Environmental Protection Administration; Jerry Mechling, also of the Environmental Protection Administration; Lew Feldstein and John Mudd in the Office of Neighborhood Government; Jon Weiner, Bureau of the Budget; Ken Harris, Human Resources Administration; and Alan Leslie, Health Services Administration were all extremely accommodating. There were many others. Particular thanks go to Andrew Kerr, who, during his tenure as Director of the Project Management Staff, First Deputy Director of the Budget, and Administrator of the Housing and Development Administration, has been a constant source of ideas and opportunities. Outside of city government, we have received significant help from Carter Bales, Robert O'Block, Gerry Hillman, and several others at McKinsey and Company, Inc.

I also want to acknowledge the Ford Foundation, whose Urban Studies grant funded much of the case development work. Mrs. Tony Wasson, who remained remarkably patient, typed many of the cases. Mrs. Gretchen Gerzina also helped with the typing task.

Finally I would like to thank Dean Lawrence Fouraker for his interest and support and the President and Fellows of Harvard by whom the cases have been individually copyrighted.

Harvard University
September 1973

John R. Russell

INTRODUCTION

This book concerns the delivery of urban services. It focuses on the problems faced by those urban executives who are responsible for managing the city's housing stock, its sanitation services, its public assistance programs, and the host of other services that cities are called upon to provide. To a lesser extent, it focuses on the kinds of analytic staff activity that can be an effective tool in helping urban executives determine what course of action they should take. Most of the cases were developed for use in the course "Management of Urban Operations" at the Harvard Business School.

The complete course in urban operations takes thirty-two class sessions of one hour and twenty minutes each. The twenty-one cases in the book cover about two-thirds of those sessions. In the past, the balance of the course has consisted of additional cases (not included here in the interest of controlling the book's size); some technical notes on housing and public assistance that provide students with enough background to permit good case discussion; and guest speakers (most of whom were currently filling some responsible, urban management position). The cases are arranged in the same order as they are used in the course. There is a group of five introductory cases, then a series of functional modules of from two to seven cases (housing, narcotics control, public assistance, and environmental protection), and, finally, a short two-case module on the decentralization of urban services.

The introductory material is designed to accomplish two purposes. First, it examines the application of analytic techniques (cost/benefit analysis and cost/effectiveness analysis) to urban issues. "Emergency Ambulance Service (A) and (B)" and "Analysis of an Estuary" allow students to see, understand, and criticize the use of these techniques in two quite different situations, each one almost a classic of its type. Discussion can go well beyond the particular analyses into more general considerations of the usefulness and probable limitations of analytic approaches in the urban sector and, of equal importance for the class, the "proper" or most effective role for analysts in the urban setting.

The second goal of the introductory section is to give students (particularly those who have finished the first year of an MBA program) an opportunity to look at two cases in which urban line managers are, in fact, trying to manage some part of their cities. "The Boston Redevelopment Authority (A and B)" and "The 1971-1972 New York City Tax Program" offer a chance to compare, with the private sector, the opportunities and constraints that are presented to and imposed upon managers in the urban sector. More specifically, they give students a chance to reorient their thinking from private to public management in preparation for the remainder of the cases and to assess for themselves the extent to which management in the urban sector is dominated by political considerations.

The functional modules that follow the introductory cases have been selected to demonstrate the breadth of issues with which urban management is concerned. The list of functions, of course, is not complete: Criminal justice, fire, health services, education, and others are missing, either because the cases that were available would make the length of the book excessive, or because there simply were no suitable cases in existence as yet. The functions that are included provide a range between "hard" services, such as sanitation, and "soft" ones, such as public assistance. They also focus on those urban services where substantial numbers of MBAs are actually working. MBAs are not so likely, for example, to find jobs in the uniformed services such as police. Within each module, there are cases that put the students in each of two separate, but interrelated roles--that of the urban analyst and that of the urban manager. Cases of the first type ask the student to use "objective" analytic methods to develop program proposals for consideration and adoption by an urban manager. Cases of the second type examine the problems of line managers (or project managers without line authority) trying to implement changes that will improve or redirect the delivery of some urban service. It is not anticipated that discussion of the cases in a functional module will make the students expert in that urban function. Rather, as they progress from case to case, it is expected that they will become increasingly familiar with the process of developing programs, implementing change, and managing the day-to-day operations of a variety of urban services.

The last unit in the book looks at the decentralization of urban management. It turns away from the consideration of individual urban services toward the problem of integrating the delivery of many different services so that they make a sensible, effective package when viewed by a citizen from the neighborhood level. The cases in this section focus on the very real difficulties of implementing a concept--greater local control over and decentralized management of urban services--that is often lifted up as a simple solution to current inadequacies in urban management.

It goes almost without saying that there is no reason why another instructor should use the cases for the purposes intended by the author or in the manner, or order, that he has used them. I am hopeful that others will experiment with the material and, if time permits, let me know what experiments they have tried and what results they have achieved. Indeed, the cases have been selected so that subgroups of them might be used as teaching material for public sector courses whose purpose is quite different from my own course. Ten of the cases, for example, can be used to provide background in analytic techniques--cost/benefit analysis, cost/effectiveness analysis, waiting line theory, and inventory management--and to give students an opportunity to do analyses of their own in a variety of urban settings. An "analytic" case package might consist of:

Emergency Ambulance Service (A) and (B)
Analysis of an Estuary
Housing Rehabilitation in New York City
Public Assistance (A)

Addiction Control in New York City (A)
Sanitation (A), (B), and (C)
Incineration and Local Law 14 (A)

A shorter, but quite complete, unit in project management can also be put together from the cases in the book. (Assistant Professor Lawrence Bennigson and I have used this four-case package in several seminars in project management given to municipal employees and in another one offered to students at the Woodrow Wilson School at Princeton University.) The cases describe New York City's highly structured, organizationally explicit project management system; provide students with several opportunities to observe and criticize the management approaches and styles of different urban project managers responding to different situations; and, finally, present an opportunity for the class to plan the implementation of a highly complex project in command decentralization. The package consists of:

Model Cities Sanitation Project (C)
New York City Housing Authority Incinerator Air Pollution Abatement Project
Addiction Control in New York City (B)
Command Decentralization (A)

Teaching Notes

Teaching notes for the cases are available to bona fide instructors. For information, contact the author, care of the Harvard Business School.

INTRODUCTORY CASES

EMERGENCY AMBULANCE SERVICE (A)

The City of New York has been providing emergency ambulance service to residents, visitors and transients since 1870. In 1967, the Department of Hospitals provided round-the-clock service with 109 ambulances, and responded to over a half million calls.

Organization

The city was traditionally divided into 49 hospital districts for the purpose of emergency ambulance operation.

In each of 17 districts, emergency ambulance service was operated by a municipal hospital while, in the remaining 32 districts, private hospitals operated the service under contract to the Department of Hospitals. The organization of the Department of Hospital's ambulance service is indicated in Exhibit 1. Exhibit 2 summarizes ambulance deployment.

The ambulances in each district were based at the hospital, with the ambulance attendants reporting to the head of nursing, and the drivers to the garage foreman. Until 1942, a hospital intern had been assigned to each ambulance, but since then trained attendants were used. Ambulance attendants were typically Nurse's Aides who were given additional training and paid an extra $240 per month for duty on ambulances. The position was non-competitive, and did not require an examination. In 1967, 40% of the ambulance attendants were female.

The drivers normally had no medical training, and were classified as "motor-vehicle operators" in the city's civil service scheme. They were permanently assigned to a specific garage (i.e., hospital) although they reported to the Department of Hospitals rather than to any specific hospital administrator. Their work schedule differed from the attendant's schedule. Neither attendants nor drivers were paid overtime.

Operation

A typical call for service originated with the police department. The police dispatcher determined the hospital district in which the emergency was located, and contacted the hospital garage by telephone. At the same time, he also despatched a police officer to the scene. The police

---

This case is based on a report prepared for the Mayor of New York by Dr. E. S. Savas, Deputy City Administrator. The report is entitled "Emergency Ambulance Service," March 8, 1968. The case was prepared by Richard J. Gill, Management Analysis Center, Inc., under the supervision of Graeme M. Taylor, on behalf of The Ford Foundation and the State-Local Finances Project, George Washington University.

officer's main role was to render emergency aid prior to arrival of the ambulance, and to gather necessary information regarding the incident. In cases of illness, he sometimes assisted in moving the patient into the ambulance.

At the hospital garage, the ambulance despatcher (foreman) assigned the call to a particular ambulance. The ambulance could communicate with the police despatcher by radio to report its status and receive information; there was no radio communication with the hospital. (Sometimes an ambulance would be reassigned to a more urgent call while enroute.)

Upon arrival at the scene, the ambulance either picked up the patient to be taken to the hospital, (after administering necessary first-aid) or it was determined that no action was necessary, in which case he notified the police despatcher of the ambulance's availability for assignment to another call.

The patient was taken to the hospital's emergency facilities where appropriate treatment was administered. Upon completion of a standard form (requiring such information as the patient's age, nearest relative, address and telephone number), the patient was formally accepted by the hospital and the ambulance was released.

Exhibit 3 summarizes emergency ambulance calls in 1967.

Costs

The Department of Hospitals annually entered into contracts with voluntary (i.e. private) hospitals to supply emergency ambulance service. The hospitals were paid on the basis of the number of calls handled. In 1967, the city contracted for 49 ambulances from 31 hospitals at a cost of approximately $1.87 million. All operating costs including purchase of the ambulance(s) were borne by the private hospitals; they were reimbursed $35,000 annually for up to 3500 calls, $37,500 for 3501 to 5000 calls, and $40,000 for over 5000 calls.

The city spent approximately $4.3 million in 1967 to operate emergency ambulances attached to municipal hospitals.

Exhibit 1

EMERGENCY AMBULANCE SERVICE (A)

Department of Hospitals, Ambulance and Transportation Service

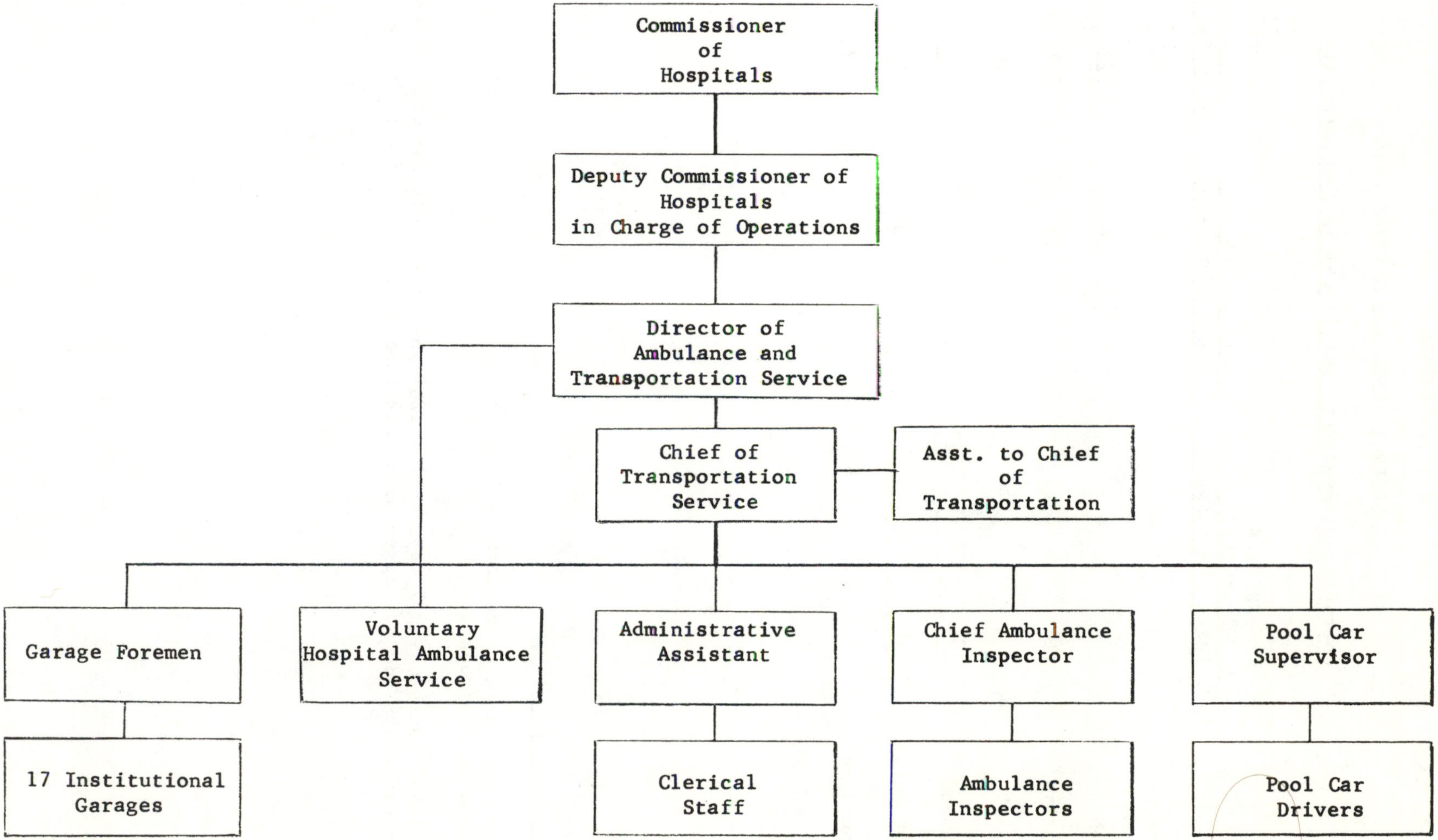

Exhibit 2

EMERGENCY AMBULANCE SERVICE (A)

Operation of Emergency Ambulances in New York City

	Hospitals (Districts)		Ambulances		Actual Reported Tours* Per Week	
	Private	Municipal	Private	Municipal	Private	Municipal
Manhattan	10	4	18	15	394	294
Bronx	1	4	1	14	21	259
Brooklyn	10	6	15	23	301	392
Queens	8	2	11	6	224	126
Richmond	3	1	4	2	84	42
Sub Total	32	17	49	60	1,024	1,113
Grand Total	49		109**		2,137	

* A tour is an operational ambulance for 8 hours (one ambulance can operate 3x7 = 21 tours/week).

** 109x3 tours/day x 7 days/week = 2289 possible tours per week. (Note: "actual reported tours" do not agree with this theoretically possible figure.)

Exhibit 3

EMERGENCY AMBULANCE SERVICE (A)

1967 Emergency Ambulance Calls (x 000)

	Emergency Room Only	Admissions	Unnecessary	DOA	Other Hospital	Not Removed	Other	Total Calls*
Manhattan								
Municipal	31.7	16.3	10.6	2.3	10.8	3.6	1.2	75.4
Private	38.1	10.8	12.7	3.6	23.7	4.1	0.8	88.8
Total	69.8	27.1	23.3	5.9	34.5	7.7	2.0	164.2
Bronx								
Municipal	42.1	10.6	12.6	2.2	12.1	2.9	0.3	81.1
Private	1.3	0.6	0.5	0.3	1.6	0.3	0.0	3.9
Total	43.4	11.1	13.1	2.5	13.7	3.2	0.3	85.0
Brooklyn								
Municipal	53.9	18.3	14.1	2.8	10.2	4.8	1.0	102.0
Private	35.7	7.4	11.4	2.7	17.5	3.6	1.6	75.1
Total	89.6	25.7	25.5	5.5	27.7	8.4	2.6	177.1
Queens								
Municipal	12.9	7.0	3.5	1.4	1.5	1.2	0.1	27.1
Private	14.7	3.5	4.2	2.0	15.2	2.4	0.2	39.2
Total	27.6	10.5	7.7	3.4	16.7	3.6	0.3	66.3
Richmond								
Municipal	0.0	0.0	0.0 **	0.0 **	0.2	0.0 **	0.0	0.2
Private	2.9	2.4	0.7	0.5	1.8	0.9	0.1	8.6
Total	2.9	2.4	0.7	0.5	2.0	0.9	0.1	8.8
Whole City								
Municipal	140.6	52.2	40.7	8.7	34.9	12.6	7.5	285.8
Private	92.7	24.7	30.1	9.1	59.9	11.3	2.0	215.7
Total	233.3	76.9	70.8	17.8	94.9	23.9	9.4	501.5

* Totals may not add due to rounding.

** Less than 51.

EMERGENCY AMBULANCE SERVICE (B)

Introduction

Emergency ambulance service has been provided by the City of New York to residents and visitors since 1870. With the growth of the city, the service is now available to approximately ten million persons daily, 24 hours a day, every day of the year. In 1967, the city's ambulance service responded to more than half a million calls for emergency assistance, an increase of more than 43 per cent in the past decade. This growing work load, together with an increasing concern about the adequacy and responsiveness of the system, led to a request by Mayor Lindsay to Dr. T. W. Costello, Deputy Mayor-City Administrator, to analyze the service and to recommend and implement significant improvements.

This case contains a report by Dr. E. S. Savas, Deputy City Administrator, Office of the Mayor, City of New York on the analysis which he performed of the city's emergency ambulance service.

Scope of the Study

Emergency Medical Care -- An Overview

Viewed in perspective, the emergency ambulance service fits within a more general framework of an overall emergency medical-care system. Such a system is composed of the following subsystems, with the first two comprising what is usually considered the ambulance system:

1. Communication
2. Transportation
3. Medical treatment

In addition, one can consider that preventive health care also enters into the total picture for it clearly affects the requirements for and the nature of an emergency medical care system. For instance, improved preventive health measures and their ready availability to the community, e.g., through neighborhood health care centers, can be expected to reduce the demand for emergency care.

This case is based on the work of Dr. E. S. Savas, Deputy City Administrator, Office of the Mayor, City of New York. The case was prepared by Richard J. Gill, Management Analysis Center, Inc., under the supervision of Graeme M. Taylor, on behalf of The Ford Foundation and the State-Local Finances Project, George Washington University.

Communication Subsystem: This subsystem includes the means by which aid is summoned for a patient and the procedure for screening, assessing, and establishing priorities for such calls. It also encompasses the requirements and means for communicating among dispatchers, ambulances, and hospitals, and possibly even for contacting the Doctors' Emergency Service, Poison Control Center, and so forth.

Transportation Subsystem: This subsystem includes the means for conveying a patient to the medical facility, or for transporting medical facilities (doctor, first-aid attendant, oxygen, resuscitation equipment, stomach pump, antidotes, and so forth) to a patient. Elements within this subsystem include such factors as the boundaries of ambulance service districts, the location of ambulances and hospitals, and the number of ambulances. Other elements might involve the use of sirens and express lanes, the design and construction of ambulances, the location of first-aid stations, devices for carrying people down stairs, et cetera.

Medical Treatment Subsystem: This area encompasses the nature, speed, and adequacy of emergency medical treatment, in terms of the qualifications of personnel, their prompt availability, the organization, procedures, and equipment in an emergency room, the equipment carried on an ambulance, the possible utility of first-aid stations, et cetera. Improvements in the transportation subsystem could be vitiated, for example, if no doctor were available immediately after the patient is carried into the hospital.

Systems Analysis of the Emergency Ambulance Service

In light of the urgent need to improve the ambulance service itself, no effort was made initially to examine the prevention or treatment subsystems. For the purposes of this report, the communication subsystem can likewise be ignored. The major effort was focused instead on particular elements of the transportation subsystem. Specifically, a quantitative analysis was made of the geographic distribution of emergency calls in the most severe problem area of the city, and the number and placement of ambulances needed to service these calls effectively. The merits of a proposed satellite ambulance station were examined in detail.

Systems analysis of a problem involves four classical steps:

(1) defining a specific objective which is to be achieved by the solution;

(2) formulating alternative ways of reaching that objective;

(3) establishing explicit criteria for evaluating the alternatives;

(4) selecting the best alternative, in terms of the criteria.

Objective: The concept of "improved ambulance service" can be described quantitatively by two related performance measures:

(1) response time -- the period between receipt of a call at the ambulance station and arrival of an ambulance at the scene;

(2) round-trip time -- the period between receipt of a call at the ambulance station and arrival of the assigned ambulance at the hospital with the patient.

Both of these related parameters are important from the public service point of view. Prompt arrival of an ambulance and trained attendant on the scene saves lives, reduces suffering, and produces confidence in the service on the part of the general citizenry. Round-trip time is the vital parameter in those cases where the patient requires prompt professional medical treatment in the emergency room of a hospital.

The objective that was adopted was to decrease the response time in the Kings County Hospital district of Brooklyn. (It follows from the above definitions that a decrease in response time produces the same reduction in round-trip time.) However, no numerical target (e.g., a five-minute reduction in response time) could justifiably be set unless it were possible to relate time savings to the saving of lives. No such study has been reported and to tackle this problem was well outside the initial scope of the project. This remains as an important topic for future medical research.

Alternatives: Three alternatives that were considered initially were the following:

(a) redistribute the existing ambulances in the district by locating some of them at a satellite garage;

(b) increase the number of ambulances at Kings County Hospital;

(c) a combination of the above two alternatives.

Criteria: Both the cost and the effectiveness of the alternatives were considered. Costs include the capital and operating costs of additional ambulances and of a satellite garage. Effectiveness was measured in minutes of average response time and also in the percentage of calls whose response time exceeded a certain level.

The Problem

Exhibit 1 portrays a typical district which is served by a hospital, indicated by H in the figure. Under the present mode of operation, the ambulances serving the district are all stationed at the hospital. The dots on the map indicate the location and relative numbers of emergency calls from different points throughout the district. Calls are not uniformly and randomly distributed throughout the area. Due to varying population density and socio-economic characteristics, certain subsections of the district exhibit rather dense clustering of dots; that is, there is a high demand for ambulance service from those areas.

A superficial look at Exhibit 1 suggests that a substantial improvement in ambulance service could be achieved by the relatively simple expedient of stationing ambulances at a satellite garage in the middle of one of the clusters, for example, at point S. Such a garage could consist of ordinary commercial garage space, or the garage of a police station or firehouse. Proponents of this idea reasoned that an ambulance located at the satellite could pick up a patient in that vicinity and deliver him to the hospital in half the time that it would take an ambulance from the hospital to go and pick up that patient and return with him to the hospital; they envisioned a 50% reduction in round-trip time. However, a closer look shows that the situation is not so simple. In the first place, not all the time that elapses is travel time; various delays contribute to the total round-trip time (Exhibit 2) and these would not be reduced by locating the ambulances elsewhere. Secondly, the ambulances will be called upon to service calls from anywhere in the district not only those in the immediate vicinity of their satellite station, and it is difficult to forecast an improvement in handling those calls. Finally, the round-trip time is very sensitive to the frequency of calls; for example, infrequent calls from the area around the satellite can be assigned to waiting ambulances and in this case a substantial improvement would be realized. However, as the frequency rises, the ambulances would be spending more and more time shuttling back and forth between the hospital and the high-demand area around the satellite, calls would queue up to await an available ambulance, and in this case it would make no difference whether the busy ambulance were nominally stationed at the satellite, at the hospital, or at any point in between.

This qualititative analysis clearly shows that the picture is not so simple as appears at first glance, and that the level of service depends in a complex way on the following five major factors:

-- geographic distribution of calls throughout the district
-- frequency of calls
-- number of ambulances in the district
-- location of hospital
-- location of ambulance garage(s)

Given the complexity of this system, no intuitive estimate can provide a sound guide. Nevertheless, the basic idea of a satellite station, that is, to put the ambulances where they are needed, is a sound one that warrants a detailed, quantitative analysis in order to provide valid estimates of the improvements to be expected.

The Approach

In light of the fact that the level of service is a complicated function of five variables, conventional computational approaches and simple mathematics will not suffice. Instead the ideal analytical tool to use in this case is computer simulation. This is the method of choice where there are many interrelated factors, where the expected effects are complex, and where trial-and-error experimentation is costly or impractical. This definition describes the ambulance system perfectly.

Exhibit 1

EMERGENCY AMBULANCE SERVICE (B)

General Representation of an Ambulance District

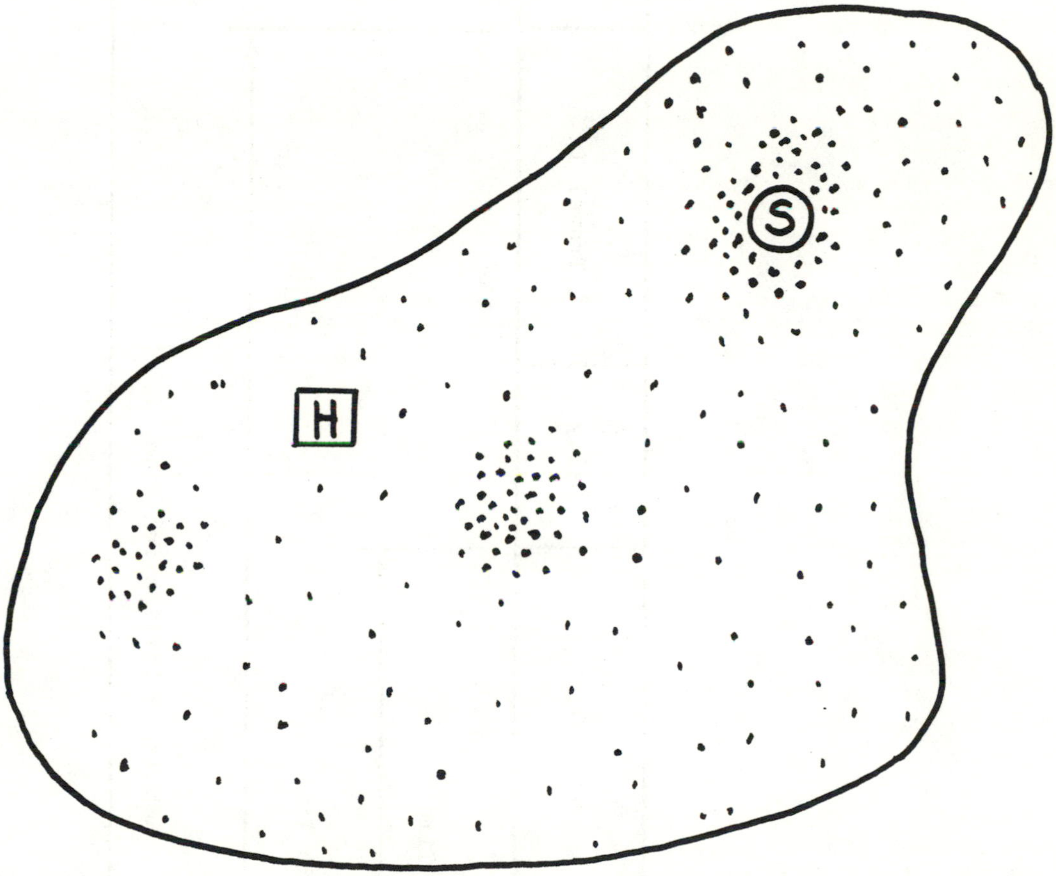

H = Location of Hospital

S = Location of Satellite Garage

• = Points Where Calls Were Made

Exhibit 2

EMERGENCY AMBULANCE SERVICE (B)

Sequence of Events During a Call, Showing Time Relationships

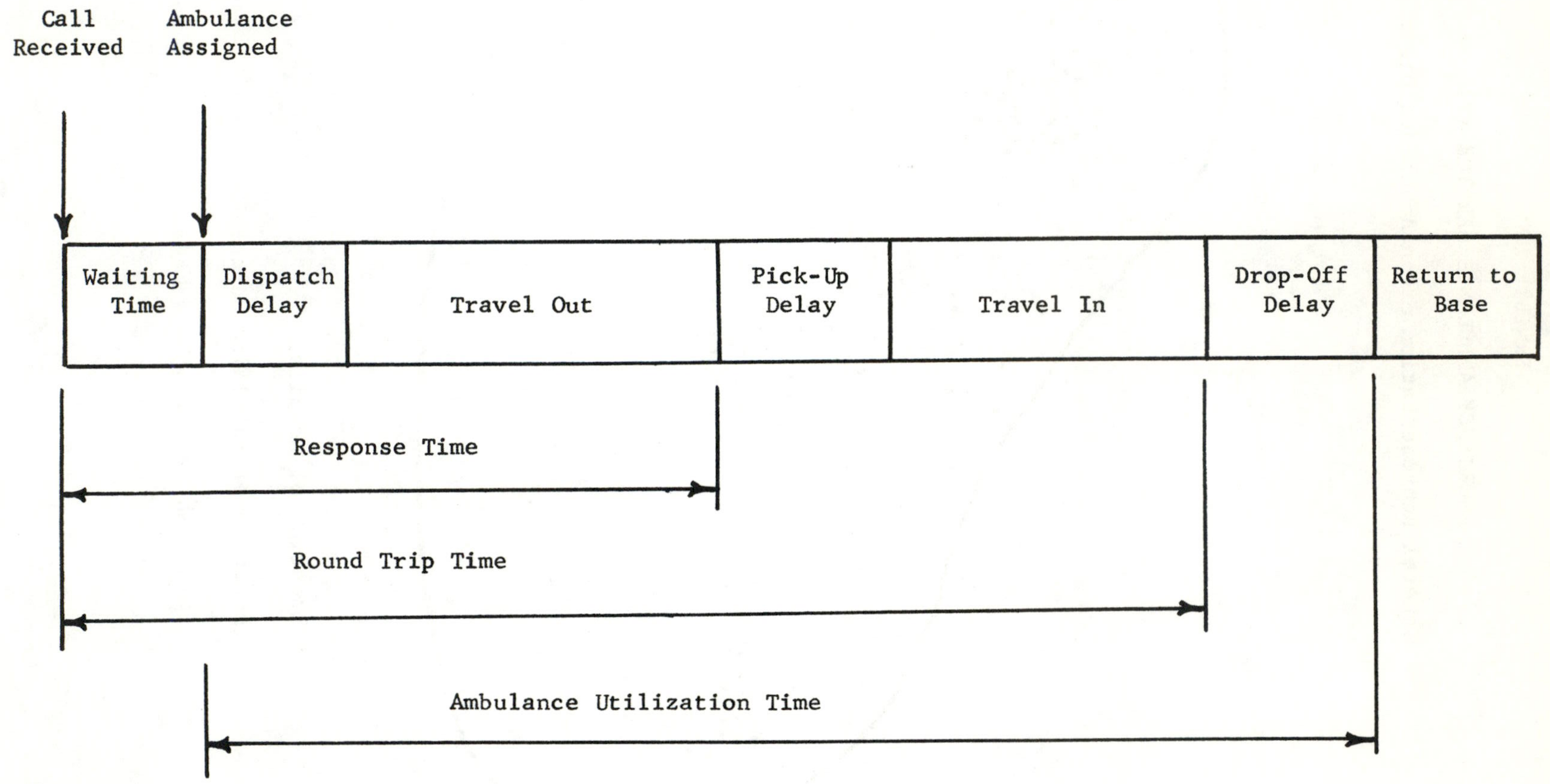

Exhibit 3

EMERGENCY AMBULANCE SERVICE (B)

Map of Brooklyn Showing Hospital District and Areas Near Hospital and Satellite

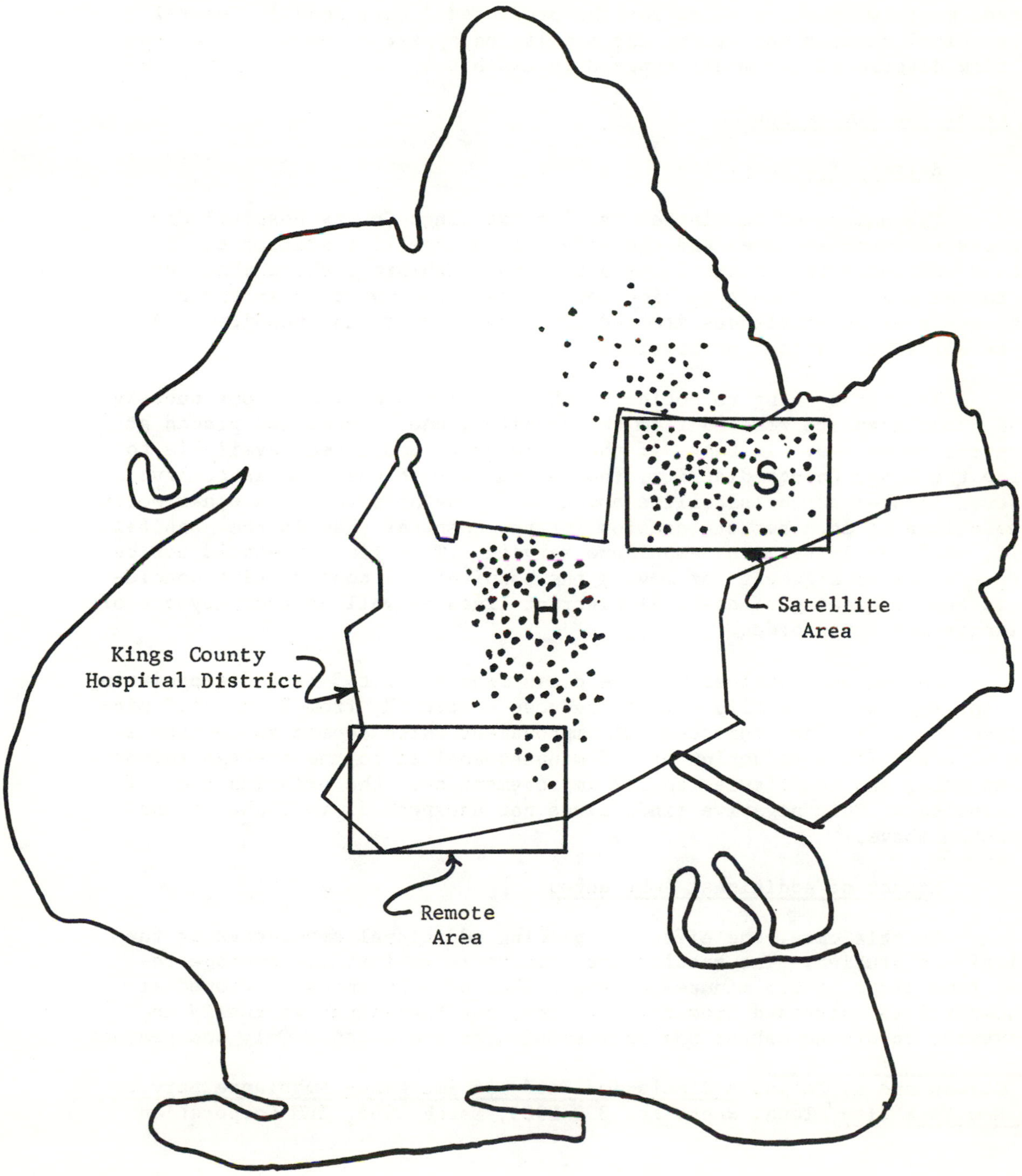

The ambulance service system in the Kings County Hospital district was simulated on a digital computer using a mathematical model of the system. A map of the district, as it was in August, 1966, appears in Exhibit 3; the hospital is located at H and the proposed satellite is at S. About 175,000 calls were simulated, corresponding to almost four years of operation of that hospital's ambulance service. Attention was focussed on the peak-load period, the 4 p.m.-to-midnight shift. The inter-arrival time was set at 7.28 min., which characterizes the peak-load period in an average month of 4570 calls. (This number of calls is 15% greater than the actual observed monthly load, to allow for the predicted future load.) General and technical details concerning the simulation appear elsewhere.[1] A general flow diagram of the model appears in Exhibit 4.

Results of the Simulation

Effect of a Satellite

The number of ambulances serving the Kings County Hospital district was retained at seven and the effect of a satellite station at the location indicated in Exhibit 3 was simulated. Exhibit 5 shows what happens to the average round-trip time and average response time in the district as the seven ambulances are redistributed between the hospital and that satellite in various proportions.

The first thing to notice is that the times decrease continuously as the ambulances are removed from the hospital, one by one, and placed at the satellite garage. In fact, if there are seven ambulances available to service the Kings County district, the optimum way to use them is to have all seven located at the satellite and none at the hospital. In other words, the satellite is at a better location for the hospital than is the hospital itself, at least in terms of ambulance service, This finding should not be interpreted as an argument for moving the hospital. A constructive conclusion is that redrawing of hospital district lines as well as redeployment of ambulances may be in order.

The second conclusion to be drawn from Exhibit 5 is a disappointing one: the average round-trip time is reduced a mere 5%, from 33 to 31.5 minutes, which is far less than the 50% improvement which seemed so obvious at first glance. (This reduction of 1.5 minutes applies to the average response time as well, and constitutes an 11% improvement over the existing time of 13.5 minutes.) This negative finding was not unexpected, in light of the discussion above.

Effect of Additional Ambulances

In this case, the effect of placing additional ambulances at the hospital was studied. The results are evident in Exhibit 6. Average response time drops by 0.3 minutes as the number of ambulances stationed at the hospital is increased from seven to ten, but thereafter virtually no improvement occurs no matter how many ambulances are added. Only one reaches

---

[1] G. Gordon and K. Zelin, A Simulation Study of Emergency Ambulance Service in New York City, Tech. Rept. No. 320-2935, March 1968, IBM Corporation.

Exhibit 4

EMERGENCY AMBULANCE SERVICE (B)

Flow Diagram of Ambulance Service Model

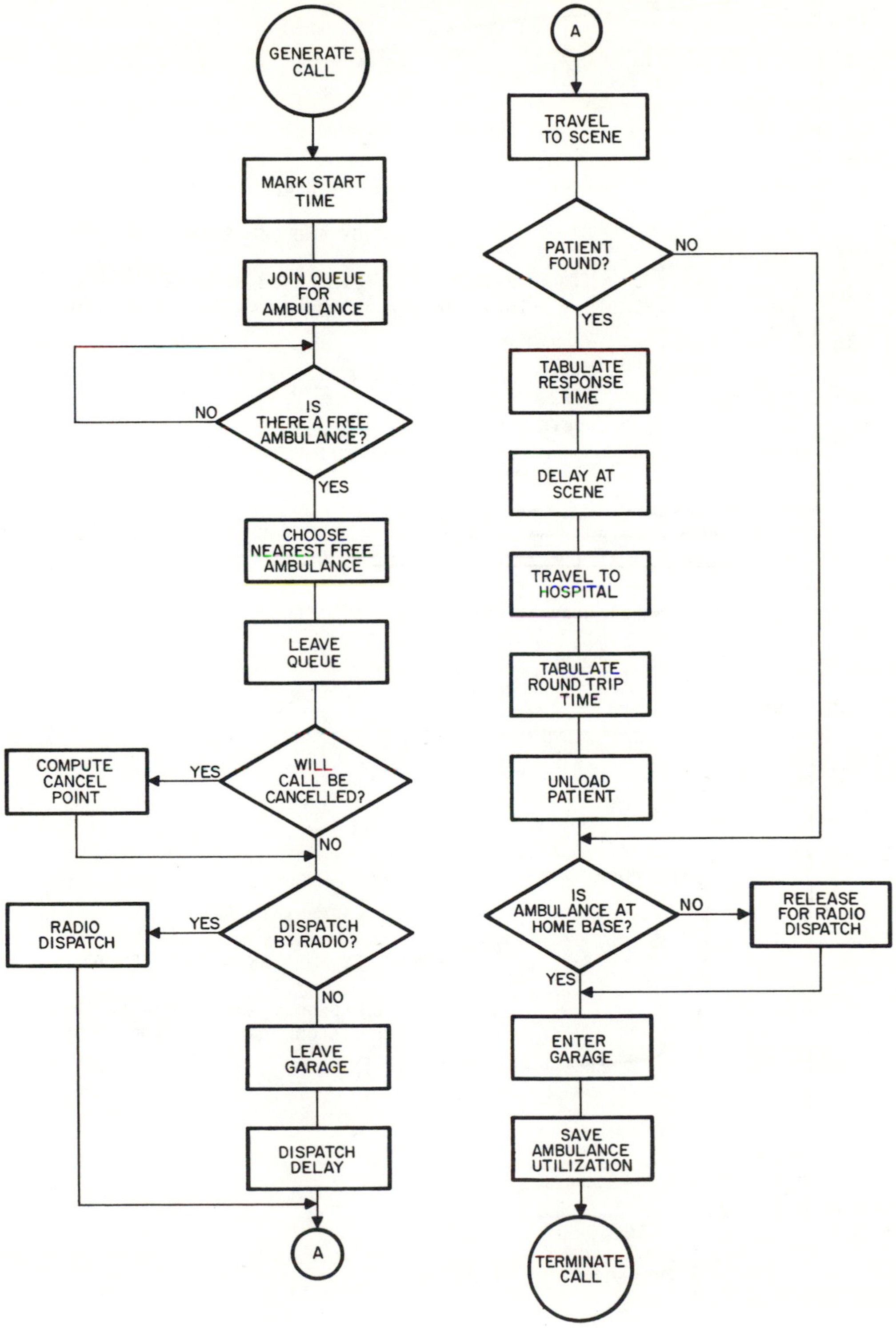

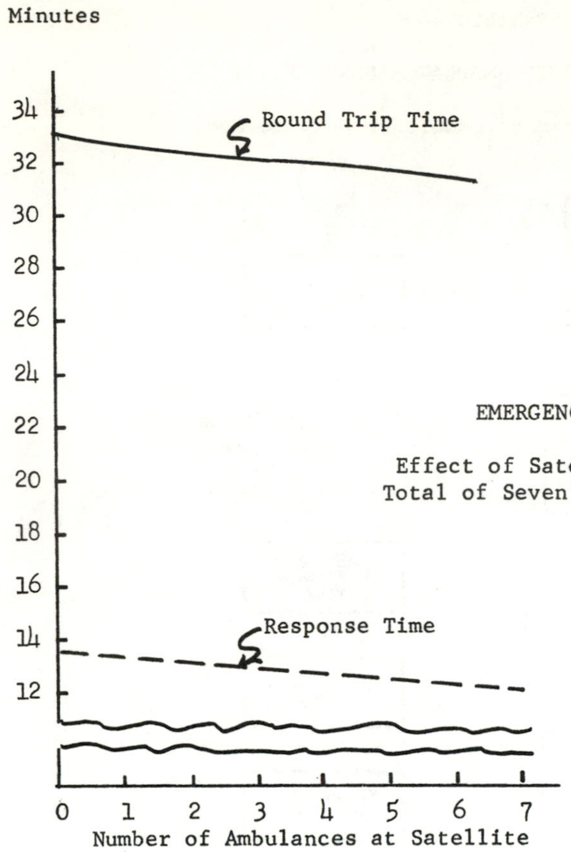

Exhibit 5

EMERGENCY AMBULANCE SERVICE (B)

Effect of Satellite on Service, With a Total of Seven Ambulances in the System

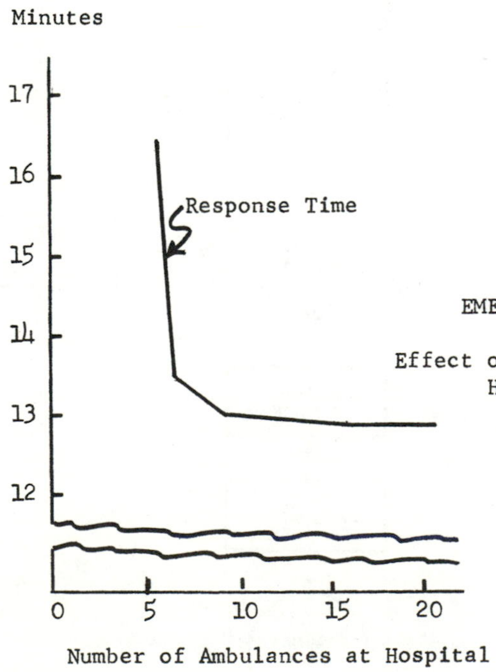

Exhibit 6

EMERGENCY AMBULANCE SERVICE (B)

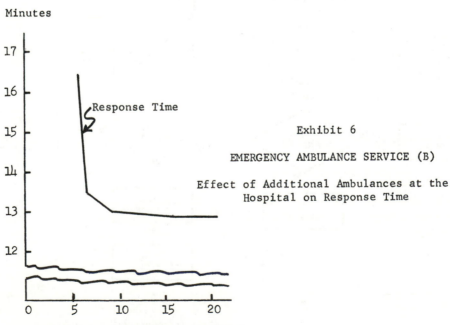

Effect of Additional Ambulances at the Hospital on Response Time

the "elbow" of the curve, one is operating on a plateau and additional ambulances are wasted.

<u>Waiting Time</u>: The reason for this effect becomes clear upon inspecting Exhibit 7. The solid line shows the average waiting time as a function of the number of ambulances at the hospital. Waiting time is the period between receipt of a call at the ambulance station and assignment of an available ambulance to that call. (See Exhibit 2.) Waiting time constitutes one identifiable segment of the response time. As more ambulances are added to the system, the waiting time drops essentially to zero and the response time therefore levels off (as in Exhibit 6) at a value which depends almost exclusively on the travel time. Travel time, in turn, is a fixed characteristic of a given district and depends upon its geometry (size and shape, and the location of its ambulances) and its traffic (routes and conditions).

<u>Ambulance Utilization</u>: The dashed line of Exhibit 7 shows how ambulance utilization declines as more ambulances are added. (Utilization is the fraction of time that an ambulance spends on a call; see Exhibit 2 for a graphic definition.) The increase in idle time (decreased utilization) is the price paid for reducing the average waiting time, that is, for assuring that an ambulance will be available for prompt assignment when a call comes in.

It should be noted that the minimum response (at the "elbow" of Exhibit 6), which is achieved when the waiting time approaches zero (in Exhibit 7), corresponds to a utilization of 42%. This compares to the actual current utilization of about 60%.

This utilization factor is an important indicator of service, and because it is relatively easy to measure, it can be used to manage the ambulance system. For example, given the existing boundaries for Kings County Hospital (and no satellite), this analysis shows that if utilization is greater than 42%, improved service can be obtained by adding ambulances. On the other hand, if utilization is less than 42%, ambulances can safely be released from the district without fear that the level of service will be degraded. Furthermore, simple arithmetic suffices to calculate how many ambulances to add or remove in order to arrive at the 42% utilization figure.

<u>Economy of Large Districts</u>: Exhibit 8 displays the relationship between work load (in calls per month) and "ideal utilization" (the utilization corresponding to negligible waiting time, e.g., 42%). The significant observation here is that ideal utilization is not constant and independent of the load; as the load increases, the ideal utilization rate also increases. In essence, this says that if the load were to be doubled, one would need less than twice as many ambulances in order to continue providing ideal service. This result has important policy ramifications. It means that a group of small districts, each with a small load and one or two ambulances, requires more ambulances to provide a given level of service than would be required if the districts were consolidated into a single large district with the ambulances pooled under a unified command in that district. The same effect is achieved by ignoring district lines and simply assigning the nearest available ambulance.

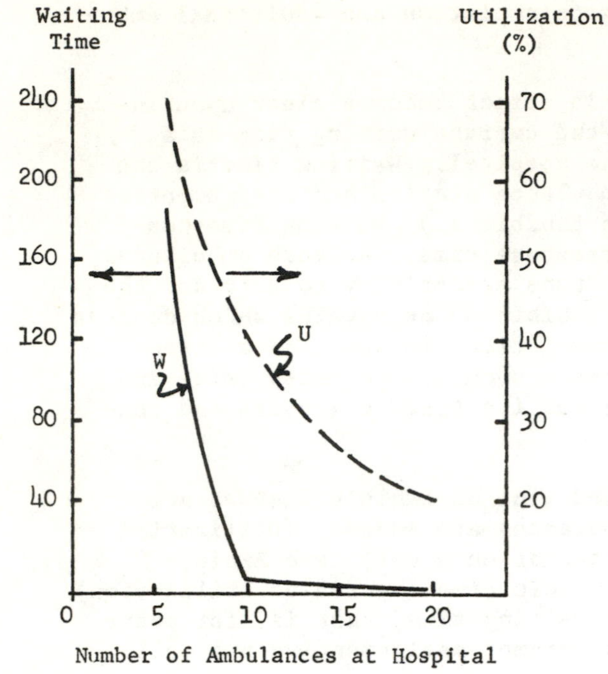

Exhibit 7

EMERGENCY AMBULANCE SERVICE (B)

Effect of Additional Ambulances On Waiting Time and On Ambulance Utilization

Exhibit 8

EMERGENCY AMBULANCE SERVICE (B)

Relationship Between Ideal Ambulance Utilization and Work Load

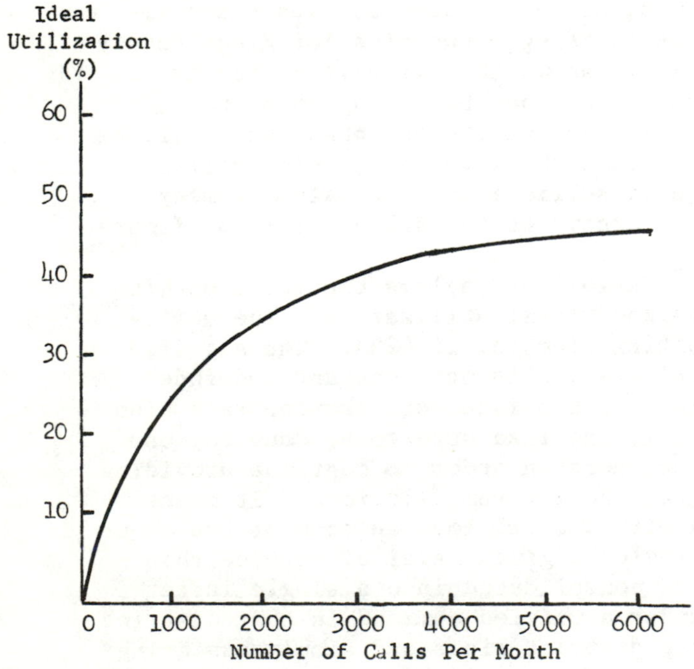

Exhibit 8 could be used to adjust the number of ambulances in the Kings County Hospital district as the work load fluctuates over time. With minor modification, the data could also be used to guide the staffing patterns at the three work shifts.

Effect of Satellite with Additional Ambulances

The number of ambulances serving the district was increased to ten and their effect, with a satellite, was simulated.

Exhibit 9 shows the results for various distributions of the ten ambulances between the hospital and the satellite. The corresponding curve for seven ambulances, taken from Exhibit 5, is also displayed here for comparative purposes.

The most important feature to observe is that the response time drops to a minimum of 10.9 minutes (with six ambulances at the satellite and four at the hospital), a reduction of 19% from the pre-existing 13.5 minute average. When more than six ambulances are at the satellite, the service gets worse, that is, the area near the satellite becomes oversaturated with ambulances, just as too many ambulances at the hospital also wastes resources.

Services in Subareas: Up to this point, the discussion has centered on average response time for the entire district. The question can be raised whether certain subareas of the district will experience a decline in service, a decline which might be masked in the district average because of a more-than-compensating improvement in service in the subarea near the satellite. Accordingly, the remote subarea and the satellite subarea indicated by the two rectangular areas on the map of Exhibit 3 were examined. The results are shown in Exhibit 10. As would be expected, the satellite subarea has better service than the district average; with the six ambulances at the satellite station, the satellite subarea has an average response time of 10.1 minutes, a 21% improvement over its pre-existing value of 12.8 minutes.

Even for the remote subarea, however, it was gratifying to note an improvement of 6% over the pre-existing situation, a drop from 16.1 to 15.1 minutes when the ambulances are divided 4:6 between the hospital and the satellite.

Proposed System

On the basis of the simulation results it was concluded that the proposed satellite station, with additional ambulances, could be justified as an immediate way to realize substantial improvements. This satellite was in fact placed in operation on a pilot basis. However, it was felt that further improvements were possible.

It was shown earlier in this report that Kings County Hospital is not particularly well situated with respect to the district that its ambulances service. Undoubtedly, this is true of many other districts in the city as well. This suggests that one source of improvement would be to redistrict the city, taking into consideration the locations of the hospitals and the distributions of calls in order to draw more rational district boundaries.

Exhibit 9

EMERGENCY AMBULANCE SERVICE (B)

Effect of Satellite on Response Time

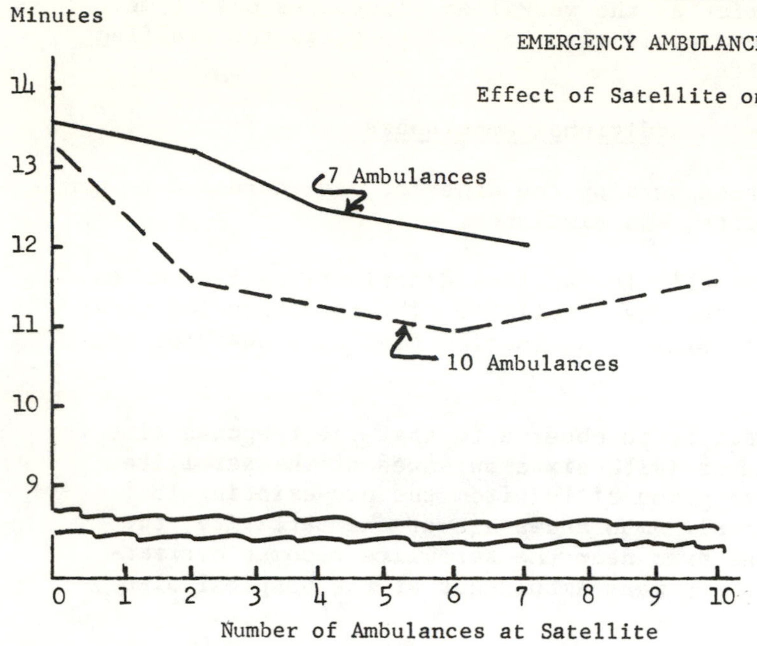

Exhibit 10

EMERGENCY AMBULANCE SERVICE (B)

Effect of Satellite on Service To Remote Area and to Area Near Satellite (10 Ambulances)

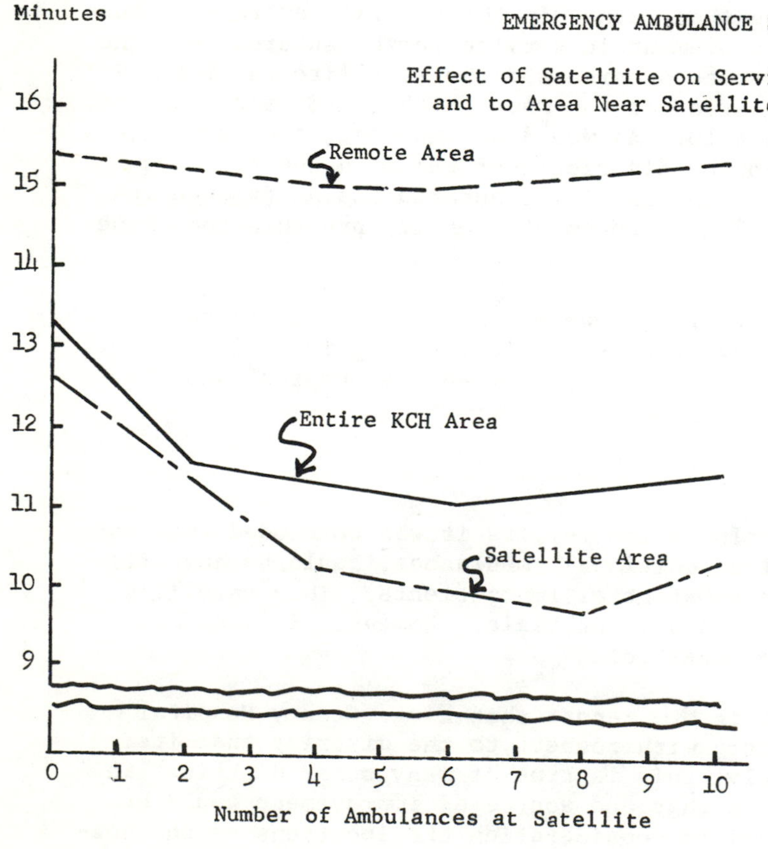

In considering this suggestion, however, a different and more fundamental recommendation emerged. Simply stated, ambulances ought to be stationed where the patients are, without regard to hospital locations and, an ambulance ought to bring a patient to the nearest appropriate treatment center, without regard to the ambulance's home station. In other words, the transportation and the treatment subsystems should be separated ("de-coupled"). The problem can therefore be stated as:

(a) where to locate ambulances so that they reach patients promptly; and

(b) where to deliver patients.

Location of Ambulances

Practically speaking, this recommendation to divorce the transportation service from the treatment service means that ambulances should be operated centrally, for example, by the Department of Hospitals. They should be distributed throughout the city in accordance with the observed demand, and they should be redistributed periodically as the geographic pattern of demand changes due to changes in the population. Hospitals are relatively permanent installations with no mobility and therefore it makes little sense for the transportation service to be attached so inflexibly to such facilities.

These statements should not be interpreted to mean that ambulances should not be stationed at hospitals; if the distribution of calls indicates that a particular hospital is well-situated to serve as an ambulance station, of course it should be used as such.

Furthermore, it is evident that to reduce response time ambulances should be completely dispersed; that is, rarely should there be two or more ambulances stationed at one location. The simulation showed clearly how the response time improves as existing ambulances from one station are apportioned properly among two stations to put them closer to high-demand areas. Further dissemination will result in further improvement, and the maximum decentralization, one ambulance per station, will probably produce the maximum improvement. This statement is in no way inconsistent with the statements made concerning the economy of large districts. The crucial point here is the elimination of the entire concept of districts as far as the transportation subsystem is concerned. The nearest available ambulance will be assigned to a call, without regard to any real or hypothetical district boundaries. In fact, this approach is completely equivalent to making the entire city a single district, and having all the ambulances serve that district. This is in perfect harmony with the comments about the savings associated with large, multi-ambulance districts.

Satellite garages, provided they entail only short-term commitments in terms of leases and amortization of capital conversion costs, offer one relatively inexpensive way to provide a more rational dispersion and distribution of ambulances, as has been shown. However, a further extension of this concept is suggested. It is not at all clear that ambulances must be inside a garage while awaiting assignment. Just as there are taxi stands, bus stops and reserved parking places in front of hotels, consulates, hospitals, and post offices, one can conceive of on-the-street ambulance stations. Besides permitting optimal placement of ambulances, this would reduce costs, increase the visibility of the service, and probably reduce the dispatching delay. (On the other hand, additional unnecessary calls might be generated by virtue of the high visibility.) The problem of comfort facilities for the ambulance crew can be handled in the same way that it is handled for radio patrolmen, bus drivers, sanitationmen, and taxi drivers. The problem of keeping warm in a standing ambulance in the winter should be surmountable; at worst it will be necessary to keep the motor running, although recognizing the cost in gasoline, noise and air pollution.

Dispatching of ambulances in such a highly decentralized system must be performed centrally, as it is now, by the Communication Bureau of the Police Department, but without going through an intermediary dispatcher at a garage. This capability exists today. Each ambulance is already equipped with a two-way radio and is in communication with the police dispatcher. The forthcoming computer-based command-and-control system ("SPRINT") at the Communications Bureau will enable the ambulance dispatcher to provide even closer, minute-by-minute control over the status and activity of each ambulance in the city system. Furthermore, SPRINT can automate the process of selecting and assigning the nearest available ambulance to each call, despite the wide dispersion of ambulances among many individual locations.

In addition, by employing statistical estimates for the length of time that an ambulance is assigned to a call, the computer might even be able to advise the dispatcher whether to assign a call immediately to a relatively distant but available ambulance, or to wait a few minutes for another ambulance, currently on assignment, that is likely to become available at a location sufficiently close to the point of demand to warrant a brief delay in making the assignment.

Supervisory control, as distinguished from dispatching, would be exercised by the Department of Hospitals by matching information reports on each call from the police dispatcher, the ambulance crew, and the hospital emergency room. SPRINT makes such detailed reporting practical, and such reporting is strengthened by the accurate and prompt feedback on ambulance service that the public provides when it calls in to complain that no ambulance has yet arrived on the scene. This opportunity for feedback control, which is absent in the case of routine preventive police patrol and in the case of sanitation trucks, minimizes the need for on-site supervision. However, such supervision, if deemed necessary, could be performed by a borough commander driving around on inspection in a sedan, in the manner of a district sanitation superintendent.

This tentative recommendation for garage-free satellite operation requires more careful evaluation to determine its feasibility and to see if any necessary functions of a garage have been overlooked. For example, some garage space would still be needed for parking excess ambulances during low-load shifts. In any event, an ambulance from a street station will have to be driven back to a garage at shift change. Refueling and minor maintenance could be performed there. Locker facilities at that garage enable the attendants to change into uniforms and store personal belongings, just as they do now.

Delivery of Patients

The above recommendations, when implemented, will tend to minimize the response time--the time required for an ambulance to reach the scene. The next question is where to deliver the patient so as to minimize round-trip time. The ideal answer is to deliver him to the nearest appropriate treatment center. (The general phrase "treatment center" is used here in order to leave open the possibility of providing some types of emergency medical care at neighborhood health clinics or first-aid centers. The term "hospital" will be employed for the sake of convenience, although the above option should be borne in mind.) The appropriateness of a hospital as a delivery point for ambulance patients depends on the following major factors:

(1) adequacy of its emergency room,

(2) if not a municipal hospital, its selectivity in terms of "interesting cases," a patient's economic resources, and other possible factors,

(3) capacity or bed availability,

One area of possible improvement lies in the first factor. If study shows that average round-trip time in an area could be reduced by bringing patients to a hospital which is not qualified at the present time solely because of inadequate emergency room facilities, the possibility, cost, and effectiveness of upgrading those facilities should be explored. (If such a hospital is too small to accept many emergency patients, it should not be considered, as the <u>average</u> round-trip time will not show a marked improvement.)

The second factor, a non-municipal hospital's policy of selectivity is outside the realm of practical systems analysis. Existing hospital district lines in some cases result from such selection criteria. Analysis can serve to identify those hospitals whose participation, or fuller participation, in the system would substantially improve the emergency ambulance service, thereby providing some direction for policy-making officials to negotiate and otherwise bargain with the private institution to secure its participation on mutually acceptable grounds.

It is the third factor, hospital capacity or bed availability, which presents the greatest problem. For the most part, the whole concept of a hospital's ambulance district is a crude attempt to match the hospital's capacity with the expected number of emergency cases in an area. Because it is such a round approximation, patients are sometimes re-transferred elsewhere when there is no space, and, conversely, overcrowding occurs despite available beds at a nearby hospital. The ideal situation would be for the central dispatcher to have up-to-the-minute information on the actual number of beds available in each hospital in the system. In that case the following ideal sequence of events would occur:

(1) the dispatcher assigns the nearest available ambulance to a call;

(2) after picking up the patient, the ambulance driver informs the dispatcher whether hospitalization is required and if a specialist or particular equipment is needed immediately upon arrival at the hospital (to the extent that he is able to make such determination);

(3) if a hospital bed is required, the dispatcher determines the nearest hospital with an available bed;

(4) the dispatcher instructs the ambulance to proceed to that hospital;

(5) if the driver has requested special aid to be on hand, the dispatcher so advises the hospital.

The Department of Hospitals has already started developing a computer-based inventory system covering the municipal hospitals. Depending on the implementation timetable of various recommendations, the inventory could be made available initially to "its ambulances" and then, as decentralization of ambulances is carried out, the dispatcher at the Communications Bureau would receive this information, probably by telephone. When SPRINT is in operation, on-line input from the various municipal hospitals to the SPRINT computer can be considered. Extension of such an inventory system, where it does not yet exist, to non-municipal hospitals which provide emergency service would be encouraged.

Increased Availability of Ambulances

The simulation study showed that the combination of adding ambulances in a district and shifting ambulances closer to the point of demand produces improved service. The discussion here centers on low-cost means for increasing the effective number of ambulances. The alternative of simply buying more ambulances is an obvious one that will be excluded from the discussion.

Improve Screening of Calls: About 15% of all calls turn out to be "unnecessary," according to a recent statistical study of New York's emergency ambulance service.[1] More diligent efforts by personnel at the Communications Bureau to question the caller before deciding to dispatch an

---

[1] D.C. Dimendberg, An Analysis of the Ambulance Service, Department of Hospitals, City of New York, June, 1967.

ambulance is likely to reduce substantially the number of cases where ambulances are sent out on unnecessary calls. (This is the procedure followed in Baltimore, where only 8% of the calls turn out to be unnecessary.) By decreasing ambulance utilization in this way, service on true emergency calls will be improved.

Overtime Pay: Because drivers and attendants do not receive pay at overtime rates, crews are said to be reluctant to accept assignments a few minutes before their normal quitting time. If this is true, it would seem that the marginal cost of overtime labor is an inexpensive way to buy, in effect, more ambulances. In addition, by being able to offer overtime pay, an employee finishing one shift can be induced to work a second shift if his relief man fails to report to work. Such absenteeism effectively results in ambulances out of service.

Interchange of Crew Members: At present, ambulance attendants report to the nursing service in hospitals while the drivers are responsible to a garage foreman. This divided allegiance results in inflexible scheduling; for example, it is not possible to shift crews from one garage to another when there is a local shortage. Furthermore, if only a driver reports to work at one hospital, and only an attendant at another, pairing the two men to provide one ambulance, instead of keeping two ambulances idle, is administratively awkward. By divorcing the ambulance service from the hospital itself, the resulting centralized authority over crew members should simplify the handling of such problems.

The suggestion has also been made to provide the same training for both driver and attendant. This will permit complete interchangeability and, together with the change in policy on overtime pay, will result in fewer ambulances standing idle due to personnel absences.

Patient Acceptance Procedures: On certain classes of calls (e.g., psychiatric cases), the ambulance crew must wait at the hospital, after delivering the patient, for an inordinately long time before the ambulance is released and becomes available for reassignment. A change in the admission/acceptance procedure in such cases will increase the effective availability of ambulances.

Cost-Effectiveness Evaluation

Effectiveness

Average Response Time: Several simulation runs were conducted with ambulances stationed at various points in the district in order to compare the proposed system of dispersed ambulances to the other alternatives. The results are summarized in Exhibit 11.

It is clear that the dispersed system is superior to the other alternatives in terms of the improvement attainable; for example, ten dispersed ambulances will reduce the response time by 30% (from the base case) whereas the same ten ambulances distributed in optimal fashion (4:6) between hospital and satellite will produce only a 22% improvement. (Due to an adjustment in the mathematical model, the absolute values of the response times are not identical to the values shown on the figures and discussed earlier for identical ambulance configurations. This improvement does not change the earlier conclusions nor do they alter significantly the percentage improvements.)

Reduction of Long Delays: The average response time in itself is insufficient to portray the effect of the alternatives on reducing the frequency of those unfortunate occurrences where a patient waits for an excessively long time before an ambulance appears. Because of the great desirability of reducing the fraction of calls which are subject to long delays, the effect of the alternatives on this factor was also examined. The findings are summarized in Exhibit 12. Again, the dispersed pattern of operation is best by far: ten dispersed ambulances can be expected to reduce this fraction by 69% compared to a 48% reduction with a satellite.

Inasmuch as mathematical models never duplicate the real world exactly and because of statistical uncertainties in the findings, it is felt that although the absolute fractions of delayed calls, shown on Exhibit 12, are not necessarily accurate, the relative improvements shown for the alternatives are indeed meaningful.

Costs

The simulation results presented in the preceding section were devoted exclusively to portraying the effectiveness of the different alternatives. Now the reverse side of the coin, the costs, must be examined. Exhibit 13 displays the capital and operating costs for the various resources required. Using Exhibit 14, which indicates the staffing patterns, the costs shown on Exhibit 13 can be combined to reflect the incremental costs involved in going from the present configuration to each of the three alternative configurations; these are shown in Exhibit 15.

It is assumed that:

(1) on-the-street stations, with zero cost, are used for the dispersed ambulance systems;

(2) equivalent levels of supervision are employed for all alternatives, thus permitting accurate and fair comparisons to be made;

(3) shift-to-shift staffing patterns are the same for each alternative, as shown in Exhibit 14.

Cost-Effectiveness

The cost-effectiveness of alternative ways to reduce response time and to reduce excessive delays are shown in Exhibits 16 and 17. The dramatic superiority of the dispersed configurations is self-evident; eight dispersed ambulances (alternative D) are as effective as ten ambulances in a satellite system (alternative B) at about one-fourth the incremental cost per call. This is a significant conclusion and a compelling argument for a dispersed system. Furthermore, the relative ranking of the alternatives is clear and unambiguous even though the actual dollar figures in the cost/effectiveness columns of the exhibits may not be accurate enough for budgetry or accounting purposes.

These exhibits give the policy maker the opportunity to make an enlightened choice as to the degree of improvement he wishes to aim for, and the most efficient (least expensive) way to achieve that objective. Work is now underway to examine other areas of the city and to take the administrative steps necessary to translate these analytical findings into public policy.

Exhibit 11

EMERGENCY AMBULANCE SERVICE (B)

Average Response Time

Alternatives	7		10	
	Average Response Time	% Improve-Ment	Average Response Time	% Improve-ment
a. All Ambulances at Hospital	11.9'	0		
b. Optimal Allocation of Ambulances between Hospital and One Satellite	10.2'	14%	9.3'	22%
c. Totally Dispersed Ambulances	9.7'	18%	8.4'	30%

Exhibit 12

EMERGENCY AMBULANCE SERVICE (B)

Fraction of Calls With Response Time Greater Than Twenty Minutes

Number of Ambulances

Alternatives	7		10	
	Fraction	& Improve-ment	Fraction	& Improve-ment
a. All ambulances at Hospital	.099	0		
b. Optimal Allocation of Ambulances between Hospital and One Satellite	.073	26%	.051	48%
c. Totally Dispersed Ambulances	.065	34%	.03	69%

Exhibit 13

EMERGENCY AMBULANCE SERVICE (B)

Estimated Costs

		Purchase Price	Annual Cost	Total Annual Cost[1]
I.	Vehicle (ambulance)	$5,700	$950	$950
	Ambulance (6 yr. life)	4,900		
	Equipment (6 yr. life)	800		
II.	Vehicle (supervisory)		3,040	3,040
	Sedan (2 yr. life)	2,000	1,000	
	Equipment (5 yr. life)	200	40	
	Maintenance & Supplies		2,000	
III.	Vehicle Maintenance and Supplies		1,958	1,958
	Maintenance and Repair Supplies		657	
	Mechanics' Labor		505	
	Gasoline and Oil		296	
	Oxygen and Medical Supplies		500	
IV.	Ambulance Crew		14,505	72,525
	Motor-Vehicle Operator		8,175	
	Salary		6,500	
	Overhead (22%)		1,430	
	Uniform (allowance)		65	
	Food Allowance		180	
V.	Garage		13,600	13,600
	Rent		12,000	
	Heat		1,100	
	Light		300	
	Telephone		200	
VI.	Garage Staffing		14,516	72,580
	Foreman		9,395	
	Salary and Overhead		9,150	
	Uniform and food allowance		245	
	Clerk		5,121	
	Salary and overhead		4,941	
	Food Allowance		180	
VII.	Cruising Supervisor		9,395	46,975

1 For three shifts per day, seven days per week.
Allowing for vacations, illnesses, etc., five crews are required to staff three shifts per day, seven days per week.

Exhibit 14

EMERGENCY AMBULANCE SERVICE (B)

Deployment of Ambulances

Alternative	Tour 1		Tour 2		Tour 3		Total No. Ambulances In System	Additional Ambulances	Total Tours*	Added Tours
	E	T	E	T	E	T				
Seven ambulances (original pattern)	6	0	7	2	7	0	9	-	20	-
Eight ambulances	6	0	7	2	7	0	9	0	21	1
Nine ambulances	6	0	7	2	7	0	9	0	22	2
Ten ambulances	6	0	7	2	7	0	10	1	23	3

E = Emergency service   T = Transfer service

* Does not include transfer service

Note: A tour is defined here as an 8-hour work period for each of seven days.

Exhibit 15

EMERGENCY AMBULANCE SERVICE (B)

Incremental Costs of Alternatives

Alternative	Annual Cost	Monthly Cost
(A) 7 ambulances with a satellite	$86,180	$7,182
garage	13,600	
garage staffing	72,580	
(B) 10 ambulances with a satellite	161,613	$13,468
garage and garage staffing	86,180	
additional ambulance	950	
maintenance and supplies	1,958	
ambulance crews (5)	72,525	
(C) 7 ambulances dispersed	16,700	$1,400
cruising supervisor and vehicle	16,700*	
(D) 8 ambulances dispersed	40,800	$3,400
cruising supervisor and vehicle	16,700*	
ambulance crews (1-2/3) (to staff one seven-day tour)	24,100	
(E) 9 ambulances dispersed	64,900	5,408
cruising supervisor and vehicle,	16,700*	
ambulance crews (3-1/3) (to staff two seven-day tours)	48,200	
(F) 10 ambulances dispersed	92,133	7,700
cruising supervisor and vehicle	16,700*	
additional ambulance	950	
maintenance and supplies	1,958	
ambulance crews (5) (to staff 3 seven-day tours)	72,525	

*Because a supervisor can cover 20-30 ambulances, a district of 7-10 ambulances requires only one-third of his time; hence, only one-third of the cost is charged to this district.

Note: The cost of a dispersed system does not include credit for savings due to staff space, and equipment reductions at the base garage.

Exhibit 16

EMERGENCY AMBULANCE SERVICE (B)

Cost Effectiveness of Alternative Ways to Reduce Response Time

ALTERNATIVE	Effectiveness: Minutes Saved	Cost: $/Month	Cost/ Effectiveness: $ Per Minute	Cost Per Call
(A) 7 Ambulances with a Satellite	1.7	$7,182	$1.16	$1.96
(B) 10 Ambulances with a Satellite	2.6	$13,468	1.42	3.68
(C) 7 Ambulances Dispersed	2.2	1,400	.17	.38
(D) 8 Ambulances Dispersed	(2.6)	3,400	.36	.93
(E) 9 Ambulances Dispersed	(3.0)	5,408	.49	1.48
(F) 10 Ambulances Dispersed	3.5	7,700	.60	2.10

Exhibit 17

EMERGENCY AMBULANCE SERVICE (B)

Cost Effectiveness of Alternative Ways to Reduce Excessive Delays

ALTERNATIVE	Effectiveness: Percentage Points Reduced Below 20 Minutes	No. Calls Per Month Reduced Below 20 Minutes	Cost: $/ Month	Cost/ Effectiveness $ Per Call Reduced
(A) 7 Ambulances with a Satellite	2.6	95	$7,182	$75.50
(B) 10 Ambulances with a Satellite	4.8	176	13,468	76.50
(C) 7 Ambulances Dispersed	3.4	125	1,400	11.20
(D) 8 Ambulances Dispersed	(4.6)	168	3,400	20.20
(E) 9 Ambulances Dispersed	(5.8)	222	5,408	24.40
(F) 10 Ambulances Dispersed	6.9	252	7,700	30.60

Note: Figures in parenthesis are obtained by interpolation.

ANALYSIS OF AN ESTUARY[1]

For three generations pollution of the Delaware /Estuary/ has been self-evident. However, up to now there has never been available a detailed analysis of that pollution; what it is, who is responsible for it, what might be done, and what it would cost to abate it.[2]

The Delaware River Basin Commission

In 1961, Congress approved a federal-interstate compact establishing the Delaware River Basin Commission (DRBC). The Commission has five members, one each from the four signatory states (Delaware, Pennsylvania, New Jersey, and New York) and one from the Department of the Interior. Officially the DRBC members are the four governors and the Secretary of the Interior but, in fact, each can and does designate a voting alternate. The Commission - the only federal-interstate compact agency in the country - is charged with the formulation and implementation of a comprehensive plan for the long- and short-range development and use of the water resources in the Delaware River basin. Broad powers are delegated to DRBC.

> .../With/ regard to water quality management, the Commission is given the powers to undertake investigations and surveys and acquire, construct, operate, and maintain projects and facilities to control potentially adverse waste discharges and abate or dilute existing waste discharges affecting quality of the water resources of the basin. It may invoke, as complainant against waste discharges, the power and jurisdiction of water quality control agencies of the signatory parties. The Commission may assume jurisdiction to control future waste discharges whenever it determines after investigation and public hearings that the comprehensive plan requires it. The Commission, after public hearing, may also classify the waters of the basin

---

[1] Sources used in preparation of this case are listed in Appendix 2.

[2] U.S. Department of the Interior, Federal Water Pollution Control Administration, Delaware Estuary Comprehensive Study, Preliminary Report and Findings, 1966, p. i.

and establish standards for treatment of municipal, industrial, or other wastes. It also has the power, after hearings, to amend and repeal rules, regulations and standards. The signatory parties also pledge themselves to pass whatever legislation may be necessary to control wastes in accordance with the comprehensive plan. The Commission also has direct enforcement powers and may, after investigation and hearing, issue orders to any persons or person or public or private corporation to cease any discharge which it determines to be in violation of the rules and regulations that have been adopted. The orders are subject to appeal in any court of competent jurisdiction.[1]

Shortly after its formation, the DRBC requested that the Water Supply and Pollution Control Division[2] of the Public Health Service conduct an extensive study of the estuary that would provide the Commission with guidance in developing its comprehensive plan. The resulting analytic effort lasted over five years and utilized a core staff of over twenty engineers, scientists, and economists at FWPCA. When its Preliminary Report and Findings was published in June 1966, an estimated $1.2 million had been spent on the project. Efforts to refine and update some parts of the analysis are still underway.

The remainder of this case describes the procedures used and the conclusions reached by the FWPCA in its conduct of the Delaware Estuary Comprehensive Study (DECS). The objectives set for DECS were:

1. To determine the relationship between pollution sources and water quality,

2. To develop methods for managing water quality, and

3. To prepare a comprehensive program for the improvement and maintenance of water quality in the estuary.

Geographically, the study area covered the Delaware River from Trenton, New Jersey, to Liston Point, Delaware (extending far enough inland from the banks of the river to include all major water users and waste dischargers). This 86 mile stretch of the river encompasses one of the most heavily populated and industrialized areas in the country. (See Figure 1.)[3] The DECS staff took as its first task the evaluation of existing conditions in the estuary.

---

[1]Allen V. Kneese and Blair T. Bower, Managing Water Quality: Economics, Technology, Institutions (Johns Hopkins Press, Baltimore, 1968), pp. 280-281.

[2]This division has since been transferred to the Department of the Interior and renamed the Federal Water Pollution Control Administration (FWPCA).

[3]The thirty sections into which the estuary was divided for computational purposes are shown in Figure 1 and will be explained more fully below.

Figure 1

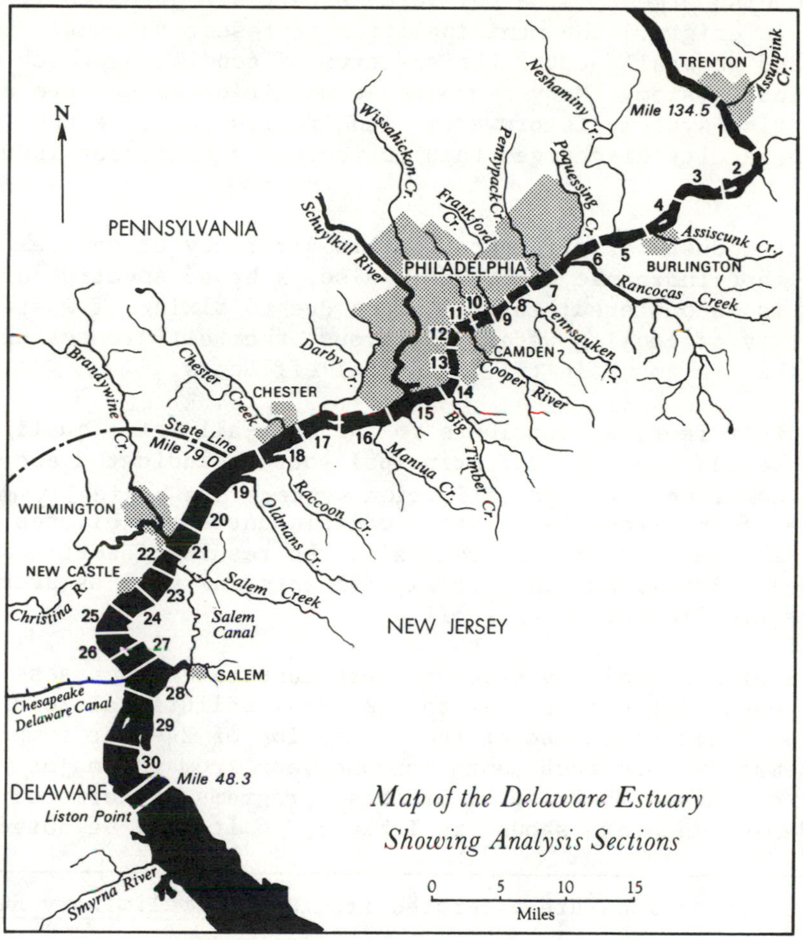

Map of the Delaware Estuary Showing Analysis Sections

Source: <u>DECS, Preliminary Report and Findings</u>.

Conditions in the Estuary

Present Waste Loads[1]

Waste discharges to the Delaware Estuary are principally municipal and industrial in origin. The municipalities represent the most significant waste sources and generally cover the spectrum of conditions which may exist within a municipal system. Many represent communities which have combined sewerage collection systems (stormwater runoff plus domestic and industrial waste). The large city discharges tend to include significant industrial waste loads.

Direct industrial effluents contain a variety of complex and unusual organic and inorganic compounds. Also, a broad spectrum of waste concentrations is encountered; this is often due to mixing of waste material with some quantity of cooling water. Numerous other differences due to production processes are found in the industrial effluents.

Two other factors contribute to the over-all water quality situation, but both result from the two principal sources indicated above. Stormwater overflows from combined sewerage collection systems are basically municipal in origin, and are of importance since they contain untreated diluted municipal waste. Bottom sludge deposits are generally the result of settleable solids discharged from municipal and industrial effluents, as well as storm water overflow and return from dredging spoil areas.

Sampling and analysis programs were undertaken to assess the contribution from each of these sources to the total pollutional loading to the estuary. The programs consisted of the collection of 24-hour composite samples approximately once each month for one year from the major waste sources to the estuary. The results of these programs in terms of carbonaceous oxygen demand load are shown in Table 1.[2] It will be noted that the

---

[1]The next three subsections are excerpted from DECS, Preliminary Report and Findings.

[2]One of the most significant relationships in water pollution is that between biochemical oxygen demand (BOD) and dissolved oxygen (DO). BOD is a measure of the quantity of dissolved oxygen removed from the water by the metabolic activity of microorganisms oxydizing materials in the water and can be expressed in lbs/day of oxygen demanding load. DO, in turn, is a commonly used index of water quality. Reasonably high levels (> 4.0 mg/l) are required to maintain a suitable population of organisms, including the aerobic bacteria that consume waste material in the water. When the DO drops to levels of less than 1.0 mg/l, conditions are likely to become anaerobic; that is, the decay of organic material takes place by means other than oxidation. The results are odors of hydrogen sulfide, the presence of organic sulfides, blackening of the water, and the destruction of fish and other aquatic organisms.

Table 1

Carbonaceous Biochemical Oxygen Demand Discharges to the Delaware Estuary - 1964

Source	Carbonaceous Oxygen Demand (lbs/day)	Per Cent
Philadelphia	450,000	
Other Municipal	210,000	
Stormwater Overflow	76,000	
Total Municipal	736,000	66%
Petroleum	99,000	
Chemicals	212,000	
Paper	33,000	
Other	26,000	
Total Industrial	370,000	34%
Total All Sources	1,106,000	100%

waste discharge is approximately 65% municipal and 35% industrial. On the other hand, the municipal discharges appear much less variable in flow and waste concentration than their industrial counterparts.

The geographical distribution of discharged load is presented in Table 4. The breakdown between municipal and industrial direct discharge can be examined along the length of the estuary.

At certain time of the year in specific areas of the estuary, a nitrogenous oxygen demand from municipal and industrial sources is estimated at about 600,000 lbs/day.

An additional oxygen demand is exerted on the estuary by bottom deposits of sludge. This demand is not shown in [Table 1].... The magnitude of the bottom deposit load is approximately 200,000 lbs/day.

Aside from the oxygen demand characteristics, several industrial discharges are contributing significant quantities of acidity to the estuary.

The major portion of the loads are discharged to the estuary after some waste reduction has taken place. Substantial differences may again be found among waste sources. On the one hand, the municipal treatment processes are relatively well defined. All municipal sources along the estuary possess at least primary treatment (about 30-39% removal of oxygen demanding load). The industrial situation is not as well defined. The process that constitutes "reduction" may cover in-plant modification, separation of cooling and process water, as well as a number of techniques designed to reduce wastes peculiar to a given industry: all these processes may be subsumed under the category of waste reduction. Using this definition, industrial waste reduction along the estuary ranges from none (zero per cent removal) to high secondary-tertiary (90-98% removal). Recognizing the highly variable nature of treatment, it is still possible to evaluate an effective system per cent removal of raw waste for the sources along the estuary taken as a whole. At present (1964) this estimated system per cent removal is about 50%.

The stormwater overflow discharges were found to possess a distinctly individual character. In terms of absolute magnitude, the load does not appear large. However, the input to the estuary is through a series of impulses approximately random in both magnitude and interval of recurrence. Hence it may be responsible for some oxygen depletion for short periods of time. The stormwater discharge contains high concentrations of coliform bacteria that are also discharged on an intermittent basis. Another more important factor, which is not readily quantified, is the esthetic effect attributable to these overflows. The occurrence of overflows results in the discharge of solids, floating material, and miscellaneous flotsam which are normally trapped by the treatment plant. Although this material may not constitute a large source of oxygen demanding pollution, its presence is quite objectionable and certainly may be termed pollution by the general public.

Future Waste Loads Before Processing

[Projections of future loads as derived by the DECS staff are shown in Table 2.]

Table 2

Projected Waste Loads Before Reduction

	Carbonaceous Oxygen Demand (lbs/day)		
	1964	1975	2010
Industrial	700,000	1,200,000	4,600,000
Municipal	1,200,000	2,800,000	6,100,000

The future municipal loads are principally caused by the discharges from eight waste treatment plants along the estuary. [A] municipal population projection provides the basis for estimating the increased load over time. Certain municipal trends are assumed to exist. For example, the service area of the plants is assumed to expand over the years; in addition, it is postulated that at irregular, but distinct intervals in time, new political subdivisions will be added to the municipalities. Such considerations lead to a dynamic concept of the ratio of served to total population.

Consideration is also given to two effects which cause an increase in per capita domestic load over time. One of these is the growing use of domestic garbage disposal units, and the second is the trend toward more utilization of significant water-using home appliances such as dishwashers and automatic washers by the general public.

Finally, account is taken of the increasing numbers of municipally-served industries. The load from these is also reflected in the municipal projections as a factor acting to increase per capita daily load.

The future industrial loads were obtained from an analysis using Standard Industrial Classifications (SIC's).... Statistical estimates of production in dollars/year have been made for industries discharging directly to the estuary. The future production for direct discharging industries in the SIC's is then projected over time. A further consideration is the change over time of waste load per unit of production due to many factors affecting trends in technology. From this trend the future waste load before treatment was derived.

Present Water Quality

The present (1964) water quality of the Delaware Estuary was determined from a series of weekly sampling runs, made by the DECS staff, together with data collected by the U.S. Geological Survey, the city of Philadelphia, and the State of Delaware. A number of water quality parameters were investigated, including water temperature, dissolved oxygen, nitrogen constituents, alkalinity and coliform bacteria.

On the basis of these data, a summary of present water quality is given below. For purposes of this summary, dissolved oxygen, coliform bacteria, chlorides, and alkalinity are used as primary indicators of water quality.

In general, the water quality at the head of tide at Trenton, N.J., is excellent, but begins to deteriorate immediately. From Torresdale, Pa., Section 7, to below the Pennsylvania-Delaware state line, Section 19, the deterioration is extreme; as a result of waste discharges, dissolved oxygen is almost completely depleted in some locations and production of gases from anaerobic organic deposits is sometimes noted. The concentration of coliform bacteria resulting primarily from unchlorinated municipal wastes is very high in the same stretch of river. Surface discoloration due to the release of oil from vessels and surrounding refineries is a common occurrence from Philadelphia to below the state line. Acid conditions due to industrial waste discharges have been observed for several miles above and below the Pennsylvania-Delaware state line.

Dissolved Oxygen (DO)

The most critical period [for dissolved oxygen] is the July-September summer months during which the average dissolved oxygen was below 4.0 mg/l from about Section 8 to Section 20 and below 3.0 mg/l between Section 10 and Section 19. On any given day, the dissolved oxygen can be considerably below these averages: the continuous water quality monitor records of the U.S.G.S. indicate that complete exhaustion of the oxygen often results during this period in the critical sections. The DO variability both within a day and throughout the year is due to many factors including tidal and wind phenomena which can cause short-term changes ... and the seasonal variation of water temperature. This latter is most important....

Coliform Bacteria

The coliform group is used as a general bacterial indicator and is composed of usually nonpathogenic organisms always found in sewage. Coliform bacteria are also found in soil and vegetation, so that the presence of this group does not necessarily indicate that disease producing organisms are present, but that they may be. High counts are generally found in the same 40 mile stretch from Torresdale to the Delaware Memorial Bridge in which the major DO problem exists.

Alkalinity

[Alkalinity was found to be substantially below expected levels because of acid discharges. This discrepancy was most pronounced in the area immediately above and below Section 22.]

Chlorides

Salt water intrusion which limits the use of water in the portion of the estuary below Philadelphia is a serious problem whenever low flow conditions persist for relatively long periods of time.

Effects of Existing Water Quality

The more readily observable effects of current water quality in the estuary can be catalogued as follows:

1. Municipal: Three municipalities maintain treatment plants that withdraw water from the estuary and process it for drinking purposes. All risk contamination from excessive salinity and high levels of municipal and industrial waste.

2. Industrial: Industry withdraws almost 5 billion gallons of water per day from the estuary primarily for cooling purposes. Too much dissolved oxygen or high level of salinity are both detrimental because they encourage corrosion. Other water quality characteristics may be important to particular industrial processes.

3. Recreational: Residential and industrial development along the estuary have severely limited its development for recreational purposes. Present use of the estuary for swimming, boating, water skiing, and sport fishing is only a small fraction of its potential. This is attributable to both poor water quality and limited access. Boating and fishing are the main noncontact activities. High concentrations of coliform bacteria prohibit officially sanctioned water contact sports in many locations. Many persons disregard these conditions, however, and some swimming and water skiing occur throughout the estuary.

4. Fish: Commercial fishing activity in the estuary has declined from a peak estimated at 25 million pounds in 1900, to about 1.5 million pounds in 1920, to only 80,000 pounds in recent years. Shad, sturgeon, striped bass, weakfish, and white perch were all important commercially. (Estuary sturgeon once supplied much of the world's caviar market.) Exact reasons for the decline in the fish population are hard to pinpoint. There are several possibilities: (2) excessive waste discharge into the estuary, (b) overfishing so that effective breeding levels no longer exist, (c) introduction of predaceous fish in the upper river, (d) siltation from farmland, suburban development, and river dredging covering spawning grounds.

The DECS Committee Structure

Early in the project, the DECS staff enlisted the help of various groups in forming three advisory committees to assist in development of the over-all comprehensive plan and to provide feedback as the work progressed. The three committees were the Policy Advisory Committee (PAC), the Technical Advisory Committee (TAC), and the Water Use Advisory Committee (WUAC).

The membership of PAC included representatives from the various agencies that have legal power to abate pollution and implement a comprehensive plan: FWPCA, DRBC, the Pennsylvania and New Jersey Health Departments, and Delaware's Water Pollution Commission. Its functions were to obtain the support of state agencies for pollution abatement plans, to represent the interests of the individual states (and the Federal Government) during the development of those plans, and to ensure that existing state abatement programs were integrated into the comprehensive plan where possible. The committee also agreed to make specific recommendations to DRBC on a final set of water quality objectives for the estuary when the analysis was completed. From July 1963 to June 1966, PAC met seventeen times. Members agreed that their activities produced a regional consciousness that had not previously existed.

TAC consisted of representatives of agencies participating directly in the study work, together with individual technical experts on particular aspects of water quality control. Its primary activities included technical review of DECS reports, providing technical assistance to PAC and WUAC, and helping FWPCA plan each stage of the study. It also was responsible for obtaining cost estimates from local industry and arranging the sampling program of river water quality. Both these efforts provided vitally needed information to the DECS staff. Meetings were held once a month.

Of the three committees, WUAC was by far the largest. Its objectives were to advise DECS on the water use and water quality needs and desires of the people, to act as a public relations group, and to perform other nontechnical tasks. Four subcommittees made up the over-all WUAC. The first, Recreational, Conservation, Fish, and Wildlife, had representatives from sixteen organizations such as the Audubon Society, Pennsylvania Federation of Sportsman's Clubs, and the Wilmington Garden Club. The General Public Subcommittee was more diverse. Twenty-four organizations were included, ranging from the League of Women Voters and the Neshaminy Watershed Association to the American Society of Civil Engineers and a number of state and local chambers of commerce. The Industry Subcommittee was made up of representatives from forty-five large companies in the area. The fourth subcommittee, Local Governments and Planning Agencies, consisted of representatives of all major cities in the study area, several regional associations of smaller municipalities, and a number of planning commissions.

WUAC began its work with two formal meetings held with each of the four subcommittees. At these meetings the DECS Project Director and Technical Director outlined the objectives of the study, the methodology being used, and the functions of WUAC. Each subcommittee then elected a chairman to be its representative to WUAC. This central WUAC group met every two to three months for the remainder of the study. Usually the Industry Subcommittee met once or twice before each WUAC meeting. Meetings of the remaining subcommittees were held much less frequently, most of their work being done through correspondence. This reflected the fact that most members of these three subcommittees were volunteers who had to take time off from their jobs to attend meetings. Participation by the industry representatives, on the other hand, was part of their normal work.

Setting Objectives

From the beginning, the DECS project staff believed that its work would be more readily accepted if it dealt with the costs and effectiveness of a number of different water quality objectives for the estuary. A lower bound on the range of possible objectives was set at the quality levels then existing (1964). An upper bound was established by estimating what water quality levels would be achieved if all sources processed their waste discharges to the maximum feasible extent. WUAC's help was then obtained to determine a suitable set of intermediate objectives to be considered by the analysis.

WUAC divided its work into two phases. The first consisted of soliciting from each subcommittee member, in narrative form, his water use needs and desires. The narratives were summarized by the subcommittee chairmen and these four responses condensed to one report by the DECS staff. The second phase was designed to provide more specific information regarding where, along the estuary, the members of WUAC wanted the water suitable for various uses and what specific levels for water quality parameters would have to be met for each use.

The first part of the second phase was accomplished without difficulty although there was little over-all agreement between WUAC members on what uses should be possible at each location. Developing specific quality standards for each use was quite another matter. The Local Governments and Industry subcommittees were able to develop these standards with relative ease since they included professionals in their membership. Many of the organizations in the other two subcommittees, however, were not even familiar with the language of water pollution control. DECS staff members, therefore, worked closely with these two subcommittees to help them prepare numerical standards.

On the basis of WUAC's completed reports, DECS developed five specific objective sets as follows (the water quality goals for each objective set are shown in Table 3):

Objective Set I. This set represents the greatest increase in water use and water quality among all of the objective sets. Water contact recreation is indicated in the upper and lower reaches of the estuary. Sport and commercial fishing was set at relatively high levels consistent with the make-up of the region. A minimum daily average DO goal of 6.0 mg/l is included for anadromous fish passage during the passage periods. Thus anadromous fish passage is included as a definitive part of the water quality management program. Fresh water inflow control will be necessary to repulse high chloride concentrations to Chester, Pa., thereby creating a potential municipal and industrial water supply use.

Objective Set II. The area of water contact recreation is reduced somewhat from that of Objective Set I (OS-I). A reduction in dissolved oxygen (DO) is considered to result in a concomitant reduction in sport and commercial fishing. DO goals for anadromous fish passage remain as in OS-I. Chloride control would be necessary to prevent salt water intrusion above the Schuylkill River.

Objective Set III. This set is similar in all respects to OS-II except for the following three changes. First, the specific DO criteria for anadromous fish passage is not imposed. However, substantial increases in anadromous fish passage will result from the treatment requirements imposed to control DO during the summer assuming that the waste load reductions are carried out during the anadromous fish run periods. Second, a general decrease in the sport and commercial fishing potential is imposed through a lowering of the DO requirements. Third, the quality at points of municipal water supply were reduced.

Objective Set IV. This set represents a slight increase over present levels in water contact recreation and fishing in the lower reaches of the estuary. Generally, quality requirements are increased slightly over 1964 conditions (OS-V) representing a minimally enhanced environment.

Objective Set V. This set represents a maintenance of 1964 conditions, i.e., a prevention of further water quality deterioration.

The water uses protected by each objective set are presented graphically in Figure 2. This chart indicates the sections of the estuary for which the various water uses were considered.

A Model of the Estuary

The underpinnings of any successful analysis were believed by the DECS staff to be the development of a clear understanding of the cause and effect relationships between waste discharges and water quality that exist in the estuarine environment. Thus, under the supervision of the DECS technical director, work was begun on a mathematical model that would trace the impact on water quality of various organic waste loads introduced at different points in the estuary. The task was greatly complicated because the estuarine environment is characterized by tidal action, large expanses of air-water interface, complex hydraulic characteristics, and involved patterns of inflow. It is suspected, moreover, that photosynthesis may affect an estuary's characteristics more than those of a simple flowing stream.

The model that was developed focused on dissolved oxygen (DO) and viewed the "system" as a composite of two subsystems; the biochemical oxygen demand (BOD) subsystem and the dissolved oxygen subsystem (Figure 3). In any part of the estuary, the level of BOD is determined by several considerations. Most obvious, of course, is the amount of waste material dumped into that part of the estuary. Also of importance are the addition and removal of BOD by the unidirectional flow of the river and the addition and removal of BOD by oscillation of the tides. In addition, BOD is transmitted from one part of the estuary to another by eddy currents. Finally, BOD decreases through natural decay processes. The level of DO in any part of the estuary is determined by these same factors plus the rate of reaeration (through turbulence, for example) and other influences such as photosynthesis. The model was intended to replicate the effect of these physical processes at given water temperatures and waste load inputs.

To do this, the model builders considered the estuary in sections. (Thirty sections were used between Trenton, New Jersey, and Liston Point, Delaware. This represented a compromise between the requirement that conditions within a section be essentially uniform and the need to keep the total number of sections acceptably low for computational purposes. Each section was either 10,000 or 20,000 feet long.) For each section, two mass balance equations were written, one for the BOD subsystem and one for the DO subsystem. In somewhat simplified form, these equations are as follows:

Table 3

Comparison of Water Quality Goals for Objective Sets 1-5
(Set 5 represents conditions in 1964)

WATER QUALITY PARAMETER:	SET:	1	2	3	4	5	6	7	8	9	10	11	12	13	14	15	16	17	18	19	20	21	22	23	24	25	26	27	28	29	30
SECTION:		Trenton			Bristol		Torresdale	Philadelphia					Camden						Chester			Wilmington			New Castle						Liston Point
Dissolved oxygen, mg/l, summer average	1	6.5						6.5		5.5		4.5						4.5	5.5		5.5	6.5						6.5	7.5		7.5
	2	5.5						5.5	4.0											4.0	5.0							5.0		6.5	
	3	5.5						5.5	3.0													3.0	4.5					4.5	6.5		6.5
	4	4.0						4.0	2.5														2.5		3.5					5.5	
	5		7.0		5.1			5.8							1.0					1.0				4.2						7.1	
Chlorides, mg/l, max. 15-day mean	1																50		250												
	2														50		250														
	3														50		250														
	4												50			250															
	5							50				100			250	400			1,340			2,400									
Coliforms, #/100 ml, 5/30 - 9/15	1	4,000[a]					4,000[a]	5,000[a]										5,000[a]			5,000[b]			4,000[a]							4,000[a]
	2	4,000[a]			4,000[a]		5,000[a]		5,000[b]																		5,000[b]			4,000[a]	
	3		4,000[a]			5,000[b]																						5,000[b]		4,000[a]	
	4	5,000[b]																									5,000[b]			4,000[a]	
Monthly geometric mean →	5		2,600		2,700		6,800			25,000				63,000			66,000		51,000		22,000			7,000				1,900		700	
Turbidity, turbidity units, 5/30 - 9/15	1	N.L.					N.L.	N.L.+30															N.L.+30	N.L.							N.L.
	2	N.L.			N.L.	N.L.+30																					N.L.+30			N.L.	
	3		N.L.			N.L.+30																						N.L.+30	N.L.		
	4	N.L.+30																									N.L.+30			N.L.	
Maximum level →	5		23		28		29		24					22			24		27		27			37			43			43	
pH, pH units, desirable range, 5/30 - 9/15	1				7.0-8.5			6.5-8.5															6.5-8.5					7.0-8.5			
	2		7.0-8.5			6.5-8.5																					6.5-8.5			7.0-8.5	
	3		7.0-8.5			6.5-8.5																						6.5-8.5		7.0-8.5	
	4	6.5-8.5						6.5-8.5	Present levels													Present levels			6.5-8.5					7.0-8.5	
Present range →	5			7.0-8.7					6.9-7.6							6.6-7.3				6.4-7.0						5.6-7.6				6.1-7.8	
Alkilinity, mg/l, desirable range	1	20-50						20-50	20-120																						20-120
	2	20-50						20-50	20-120																					20-120	
	3	20-50						20-50	20-120																						20-120
	4	20-50						20-50	Present levels																						Present levels
Present range →	5		25-51					33-46								34-50				13-41						4-25				10-49	
Hardness, mg/l, monthly mean	1	95						95	150										150												
	2	95						95	150								150														
	3	95						95	150								150														
	4	95						95	150						150																
	5		83										122						467												
Phenols, mg/l, monthly mean	1	.001																	.001	.01											.01
	2	.001						.001	.005								.005	.01													.01
	3	.001						.001	.005								.005	.01													.01
	4	.005													.005	.01															
	5		.01		.02		.03			.04					.03		.05		.05			.06									
SECTION:		1	2	3	4	5	6	7	8	9	10	11	12	13	14	15	16	17	18	19	20	21	22	23	24	25	26	27	28	29	30

a. Maximum level. *b. Monthly geometric mean.* N.L. = *Natural levels*

Source: Kneese and Bower, Managing Water Quality: Economics, Technology, Institutions.

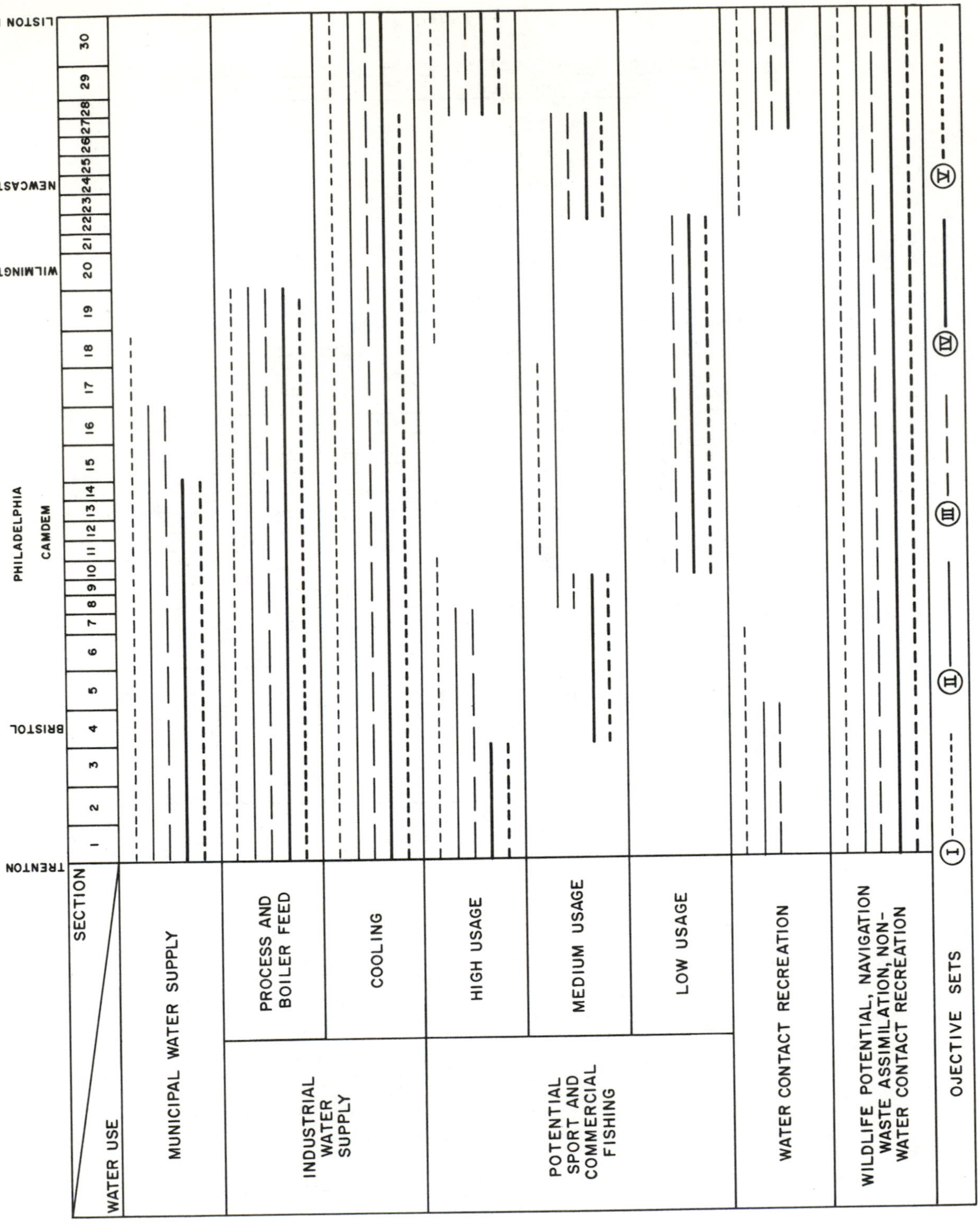

Figure 2 WATER USES FOR OBJECTIVE SETS I - V

Figure 3

Model of Dissolved Oxygen System, Delaware Estuary

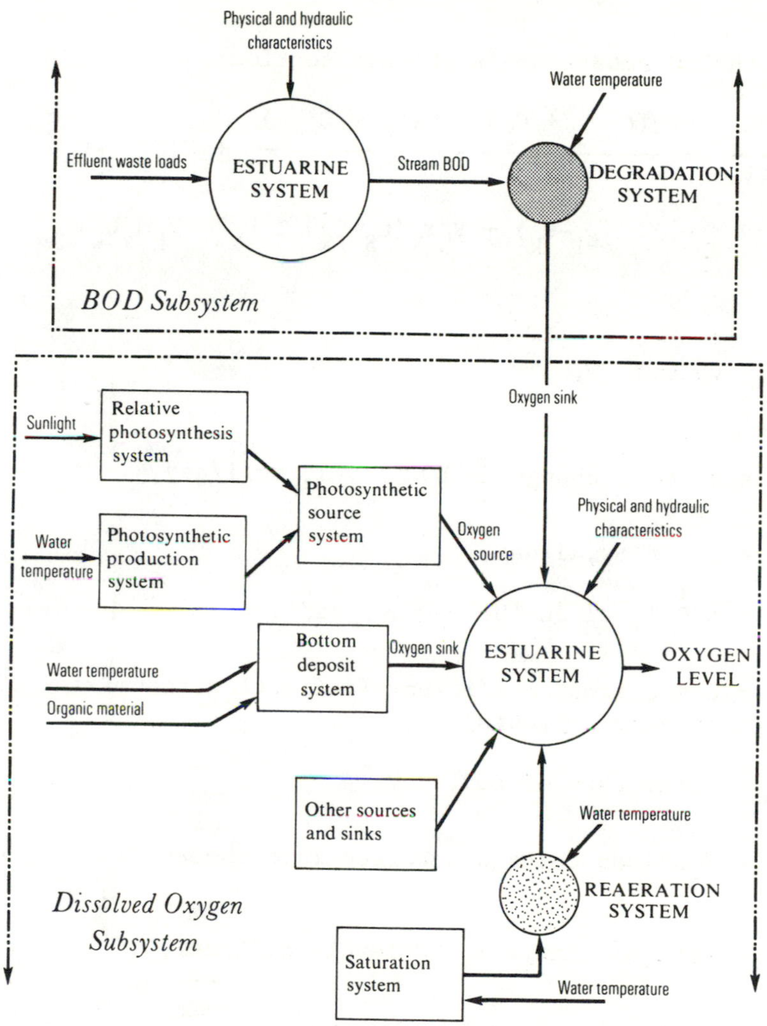

Source: Kneese and Bower, Managing Water Quality: Economics, Technology, Institutions.

(a) For the BOD subsystem in the kth section:

$$V_k \frac{dL_k}{dt} = \frac{Q(L_{k-1} + L_k)}{2} - \frac{Q(L_k + L_{k+1})}{2} + E(L_{k-1} - L_k)$$

$$+ E(L_{k+1} - L_k) - V_k d_k L_k + J_k .$$

(b) For the DO subsystem in the kth section:

$$V_k \frac{dC_k}{dt} = \frac{Q(C_{k-1} + C_k)}{2} - \frac{Q(C_k + C_{k+1})}{2} + E(C_{k-1} - C_k)$$

$$+ E(C_{k+1} - C_k) + V_k r_k (C_S - C_k) \pm P_k - V_k d_k L_k$$

where

V_k = volume, l,

$\frac{dL_k}{dt}$ = rate of change in BOD level, mg/l/day,

Q = net flow, l/day,

L_k = BOD level in the section, mg/l,

E = dispersion coefficient (reflecting the mixing effect of eddy currents), l/day,

d_k = decay rate of BOD, days^{-1}

J_k = BOD load being discharged into the section, mg/day,

$\frac{dC_k}{dt}$ = rate of change in DO level, mg/l/day,

C_k = DO level in the section, mg/l,

r_k = reaeration rate, days^{-1},

C_S = saturation level of DO, mg/l, and

P_k = other sources or sinks of DO acting on the section, mg/day.

To clarify the physical meanings of the various terms in these two equations, the equation for DO has been separated into its constituent parts and each part identified on the block diagram shown in Figure 4. The entire system consists of two sets of thirty (linear differential) equations.

The model was calibrated by testing its predictions against actual observations of DO. Values for C_S, E, d_k, and r_k were taken from various engineering studies. (C_S, d_k, and r_k are dependent on water temperature.) The waste load, J, for each section was obtained by sampling the large municipal and industrial plants for one year and adjusting the figures upward based on estimates for the smaller plants. Also included in the total load were estimates of the BOD contribution of tributaries and stormwater runoff. P loads were estimated from a program of bottom sampling. (Photosynthesis was neglected since preliminary data indicated that its effects were negligible.) The waste loading and DO sink estimates are shown in Table 4. Using these various values in the model produced computed levels of DO that compared with actual levels as shown in Figure 5.

If the simplifying assumption is made that the mass balance equations do not vary with time, then one output to the process of solving the model is a matrix of transfer functions. These functions enable the analyst to determine what effect a change in waste load in one section will have on either the BOD or DO in any other section. And because the basic equations are linear, the impact of waste loadings from each of several (or all) sections on any one section can be added to determine the total effect on that one section. Using the transfer functions, therefore, makes it possible to calculate simply and rapidly the effects on DO (or BOD) throughout the estuary of various levels of waste load control in the thirty sections. Numerous sets of these transfer functions were computed for different fresh water inflow conditions, decay rates, and reaeration rates.

In addition to developing the "steady-state" transfer matrices, the DECS staff also took steps to make the model time dependent. By introducing empirically derived lag factors between the time a waste load was introduced in one section and the time that it had an impact on each other section, they were able to test the effect of periodic, transient, or random waste loads. These considerations are important because aquatic life may suffer from temporary conditions that are not reflected in the steady-state analyses.

A final feature of the model was its usefulness in investigating aspects of water quality other than DO. If, for example, the decay mechanism is removed in the equation for BOD, then it becomes suitable for such nondecaying variables as alkalinity, pH, and chlorides.

Figure 4

Simplified Mass Balance on Section k

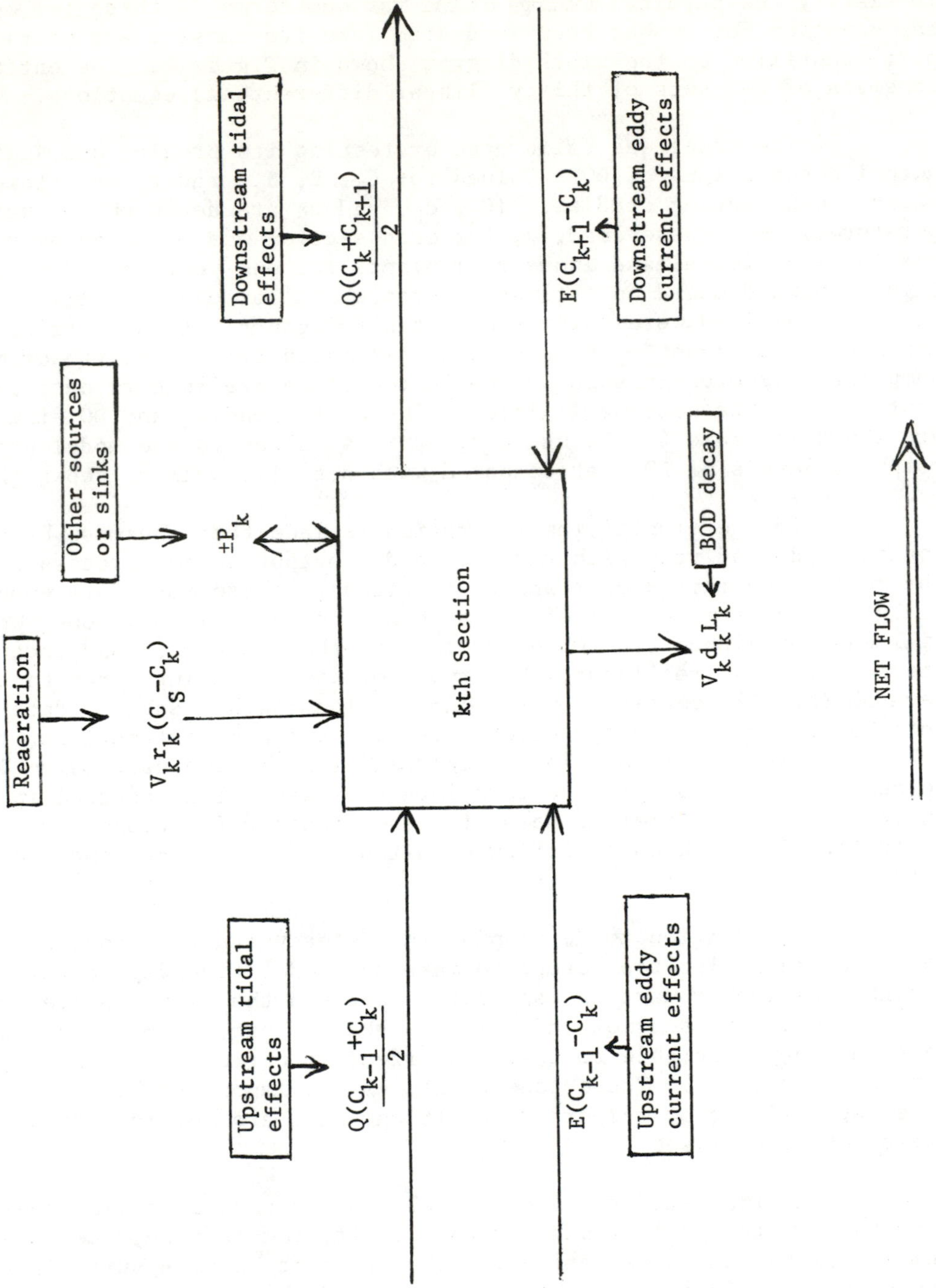

Figure 5

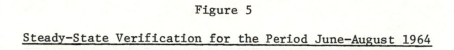

Steady-State Verification for the Period June-August 1964

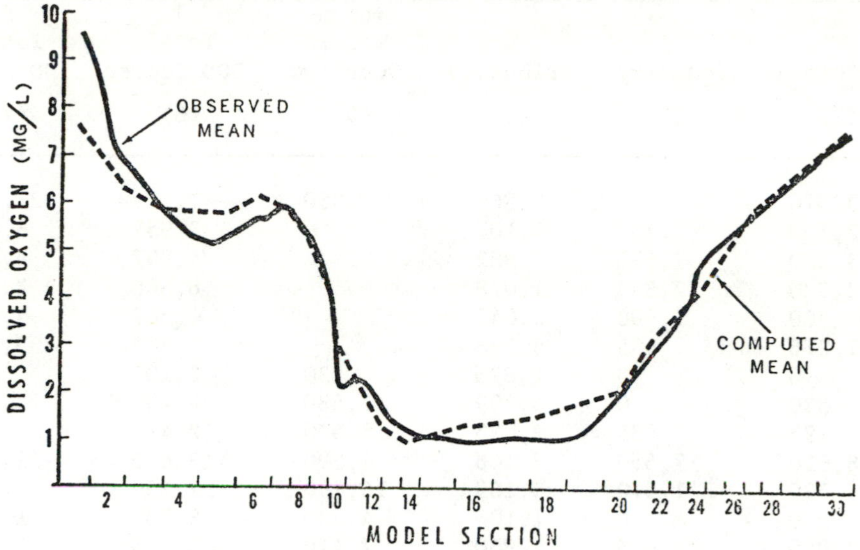

Source: Smith and Morris, "Systems Analysis for Optimal Water Quality Management."

Table 4

1964 Waste Loading in the Delaware Estuary, in Pounds per Day of Carbonaceous Biochemical Oxygen Demand

Section	Municipal	Industry	Tributary	Storm-Water Overflow	J, Total BOD Source	P, Total DO Sink
(1)	(2)	(3)	(4)	(5)	(6)	(7)
1	3,570	0	2,869	1,360	7,799	22,280
2	2,100	2,750	4,107		8,957	8,622
3	3,380	1,635	982		5,997	4,140
4	2,720	2,850	1,078		6,648	2,700
5	900	1,400	2,047		4,347	4,800
6	1,075	435	5,798		7,308	5,040
7	0	0	1,875	230	2,105	890
8	520	0	4,309	1,580	6,409	2,125
9	795	35	3,095	8,570	12,496	2,250
10	128,610	7,550	3,146	4,390	143,695	2,250
11	720	1,570	3,189	16,780	22,259	5,760
12	0	0	1,105	4,480	5,585	1,350
13	62,080	13,925	1,800	7,410	85,215	3,240
14	174,520	19,670	1,566	2,080	197,836	3,960
15	3,330	39,550	17,649	18,860	79,389	14,700
16	158,070	25,650	3,761		187,481	6,750
17	14,575	42,420	8,678	1,950	67,623	11,475
18	10,185	14,535	6,003		30,723	7,200
19	1,820	64,360	1,668		67,848	16,200
20	0	0	1,071		1,071	15,750
21	87,400	8,480	6,848	8,320	111,048	6,930
22	0	116,755	294		117,049	6,000
23	1,870	0	306		2,176	13,050
24	0	370	421		791	11,000
25	0	0	855		855	9,300
26	0	2,500	1,416		3,916	12,000
27	660	0	322		992	15,000
28	1,730	0	9,078		10,808	15,000
29	0	0	5,011		5,011	0
30	0	0	5,509		5,509	0
Totals	660,630	366,440	174,719	76,010	1,277,799	229,762

Source: Pence, Jeglic, Thomann, "Time-Varying Dissolved-Oxygen Model."

Alternative Programs[1]

The methods by which water quality may be improved include: 1) limiting effluent discharge to the estuary by requiring reduction of wastes before discharge, 2) piping of the wastes to a place or places where the discharges will have a reduced economic and/or social effect, 3) flow regulation, 4) removal of benthic sludge deposits, 5) in-stream aeration, and 6) control of stormwater discharges. A successful comprehensive program to achieve a particular water use and water quality objective set might incorporate several of these possibilities but in the final analysis should depend primarily on reduction of waste at the source since this has a higher assurance of successful control. Piping of wastes creates chloride control problems by diverting flow from the estuary and new pollution problems in the discharge area. Maintenance of minimum flows has important chloride control effects but does not significantly alter summer average dissolved oxygen levels. However, transient releases of significant amounts of fresh-water inflow can be beneficial in specific instances. Little is known of the practicability of the in-stream aeration of an estuary. The size of the operation may cause difficulties in terms of other uses of the estuary (i.e., navigation, recreation) and in any event would only improve DO without improving other water quality parameters. In-stream aeration can be considered, however, as a transient supplement to effluent waste removal. Sludge removal and stormwater overflow control also fall into the category of supplemental control measures to be considered in conjunction with effluent control.

There are many ways of controlling the discharge of waste to the estuary to satisfy a specified water quality objective. Several different categories have been investigated. All relate primarily to the control of waste sources to improve DO. If the control scheme to meet a specific DO objective did not meet all other variables (e.g., bacteria) separate control procedures (e.g., disinfection) were then imposed. The control programs investigated are:

1. Uniform Treatment - Each waste discharger must remove the same per cent of the "raw" load (the load before any waste reduction). [This is the most commonly used approach in existing programs of water quality management. Another common scheme is to have the largest sources remove the maximum possible amount of their load.]

2. Zoned-Uniform Treatment - The estuary is divided into a series of zones and a uniform treatment level (same percentage reduction of the "raw" load) is found for each of the zones that will satisfy the DO goal at least cost to the region.

3. Municipal-Industrial Category - A uniform treatment level is found for all municipalities and another is found for all industries that will satisfy the DO objective at least cost to the region.

---

[1] The next three sections of the case are excerpts from DECS, <u>Preliminary Report and Findings</u>.

4. Cost Minimization - This program computes the amount of waste to be removed at individual effluent sources so as to secure the DO objective at least cost to the region.

In all of these programs it is assumed that no source will discharge any more waste than is presently being discharged and that all sources which are now below primary treatment (35% removal) will be raised to at least that level.

Program Costs

Forty-four industries and municipalities which comprise approximately 97% of the 1964 carbonaceous oxygen demand waste discharge to the estuary were included in the evaluation of the alternative programs. The underlying systems on which these analyses were based are for steady-state flows of 3000 cfs at Trenton. Some additional estimates were made for flows of 4000 and 6000 cfs at Trenton.

Table 5 shows the estimated costs (construction cost plus the present value of operation and maintenance costs at a 3% discount rate and a 20-year time horizon) to reach the DO objectives under each of the alternative control programs. [See Appendix 1 for a discussion of the procedures used in deriving these costs.] Table 6 shows the waste reduction requirements for reaching the DO objectives. . . . Since the waste removal programs were based on DO improvement, the pH and bacterial objectives were not met in all cases. The additional cost of neutralization and chlorination in these cases was also calculated. However, the cost of additional reservoir storage for flow regulation to control chloride levels in the estuary is not included. Table 7 shows the total costs of the alternatives when the costs of chlorination and pH control are added.

The DO objective for Objective Set I can be reached only by 92%-98% removal of all carbonaceous waste sources plus in-stream aeration and dredging of sludge deposits at an estimated cost of 460 million dollars. However, estimating the cost of removals above the 85%-90% removal level is difficult since only pilot tertiary treatment plant data exist. Thus a program recommending 92%-98% removal would require additional work on large-scale advanced treatment processes and costs. The cost of attaining the other objective sets differ due to the type of program used. In OS-II and OS-III about 1 to 2 million dollars were necessary for stream aeration in some upper sections to cope with natural undesirable quality conditions. Many sources would have to make improvements to keep their present level of discharge as is required for Objective Set V. This cost is approximately 30 million dollars. Five sources must raise their treatment to primary treatment at a total cost of 10 million dollars. These costs of maintaining existing conditions are included in the tables. Studies of these alternatives at different steady fresh-water inflows showed changes in costs as the flow increased. Under certain water quality objectives and types of waste reduction program the cost of achieving the DO goal was higher at 6000 cfs than at 3000 cfs. This is basically due to a "shift" in the DO profile requiring certain waste sources to remove additional amounts of waste load at a subsequent additional cost.

Table 5

Summary of Total Costs of Dissolved Oxygen Objectives* **
Flow at Trenton = 3000 cfs

Estimated Costs in Millions of Dollars (Present Value)

Obj. Set	Uniform Treat.			Zoned††			Municipal Industrial Category			Cost Minimization		
	Cap.***	O&M#	Total	Cap.	O&M	Total	Cap.	O&M	Total	Cap.	O&M	Total
I	180	280 (19.0)##	460###	180	280 (19.0)	460	180	280 (19.0)	460	180	280 (19.0)	460
II	135	180 (12.0)	315†	105	145 (10.0)	250	135	180 (12.0)	315	115	100 (7.0)	215
III	75	80 (5.5)	155	50	70 (4.5)	120	75	45 (3.0)	120	50	35 (2.5)	85
IV	55	75 (5.0)	130	40	40 (2.5)	80	50	30 (2.0)	90	40	25 (1.5)	65

Notes:
- * Costs include cost of maintaining present (1964) conditions.
- ** Costs reflect waste load conditions projected to 1975-1980.
- *** Capital costs
- # Operation and maintenance costs - discounted to present value at 3% - 20 yr.
- ## Annual operation and maintenance costs in millions of dollars/year.
- ### HISEC-TER (92-98% removal) for all waste sources for all programs. Includes in-stream aeration cost of $20 million.
- † OS-II & OS-III for all programs include $1-2 million for either sludge removal or aeration to meet goals in Sections #3 and #4.
- †† The zones correspond to the sections shown in Figure 1 as follows:

Zone	Sections
I	1 - 6
II	7 - 14
III	15 - 18
IV	19 - 30

Table 6

Summary of Waste Reduction Requirements to Meet Dissolved Oxygen Objectives
Flow at Trenton = 3000 cfs

% Removal Based on 1964 Waste Loads

Obj. Set	Uniform Treat.: No. of Waste Sources Involved	Uniform Treat.: Minimum* Treatment (Computed % Removal)	Zoned: No. of Waste Sources Involved	Zoned: Minimum* Treatment (Computed % Removal)	Industrial Category: No. of Waste Sources Involved	Industrial Category: Minimum* Treatment (Computed % Removal)	Cost Minimization: No. of Waste Sources Involved	Cost Minimization: Treat.** Range (Computed % Removal)
I	22M-22I***	HISEC-TER (92-98%)#	22M-22I	All Zones HISEC-TER (92-98%)#	22M-22I	HISEC-TER (92-98%)#	22M-22I	HISEC-TER (92-98%)#
II	22M-22I	HISEC-TER## (90%)	1M-1I 5M-4I 9M-10I 4M-6I	Z-I-SEC## (85%) Z-II-SEC (85%) Z-III-HISEC-TER (90%) Z-IV-SEC (85%)	22M 22I	Municipal HISEC-TER (90%) Industrial HISEC-TER (90%)	15M-16I	PRIM to TER## (35-98%)
III	15M-20I	SEC (75%)	1M-1I 2M-4I 7M-10I 4M-4I	Z-I-SEC (85%) Z-II-INT-IS(70%) Z-III-SEC (80%) Z-IV-MI PRIM-LS (50%)	17M 16I	Municipal SEC (85%) Industrial	5M-10I	PRIM to SEC## (35-85%)
IV	14M-19I	INT-LS (70%)	1M-1I 5M-4I 7M-7I 0M-1I	Z-I-SEC (85%) Z-II-SEC (80%) Z-III-INT-LS(50%) Z-IV-PRIM (35%)	17M 5I	Municipal SEC (80%) Industrial PRIM (35%)	7M-10I	PRIM to SEC (35-85%)

NOTES:
* Minimum treatment required by solution but not below present treatment level.
** Treatment range is for all 44 sources. Sources not in solution remain at present level.
*** M=Municipal waste source, I=Industrial waste source (total # of sources = 44)
# Also requires additional control measure such as stream aeration.
Requires aeration or sludge removal to meet DO goal in Sects. #3&4.

Table 7

Estimated Total Costs of Objective Sets (Millions of Dollars)
Flow = 3000 cfs at Trenton

OS		Uniform	Zoned	Municipal-Industrial	Cost Minimization
I	DO Cost***	460	460	460	460
	Bact.	30	30	30	30
	Total	490	490	490	490
II	DO Cost***	315	250	315	215
	Bact.	20	20	20	20
	Total	335	270	335	235
III	DO Cost***	155	120	120	85
	Bact.	20	20	20	25*
	pH	-	15**	25**	25**
	Total	175	155	165	135
IV	DO Cost***	130	80	90	65
	Bact.	15	15	15	20*
	pH	-	15	15	15**
	Total	145	110	120	100

Notes: * To meet bacterial goals, additional chlorine dosages needed by several sources not in DO program.

** To meet pH goals, pH control needed by several sources not in DO program.

*** Other water use goals (except chlorides) assumed to be met by DO, pH and bacterial control measures. Chloride goal requires fresh water flow regulation. Meeting the phenol goal for OS-1 in sections 18-22 may require supplemental phenol control measures. All DO costs include $30 million cost of maintaining OS V.

If an assured high level (90%-95% survival) of anadromous fish passage is desired, while all other water uses are satisfied by OS-III quality goals, DO levels must be raised to OS-II goals approximately 6 months of the year. It is estimated that for 50% of the years, this requirement could be met by fresh-water inflow controls. At most, the level of this augmentation would be about **1,000** cfs for 30 days. The other 50% of the years, the DO objectives could be met in either of two ways: 1) in-stream aeration at an estimated total cost (OS-III, Zone + assured anadromous fish passage) of 145 million dollars or 2) by requiring waste reduction facilities that are sufficiently flexible to enable operation at OS-II levels during the critical periods and at OS-III levels during the rest of the time at a cost (OS-III, Zone + assured anadromous fish passage) of 195 million dollars.

The cost of piping wastes out of the study area was also investigated. Two problems are apparent in the design. The first is that not enough is known of the Delaware Bay environment to assure that the piping of wastes to that area would not create new pollution problems.

Thus more time and money would have to be spent to determine the outfall location. An undesignated area off the coast of New Jersey was therefore used for design purposes. Second, when ocean disposal is considered, a pipeline would divert flow from the estuary which would normally help control chlorides. This would result in an additional cost for chloride control in the form of additional storage in upstream reservoirs. Table 8 presents the capital costs for chloride control as well as for piping of all wastes to the ocean. No estimates have been made of additional costs incurred by the increased pollutional load in the ocean disposal area.

Rough estimates of the total cost (including capital and operation and maintenance) of reaching the various DO objectives by mechanical aeration based on the scale-up of pilot plant data [indicated costs of 70, 40, 12, and 10 million dollars to meet Objective Sets I, II, III, and IV, respectively].

It should be noted that this meets DO objectives only and additional expense would be necessary to meet other parameter objectives. Since a large scale in-stream aeration such as would be required for the Delaware has never been attempted, considerable study would have to be devoted to the feasibility of the size of the system that is required. It is anticipated that some problems may also develop in interferences with navigation and recreation as well as the creation of nuisance conditions (foaming, etc.).

Maintenance of Objectives

If the waste loadings to the stream that are prescribed for each objective set are held constant, that particular objective set will always be maintained.

Table 8

Capital Costs for Attainment of Objectives
(Millions Of Dollars)

1) By Piping Of Wastes Out Of The Estuary
2) By Reduction Of Wastes At The Source

Obj. Set	Estimated(*) Diverted Flow (cfs)	1) Piping of Wastes Out of the Estuary			2) Waste Removal
		Piping	Chloride Control**	Total	
1	1200	125	40	165	180
2	1150	120	35	155	115
3	800	90	25	115	50
4	650	65	20	85	40

* It is assumed that industrial waste streams will be separated to allow cooling water to return to the stream.

** Estimated Capital Cost of additional storage necessary to counteract effects of diverted flow.

The costs shown in Table 5 for achieving the various objectives show estimates of costs of maintaining these discharges for the time period up to 1975-1980. Estimates of future loadings based on economic projections show a substantial increase in waste production in the estuary. To maintain the objective under these increased waste loadings will increase the program cost. To maintain the objectives from 1975 to 1985, it is estimated that the region would have to spend an additional 5.0 to 7.5 million dollars/year.

By 1975, over-all treatment levels to maintain OS-IV would approach 80%, for OS-III about 90%, and for OS-II, 93% removal of the estimated waste loads will be necessary. By 2010, the estimates of waste loadings before treatment or reduction are so large that 96%-99% waste removal will be necessary to maintain the objectives. An estimate of the treatment costs for that time would be misleading for several reasons. First, as waste removal requirements to meet the necessary levels of discharge become more stringent and expensive, other alternatives such as piping of wastes out of the critical areas, water recycling, and reuse, and in-stream aeration may become more economically feasible alternatives than attempting to achieve higher treatment levels. Second, some industrial waste sources faced with discharge limits might turn to in-plant changes, more efficient process due to advanced technology or perhaps shift production to products which create less waste load in their manufacture. Thus, the means by which the objective selected will be maintained will be largely a function of the future economic alternatives. At the present time the reduction of waste at the sources appears to be the least expensive and most feasible alternative. By 1985-1990 additional treatment to maintain an objective may be more expensive than some other schemes and a new look may be needed at the various alternatives available at that time.

Benefits of Improved Water Quality

The third major analytic task carried out by the DECS staff was the quantification of benefits that would accrue under the various objective sets. It was not expected that all benefits could be expressed in dollar terms. Philadelphia's largest water treatment plant, for example, was already producing potable water from the estuary at relatively low cost. Improvement in the quality of its intake would have little effect on the cost of operating the plant, but it might improve both the taste and odor of the drinking water produced. Quantifying this kind of benefit was considered impossible. For study purposes, therefore, only three kinds of benefits were investigated; those accruing to industry, those enhancing commercial fishing activities in the estuary, and those permitting increased use of the area for recreational purposes. The last of these was the subject of a study contract awarded to the Institute for Environmental Studies at the University of Pennsylvania.

Industry Benefits[1]

The estimation of industrial water quality benefits is a complex process under the influence of many factors. Among industrial plants,

[1] Excerpted from the DECS, Preliminary Report.

variations in operating policy, type of construction, method of water use, and degree of water treatment must all be considered.

In an attempt to account for these factors, information was obtained from the major water using industries along the estuary. Data were received on the cost effect of variation of dissolved oxygen and chloride levels in the intake water. These two variables were found to be the most important quality parameters to industrial water users. In most industrial plants, the chain of cause and effect relationships linking river water and monetary savings had not been previously quantified. In spite of the difficulty of such estimates, a number of positive replies were received; many of the non-zero responses were in the petroleum refining, chemical industry, and paper products categories. Other industries such as the electric power utilities indicated no effect for the quality characteristics.

The information supplied by these industries was used to compute statistical estimates of benefits (or costs) for the major water using industries, including those unable to determine their own cost response. For this latter group the annual benefit (dollars per year) was considered to depend on the following variables:

1. Dissolved Oxygen or chloride level, each a function of the objective set,

2. Location,

3. Quantity of estuarine intake water,

4. Industrial type,

5. Type of use.

In terms of location, benefits (or costs) are considered to accrue only in those areas of the estuary exhibiting significant dissolved oxygen increase or chloride depression. These areas are determined primarily by the objective sets.

The total benefit in annual terms is then the sum of individual industry values, where some are based on original interview data and others on the statistical estimates. . . . In all cases the benefits (costs) represent a dollar value which would accrue as a result of steady-state (long-term) conditions. The inputs are assumed to be relatively stable at the levels indicated by the objective sets over a number of years, with the exception of water use. . . . The estimated present (1964) value of the benefits (costs) of achieving new dissolved oxygen levels are approximately 14.5, 13, 10, and 1 million dollars for Objective Sets I, II, III, and IV, respectively. It will be noted that these are negative benefits. This is primarily due to increased corrosion rates at the higher oxygen levels.

Benefits to Commercial Fishing[1]

Although the estuary proper no longer supports a substantial commercial fish harvest, its water quality does influence commercial fish production in adjacent areas.

For shad and other migratory fish, the estuary serves as a passage between their spawning grounds in fresh water and their primary habitat in the sea; it is a place of temporary residence possibly once or twice in a lifetime. For the menhaden the estuary is also a temporary residence; as juveniles, the menhaden move from the ocean into the lower portion of the study area where they grow substantially during their two- to three-month stay. Finally, the study area is important to the large number of other species which spend most of their lives therein and are considered permanent residents.

When calculating benefits, a given species was considered to be beneficially influenced by improved water quality if it must depend on water within the study area for survival at some period in its life cycle. The commercial fishery attributable to the study area contains three components, the menhaden, the shad, and a composite group of all other commercially harvested species. It is assumed that an increase in the volume of good quality water will support an enlargement of the above fish populations which, in turn, will be reflected in greater commercial fish harvests.

Menhaden are the basis of the largest commercial fishery in the United States. The Delaware and southern New Jersey fishing industry average about $4,000,000 annually of which approximately $1,400,000 is attributable to fish from the Delaware. Virtually all menhaden caught are reduced to fish meal, condensed solubles, or oil.

As the water quality improves with each objective set, the volume of water inhabitable by menhaden will also increase. For this estimate, it was assumed that the dollar value of the catch attributable to the Delaware River would increase in proportion to the volumetric increase in inhabitable water. The results are presented in Table 9.

Shad fishery benefits were calculated under two primary considerations, (1) the suggested fishway at the proposed Tocks Island Dam will not be successful,[2] (2) the fishway will be successful or alternative spawning grounds will evolve. The proposed Tocks Island Dam will probably be a hindrance to the normal migration of shad to and from the principal spawning areas above the dam site. Because of this obstacle, it is the general opinion of biologists that shad spawning success will be considerably reduced in the Delaware River. When developing estimates of the shad fishery under the water quality conditions represented by the different objective sets, the following items were considered: probable size of the attainable harvest, the effect of good fishery management, research into anticipated markets, opportunity to develop new markets, water quality under various flow and waste load combinations, time of year and duration of the annual shad migration, and the dissolved oxygen tolerance of shad. The estimated value of the annual commercial shad harvest is given in Table 9.

[1]Excerpted from DECS, Preliminary Report.

[2]The Tocks Island project involved damming the river upstream from the study area to create a lake over 20 miles long.

Table 9

Estimated Net Commercial Fishing Benefits

Present Value

(millions of dollars)

	Menhaden	Shad: Unsuccessful Fishway	Shad: Successful Fishway	Other Finfish	Total: Minimum	Total: Maximum
OS- I	7.4	1.3	4.0	.3	9	12
OS- II	7.4	1.3	4.0	.2	9	12
OS-III	3.7	1.1	3.3	.2	5	7
OS- IV	1.9	.9	2.5	.1	3	5

In the final category of commercial fisheries are all the remaining species that are harvested on a commercial basis, e.g., croaker, striped bass, weakfish, blue fish, and white perch. The value of these fish caught within the study is quite small, being in the order of $12,000 annually. With pollution abatement programs, new areas of good quality water will be available and in turn should produce more fish. The increased volume of good quality water under various objective sets is reflected in the anticipated harvests for "other finfish" as given in Table 9.

It is anticipated that commercial fishing within the study area will be quite limited primarily because of competing uses such as recreational boating, sport fishing, commercial shipping, and waste disposal. However, with improved water quality conditions the lower portion of the study area will increase in value for its two most important functions: (1) a nursery area for juvenile fish and (2) an area with a very high production of aquatic organisms which serve directly and indirectly as food for fish which are harvested in abundance elsewhere.

Recreational Benefits

The University of Pennsylvania research team evaluated four kinds of recreational benefits; swimming, boating, fishing, and picnicking. Several other river-oriented recreational activities were noted but felt to be unquantifiable. These included nature walks, aesthetic enjoyment, and the pleasure of cleaner air. The research plan was cast in the following format: First, total demand for the four recreational activities would be forecast into the future. Next, this total demand would be adjusted downward to reflect the expected availability of recreational facilities not associated with the estuary. These two steps would provide an estimate of the unfilled recreational demand that might be satisfied by the estuary. The third step would be to estimate the amount of recreational activity that could be supported by the estuary under each of the five objective sets. Finally, the total value of the benefits under each objective set would be determined by multiplying either the unfilled demand or the capacity of the estuary to meet demand (whichever was smaller) by the dollar value placed on satisfying a unit of demand.

As a preliminary step, the research group first made an inventory of the already available recreational facilities in the area. They found that the water acreage for recreational purposes, in general, and for boating, in particular, was minimal. Delaware Bay and the New Jersey shore were the closest areas used for such purposes. Both these areas had substantial room remaining for the development of water recreation facilities. Most inland fresh waters were already fully developed leaving only the Delaware River as a large potential source of inland water for recreation.[1]

The demand for recreation is generally believed to be a function of two groups of factors: user-oriented factors which are closely interrelated with one another and environmental influences which tend to act independently. The first group includes income, education, occupation, age and place of residence. The second consists of the amount of leisure time, and proximity to recreation facilities. The task of projecting future demand for recreation, then, required that specific relationships be established between the two groups of factors and the demand for recreation and that the factors be estimated for future years. To do this the University of Pennsylvania research group relied heavily on work done earlier by the Outdoor Recreation Resources Review Commission (ORRRC) a group established by Congress in 1958 to determine what the nation's recreational needs would be in 1976 and 2000, what recreational resources were available, and what recreational policies and programs should be adopted nationally.

ORRRC's findings, in turn, made substantial use of a special survey of 16,000 respondents conducted for it by the Bureau of the Census. The survey provided data such as that shown in Figure 6 which relate the percentage of persons 12 years and older who participate in various activities to annual family income. Similar data were obtained for the other six factors listed above. Regression analyses then provided ORRRC researchers with a mathematical relationship between the seven factors and the participation <u>rate</u> for persons 12 years and older. An identical procedure was used to determine the relationship between the seven factors and the number of activity days per year that a person would participate <u>if</u> he chose to participate at all. The final step in ORRRC's procedure was to estimate the changes that would take place in the seven factors on a population-wide basis by 1976 and 2000. For the five user-oriented factors, demographic projections developed by the National Planning Association were used. For leisure time and proximity to recreational facilities, ORRRC developed its own estimates of change by extrapolating past trends and making judgmental

---

[1]In addition to the estuary, considerable water acreage would become available if the Tocks Island project materialized.

Figure 6

INCOME AND PARTICIPATION IN THE NORTHEAST U.S.

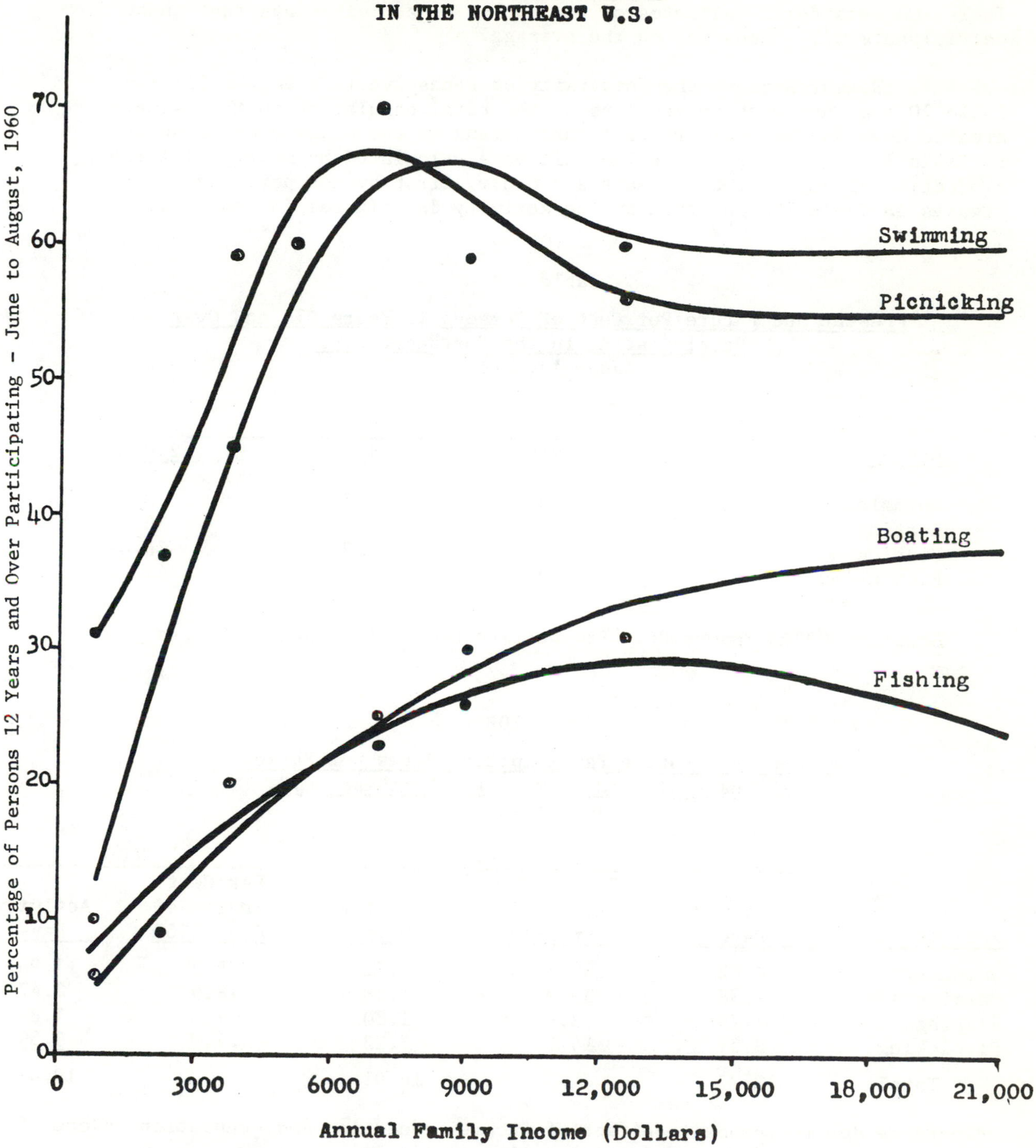

Source: ORRRC Report 19, National Recreation Survey.

adjustments. The results are shown in Tables 10A and 10B. Table 10A shows the percentage of all persons 12 years and older that were expected to participate in swimming, boating, fishing and picnicking in 1976 and 2000. Table 10B sets forth estimates of the number of activity days that these participants will "consume" on the average.

Researchers at the University of Pennsylvania used the figures in Table 10 together with projections of the total population in the estuary area to develop the total recreational demand in the study area as shown in Table 11. (The figures in Table 11 were calculated by multiplying the projection of population 12 years and older, first by the percentage figures in Table 10A and then by the activity day figures in Table 10B.)

Table 10A

Present and Future Per Cent of Persons 12 Years Old and Over Participating in the Northeast U.S.
(June-August)

	Year		
Activity	1960	1976	2000
Swimming	45	55	63
Boating	22	28	38
Fishing	29	32	36
Picnicking	53	57	61

Source: ORRRC Report 26, "Prospective Demand for Outdoor Recreation."

Table 10B

Present and Future Participation Rates per Person 12 Years Old and Over in the Northeast U.S.
(June-August)

	1960	1976		2000	
Activity	Activity Days	Per Cent Increase* Over 1960	Activity Days	Per Cent Increase* Over 1960	Activity Days
Swimming	6.82	33.7	9.12	75.3	11.96
Boating**	1.38	35.9	1.88	78.9	2.47
Fishing	1.76	2.4	1.80	2.3	1.80
Picnicking	2.81	14.1	3.22	27.9	3.59
Total	12.77		16.01		19.82

*Increase due to composite effect of income, education and occupation, place of residence, age and sex, and leisure time available.
**Other than sailing or canoeing.

Source: ORRRC Report 26 "Prospective Demand for Outdoor Recreation."

Table 11

Present and Future Activity Days in Millions
in the Study Region

Activity	1960	Year 1976	2000
Swimming	26.8	45.4	79.3
Boating	5.4	9.4	16.4
Fishing	6.9	9.0	11.9
Picnicking	11.0	16.0	23.8

Source: Institute for Environmental Studies, Water-Oriented Recreational Benefits.

The next basic step in the University of Pennsylvania study was to determine the number of activity days that could be satisfied by the estuary under each of the five objective sets. For swimming, this was done by noting those sections of the estuary where water contact sports would be permissible - e.g., sections where the coliform bacteria count was less than 5,000/100 ml. In each of these sections, the shore line was assumed to be a simple line of which 25% would be a suitable location for swimming. It was also assumed that each 25 feet of this shore could accommodate 150 people per day during a swimming season whose duration was estimated to be 100 days. This resulted in yearly swimming activity days that the estuary could supply as follows:

Objective Set	Activity Days per Year
I	48.0×10^6
II	29.8×10^6
III	29.8×10^6
IV	8.25×10^6
V	3.96×10^6

Estimates were then made of the number of activity days of swimming that would be satisfied by facilities outside the estuary (other fresh water facilities and private and public pools). The three types of information about swimming, then, were combined to determine swimming benefits in terms of activity days. Similar procedures were used to estimate the benefits from boating and fishing. The over-all benefits are summarized below.

Future Participation in Water-Oriented Recreation Activities in Millions of Activity Days by Objective Set*

O.S.	Swimming 1976	Swimming 2000	Boating 1976	Boating 2000	Fishing 1976	Fishing 2000	Total 1976	Total 2000
I	3.9	18.0	4.0	4.0	1.17	1.17	9.07	23.17
II	3.9	18.0	3.3	3.3	0.68	0.68	7.88	21.98
III	3.9	18.0	2.9	2.9	0.68	0.68	7.48	21.58
IV	3.9	8.25	2.6	2.6	0.40	0.40	6.90	11.25
V	3.9	3.96	1.4	1.4	0.39	0.39	5.19	5.75

*Picnicking was treated separately.

Source: Institute for Environmental Studies, Water-Oriented Recreation Benefits.

This left only one remaining task for the University of Pennsylvania study group; the translation of activity day benefits into estimates of their dollar value. This was accomplished by using "standard" benefit values recommended by the Ad Hoc Water Resources Council of the Department of the Interior in 1964. The Ad Hoc Council had divided outdoor recreation into two categories: A "General" recreation day involved those activities attractive to a majority of outdoor recreationists and included swimming, picnicking, hiking, small game hunting, water skiing, motor boating, sailing, most warm water fishing, and other activities. A "Specialized" recreation day involved activities where opportunities are, in general, more limited and the intensity of use is lower. These include big game hunting, white water canoeing and boating, and others. The council recommended that the benefits for a General activity day be set between $0.50 and $1.50 and for a Specialized day between $2.00 and $6.00. These ranges reflected the answers received to a questionnaire sent to a number of privately owned and operated recreational facilities asking them for data on their daily admission fees. To select a particular value within these ranges, the council suggested that weight be given to the amount that participants customarily spend to take part in the activity including the cost of equipment purchase, maintenance and operation.

Using these guidelines, the University of Pennsylvania team selected the following benefit ranges as being "reasonable" for the estuary:

	Minimum	Maximum
Swimming	$ .75	$1.25
1/4 of Boating (Specialized)	3.00	5.00
3/4 of Boating (General)	.75	1.25
Fishing	.75	1.25

When applied to the activity day estimates shown in Table 11, and discounted over 20 years at 3%, the minimum and maximum net total benefits for the objective sets are as shown in Table 12.

Table 12

Estimated Recreational Benefits (1975-1980)
Present Value

(millions of dollars)

O.S.	Net Benefits* Maximum	Net Benefits* Minimum	Net Marginal Benefits Maximum	Net Marginal Benefits Minimum
I	355	155		
			35	20
II	320	135		
			10	10
III	310	125		
			30	10
IV	280	115		

*Net Benefits above OS-V.
Source: DECS Preliminary Report and Findings.

Other Benefits[1]

Another type of benefit results from the effect of the preceding quantifiable direct benefits on the regional economy. These benefits included: (1) "induced" benefits that are realized by new or expanded activities in the region and, (2) secondary benefits that are realized by a large number of trade and service industries. These extra benefits are estimated to be in the range of at least 15% of the direct quantifiable benefits.

In addition to the measurable benefits there are numerous other uses that will be improved as a result of increased water quality. The water quality levels presented in the four objective sets would reduce the rate of delignification, corrosion, and cavitation of piers, wharfs, buoys, bridge abutments, and boat engines and hulls. Debris, silt, oils and grease that settle and block channels and intake devices and clog cooling systems in boat engines would be reduced substantially. The dollar benefits attributable to these effects, however, remain undefined.

Another important benefit of increased water quality is the improved aesthetic value of the river. Part of these benefits are reflected in the estimates of increased recreational value. However, these estimates do not include the increase in value of property adjacent to the estuary that will occur by providing a watercourse that is more aesthetically pleasing; nor do the quantifiable benefits include the enhancement of parts and picnic areas adjacent to this watercourse.

[1]Excerpted from DECS, Preliminary Report and Findings.

Recommendations

With its analytic tasks largely completed, the DECS staff turned its attention to developing a recommended course of action for FWPCA to present to the Delaware River Basin Commission. To assist in this task, the various subcommittees of WUAC were asked to express their preferences among the five objective sets. The DECS staff planned to form its own conclusions after reviewing the results of their canvass of WUAC.

APPENDIX A

ANALYSIS OF AN ESTUARY

Derivation of Program Costs for Alternate Means of Waste Discharge Control

The data in case Table 5 were derived through solutions to a cost minimization formulation of each of the four basic control programs (Uniform Treatment, Zoned, Municipal-Industrial and Minimum Cost). Input data to each formulation included:

1. The transfer coefficients generated by solution of the mass balance equations for the estuary.

2. Estimates of current waste loads as shown in Table 4.

3. Differences between the observed DO levels in the 30 zones and the levels required by various objective sets, and

4. An estimate of the costs to reduce waste loadings. These were supplied voluntarily by most of the major dischargers who were asked to reflect in their estimates the impact of load increases from expanded operations up to 1980. The costs reported were nonlinear, rising more steeply as the percentage waste removal increased. (For computational purposes, these cost curves were approximated by linear segments.)

Using these inputs, the Minimum Cost program was stated and solved as a linear programming problem. Total costs were minimized subject to constraints as follows:

1. DO levels in each section must equal or better those required by the particular objective set under investigation.

2. No waste source will treat to a level less than its current practice.

3. No source is asked to treat to levels that are not technically feasible.

4. No source treats to less than the primary level (i.e., 35%).

Appendix A (continued)

The Uniform Treatment program was stated in much the same way as the Minimum Cost program except that an additional constraint was added - i.e., all sources must remove an equal percentage of their carbonaceous wastes (subject still, however, to the provision that no source will remove less waste than it is doing already). The problem was solved by a simple search technique in which successively higher trial values of the uniform treatment level were selected until the DO requirements were met in all 30 sections. Because costs are known to increase with the level of waste removal, the solution thus derived for the uniform treatment level is also the minimum cost solution for that control program. The cost of the program will always exceed the over-all Minimum Cost program and will result in DO levels in one or more sections that exceed the requirements of the particular objective set under investigation.

The concept of zoned treatment covers both the case of Zoned Uniform Treatment and Municipal-Industrial. In the former, "zones" are geographic sections; while in the latter all municipalities are taken as one "zone" and all industries as another. The problem for both is stated like the Uniform Treatment program except that the solution is constrained to require uniformity only within zones. (In fact, the Cost Minimization program and the Uniform Treatment program are merely special cases of the zoning approach. Cost Minimization treats each source as a separate zone; Uniform Treatment considers the entire estuary as one zone.) Because of discontinuities and nonlinearities in the constraints, neither the Zoned Uniform Treatment nor the Municipal-Industrial problem can be solved by conventional linear programs; hence, a system of bounded enumeration was used.

The general shape of the waste removal requirements for each of the four programs is shown in Figure 7. (The graphs are not to scale.) For the Municipal-Industrial program costs were divided about 60%/40% between municipalities and industry, respectively. Some additional computer runs which divided the industry "zone" into chemical, petroleum, and other industrial (steel, paper and so forth), showed that practically no additional cost would accrue to any but the chemical industry for objective sets up to OS-II. In other words, the total cost of meeting these objectives would be borne 60% by municipalities and 40% by the chemical industry alone.

Appendix A (continued)

Figure 7 WASTE REMOVAL REQUIREMENTS UNDER VARIOUS POLLUTION CONTROL PROGRAMS

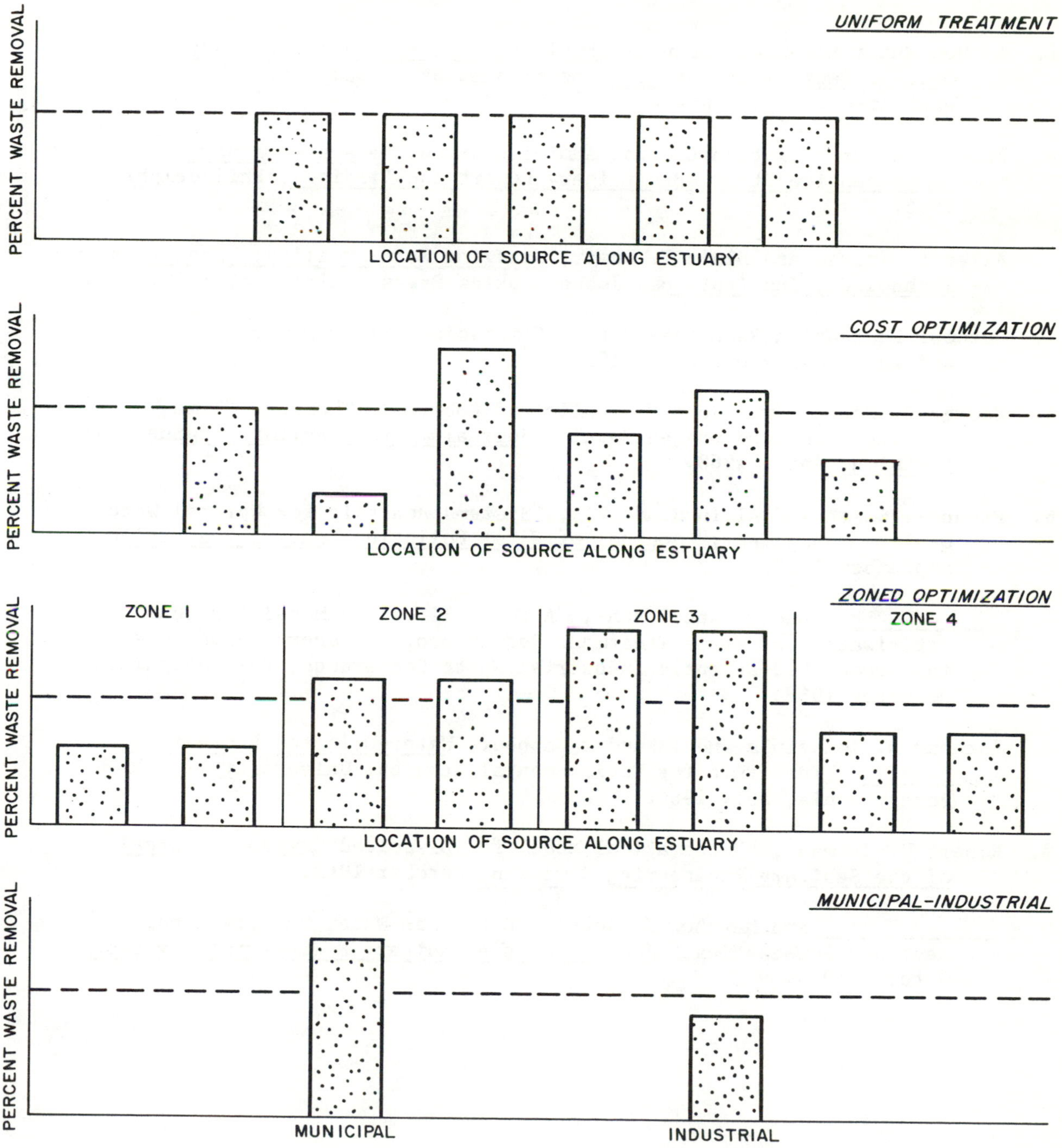

APPENDIX B

ANALYSIS OF AN ESTUARY

List of Sources

1. Ad Hoc Water Resources Council, Evaluation Standards for Primary Outdoor Recreation Benefits, Memorandum 64-8, Supplement No. 1, Washington, D.C., June 4, 1964.

2. Federal Water Pollution Control Administration, Delaware Estuary Comprehensive Study, Preliminary Report and Findings, Philadelphia, 1966.

3. Allen V. Kneese and Blair T. Bower, Managing Water Quality: Economics, Technology, Institutions, Johns Hopkins Press, Baltimore, 1968.

4. Outdoor Recreation Resources Review Commission, Study Reports 19, 21 and 23, Washington, D.C., 1962.

5. George D. Pence, Jr., John M. Jeglic and Robert V. Thomann, "Time-Varying Dissolved-Oxygen Model," Journal of the Sanitary Engineering Division, April 1968.

6. Ethan T. Smith and Alvin R. Morris, "Systems Analysis for Optimal Water Quality Management," Journal of Water Pollution Control Federation, September 1969.

7. ____________ and Emmanuel Mehr, "A Cost Allocation Model for Zoned Optimization of Waste Treatment Requirements." Paper presented at the Second Mid-Atlantic Industrial Waste Conference, Philadelphia, November 1968.

8. Anthony R. Tomazinis and Iskandar Gabbour, Water-Oriented Recreation Benefits, Institute for Environmental Studies, University of Pennsylvania, July 1966.

9. Robert V. Thomann, "Mathematical Model for Dissolved Oxygen," Journal of the Sanitary Engineering Division, October 1963.

10. ____________ and Matthew J. Sobel, "Estuarine Water Quality Management and Forecasting," Journal of the Sanitary Engineering Division, October 1964.

THE 1971-1972 NEW YORK CITY TAX PROGRAM

The Budget Gap

The same problems that plague most large cities - rising costs, a slowly growing revenue base, poor housing, a large indigent population - also plague the City of New York. But as with everything else that has to do with the Empire City, its problems seem somewhat larger than life. In January of 1971, Mr. Edward K. Hamilton, the Director of the city's Bureau of the Budget informed Mayor John V. Lindsay that without additional revenue, the city would be faced in the next fiscal year with a "budget gap," that is, a gap between expenditure and revenue. The size of the gap, Hamilton asserted, would be $1.14 billion on a budget estimate of $9.2 billion.

This fiscal crisis was by no means a sudden surprise. For most cities - and New York was no exception - it had been coming for some time. Over the past several years expenditures had been rising at a rate far greater than revenues. In 1965, the last year of Mayor Robert Wagner's administration, the Executive Budget was $3.9 billion. In 1970-1971, it was $7.7 billion, almost double the 1965-1966 figure. Only one-tenth of the $3.8 billion increase went to "discretionary items" - programs that the city <u>could</u> have elected to do without. The rest went for "mandatory and inescapable" costs.

The most important cause of the increase was inflation. The consumer price index in New York rose 26% between 1965 and 1970. A dollar earned in 1970 had the buying power of only 79 cents compared with 1965. It cost $500 million more in 1970 to keep the purchasing power of the city's 1965 work force constant. Along with the increased salaries went $100 million in automatic pension costs. One hundred and fifty million dollars of the interest on the city's debt was attributable to the effect of inflation on the bond markets. Well over $600 million in Welfare and Medicaid payments went, in 1970-1971, to offset cost-of-living increases and price inflation in medical services since 1965. City supplies cost $80 million more due to inflation.

Large budget increases had also occurred at the negotiating table. Despite some extravagant miscalculations made by city negotiators, however, the contract settlements between 1965 and 1970 were not as outrageous as some observers claimed. Although the total outlay for wages, pensions, and other benefits went up 38% between 1968 and 1970, the "real" payroll, (after deductions for inflation) grew only 18.8%, or 9% yearly. Of that, 4.8% came through union contracts; the remainder came from paying higher salaries to workers who grew in seniority and from paying additional employees hired during the period.

An annual increase of 4.8% in "real" salaries seemed high compared to annual increases of 2.8% for construction workers and only 1.1% for industrial workers between 1965 and 1970 until one looked at where municipal employees had started from. In 1965, the average teacher in New York earned $5,300 and a policeman with three years' experience earned $8,483. The average construction worker earned $11,200. In that year the Bureau of Labor Statistics estimated that a salary of $9,412 was necessary to maintain a "moderate" standard of living for a family of four in New York City (meat once a day and a movie once a month). In 1970 the teacher earned $11,544, the policeman $10,950, and the construction worker $13,000. However, the cost of a moderate standard of living had increased to $12,134 in 1970, so that municipal workers were still below that level.

The third major cause of the budget increase was the growing load of welfare and Medicaid payments. One-fifth of the families in New York earned less than $4,000 in 1960. In 1970, one-third of the families fell below that income level. In 1965 there were 574,000 people on the welfare rolls; by 1970 there were 1.2 million. Welfare cost $494 million in 1965; in 1970 the cost had climbed to $1.9 billion. Of this, the city paid $543 million. The major reason for the phenomenal increase was migration. Four hundred thousand people migrated from the South to New York and almost as many came from Puerto Rico.

The same story was true of Medicaid. Costs jumped dramatically with the inflow of eligible poor and the substantial rise in the cost of medical care. In 1970, the city's share of the Medicaid bill was $270 million.

The final major reason for budget increases was the addition of staff and the expansion of services. Between 1965 and 1970, the city hired 66,000 new employees. Many of these were mandatory or paid for by outside funds:

- 17,500 paraprofessional school workers paid entirely by federal funds.

- 4,600 school lunch aides also paid by federal funds.

- 10,300 caseworkers and other welfare employees to meet the 1 caseworker to 60 cases ratio required by the union contract.

- 7,800 teachers to accommodate 75,000 more pupils and to reduce the pupil-teacher ratio in accordance with the union contract.

- 6,000 miscellaneous positions, also mandatory.

The remaining 20,000 new employees were hired (at the city's discretion) to meet increased demands for services:

- 4,000 police. Robberies alone had increased 70% from 1967 to 1969.

- 1,500 sanitation men. Five thousand additional tons of garbage were collected daily in 1970 compared to 1965.

- 1,200 firemen. Fire alarms doubled in the five years.

- 400 correction officers. The prison population had swollen.

- 7,500 City University employees to cope with an open admissions policy that guaranteed every graduate of a city high school a place in the University's freshman class.

The school and hospital systems were also expanded and several new agencies were formed such as the Department of Air Resources to deal with air pollution and the Addiction Services Agency to attack the narcotics problem.

In summary, the $3.8 billion increase could be broken down as follows: Inflation was responsible for $1.4 billion. Next came Welfare and Medicaid: $1.3 billion, excluding inflation. Then collective bargaining which, excluding inflation, cost $570 million. Finally, there was the cost in real wages and pensions of new employees, many of them mandatory ($130 million). Less than $400 million was attributable to choices clearly under the city's control.[1]

On the other side of the budget gap, revenues were not increasing nearly as fast as expenditures. Officials at the Bureau of the Budget estimated a revenue growth of 4%-5% and an expenditure growth of 12%-15%. The reason for this discrepancy was fairly simple. The city's tax system had approximately "unit elasticity" - that is, without any change in rates, it yielded revenue increases that corresponded roughly to the growth in the city's economy.[2] This growth had not kept pace with the increased demand for municipal services. Not even the massive infusion of external aid from the federal and state levels has been able to offset the effect completely. And the aid <u>had</u> been massive in recent years. From 1960 to 1965 the average annual increase in external aid was $75 million; between 1965 and 1969, over $400 million annually. While the budget tripled between

---

[1]Data on the growth of New York City's expense budget was taken from "Why the City Went Broke" an unpublished paper by Carter F. Bales of McKinsey & Company, Inc.

[2]Exhibit 1 shows a breakdown of revenue sources for fiscal year 1969-1970.

1959-1960 and 1969-1970, the amount of external aid increased more than sixfold, from $471 million to $2,833 million. Aid financed 21% of the budget in 1959-1960 but 41% in 1969-1970. Of this, the State of New York provided about 60% (or 25% of the budget) and the Federal Government provided the rest. A large part of the aid money was earmarked for Welfare and Medicaid. In 1970-1971, only $1,485 million of the $2,044 million in state aid and $551 million of the $1,321 million in federal funds were for purposes other than these two categories. Indeed, none of the federal funds and few of the state funds were unrestricted. Federal money not designated for either welfare or Medicaid came largely in the form of grants for such things as education and crime control, while state aid was largely for education. Since 1969, the state had had a revenue sharing plan, and in 1971 this plan was cut from 21% of the state income tax to 18%, costing New York City $75 million in aid.

In recent years the rate of growth of external aid had slowed. Between 1964-1965 and 1968-1969, aid grew at an average annual rate of over 31%. In 1969-1970 it grew only about 12%; in 1970-1971, 18.78%; and in 1971-1972, the growth was expected to be negligible. Even if the rate of increase should revert to 30%, however, it would be some time before it would be enough.

The Mayor's Options

Since the 1970 budget negotiations with the state legislature had been highly successful for the city, the Bureau of the Budget suspected that the 1971 negotiations might be very tough, a fact that the people of the city and even some of the city leadership did not realize. In an effort to prepare people for the battles that would come in the spring, BoB started talking about a large budget gap as early as September 1970. In October, it began estimating the possible size of a revenue short fall. In November, 500 city employees were laid off in an effort to drive home the message that 1971 would be a tough year financially. Since the lay-offs were the first since the depression, the message carried weight.

In December, BoB was able to flesh out its earlier estimates as the various departments submitted budget requests for 1971-1972. These requests were, essentially, the outside limits of expenditures. They represented what departments would like rather than what they realistically expected to get. BoB made its own evaluation of the requests and attempted to negotiate (and/or recommend to the mayor) any modifications that it felt were appropriate. It also calculated the cost of maintaining this year's level of activity (plus any unavoidable increases) at next year's salaries and fringe benefits, and thereby developed the "mandatory budget." For the 1971-1972 year this budget was $9.2 billion - an increase of $1.4 billion over 1970-1971. According to the Budget Bureau and subsequently the mayor, this amount represented the minimum expenditure necessary in 1970-1971. The gap between $9.2 billion and the revenue expected from existing sources amounted to $1.14 billion.

In early January 1971, Budget Director Hamilton informed the Mayor of the size of the 1971-1972 budget and the size of the "budget gap." According to Jon Weiner, the official at BoB who coordinated the design and development of the tax package, Mayor Lindsay, initially was very strongly of the opinion that the Bureau had to do something about the expenditure side of the budget. This meant cutting services and, if the entire gap had to be eliminated in that way, probably courting disaster. BoB estimated that a reduction in expenditures approaching $1 billion would require laying off 90,000 city employees and eliminating the services they provided. Even smaller cutbacks -- far less than $1 billion -- could be politically dangerous. The dislocations caused thereby are an ever-present irritant to the populace and, for a politician, that has to be a consideration. When it is added to the fact that cutting services is moving backward, the concept becomes very unpopular. No mayor wants his city to step backward. Mayor Lindsay turned his attention to other possibilities.

The first of these possibilities was to get more state and federal aid. In fact, the Mayor had been attempting to get this aid for several months in a nationwide campaign in favor of revenue sharing; but, so far, the campaign had not been a great success. In the state, Lindsay faced a very conservative and generally unsympathetic legislature whose membership tended to be skeptical about the seriousness of New York City's fiscal plight. In Congress, President Nixon's revenue-sharing scheme had been criticized and held up by Representative Wilbur Mills. There would amost certainly be some amount of aid forthcoming but it seemed very unlikely that it would approach the amounts that New York City needed. Accordingly, the Mayor could not count on aid as his principal means of salvation.

A second option was one rarely considered in the past but gaining acceptance in the academic community. That alternative was to accept a more modest role for city government, acknowledge the fact that there are some things city governments are not equipped to do, and relinquish them to other levels of government that can do the job effectively. As Dick Netzer, Professor of Public Finance at New York University, points out:

> If the city government cannot finance a service adequately or administer it effectively, this does not mean that other levels of government or other governmental entities face similar disabilities. If there are public entities that can do better, the city government should take some initiative in the transfer of responsibilities. The goal is not merely fiscal relief, but better performance of the service.[1]

The kinds of services that are appropriate for such a transfer, Netzer says, have one or both of two characteristics: their primary purpose is income redistribution and the services can be effectively provided and planned only over geographic areas that go beyond one city. Gerald Hillman, who headed McKinsey and Company's task force on the New York City tax package, says:

> It is weird that in the United States, many activities that are of national benefit and are essentially income redistributional - welfare, health and education - are local responsibilities. Since they are of national benefit one would assume that they should be treated to greater subvention in terms of federal fiscal responsibility than they now get and that we should at least consider as a partial alternative to revenue sharing, the shifting of funding responsibility for such activities to higher tiers of government.

By "income redistributional," Hillman means programs like welfare, Medicaid and free public education are income redistributional because they provide income, health care and education to the poor, thus helping to bridge the gap between the well-off and those less so.

There is, of course, a counter argument to Netzer's position. If the provision of certain services is left to levels of government whose constituencies are, for the most part, unconcerned about them, it is questionable whether adequate levels of those services will be provided to those who need them. Because, for example, the poor are so heavily concentrated in the cities, city politicians must be responsive to their needs. The same is not necessarily true for state officials whose constituency may be predominantly rural and/or suburban. In any case, it would be impossible for New York to transfer sizeable parts of its current burden of services in time to help the 1970-1971 budget. Attempts to do so would amount simply to cutting services.

Since substantial budget-cutting was not possible, large amounts of aid were not forthcoming despite appeals, and transferring responsibilities to others was not practicable, at least in 1971-1972, there remained only one other option - cutting the budget somewhat and raising taxes by a large amount. No politician likes to raise taxes and Mayor Lindsay was no exception. Taxes are politically unpopular and a tax package of $900 million would be especially dangerous politically. In this case, however, raising taxes seemed the only viable course of action. To quote Jon Weiner:

> I think it was clear fairly early that although this was a fairly stiff package. . .that the alternative of cutting seriously into expenditures was even more obnoxious. We felt that, by and large, business and most residents would be more put out by a reduction in city services than they would by fairly stiff increases in city taxes at this point. . . .

[1] Netzer, Dick, "The Budget: Trends and Prospects," in L.C. Fitch and A.H. Walsh, ed., Agenda for a City, (Beverly Hills, California: Sage Publications, 1970), p. 708.

So having decided reluctantly to ask for a huge tax package, it remained to decide on the components of that package.

The Tax Package

Initial planning for the tax package had begun well before the Mayor's decision. A team headed by Budget Director Hamilton and consisting of representatives from BoB, the Finance Administration, the Corporation Counsel, and the Mayor's Office had started investigating various tax alternatives early in the fall. They were assisted by a team from McKinsey & Co. led by Gerry Hillman. Jon Weiner of BoB acted as liaison between the city and its consultants.

The process of developing the package required frequent discussions with the Mayor, in which the team worked with him to create an over-all tax strategy and to test his reaction to specific tax options. When the Mayor had selected the taxes he wished to ask for, the revised package would be circulated within the City Administration and among business and political leaders in order to bring fundamental objections to the surface quickly. The newly revised package would then be given to the City Council. Although the law did not require it, the Legislature wanted the Council to send a "home rule message" to Albany - a message that asked the Legislature to "review a bill of importance to the city." In recent years the Council had sent the home rule message to Albany without making any attempt to cut the tax package down beforehand and leaving it to the Legislature to do so. The State Legislature would, when it got the package, determine the taxes that it thought necessary and would pass a still further revised tax package. Finally, the City Council would be asked to enact the taxes that the Legislature had passed. In recent years, the Council had made some last minute budget cuts that enabled it to kill some of the taxes that the Legislature had passed. The Legislators felt that this behavior gave the people of the city the impression that the Council had "saved" the city from the Legislature, an impression that was unfair and irked the Legislature. The team's task while this activity was going on was to prepare material in support of the Mayor's proposals, do variance analyses, and evaluate new suggestions and new combinations as they developed, especially during the negotiations in Albany.

In designing a tax package, the Bureau of the Budget and the team from McKinsey had certain things it wished to do. Jon Weiner recalls:

> What we wanted to do, first of all, was raise the revenue and do it in a way which would increase the elasticity of our tax base in the future. Second, we wanted to impose as great a burden as possible on out of city residents as opposed to residents of the city. . . . Third, we did not at this point want to impose any major taxes on business. That was a mayoral decision and, I think, a sound one. . . . Those were the guidelines. There was another guideline that was not set right at the beginning, but became a subsidiary and important one, and that was if we're going to have taxes, in addition to raising revenue, we'd like to use the taxing mechanism as a means of achieving other socially desirable ends.

Another aspect of developing a tax package also became clear to the team. Gerald Hillman says:

> If the package had to be very, very large, it was clear that there was no way to have a large income generated from taxes unless you were going to go after the large tax bases -- income, wealth and expenditure -- and these bases are very hard to hit. . . . Two other things. One is you need several taxes. You can't go with just a few because you can't afford a loss if you go with just a few in a negotiation. The second is that your taxes have to be a mixture of the traditional and untraditional. You cannot give people only what they have never heard before. You have to let them hang their hats on issues that have been raised before. You never concede that issues of taxation that you lost in the past are dead issues. . . .

Hillman's untraditional taxes found expression in what he called "programmatic taxes." Most taxes, he said, were offered in terms of three criteria: their revenue generating capacity, their progressivity (i.e., their ability to tax the rich at a progressively higher effective rate than the poor, instead of at a flat rate), and their elasticity (defined as the rate of growth of taxes as a function of the rate of growth of income or tax base). Beyond this, however, they were expected to be neutral in their effect on the choices made by business and individuals. A programmatic tax, on the other hand, is an "excess benefits tax, a deliberate attempt to affect choice," in Hillman's words. Thus someone might be rewarded for doing "good things" or preemptively penalized for not doing "good things." Or such a tax might be used as a market correcting mechanism in order to raise the price of a socially undesirable product so as to shift consumer choice towards more desirable products, e.g., taxing leaded gasoline so that motorists use unleaded gasoline. Says Hillman:

> I think the future of cities, which in this country have had major tax bases pre-empted by higher levels of government or have exhausted their capacity to increase rates on local bases, is in the area of programmatic taxes - taxes that correct behavior in the cities and, in effect, are administered as programs.

With these guidelines, the team set out to develop the tax package. They had a series of about ten meetings with the Mayor on the tax package, each about an hour to an hour and a half long. Recalls Jon Weiner:

> We had to construct a tax package to his specifications and they were his specifications. . . . Our major client was the Mayor and I think that through the series of meetings we satisfied him that we had an equitable tax package and one that could bring in the revenues that we needed.

A description follows of each new tax finally recommended by the Mayor to the council and the legislature in their initial tax proposal.

1. Extension of the Unincorporated Business Tax to Self-Employed Professionals. The Unincorporated Business Tax is a tax levied on the gross income of unincorporated business. The tax was now to be levied on self-employed professionals such as doctors, lawyers, accountants, architects, engineers, and so forth. There are 56,000 such professionals practicing in the city. The tax rate would be 4% of gross income. Before levying the tax, however, certain deductions and exemptions would be applied: operating expenses and business losses incurred since January 1, 1966; a $5,000 flat exemption; up to $5,000 per owner or partner with a maximum limit of 20% of total taxable income; depreciation allowances and special credits for research. In general, sole professionals with incomes under $20,000 would not be liable for the tax because of the deductions. The yield of such a tax was estimated at $25 million. There were several potential problems with this tax; it had been defeated the previous year by the state legislature, it might increase the cost of professional services, and it might discourage some young professionals from moving to the city.

2. Extension of Sales Tax.

a. Personal Services: The base would be all expenditures in the city on services at the city's 24,500 barber shops, beauty parlors, cleaning establishments (automatic or manual), tailor shops, photographic studios and shoe repair shops. The yield would be $24 million. The possible problems were that such proposals had failed in the legislature in the past, that most barber shops were already experiencing a decline in business, and (as is usual with a sales tax differential) that establishments on the fringes of the city might be hurt.

b. Admissions to movies: The yield from the tax would be $4 million. The possible problems were that this tax had been defeated by the legislature before and that the rise in price might exceed the amount of the tax.

c. Restaurant sales of under $1.00: The so-called "hot dog tax." The yield from this tax would be $20 million.

d. Drug sales: The base would be all non-taxed expenditures for drugs in the city excluding tax exempt sales by institutions. A yield of $10.3 million was anticipated. It could be an extremely unpopular tax politically, however, even though its cost would be covered by Medicare and Medicaid. Furthermore, it would complicate the already difficult administration of state drug taxes since some drugs would have state and city taxes and others would have only city taxes.

3. Change Sales Tax Collection from Point of Delivery to Point of Sale. At the present time, the sales tax on an item purchased in the city, but delivered outside the city limits, is levied at the rate applicable at the point of delivery and paid to the municipality where the item is delivered. This results in a large loss of revenue to the city. Simply by shifting the allocation point of the tax from the point of delivery to the point of sale, New York City could gain about $45 million. Also, the state, which collects and distributes the sales tax, returns the money only quarterly.

By filing the returns monthly, the city would save an additional \$1.1 million in interest charges and also gain \$1.2 million in interest that the state currently keeps. However, the state might resist a monthly filing since its administrative costs would go up and it would lose interest payments. Nassau, Suffolk, and Westchester counties would probably oppose the change in collection point since they would lose heavily in revenue.

4. Taxing Advertisers: This tax would be levied on companies whose products are advertised in New York City. The amount would be based on that portion of the company's total advertising budget that could be reasonably prorated to New York. A yield of \$57 million was estimated. There was some concern that this tax would be challenged in court on one of three bases; its denial of free speech, its violation of interstate commerce provisions, or the absence of city jurisdiction. In addition, the tax could result in a fall of media receipts and thus threaten marginal media companies.

5. City Tax on Beer and Liquor. The state excise tax would be increased by \$0.12 per gallon of beer (which would amount to 1.5 cents per can) and by \$1.00 per gallon on liquor and the proceeds distributed to the city. The yield would be \$37 million.

6. Increasing the Vault Charge Rate. The annual vault charge rate would increase to \$1.00 per square foot of plane or surface area of underground vaults. The present tax is \$0.35 per square foot per the first 250 square feet and \$0.60 for each additional square foot. In addition, the collection date of this charge would be moved up to June 15 from July 15. The yield from the increase in the tax would be \$2.0 million and in fiscal 1971-72 there would be a gain of \$4.0 million from the change in collection date.

7. Increase the Staten Island Passenger Fare. Foot passengers of the Staten Island Ferry would pay a fare of 25 cents. The present fare, unchanged since the last century, is 5 cents. The yield from the fare increase would be \$4.0 million and despite the increase, the city would have to subsidize about half the cost of the ferry operation. (This "tax" did not require authorization by the legislature.)

8. Auto Use Tax. A tax of \$10 would be imposed by the city, payable at the time of registration. The yield would be \$17.5 million and, it was hoped, car ownership in the city would be discouraged to a limited extent. This tax, like the Staten Island Ferry fare increase, could be imposed by action of the City Council.

9. Tax on Leaded Gasoline. All gasoline with more than 0.5 grams of lead per gallon would be taxed at a rate of 4 cents per gallon. The yield would be \$46 million. Hopefully, motorists would shift to less polluting gasolines and the tax revenue would drop in future years.

10. Tax on Non-recyclable Containers. The city would impose a tax on specified containers. Containers of food items not subject to the sales tax would be exempt from the container tax. The tax would be as follows:

Plastic bottles	3 cents a container
Other plastic containers	2 cents
Glass containers	2 cents
Multi-metallic containers	2 cents
One metal containers	1 cent
Paperboard containers	1 cent

A one cent credit against the tax rates would be applied for containers composed of the following minimum amounts of recycled material:

Plastics	30%
Glass	20% cullet in 1971-72; 30% cullet thereafter
Metals	30% in 1971-72 and 40% thereafter
Paperboard	80% if boxboard; 30% if other paper material

Cullet is broken or refuse glass, used to facilitate melting in making glass. In those instances in which reused containers make up at least 60% of the shipment, a one cent credit would be granted against the appropriate tax on each container. The yield from the tax would be $33 million. The tax was intended to help relieve the solid waste disposal problem in the city by reducing the number of containers that are used only once before being disposed of.

11. Tar and Nicotine Tax. The tax rate would be at 4 cents per pack of cigarettes which contain more than 17.0 mg. of tar and 1.1 mg. of nicotine per cigarette. Cigarettes that meet one of the two standards but not the other would be taxed at 3 cents a pack and cigarettes that meet the standard for both tar and nicotine would not be taxed at all. The yield from this tax would be $23.0 million. It is intended to encourage smokers to shift to less dangerous brands and to induce manufacturers to lower tar and nicotine content in their cigarettes.

12. Increasing the Income Tax. The first issue that the team and the Mayor had to decide was how to treat the commuters. Over six hundred thousand commuters come into New York City each morning, earn their living and leave for the suburbs each evening, leaving the city's problems, and, more importantly, its tax rate behind. At the present time commuters pay about an eighth the taxes on the same income as a resident of New York City. To the commuters' argument that they do not use as many of the city's services, Pete Hamill, a New York Post columnist had a simple answer:

> The heart of our area is New York City. You could not have Oyster Bay or Massapequa outside the city limits of Cheyenne, Wyoming. They are there because New York is the heart of this region; they are there because thousands of the inhabitants depend on employment in New York City to keep them going. They are going to have to start sharing the cost of maintaining the city's health; no New York, no suburbs. The sooner the suburbs understand that the better. The continuing ability of the suburbanites to escape responsibility for the city which provides them sustenance is an insult to all the people who have stayed on and tried to make the city work.[1]

[1]Pete Hamill, "The Outlanders," New York Post, 3/15/'71.

New York is not unique in taxing residents at a higher rate than it taxes commuters, but it is one of only a few such cities. Most tax residents and commuters at the same rate. The only other state in the union that has a different tax rate for commuters is Michigan and one city in Pennsylvania taxes its commuters more than its residents. Even in Michigan, the commuter tax is half the resident rate while in New York commuters pay only one-eighth as much as residents. Since New York City is the only city in the state with an income tax, the differential is directed at the city.

When the question was raised in the meetings with the Mayor, there was no doubt as to where he stood. Jon Weiner recalls that Lindsay was quite emphatic in his support of the Bureau's recommendation that commuters be treated on an equal basis with residents and that the nominal rates on commuters at least be the same as on residents. The rates would be only nominal because commuters could be taxed only on their earned income, that is, their salaries. Their unearned income - the interest on savings accounts, dividends, capital gains and so forth, cannot, for the most part, be taxed by the city.

Another factor that the team considered was the threshold at which to begin taxing residents. At present, taxation begins at $600 in annual income. Gerald Hillman:

> Another anomaly . . . was the fact that you had the tax running all the way down the distribution. You can't tax incomes down there in good conscience. By taxing them, now, we're getting about $3.3 million, or just a couple of percentage points of yield, and what are you taxing? You're taxing the . . . working income of your social security recipients and the aged. You're taxing the supplemental income of welfare recipients. You've got a real case, with a third of your distribution down there, for relieving that taxation. You don't lose any money. You pick up in administrative gain (from not handling the returns) what you lose from not collecting the $3.3 million in taxes.

Accordingly, most of the options that were offered the Mayor for a change in the income tax structure treated commuters the same as residents and began taxation at an income level of $6,000. They also eliminated the difference between commuters and self-employed commuters. McKinsey's computer was used to develop several hundred combinations of rates of which ten were presented to the Mayor. The options varied with respect to progressivity (from a flat rate to a highly progressive one), credits, exemptions, and deductions, but did not vary much with regard to the target yield. They were all aiming for a yield of $700 million. An early version of nine of these options is shown in Exhibit 2. The Mayor eventually picked a variation of Option 8 that was highly progressive and was organized in such a way that with a slight change in its tax form, the state could collect the tax for the city. (The state had agreed to do this in the past but had never done so.) The yield from the tax was expected to be $700.2 million, of which $520 million would be new revenue. Residents would provide almost 70% of the revenue and commuters the rest. (At present commuters provide 15% of a smaller yield.) All the options had a yield of $700 million because it was felt that such a large tax package should hit the most elastic and potentially most progressive base the hardest and $700 million was the most that could be raised from the income tax.

* * * * *

In addition to the twelve taxes discussed above, three other major levies were evaluated and discussed at length before being dropped from the package. They were:

13. <u>Food Purchased for Off-Premises Consumption</u>. This would be a tax on food bought in markets for home consumption. The yield from this tax would be $80 million or $61 million with off-setting credits for low-income families. The problem with this tax, apart from its extreme unpopularity, was that it would be extremely regressive by income and family size, a regressivity that would be only partially mitigated by the credit.

14. <u>Parking Sticker</u>. A tax designed to discourage parking in downtown Manhattan. Each car that parked in Manhattan below 96th Street would require a parking sticker. The sticker would apply for both on and off street parking. From 96th Street to 59th Street and below 34th Street the sticker would cost $150 a year for non-residents and commercial (including passenger) vehicles and $75 for residents. Between 59th Street and 34th Street the stickers would cost $200 and $100 respectively. The tax would raise about $36 million but would pose several problems. It would be difficult to enforce for transients; it might hurt the tourist trade and would require more enforcement and administrative personnel. The increased administrative costs would be $6.4 million but it would be more than offset by $25 million in revenue from parking tickets.

15. <u>Rents</u>. Under the provisions of this tax, the real-estate tax portion of rents would be made deductible on federal income tax returns, thus saving renters a great deal in taxes. Part of this saving would be returned to the city in the form of a sales tax on the non-real-estate tax portion of the rent. Total savings to renters in federal income taxes would be $165 million. A city tax of 6% would bring $115 million of this saving to the city; a 7% rate would yield $134 million. The problems, however, might be immense. The real-estate tax deductions might be challenged by the Internal Revenue Service and the tax might run into legal problems in New York if it were interpreted as a real property tax and therefore subject to constitutional limitations. Nevertheless, with over two-thirds of the city's population renting their dwellings, the tax represented a base that would be hard to resist. "The Mayor liked it a great deal," says Jon Weiner, "because it was directly a revenue sharing scheme and one which had such a differential impact on urban areas."

The taxes considered thus far (together with their yields) are summarized in Exhibit 3.

The Legislative Battle

Having decided on the tax package he wished to ask the legislature for, the Mayor had to decide on his approach. He knew that he would be facing an extremely budget-conscious legislature.[1] To quote Jon Weiner:

> We were at the point of realizing that the state was at the end of its rope fiscally, something which had not been the case at any other time during the Lindsay administration. We'd always felt that there was some give at the state level come the spring and they'd always been able to bail us out. And I think it was this year that in fact the state really did not have the fiscal wherewithal to do so from its own resources. . .and we did have the prospect of a fairly conservative legislature.

Indeed it was the first time during the Lindsay administration that both the state and the city were in deep financial trouble and had to ask the legislature for large tax packages. The legislature had been faced with substantial tax increases before but never with two at once from the state and the city and never in an amount exceeding $2 billion.

Weiner felt that for the first time, the Governor and the legislative leadership did not have complete political control over the legislature and that the city would have to deal with a wider circle of decision makers. The prospects did not seem encouraging, particularly since there was uncertainty regarding the Governor's willingness to back the city. Rockefeller and Lindsay were not noted for their mutual support of one another. Since 1963, their relationship had deteriorated in a series of incidents until, in 1969, the Governor refused to endorse Lindsay's bid for re-election and, in 1970, the Mayor backed Arthur Goldberg's campaign to unseat Rockefeller. The 1971 legislative session would be Rockefeller's chance to retaliate if he chose to do so. Republicans controlled both houses of the legislature and were so dominant that the state budget was negotiated and passed without the help of the Democrats. Rockefeller could have smoothed the path for the city, but Jon Weiner feels that he chose not to use whatever influence he had. That left the city at the mercy of the legislature whose conservatism worried the Budget Bureau and the Mayor. In Jon Weiner's words:

> We felt that we were in an embattled position, that we were dealing with a very conservative and hostile legislature, and that moreover, we were dealing with a governor who might not choose to help us out on this go around, for whatever reason. The point is that we came up to Albany feeling that we didn't have friends, and no action in the first week and a half convinced us that it was any different. I think the mayor was terribly concerned that we would come out of this facing a very major budget disaster.

Another fact was noteworthy: 1971 was the first year that Mayor Lindsay would not be dealing with the Republican leaders in Albany as a fellow Republican. In previous years there had been advance discussions and substantive negotiations between the Mayor and his staff on one hand and the Governor, his staff and the legislative leadership on the other. This year there was no advance discussion.

---

[1]The legislature's budget consciousness was shown about a month after the Mayor released his tax package when it cut $760 million out of Governor Rockefeller's tax request of $1.1 billion. As a result of the cuts in the state tax package and the state budget, welfare grants were cut by close to 10% per person. Medicaid eligibility was tightened considerably and while this saved the state some money, it increased the cost to the city since the ineligible people would be treated at city expense in municipal hospitals. Finally, the state revenue sharing scheme was cut from 21% of the state income tax to 18%, costing New York City at least $75 million.

On April 19, 1971, John Lindsay sent a 168-page letter to the Governor, the members of the state legislature, the City Council and the Board of Estimate outlining four alternative budgets and the effects of each. Under Option I, the budget would be $7.8 billion, the same as 1970-71. It assumed that the legislature would refuse to rescind $500 million in state aid cuts (that had taken place midway through fiscal year 1970-1971), and would refuse the city any new taxing authority. Under this option, the city would have to lay off 60,000 people and leave 30,000 other jobs unfilled as they became vacant. The cutback would represent almost 25% of the city's work force of 381,000. Of these 21,000 would be from the health and hospital services, 19,700 in education (9,422 teachers), 14,287 in police (of a force of 32,000), 15,000 in welfare, 3,227 in the fire department, and more than 4,500 in the Environmental Protection Administration (responsible for sanitation). Eight municipal hospitals of eighteen would be closed, all remedial and special education would cease, no freshman class would be admitted to City University (under open enrollment, 35,000 would be admitted) and 2,400 faculty and other jobs would be eliminated at the university, and park maintenance would be virtually halted. Under civil service regulations, layoffs must start with appointees and then go through the probationers before reaching the civil service itself. Within the service, layoffs occur in inverse order of entry. The effect is that the youngest and freshest people, and members of minority groups (who entered in large numbers only recently) are the first to be laid off.

Option II assumed that the $500 million aid cut would be restored and that the city would get $400 million in new taxes. Even so, 50,000 jobs would be eliminated (including 30,000 layoffs); 11,200 jobs in the police department would go; 12,000 in health and hospitals; 10,800 in education; 10,750 in welfare; 3,630 in sanitation; and 2,500 in fire. Five municipal hospitals would close, park maintenance would be cut 50%, all extracurricular school activities would end and open enrollment would be stopped at City University.

Option III assumed a restoration of aid and a tax package of $880 million. It was a $9.2 billion budget and under it, the city would cut back 6,000 jobs through attrition, with 3,750 coming from education, 1,800 from police, and 410 from fire. No new programs would be added and there would be no major expansions.

The Option IV budget was the one the mayor wanted. In it, state aid cuts would be restored, the $880 million tax package approved, and an additional $115 million provided. The result would be a $9.3 billion budget that would operate the fire department at full strength, put more policemen on the streets, institute a free breakfast program, start programs to control venereal disease, and open a new prison ward in a Bronx hospital.

The option budgets created tremendous publicity all over the state and the nation. They became a major rallying point for the people of New York City, many of whom travelled up to Albany to show their support of Mayor Lindsay's position.

The Governor's initial response was to comment that a cutback of 90,000 "would about bring the city back to where it was when he (Lindsay) took over."[1] Between 1966 and 1971 the mayor had added about 70,000 jobs. Almost half this increase, the mayor's staff noted, was mandated under new or expanded federal and state programs; and some of the remainder, such as the hiring and training of paraprofessionals, was designed to reduce costs from what they otherwise would be. In a formal response - a letter to the Mayor on April 24 - Rockefeller stated:

> Just as the state found it necessary to face the harsh realities, so must every other unit in the state - from the smallest school district to the largest urban center - exercise a comparable discipline in the light of the present fiscal crisis.[2]

On April 28, Lindsay altered his position from open support of the Option IV budget to backing the Option III budget. Even so, few people in City Hall expected to get anything like an Option III tax package. One aide described such a package as "nirvana."[3]

On April 29, the City's Controller, Abraham Beame got involved in the argument over the size of the budget gap. A Democrat who had been defeated by Lindsay in the mayoral election of 1965, Beame is generally regarded as having his eye on the mayoralty in 1973. Beame now claimed to be able to cut the city's budget gap by $276.9 million. He claimed that Lindsay's aides had underestimated General Fund revenues by $183.7 million and that, in addition, the state could help through roll-overs (early payments) to the tune of $66.7 million. The General Fund consists of taxes collected for unrestricted purposes, that is, not earmarked for some specific use such as highway maintenance. Finally, Beame said, the Teacher's Pension Fund had a surplus of $26.5 million that Beame could release. The Teacher's Pension could have a surplus by dint of an overpayment that only the Controller could release. It is an intentional overpayment.

Of all the charges, Budget Director Hamilton accepted only the statement about the Teacher's Pension Fund. It was a transfer that was "something the controller can do - I'll defer to him on that."[4] As for the rest, Hamilton said: "This is a very bad time to phony up General Fund estimates. I'm saying that our projections are conservative and sound. His (Mr. Beame's) leave a great deal of professionalism to be

---

[1]Rockefeller's quotation and material on the Option budgets came from the New York Times, 4/20/71.

[2]Rockefeller, quoted in the New York Times, 4/25/71.

[3]Quoted, New York Times, 4/29/71.

[4]Quoted, New York Times, 4/30/71.

desired."[1] Nevertheless, Beame's projections were used by the legislative leaders as an indication that the Mayor was exaggerating the extent of the fiscal crisis and using unfair tactics by publicising the option budgets so heavily. Jon Weiner says:

> I think originally . . . the state people - including the professionals: the State Budget Bureau, the Governor, certainly the legislative leaders - did not actually believe the size of that (budget) gap, and I think were a bit put off by the intense publicity that we gave the option budgets and believed that we were engaging in the worst kind of scare tactic. It was certainly clear that the two legislative leaders (Assembly Speaker Perry B. Duryea, Jr., of Montauk, L.I. and Senate Majority Leader Earl W. Brydges of Buffalo) certainly did not believe it. . . .

Once the legislature began discussing the tax package, it became even more clear that the city was in a bad predicament. Part of the problem had to do with Lindsay himself rather than with the issue at hand.

"John Lindsay doesn't have a party - he's a man without a party," Governor Rockefeller told a group on May 21. As Martin Tolchin has pointed out, "in a two party system, the man without party lacks a friend at court."[2] The Republicans in Albany couldn't forgive Lindsay for supporting Goldberg, and the Democrats were powerless to help him. The result was a constant needling, especially by the Governor. In one meeting the Governor prefaced all of his comments with "Now John, I'm not being critical" and proceeded to criticize strongly. "It reminded me of a surgeon performing an operation," said City Councilman Matthew J. Troy. "The Governor never once showed blood, but he let it be known he was doing the cutting."[3]

When the negotiations really began, the city found itself completely cut out, as did the Democrats. Jon Weiner says:

> The negotiations were actually between the governor and the State Budget Bureau and the Republican leadership for a while, and the city of course was rather much out of it - we didn't have much to say. We just literally sat in Albany waiting for someone to call us and very much on the outside of negotiations.

On May 24, another city official complained that "apparently our fate is being decided behind closed doors without our involvement by people who are largely from outside the city."[4]

---

[1]Quoted, New York Times, 4/30/71.

[2]New York Times, 5/24/71.

[3]Quoted, New York Times, 5/28/71.

[4]Quoted, New York Times, 5/27/71.

Nevertheless, city officials did not stop trying, although without much conspicuous success. Said Jon Weiner:

> What we did was literally go around with a chart show. It was very much a question of lengthy, continuous exposition of our problem. One of the reasons we were despondent was that we realized that even though we did begin our campaign of public education in March, that we didn't have the legislators' understanding, in the most general way, what the dickens these taxes were!

Despite the statements that they had been cut out, city officials did have some idea of what was going on. Sympathetic legislators acted as bridges between the conclave of the Governor, his aides, and the legislative leaders on the one hand and Hamilton and his staff in Albany on the other. The professionals on the Governor's staff also kept Hamilton informed by briefing him every two hours so that although Hamilton was not involved in the negotiations, he knew what was going on. Frequently, city officials then communicated with the consultants in New York who evaluated each offer, provided supporting data, and performed variance analyses.

It appeared, for a while, as though the city would be able to get only about $300 million in new taxes, which the Mayor and his aides felt would be a fiscal disaster. Then it looked as though either $300 million in taxes or $600 million was practicable, but nothing in between. The reason for this was fairly simple. The Republican majority could have rammed through a $300 million package without Democratic help. If they needed Democratic help, however, the package would have to jump drastically since the Democrats wanted the full $900 million package. The Democrats represented largely urban districts and were, therefore, somewhat more sympathetic to New York City's problems and well aware that their constituencies might need similar help some day. Besides, as Democrats, they would be philosophically more inclined to aid cities and increase taxes. With one group asking for a $300 million package and another holding out for $900 million, $600 million seemed a logical compromise.

It was at this point that the intense publicity surrounding the option budgets began helping the city. Some observers felt that the care with which the city had prepared the budgets, the work involved and the degree of exactitude in the budgets (down to the last hundreds of thousands of dollars) impressed the Governor. These observers felt that the Governor genuinely began to feel that New York's fiscal position was severe and could not be helped sufficiently by a $300 million package. It may also have been the intensity of the publicity that changed his mind forcing the discussion out of the back rooms in Albany and making it politically expedient for Rockefeller to support a larger package. While some believe the change of heart to be genuine, if somewhat skeptical, no one except the Governor really knows for sure.

In any case, on May 27, the Governor acknowledged that he and the Republican leadership had decided on a tax package in the neighborhood of $450 million. Two days later, the Mayor labeled it "not enough" and stated that the state was acting with "a combination of arrogance and contempt."[1] On May 31, he called the package "part sham and part bad policy."[2] Yet even with a $450 million package, the Governor found his majority slipping away. The conservative Republicans would not follow him.

Observers said that for days Rockefeller had been trying to get the Republicans to authorize a state Real Property Tax that would apply only to New York City. It was an attempt to get around the constitutional limits on city real property taxes and would raise $70 million for the city in the first year. Rockefeller tried hard to get this tax but Republican legislators would not accept any increase in real property taxes. According to an observer, "It's one of the few sacred cows they have in Albany." Failure to get this tax through was one reason the Governor finally decided that he would have to deal with more than the Republican majority. Another, observers claim, was his concern that the legislative leadership would intentionally delay passage of a tax program until the City Council was forced to pass a final budget. This would shift the onus of new taxes and/or service cuts to the City Council. In addition, the legislature might not have to pass such a large package. If the legislature were to adjourn in the midst of such a process, the result could have been disastrous. In hopes of getting the negotiations going again, the Democratic minority was brought in on June 2. The new arrivals immediately demanded a package of $700 million. In asking the aid of the Democrats, the Governor tacitly acknowledged the fiscal plight of the city. Jon Weiner concluded that "the Governor was genuinely impressed, after a week or two, with our fiscal situation." But Rockefeller also felt, according to Weiner, that "the Mayor was using unfair publicity with budget options and one thing and another." On June 3, Rockefeller, Duryea and Brydges, in a joint statement, charged that Lindsay was "inept and extravagant" and that their efforts to help the city had been "hindered by a growing loss of confidence in the Mayor's administration of the city."[3] In a sharp rebuttal, a City Hall spokesman said:

> The same Albany leaders have the colossal nerve to attack the Mayor for failure to negotiate - in negotiations from which he has been systematically excluded.[4]

The $700 million package that earned the support of the Democrats included eight new taxes that had not been in the city's original proposal. The taxes had come out of a Democratic caucus with Budget Director Hamilton; Deputy Director of BoB Jim Cavanaugh; and Deputy Mayor Richard R. Aurelio. It was the first time city officials of the Lindsay administration had negotiated with the Democrats. The eight new taxes were:

---

[1] Quoted, <u>New York Times</u>, 5/29/71.

[2] Ibid., 6/1/71.

[3] Ibid., 6/4/71.

[4] Ibid.

16. Increase in City General Corporation Tax. The city tax rate on the net income of corporations would be raised from the present 5.5% to 6.7% - a rise of 21.8%. The yield would be about $45 million.

17. Increase in City Financial Corporation Tax. The city's tax rate on the income of banks and other financial institutions would be increased from 4.5% to 5.63% - an increase of 25%. The minimum bank tax would be increased from $10 to $12.50. In other words, if, after all the deductions, a financial corporation's tax liability was less than $12.50, the corporation would nevertheless have to pay $12.50. The estimated yield of the increase in the tax rate was expected to be $10.5 million.

18. City Mortgage Recording Tax. A city tax on the recording of mortgages would be imposed at the rate of 50 cents per $100 of debt secured by the mortgage. The new tax would double the rate prevailing in the city at present. The present tax is imposed by the state and all revenues are returned to the city. The yield from the new tax would be $11.0 million.

19. Increase in City Real Property Transfer Tax. The city's tax on the conveyance of real property would be doubled from 0.5% to 1.0%. The tax would apply only to transfers in excess of $25,000. The yield from the tax would be $7.0 million.

20. Rescinding Exemptions from the Real Property Tax. Rescind exemptions from the tax of all classes of property whose exemption is not based on constitutional provision. These organizations would include medical, dental and pharmaceutical societies, a range of patriotic and historical societies and improvement societies of various kinds. The yield would be $12.0 million.

21. Service Charges for Tax Exempt Property. The city would impose service charges for police and fire protection; street and highway construction, maintenance, and lighting; and sanitation and water supply on a variety of properties now exempted from the real property tax. Properties subject to the tax would be those whose tax exempt status is not based on constitutional provision. These would include properties of scientific and professional societies, benevolent associations, organizations for the moral or mental improvement of men and women, and others. Property of charitable, educational, religious and cemetery organizations (who are constitutionally exempted), which is not used for the exclusive purposes of the organization would also be subject to the service charges. The amount of the service charge would be a fraction of the real property tax levied were the property subject to the property tax. The fraction is determined by the proportion of the city's real estate tax levy that can reasonably be prorated to the cost of supplying the services listed above. In 1971-72 that fraction was expected to be slightly greater than one-third. The yield from these charges would be $5 million.

22. Increased Commercial Vehicle Tax. The city's tax on commercial vehicles, excluding taxis, buses and other passenger carriers would be doubled. The yield would be $2.9 million.

23. Manhattan Garage Tax. The city's 6% garage tax would be increased by an additional 8% on the sale of any garage space in Manhattan. The incremental tax would not apply in less congested boroughs. The yield of the tax would be $8 million. It should help to reduce the congestion in Manhattan as well as some of the pollution caused by automobiles.

On June 9, the tax package passed the legislature. It amounted, in all, to an $861 million package composed of $525 million in new taxes; a $100 million revenue sharing guarantee (that is, if the Federal Government did not provide it, the state would); $87 million in deferred payments to the Teachers' Pension Fund; $81 million in deferred payments to the General Fund Stabilization Reserve (the "Rainy Day Fund"); and $68 million in Welfare and Medicaid payments. The Teacher's Pension Fund was the only pension fund that was on a current basis. All other pension funds were lagged two years. By lagging this final fund by two years, the city saved itself $87 million in 1971-1972 and 1972-1973 since it need not pay for two years. The deferral does not hurt the Fund and since the city is a continuing entity, the Fund will simply be perpetually lagged two years. The "Rainy Day" fund is exactly what it sounds like - a fund to build up reserves in case of financial emergencies such as a serious fire. It is built up in good years and borrowed against in bad years. By deferring payments, the city is left in a more financially precarious position and less able to respond adequately in an emergency. In developing the tax package, the state left the same income tax structure as currently prevailed, that is, taxes all the way down the distribution, a resident tax that was eight times the commuter tax and a tax organized so that it was quite different from the state's, so that the state could not collect it for the city. The yield from the income tax was cut to $190 million (with commuters paying $37 million more). The Leaded Gasoline Tax was reduced to 1¢ a gallon, cutting the yield to $12.0 million and three taxes were cut out. The three were the sales tax on drugs, the sales tax on city-directed advertising and the change in collection point for the sales tax. The latter was cut out because it would cost the suburban counties a great deal of money without returning anything to them.

After all the negotiations and all the recrimination the final package passed the legislature without debate and with no more than five minutes spent on each new tax provision.

The biggest loss in revenue was the income tax cutback. That commuter-resident equity was not realized was not really a surprise. There had, however, been a reason for the city's big push for equity. Said Jon Weiner:

> We were forced to make a very strong pitch for equal treatment of commuters if only for the politics involved. With the legislature heavily weighted with suburban and upstate voters, it would tend to give us an income tax package that placed a very heavy burden on New York City residents but did not do very much with commuters. If we got that from the state, then I think we would have had very serious trouble getting it through the City Council, because Councilmen feel _terribly_ vulnerable to passing a _very_ substantial increase in the income tax if there were not an even more substantial rise in the tax that commuters pay. So I think we were stuck in political crossfire in proposing an income tax that was heavily weighted towards commuters. I don't think we _ever_ expected to get it. It was proposed as an educational device.

The legislature extracted a price for its tax package. City officials concluded that the bargain for $525 million in new taxes was an agreement not to conduct massive layoffs that could be blamed on the governor and the legislature.

After the legislative session ended, the Mayor told a meeting of the New York State Conference of Mayors that he could not recall a session "more chillingly anti-city. . .as blindly partisan. . . . I cannot recall any leadership in this great state so opposed to progressive change, so ready to punish the poor. . .and so determined to extract the last pound of flesh from its opponents."[1]

Lindsay now had to get the City Council to enact the taxes that the legislature had authorized. His task was not made easier by Controller Beame, who claimed on June 15 that the Bureau of the Budget had made errors totalling $330 million in the budget. He stated that the Bureau's estimate that the increases in the income tax, the unincorporated business tax, the general corporation tax and the financial corporation tax would raise $270.5 million was $135 million short since the tax increases were retroactive to January 1, 1971, and therefore were voted for 18 months instead of 12. In addition, Beame said, the Bureau had underestimated General Fund revenues by $108.5 million and overstated expenditures by $76.6 million.

The City Council's response was that if Beame was correct they would "slash the Mayor's tax package to ribbons."[2] The Mayor responded by saying that the Controller's "recklessness was doing untold damage to the city,"[3] and Ed Hamilton said that "his track record estimating budgets is so bad that you'd think it ought to sober him a bit."[4] Hamilton said that the tax revenues had been calculated on an 18-month basis and that the Bureau's other figures were just more realistic estimates than Beame's. Hamilton said that a large part of the 1970-1971 budget deficit could be attributed to the fact that Beame had succeeded in pushing revenue estimates up.

On June 14, Mayor Lindsay reduced his $9.1 billion "survival budget" to $8.75 billion, largely by deferring payments rather than cutting services. On June 22, the City Council cut $187 million from the revised Expense Budget and passed an $8.56 billion budget. The Council also induced the Mayor to revise upward the yield from some revenue measures by $77 million and compromised on a change in the expected increase in welfare case load. The Bureau of the Budget had estimated a monthly increase in the case load of 12,000. After discussions with the Council, the estimated increase was reduced to 5,000 new cases a month. The savings from this maneuver were $43 million. Miscellaneous small changes saved $7 million more. Accordingly, the Council eliminated $127 million in taxes authorized by the legislature. It eliminated the sales tax on movies; the tax on beer and liquor and the liquor licensing surcharge; the increase in the Staten Island Ferry fare; the Auto Use Tax and the Manhattan Garage Tax. The Council also refused to tax metal and glass containers but imposed a 2¢ a container tax on plastic containers. This tax was now expected to yield $10.0 million since even plastic blade dispensers would be taxed, as would items encased in a plastic bubble. (The casings for ball point pens and so forth.) Considering the fact that no changes had been made in the structure of the income tax, it was perhaps a surprise that the income tax passed the City Council. The reason, according to Jon Weiner, is quite simple:

---

[1]Quoted, New Yorker, 6/26/71.

[2]Quoted, New York Times, 6/16/71.

[3]Ibid.

[4]Ibid.

> It passed the City Council because, I think, at that point they were really up against a wall. They realized that if they didn't pass this in some form or another that it would mean layoffs and I think the Council was in the position, even more than the executive, of assuming that layoffs would be politically disastrous, and so we did get a very unsatisfactory income tax (i.e., without any reforms in the system).

The final budget of $8.56 billion was described by one Budget Bureau aide as an "Option 2.8 budget." It called for a reduction of 19,333 jobs solely by attrition. Five thousand jobs that were presently unfilled would be abolished, while 14,320 other jobs would not be filled as they became vacant. By June 30, 1972 there would be at least 4,580 fewer employees in education (of whom 3,500 would be teachers), 1,300 fewer policemen, 1,000 fewer welfare workers, 960 fewer sanitation men, 620 fewer employees in health and hospitals, and 360 fewer firemen. The rest of the attrition would come from whatever departments had workers leave because of retirement, deaths and resignations. There would be some dislocations but not even close to the fiscal disaster the Mayor had predicted.

In each year since 1967 (except for 1970) Mayor Lindsay had threatened disaster unless his full tax package was passed. Each time he succeeded in getting only about half his package. Yet, despite all the warnings, the disaster had somehow been averted each year. Perhaps understandably, the Mayor was being accused of crying "wolf" too often. The prediction was made that the legislature would be much more skeptical next year.

Exhibit 1

THE 1971-1972 NEW YORK CITY TAX PROGRAM

Sources From Which City's Income was Derived (1969-1970)*
(millions)

Source of Income	Amount	Per Cent of Total
Tax Levy	$1,893	28.2
State Grants	1,738	25.9
Federal Grants	1,074	16.0
Sales Tax	467	7.0
Stock Transfer and Mortgage Tax	255	3.8
General Corporation and Financial Corporation Tax	245	3.7
Other Special City Taxes	217	3.2
Personal Income and Earnings Tax	206	3.1
Fees, Fines, Licenses, Permits, etc.	119	1.8
Rental, Interest, Services, Ferry Fares, In Rem, etc.	112	1.7
Water Charges	104	1.5
Cash Carryover	104	1.5
Other Income	87	1.3
Transfers and Borrowings	84	1.3
	$6,705	100.0

*Source: Controller's Report for 1969-1970.

Exhibit 2

THE 1971-1972 NEW YORK CITY TAX PROGRAM

Effective Tax Rates on Earned Income 1971-1972

	Income Level	$500	$1,500	$2,500	$3,500	$4,500	$5,500	$6,500	$8,500	$12,500	$17,500	$22,500	$27,500	$40,000	$75,000	$150,000	$250,000	Yield 1971-72 $(Mill.)	%
Current Tax Structure	Residents		0.07%	0.10	.19	.26	.31	.34	.39	.51	.65	.76	.83	1.00	1.28	1.43	1.48	192.8	89.1
	Commuters								.16	.21	.22	.23	.24	.25	.25	.25	.25	19.1	8.8
	Self-Employed Commuters								.24	.31	.33	.35	.36	.37	.37	.37	.37	4.5	2.0
Option 1	Residents							2.10	2.10	2.10	2.10	2.10	2.10	2.10	2.10	2.10	2.10	493.5	69.9
	Commuters							2.10	2.10	2.10	2.10	2.10	2.10	2.10	2.10	2.10	2.10	212.6	30.1
2	Residents							1.97	1.98	2.03	2.08	2.11	2.13	2.15	2.17	2.19	2.20	492.8	70.1
	Commuters								1.98	2.03	2.08	2.11	2.13	2.15	2.17	2.19	2.20	210.3	29.9
3	Residents							2.15	2.16	2.21	2.27	2.30	2.32	2.34	2.37	2.38	2.40	528.6	77.4
	Commuters								1.07	1.11	2.27	2.30	2.32	2.34	2.37	2.38	2.40	154.4	22.6
4	Residents							1.02	1.11	1.30	1.53	1.76	1.95	2.39	3.02	3.48	3.70	499.8	71.1
	Commuters								1.14	1.35	1.61	1.86	2.10	2.65	3.27	3.63	3.78	201.0	28.9
5	Residents							1.53	1.61	1.82	2.02	2.20	2.36	2.77	3.53	4.20	4.54	497.0	71.1
	Commuters								2.00	2.00	2.00	2.00	2.00	2.00	2.00	2.00	2.00	202.5	28.9
6	Residents							1.53	1.61	1.82	2.02	2.20	2.36	2.77	3.53	4.20	4.54	579.5	82.6
	Commuters								.81	.91	1.01	1.10	1.18	1.39	1.77	2.10	2.27	121.5	17.3
7	Residents							.96	1.04	1.23	1.46	1.68	1.85	2.29	3.22	4.01	4.48	520.0	74.1
	Commuters								1.02	1.22	1.47	1.68	1.85	2.28	2.13	3.86	4.49	181.9	25.9
8	Residents					.24	.58	.63	.73	1.01	1.40	1.77	2.06	2.77	3.89	4.51	4.73	487.7	69.6
	Commuters								.75	1.06	1.48	1.89	2.24	3.12	4.25	4.72	4.85	212.5	30.4
9	Residents							.88	1.03	1.40	1.95	2.47	2.81	3.29	3.75	3.87	3.86	546.6	71.2
	Commuters								1.03	1.40	1.95	2.47	2.81	3.29	3.75	3.87	3.86	221.4	28.8

Exhibit 3

THE 1971-1972 NEW YORK CITY TAX PROGRAM

Evolution of the 1971-1972 Tax Package

(X = Eliminated; * = Introduced in Albany)	Reviewed by City	Proposed by City	Authorized by State Legislature	Enacted by City Council
		Yield in $ Millions		
1. Extension of Unincorporated Business Tax	25.0	25.0	25.0	25.0
2. Sales Tax Increases				
a) Personal Services	24.0	24.0	24.0	24.0
b) Movies	4.0	4.0	4.0	X
c) Restaurant Sales Under $1.00	20.0	20.0	20.0	20.0
d) Drugs	10.3	10.3	X	-
3. Sales Tax Allocation Point	45.0	45.0	X	-
4. Tax on Advertisers	57.0	57.0	X	-
5. City Tax on Beer and Liquor	37.0	37.0	37.0	X
6. Increase in Vault Charge Rates	6.0	6.0	6.0	6.0
7. Increase in Staten Island Ferry Fare	4.0	4.0	4.0	X
8. Auto Use Tax	17.5	17.5	17.5	X
9. Leaded Gasoline Tax	46.0	46.0	12.0	12.0
10. Recycling Incentive Tax	33.0	33.0	33.0	10.0
11. Tar and Nicotine Tax	23.0	23.0	23.0	23.0
12. Changes in Income Tax Structure	Many	520.0	190.0	190.0
13. Food Purchases	61.0	X	-	-
14. Parking Sticker & Fines - Administrative Costs	30-70	X	-	-
15. Tax on Rents	134.0	X	-	-
16. Increase in General Corporation Tax	-	*	45.0	45.0
17. Increase in City Tax on Financial Corporations	-	*	10.5	10.5
18. City Mortgage Recording Tax	-	*	11.0	11.0
19. Increase in Real Property Transfer Tax	-	*	7.0	7.0
20. Rescinding Real Property Tax Exemptions	-	*	12.0	12.0
21. Service Charges on Tax Exempt Property	-	*	5.0	5.0
22. Commercial Vehicle Tax	-	*	2.9	2.9
23. Manhattan Garage Tax	-	*	8.0	X
Total Number of Taxes	18	15	20	15
Total Yield	-	871.8	496.9	403.4

THE BOSTON REDEVELOPMENT AUTHORITY (A and B)

On January 15, 1968 Hale Champion was appointed by Mayor Kevin White to the $35,000 a year post of development administrator of the Boston Redevelopment Authority (BRA). In assuming the leadership of the Authority, Champion was faced with the difficult problem of deciding what the BRA ought to be doing and how it should go about doing it. Established in 1957, the BRA had the sole responsibility for urban renewal activities in the City of Boston. Moreover, the Boston City Planning Board had been abolished in 1960 and its duties and responsibilities given to the BRA. For example, in addition to the federal urban renewal areas, the BRA was involved in programs such as planning of a new sports stadium, securing money for Model Cities Programs, and improving the city's transportation system.

Champion had been graduated from Stanford University in 1951, had served as an assistant to a Congressman for a year, and then became a newspaper reporter until 1958. (In 1956-1957, he was a Nieman Fellow at Harvard.) From November 1958 until appointed director of finance for the State of California in 1961, he had been press secretary and then executive secretary to Governor Pat Brown. He had helped manage Brown's successful campaign for governor against Richard Nixon in 1962. During 1967, he was a Fellow at the Kennedy Institute of Politics at Harvard.

At the time of Champion's appointment to the BRA, Boston had just elected a new mayor and a new city council. Residents of the city were demanding a greater voice in the planning and execution of programs that affected them. And the war in Vietnam had greatly reduced federal funds available for urban renewal projects while riots of the previous summer in cities such as Detroit argued for immediate action.

Commenting on Boston's urban renewal efforts in an interview published in <u>Boston</u> magazine, Mayor White said:

I think you have to view a city like a human being...a city has both its physical needs and its psychological needs. We've been reacting only to its physical needs....

/Ex-Mayor/ John Collins made the assumption, and it was a valid one at the time, that if he could rebuild the face of the city, give it a feeling of economic rejuvenation, and keep the tax rate down, that was the happy formula. Well, I'm not sure any of us has the formula, but anyway that didn't prove to be it.

My battle is on another front (neighborhoods).... When you're building a city, you can see the construction and renewal--you can add and subtract; like painting a fence, you know what you've done and what you have yet to do. But when you're dealing with the psychological sustenance of people, trying to communicate with them, trying to educate them as you execute a program, it's hard to measure what progress you are making. That is the more difficult fight, I think, but maybe because I'm subjective and I'm doing the fighting.

Urban Renewal

What was it?

Under the provisions of the Housing Act of 1949, as amended, the Federal Housing and Urban Development Department (HUD) was authorized to enter into contracts with local redevelopment authorities (the BRA was such an authority) to finance slum clearance, urban renewal projects, and other programs designed to prevent the spread of urban blight and to improve the quality of the urban environment.

Thus the urban renewal program was a means for augmenting virtually any objective. Its mode of operation was totally dependent on the purposes for which it was utilized. It could, for example, be used to generate land for low-income public housing, moderate-income housing and/or luxury housing; rehabilitate or clear sizable areas; change land uses and assemble land; conserve, upgrade, alter, or restructure areas and neighborhoods by providing land for a central business district, industrial, and related economic development for the purpose of revitalizing core cities and enhancing their tax base; produce sites for and/or subsidize public facilities (schools, libraries, streets, sewer and water systems, parks, fire and police stations, civic centers, off-street parking, etc.).

As such, urban renewal was a program which raised many of the questions disturbing the United States in the 1960s: What was the purpose of a city? Whose values were to be served? What sacrifices should citizens make for the common good, somehow defined? What parties required government subsidies and why? To what extent did democracy require citizen participation in--and a veto over--decisions about the future of neighborhoods and the disposition of private property?

Considerable debate raged around these questions. Representative of those who opposed the Federal Urban Renewal Program were the views of Martin Anderson.

> Since 1949 two different methods have been used to grapple with the "problems" of housing and cities. One of these is basically the system of free enterprise, guided by the complex interplay of the marketplace. The other force is the federal urban renewal program, guided by over-all plans prepared by city planning experts and backed up with the taxpayers' money and the police power of the government.
>
> The facts tell us that private enterprise has made enormous gains, while the federal program has not. Contrast, for example, the fantastic increase of 18 million homes in areas outside urban renewal projects with the net decrease of homes within urban renewal projects. Consider also the decrease in low-rent housing and the increase in high-rent housing in the urban renewal areas; urban renewal actually subsidizes high-income groups and hurts low-income groups. Add to this the destruction of businesses and the forcible displacement of people from their homes. The program endangers the right of private property--commercial and residential--in its equating of public interest with public use.
>
> The over-all results of the government program, when compared to the results of private forces, are negligible. Its over-all costs, when compared with its results, are high. On balance, the federal urban renewal program has accomplished little of benefit in the past, and it appears doubtful that it will do better in the future.[1]

A more favorable view of urban renewal was provided by Charles Abrams.

> The mass displacements of the renewal program have led to an increasing barrage of criticism that could be satisfied by nothing short of the program's repeal. These critics are as naive as those who unconditionally defend the program in its every aspect. A program which siphons federal money into our languishing cities would be a legislative curiosity if it did no good at all. If it did no more than incite some eight hundred cities (not to mention the thousands of other communities receiving planning grants) to take a constructive look at their environments and replan them, it could not be rated a total loss.

---

[1] James Q. Wilson, Urban Renewal: The Record and the Controversy, (MIT Press, 1965), pp. 506-507.

The renewal law has virtues as well as vices, and the vices exist largely because the measure is actually a half-measure. What the program needs is amplification, not abolition, a complementary housing program to make it workable, and an enlargement of its basic concept to do what its name implies. In a nation whose affection for its cities is inconspicuous, it makes no sense to scuttle any program, however imperfect, that aims to help them.[1]

What major external constraints faced renewal authorities?

A rational strategy of priorities and goals for urban renewal had to recognize the constraints which operated within the older metropolitan area core cities. The following is a summary of those constraints.

A. Scarcity of Land: Older metropolitan core cities were built up border-to-border with an absence of available undeveloped land. This produced an inflexibility in any program of physical change since every action resulted in disruption of existing residential and/or nonresidential functions and activities.

B. Nature of Housing Market: The central city housing market all too frequently: (1) had a critically short supply of standard housing, particularly in the size and price levels available to low-income persons and families; (2) had large numbers of dwellings which were aged, dilapidated, and economically and functionally obsolete; (3) contained large numbers of families unable to bear the economic rent of standard housing; and, (4) was compartmentalized along racial lines.

C. Lack of Residential Alternatives: Most non-Whites were denied access to both the full city-wide housing market and to virtually all of the much larger suburban stock. Out of this pattern emerged a phenomenon where low-income non-White families paid substantially more for substantially worse housing.

D. Rural to Urban Migration: Since 1930 the U.S. had seen continuing rural to urban migration, primarily comprised of poor Blacks and Whites.

E. Outmigration of Middle- and Upper-Income Strata: Aggravating the problems imposed by the constraints listed above was a simultaneous departure from the city of the upper-income strata (overwhelmingly White, but increasingly Black). Thus the concentration of "expensive-to-service" population in the inner city had been compounded by the departure of the affluent population.

[1] Ibid., pp. 558-559.

F. Capital Shortages: During the 1930s the nation's cities were unable to replace public or private capital facilities at a rate approaching deterioration. During the 1940s capital was largely preempted by the war effort. During the 1950s the great surge of capital reinvestment went to the suburbs. This had produced increased deterioration and functional and economic obsolescence of much of the public and private plant of urban core cities. This pattern was augmented by the constraints discussed here, particularly by the massive inflow of new populations that utilized this plant stock more intensively and accelerated wear and tear.

G. The Decentralization of Jobs: Job opportunities were opening up at a much faster rate in suburban fringe portions of metropolitan areas. Moreover, this trend was even sharper in the unskilled, semiskilled, service, clerical, operative, laborer and other low-threshold jobs which were most suitable to present underemployed and unemployed. Central cities tended to be made up of sizable increases in professional, managerial, technical, financial, and other high threshold jobs coupled with losses of occupations with low entry requirements.

H. Continuation of Stated Constraints: It was generally assumed in 1968 that there would be no significant "metropolitanization" of solutions to the most critical and urgent problems of slums, blight, and poverty. It was not anticipated that major federal or state policies or statutes would be promulgated to induce suburban committees or metropolitan planning bodies to deal with these issues on a metropolitan basis. Neither was it likely that suburban fringe communities would voluntarily develop the massive, expansive, and politically unpopular programs to significantly contribute to their solution.

What were the formal procedures?

The Federal Government paid for two-thirds of the net cost of an urban renewal project. The local community provided the remaining one-third in either cash or "noncash grants-in-aid." (In Massachusetts, the state paid one-sixth of the project cost and the local community provided one-sixth.) Noncash grants-in-aid included items such as site improvements (streets and sidewalks). The term also included public facilities to support the new uses of the project area (such as schools, police stations, libraries, and parks) to the extent they served and benefited the project, and certain statutory credits such as those related to the acquisition of land by colleges, universities, and hospitals, or the provision of land for low-rent public housing.

In launching a renewal project, the first formal finding made by a local governing body (in Boston, the city council) was that the area selected was a slum, blighted, deteriorated, or deteriorating. This finding was supported by data on buildings and environmental conditions. This and other information was included in a survey and planning application to the Renewal Assistance Administration (RAA) of HUD. Upon approval of this application, the community began its project planning.

The major product of the planning period was the urban renewal plan. A typical urban renewal plan identified the area covered and indicated in general terms the public actions to be taken to achieve the objectives of the project. It established land uses in the area, identified the changes to be made to the streets, other public rights-of-way, and utilities; and established the controls to be applied to new development. Properties to be acquired were identified or the conditions under which they were acquired were established.

After approval of the urban renewal plan by the local governing body, the State of Massachusetts and the RAA, federal financial assistance for a renewal project was made available. The locality then began project execution activities.

Normally, the first phase of project operations was the acquisition of project properties, either through negotiation with the owners, and if necessary, by court condemnation proceedings. While the acquired properties were still occupied, the local planning agency (in Boston, the BRA) continued to manage and maintain the buildings and collect the rentals. A relocation service had to be established to provide displaced families with suitable housing within their means.

The removal of structures was normally done under a contract with a private contractor, as was the work involved in preparing the site and installing necessary streets and other site improvements. At the same time the city was engaged in providing the public facilities to support the new uses.

When the site was cleared, the land available for new development was publicly advertised to develop the market. Finally, as new private construction took place, it was inspected to assure that it was being carried out in accordance with the standards established in the project plan.

It should be emphasized that while the Federal Government did have national goals (see Exhibit 1), it did not prescribe the specific approach that a community should take to urban renewal. For example, one federal official commented: "My staff wanted to turn down a project which planned to rehabilitate some buildings and demolish others. I took the position that we should let the community go ahead. It's their town...."

Boston

Population

In 1960, the City of Boston had 697,197 residents, a decline of 13% from 1950. During the 1950s Boston's Black population increased from 5% of the total population to 9%, a figure that placed Boston twenty-third on a list of the thirty largest U.S. cities when ranked by the proportion of Blacks in each.[1] (Washington, D.C., ranked first with 54%.) However, the per cent of Blacks in Boston increased to 17% in 1965 while the city's population dropped to 616,326.[2]

Construction

From January 1, 1950 to January 1, 1968, the assessed value of Boston real estate increased from $2.1 billion to $2.7 billion. However, the value of taxable real estate declined from $1,429 million to $1,424 million during this period. Total value of new construction started in Boston from January 1, 1950 to January 1, 1968 was $1,089 million, $755 million of which was started after 1959. (See Exhibit 3.)

Housing

Housing starts from 1955 through 1967 were valued at $233 million; $198 million of this construction was begun after 1960. (See Exhibit 3.) Despite an increase in the number of dwelling units each year but one after 1960 (see Exhibit 3), no new public housing was built in Boston after 1956 (except for the elderly). For example, in 1960 it was estimated that 24,100 new or rehabilitated dwelling units of low-income housing were needed in Boston. By January 1968 less than 10% of this need had been satisfied. On the other hand, the estimated need for middle- to upper-income housing in 1960 was 5,700 new or rehabilitated units. By January 1968 actual and planned projects supplied more than three times the units needed in 1960.

Political[3]

The Mayor. The mayor was elected in odd-numbered years for a four-year term. (See Exhibit 4.) He appointed and removed department heads and board members, prepared the budget, and originated ordinances. However, he had little to do with school and police matters.

---

[1]See the Kerner Commission Report, p. 248.

[2]On the other hand, it is important not to misinterpret these aggregate figures. For example, during the 1950s, three of Boston's fifteen census districts increased their populations while the West End, the location of Boston's first urban renewal project, experienced a 49.6% loss in population. Moreover, while the percentage of Blacks in Boston had been increasing, the area in which they live had not: 90% of Boston's Blacks lived in three census tracts. (See Exhibit 2.)

[3]Much of the material in this section is drawn from E.C.Banfield, A Report on Politics in Boston, (Cambridge, Mass., Joint Center for Urban Studies, 1960).

The City Council. The council was a nine-member body elected at large[1] in odd-numbered years for two-year terms. The mayor could summon the council and address it when he pleased, and the council could require him or his department heads to furnish information in writing or to appear in person to answer questions. In practice the mayor rarely asked to see the council, whereas it called upon the administration for information fairly often. Both the mayor and the council could initiate ordinances, loans, land sales, and other measures "for the welfare of the city." The council could refuse to accept recommendations made by the mayor, but it could not appropriate out of general revenues more than he recommended. The mayor, on the other hand, could veto acts of the council. In matters involving money, the mayor had an item veto which could not be overridden. In other matters, his veto could be overridden by a vote of six.

The council could only appoint the city clerk and a small council staff. Its power of confirmation for mayoral appointments was limited to constables, weighters of goods, and members of the Housing and Redevelopment Authorities. Much of the council's business was done in committees.

The mayor and the city council were frequently at odds. The council did not have enough weight to pull the mayor around: its legal powers were very limited; it got little attention in the press; and councillors, being elected at-large, had little strength in the wards. The mayor, moreover, had the advantage of any executive in dealing with a legislative body: superior knowledge, decisiveness, and information. On the other hand, the mayor could not prevent the council from exercising its prerogatives.

For example, the council carried on rather thorough investigations into the granting of tax abatements, the treatment of wealthy tax delinquents, garbage and parking garage contracts, redevelopment projects, the management of hospitals and housing projects, and other matters. These crusades, the crusaders admitted, didn't get very far. Publicity was needed to keep them going, and the press soon lost interest.

The 1967 Election

Mayor. On November 7, 1967, Kevin White defeated Louise Day Hicks and became mayor of Boston. White received 102,331 votes and Mrs. Hicks received 90,122. At the time of the election, Mrs. Hicks was the chairman of the school committee and White was Secretary of State of Massachusetts. Mrs. Hicks' campaign slogan was "Boston for Bostonians." Her most well-known position was that opposing the busing of Black children to achieve racial balance in the schools. Newsweek described Mrs. Hicks' campaign as "an unabashed crusade for the alienated voter (that) excluded the most alienated of all, the Negro."

---

[1]In Boston's at-large electoral system, candidates for city council positions ran in all districts (wards). Voters could vote for up to nine candidates, and the nine candidates with the greatest number of votes were elected.

Before becoming mayor of Boston, Kevin White spoke of two "priority" problems he hoped his administration would solve. White felt that too many people had lost faith that somebody at city hall cared. And that too many people had been unable to convey their sense of frustration to persons in power.

"A mayor has to be seen...a mayor has to listen a lot," White said. "And he must be able to convince people that his administration truly cares about all those mundane, inglorious, but still infuriating indignities that beset the residents of Boston."

White's other priority was to improve "visible" services: the school system was second rate,[1] the parks and recreation system was dilapidated, and the city's streets were often dangerous.

City Council. On November 7, 1967 nine men were elected Boston city councilmen. Only four of these were incumbents. One was a Black. Both facts were unusual.

As a rule, incumbent city councilmen returned year after year. However, some incumbents ran in the mayoral primary and, therefore, were unable to run in the city council primary. The one incumbent who ran and lost was Katherine Craven. (Mrs. Craven was well-known for her opposition to the urban renewal program. However, William J. Foley, Jr., was also identified as being opposed to the urban renewal program and Foley was reelected.) Only one member of the council received more than 13% of his total vote from anyone of the city's 22 wards. All received from 23% to 37% of their total vote from their three best of 22 wards.

Mr. Thomas Atkins' election to the council was the first time a Black had been elected to the city council since the at-large system was initiated in 1951. Exhibit 5 summarizes the results of the 1967 mayoral and city council elections by ward.

The Boston Redevelopment Authority

Relationship to Boston City Government

The mayor of Boston (with city council concurrence) appointed four of the five members of the board of the BRA.[2] (The governor of Massachusetts appointed the fifth board member.) However, the terms of the board members (five years) did not coincide with that of the mayor (four years). For example, there would be only one BRA board vacancy for Kevin White to fill in 1968.

The role of the mayor with respect to the success or failure of urban renewal was critical. Urban renewal was the mayor's program. It

---

[1]Over 75% of Boston's schools were built prior to 1930. Over 25% were built prior to 1900.

[2]The BRA was governed by an independent five-person board. All action taken by the BRA had to be approved by the board.

was the mayor who dealt with the city council. His political strength and wisdom determined how a project fared in the council. Moreover, many activities associated with urban renewal were outside the BRA's control, yet under the mayor's. For example, many site improvements were made by city departments which reported to the mayor, not the BRA.

In addition to confirming mayoral appointments to the BRA, the Boston city council was required by federal law to approve each urban renewal project and a yearly workable program. (This document reviewed the complete activities of the redevelopment agency and was required by the Federal Government to guarantee continuance of federal grants to all projects.)

The council usually used consideration of particular projects as a vehicle to criticize the operations of the BRA even though the council had no legal power to change them. On the other hand, during the Collins administration (1960-1967), the city council passed every project that the BRA proposed. The vote, however, was often 5 to 4.

History

While the BRA was established in 1957, the "modern" era for the authority did not begin until John Collins became mayor in 1960 and hired Edward J. Logue to be development administrator[1] of the authority. Collins promised to build a "New Boston" and Logue was to be his right-hand man in the process. Logue had previously established a national reputation for his energetic management of urban renewal in New Haven, Connecticut.

Prior to 1961, the BRA was directed by Kane Simonian. As executive director, Simonian reported directly to the BRA five-man governing board. When Logue, who was hired on a 90-day trial basis by the BRA board, demanded full control over the renewal program, Simonian objected. Simonian claimed that, if Logue were placed over him, this in effect would be a demotion and as such not permitted under the civil service tenure law. (After six months all employees of the BRA had life tenure.) On a 3 to 2 vote, the BRA board supported Logue. However, to avoid tenure problems in the future, the board established a new class of "temporary employee"[2] for all future (including Logue) employees of the BRA. Simonian brought suit against the BRA after the January 1961 board decision. On May 5, 1961, the state Supreme Court dismissed the case.

After the reorganization, Simonian was in charge of the operations department and all projects started before Logue came. The operations department was responsible for engineering, land acquisition, property

---

[1]A special position created by Collins and accepted by the BRA board on a provisionary basis in 1960.

[2]This class of employee was not covered by the civil service tenure law.

management, business relocation, purchasing, property maintenance, and site development. Millions of dollars annually were awarded in connection with operations activities. Simonian and the BRA board had offices in 73 Tremont Street.

Logue was in charge of the planning, design, family relocation functions and all projects started after 1960. Logue's office and those of the departments he directed were in the City Hall Annex. Both Logue and Simonian reported directly to the BRA board.

Hired in October 1960, Logue enlarged the 81-man BRA staff by 125 city planners, architects, engineers, and clerical workers on November 2, 1960. A _Fortune_ article in 1964 described the atmosphere at the City Hall Annex in the following terms:

> Logue's personal dash and unquenchable élan have attracted talented and zealous young people from all over the country to work for him. Like their boss, many of them work hours that proper Bostonians find quite incredible. Logue pounds his people hard, but he pays them well, particularly by comparison to the main body of Boston city employees. For example, a week before Christmas, the Boston radio broadcasters broke the news that BRA people were getting raises ranging from $250 to $2,000 per year, and an envious shudder seemed to run through the other nine floors of City Hall Annex. The other city employees were getting no Christmas raises; was Santa trapped on the top floors?
>
> The explanation was simple enough: the City of Boston wasn't providing the cash; Washington was. A full 90 per cent of Logue's large payroll is paid by normal advances made by the Federal Urban Renewal Administration on projects in the planning stages. The city, at that, pays only $5,000 of the administrator's own ($30,000) cash salary. Federal advances take care of other parts of the process, too, including 80 per cent of the cost of remodeling the BRA offices, which totaled more than $450,000 with air conditioning.[1]

Logue's relationship with the city council and the BRA board can best be described as "stormy." An October 31, 1961 _Globe_ story gives a good example of this relationship.

> The BRA board is holding up payment of $160 for moving expenses of a project manager. The treasurer, James Colbert, said he would pay expenses from Newark, not California, since the man had taken a job in Newark and a month later taken the BRA position. Logue argued that the BRA was getting a bargain and should pay the entire amount.

---

[1] Walter McQuade, "Boston: What Can a Sick City Do?", _Fortune_ (June, 1964), p. 170.

On April 13, 1962 a Globe article also illustrates the nature of Logue's relationship to the board.

> Development Administrator Edward J. Logue yesterday countermanded an order passed by three of the five-man BRA board preventing employees from making public statements on policy. He vowed he would "fight it all the way." Treasurer and board member James G. Colbert charged Logue with "insubordination."

However, in spite of the constant public sparring with city council and BRA board, Logue's final report to Mayor Collins in August 1967[1] listed considerable activity. The BRA had become the largest city agency: it had grown from 81 to 498 (125 in the operations department). The Authority's payroll was $4.6 million annually and the newspapers listed the salaries of 136 employees who received more than $10,000 a year. Thirty-two hundred acres or 11% of Boston was undergoing renewal. Total private and public investment in these areas would be more than $2 billion. A summary of BRA activity under Logue is included as Exhibits 6 and 7.

The BRA from August to December 1967

Mayor Collins appointed Francis X. Cuddy to replace Logue as development administrator. Cuddy had been commissioner of assessment for Collins. No new projects were started under Cuddy. His role was clearly that of an interim administrator, since Collins was not running for reelection.

During October, Collins shuffled the BRA board members' terms so that he could give board member James G. Colbert a new five-year term. Later during December, several top aides to Mayor Collins were given posts with the BRA.

West End Project - An Example of Renewal

The West End project was the most infamous urban renewal project ever attempted in Boston. Approved by the Boston city council in 1957, the project was still not completed by the end of 1967. During its development, 1,729 families and 300 businesses were moved out of the West End. Eight

---

[1]Logue resigned during the summer of 1967 to run in the September 1967 mayoral primaries. Logue was considered to be Kevin White's principal competition for second place in the primary. (Experts felt that Mrs. Hicks would get the most votes in the 11-contestant field.) Many top people in the BRA spent a great deal of time during the campaign working for Logue. (One person reported that the BRA was "empty" during the election.) One of the major incidents of the primary was a challenge to Kevin White's nomination papers--a challenge made with the knowledge and consent of Logue and which was unsuccessful. After his victory in November, White expressed the feeling that the BRA had been exploited politically and that he wanted to make BRA employees professionals, not politicians. Logue left the area to head New York State's Urban Development Corporation.

hundred seventy-seven buildings were demolished. Yet by 1967 only two-thirds of the property had been rebuilt. The remainder was a parking lot owned by the BRA.

The impact of the West End project on the rest of Boston's urban renewal effort was predictably negative.

> There are neighborhoods in Boston that are militantly unwilling to let the Redevelopment Authority come near them--remembering with bitter clarity what happened in the West End. One such district is Charlestown, which sits across the lower Charles River behind the Navy Yard. Except for the monument up top, Bunker Hill, and a few good residential blocks around it, Charlestown today is decaying. Because Boston's trash collectors have seldom been zealous, empty lots became car parks or dumps. There is a rat problem. The people who remain, however, are tough, determined, and insular--only a few Negro families have dared move in, for example. When, after almost two years of work within Charlestown, including 135 neighborhood meetings, the Boston Redevelopment Authority advertised a community-wide hearing, Logue and his staff walked into near riot. The fact that the head of the appointed BRA board is a popular Catholic priest, Monsignor Francis Lally--one of Cardinal Cushing's closest aides--restrained the crowd but slightly. Even he was booed, and it was necessary to clear the aisles a number of times.[1]

1961-1967 Strategy

In the view of some observers, the Collins-Logue approach to urban renewal could be characterized by the words "simultaneous" and "bricks and mortar." The BRA asked for and received planning grants from the Federal Government in 1961 to study 10 urban renewal project areas at the same time. The more usual pattern in the urban renewal area was to plan one project at a time.

Moreover, the BRA program was aimed at stimulating as much construction activity as possible--the goal was visible progress. Success seemed to be measured by the dollar value of new construction rather than by the kind of new construction. The strategy was to build Boston's spirit with bricks and mortar.

Whether the strategy is to be considered a success depends on how results are measured. From the point of view of urban designers and the business community, the Logue-Collins approach was a success. From the point of view of the residents of Boston, the verdict was not as favorable.

---

[1] McQuade, op. cit., p. 169.

In the aggregate, the tax rate continued to rise (see Exhibit 3). In immediate terms thousands of people were forced to relocate from neighborhoods in which their families had lived for generations. The breadth of the resultant discontent was best reflected by the fact that Collins lost 21 out of 22 Boston wards when he unsuccessfully ran for senator in the 1966 Democratic primary.

Moreover, critics of the Collins-Logue strategy maintained that it was able to succeed to the degree that it did only because of Collins' strong political position in Boston and Logue's influence in Washington. For example, Logue was said to have helped the director of the Urban Renewal Administration[1] get his job. Moreover, President Kennedy had more than a passing interest in the City of Boston. One critic claimed, "Logue got money for programs that we never should have done. He never had to worry about local politics because Collins was so powerful and he had so much influence in Washington. Logue could get approval for a program in Washington and then use that approval as a lever to get local approval."

1961-1967 Organization

The organization and management style of the BRA remained essentially unchanged from 1961 to 1967. Although the size of the BRA grew from 81 people to over 500 people and the nature of the organization's primary activity shifted from planning to execution, the project-type organization and the informal style of management remained. One BRA employee explained that Logue's accessibility and involvement in the planning and design activities of the BRA was a major reason why many creative and imaginative people came to work for the authority. "Logue never let red tape hold him from going ahead with his plans. If I sent a memo to Logue, I always got a prompt answer. If I had a problem, I could just walk into his office and discuss it."

On the other hand, some employees claimed that Logue would sign anything but would never take action to solve the problem. "Logue planned a lot of things and then forgot about them." One employee described the BRA organization in the following manner.

> Under Logue the BRA really had no organization. There was an organization chart, but if I found it and showed you, it wouldn't mean very much. Logue managed like the early pilots flew--by the seat of his pants--by feeling.
>
> Moreover, project directors were little tin gods. They didn't answer to anyone except Logue. And sometimes they didn't even answer to Logue. They certainly never cooperated with the few central services Logue kept.

---

[1]The Urban Renewal Administration was renamed the Renewal Assistance Administration.

The central planning function had about 65 people working in it. Then there were about 100 people in the operation function. And then the remainder of the 500 people in BRA were working for one of the project directors. Each project had its own relocation specialist, its own rehabilitation specialist, its own engineers, designers and planners.

Although it was pretty close to being a one-man show, I don't think that would be a completely accurate description of the BRA under Ed Logue. Rather, it was a one-clique show. Logue and his pets--his inner circle--really ran the BRA.

This view of the BRA was not shared by all its employees. One project director commented:

Logue sold Boston an idea--faith in him; faith in the Collins administration. Logue went throughout the country and got the best urban renewal technicians he could find. His aim was not to solve Boston's immediate problems--not the tax problem today. Rather, Logue's orientation was toward the future.

He always made decisions in light of his long-term goals for Boston. For example, the decision not to put low-income housing in the South End was the right decision. Building low-income housing in the South End would just have preserved the slum. Yet by making that decision, Logue opened himself up for a lot of criticism. It's always easier to give in to community pressure. It's difficult to do the right thing.

I think the secret to Logue's success was the way in which he organized the BRA. Logue understood that the size of the urban renewal program in Boston meant he would have to delegate authority. Therefore, he set up a project type of organization.

A project director was responsible for the BRA's program in his particular community. His office was in the field, not in City Hall. If any problems came up with respect to the project, the project director saw that they were solved.

Department heads in the central planning organization were of equal status with project directors. Thus, if a project director and a department head disagreed on a particular decision, the dispute went to Logue's office. Nine times out of ten Logue ruled in favor of the project director since the project director was in the field and really understood the community's needs. Moreover, until a decision got up to Logue, the project director was king.

Boston--January 1968--The Political and Social Climate

In addition to being familiar with the BRA's past strategy and organization, Hale Champion also had to be aware of the political and social environment in which the BRA would have to operate. Writing in the New Republic (October 26, 1968), Robert Coles said:

> It is interesting today to compare the fate of the Irish in Boston with the treatment Southern blacks received when they came north. Both groups fled hunger that bordered on starvation; both came to American cities with high hopes; and both met violent rejection at the hands of their fellow citizens, who found democratic ideals fine only in the abstract. While George Santayana was at Harvard, the Irish were considered a scourge on Boston, as much a pestilence as the one that caused them to leave their native land. They were shunned, segregated, denied employment, called every vile name imaginable, and looked upon as a threat to everything: to law and order, to stability, to the nation's racial purity, indeed to the nation's very existence. A look at old newspapers and pamphlets shows how stalemated we are historically: "Stop the flood before we are drowned," one reads, along with the following: "They are dirty and lazy. They don't know how to provide for themselves, and want only to take from others. Their arrival is our tragedy. Something must be done." That was the way it was in 1871.
>
> Anyone who has read Edwin O'Connor's novels, starting with The Last Hurrah and ending with All in the Family knows what happened later on. The scorned, helpless Irish huddled for a while: a bother, a nuisance more than a political threat. The Yankees continued to run things. But eventually the "natives" (in this case white and with a brogue for an accent) became restless, then importunate, and finally outrageously eager for power--for power that would correct injustice and power that would also exact a measure of revenge. Skeffington, O'Connor's Mayor of Boston, was a romanticized version of the old-time Irish politician who achieved that power, at least in the city of Boston, though in The Last Hurrah and the novels that followed it, another fact comes across, too: there is a limit to what Boston's mayor can do, a limit set by powers and principalities either obvious or hidden--such as the state legislature and the very discreet Yankee bankers who own money if not urban voters. By the mid-forties those bankers and others who follow their lead had made their point. Politicians like James Michael Curley--and others far seedier, far less attractive, intelligent and generous--could run the city, but the city would die if an armistice was not reached with the business and financial community, which wanted a semblance of order in City Hall, and a halt called to flagrant corruption, and the passionate attacks that came with every election. ("No more will the Yankees treat us like slaves," Curley shouted.)

By the mid-forties time had healed some of the old wounds. War had ended the depression. A solid Irish middle class had come into being, much of it outside Boston, but some of it in the city's suburban wards. And a few of the city's leading Yankees indicated a willingness to go halfway, abandon their aloofness, their arrogance, their hauteur, which actually masked a cruel spitefulness: let them all drown in their brash, ward-heeling politics--and prove us correct for having scorned them in the first place. With Mayor John Collins (1960-1968), a tentative affair turned into a firm marriage. Investments of all sorts were made in the "new Boston." Under urban renewal, old, sometimes lovely, buildings were torn down--and thousands of poor or lower-middle-class people brushed under the rugs of other, more distant slums. And today the replacements can be seen: buildings and more buildings push higher into Boston's surprised sky. Many of them are vulgar, ugly things, an awful sight in comparison to what was built in the 18th and 19th centuries; but big business, new business needed space, needed a lot of it and fast, and old dame Boston, determined to look as young as possible, was in no position to be choosy.

For all the prosperity he brought to Boston, Mayor Collins became increasingly unpopular. Downtown Boston--with its stores and banks and offices--was doing fine, but life was not going so well elsewhere. Every year more and more blacks from the rural South have come to Boston, even though it has no large-scale industries to match cities like Detroit or Chicago....As black people in the ghetto asked for more, thousands of white people began to realize how little they were getting--from the city and the liberal intellectuals, the students and professors who have indeed found it easier to establish ties with poor blacks than with poor or not-so-poor whites. The alliance between upper-middle-class whites and blacks is not new--it keeps Atlanta's excellent Mayor Ivan Allen in office--but in Boston such a political alliance is not really possible. There are simply not enough blacks, and most of the upper-middle class deserts the city after work.

Urban renewal reporter, Anthony Yudir, writing in the Boston Globe (December 24, 1967) concluded that Champion's problems would be far different from Logue's.

Former renewal director Edward J. Logue stressed the "planning with people" approach during his seven years in the city, and was successful in getting under way major neighborhood renewal and rehabilitation programs. But he also had the advantage of coming into a program when citizen groups, usually comprising mostly middle-class and long-time residents, were eager to cooperate with the city government in order to get a revitalization plan under way.

Today Logue's approach probably would not work well in winning support. In the last few years there has sprung up in many areas a widely held theory that the people on the grass-roots level, which includes a majority of the poor, should initiate their own planning, should be their own commercial and housing developers...

When Logue arrived on the Boston scene he immediately ran into strong hostility from three members of the renewal board itself who were not interested in making any changes in the renewal setup. After overcoming this hostile resistance--from members James Colbert, Melvin Massucco and Stephen McCloskey--Logue went on to rid the renewal agency of as much deadwood as possible and built the largest agency in the city with a concentration of top professional planners, architects, administrators and project directors.

The same three board members are still on the authority and it will be interesting to see what kind of a reception Champion gets. He is assured of at least the cooperation of the present chairman, Rt. Rev. Francis J. Lally and the newest board member, George Condakes.

Colbert recently was reappointed by Collins to a five-year term and in some respects can be pretty independent if he wants to be. Massucco is a state appointee. McCloskey is on unsteady ground since he is a holdover and can be replaced at any time. Colbert, since Logue resigned, has been more or less running the board.

The BRA under Champion - The Public Record (1968)

During his first year as director of the BRA, Champion took a number of actions. The following paragraphs summarize those actions as they were reported by the media.

February 16: The BRA worked out changes in some zoning statutes which cleared the way for construction of a 60-story office building for the John Hancock Insurance Company.

March 31: President Johnson announced he would not seek reelection.

May 3: The BRA was criticized at the first public hearing on the South End urban renewal project it had held in the neighborhood since 1965. Since the city council had approved the project in December 1965, no housing had been built or had been started. Councilman Thomas Atkins led the criticism of the BRA.

June 13: The city council approved Mayor White's appointment of Patrick Bocanfuso to the BRA Board of Directors.

June 28: James Colbert charged that Champion fired a former aide to Mayor Collins "without any cause except political." Champion denied the charge and was not overruled by the Board.

July 11: Champion recommended that the operations department and other activities under Kane Simonian's direction be integrated into one organization with the rest of the BRA's activities and be placed under the development administrator.

Moreover, Champion asked that more authority be delegated by the BRA Board to the development administrator. Finally, Champion said that due to pressure from the federal authorities to cut back BRA expenses, "a substantial number of economy dismissals" would have to be made. Champion promised specific proposals in the following weeks.

July 15: The BRA submitted the "infill" program to the city council for its approval. The infill program was aimed at building about 2,000 three-, four-, and five-bedroom housing units on scattered sites on vacant, city-owned land. These units were to be leased through the Boston Housing Authority to large, low-income families. When approved, the first units were to be built in Charlestown and the South End.

July 23: The city council asked the BRA to block "wholesale dismissal of employees" until the council's committee on urban renewal could hold a public meeting. All city councilors had received letters from the Italian-American War Veterans urging that council "protect the rights of Veterans."

August 4: Effigies of Champion and Walter Smart, South End project director, were burned by South End residents protesting BRA policies.

August: The BRA rejuvenated a program in which a group of local Boston banks were providing home financing loans for inner city residents.

August 25: The BRA Board approved Champion's recommendations for dismissal of 32 employees. Thirteen of these appealed their dismissals to the BRA Board and two filed complaints with the Massachusetts Civil Service Commission. The vote on the dismissals was three to one. (James Colbert was in opposition.)

September 12: Champion proposed a new BRA organization reporting through the development administrator to the BRA Board. In addition, Champion suggested that a "Cabinet" made up of five top administrators responsible for policy with respect to Planning and Design, Operations, Development, Community Organization and Relocation, and Staff Services. Below this cabinet, Champion proposed a second series of positions responsible for the operation of the BRA's major departments.

September 14: Councilor Joseph Timilty criticized the BRA for firing 32 employees in the name of austerity while (1) it proposed to give an additional $4,500 per year to members of the new cabinet and (2) it had recently allowed a $50,000 sculpture called "Cubi II" to be purchased by the city.

October 19: Councilor Thomas Atkins requested a hearing on the firings of personnel at the BRA.

October 24: Champion refused to attend the city council session to discuss the dismissals. He said he was acting with full knowledge of the mayor. Atkins refused to take action on several BRA projects, including the workable program,[1] unless Champion and the BRA cooperated.

October 30: The city council passed the mayor's infill housing program. However, the mayor termed the amendments made by the council unacceptable and, therefore, vetoed the program (as amended) and resubmitted his original infill program bill.

October 31: Mayor White charged the city council with delaying $20 million worth of urban renewal programs. White singled out the urban renewal committee headed by Councilman Thomas Atkins.

October 31: Councilman Atkins cancelled a scheduled city council hearing on the BRA's "workable program."

November 5: Richard Nixon was elected President of the United States.

December 4: After some unorthodox procedural moves freed the "workable program" from the urban renewal committee, the full city council voted to approve it. The vote was eight to one. (Councilman Foley was in opposition.)

December 12: The BRA Board unanimously approved the reorganization that Champion had requested (see Exhibit 8).

December 20: Construction on a $2.5 million building in the Government Center was started.

During 1968, $167 million of new construction was begun in Boston. (Fifty-two million dollars of this figure was for housing and $56 million for office and bank buildings.) The tax rate was $129.20. Activity in the urban renewal projects inherited by Champion is reported in Exhibit 9. The campus high project and the code enforcement project had been approved during the last days of the Johnson administration. The "infill" program and the "Faneuil Hall" project, however, had not been approved by the Johnson ad-

---

[1]The workable program was a document which reviewed the complete activities of a redevelopment authority and was required by federal law to guarantee continuance of federal grants to all urban renewal projects in a city.

ministration. And only two units of low-income housing had been completed under the "infill" program during 1968. On the other hand, the local savings bank loan program had been quite successful. The group had loaned $3.4 million from August to November and over $3.0 million of applications were in process as of December 1. This level of activity was greater than that during the six years in which the program had been operating prior to August 1, 1968.

Champion's Views on His First Year

Champion gave his views on a number of issues concerning the BRA: BRA organization, housing, planning, the community, his first six months as development administrator, and the public record of the BRA in 1968. He argued that it took time to turn an organization around and that one could not judge performance by short-term accomplishments.

Organization

When I took over the BRA, it had been drifting. There had been no central push or drive. Operations just seemed to have slackened off. Perhaps age might have gotten to it.

The organization had been under interim leadership. Few decisions had been made, and where they had, they were not of consequential character. No strategic planning had taken place, morale was down, many actions and appointments had been clearly political.

When the BRA had been an effective organization, it was a one-man band. There was only one real decision-maker, very little delegation of authority, and no real organization structure. There were no clearly understood relationships between people. Thus, the result was extreme dependency on one individual. Personnel practices and any standard of performance just did not exist.

Housing

The decisions I made at first were reflexes rather than long-term commitments to a strategic direction. For example, low-income housing was a critical problem area. Forecasts called for a need of 12 to 15 thousand units in the future. While I was not sure that this was a valid estimate, I did know that we needed 2 to 4 thousand units for large families, and that would take at least two years of work. Thus, I could go ahead on the "infill" program without committing the BRA to long-term strategic plans.

Planning

I quickly found out that there was no way to construct a logical system to deal with the problems facing a redevlopment authority. One cannot set priorities. One cannot spend time in a carefully worked out manner. You must confront issues on a day-to-day basis. It's not a progress planning job, a control or auditing job; it's just all over you all the time. It's difficult to make fundamental evaluations on what the organization should be doing.

Community

One cannot be arbitrary on what is important and what is not important. "Little things"[1] are not really distractions, they are strategic needs. The "little things" are as important in this job as the big things. Success of a program depends on the attitude of the community, and the BRA had a credibility problem--the slogan "planning with people" was only a slogan. Our relocation problems were quite severe.

My first thought was to satisfy these problems by delivery (performance). However, now I've shifted my focus. While I'm still shooting for performance on the big things, I am also trying to re-establish communication and understanding with the community. If we discuss problems along the way and do small things when we can, I believe we will be successful. For example, in Charlestown we are now trying to meet with neighborhood groups and satisfy the small complaints that they might have. I think this is the only way to approach the substantive issues.

First Six Months

During the first six months of this job, I don't think I paid enough attention to dealing with the small problems and issues confronting the community. Perhaps the reason for this relative inattention was the newness of the job. When I arrived, there were two major crises right on my desk. One program called for dislocating a number of low-income families. No advance social planning had been done. Therefore, I was on the phone to the Federal Government, to the FHA, to the developers, trying to work out a solution to the problem. We finally did get a grant to do the relocation. The other program was the Hancock building. I had to decide whether to let the structure proceed and, if so, under what conditions.

Another area that diverted my time during my first days as development administrator was establishing of relationships between myself and local, state, and federal government people. Some people have said that I spent too much time with the mayor. However, he lacked adequate personnel to deal with problems such as the budget, and by building a relationship between Mayor White and myself, I was able to get on committees that Ed Logue wasn't able to get on.

---

[1]For example, responding to a variety of complaints in Charlestown, the South End, and Roxbury concerning such matters as street cleaning, lighting and zoning.

The Public Record

The public record does not reflect the nature, relative importance, or volume of activity. It shows convenient, recognizable milestones. Over five or ten years, you can measure performance in terms of final action. However, for a year or two, so much is in the pipeline that it is a much subtler job to measure performance.

What are the things that you work at? How do you spend your time in order to get results? Let me give you an example. Infill was a complex administrative program. I had to find vacant lots, straighten out any legal constraints or problems, arrange to have the lots transferred to the BRA and then negotiate with the developers for construction. The problem is not drafting the program--the problem is executing it. These kinds of things don't show on the public record.

One the waterfront project, the union freight railroad had to be relocated. There were thousands of little regulatory roadblocks. We had to deal with the FHA and the railroads and the ICC and the Public Works Commission. We needed to get approval and releases from each of these agencies or organizations. However, now we're finally starting to drive piles for the new construction.

Another example I had in mind was the John Hancock building. That was a planned development outside the urban renewal area. However, since we were given control, it allowed us to help the developer do something he might not have been able to do. On the other hand, this involved a good amount of my time and the time of much of my top staff.

Also a lot of progress gets slowed down by the Feds. I can think of two good illustrations. First, the infill program. We're still waiting for federal approval; yet we've already spent $200,000 putting the program together. We had to gamble with time and money if we were ever going to get that program going.

A second example is our effort to revive the dormant rent-subsidized housing program. Last summer, the Federal Government told us that we could not reduce land prices below $500 per dwelling unit as we had been doing up until then. As a result, ten of these housing projects had to be delayed due to the need for contract renegotiation. At the same time, we were told, due to the sensitive political situation, to go slow of relocation in the South End project.

Exhibit 1
THE BOSTON REDEVELOPMENT AUTHORITY (A and B)

Department of Housing and Urban Development
Washington, D.C. 20410

Office of the Assistant Secretary
For Renewal and Housing Assistance

May 19, 1967

LOCAL PUBLIC AGENCY LETTER NO. 418

SUBJECT: National Goals and Urban Renewal Priorities

The urgent needs of our cities, and the ever-increasing demand for Federal urban renewal grant authority, make it necessary for HUD to adopt policies that will assure that aid is available for those projects which advance national goals responsive to those needs, and which make the most productive use of every urban renewal dollar.

These goals are:

1. The conservation and expansion of the housing supply for low and moderate income families.

2. The development of new employment opportunities.

3. The renewal of areas with critical and urgent needs.

The policy guidelines set forth in this LPA Letter reflect a reorientation of the priority criteria which HUD will use in considering new project applications....

NATIONAL GOALS

Expansion of Housing Supply for Low and Moderate Income Groups

The Department will give priority consideration to projects which contribute to conserving and increasing the existing housing supply for low and moderate income families.

* * * * *

Development of Areas of Employment Opportunity

The Department will give priority consideration to projects which contribute to the development of centers of employment opportunity for jobless, under-employed, and low income persons, through commercial or industrial redevelopment.

Renewal of Areas with Critical and Urgent Need

The Department will give priority consideration to projects which attack critical slum and blighted areas--those areas of physical decay, high tensions and great social need, and in which the locality is prepared to utilize all available resources--Federal, State, and local in improving conditions in these slum and blighted areas.

* * * * *

/s/ Don Hummel
Don Hummel
Assistant Secretary for
Renewal and Housing Assistance

Exhibit 2

THE BOSTON REDEVELOPMENT AUTHORITY (A and B)

Boston Social Statistics by Census Tract[1]

Area	1960 Population	% Change from 1950	Non-White	Foreign Stock	Median Family Income	Housing Units	Number Deteriorating	Number Dilapidated	Number New Units 1950-1960
Brighton	64,282	- 4.4	592	33,491	$6,270	23,526	961	297	1,283
Charlestown	20,147	-35.7	117	7,385	5,187	6,443	1,612	227	3
East Boston	43,809	-14.4	71	24,546	5,323	13,702	1,385	277	485
South Boston	45,766	-20.8	317	19,618	5,106	14,575	2,581	881	227
North End	13,374	-26.8	49	9,308	4,815	5,658	1,969	283	-
West End	13,718	-49.6	261	5,842	6,282	7,437	714	68	222
Back Bay	47,587	- 7.1	4,019	17,191	5,265	22,327	2,527	99	623
South End	35,082	-35.7	12,448	15,447	3,814	21,401	9,449	2,098	461
Roxbury	84,924	-24.8	37,530	28,571	4,631	29,400	8,708	3,028	945
Dorchester North	112,504	- 8.2	11,235	51,722	5,709	34,145	5,329	765	2,016
Dorchester South	74,135	- 4.0	384	39,805	6,256	22,072	1,857	102	1,748
Jamaica Plain	35,373	- 7.7	282	17,910	6,285	10,969	1,895	658	422
Roslindale	41,467	+ 4.2	403	18,900	6,734	10,831	682	65	992
West Roxbury	25,328	+ 9.9	53	11,469	7,512	7,365	169	22	1,336
Hyde Park	31,123	+14.5	112	14,675	6,498	9,292	528	81	4,452
TOTAL	697,197	-13.0	68,493	317,064	$5,747	238,547	40,366	9,306	12,815

[1]See Exhibits 10 and 11 for maps of Boston's Census Tracts.

Source: Massachusetts United Community Services Research Department.

Exhibit 3

THE BOSTON REDEVELOPMENT AUTHORITY (A and B)

Data on Boston Real Estate

Year	New Building Starts (Millions of Dollars): Housing	Offices & Banks	Public Facilities	Other	Total	Net Change in Number of Dwelling Units	Tax Rate ($ per $1,000 Valuation)
1950	-	-	-	-	32	-	$ 63.00
1951	-	-	-	-	48	-	62.80
1952	-	-	-	-	44	-	66.80
1953	-	-	-	-	17	-	70.70
1954	-	-	-	-	22	-	69.80
1955	8	-	-	-	24	+ 526	69.80
1956	5	-	-	-	35	- 296	78.00
1957	4	-	-	-	27	- 979	86.00
1958	6	-	-	-	36	-1,352	93.00
1959	6	61	0	11	79	- 661	101.20
1960	16	4	0	16	36	- 111	100.70
1961	16	3	0	30	49	+ 966	100.60
1962	16	6	1	39	64	+2,356	99.80
1963	24	55	22	44	145	+2,450	96.00
1964	75	2	10	39	126	+8,150	99.80
1965	35	24	0	36	95	+1,998	115.00
1966	6	1	14	41	62	- 200	101.00
1967	16	112	17	33	178	+2,439	117.80

Exhibit 4

THE BOSTON REDEVELOPMENT AUTHORITY (A and B)

ORGANIZATION OF BOSTON'S CITY GOVERNMENT

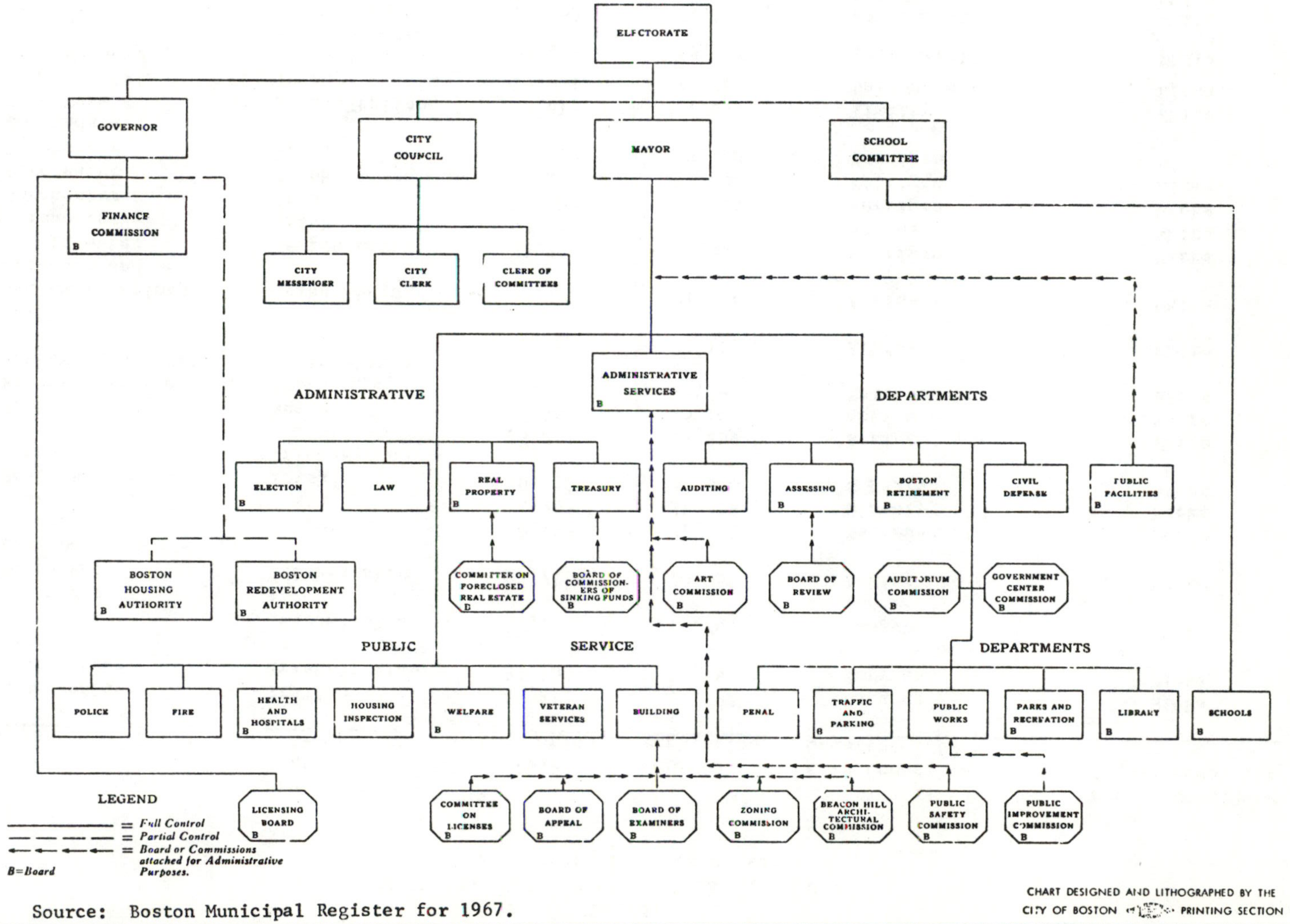

Source: Boston Municipal Register for 1967.

Exhibit 5
THE BOSTON REDEVELOPMENT AUTHORITY (A and B)
Characteristics of Boston Wards

Ward[1]	Location	Predominant Ethnic Group	1959 Population	1965 Population	City Council with Greatest 1967 Votes	Mayoral Candidate with Greatest 1967 Votes
1	East Boston	Italian	48,813	39,792	Langone	Hicks
2	Charlestown	Irish-Italian	23,306	16,381	Kerrigan	Hicks
3	West End North End	Irish-Italian	40,174	20,761	Langone	White
4	South End South End	Irish-Yankee	27,743	20,055	Atkins	White
5	Back Bay Beacon Hill	Yankee	30,723	22,715	Saltonstall	White
6	South Boston	Irish	26,293	21,658	O'Leary	Hicks
7	South Boston	Irish	30,352	25,030	O'Leary	Hicks
8	Roxbury	Irish-Negro-Italian	25,812	17,239	Atkins	White
9	Roxbury	Negro	26,447	15,141	Atkins	White
10	Roxbury-Mission Hill	Irish	28,293	23,297	Saltonstall	Hicks
11	Roxbury (Fort Hill)	Jewish-Negro-Irish	27,582	22,178	Atkins	White
12	Dorchester (Columbia Point)	Irish-Negro	32,003	21,654	Atkins	White
13	Mattapan and Dorchester	Jewish-Negro	32,257	28,852	Kerrigan	Hicks
14	Dorchester	Irish	50,088	46,751	Atkins	White
15	Dorchester	Irish	24,409	22,714	Kerrigan	Hicks
16	Dorchester	Irish	31,116	29,232	Kerrigan	Hicks
17	Dorchester	Irish	30,830	30,108	Kerrigan	Hicks
18	Roslindale Hyde Park	Irish-Italian	50,413	57,548	Timilty	White
19	Jamaica Plain	Irish	29,601	29,267	Saltonstall	Hicks
20	West Roxbury	Irish-Italian Yankee-Jewish	39,431	45,065	Saltonstall	White
21	Allston	Irish-Jewish	39,752	31,678	Saltonstall	White
22	Brighton	Irish-Jewish	32,264	29,210	Saltonstall	White

[1] See Exhibit 11 for a map of Boston's wards.

Source: Boston Globe.

Exhibit 6
THE BOSTON REDEVELOPMENT AUTHORITY (A and B)
Changes in Housing Stock in Urban Renewal Areas[1]

	Clearance			Construction			Low-Moderate Income Housing Construction in Urban Renewal Areas: June 30, 1967		
	Number of:			Number of:			No. of 221 (d)(3) Units:		
Federally Assisted Projects	D.U.s* Cleared	D.U.s* to be Cleared	Total No. of Units to be Cleared	New Units Constructed	New Units Under Construction	Total No. of Units to be Constructed	Constructed	Under Construction	Committed
New York Streets	998	-	998	-	-	-	-	-	-
West End	3,510	-	3,510	1,440	-	2,400	-	-	-
Washington Park	2,453	117	2,570	482	582	1,550	482	582	194
Government Center	989	-	989	-	-	-	-	-	-
North Harvard	59	-	59	-	-	140-280	-	-	200
Charlestown	-	925	925	-	-	1,400	-	-	318
Waterfront	-	-	-	-	32	1,960	-	-	350
South End (Inc. Castle Square)	988	4,262	5,250	500	96	4,100	500	-	1,160
South Cove	281	281	-	-	-	600	-	-	350
Fenway	-	810	810	-	-	3,500	-	-	-
Central Business District	-	-	-	-	-	450-1,000	-	-	-
Campus High Early Land	-	632	632	-	-	400-600	-	-	-
Subtotal	9,278	7,027	15,743	2,422	710	16,500-17,390	982	582	2,572
Nonfederally Assisted									
Whitney Street	437	-	437	422	-	632	-	-	-
Prudential	-	-	-	-	542	812	-	-	-
Tremont-Mason	-	-	-	378	-	378	-	-	-
Jamaicaway	3	-	3	282	-	282	-	-	-
Allston-Waverley	-	-	-	-	-	102	-	-	-
Back Bay	-	-	-	-	130	230	-	-	-
Subtotal	440	-	440	1,082	672	2,436	0	0	102
Grand Total	9,718	7,027	16,183	3,504	1,382	18,936-19,826	982	582	2,674

*D.U. = Dwelling Unit

[1]See Exhibits 10 and 11 for maps of Boston's urban renewal project areas.

Source: Boston Redevelopment Authority.

Exhibit 7

THE BOSTON REDEVELOPMENT AUTHORITY (A and B)

Status of Federally Assisted Urban Renewal Projects in Boston at the End of 1967[1]

December 31, 1967	Project Approved by Federal Government	Federal Capital Grant	Number of Structures to be Rehabilitated: Planned	Completed	Number of Parcels to be Acquired: Planned	% Acquired	Number of Families to be Relocated: Planned	Relocated	Number of Structures to be Demolished: Planned	Demolished	Number of Acres to be Sold: Planned	% Sold	% Site Improvements Completed	Scheduled Completion Date
Campus high school (M.C.)[2]		$ 8,524,304[3]	-	-	-	-	-	-	-	-	-	-	-	-
Code enforcement		3,159,118[3]	-	-	-	-	-	-	-	-	-	-	-	-
Charlestown	Oct. 1965	26,628,302	2,296	-	717	-	525	81	514	-	119	-	-	Sept. 1969
Central business district	-	19,460,880	662	-	42	-	-	-	29	-	27	-	-	-
South Cove	Apr. 1966	11,507,235	233	-	223	-	234	79	237	-	27	-	-	Apr. 1970
Government Center	July 1964	33,957,391	-	-	332	99	262	262	364	295	38	50	5	July 1968
Waterfront	Aug. 1964	16,485,200	222	-	211	45	-	-	211	-	61	11	-	Aug. 1969
New York Streets	Apr. 1955	3,194,033	-	-	292	100	368	368	321	321	15	100	100	Completed 4/1964
North Harvard Street	July 1964	396,122	-	-	42	100	51	41	52	-	7	-	-	July 1968
Fenway	Feb. 1967	9,370,943	280	-	115	-	460	-	181	-	28	-	-	-
Washington Park	Apr. 1963	25,081,775	1,165	595	1,250	66	1,853	1,811	1,257	1,180	135	14	10	Dec. 1968
South End	June 1966	37,165,309	3,458	-	267	64	3,209	496	1,387	308	154	6	-	May 1973
West End	Dec. 1957	11,774,918	-	-	716	100	1,729	1,729	877	877	36	67	70	Mar. 1968

[1] See Exhibits 10 and 11 for maps of Boston's urban renewal project areas.

[2] Model Cities Program.

[3] Requested.

Source: Casewriter's notes.

Exhibit 8

THE BOSTON REDEVELOPMENT AUTHORITY (A andB)

Revised BRA Organization

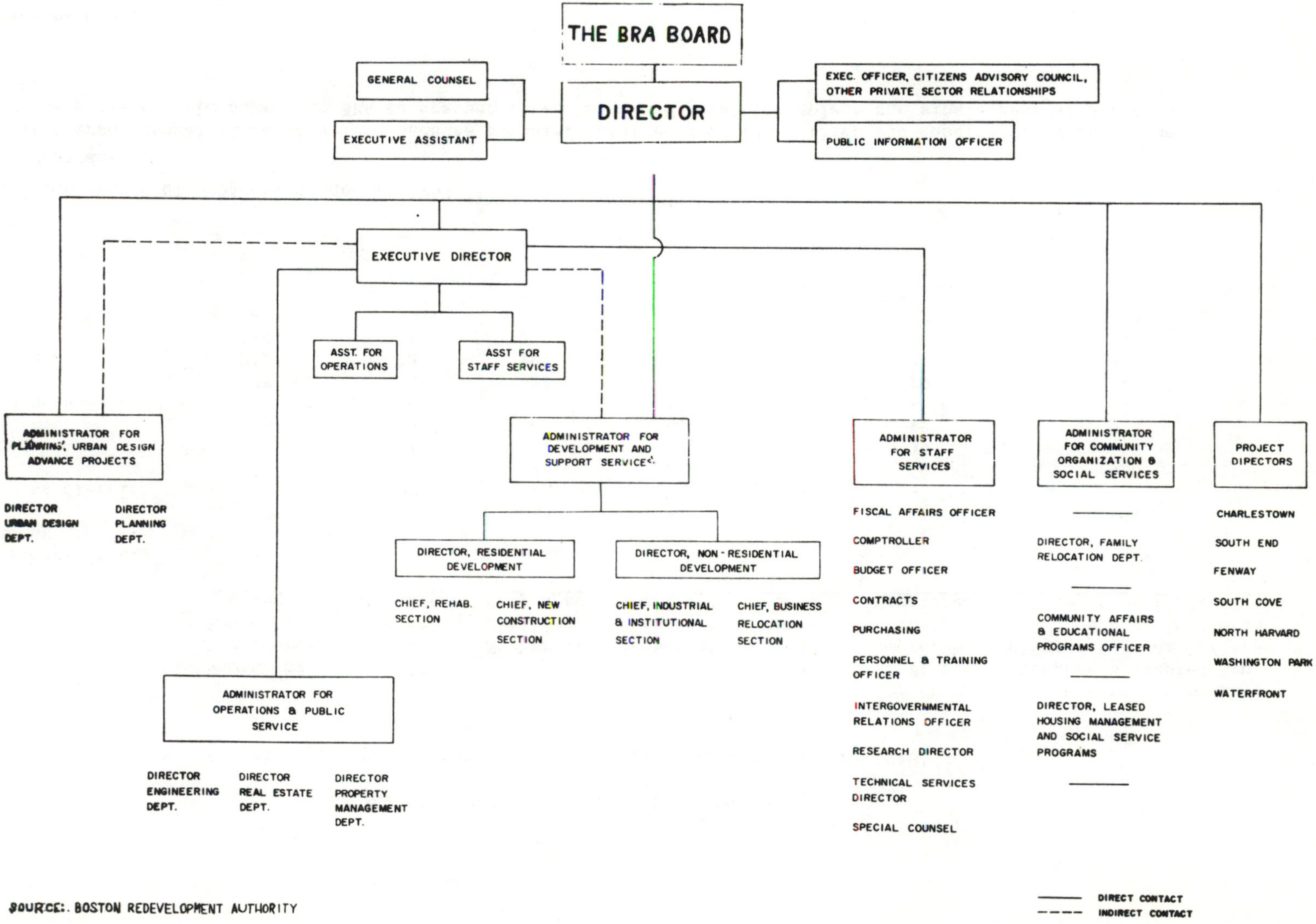

SOURCE: BOSTON REDEVELOPMENT AUTHORITY

Exhibit 9

THE BOSTON REDEVELOPMENT AUTHORITY (A and B)

Activity in Federal Urban Renewal Projects in Boston during 1968[1]

	Number of Structures Rehabilitated	% of Project Area Acquired	Number of Families Relocated	Number of Structures Demolished	% of Project Area Sold	% Site Improvements Completed	Difference (in months) between Scheduled Completion Date on 12/31/68 and Scheduled Completion Date as of 12/31/67
Campus high school (M.C.)[2]							
Code enforcement							
Charlestown	177	43	115	66	-	31	+21
Central business district[3]	-	90	-	24	-	-	-
South Cove	25	75	75	23	-	44	+30
Government Center	-	1	-	67	30	39	+12
Waterfront	5	40	-	24	2	19	+16
North Harvard Street	-	-	-	35	-	-	+17
Fenway	38	5	20	-	-	10	-
Washington Park	212	28	199	92	36	89	+13
South End	110	25	229	59	2	8	-
West End	-	-	-	-	-	13	+18

[1]See Exhibit 7 for status of projects at end of 1967.

[2]Model Cities Program.

[3]Remaining capital grant cancelled January 1968 because proposed total need of $70 million was considered by HUD to be excessive for one project. HUD asked the BRA to present three "mini-projects" to replace the single central business district project.

Source: Casewriter's notes.

Exhibit 10

THE BOSTON REDEVELOPMENT AUTHORITY (A and B)

FEDERAL URBAN RENEWAL PROJECT AREAS IN RELATION TO BOSTON CENSUS TRACTS

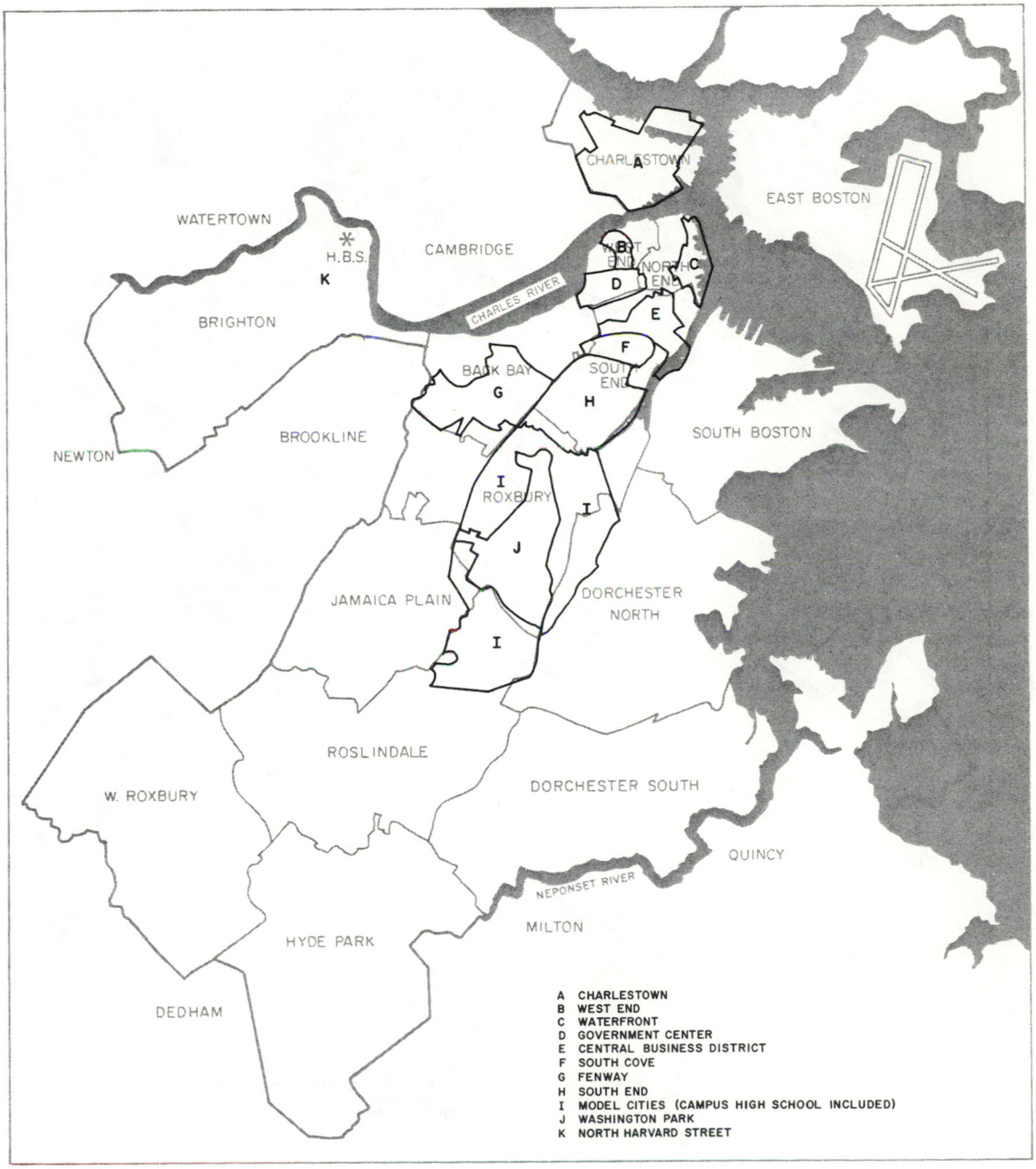

Exhibit 11

THE BOSTON REDEVELOPMENT AUTHORITY (A and B)

FEDERAL URBAN RENEWAL PROJECT AREAS IN RELATION TO BOSTON POLITICAL WARDS

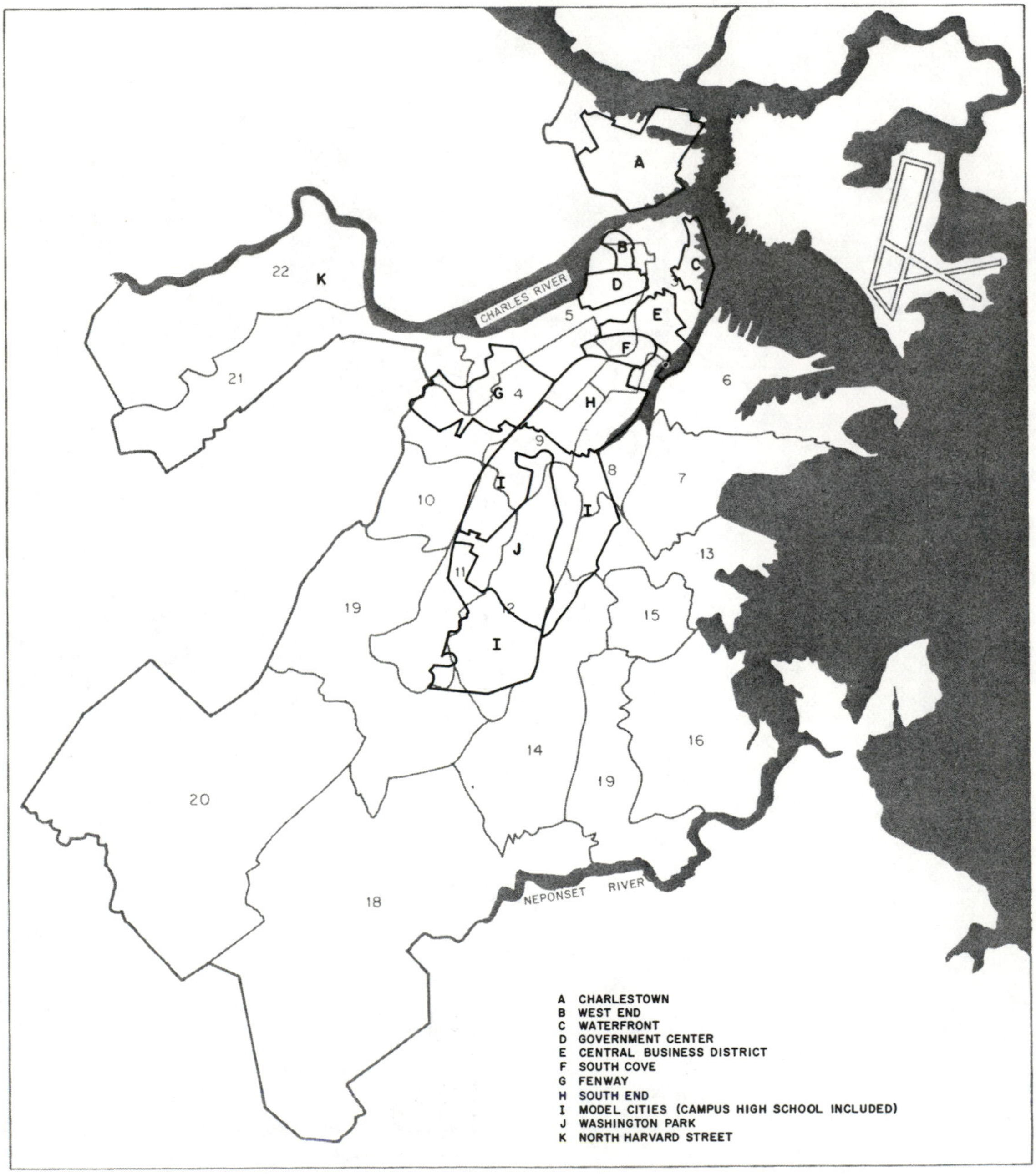

HOUSING

CONFRONTING THE HOUSING CRISIS

Introduction

The joint analytical work performed by the City of New York's Housing and Development Administration (HDA), the New York City-Rand Institute, and McKinsey and Company on the city's housing problems was the most comprehensive and careful look at an urban housing system ever undertaken. The effort began in early 1968 when several factors combined to set the stage for a more analytic approach to developing housing policy. To begin with, Mayor Lindsay and his Budget Director were enthusiastic proponents of an increased use of analysis in urban government and were giving strong backing to the development of an in-house analytic capability in the city's agencies. Second, a major reorganization had changed the nature of the agencies, drawing together groups with related and overlapping functions into "super agencies" such as HDA. Third, within HDA, a young, "analysis-oriented" man had been appointed director of the agency's Office of Programs and Policies (OPP). Finally, surrounding all these other developments was a growing consensus that the city's housing problems were both poorly understood and reaching crisis proportions. HDA administrators concluded that thorough analysis might help to develop understanding and point the way to effective action.

In February 1970 Rand published a report entitled "Rental Housing in New York City, Volume 1, Confronting the Crisis" which summarized the HDA/Rand/McKinsey work to date. The Rand project leader described it as "our first crack at synthesizing our research." A second purpose, according to the director of HDA's OPP, was to "spark public discussion and provoke controversy." Excerpts from the report are set forth in the following pages.

Dimensions of the Crisis

The rental housing market in New York City is in a state of crisis. Vacancies are acutely scarce, construction is at its lowest level in many years, rents in [apartments not subject to rent control rose substantially in 1969], and large numbers of recently habitable buildings have been reduced to shambles or withdrawn entirely from the market. Tenants are deeply dissatisfied either with the quantity of service provided by their landlords or with the rents demanded, or both. Landlords are equally dissatisfied with the yields of their property, the behavior of their tenants, the burdens of public regulation, and the illiquidity of their investments. Housing issues have been politicized to such an extent that parties to housing disputes frequently ignore market channels in favor of pressure on public officials to provide lopsided remedies favoring one side or the other. Until recently, most public discussions of the city's housing problems have paid scant attention to available facts, and indeed, much information needed for rational discussion of current problems was lacking or inaccessible.

In 1968, there were 2.8 million occupied housing units in New York City, of which 623,000 were occupied by owners. Among the 2.2 million rental units, the following divisions are most important:

Private rental housing units		1,952,000
Under rent control*	1,340,000	
Not controlled	612,000	
Publicly aided rental housing units		229,000
Publicly owned and operated**	144,000	
Publicly aided and regulated***	85,000	
Total		2,181,000

*Includes 74,000 single-room occupancy units (lacking private bath or kitchen), illegal for family occupancy.

**New York City Housing Authority projects.

***Limited profit, limited dividend, and redevelopment company projects, including 47,000 "cooperative" units whose tenants' equities are nominal.

The current crisis in rental housing involves all of these groups though the most visible symptoms of the crisis are different for each.

The Shortage of Rental Housing

In 1965 the city's rental vacancy rate reached 3.2 per cent, the highest value of the postwar period. The 1969 Housing and Vacancy Survey reported a rental vacancy rate of 1.2 per cent. Under these market conditions, rents on [apartments not subject to rent control] began to rise sharply. Increases of 25 per cent on two-year leases negotiated in 1968 were not uncommon.

This shortage of rental housing is clearly not attributable to any rapid or unusual growth in demand. The city's population has not grown significantly since 1950, and may be declining. However, a trend of decreasing family size and increasing numbers of unrelated individuals has resulted in net growth in the number of households, despite the lack of population growth. The rate of net household formation has been falling steadily since the early 1950s and currently amounts to about 13,000 additional households per year (as compared with 22,000 per year, 1950-60). The primary reasons for the housing shortage are a decline in the rate of new construction, and ... withdrawal of housing from the active inventory.

These events are illustrated in Figure 1. The left-hand panel shows the average annual numbers of units added to the inventory in each of two periods: 1960-64 and 1965-67. The right-hand panel shows the average annual number of units withdrawn from the housing inventory for the same two periods. These include units demolished, units lost by structural merger with other units, and a large category of "unrecorded" losses. They include units converted to nonresidential uses, units merged without structural alterations use, i.e., units in buildings that are vacant and have been boarded up, vandalized, burnt out, labeled "unsafe" by the Department of Buildings, or scheduled for demolition.

During the first half of the decade, the housing inventory was growing at an average rate of 22,000 units a year - well above the rate of household formation. That is why the rental vacancy rate rose to 3.2 per cent in 1965. Since 1965, losses have exceeded additions by more than 7,000 units a year, so the inventory has been shrinking. Since the number of households continues to grow (though at a very modest rate), the vacancy rate has plummeted.

Deterioration of the Housing Stock

Despite the addition of 334,000 new housing units and the demolition of 84,000 older units in the period 1960-67, the incidence of structural deterioration in the housing stock rose sharply.

The Census divides residential buildings into three categories of structural quality: sound, deteriorating, and dilapidated. Counting only those housing units with full plumbing facilities, there were 117,000 dilapidated units and 371,000 deteriorating units in the city in 1968, about 18 per cent of the family housing stock. While the inventory of sound housing grew by 2.4 per cent, 1960-67, the dilapidated inventory grew by 44 per cent and the deteriorating inventory grew by 37 per cent.

Figure 1

Additions and Losses to New York City's Housing Inventory, 1960-1967

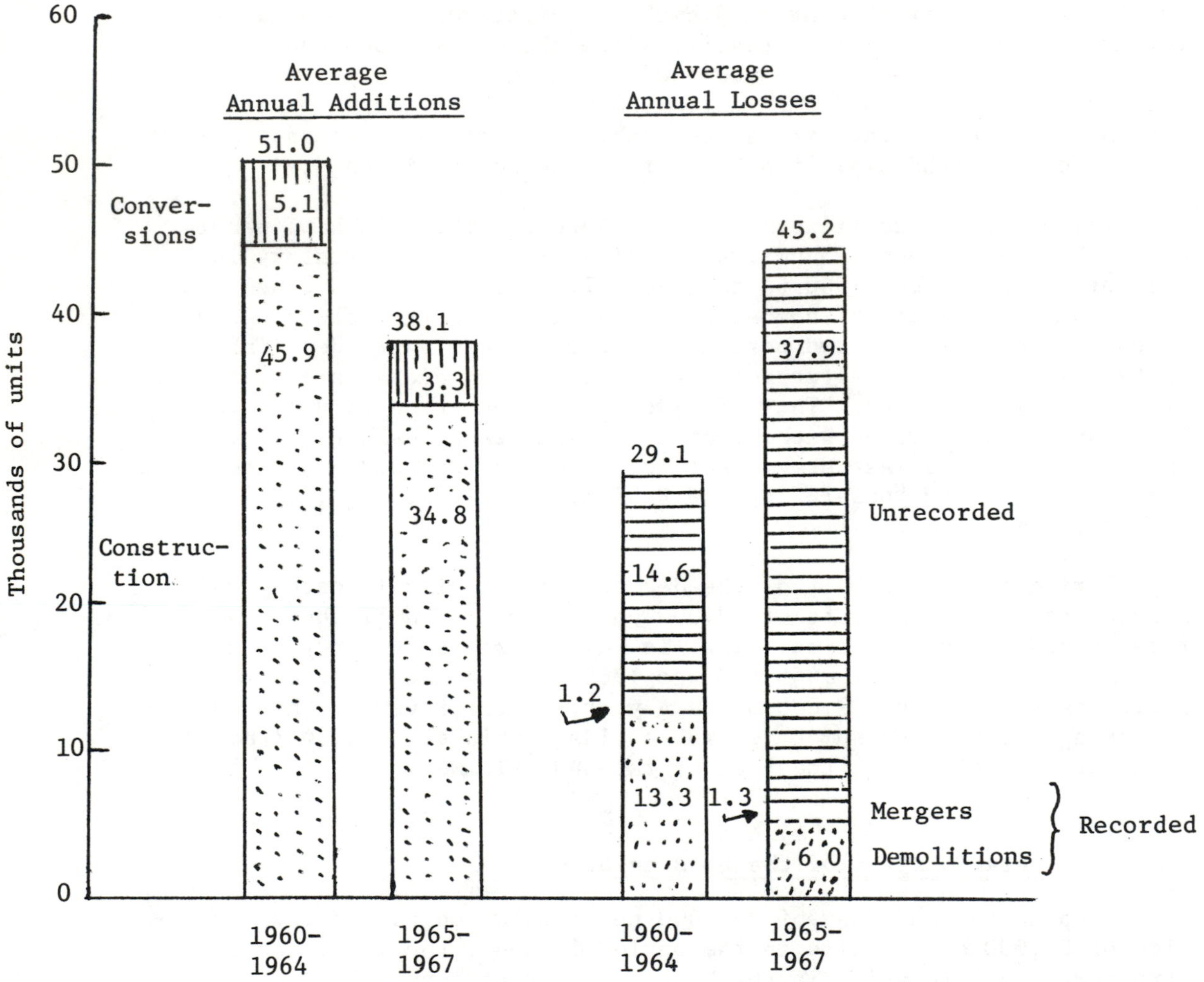

Units subject to rent control were much more likely to show evidence of deterioration (29 per cent) than units not subject to control (8 per cent).

Building Abandonment

The term "abandoned buildings" is currently applied to a variety of situations, and the incidence of building abandonment is correspondingly ambiguous. But a search of HDA records in 1968 turned up 7,100 buildings that were officially recorded as vacant and boarded up, vandalized, or burnt out. These contained an estimated 57,000 housing units. The list is believed to be far from complete.

Comparing successive inventories of the housing stock, we estimate that 114,000 housing units were withdrawn from the market in only three years, 1965-67. Foreclosures for nonpayment of taxes doubled between 1965 and 1967. Of the 126 buildings taken under city receivership since 1962 because of hazardous code violations, only 17 have been reclaimed by their owners.

At least 80 per cent of the unrecorded losses of the last three years were units in buildings classified in 1965 as either sound or deteriorating but not dilapidated.

Housing Costs and Rental Revenues

Since 1945, the cost of supplying well-maintained rental housing has risen at an average rate close to 6 per cent per year.

In the sector of the market [not subject to rent control], landlords have generally been able to increase rents to cover rising costs and protect their yields, except during the building boom of the early 1960s, when high vacancy rates in newly constructed buildings forced them to set rents below full costs in many cases. A number of these buildings fell behind in their mortgage payments. As the market has tightened and leases have expired, they have attempted to recoup these losses and cover subsequent cost increases. In 1968-69, rent increases of 25 per cent on two-year leases were not uncommon. As a result of [the Rent Stabilization] legislation adopted in 1969 by the City Council, these increases are being scaled down to a maximum of 10 per cent on two-year leases and 15 per cent on three-year leases.

In the [rent] controlled sector, rent increases have fallen far short of cost increases. For units continuously in the inventory since 1943, we estimate that the average annual increase in rents has been about 2 per cent per year.

Friction Between Tenants and Landlords

In many parts of the market, relations between landlords and tenants have deteriorated to the point of open hostility. The city is increasingly under pressure to intervene in their disputes and to provide lopsided remedies for real or fancied wrongs.

In the uncontrolled inventory, the principal tenant complaint has been the unexpected and large rent increases demanded for renewal of recently expired leases, complaints to which the city has responded by imposing a modified form of rent control [as described above].

In the [rent] controlled inventory, the principal tenant complaints relate to attempts by landlords to reduce maintenance or building services, or failure to remedy housing-code violations. Between 1962 and 1968, the number of such complaints increased by 240 per cent. On the one hand, there is evidence that tenants often create violations for the specific purpose of obtaining rent reductions. On the other hand, there is evidence that landlords frequently resort to harassment of statutory tenants in order to force them to vacate an apartment (thereby enabling the owner to secure a "turnover" rent increase), or to agree to support the landlord's petition for rent increases under the various provisions of the rent control ordinance.

Especially in low-income neighborhoods, tenants have become increasingly militant, organizing rent strikes and otherwise rejecting the traditional prerogatives of existing ownership.

Family Incomes and Housing Expenditures

Both real incomes and rents in New York City have risen substantially since 1950; the share of family budgets allocated to housing has gone up very little, but space consumption per capita in rental housing has increased by 18 per cent.

After adjusting for changes in the value of the dollar, and taking into account changes in family-size distributions, it is clear that the level of living within financial reach of families in New York City rose sharply and across the board between 1950 and 1960. Since 1960, further improvement has occurred, but mostly at the lower end of the income scale; higher standards and broader coverage of public assistance undoubtedly play a substantial role in these recent improvements.

With more real income the city's families have bought steadily increasing quantities of housing. Whereas the size of the city's population changed very little in those 18 years, the total number of occupied rooms increased by 1.8 million.

Largely because of rent control and welfare payments, this expansion in space consumption has been accompanied by relatively little strain on the tenant's pocketbook. One measure of budgetary strain is the ratio of gross rent to household income. In 1950, the median value of this ratio was .19; it was about the same in 1960 and slightly higher in 1968 - less than .21.

Actually, even that increase is deceptive. About 550,000 families paid less than 15 per cent of their incomes for rent. At the other end of the scale, nearly 420,000 families paid 35 per cent or more. But we estimate that over a third of these were welfare recipients whose rent allowances are not functionally related to their incomes. If welfare cases are excluded, 1968's median rent/income ratio was about .19.

Disinvestment in Rental Housing

Faced with declining yields even when their buildings are fully occupied, and often with negative cash flows when vacancies occur, the owners of rental housing in many areas of the city can see little prospect for future gain. Such buyers as they can find insist on purchase-money mortgages with the expectation of milking the property for a few years, then forfeiting title.

Interviews with banks and other mortgage lenders confirm our general impression that institutional investors are, as rapidly as possible, reducing their portfolios of controlled housing and of housing in deteriorated neighborhoods.

While these conditions are widespread, they are not all-pervasive. Market conditions vary considerably by neighborhood. The West Side of Manhattan is a prime example of an area increasingly popular with middle- and upper-income families. Owners of rent controlled buildings consequently retain a strong interest in the long-term future of their properties despite low current yields.

In Harlem and Bedford-Stuyvesant, and in neighborhoods on their fringes, the prospects are bleak. With or without rent control changes, the prospects for obtaining higher revenues from low-income tenants are slim. Because of the high incidence of fires and vandalism, insurance is seldom obtainable. Rehabilitation capital is unobtainable from private sources; and in any event is not amortizable out of anticipated postrehabilitation revenues. Even existing mortgages are usually nonrenewable. Given the characteristically short term (five or ten years) of such mortgages in New York City, and the unwillingness of existing mortgage-holders to foreclose and assume responsibility for the property, there is every prospect that the rate of building abandonment will continue to rise.

Limitations of Existing Programs

City, state, and federal contributions to housing and urban renewal programs in New York City amounted to about $800 million in fiscal 1968, including capital investment, contributions to annual operating costs of public-assisted housing, rent assistance to welfare clients, and regulatory programs such as rent control and code enforcement.

This [part] deals with inventory management programs impinging directly on the existing stock of private rental housing through regulation of rents and standards of property management, financial or other assistance to landlords or tenants, and real estate taxation.

The specific programs reviewed here are listed in Table 1; for each program we have provided indicators of the amount or kind of housing within its scope.

Rent Control

The rent ceilings now imposed [by the rent control law] on most multiple dwellings built prior to 1947 are based on rents charged in 1943, with one 15 per cent increase granted across the board in 1963. Current ceiling rents for individual apartments are not systematically related to the quality of housing provided, the tenant's ability to pay, or the long-run costs of supplying such housing.

Over the years, the basic rent control ordinance has been amended to permit correction of the worst inequities. Today, rent ceilings may be raised or lowered on a case-by-case basis for various reasons. Over 450,000 units - a third of the rent controlled inventory - were granted some form of increase in 1968 and rents were reduced on 57,000 units.

Some rent-increase provisions work fairly well at compensating landlords for cost increases. Others do not. The New Lease[1] provision accounts for more than half the dollar value of increases granted in recent years. But increases granted under this provision are in no way based on actual cost changes. Landlords with the greatest turnover in tenants get increases, while those with stable tenantry do not.

If landlords allow service levels or building quality to decline, rent ceilings may also be reduced.

---

[1] The rent control law allowed a landlord and a new tenant to enter into a lease that provided for an increase in the maximum legal rent not exceeding 15 per cent and for a term of at least two years.

Table 1

Summary of City Programs Affecting Private Rental Housing

Program Name	Function	Applicability
	General Programs	
Rent Control	Control rent increases and decreases	Most pre-1947 multiple dwellings
Rent Stabilization	Limit rent increases	Most post-1946 multiple dwellings
Welfare Rents	Rent assistance to welfare recipients	Housing occupied by welfare recipients
Rent Supplements	Federal rent assistance to low-income families	Housing financed under 221(d)(3)
Assessed Value Protests	Assessment appeals	All taxable real estate
	Problem Building Programs	
Code Enforcement	Detection and correction of violations and punishment of violators	All multiple dwellings
HRM-RSK	Management counseling to assist owners in removing code violations	All rent-controlled housing scheduled for rent reductions
Municipal Loans	Low interest financing of capital improvements	Controlled pre-1929 multiple dwellings
Federal 221(d)(3)	Low interest financing of capital improvements	Most pre-1947 multiple dwellings
J-51	Tax exemption and abatement for capital improvements	Controlled pre-1929 multiple dwellings
Major Capital Improvements	Permits rent increases in controlled buildings for major capital improvements	Controlled, violation-free housing
Emergency Repair Program	Provides emergency repairs for conditions that jeopardize tenants' health or safety	Buildings with emergency code violations
Emergency Vacates	Relocation of tenants	Buildings declared unsafe for occupancy
Unsafe Demolitions	Demolition of unsafe buildings	Vacant buildings declared unsafe for occupancy
In Rem	Public acquisition and management after tax foreclosure	Buildings with 4-year tax arrears
Receivership	Public management for purposes of tenant protection	Buildings with hazardous code violations

The lowest rents accrue to families of long tenure, whose housing is in effect subsidized by their more recent neighbors. To retain the benefits of controlled rents, many families have held onto large controlled apartments despite departure of some family members from the household.

Rent Assistance

Rent allowances paid to welfare clients amounted to at least $235 million in calendar 1969.

The Department of Social Services pays all or part of the rent for nearly 15 per cent of all renter households in New York City, and for at least 40 per cent of those with incomes under $4,000. (Other rent assistance programs are in operation, but their volumes are comparatively insignificant.)

The Department of Social Services imposes administrative ceilings on rent allowances, varying with the number of persons in the household. Within these limits, the department pays the contract rent of the dwelling actually occupied by the client and adds an allowance for utilities when these are not included in the rent. Welfare centers are not supposed to refer clients to buildings with hazardous code violations, but most clients find their own housing and its condition is not investigated.

About 60 per cent of all welfare households occupy Old Law or New Law tenements,[1] and those buildings containing welfare families are typically in worse condition than buildings without welfare tenants. Thus, welfare-occupied buildings of each type have two or three times the average number of uncorrected housing code violations for all buildings of that type. The rents per room paid by welfare households, however, are not substantially different in their distribution from those paid by nonwelfare tenants of controlled housing.

One striking feature of welfare housing is overcrowding. Even large welfare families tend to occupy small apartments, with households of five or more persons averaging less than one room per person. Another striking feature is instability of tenure; about a fourth of all welfare cases move each year.

Real Estate Taxation

Current city taxes on residential real estate add roughly one-third to the typical family's rent bill. Taxes on existing structures have been increasing at the rate of 4 to 6 per cent annually, and

---

[1]Old Law tenements were built before 1901; New Law tenements between 1901 and 1929.

account for a substantial portion of the rise in rents on uncontrolled housing. In the controlled sector, tax increases are partly absorbed by the landlord.

The total assessed value of rental housing amounts to $12 billion. The 1968 tax yield from rental property was about $600 million, a figure that may be compared with aggregate gross rent payments of $2.6 billion in that same year.

The city has made extensive use of tax exemptions and abatements as incentives for new construction and for building improvement. In 1968, about 230,000 units of public and publicly assisted housing received tax benefits amounting to $64 million, and over 100,000 private rental units received tax benefits (under the J-51 program) amounting to roughly $7.6 million. The incentives offered are substantial and it is often argued that these tax benefits cost the city very little because they induce construction and improvements that otherwise would not have occurred. Whatever the merits of this argument, it is clear that these tax benefits are unevenly distributed among the city's residents.

Problem Building Programs

The workloads of programs for detecting and treating problem buildings have grown rapidly. ... Some city responses are designed primarily to protect tenant health and safety; others to protect tenants from unfair treatment; others to protect the housing stock from deterioration.

Detection and Diagnosis of Problem Buildings: Under the present system, the symptoms of trouble most likely to bring a building to the city's notice are complaints of deficiencies in building services or maintenance, and failure to pay taxes. Other symptoms, such as high vacancy rates, rapid turnover of tenants, or failure to meet mortgage payments, do not usually engage the city's attention. Tenant complaints ... are the main sources of entry. City-initiated searches account for only a small fraction of the total.

Primitive Responses: Punishing the owners of badly maintained buildings has not proven to be a very effective way of inducing better maintenance. When applied to neglected buildings already in financial difficulties, heavy fines or rent reductions are more likely to result in building abandonment than building improvement.

When a landlord fails to correct a violation of the housing maintenance code, the city's first line of response has been to refer the case to the Criminal Court. The annual number of such referrals has roughly doubled since 1962, with about 30,000 cases tried in 1968. Once in court, an offender is, almost always, convicted, but the fine is usually trivial. In 1968 the average fine was $12.32.

The city's other major form of punishment [is] rent reduction. The Office of Rent Control is empowered to reduce rents when customary services are discontinued or when hazardous violations of the housing maintenance and building codes go uncorrected. Some 348,000 applications for rent reduction were filed in 1968, about 85 per cent of which originated in tenant complaints and 15 per cent in referrals from the Office of Code Enforcement and the Department of Buildings. In 292,000 cases the application was disallowed or the violation corrected prior to rent reduction; only in 57,000 cases were rents actually reduced. Reductions, however, were quite substantial, averaging $11 per month for units whose rents were mostly in the $70-$110 range. The threat of reduction appears to have been an effective inducement to corrective action; but actual imposition of a rent reduction does not appear to induce compliance; in contrast to the 57,000 rents reduced, only 3,000 rents were restored in 1968.

Assistance Programs: Several forms of financial assistance are available to owners of rental property who agree to make capital improvements. Both city and federal loan programs have been restricted to major rehabilitation of a very small number of housing units. The only program that has affected a large number of housing units has been [the Municipal Loan program] in which the city bears the full cost of improvements. The principle of the Municipal Loan program is quite simple: the city's borrowing power is made available to landlords who could not obtain capital in the private market at a comparable interest rate.

Both the Municipal Loan and Federal 221(d)(3) programs provide low-cost financing for major rehabilitation of rental housing; together, these programs committed $39 million of public funds in 1968 to provide for the rehabilitation of 2,800 housing units. Municipal loans averaged over $9,000 per unit in 1968; federal loans averaged over $15,000.

The Tax Exemption-Tax Abatement (J-51) program has had a much wider impact. Tax benefits have been conferred on more than 100,000 housing units since 1955; in 1968, the program covered $20 million in capital improvements on 34,000 housing units (about $600 per unit). Review of J-51 applications suggests that many buildings receiving tax benefits under this program would have been improved even without this assistance, the tenants bearing the costs in the form of rent increases granted [for major capital improvements under the rent control law].

An attempt was made in 1966 to provide city assistance specifically to buildings that were threatened with rent reductions due to code violations. Under the Housing Repair and Maintenance (HRM) program, the city can contract with the building owner to suspend punitive action for 3 to 9 months. During this period, rents are placed in escrow until repairs are made. While under contract, the owner is given management counseling. Buildings with less serious problems may be referred to a companion Landlord Repair Schedule (RSK) program, which lacks rent escrow powers.[1]

Takeover Programs: The principal means by which the city acquires problem buildings is through foreclosure of tax liens, a step that can be taken no less than four years after the owner has signaled his loss of interest by failure to pay taxes. In 1968, nearly 700 buildings were thus acquired, and about 300 previously acquired buildings were sold at public auction. As these figures suggest, the inventory of buildings under city management is growing rapidly; by the end of 1968, it approached 1800 buildings. During the 1969 fiscal year, the cost of operating and repairing these buildings amounted to $2 million. Rental receipts amounted to roughly $1 million.

The city is also empowered to take over the management of buildings with persistent and serious code violations. Since 1962, 126 buildings have been taken under city receivership. Although owners may redeem these buildings by reimbursing the city for its net expenditures under receivership management, only 17 have done so.

Buildings taken under receivership typically have high vacancy rates and need extensive repairs to meet code standards. Their owners were unable to operate the buildings profitably and the city's experience has been no better.

Cost Considerations

For multiple dwellings built before 1947 but kept violation-free, maintenance and operating costs, real estate taxes, and an 8 per cent return on capital averaged about $25 per room per month in 1968. We do not propose this average figure as an operational standard to apply to all buildings, nor as one that would be equally applicable to market conditions in 1970. ...[The first section of Table 2 contains estimates of the number of apartments needing additional revenue to meet the standard of $25 per room per month.]

---

[1] There is also an Emergency Repair Program (ERP) covering housing with code violations that endanger the health or safety of the tenants. Under its provisions, the city makes the needed repairs at the owner's expense.

Table 2

Costs in 1968

Item	Thousands of Cases	Amount Needed Per Year: Total ($ millions)	Per Case ($)
Apartments needing more revenue	722	255	353
Controlled	627	225	359
Not controlled	95	30	316
Households needing rent assistance*	621	410	660
Welfare clients	269**	284	1,056
Present program	(269)***	(214)	(796)
Additional need	(156)***	(70)	(450)
Other low-income households	352	126	358
Households able to pay more rent	290	91	314
Living in controlled housing	248	79	319
Not in controlled housing	42	12	286

*Excludes public housing tenants except for 18,000 welfare families living in public housing. In 1968 there were about 144,000 families living in public housing at a public cost (including real estate taxes foregone) of $104 million.

**Excludes welfare households not paying cash rent.

***All 269,000 welfare families received some rent assistance. However, 156,000 of them did not receive enough to meet the space and rent standards discussed in the text.

The second section of Table 2 presents estimates of the number of households unable to afford well-maintained housing in 1968. Ability to pay and housing needs vary with income and family size. The ability-to-pay standard currently used by the Federal Rent Supplement program is 25 per cent of gross income; housing standards of the American Public Health Association call for space allowance of one room plus one room per person for all except the largest families. If these standards are applied to New York City's residents in 1968, about 621,000 households in private rental housing were unable to afford $25 per room per month.

[The third section of Table 2 provides estimates of the number of families who could be paying more rent.] We think they were mostly long-term middle-income tenants of rent controlled apartments. Applying the same standards as before (one room plus one room per person and a maximum rent-income ratio of .25), we find about 290,000 families who could have afforded $25 per room but actually paid less.

RENT CONTROL (A)

The Stage Is Set

As 1969 drew to a close, pressure mounted for change in New York City's World War II Rent Control Law. Landlords, looking forward to the April 1970 expiration of their contract with building service employees (and noting that the City Council would be considering whether or not to renew the rent control law after it ran out on March 31), served notice on the Mayor that rents in the controlled sector must be increased. Unless the law was modified to improve the rate of return on their buildings, the owners threatened to refuse any wage hikes. This could mean a prolonged strike, one that would stop services in over 5,000 apartment buildings throughout the city.

Concurrent with these rumblings, the tentative results of housing studies under way at McKinsey & Company and the New York City-Rand Institute, began to reach the Mayor's office. McKinsey's analysis of the city's rehabilitation programs suggested that there was little incentive in New York for owners to improve deteriorated or dilapidated buildings since the imposition of rent control frequently prevented the required investment from earning a reasonable rate of return (if any). Rand, conducting a broader-based study of the city's housing problems, had concluded, among other things:[1]

> We think that the first priority of city housing policy should be to redress the existing imbalance between rental revenues and costs in a way that provides long-run incentives for preventive maintenance. Unless this is done, we anticipate continued decline in housing quality, continued high rates of inventory loss, intensification of landlord-tenant antagonisms, and a permanent shortage of rental housing.

---

[1] See Housing Rehabilitation in New York City and Confronting the Rental Housing Crisis.

Other events focused attention on rent control. During the fall, three key positions in the Housing and Development Administration (HDA)[1] were vacated through resignations; the Administrator of HDA; the Commissioner of Rent and Housing Maintenance; and the Deputy Commissioner for Rent Control (see Exhibit 1). These vacancies left the entire policy making and operating chain of command for rent control open. In particular, it removed from the scene Commissioner of Rent Control Berman, long a staunch proponent of existing rent control legislation and firm in the belief that it was not change that was needed but extension of the law to cover more of the uncontrolled housing sector.

In January and February 1970, the issue intensified. Articles appeared in the press highlighting various aspects of the housing "crisis" and carrying such headlines as "Housing Supply in City Eroding Amid Construction Standstill," "Private Sector is Paralyzed in Housing Slump Here," and "Crisis in Housing Demands Action." Rand's findings were published, including their conclusion that rent control was largely responsible for the deterioration and abandonment of rental housing. Albert A. Walsh, the new Administrator of HDA, and Benjamin Altman, his recently appointed Commissioner of Rent and Housing Maintenance, responded by issuing a joint statement criticizing the Rand study for "incomplete data and certain untested assumptions."[2] They suggested that the report made all landlords seem well intentioned when, in fact, "some are not."

On February 9, in the wake of these statements, four landlord organizations announced their plan for altering the rent control law. They labeled it a way to "stem the flood of abandoned buildings, halt the massive decay of housing, and start to solve the worst housing crisis in the history of the city." Under the landlords' proposal, rents would be raised an average of 25% in each controlled building and the increase apportioned among units so that the most expensive apartment received the least increase and the least expensive apartment the greatest rent rise. If this formula failed to lift all rents to a minimum of $30 per room per month, an additional increase would be allowed. After the initial rent hikes, landlords would be permitted 10% and 15% rises at the expiration of two-year and three-year leases, respectively. In return for higher rent levels, the owners would pledge themselves to spend one-fourth of the rent increases on improved maintenance and more rehabilitation. An association of owners would be formed with the power to expel members (thereby returning their buildings to the old rent levels) if they did not keep their structures free of code violations.

Jane Benedict, director of the Metropolitan Council on Housing, a city-wide organization of tenants, called the landlords' proposal a "tremendous swindle." "It's like asking the Mafia to police itself," she said.

---

[1]HDA was the agency responsible for the management of all the city's housing and renewal programs. Its administrator reported directly to the Mayor.

[2]The position of Deputy Commissioner for Rent Control had also been filled, by a former associate of Commissioner Altman's.

On February 10, Mayor Lindsay announced that his administration was reviewing the "whole matter of rent control" before the law's March 31 expiration. The review would be the responsibility of Administrator Walsh and Commissioner Altman. Within HDA, Arthur Spiegel, Director of the Office of Programs & Policy, was given direct responsibility for the project. He was to be assisted by Nat Leventhal from the Mayor's office and by a consulting team for McKinsey, headed by Robert O'Block. On February 14, Walsh and Altman issued another statement indicating their support for some program that would relax rent controls provided adequate protection was afforded to tenants unable to pay any more. As O'Block put it, "[at this point] almost everyone agreed that reform was needed. The major question was, 'What kind of reform are you talking about?'; and, on that point, everyone had their own ideas."

History and Scope of Rent Regulation [1]

History

Government controls on rent levels, a wartime price stabilization measure, became effective in New York City in 1943. The legal justification for keeping rents below market levels was a shortage of rental housing severe enough to constitute a public emergency. Federal rent control terminated in 1950, but New York State continued the program under state law. Only buildings constructed prior to 1947 were covered. Then, in 1962, administration of rent control was transferred to the city pursuant to a state law which allowed the city to create its own rent control program. The city rent control law was closely modeled on the state's, and except for a few special cases, this law also covered only rental structures built before 1947. In 1970, it affected about 1.3 million units, including apartments and single-room occupancy units.

Since 1964, the retention of rent control had been contingent upon the City Council's determination that a public emergency in rental housing persisted: a vacancy rate of less than 5% was the criterion for such a finding. But in 1965 the net vacancy rate was only 3.2% - the highest vacancy rate recorded since the end of World War II - and in 1968 the United States Census Bureau reported that the rate had dropped to 1.2%. There was no evidence that it had increased since. Nevertheless, portions of the controlled stock with higher vacancy rates could be selectively decontrolled. Stock was also removed from the controlled sector due to demolition. As a consequence, the number of controlled units was steadily decreasing. In 1960, about 77% of all rental households occupied controlled units - about 1.60 million. By 1968 these totals had fallen to 64% and 1.34 million, respectively.

---

[1] Adapted from Rental Housing in New York City, Volume IV, Chapter II, The New York City-Rand Institute and McKinsey & Company, Inc.

In 1969, the city established a second control mechanism for its rental housing stock: The Rent Stabilization Law was enacted in response to the large rent increases that occurred in uncontrolled housing in 1968 and early 1969. This measure extended control over the rate of rent increase to almost all previously unregulated rental units in the city and created new administrative machinery to manage the program. (In it the increases allowed during 1969 were 6%, 9%, and 11%, on 1-, 2-, and 3-year lease renewals, respectively; and 16%, 19%, and 21% on 1-, 2-, and 3-year new leases, respectively.) The law, which covers approximately 353,000 rental units, was administered by an association to which owners of buildings constructed after 1946 had to belong to avoid transfer of their property to regulation under the 1962 Rent Control Law.

Administration of the Law

The 1962 Rent Control Law delegated responsibility for implementing its various provisions to the Housing and Development Administration. Within HDA, operational control was exercised by the Office of Rent Control (ORC), a division of the Department of Rent and Housing Maintenance (see Exhibit 1). By establishing general rules and guidelines for rent changes, and through the processing of applications for changes by tenants and owners, ORC influenced a major proportion of housing units in the city. It handled almost 1 million transactions per year, and the number had been growing despite the declining number of controlled units. In 1969, ORC acted upon over 414,000 applications for rent increases, 389,000 applications for decreases, and about 88,000 other applications.

The administrative structure of the Office of Rent Control comprised five divisions under the office of the Assistant Commissioner. Four of the divisions - Research, Property Improvement, Legal and Accounting - were centralized and served the entire office. The fifth division - Operations - oversaw the activities of six District Rent Offices (DROs) (two in Manhattan and one in each of the other boroughs). ORC's operations were characterized by tight and methodical procedures and meticulous recording and storage of data. The records were maintained manually, and rent change operations were decentralized to the DROs.

ORC's workload was handled by a staff of about 900 people. More than three-quarters of them worked in the District Rent Offices handling the constant flow of incoming cases. Although responsibility for administering the rent control program was transferred from the state to the city in 1962, almost all the costs of the program continued to be paid by the state. Personnel costs accounted for almost 90% of the total budget. Thus, although the staff had not increased significantly, rising wages and salaries caused administrative expenses to climb from about \$5.5 million in fiscal year 1963-1964 to \$9.1 million in 1968-1969.

Objectives of the Law

The 1962 Rent Control Law had several broad objectives:

1. To ensure that rent increases over time were equitable for both tenants and landlords. Tenants should be protected from excessive increases and landlords should receive sufficient revenues to cover the costs of maintaining their buildings properly.

2. To encourage new landlord investment to improve the quality of the controlled stock and discourage undermaintenance.

3. To protect tenants from unfair treatment.

To achieve these objectives, the law established maximum rents based on the 1943 rent and service levels of all registered units and set forth conditions governing changes in these maximum rents. The most important were:[1]

Provisions to Govern Rent Increases: These provisions permitted rises in ceiling rents for individual buildings or apartments to cover increases in the costs of maintaining a building and providing the same level of services as in 1943. The most important were New Lease, Hardship, and Equalization and Labor Cost Passalong. In addition, the City Council had the power to increase rents, but had done so only once: In 1953 a 15% increase was given to all controlled units whose rent ceilings had not been raised by at least 15%, since March 1, 1943, (excluding rent adjustments due to changes in services and facilities). The effects of actions taken under the rent increase provisions between 1962 and 1969 are summarized in Exhibit 2.

Provisions to Maintain and Improve Housing Quality: The 1962 Rent Control Law contained two main provisions intended to upgrade housing quality by allowing increased rents for improvements: the Increased Services and Facilities provision and the Major Capital Improvement and Substantial Rehabilitation provision. Actions under these two provisions are also shown in Exhibit 2. In addition, the law set forth conditions under which rents could be reduced if services or maintenance fell below 1943 levels.

Provisions to Protect Tenants from Unfair Treatment: Because the rent control law provided for automatic rent increases for vacated units, it also limited the landlord's right to evict tenants and protected tenants from landlord harassment which might otherwise drive them from their apartments. Tenants were also protected from overcharging.

---

[1] These provisions are discussed in more detail in Appendix A.

Despite the existence and careful application of these provisions, there was substantial evidence by 1969 that the 1962 law was failing to meet most of its objectives. To some extent, tenants were being protected from excessive rent increases. Between 1960 and 1968, the median contract rent for controlled housing grew at a rate of only 2.3% a year - from $65 per unit per month to $78 per unit per month. During the same period, median contract rents in uncontrolled housing grew 4% per year. The ratio between rents and incomes also remained relatively constant in the controlled sector. The median rent-income ratios were 0.19, 0.18, and 0.20 in 1950, 1960, and 1968, respectively. In uncontrolled housing, the ratio was .22 in 1968. (Most standards established for public assistance in housing use rent ratios between 0.20 and 0.25 as guides to reasonable rent levels.) Median ratios, however, do not tell the full story. Over one-third of the households in the controlled stock had ratios of 0.25 or more. About 150,000 of these were welfare households whose rent was paid for them and whose nonrent income is not affected by the amount of rent assistance received. The remaining 240,000 were not on welfare, but almost all had incomes of less than $4,000 per year (see Exhibit 3).

Moreover, the pattern with which protection was provided was highly uneven. The greatest freedom from rent increases was given to long-tenure tenants. This included not only many low-income, elderly persons, but also substantial numbers of higher income households who could afford to pay the full cost of their housing. New arrivals in the city and those who tended to move frequently (Puerto Ricans and Blacks) were more likely to be subject to rent increases under the new lease provisions. In addition, these provisions, which accounted for over half the dollar amount of rent increases, recognized neither cost nor quality differences (or similarities) between units. Desirable apartments would remain free of rent increases because turnover would be low; the converse would be true of undesirable apartments. Similar units in the same building could command substantially different rents because of differences in turnover. Finally, families whose housing needs diminished as their children left home found it advantageous to go on occupying large apartments in order to avoid new lease increases in rent.

As to the objective of providing sufficient revenue to cover the cost of maintenance, the picture was even less favorable. While median rent levels were increasing 2.3% per year, the cost of providing well-maintained housing grew 4 to 6% annually. The result was a cost/revenue squeeze and an estimated rent "gap" of $260 million per year.

(This amount equals the difference that would exist between cost increases and revenue increases since 1943 if landlords were maintaining their buildings at 1943 standards.)[1] The gap was apportioned between housing units as shown below. In addition, by 1969, twenty-nine per cent of the controlled stock was considered unsound compared to nine per cent of the uncontrolled housing.

Monthly Rent Level	1969 Rent Gap (Millions)
Less than $60	$ 74.7
60 - 79	119.6
80 - 99	54.0
100 - 125	10.6
125 - 150	0.8
More than 150	-
	$259.7

Drafting the Administration's Proposal

As Spiegel and O'Block began their investigations, O'Block's earlier comment regarding the plethora of ideas regarding rent control reform began to take on substance. At least four positions were receiving strong support. The first had already been stated by the landlords in their public announcement. The second was held by a vocal subgroup of owners and several conservative political interests. They saw rent control in any form as an anachronism, one that interrupted the free play of the market in ways that were detrimental to the long-term health of the housing stock. The only wise alternative was to eliminate it altogether. The third position was held by a substantial number of old guard civil servants in the Office of Rent Control. (In ORC, "old guard" usually meant tenure dating back to the inception of rent control in 1943, or very close to it.) They had seen an across-the-board 15% increase in 1953 and had found the change easy to administer and, apparently, a satisfactory palliative for the owners. They favored another 15% across-the-board action.

---

[1]In addition to the rent gap, there was also an "income gap" that affected housing. Demographic projections suggested that by 1972, the disparity between tenant income and the income levels required to cover the costs of acceptable housing would equal $2.8 billion per year. Only $1 billion of this gap would be filled by welfare rent assistance.

Spiegel and O'Block, together with analysts at Rand and several other staff members at HDA and in the Mayor's office, believed that none of these suggestions would solve the problems created by the city's rent control law. A fourth alternative became their goal, namely, the "rationalization" of rent control - that is, the development of some means of protecting tenants in an artificially tight housing market, ensuring the maintenance of housing quality, and providing landlords with a fair return on investment. To reach this goal, they would have to devise the concepts and components of a rational law and then present them convincingly, first to enough members of the administration so that they would be adopted as the Mayor's program and, second, to enough of the City Council to ensure the program's enactment.

During February, the two men (working with Nat Levanthal) identified a number of basic approaches to rent control change and subjected each one to preliminary analysis. They finally settled on the concept of establishing rents on the basis of a formula which would take into account operating and maintenance expenses, real estate taxes, and an appropriate return on capital. Periodic revisions would be made to the formula as economic conditions changed and, each time it was modified, the rent revenue for some, or all, of the controlled stock would also change. In O'Block's view, this approach came as close to "phasing out rent control" as was possible without resorting to complete decontrol. It also represented a unique and untried concept.

Having decided on their approach, the two men saw the next step as one of developing and refining their initial thoughts into a workable program, presenting this program to as many key members of the administration as possible, and protecting the basic integrity of the idea from the sniping of those who could not be convinced. In particular, they would need to influence five individuals or subgroups:

1. The Mayor and some of his key advisors.

2. HDA Administrator Walsh (a Republican).

3. Commissioner Altman. Support from the commissioner was especially important. Altman was a reform Democrat and reform Democrats had always favored strict rent control legislation. His switch to support of a flexible approach (as the formula represented) would be a major step for a man of his political persuasion, and a major asset to the administration when it came time to present the program to the City Council and the citizens.

4. The HDA Legal Staff. Past rent control legislation had been subjected to repeated litigation by its opponents. In fact, the recently enacted Rent Stabilization Law was in the midst of a court test on the grounds that it was patently inequitable since it placed post-1947 buildings and pre-1947 buildings under different forms of control. In view of this, it was not likely that either the HDA Administrator or the Mayor would support a formula approach unless it had been approved by HDA lawyers.

5. ORC Policy Council. This group, consisting of six, long-tenure ORC employees would be as difficult as any to convince. It was, after all, ORC that had successfully administered the old rent control law for a quarter of a century and that would contend with the upheaval accompanying the implementation of any substantially new provisions. To a man, the council favored the old ways. Yet, its cooperation would be needed if change was to be brought about quickly.

There began two months of an almost unending reiterative process. Spiegel, O'Block, and Levanthal developed the rudiments of a program of which a rent formula was the heart. McKinsey tested the impact of the formula on individual sample buildings and on the controlled stock in aggregate. Meetings were arranged with the five groups outlined above and with others. Before each meeting, key persons scheduled to attend the meeting were identified and given individual presentations in an effort to ensure their understanding and to test their reaction in advance of the "official" meeting. "We never went in cold," said O'Block. Out of these meetings, both with individuals and with larger groups, came suggestions for change and modification which in turn, were tested, assessed and presented again to the same and to different groups. By mid-April, after two months of this activity, a reasonable consensus had developed. Although the ORC Policy Council remained skeptical, the Mayor's Office, Administrator Walsh, Commissioner Altman, and most of the HDA legal staff had "syndicated" - i.e., approved - the broad outlines of a rent control reform program. Its objectives were to:

1. Establish new maximum rents that would protect tenants from paying large increases in rent or excessive rents for low-quality units, but that also would provide landlords with a fair return on capital.

2. Encourage landlords to improve building quality and maintenance.

3. Periodically adjust the maximum rent ceiling to compensate for changes in general economic conditions.

4. Create an equitable distribution of housing costs among income groups, and require that households now getting rent "bargains" pay more.

5. Provide an administrative mechanism to effectively manage, control, and monitor the rent controlled stock.

These objectives would be achieved through a program that based maximum rents on a formula; gave landlords immediate relief (while the formula approach was being implemented) by raising rents through some simple, easy to administer set of rules; required landlords to certify that their buildings were free of code violations before they were eligible for rent increases; and protected those tenants who were unable to pay any more rent.

On the basis of this consensus, the team received directions from the Mayor's office to develop a detailed proposal for presentation to the council. On May 11, work was completed and sent to Mayor Lindsay by Commissioner Altman. The Mayor added his covering letter and, on the same day, transmitted the proposal to the council and announced the new rent control program to the press. The basic provisions of the proposed program are outlined below.

Maximum Base Rents (MBR)

Maximum rents for rent controlled structures would be determined by the sum of four components: real estate taxes, operating and maintenance expenses, a collection loss factor, and return on capital value (including both interest charges and profit). The first component would be computed directly, while the others would be determined by the application of a formula. MBR's would be computer calculated for each of the 1,300,000 rent controlled units in the city. The design and implementation of systems and procedures to do this would take at least a year.

Real Estate Taxes: The real estate component of MBR would be determined by multiplying the building's assessed value (on record at the Tax Assessor's Office) by the applicable borough tax rate.

Operating and Maintenance Expenses: Preliminary recommendations were submitted for the determination of an operating and maintenance expense allowance based on analysis of a sample of 145 buildings that were known to be free of code violations and had no outstanding tenant complaints. The Mayor's proposal to the council placed in the hands of HDA the job of developing final schedules for O&M expense. (These schedules would be set after completion of a more refined analysis of 450 buildings - 26,000 units - under way at the NYC-Rand Institute.) Examination of the O&M expense history for the sample of 145 suggested that these expenses were a function of the number of units in the building, whether or not there is an elevator, and the age of the structure. Some example O&M allowances based on these factors are shown in Exhibit 4 together with the actual O&M expenses for three specific buildings. (The discrepancies between calculated and actual O&M expenses shown in Exhibit 4 were one factor that led the administration to its decision to await the results of the Rand study before firming up the formulae.)

Collection Loss Factor: An additional increment in rent would be provided to account for vacancies and withholding or nonpayment of rent, all of which were considered to be the equivalent of operating expenses. Research by Professor George Sternlieb of Rutgers (who was just completing a major report on rental housing in the city) indicated that the average vacancy loss was about 2.9% of total building rent and that bad debts averaged about 1.2% of the rent received. Accordingly, the collection loss factor was set tentatively at 4.1%. It was later reduced to 3% by HDA.

Return on Capital Value: Setting the return on capital required decisions on two issues: How to measure the capital value and what rate of return to use. The administration proposed to measure capital value by multiplying assessed value by a factor that would reflect the average difference between current market value and assessed value. A sample of over 4,000 buildings showed that the average ratio of market value to assessed value was about 1.4 and this figure was used for illustrative purposes in the proposed legislation. HDA would have the authority to determine the ratio actually used. The recommended rate of return was 9.5% based on current interest rates for residential mortgages of between 9 and 12%. The rate, like other parts of the MBR formula, would be subject to periodic change by HDA.

In summary, then, the new maximum revenue for a controlled building would be set as follows:

New Maximum Revenue	=	Real Estate Taxes	+	Operating and Maintenance Allowance	+	Collection Loss Factor	+	Return on Capital Value
		Assessed Value x Tax Rate				3.0% of Total Building Rent Roll		9.5% x City Equalized Assessed Value

Exhibit 5 shows the application of this formula to a sample building. The council was not asked to approve the specific numbers in the formula, only its general format. HDA would be responsible for setting specific formula values. The legislation provided, however, that the final MBR formula would be filed with the council for its comment prior to setting MBR's.

Several other provisions in the proposed legislation concerned MBR's. The new maximum rents were to take effect on July 1, 1971. Thereafter, apartments whose rents were below MBR levels would receive annual upward adjustments not exceeding 9.5% until the MBR level was reached. HDA would adjust the formula each year to reflect changes in economic conditions; rents would be modified accordingly. Under no circumstances, however, would a rent adjustment be allowed to exceed 15% in any one year. Any landlord who felt that the MBR formula worked an undue hardship on him could ask that his rent levels be set on the basis of actual cost experience and a return on capital of 9.5%.

First Year Increase (FYI)

Because immediate relief for landlords was one objective of the program and MBR's could not be implemented for at least one year, an interim increase, averaging 10.74%, was recommended for all units. The FYI would be applied to controlled units except those that had received no rent increase through vacancy turnover since 1953. These apartments - approximately 315,000 - would be given a 15% increase during the interim year. Different buildings would receive slightly different interim increases according to an index developed in the Sternlieb report.

Other Provisions

Other major provisions of the Mayor's proposed new rent control legislation included:

1. Exemption from rent increases for any family already paying rent above public housing levels if the family's rent-income ratio was greater than 35% or if the ratio was between 25 and 35% and the family's disposable income was particularly low or the family size large. (Exact standards would be defined by HDA before July 1 1971. Average public housing rents were about $60.)

2. Requirements that rent increases be forfeited by any owner who did not remove all serious or hazardous code violations during the first year of the new program.

3. Expansion of current provisions protecting tenants from eviction, harassment by landlords; provisions granting increased benefits for relocation when a tenant, for justifiable reasons, is forced to leave his apartment.

Impact of the New Program

The over-all effect of the proposed FYI would be to increase total rent revenue in the controlled stock by $137 million per year distributed between various units as shown in Exhibit 6. The subsequent move to MBR rent levels would produce at least another $163 million over an eight-year period (see Exhibit 7). Looking at ability to pay, Exhibit 8 sets forth the percentage increases in rent that would be sustained by various income groups under the FYI part of the program. Exhibit 3 showed the existing rent/income ratios for nonwelfare households with different incomes in both the controlled and uncontrolled stock. (For welfare clients, the Department of Social Services pays the entire rent, thus removing the onus of increases under the proposed law.) Exhibit 9 indicates the number of welfare eligibles who were living in controlled housing but not receiving welfare.

In his letter of transmittal to the Mayor, Commissioner Altman summed up his own feelings about the new law as follows:

> The program . . . is complex, as are the problems and constraints it deals with. It is a phased program, and its positive impact will be felt gradually over a period of years. It is a program which recognizes that the City must face some difficult and painful adjustments if we are to stem the tide of housing deterioration.
>
> By revoking certain provisions of the [old] law that have outlived their usefulness, and by revising and adding others, I think that we will be able to restore a sense of optimism so necessary for future private investment. I also expect that the prevalent adversary relationship between tenant and landlord will be noticeably reduced if these proposals are adopted.
>
> From now on, both landlords and tenants will know what to expect and when. There will be no "giveaways" but there will be enough revenues to insure well-maintained housing and to keep responsible owners in the housing arena. Increases will always be gradual and modest for tenants, and will be directly linked to housing quality.

The City Reacts

In the midst of HDA's study of changes in the rent control law, the April 20th expiration date for the building workers' contract had come and gone. Thanks to efforts by the Mayor and to cooperation by both owners and Local 32B of the Building Service Employees Union, a one-month extension had been negotiated that gave the union a $13 per week pay increase and the city time to complete its recommendations for rent control reform. From April 20 to May 12, the various interest groups waited. On the twelfth, they read the administration's proposals and erupted. Edward Sulzberger, head of the Combined Owners Group, labeled the program "an administrative nightmare," and predicted that it would lead to a strike by the 25,000 employees of Local 32B. "This so-called 're-structuring'," he said, "will confiscate all the owner's invested capital and destroy the private housing needed for all tenants." He termed it "the complete socialization of all of New York's housing." Jane Benedict on the other hand, called it "the abolition of rent control," "a pro-landlord thing" and a plan that would "hit hardest on the elderly." She and her group, the Metropolitan Council on Housing, vowed to fight the measure. Councilman Donald Manes, a Queens Democrat and Chairman of the Council's Housing Committee, commented that it looked like the Mayor "first decided to raise everyone's rent and then looked for justification." But a fellow councilman, Republican Vito Battista from Brooklyn, was not so mild. He characterized the package as "a farce, like offering half an aspirin to a man dying of cancer." Commented The New York Times, "this sweeping change is . . . a declaration that housing must be regarded as a kind of public utility, subject to indefinite regulation beyond the 'emergency' conditions that justified the imposition of controls during World War II."

On May 18, two days before the extension of the contract with building employees was due to terminate, negotiators for the Realty Advisory Board notified the union and the Mayor that they would make no new wage offer unless the administration modified its rent control proposals. Thomas Shortman, president of Local 32B, declared, in response, that without an offer, his union would have no choice but to strike. The next day, under pressure from Deputy Mayor Richard Aurelio and Thomas J. Cuite, majority leader of the City Council, negotiators representing uncontrolled and cooperative apartments agreed to another thirty-day extension of the contract to allow the council more time. Representatives of the 3,000 rent-controlled buildings broke ranks, however, and refused to endorse the extension. At a raucous meeting in the Hotel Commodore that evening, 1,300 owners of controlled buildings chanted "strike, strike, strike!" when asked what they wished to do. Still, the following morning, they, too, acquiesced to the 30-day extension and, once again, a major strike was averted.

But the battle was just beginning; at hearings held by the council, emotions rose and positions hardened further. On Monday, May 25, the landlords presented their case, to the councilmen. "This is a communistically created and socialistically executed bill," shouted Mrs. Grace Liotta, a landlord from the Bronx, standing on tiptoe to see over the lectern. "We need an American bill based on the American heritage of free enterprise." The crowd of 200 landlords roared its approval. Pressed for particulars instead of rhetoric, Mr. Sulzberger criticized the provision for a 9.5% profit rate as far too small unless the owners were not expected to pay mortgage interest from that amount. He demanded that real estate taxes be reduced by the same dollar amount that each owner lost through renting to families that would be exempted from rent increases. "The real estate industry cannot perpetually be the second welfare department," he said.

On Wednesday, 200 tenants, charging that landlords would put rent increases into their own pockets rather than their buildings, flooded the council hearing room to have their say. They labeled property owners "slumlords," "vultures," and "millionaires" and urged a complete government takeover of the city's housing. "We believe it's about time the real estate industry is destroyed," shouted the Reverend Louis Gigante, a Roman Catholic priest and candidate for the U.S. House of Representatives. Jane Benedict assessed the Mayor's contention that the new program would foster better maintenance as "hogwash." She, too, advocated public ownership of housing. Former Bronx president, Herman Badillo, warned:

> Unless the city comes up with more reasonable proposals that take the serious problem of tenants into account, we are likely to see the outbreak of rent strikes throughout the city.

Assemblymen Katz, DeMarco, and Manes all came under fire as "slumlords" whose interests lay clearly with the landlords, not the tenants.

During the hearings, however, a few pockets of support emerged for the new program. The Citizens Planning Council, a leading civic group, called the proposal a "gigantic step forward" although they were critical of certain aspects of the new law. Dr. Frank Kristof, an economist with the State Urban Development Corporation endorsed the plan and called for its adoption with certain modifications and simplifications. The League of Women Voters supported the Mayor's proposal.

As the hearings progressed, Spiegel and O'Block, with the help of Levanthal turned their attention to educating and convincing as many members of the 37-man City Council as they could. Their tactics were much the same as they had been when dealing with members of the administration. Frequent meetings were called with various subgroups in the council and preliminary sessions held with key individuals within each subgroup. Councilmen Manes and Cuite were singled out for particularly detailed attention. "We had to sell them on two issues" commented O'Block, "the concept of using a formula to determine rents and the fact that computerizing the system was both feasible and economically reasonable. One of the tactics we used was to select buildings actually owned by some of the councilmen for our illustrative examples. That way, they could see exactly what would happen to their income and when it would happen." On May 26, immediately following one of the more raucous hearings on the bill, Councilman Manes commented, "There are a lot of flukes and a lot of flaws in the law. And there will have to be substantial changes before it gets through."

The directions that those changes might take began to take shape a few days later. Councilman Katz issued a detailed criticism of the Lindsay proposals (see Exhibit 10). More important, on June 3, twelve councilmen offered their own plan for changes in rent control. The group, which included eight reform Democrats and four Liberals, dubbed the administration's program "a cure worse than the disease." The twelve men rejected the concept of "economic rent levels" calculated by computer and suggested, instead, that rents be allowed to rise each year in response to actual increases in cost. These increases would be determined by an index that would reflect taxes, operating costs, and interest charges. Apartments would be broken down into eight categories according to age and size for purposes of determining and applying the index. In addition, their bill proposed that owners who could prove that they were not making a return of 8% on their equalized assessed valuation each year would be entitled to rent increases not to exceed 7.5% annually. Finally, they wanted to extend rent control to all rental housing and to secure rent subsidies totalling $50 million per year for tenants who were not on welfare but whose rent/income ratios exceeded 25%.

As June wore on, the polemics abated and the council deliberated. Over the weekend of June 20, Councilman Manes stated, in an interview, that he hoped the council would act no later than July 1. He said he wanted to "put teeth" in the bill to "make sure that a major proportion of any rent raises" would go into "maintenance, decoration, and repair." He also stated that the greatest difference of opinion on rent control that now existed in the council was what constituted a fair rate of return. The same weekend, Commissioner Altman, talking with newsmen in a television interview, praised council majority leader Cuite for a "remarkable job of unearthing a lot of problems" and for a nonpolitical approach to a very difficult set of issues.

The following Wednesday, owners of rent controlled housing - fearing that the council would dilute the administration's program too far - threatened to rescind the $13 per week raise that building employees were receiving. The union called a strike for 12 midnight on Friday. Then, on the eve of the strike deadline, Councilman Manes' Housing Committee ended two days of closed-door sessions and reported its rent control bill to the full council. Early Saturday morning, the council met. Local 32B postponed strike action until 7, Sunday morning, and at 3:30 a.m., after 16 hours of deliberation, a tired and angry council passed the first major revision to New York City's rent control legislation since the law's establishment in 1943. The vote was 27 to 10, two more than needed for a two-thirds majority.

As the council adjourned and some councilmen headed for an all-night restaurant in Queens and others to a similar spot in Chinatown, the Mayor commented:

> The council has taken a giant stride toward ensuring that the law fulfills its original purpose - equitable rents combined with proper housing maintenance.

What the Council Passed

The council's bill was almost identical in concept to the Mayor's proposals; only the details were changed.

Maximum Base Rents

MBR's would be calculated in accordance with the formula recommended by the Mayor, but its application would be modified as follows:

(i) MBR levels would take effect January 1, 1972 instead of July 1, 1971.

(ii) Rent increases resulting from MBR would be limited to 7.5% per year (instead of 9.5%).

(iii) The rate of return on capital was reduced from 9.5% to 8.5% and the council retained its power to make adjustments to this figure.

(iv) The equalization factor to be applied to assessed values would be based on the average for all properties, not just residential. (This had the effect of increasing the multiple from about 1.4 to a little over 1.6.)

First Year Increases

FYI provisions, while retained in concept were modified substantially. FYI increases would be determined by the number of rent increases received under the old law by individual units, current rent levels of individual units, and the owners' increased operating costs resulting from new labor contracts negotiated during the interim period. On July 31, 1970, rents could be raised in accordance with the provisions shown in the table below.

	ALLOWABLE MONTHLY RENT INCREASE
Rent history	
Number of full 15 percent lease increases since 1953	
• Two	None
• One	8%
• None	15%
Rent level: Units under $60 per month	
Units with 3 rooms or less	$10
Units with 4 rooms or more	$15
Labor cost recoupment	
Buildings with more than 20 units	Up to 4% and, in addition, up to 4% in April 1971 if required
Buildings with less than 20 units	5%
Owner-serviced buildings	$1.40 per unit

Two certifications would have to be filed by a landlord receiving a first year increase. The first would state that he was spending for services, operations, and maintenance, an amount equal to his average annual expenditures during the preceding five years plus 90% of the interim increases collected. The second was a statement that the building was not being "warehoused" - that is, did not contain units that were deliberately being kept vacant for periods exceeding six months.

Other Provisions

The most substantial change in the remaining provisions of the rent control law concerned the circumstances under which tenants would be exempted from rent increases. The council scrapped the Mayor's proposals and provided, instead, that exemptions would be given only to persons who were 62 years of age or older, and whose family income did not exceed $4,500. Eligible households would not be required to pay more than one-third of their income in rent.

Impact of the Council's Bill

The impact of the council's FYI program on apartments of various rent levels is shown in Exhibit 11. The effect on tenants of the MBR provisions (through the end of 1973) is set forth in Exhibit 12.

Exhibit 1

RENT CONTROL (A)

Organization Chart for Housing and Development Administration

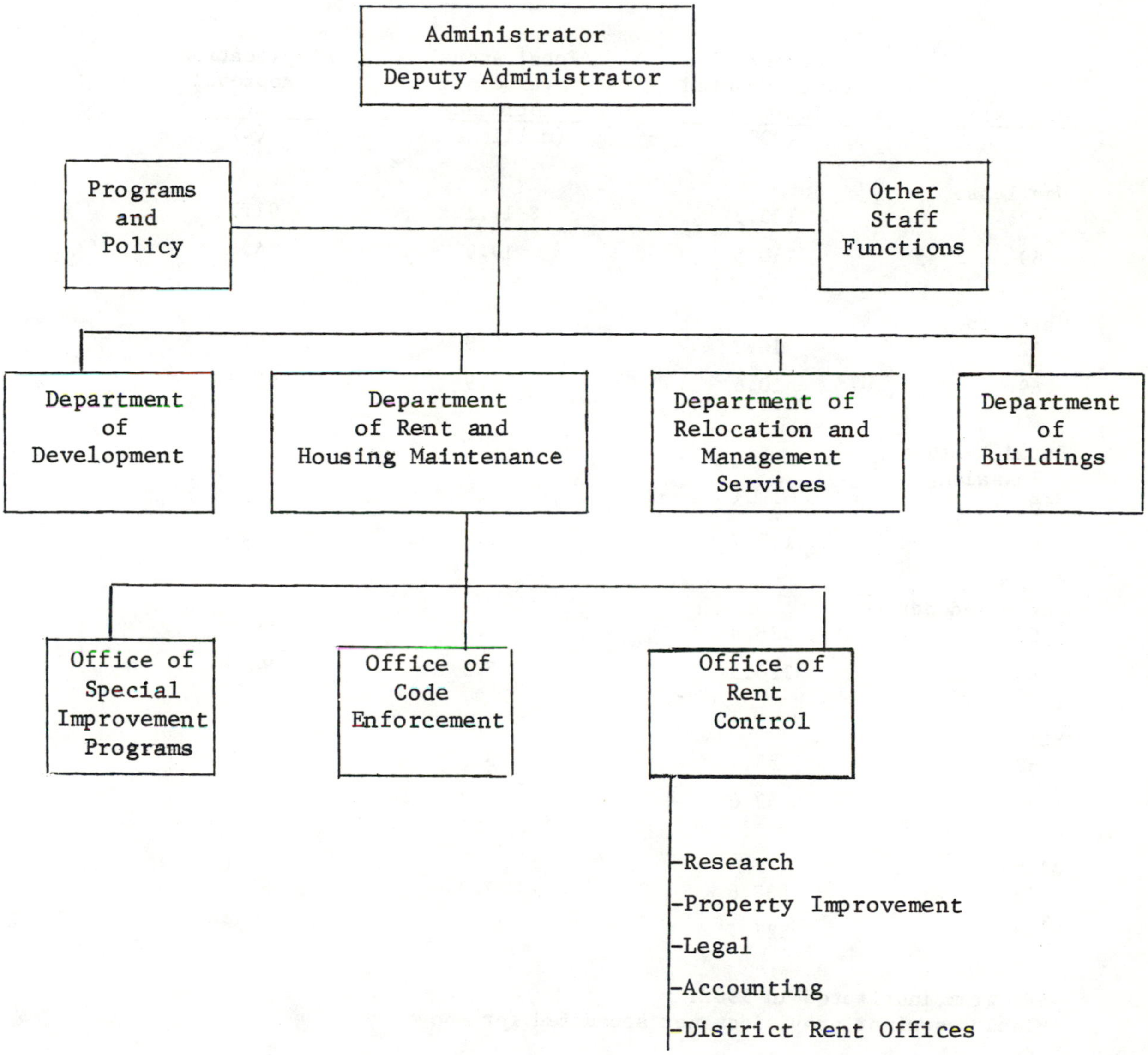

Exhibit 2

RENT CONTROL (A)

History of Rent Increase Action under the 1962 Rent Control Law

Provision	Number of Units Granted Increases (000)	Total Annual Value of Increases (millions)	Application Approval Rate (%)
New Lease			
62	135.3	$ 14.1	91.5
69	150.5	19.9	94.4
Hardship			
62	16.3	1.9	29.1
69	20.6	2.9	68.9
Equal & Labor Passalong			
62	-*	-	-
69	185.7	2.8	93.8
Increased Service			
62	128.4	7.3	89.1
69	120.9	7.5	88.5
MCI			
62	55.7	3.5	88.0
69	42.0	2.2	90.8
All**			
62	337.6	27.0	81.4
69	521.7	35.6	89.8

*Program instituted in 1967.
**Includes minor provisions not accounted for above.

Exhibit 3

RENT CONTROL (A)

Rent Income Ratios for Nonwelfare Households
in New York City

Controlled Housing Sector

Annual Income (Dollar)	Rent/Income Ratio (%) <15	15-19	20-24	25-34	≥35	Total Number of Households
< 2,000	0	0	0	0	102,027	102,027
2,000- 2,999	264	0	3,140	13,558	54,572	71,534
3,000- 3,999	2,451	11,689	22,104	44,782	28,634	109,660
4,000- 5,999	24,310	78,407	78,049	58,086	11,883	250,735
6,000- 7,999	70,705	76,246	36,618	15,113	3,235	201,917
8,000- 9,999	80,013	35,846	9,766	2,430	994	129,049
10,000-14,999	98,028	21,903	7,699	3,523	131	131,284
≥ 15,000	51,104	4,828	0	0	0	55,932
				137,492	201,476	
				338,968		1,052,138

Uncontrolled Housing Sector

Annual Income (Dollar)	Rent/Income Ratio (%) <15	15-19	20-24	25-34	≥35	Total
< 2,000	0	0	0	1.2	98.8	100%
2,000- 2,999	0	0	.9	2.9	96.2	100
3,000- 3,999	.7	2.0	5.3	24.8	67.3	100
4,000- 5,999	1.4	7.2	17.6	40.9	32.9	100
6,000- 7,999	7.6	16.6	27.7	40.0	8.0	100
8,000- 9,999	14.3	28.3	37.7	15.3	4.4	100
10,000-14,999	33.1	39.1	17.9	6.8	3.2	100
≥ 15,000	61.9	22.3	8.8	4.8	2.3	100
Total	22.0%	21.5%	19%	8.7%	18.8%	100%

Exhibit 4
RENT CONTROL (A)

Schedule of Proposed Operating and Maintenance Expense Allowances

Basic O & M Cost per Room

BUILDING TYPE	NUMBER OF UNITS	ANNUAL COST PER ROOM*
Walk-up	All sizes	$100
Elevator	50 or less	110
Elevator	51 to 100	115
Elevator	101 to 150	120
Elevator	151 to 200	125
Elevator	201 or more	130

Added O & M Cost per Unit (Older Buildings)

AGE OF BUILDING	ANNUAL COST PER UNIT*
31 to 40 years	$2 for each year over 30
41 to 50 "	$ 20 + 4 " " " " 40
51 to 60 "	60 + 6 " " " " 50
61 to 70 "	120 + 8 " " " " 60
71 or more	200

*In 1965 dollars.

Examples of O & M Allowance Calculations

	BUILDING A	BUILDING B	BUILDING C
Building Description			
Type of building	Elevator	Walk-up	Elevator
Number of units	124	24	48
Number of rooms	443	78	184
Rooms per unit	3.57	3.25	3.83
Age of building	29	41	30
Estimated Annual Cost			
Basic cost per room	$ 120	$ 100	$ 110
X number of rooms	x 3.57	x 3.25	x 3.83
Basic cost per unit	$ 428	$ 325	$ 421
Added cost per unit (older buildings)	0	+24	0
Total cost per unit	$ 428	$ 349	$ 421
Total cost per building	$ 53,160	$ 8,376	$ 20,222
Audited Annual Cost*			
Total cost per unit	$ 460	$ 387	$ 438
Total cost per building	$ 57,072	$ 9,295	$ 21,027
Percentage error	(7)%	(10)%	(4)%

*Certified costs submitted to Office of Rent Control.

Exhibit 5

RENT CONTROL (A)

Sample Calculation of Maximum Base Rent

BUILDING CHARACTERISTICS

Year of Construction	1937
Total Number of Units	48
Total Number of Rooms	184
Building Type	Elevator
Assessed Value	$380,000

+

ASSUMPTIONS

Rate of Return on Capital	9.5%
"Equalization" Factor for Assessed Value	1.4
Collection Loss Factor	3.0

=

COMPUTED VALUES

	COMPUTED	ACTUAL
3.0 Percent Collection Loss	$ 2,908	–
Real Estate Taxes	22,610	$17,594
Operating and Maintenance Allowance	20,907	21,027
Return on Capital Value	50,540	28,090
New Maximum Building Rental	96,966	66,711
New Maximum Rent Per Unit		
3.0 Room	$144.29	$ 86.55 – $133.59
4.0 Room	173.17	101.98 – 161.41
5.0 Room	202.01	115.90 – 139.30
6.0 Room	230.87	147.21 – 164.35

Exhibit 6

RENT CONTROL (A)

Gross Impact of Proposed First-Year Moves on Rent Revenues

Current Controlled Rent Level
(Dollars/Unit/Month)

	< 40	40-59	60-79	80-99	100-124	125-149	150-199	≥ 200	TOTAL
Number of Units (000)	11.5	136.2	334.6	352.7	223.6	96.2	54.1	27.9	1,266.8
Annual Revenue (Millions of Dollars)	$4.84	$89.38	$281.10	$381.10	$301.90	$159.10	$113.70	$73.40	$1,401.00
Rent Increase (Millions of Dollars)	$0.73	$12.60	$ 34.19	$ 38.44	$ 26.58	$ 12.24	$ 8.23	$ 4.10	$ 137.11
Percentage Rent Increase	15.0%	14.1%	12.2%	10.1%	8.8%	7.7%	7.2%	5.5%	9.8%
Rent Gap Before FYI (Millions of Dollars)	$74.7 (< 40 and 40-59 combined)		$119.6	$ 54.0	$ 10.6	$ 0.8	0	0	$ 259.8

Exhibit 7

RENT CONTROL (A)

Impact of the Proposed FYI and MBR Programs on Units With Different Current Rent Levels*

Current Unit Rental	First-Year Increase (Millions of Dollars)	Revenue Required to Reach MBR (Millions of Dollars)			
		1971-1973	1973-1975	1975-1977	1977-1979
Less than $ 60	$ 13.3	$15.3	$15.3	$15.3	$15.3
$ 60 - $ 79	34.2	42.7	42.7	-	-
$ 80 - $ 99	38.4	15.6	-	-	-
$100 - $124	26.6	-	-	-	-
$125 - $149	12.2	-	-	-	-
Greater than $150	12.3	-	-	-	-
Total	$137.1	$73.6	$58.0	$15.3	$15.3

Total Revenue over 9 years - $299.3 million

*Assuming all parameters in the MBR formula remain at 1970 values.

Exhibit 8

RENT CONTROL (A)

Percentage Increase in Rent Levels Under Proposed FYI
for Different Income Groups

Annual Income	Number of Nonwelfare Households (000)	FYI Average Percentage Increase
Less than $2,000	111.1	11.9
$ 2,000 - 2,999	74.2	11.1
$ 3,000 - 3,999	110.9	11.0
$ 4,000 - 5,999	251.8	10.7
$ 6,000 - 7,999	202.0	10.2
$ 8,000 - 9,999	129.0	9.9
$10,000 - 14,999	131.1	9.3
More than $15,000	57.5	8.5
Total	1,067.6	10.3

Exhibit 9

RENT CONTROL (A)

Welfare-Eligible Households in Controlled Housing

Annual Income (Dollars)	Household Size (Number of Persons)								TOTAL
	1	2	3	4	5	6	7	8+	
Less than $1,000	19,089	6,053	1,560	219	389	103	200	-	27,613
$1,000-$1,999	28,681	28,464	6,011	3,516	1,211	569	49	39	68,540
$2,000-$2,999		13,067	743	5,705	4,577	2,629	522	645	27,888
$3,000-$3,999			754	-	3,214	2,389	1,688	1,225	9,270
$4,000-$4,999					288		586	2,570	3,444
$5,000-$5,999						31		180	211
Total	47,770	47,584	9,068	9,440	9,679	5,721	3,045	4,659	136,906

Exhibit 10

RENT CONTROL (A)

Councilman Katz' "Fact" Sheet on the Proposed New Rent Control Provisions[1]

The Lindsay "Rent Control Modifications" are supposed to provide landlords with enough rents to guarantee better building maintenance and stop building abandonment.

They cannot accomplish that purpose because:

FACT 1. By excluding mortgage interest completely, the "formula" fails to provide building owners with enough cash income in 1970 to even make repairs, let alone, building improvements.

WHY - Before 1970, every apartment building paid about 35 cents of every rent dollar for debt service on building mortgages. Today that amount has been substantially increased because of current interest rates. The rent control formula completely ignores interest as a building operating expense so that the amount of rent a landlord can charge will be insufficient to provide enough money to pay the mortgage and make repairs or improvements. So just as before these charges on buildings mortgage will be paid and without enough money, repairs cannot be made.

FACT 2. The Lindsay "proposals" actually destroy any "market for real estate" and means that older buildings in ghetto areas will eventually be abandoned.

WHY - By permitting all rent controlled apartment buildings to make only one yield, the same profit, (9.5%) without recognizing a basic market difference, will mean that no one will purchase any real estate except the best, no risk midtown realty. All other apartment houses, older buildings, more run down properties etc., buildings, where problems keep cropping up etc., will have no sales or market value because no reasonable buyer would purchase such property when they can earn the same percent of profit on the finest building in New York as from the worst building in Hunts Point or Brownsville.

FACT 3. People on fixed incomes, people on pensions, poor people will be unable to obtain a better rent controlled apartment.

WHY - Since the landlord obtains no reduction in assessed valuation or in taxes when tenants income is less than the percentages described in the "exemption" statute or when the apartment MBR exceeds public housing

[1] Only eight of Mr. Katz' ten facts have been reproduced.

Exhibit 10 (continued)

rents, landlords just will refuse renting to these tenants. A landlord cannot apply for real estate building assessment reductions, because by doing so he reduces the amount the building can earn. The landlord is better off simply not renting to people who cannot pay because of economics.

FACT 4. Homeowners and commercial tenants will be paying higher taxes if these proposals are enacted into law.

WHY - The amount of money New York City borrows depends on the total amount real estate is assessed in this city. Since landlords can never bring actions to reduce building assessed valuations, the total sum of real estate assessed valuations will rise. This automatically expands the city's borrowing ability. Since real estate taxes must pay the interest and principal for all city borrowing, the total real estate taxes must be increased to raise the funds to pay for the total city borrowing.

FACT 5. Only landlords who cheat and do not make repairs or improvements can earn more than a maximum 9 1/2% return

WHY - Since the "formula" includes a precise amount for repairs, a landlord cutting back on improvements can earn more than what he should otherwise earn. Therefore, those landlords who "cheat," benefit, those who spend the prescribed amounts make only 9 1/2%, and those who would spend more, can only make less than 9 1/2%.

FACT 6. The effect of eliminating the 15% new lease increase will mean that many landlords and tenants can never reach agreement on new apartment improvements.

WHY - Many landlords and tenants often agreed on apartment improvements if tenants agreed to pay 15% lease increases on top of new kitchen equipment service increases. Since there will be no more lease increases after July 1, 1970, landlords will not make any kitchen service improvements in apartments as before.

FACT 7. These proposals will lead to increased building destruction by destructive tenants.

WHY - Professor Sternlieb established that the complete lack of landlord control on destructive tenants led to building abandonment. Sternlieb said that "one bad tenant in an apartment building could force 50 tenants to lose their apartments." Since absolutely no legal restraints are being placed on destructive tenants and when the frequency of these kinds of social mis-behaviour is increasing, more buildings will be abandoned and destroyed by the absence of any controls on disruptive tenants.

FACT 8. What will be the result if the Lindsay proposals do not work and the city continues losing housing stock?

Exhibit 10 (continued)

Since the "mean" rents in non-controlled housing is three times more than "mean" rents in rent controlled housing, and since 68.5% of all welfare tenants live in the most poorly maintained and least profitable buildings, and since only 11% of welfare families live in public housing, a loss of more rent controlled buildings that "house" welfare tenants, will be at tremendous cost to this city.

In addition, the city pays each person on welfare in hotel accommodations \$8 daily, or \$240 monthly, for food allowances. Today, the total of these payments exceeds \$15 million annually.

If this city continues to lose the rent controlled buildings which now house this number of welfare tenants, New York's Department of Social Services will be compelled to budget a billion dollars annually for housing and food, for welfare tenants forced into hotels or non-controlled accommodations.

Exhibit 11

Gross Impact of Actual First-Year Moves on Rent Revenues*

	$ Rent/Month/Unit						
	Total	< 60	60-79	80-99	100-119	120-149	≥ 150
Gap Before FYI (million)	$274.0	$62.6	$105.5	$69.9	$27.4	$ 9.0	0
Percent of Rent Gap Filled by FYI	32.8%	43.9%	22.7%	35.1%	26.4%	80.0%	-**

*Figures for existing rent gap differ from those shown in Exhibit 6 because a larger sample of buildings has been used.

**Rent increases in this category totalled $8.3 million.

Exhibit 12

RENT CONTROL(A)

Impact of City Council's Rent Control Program

AVERAGE RENT INCREASE BY INCOME LEVEL

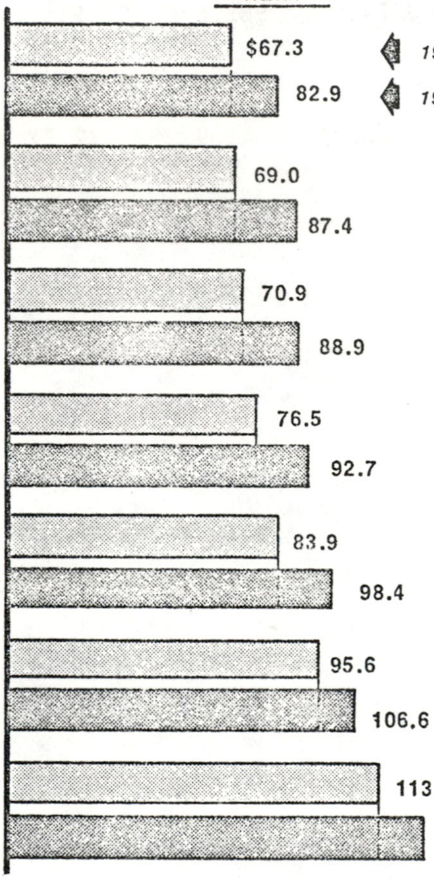

INCOME LEVEL	PERCENTAGE OF ALL HOUSEHOLDS*		AVERAGE RENT/INCOME RATIO	AVERAGE MONTHLY RENT	PERCENT INCREASE 1970-1973**
Less Than $2,000	9.1%	1970	65.3	$67.3	
		1973	86.7	82.9	23.2%
2,000-3,999	16.5	1970	28.4	69.0	
		1973	36.0	87.4	26.7
4,000-5,999	17.8	1970	17.0	70.9	
		1973	21.3	88.9	25.4
6,000-7,999	17.5	1970	12.8	76.5	
		1973	15.7	92.7	21.2
8,000-9,999	13.0	1970	11.1	83.9	
		1973	13.0	98.4	17.3
10,000-14,999	13.9	1970	10.3	95.6	
		1973	11.6	106.6	11.5
15,000 Or More	12.2	1970	6.7	113.4	
		1973	7.4	126.8	11.8

AVERAGE RENT/INCOME RATIOS BY HOUSEHOLD SIZE

NUMBER OF PERSONS PER HOUSEHOLD	AVERAGE RENT/INCOME RATIO 1970	1973
1	21.4%	32.0%
2	21.8	22.3
3	22.8	28.7
4	16.0	23.4
5	24.9	30.6
6	25.3	30.8

* *100% = 1,266,800 households.*

** *Change projected from August 1, 1970, to December 31, 1973 — this includes the interim increases and the first two rounds of MBR increases.*

APPENDIX A

RENT CONTROL (A)

Description of the Major Provisions of the 1962 Rent Control Law

Provisions to Govern Rent Increases

New Lease

The 1962 law allowed a landlord and a new tenant to enter into a valid written lease providing for an increase in the maximum legal rent not exceeding 15% and for a term of at least two years. Once both parties signed the lease, the increase was automatic, provided the owner filed a lease report with the Office of Rent Control. A unit could receive a new lease increase only once every two years. Once a tenant had signed the initial lease, he became a "statutory tenant" and was not required to renew his lease. Because the new lease program offered fairly sizable increases without placing a burden on tenants in occupancy, some of the problems of landlord-tenant relations associated with the granting of rent increases by a regulatory agency were avoided. Moreover, the program's simplicity was a major advantage - it was readily understood by landlords and tenants and easy to administer.

The impact of the new lease provision was highly dependent on patterns of apartment turnover. These patterns were examined for a substantial sample of units for the years 1960-1968 with the results shown below.

Turnover Frequency 1960-1968	Percent of Units		Potential Rent Increase
0	40%		0
1	37		15.0%
2	17		32.3
3	5		52.1
4 or more	1		74.9
		Average =	14.4%
		=	1 3/4%/year (approx.)

The rate at which apartments turned over was closely tied to tenant characteristics and building conditions. New York's minority group families, who have lower incomes and live in older, more dilapidated buildings, moved more often than more prosperous tenants. Nonwhites moved more often than Whites; Puerto Ricans moved most of all. Turnover was higher in older buildings than in new ones, and higher in dilapidated and deteriorating units than in sound ones. At the extreme, however, mobility rates were lowest when rent-per-room

Appendix A (continued)

was low, reflecting the desirability to tenants of low-priced units. Rents of less than $15 per room were paid by 24% of tenants who moved in prior to 1954; while only 10% of those who moved in after 1954 paid rents that were that low. For the most part, these long-tenure families were old, poor, White, and comprised of one or two persons (44% were over 65 years old, 21% had incomes less than $2,000 per year, 87% were White.

Hardship

The Hardship provision of the 1962 law was one basis for court decisions that rent control was not unconstitutional as an unwarranted deprivation of private property. It was also one of the law's most frequently litigated provisions. The purpose of the Hardship provision was to allow increases in rents where individual buildings were not yielding a fair net annual return. The law defined a fair net annual return as 6% of a building's fair value plus a 2% depreciation allowance. "Fair value" was equal to assessed value (structure plus land) for buildings last purchased prior to 1961 or, for buildings acquired after 1961, the purchase price could be used as the measure of fair value.

The process for obtaining hardship increases was a complex and lengthy one. Substantial numbers of applicants found it necessary to utilize private lawyers and accountants whose business consisted solely of obtaining hardship increases - and their services were a considerable expense for the landlords. Small owners with little business background found the procedure especially difficult. Furthermore, the evaluation of the applications in HDA was time-consuming. Unless a very recent inspection had occurred, a city inspector had to examine the property and certify that the building was violation-free and that all tenant appeals had been resolved. Actual increases allowed could not exceed 15% even though the hardship formula indicated a larger one (as was true for 25% of a sample of 145 cases).

Equalization and Passalong

Because of disputes over rising labor costs in building operation, the law was amended in 1967 to include two additional rent increase provisions. Rent Equalization granted automatic increases in rents if the current rental income for a building was less than 32.25% above the maximum rent of March 1, 1943.

The Labor Cost Passalong provision permitted rent increases for a property that "has not received increases in rental income sufficient to offset an increase in labor costs resulting directly or indirectly from industry-wide collective bargaining agreements." The adjustment in a unit's rent for any 12-month period could not exceed 2.5% of the rent in effect when the increase application was filed.

Appendix A (continued)

Provisions to Maintain and Improve Housing Quality

Increased Services and Facilities

The Increased Services provision allowed landlords and tenants to negotiate improvements in services (e.g., security, extermination, janitorial, garbage collection) and facilities (e.g., stoves, refrigerators, flooring, new kitchen cabinets) beyond those that were registered with the Office of Rent Control in 1943. The proposed improvement had to constitute "a substantial increase or decrease in dwelling space or a change in the services, furniture, furnishings, or equipment provided in the housing accommodations."

A "schedule of rental values" developed by HDA covered most of the improvements which required tenant consent or were allowed by law, so both the tenants and the landlord knew in advance the amount by which rents would be adjusted for any proposed improvement. No rent increase greater than 15% was permitted unless the tenants agreed to a higher percentage.

Major Capital Improvements and Substantial Rehabilitation

Improvements approved under this provision did not require tenant consent. The Major Capital Improvements (MCI) section allowed rent increases if the landlord had made "a major capital improvement required for the operation, preservation, or maintenance of the structure" (e.g., rewiring, replumbing). The Substantial Rehabilitation section of the law permitted rent increases where there had been "an increase in the rental value of the housing accommodations as a result of substantial rehabilitation of the building or housing accommodation therein which materially adds to the value of the property or appreciably prolongs its life, excluding ordinary repairs, maintenance, and replacements" e.g., redesign of apartments, replacing interior staircase). The law allowed ORC to determine the increases in legal maximum rents that would be allowed for both MCI's and substantial rehabilitation.

The MCI program had a substantial impact on the housing stock - nearly 800,000 units underwent some improvement under this provision after 1959. (Rewiring was the improvement for more than 360,000 units.) However, since the mid-1960s, the provision's impact on the quality of the housing stock had steadily diminished.

Rent Reduction Provisions

Just as maximum rents could be increased when landlords improved their buildings, rents could be decreased if owners allowed building quality to decline and tenants filed complaints. The ORC had the power to reduce

Appendix A (continued)

rents if it found that the "living space, essential services, furniture, furnishings, or equipment" provided on the date fixing the maximum rents had been diminished. However, before rents could be reduced, landlords were permitted a grace period during which they could correct violations. The size of the decrease depended upon ORC's evaluation of the amount by which rental value was reduced by the decreased services, space, or equipment.

The volume of applications for decreases quadrupled between 1962 and 1969 (from 90,000 to over 380,000) mostly due to an increase in the number of tenant complaints. The approval rate remained constant at about 70%. Along with the number of applications, the annual value of rent reductions grew from \$1.8 million to \$7.7 million between 1962 and 1969. The fraction of rent decrease applications that ultimately resulted in rent reductions rather than service restoration declined from 33% in 1965 to 24% in 1969. Most owners (more than two-thirds) responded to the threat of a reduction in income by carrying out the required repairs. However, if the case progressed to an actual rent reduction, repair was unlikely. Only 6% of these units were restored.

Provisions to Protect Tenants from Unfair Treatment

Statutory Tenancy and Legal Evictions

Under the law, a tenant whose lease has expired could continue to occupy his apartment indefinitely as a statutory tenant. The rent control law allowed evictions only for (i) specified tenant infractions and (ii) carefully circumscribed situations where the landlord could show that the apartment in question would be put to an alternative use recognized under the law as sufficient to justify eviction.

In no year after 1962 were more than 2,000 eviction certificates granted. Generally, about 40% of the applications were approved (ORC's approval process was careful, thorough, and slow). One-third to one-half of the eviction certificates issued between 1962 and 1969 were based on demolition for new construction.

Noncompliance: Illegal Eviction, Harassment, and Overcharging

If a landlord wished to evict a tenant, but lacked legal grounds or found legal proceedings too slow, he might be tempted to resort to harassment or illegal eviction. Or he might attempt to charge a rent higher than the legal maximum registered for an apartment. The law provided penalties to discourage such behavior.

The volume of noncompliance activity fluctuated between 15,000 and 22,000 cases per year after 1962. The great majority of cases were dismissed following investigation. Noncompliance applications granted in 1969 had fallen to just over 1,100 and constituted only 7% of applications disposed.

HOUSING REHABILITATION IN NEW YORK CITY

Introduction

There are three methods of increasing the quality and availability of housing: maintenance of the existing stock, rehabilitation of the existing stock, or new construction. The thoughts and actions of housing officials in New York City, as in other municipalities, have been dominated, traditionally, by a "new construction philosophy" -- despite the existence of financing and tax-incentive programs for rehabilitation and a large code enforcement program designed to encourage preventive maintenance. As one analyst from the NYC-Rand Institute observed, new construction was "the single, permanent issue in the city's interminable housing debate."

Of late, however, this debate has been widening. The Housing and Development Administration (HDA), New York's "superagency" for housing, undertook in 1968 a broadbased, long-term study of the city's housing problems. HDA's internal staff was assisted by consultants from both McKinsey and Company, Inc. and the NYC-Rand Institute. Early feedback from the project suggested that far greater attention should be paid to the potential benefits of rehabilitation. During 1969 and 1970, therefore, further investigations were conducted in preparation for recommending a practicable citywide rehabilitation program. The information developed in those investigations is summarized below.

Strategic Questions

Rehabilitation decisions are made within the context of four closely interrelated strategic questions (Exhibit 1). First there is the question of investment: How much of its resources can and will the city allocate to a rehabilitation program? The answer will determine how much rehabilitation can be accomplished under various alternative programs. Second, an inventory or quality control strategy is required. This involves setting the housing standards that the city will demand. Higher standards imply a lower rate of "capital consumption" (deterioration), higher rehabilitation costs, and higher rents or larger rent subsidies. The third strategic consideration is price. New York is one of the few cities to apply rent control and stabilization measures, and the pricing strategy determines the rents that will be permitted, or approached through the free market, relative to the tenants' ability to pay. Finally, the city must decide which income group, or groups, should be served by its rehabilitation programs. Should it concentrate primarily on low-income households, direct its efforts at the larger group of middle-income households, or pursue some compromise between these two extremes?

Flows in the Housing Stock

The role played by rehabilitation programs can be viewed in terms of the flows that take place in the housing stock (Exhibit 2). The total stock is divided into two inventories -- sound housing and unsound housing -- and the level of these inventories is determined by four flows: new construction, deterioration, removals, and rehabilitation.

New Construction: The effect of new construction is to increase the supply of sound housing and, by replacing units that have been removed from stock, to upgrade or improve the quality of the total stock. Exhibit 3 summarizes the number of units in new construction projects in the city since 1966. The number of privately financed units has shown a consistent downward trend. On the other hand, publicly assisted projects have supplied an increasing, though variable, number of units each year.

Analysts at McKinsey believed that the factors that prevented any substantial increase in private starts, such as zoning laws, carrying costs, rising labor costs, and an uncertain market for units with unsubsidized rents, would probably continue to deter any dramatic change in this component of the new construction flow over the next five years. Barring some major new program(s), severe constraints on the various sources of funds were also expected to prevent any large expansion in the rate of publicly supported new construction starts.

Deterioration: The effect of deterioration is to reduce the number of housing units in the sound housing inventory and to increase the unsound inventory. The impact of this process was more pronounced in the rent controlled portion of the city's housing stock; the incidence of unsound housing in the noncontrolled stock was only 9.3 percent, while in the rent controlled portion of the stock, it was 28.8 percent.

Although the effect of deterioration was clear, it was difficult to determine the exact rate at which it was proceeding.[1] Several independent estimates suggest a figure of about 32,000 per year but this may be low because the factors that cause deterioration have become more pronounced in recent years.

Deterioration is the result of inadequate building maintenance for the level of use over a period of time. Typically, the costs of operating and maintaining a building are passed on to tenants through rents. During the first half of the 1960's, operating and maintenance costs increased, but not much faster than the rate of increase in rents in the rent controlled stock. After 1965, however, the cost of skilled labor climbed at about 10 percent a year, the cost of unskilled labor about 6 percent a year, and materials costs (such as fuel oil) and other operating expenses (such as taxes) from 3 to 6 percent a year. At the same time, increased rents permitted under the city's rent control laws did not keep pace; the average annual increase in rents from 1960 to 1970 was about 2 percent.

Thus, the margin between revenues and operating costs shrank for many building owners; and this cost-revenue squeeze (together with the attractiveness of alternative investments) tended to keep the rate of deterioration high. The new rent control law, passed in 1970, was expected to reduce this rate by adjusting rents upward to keep pace with increased operating and maintenance expenses; but the full impact of these rent increases would not be felt for 3 to 5 years.

Removals: Dwelling units are removed from the housing stock through demolitions (either public or private) and abandonments. The effect of removals is to reduce the size of the total housing stock. The rate of removal in the late 1960's was about 45,200 units a year, and was closely tied to the economic viability of buildings. If a building provided an adequate return to its owner, he would not want to walk away from it. The new rent control law (by raising rents) was expected to improve the financial attractiveness of some marginal buildings enough to reduce the rate of removals. This effect, however, was still uncertain.

---

[1] For the purpose of measuring the structural quality of the housing stock, the terms "sound," "deteriorating," and "dilapidated" were used as follows:

Sound housing . . . has no defects, or only slight defects which are normally corrected during the course of regular maintenance . . . (defects are understood to be "slight" only if they do not affect the weather tightness of the housing unit or endanger the safety or health of the occupants).

Deteriorating housing needs more repair than would be provided in the course of regular maintenance . . . (it has one or more "immediate" defects which need to be repaired if the unit is to continue to provide safe and adequate shelter).

Dilapidated housing does not provide safe or adequate shelter and in its present condition endangers the health, safety, or well-being of the occupants.

Rehabilitation: Rehabilitation has several effects on the size of the total housing stock and unsound housing inventories. It increases the size of the sound housing inventory, reduces the size of the unsound inventory, and may either reduce or maintain the size of the total housing stock, depending on the characteristics of the particular rehabilitation project.

For example, if a building that has been abandoned by its owner and vacated by the tenants is then rehabilitated, that rehabilitation restores housing units to the sound housing inventory by reducing removals. If a still occupied building is rehabilitated, this rehabilitation is in fact the reverse of the deterioration process, reducing the unsound inventory and increasing the sound inventory. If several smaller apartments are combined to form a larger unit, some removals occur since fewer units are returned to the sound housing inventory than once existed. But if a few large apartments with large rooms are redesigned into a greater number of smaller apartments with smaller rooms (as frequently is the case), new dwelling units have actually been added to the inventory of sound housing and to the total housing stock.

Average annual rates for rehabilitation were difficult to determine with precision, in part because different kinds of rehabilitation were possible and in part because some rehabilitation went unreported. Over the 5-year period 1965 to 1969, the average was probably about 6,900 units per year under privately sponsored projects and 2,300 with public funding for an annual total of 9,200.

Net Impact of Housing Flows: Without question, the net loss of sound housing and the decline in size of the total housing stock (both sound and unsound) as shown in Exhibit 2 were New York City's most pressing housing problems. One manifestation of the loss of housing was a decline in vacancy rates from 5 percent in 1965 to less than 1 percent in 1970, a condition that placed strong upward pressure on rent levels. Another result was that many of the poor, particularly those on welfare, were housed in unsound buildings.

The Environment for Rehabilitation

Five environmental influences were identified that lay beyond the city's control but exerted a strong impact on the effectiveness of any rehabilitation program. They were:

1. The cost of rehabilitation
2. The availability and cost of capital
3. The characteristics of building owners
4. The managerial and financial capabilities of would-be rehabilitation project sponsors, and
5. Neighborhood expectations.

The Cost of Rehabilitation: The cost of a rehabilitation project is determined by the extent of work done, the type of building, the quality standards that are imposed, and the basic costs of such items as labor, material, and project management.

The extent of rehabilitation work may be usefully defined in terms of four points on a spectrum:

Minimum - includes the repair and/or replacement of some major housing subsystem components (e.g., plumbing), selective replacement of accessories, structural repairs, cleaning-patching-painting, and possibly the addition of amenities (e.g., television antennas, parquet floors).

Moderate - includes the same components as minimum but more work is required on each; major repair and/or replacement of subsystem components, repair and/or replacement of carpentry items, and major replacement of accessories.

Layout change - includes a greater degree of work on some or all of the components of the minimum and moderate levels plus the rearrangement of apartments and new apartment and room size designs.

Gut - the most extensive and costly level - includes stripping the entire building down to joists and headers, replacing all building subsystems, rearranging apartment layouts, and replacing all accessories and carpentry items. New amenities are added where desirable.[1]

Building type influences rehabilitation cost in several ways. Some buildings are inherently more attractive for investment purposes -- e.g., masonry or brick structures are preferable to wood frame buildings. An equivalent investment in two different buildings can produce different quality results and different levels of return. In some cases, even extensive rehabilitation cannot bring a building up to code standards and, thus, the investment required would not generate an adequate return nor produce an acceptable structure.

The four most common building types found in New York City were Old and New Law tenements, post-1929 buildings, and 1- and 2-family houses converted to apartments (see Exhibit 4). Old Law tenements (built before 1901) had the least rehabilitation potential because some undesirable building features such as inadequate courtyard ventilation and narrow building width could not be altered, while others could be improved only at

[1] Layout change and gut rehabilitation require that tenants be relocated while work is in progress; minimum and moderate projects do not. When relocation is required, it adds about $500 to the total cost of a project.

excessive cost. New Law tenements (built between 1901 and 1929) had better potential because of more adequate lighting and ventilation and greater building width, which allowed better apartment layout and larger room size. Post-1929 buildings and 1- and 2-family houses converted to apartments had higher rehabilitation potential than either Old or New Law buildings. Although they might require modernization, most were structurally sound and were built in a large variety of shapes and sizes. The distribution of the city's 438,000 substandard units among the four building types is shown in Exhibit 5.

The third consideration that influences the cost of rehabilitation is the desired quality of the finished work. At a minimum, the building must meet the health and safety standards established through legislative enactments such as the New York City Building Code, the Housing and Maintenance Code, and the State Multiple Dwellings Law. In addition, it must meet minimum construction standards specified by the lender, whether it is the city, the Federal Government, or a private source. These standards are designed to ensure that the physical and economic life of the building will at least equal the payback period of the mortgage. For example, a building with a 30-year loan would require higher construction standards than one with a 20-year loan.

The last determinant of rehabilitation cost is the labor, material and project management costs. Both labor and material have been subjected to strong inflationary pressures in recent years - 10% annually for labor and 7% for material. As is true throughout the construction industry, union pressure has made it difficult to respond to this inflationary trend with cost saving innovations in design and processes. Project management costs are particularly high due to several characteristics of the rehabilitation industry. To begin with, most projects are small scale, typically only one building. Even when a company is working on several buildings, they are usually scattered throughout the city. Thus, economies of scale are difficult, if not impossible, to achieve. Second, owners of buildings to be rehabilitated frequently have difficulty dealing with contractors. With little or no previous experience, the average owner lacks the knowledge to evaluate materials, costs, and contractors or to supervise the quality and progress of the work. Third, the lack of an established rehabilitation industry contributes to higher costs since few firms (about five in Manhattan and fewer in other boroughs) have built up expertise and experience in the field.

Exhibit 6 is a table of recent project cost experience broken down by level of rehabilitation and building types.

The Availability and Cost of Capital: All of the 438,000 substandard units counted in the 1968 Housing and Vacancy Survey required some rehabilitation to bring them up to the standard of safe and dependable living accommodations. The cost of this undertaking would have been equal to the construction costs plus an allowance for financing and carrying charges, fees and administrative costs, and allowances for land and/or building acquisition and refinancing. Construction costs could be estimated by (i) assessing the number of unsound buildings that required each of the four levels of rehabilitation and (ii) multiplying these numbers by the cost per unit for the level of rehabilitation needed. Exhibit 7 shows a likely distribution of unsound dwelling units by level of rehabilitation required to return them to the inventory of sound housing. The total construction costs for this effort would have been approximately $4.4 billion; and since total project costs are typically 168% of construction costs, the capital cost for complete rehabilitation would have been more than $7.4 billion (in 1969 dollars).

At the time, the private sector was not a promising source for this amount of funding. Discussions with bankers and other mortgage lenders suggested that private mortgage money for rehabilitation was extremely limited, particularly in transitional and core areas where most private institutions were not making or even renewing mortgages. This reluctance to invest in rehabilitation had placed a large portion of the work load on the public sector. But, compared to the need, public resources for rehabilitation had been inconsequential. The public sector had provided approximately $136 million of mortgage funds for the rehabilitation of about 6,444 completed units since 1964. This funding came from several sources: New York City's own debt capacity, State Housing Finance Agency (HFA) bond issues, and Federal Government appropriations for the Department of Housing and Urban Development, (HUD) and the Federal Housing Administration (FHA).

The city's borrowing power for capital projects was limited by 2 percent and 10 percent debt limits. The state constitution permitted the city to incur debt equal to 2 percent of the 5-year average of the assessed valuation of taxable real estate for the funding and assistance of low-rent housing. The city's rehabilitation programs -- to be discussed later -- had to compete with several other new construction and urban renewal programs for funds available under the two percent limit. This limit ($680 million) was fully committed by the end of 1970.

The state constitution also permitted the city to incur general capital debts equal to 10 percent of the five-year average full valuation (as opposed to the assessed value used for the 2 percent limit) of taxable real estate. Funding for all city housing programs that were capital improvement programs, as well as all other projects included in the capital budget, were charged against the 10 percent debt limit. Thus, rehabilitation financing had to compete with other housing programs, as well as all of the city's other capital projects like schools and hospitals. Additional factors, such as the marketability of municipal bonds, and the capacity of the expense budget to pay for debt service, constrained the amount actually useable under the 10 percent limit.

State and federal funding sources had contributed much less to the rehabilitation of the city's existing housing stock than to programs for new construction. Federal loan resources committed to rehabilitation in fiscal 1971 were less than 4 percent of the amount directed toward new construction. (City resources were split between new construction and rehabilitation in about the same proportion.) Federal funding was usually channeled through HUD. (The level of this support is discussed below.)

No state resources were allocated to rehabilitation. One possible source -- bond issues of the State Housing Finance Agency -- had not been used because of decisions, at the state level, to channel these funds to new construction. Although about $900 million of HFA bond-issuing authority remained available, there were no plans to finance rehabilitation projects in the city with any part of this money.

Other Environmental Factors: Three other environmental factors (characteristics of building owners, managerial and financial capabilities of project sponsors, and neighborhood expectations) are important to the effectiveness of rehabilitation programs.

Building owners may generally be differentiated by their financial strength and sophistication in real estate matters. Operators of the city's worst housing tended to be absentee owners who held single parcels, derived little income from real estate, and lacked the resources for adequate maintenance. Conversely, resident owners and landlords who secured the bulk of their income from real estate, who were at least medium-scale operators, and who had held their properties for relatively long periods of time tended to maintain their properties in much better condition and to be more responsive to outside financial incentives for rehabilitation. In New York, more than one-half of the rent controlled buildings were owned by persons who received only a minor portion of their income from real estate. The typical owner had fewer than three buildings and these were likely to be older (pre-1929) and relatively small in terms of the number of dwelling units per building.

The capabilities of sponsors of rehabilitation projects impinge on program effectiveness in much the same way as owner characteristics - indeed, the sponsor may be the owner. Many rehabilitation funding programs are available only to nonprofit or limited profit organizations who often lack the resources either to launch substantial rehabilitation efforts or to manage projects well.

Neighborhood expectations play a key role in a sponsor's willingness to support a rehabilitation project. If the neighborhood is expected to improve, the strong investor - one looking primarily for capital gain - will buy a building or, if he already owns it, will hold onto or even upgrade it. On the other hand, the weak investor - one interested mostly in current income - will not be likely to buy a building or, if he already owns one, may try to sell it to someone who can forego current income and wait to take advantage of the expected price appreciation. If the outlook for the neighborhood is pessimistic, and an owner cannot sell his building, he will be unlikely to upgrade it. Rather he will skimp on operating and maintenance expenses to increase his current income, thus contributing to the physical deterioration of the building and the neighborhood.

Rehabilitation Programs

The city's publicly supported rehabilitation efforts encompassed a number of programs established by approximately twenty federal, state, and city laws serving the same broad objective - to lend capital funds and provide subsidies to stimulate rehabilitation. Of the twenty, however, only five were important in terms of the amount of money committed and the number of dwelling units treated.[1] The programs fell into three categories:

Program Category	Responsible Public Body	Program Name
Interest-subsidized loans	Federal	Section 221(d)3, Section 236
Direct loans	Federal, City	Section 312, Municipal Loan (including Mini-Loan)
Direct grants	Federal	Section 115

The impact of these five rehabilitation programs may be summarized under four headings: volume, cost, subsidy requirements, and leverage.

The volume of units rehabilitated under the five programs since 1965 is shown in Exhibit 8. Only two rehabilitation programs, Municipal Loans and Section 221(d)3, had produced a substantial number of completions since 1965, accounting for over 90 percent of all publicly assisted rehabilitation completions. The Municipal Loan program alone accounted for 52 percent of them. In terms of funds committed, the 6,444 units represented mortgages of $136 million, of which Municipal Loans accounted for about $67 million.

Costs for four of the programs are summarized in Exhibit 9. (Section 115 has been omitted.)

Subsidy requirements arise when tenants cannot afford to pay post-rehabilitation rents. A completed rehabilitation project has an economic rent equal to the sum of debt service, real estate taxes (if any), and operating and maintenance costs.[2] The rent that a tenant is capable of paying, however, is typically 25 percent of gross income, an amount that may not cover the economic rent. When this is the case, some form of rent subsidy is required. For example, as Exhibit 9 shows, a two-bedroom unit rehabilitated for $22,000 under the Municipal Loan program had a "market" rent

---

[1] Appendix A contains descriptions of each of the five programs.

[2] Financing terms affect the level of the economic rent as explained in Appendix B.

(fully tax paying) of $319 a month. But based on the income distribution of the families served by this program the typical family in a Municipal Loan unit could afford a rent of about $66 a month. The difference between the market and the affordable rents is the subsidy required.[1]

One kind of subsidy (for which projects under Sections 221(d)3, 236, and 312 and Municipal Loans all qualified) was real estate tax exemption and abatement under Section J51-2.5 of the New York City Administrative Code. Tax exemption applied only to tax increases caused by an increase in assessed valuation resulting from improvements. An exemption remained in effect for 12 years. Tax abatement applied to the real estate taxes levied on the net post-improvement assessed valuation after the exemption is credited. Abatements could be granted for periods up to 20 years.

As Exhibit 9 shows, tax subsidies could reduce the rent on a typical Municipal Loan unit by $1,090 a year and on a Section 236 unit by $1,480 a year. For the 1,900 Municipal Loan and Section 221(d)3 and 236 units that were completed in 1970, this meant an annual loss of tax revenue of over $2 million. Even with full tax exemption and low-interest mortgages, however, postrehabilitation rents might be too high for tenants to afford.

Additional subsidies were available under several publicly sponsored rent assistance programs. Welfare rent payments contributed the major portion of this assistance, with the Federal Rent Supplements contributing a lesser portion and public housing leasing the least. These forms of assistance added about $2.5 million a year to the cost of Municipal Loan and Section 236 projects completed in 1970. On the average, rent assistance was $123 a month for a Municipal Loan unit and $73 a month for a Section 236 unit.

The annual burden of subsidy costs should be included as part of the full cost of a rehabilitation project. Providing funds for a mortgage is a one-time expenditure, but it may commit the city to a series of annual subsidy payments that significantly increase the overall cost of the project. For the vast majority (over 90 percent) of units completed after 1965, the subsidy requirements were very high. For those projects finished in 1970 alone, the tax and rent assistance subsidies amounted to about $4.5 million.

---

[1] Average rent subsidy figures here and in Exhibit 9, are calculated for welfare plus nonwelfare households. Welfare-supported households are assumed to be 33 percent of the tenantry in publicly supported rehabilitation projects. This estimate is based on reports from HDA and corresponds to experience during the first 6 months of 1970. For the remaining 67 percent of the tenants, it is necessary to assume an income distribution and an appropriate rent-to-income ratio. For this calculation, the results of a survey of incomes for households in rent controlled housing carried out for the city Bureau of the Budget in late 1969 were used; the rent-to-income ratio and the income distribution imply an average rent-paying capability. The difference between this average figure and the average postrehabilitation rent is the implied rent-subsidy estimate.

Leverage of city money invested in rehabilitation can be obtained in two ways. First, these funds can serve as an attraction for additional rehabilitation funds from the private sector. The estimated annual rate of privately sponsored rehabilitation was 6,900 units. None of this work however, was explicitly coordinated with publicly sponsored rehabilitation and none had been located in areas served by the public programs. Apparently this form of leverage had not been very great.

The second means of leveraging city funds is to use other city programs to force owner-sponsored rehabilitation efforts. For example, the building code violations removal provision of the new Rent Control Law required that violations must be corrected before rent increases were permitted. The major capital improvements schedule was another important part of rent control that encouraged rehabilitation. Proof of such improvements was grounds for increasing rents.

Recent Developments

In June 1971, as the rehabilitation studies were drawing to a close, the State Legislature authorized the creation of a New York City Housing Development Corporation. The objective of this new agency would be to deliver sound housing for low- and middle-income occupants. To do this, it was authorized to sell tax-exempt bonds in major money markets and to lend the proceeds, at the tax-exempt borrowing rate, to sponsors of new construction or rehabilitation projects. (The actual rate paid by mortgagees would be somewhat greater than the corporation's borrowing rate because of discounts and fees needed to cover administration and servicing costs.) The corporation's lending ceiling was set at $700 million. No firm requirements were imposed on the division of these funds as between new construction and rehabilitation. Early discussions within HDA, of which the new organization would become a part, indicated a tentative consensus on an allocation of between $200 million and $300 million for rehabilitation.

Exhibit 1

HOUSING REHABILITATION IN NEW YORK CITY

Elements of a Rehabilitation Strategy

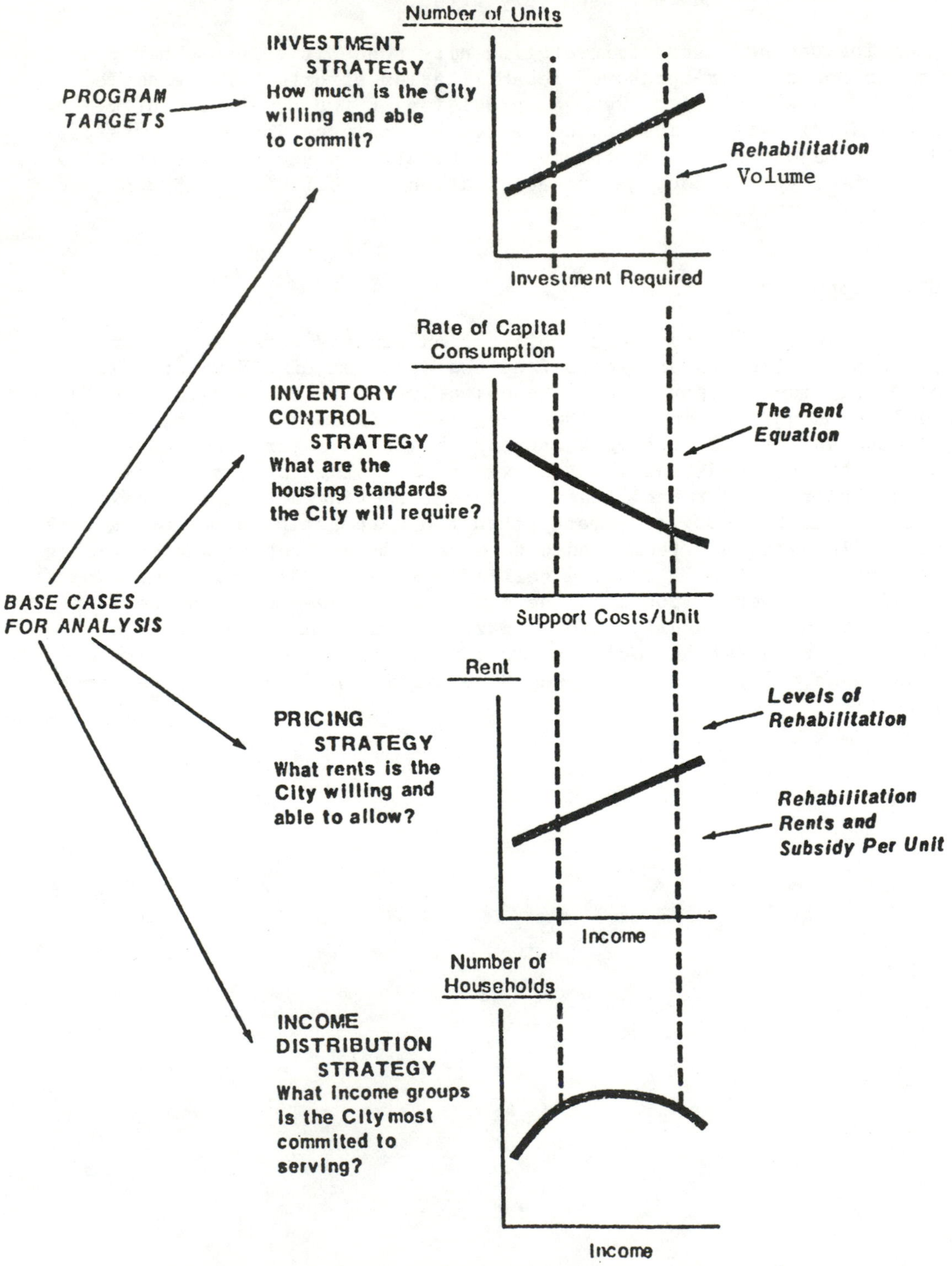

In Addition The City Must Consider What Types of Ownership It Should Encourage . . . .

Exhibit 2

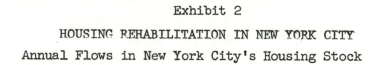

HOUSING REHABILITATION IN NEW YORK CITY

Annual Flows in New York City's Housing Stock

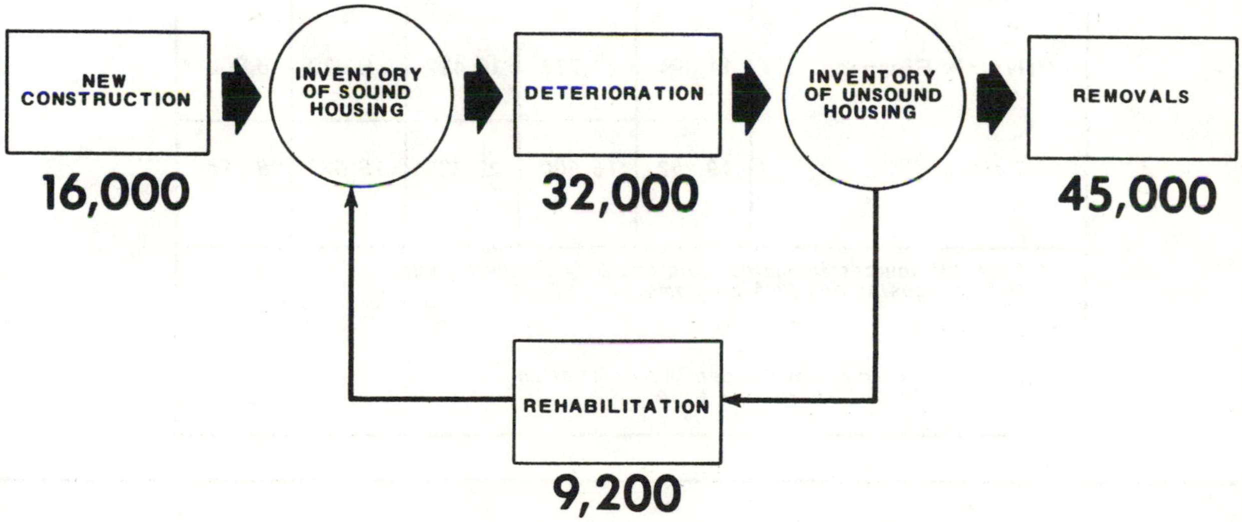

Exhibit 3

HOUSING REHABILITATION IN NEW YORK CITY

New Construction Starts

	1966	1967	1968	1969	1970
Publicly Assisted*	8,458	4,722	12,215	6,006	20,714
Privately Financed	11,394	11,778	10,422	9,670	8,000**
Total	***19,852***	***16,500***	***22,635***	***15,676***	***28,714***

* *From all sources including State and City Mitchell-Lama. Public Housing and FHA programs.*

** *Estimated.*

Source: *Housing & Development Administration, Office of Programs & Policy.*

Exhibit 4

HOUSING REHABILITATION IN NEW YORK CITY

Characteristics of Four Major Building Types

Multiple Dwellings (Post-1929) and Other

- Large variety of shapes and sizes
- Predominately sound buildings

Old Law Tenements

- Small room size
- Inadequate lighting and ventilation
- Lack of closet space
- Narrow railroad flats predominate
- 2 to 3 apartments per floor
- Ground floor commercial use

Questionable rehabilitation potential ....

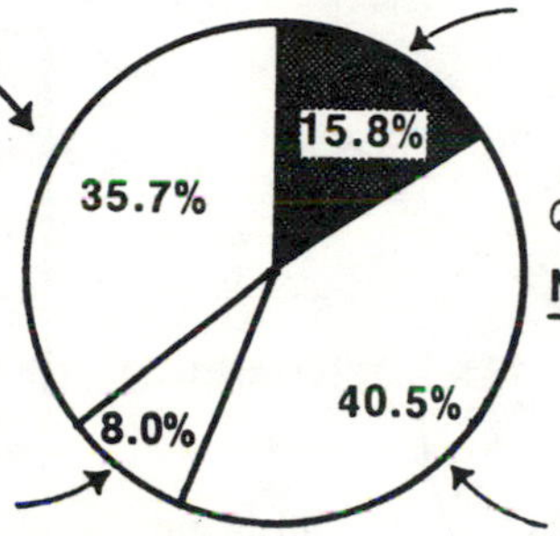

1-2 Family Converted to Apartments

- Includes frame, masonry and brownstones
- Illegal to convert frames to multifamily
- Others have adequate interior space but lack adequate kitchen and bathroom facilities
- Room rearrangement necessary
- Sound construction

New Law Tenements

- Larger room sizes
- Adequate lighting and ventilation due to larger courtyard requirements
- Wider buildings
- 3 apartments per floor
- Room rearrangement problems

Source: *Percentage of housing stock based on the 1968 Housing and Vacancy Survey.*

Exhibit 5

HOUSING REHABILITATION IN NEW YORK CITY

Condition of the Housing Stock

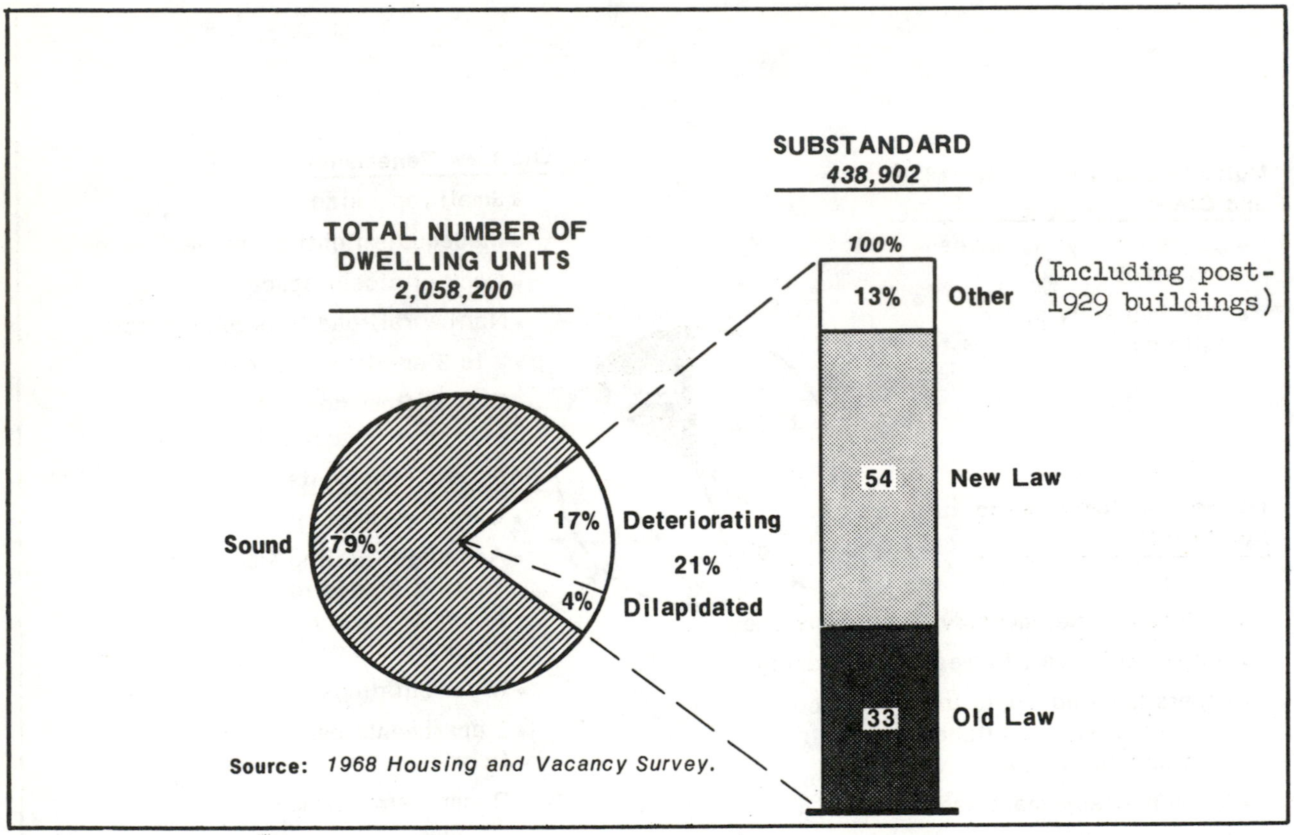

Source: *1968 Housing and Vacancy Survey.*

Exhibit 6

HOUSING REHABILITATION IN NEW YORK CITY

1969 Rehabilitation Construction Costs by Level of Rehabilitation and Building Type

Level of Rehabilitation	"Average" Unit	New Law Unit	Old Law Unit
Minimum	$1,796	$ 1,569	$ 1,754
Standard error*	(0.45)	(0.63)	(0.32)
Moderate			
Standard error*	N.A.**	N.A.**	N.A.**
Layout	7,863	7,196	8,007
Standard error*	(0.19)	(0.14)	(0.14)
Gut	10,980	10,532	12,965
Standard error*	(0.24)	(0.09)	(0.25)

*Standard Error = $\frac{\text{Standard Deviation}}{\text{Mean}}$ where the standard deviation is equal to the average deviation from the mean.

**No figures are available because of the city's limited experience in this area. More recent data suggest that a typical moderate rehabilitation project costs about $4,500.

Source: Sample of 155 rehabilitation projects from the 1960 Rehabilitation Financing study.

Exhibit 7

HOUSING REHABILITATION IN NEW YORK CITY

TOTAL REHABILITATION CONSTRUCTION COSTS BY LEVEL OF REHABILITATION AND BUILDING CHARACTERISTICS

(NUMBER OF UNITS)

BUILDING CONDITION AND TYPE	LEVEL OF REHABILITATION			
	MINIMUM	MODERATE	LAYOUT	GUT
Sound*				
Old Law units (5 percent) **		8,807		
New Law units (3 percent)	8,727	8,727		
Others (1 percent)	8,581			
Deteriorating				
Old Law units (100 percent)		27,622	27,623	55,245
New Law units (100 percent)		47,340	47,340	94,680
Others (100 percent)		11,900	11,900	23,800
Dilapidated				
Old Law units (100 percent)				35,482
New Law units (100 percent)				50,755
Others (100 percent)				5,213

*Some sound units require preventive maintenance to forestall deterioration in the near future.

**Percentages refer to percentage of units in each category which will be rehabilitated.

Exhibit 8

HOUSING REHABILITATION IN NEW YORK CITY

Volume of Units Rehabilitated

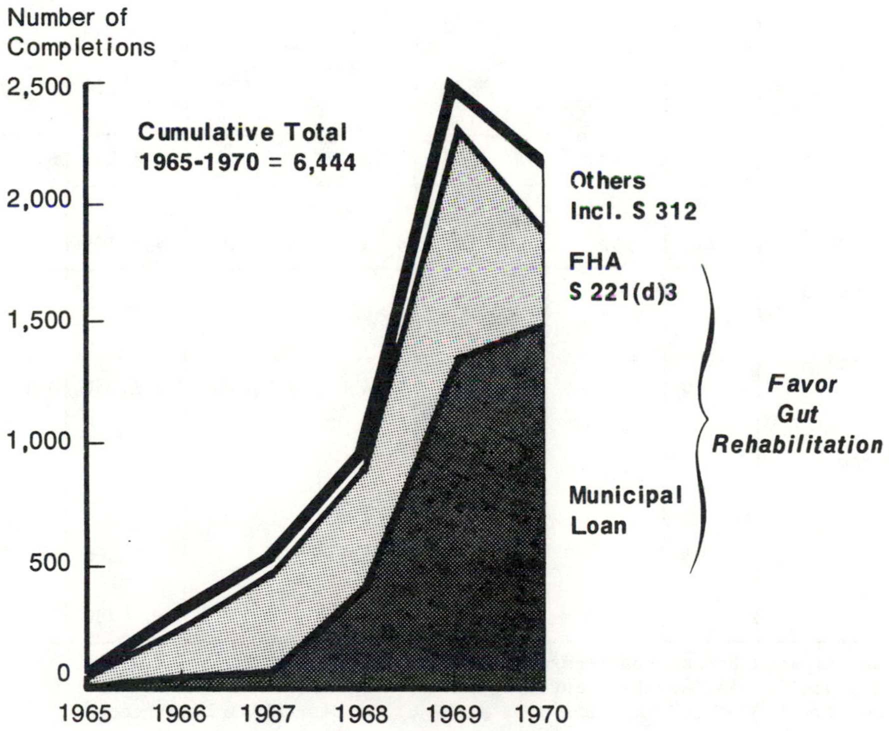

Exhibit 9
HOUSING REHABILITATION IN NEW YORK CITY
1970 COST DATA FOR THE
CITY REHABILITATION PROGRAM*

	Minimum Rehabilitation		Moderate Rehabilitation		Gut Rehabilitation			
	312 (1969 Costs)	Miniloan (1970 Est.)	Municipal Loan	312 (1969 Costs)	Municipal Loan	236		221(d)(3)
Development Costs/Unit								
Construction	$1,850	$870	$10,000	$4,600	$17,600	$16,000	$18,000	$11,300
Site acquisition or refinancing	0	0	2,500	0	2,500	3,500	4,000	2,400
Fees, etc.	150	100	1,500	1,000	3,500	7,500	8,000	5,100
Total	$2,000	$970	$14,000	$5,600	$22,000	$27,000	$30,000	$18,800
Rent Components (Per unit)								
Debt service			$ 1,140		$ 1,920	$ 820	$ 912	$ 810
Taxes**			0		0	0	0	0
Operating and maintenance			675		675	750	750	675
Profit			150		150	0	0	0
Total	N.A.	N.A.	$ 1,965	N.A.	$ 2,745	$ 1,570	$ 1,662	$ 1,485
Rent**								
Dollars/unit/month	N.A.	N.A.	$ 163	$ 110	$ 229	$ 131	$ 139	$ 124
Public Program Costs								
New York City								
Tax abatement/ unit/year	$ 370	0	$ 865	$ 430	$ 1,090	$ 1,330	$ 1,480	$ 860
Capital	0	$970	14,000	0	23,600	0	0	0
Federal Government								
Interest subsidy/ unit/year	36	0	0	112	0	980	1,090	430
Capital	2,000	0	0	5,600	0	27,000	30,000	18,800
Rent supplement and welfare/unit/year	0	0	1,080	0	1,550	780	880	760

* All figures computed for a 2-bedroom unit.
** Assumes full use of J51 Tax Abatement program.
Source: HDA survey of Sections 312, 221(d)3, and 236, and Municipal Loan records.

Appendix A

HOUSING REHABILITATION IN NEW YORK CITY

Descriptions of Major Rehabilitation Programs

Sections 221(d)3 and 236

Under Section 236 and its predecessor, Section 221(d)3 Below Market Interest Rate (BMIR), the Federal Government provides interest-subsidized mortgages to private project sponsors.

Between 1965, when the Section 221(d)3 BMIR program was first used for rehabilitation in New York, and June 30, 1970, 2,209 units were rehabilitated under its provisions. Another 138 units had been granted mortgage insurance under the Section 221(d)3 MIR program. In addition, 1,211 units supported by Sections 221(d)3 or 236 were under construction. (1970 starts included both Section 236 and Section 221(d)3 projects. Since May, however, Section 221(d)3 had been terminated and all future starts would be initiated under Section 236.)

All completed Section 221(d)3 BMIR and Section 236 rehabilitation projects consisted of gut level work, except for two buildings. The focus on gut rehabilitation had resulted in part from the high legal mortgage ceilings (up to $37,934 per unit), the long maximum financing period (40 years), and FHA-established architectural standards. Most administrators felt that gut rehabilitation was necessary to ensure an economic life equal to the term of the mortgage.

Because of the high costs of gut rehabilitation, however, HDA had begun to favor the use of Section 236 for new construction rather than rehabilitation.[1] Some sponsors and community groups were supporting this trend, apparently feeling that new construction produced higher quality units and that this quality was worth the additional cost.

Consistent with the targeted rehabilitation levels, Sections 221(d)3 and 236 had been directed toward areas with poor housing conditions. Although not legally required, the program had been used primarily on the fringes of urban renewal areas. Fifty-four percent of the Section 221(d)3 units completed, accounting for 30 percent of the projects, had been in these areas; and most of the remaining projects clustered around them. In other words, the program had been used to supplement renewal efforts and to supply funds where private-market financing was difficult, if not impossible to obtain.

---

[1] Total development costs for new construction, during the same period, were between $30,000 and $35,000 per unit for public and middle-income housing.

Appendix A (continued)

Postrehabilitation rents charged in Section 221(d)3 and Section 236 projects were fairly low (see Exhibit 9). These low-rent levels stemmed from both the legally defined provisions and the administrative targeting of Sections 221(d)3 and 236. By law, the programs provided for tax abatement on rehabilitated buildings, allowed a mortgage term of 40 years, and provided favorable financing terms. Administratively, HDA had targeted the program to nonprofit sponsors. This lowered the effective postrehabilitation rent levels even further and enabled the Section 221(d)3 and 236 programs to serve low-income tenants, although rent subsidies often had to be provided. The Federal Government bore most of the costs, including the cost of purchasing the mortgage, paying the interest,providing rent subsidies, and assuming its share of welfare rents.

Section 312 and Section 115

Under Sections 312 and 115, federally funded loans and grants, respectively, are provided to sponsors of rehabilitation projects in federal code enforcement and urban renewal areas. Section 312 provides loans to low-income owner-occupants. The maximum interest rate is 3 percent and the maximum term 20 years. Section 115 provides grants up to $3,000 to owner-occupants who lack the financial resources to repay a loan even under the generous terms offered by other programs.

Since the program's inception in 1964, loans and grants had been made to 79 projects that included 435 dwelling units. Of this total, 303 units were completed and 132 were under construction as of June 30, 1970. Of the $96 million in Section 312 funds loaned nationwide (to June 30, 1970), $16 million had been loaned in the New England region and, of this, New York City had received $54,000. (One federal official commented that enough federal money was available to finance the rehabilitation of as many as 2,500 units a year in New York City through Section 312).

While Sections 312 and 115 are legislatively targeted to both urban renewal and federal code enforcement areas, most loans had been made in the latter areas. Among other requirements, candidate buildings in these areas had to require less than total rehabilitation in order to qualify for Section 312 or 115 funds. Grants and mortgages were designed to upgrade an area before disinvestment and deterioration made it a slum. Thus, the levels of rehabilitation most often funded were minimum and moderate rehabilitation, even though the legal mortgage limits were sufficient to cover more extensive work. Both loans and grants served a wide range of income groups. In both code enforcement and urban renewal areas, they were typically aimed at the owner-occupants of small buildings (about 6 units). Building owners had incomes ranging from $7,000 to $12,000 a year, while tenants typically had incomes between $4,000 and $8,000 a year. In other words, the program served middle- and lower-middle income families, usually without the need for rent subsidies.

Rent levels in completed projects were not substantially more than the rents charged before rehabilitation. The typical rent on a two-bedroom unit was $110 a month, although they ranged from about $75 to $150 a month, depending on the prerehabilitation rent and the level of work undertaken.

Appendix A (continued)

Construction costs averaged $14,300 per building, or $2,200 per dwelling unit. In 1969, the average total development cost ranged from $2,000 to $5,600 per unit. These low costs reflected the emphasis on minimum and moderate rehabilitation that resulted in lower construction costs and several other savings as well. First, with low-level rehabilitation, there were no acquisition costs and carrying costs, therefore, were eliminated. In addition, because processing and construction periods were short, there was little time for inflation to increase the cost of the project. Besides keeping rents low, these savings reduced the public cost per unit. In 1969, the typical cost to the city was $430 a year per unit for moderate rehabilitation (to cover the cost of tax abatement). The cost to the Federal Government was $112 per unit for interest subsidy and $5,600 per unit for capital.

Municipal Loan Program

Under the Municipal Loan program, the city provided below-market-interest-rate loans to building owners and other eligible sponsors for the rehabilitation of multiple dwellings built before 1929. The interest rate charged was 1/2 percent above the city's tax-exempt borrowing rate -- about 5 to 6 percent. After 1968, the number of completed Municipal Loan projects grew rapidly, although the total volume remained low. As of June 30, 1970, 2,545 units had been renovated since January 1963 and 3,751 units were in process. Between June 30 and December 31, 1970, 825 additional units were completed, bringing the cumulative total to 3,370 units. Continued expansion of HDA's mortgage lending power would be curtailed, however, since no borrowing power remained under the 2 percent debt limit.

For the most part, Municipal Loans had been used for gut rehabilitation. To avoid relocation problems and costs, abandoned buildings had often been selected. They were among the most deteriorated in the city and generally required extensive rehabilitation. To reduce monthly debt service payments and keep rents low, the maximum mortgage term of 30 years had been granted, thereby making gut rehabilitation necessary to ensure a building life expectancy greater than the mortgage term.

Most Municipal Loans had been granted to sponsors in urban renewal areas. This focus was administratively, not legislatively, determined on the basis of area need. Sixty-seven percent of the completed projects and 59 percent of the completed units were in these areas. This trend held for projects still under construction: 65 percent of the projects and 67 percent of the units were in renewal areas. These core areas generally attract little private rehabilitation investment and the Municipal Loan program, therefore, was providing funds that otherwise would have been unavailable.

The rents that must be charged for a given level of rehabilitation under the Municipal Loan program are considerably higher than those under other programs. For the most part, these rents are the result of relatively high interest rates charged for Municipal Loans -- 5.5 percent in 1969 and 6.5 percent in 1970 -- as compared with 3 percent under Section 221(d)3.

Appendix A (continued)

Legally, the Municipal Loan program is targeted to low-income families. The legislation limits a household's annual income to seven times its annual rent. As rehabilitation costs and therefore rents increase, however, the maximum allowable incomes increase and low-income families can no longer afford the rents. For example, the typical rents in gut rehabilitation projects in 1970 implied a maximum family income of $18,000. Therefore, rent subsidies had to be provided to enable low-income families to live in units rehabilitated with Municipal Loans.

The city bears the full cost of the Municipal Loan program, excluding federal rent supplement and welfare payments. In total, HDA had requested $86 million in city mortgage-lending power.

In the spring of 1970, the city developed a Mini-Municipal Loan program in response to the need and demand for minimum levels of rehabilitation. Starting in 1971, this program began offering loans of up to $1,000 per unit with a maximum term of 15 years to owners who could not obtain favorable financing elsewhere. The interest rate charged was the same as for regular Municipal Loans.

The Mini-Municipal Loan program was less expensive on all accounts than regular Municipal Loans. Based on 1970 financing terms and costs, the average total cost to the city was $970 per unit -- the amount of the mortgage. The program does not support refinancing or acquisition costs and rents are low enough that rent subsidies are not required.

Appendix B

HOUSING REHABILITATION IN NEW YORK CITY

The Effect of Financing Provisions on Postrehabilitation Rents

The use of appropriate mortgage interest rates and repayment terms and tax exemption and abatement constitute one approach that the city can take to hold down rehabilitation-caused rent increases without direct rent assistance.

To illustrate the impact of financing terms on rent increases, a typical moderate rehabilitation project on a deteriorating New Law tenement will be examined. Exhibit B-1 breaks down the pre- and postrehabilitation rents showing the portion spent on the operation and maintenance of the building, real estate taxes, debt service and, after the property has been improved, profit. The postrehabilitation rent of $183 a month is based on using a conventional mortgage to finance 70 percent of the cost of rehabilitating the building -- in this case, $6,666 per unit.

These terms and the consequent rent form the bench mark against which alternative financing terms can be measured. For example, the Municipal Loan program offers funds at 6.5 percent over 10 years plus tax exemption and abatement, resulting in a rent of $138.40 a month -- a reduction of almost $45 a month, or about $535 a year. The cost to the city, however, is only the cost of the foregone tax revenue because the 6.5 percent interest rate is the city's borrowing rate and is not an actual interest-subsidy cost. In this case, the foregone tax revenue is $228 a year, which buys a yearly rent reduction of $535. Therefore, the ratio -- or efficiency -- of rent reduction to city cost is 2.3 for this program.

Using this "efficiency" measure, it is possible to test a number of combinations of financial terms as shown in Exhibit B-2. One program in the exhibit has an efficiency rating of 3.3. With the same $228 in foregone tax revenues, it buys $744 in rent reduction. It achieves this high efficiency by extending the payback period to 20 years, offering 100 percent financing of the project (no equity required of the project sponsor), and eliminating the allowance for profit.

The number of rehabilitation projects that can be undertaken with a given amount of funds is quite sensitive to financing terms. If a publicly funded mortgage program offers 100 percent financing to a project instead of 70 percent, for example, the number of units that can be financed is reduced by about one-third. If a program offers 20-year terms instead of 10-year terms, the money lent out will be much slower to return and hence less available for reinvestment. Tax exemption and abatement lowers revenues and interest subsidies (for interest rates under 6.5 percent) raise costs in the expense budget, thus competing with all of the other operating programs in the city for support.

Exhibit B-1

Pre- and Postrehabilitation Rents for a Sample Project (Deteriorating New Law; Moderate Rehabilitation at $6,666/D.U.)

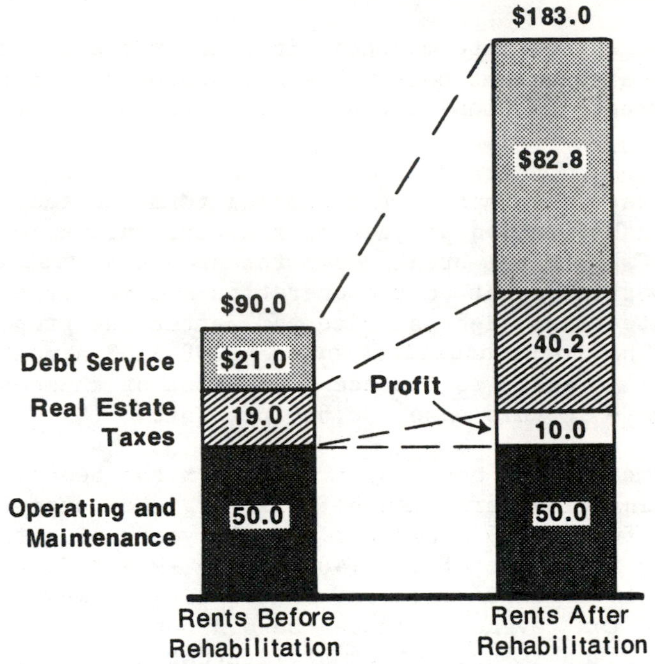

ASSUMPTIONS

PREREHABILITATION BUILDING AND FINANCING CHARACTERISTICS

Rooms/D.U.: 4.5

Market value/D.U.: $6,040

A.V.*/Market Value: 0.70

A.V./D.U.: $4,228

Debt/D.U.: $3,571

Mortgage Terms: 5% – 25 years

REHABILITATION

Cost/D.U.: $6,666

Debt/Equity: 0.70

Debt/D.U.: $4,666

Mortgage Terms: 9½% – 10 years

Profit/Equity: 6%

* *A.V. = assessed value.*

Exhibit B-2

HOUSING REHABILITATION IN NEW YORK CITY

Alternative Rehabilitation Programs

Deteriorated New Law

Moderate Rehabilitation at $6,666/D.U.

	PROGRAM SPECIFICATIONS					PER UNIT IMPACT				
EXISTING PROGRAM	INTEREST RATE	TERM	D/E	PROFIT	TAX EXEMPTION ABATEMENT	RENT/MONTH (After Rehabilitation and Financing)	YEARLY RENT REDUCTION (Resulting from Program)	REFERENCE INCOME GROUP[1]	YEARLY CITY COST (Abatement and Interest Subsidy)	EFFICIENCY MEASURE RENT REDUCTION/ CITY COST
Conventional	9½%	10 Yrs.	70%	6%	None	$183.00	Base Case	$ 8,800	0	—
312	3	10	100	0	J 51	136.00	564	6,500	$228	2.5
Municipal Loan	6½	10	70	8	J 51	138.40	535	6,600	228	2.3
J-51	9½	10	70	6	J 51	144.50	462	7,000	228	2.0
New	6½	10	100	0	None	188.40	(65)	9,000	0	—
Financing	6½	10	100	0	J 51	148.30	416	7,100	228	1.8
Programs	6½	20	100	0	None	161.20	262	7,700	0	—
	6½	20	100	0	J 51	121.00	744	5,800	228	3.3
	6½	20	70	6	None	156.20	322	7,500	0	—
	1	10	100	0	None	169.50	162	8,100	227	0.7
	1	10	100	0	J 51	129.30	644	6,200	455	1.4
	1	20	100	0	None	141.80	494	6,800	233	2.1
	1	20	100	0	J 51	101.60	977	4,900	461	2.1
	1	20	70	6	None	142.60	485	6,800	163	3.0

1. "Reference income group" designates the annual income level required to support a rent expenditure of 25% of annual income.

NARCOTICS CONTROL

ADDICTION CONTROL IN NEW YORK CITY (A)

In July 1970, the Mayor's Narcotics Control Council (NCC) met to discuss and review the status of New York City's narcotics problem and to evaluate current efforts to combat it.[1] It was becoming apparent to those involved that the work presently being done in the city was not sufficient and that stepped up efforts would be needed to respond to the increased political and social demands being placed on the city's administration. A recent report issued by the Department of Social Services (the organization responsible for administering public assistance programs) had concluded:

> Along with the growing concern over the abuse of narcotics, not only within the public assistance population, but throughout the general community, there is also a growing awareness that there is very little known about the large number of treatment facilities available to the addict. Not only is there no information concerning the size and capacity of these agencies, the types of rehabilitation and other programs that they offer, but in many cases (with the exception of certain well-known agencies), the general public does not even know names and addresses of these local facilities.

The political potential inherent in the drug abuse issue had been underscored by a Gallup poll in which city residents had ranked it as the nation's third most critical problem - preceded only by the Vietnma War and the sluggish state of the economy.

NCC's function was to gather and disseminate information and to provide a forum for the discussion of drug-related problems. It had been

---

1 While the word "narcotics" may be used to designate any of the opiates (heroin, morphine, opium, codeine, and others), it will be used in this case to denote only heroin.

created by Mayor Lindsay, who sat as its chairman. Membership included people in the administration who were responsible for developing city policy and managing its programs for dealing with narcotics abuse. These were: the Administrator of the Health Services Administration (HSA), the Commissioners of the Departments of Health and Mental Health; the Administrator of the Human Resources Administration (HRA), the Director of the Addiction Services Agency (ASA), the Police and Corrections Commissioners, and representatives of the Mayor's Office, the Board of Education, the Criminal Justice Co-ordinating Council (CJCC), and the Vera Institute of Crime. (An organization chart of the city administration is shown in Exhibit 1.) Spokesmen for various interested private groups also sat on the Council. There was a growing consensus in the Council that the city's goals with regard to narcotics abuse needed clarification, that improved resource allocation policies were needed, and that more effective control of existing treatment facilities should be instituted.

Dimensions of the Problem

HSA reported that as of the middle of 1970, there were over 65,000 heroin addicts known to the city's Narcotics Register.[1] From this, it was estimated that the total addict population was more in the vicinity of 100,000 to 150,000 - that is, from 1.3% to 2% of the city's total population. Projections showed a compound growth rate of 10% per year and suggested that the 1978 addict population would be close to 250,000. (This would approach the 1970 addict population of the entire United States.) In 1969, there were 900 heroin-related deaths in New York, 25% of them teenagers. Indeed, drug abuse was the largest single cause of death for males between the ages of 15 and 35. (Administered in overdose levels, heroin kills by stopping the heart and respiratory mechanisms. Prolonged usage often leads to malnutrition resulting from the addict's life style or to disease and infection from dirty apparatus.) Doctors estimated the life expectancy of a 20-year-old heroin addict to be comparable to that of a 55-year-old man.

The addiction problem, however, extended far beyond the physical and mental health of the user. The economic, social, and moral costs of drug addiction presented a threat that permeated every aspect of society from the

---

[1]The Narcotics Register collected data used to evaluate the extent of narcotics addiction in the city. It had been operational since 1966 in the Department of Health. The purposes of the Register were to establish and maintain an unduplicated count of drug abusers; to estimate the incidence and prevalence of drug abuse in the city; to investigate the demographic and social characteristics of the addict population; and to conduct studies on the epidemiology of drug abuse. Data collected by the Register included the name, birthdate, birthplace, residence, sex, ethnic group, and drugs of abuse for each addict. Its sources included private M.D.'s, hospitals, clinics, social service agencies, the Police Department, the Poison Control Center, the Office of Vital Statistics, the Bureau of Preventable Diseases, and private industry.

The Register was used for statistical purposes only. Under no circumstances were individual names made available to anyone. The Register released routine reports and the results of special statistical work.

individual to the Federal Government. With the price of a "bag" (the one-ounce retail package) around $5.00, an average user spent between $25 and $30 per day to support his "habit." Most of this money was obtained through theft and, since stolen goods sold at a substantial discount, the necessary level of this activity was multiplied. The Vera Institute and the Police Department estimated that between $1 billion and $1.5 billion per year was stolen in cash and property in narcotic-related crimes. The Police Department believed that 40% of its budget was spent in drug-related activity including over 50,000 arrests per year. Even when an addict obtained his money legally, there was often a direct cost to society. There were, for example, 19,000 addicts receiving $58.3 million in public assistance each year. Moreover, the Department of Social Services reported that 1,200 new addicts were joining the welfare roles every month.

Exhibit 2 is a summary of income sources used by various types of addicts. Appendix A develops an estimate of the monetary benefits that would accrue to society for each man-year of heroin addiction that could be avoided. In summary, these benefits are:

Increased employment earnings	$ 3,260
Reduction in premature deaths	1,510
Reduction in morbidity	384
Reduction in crime	4,100
Reduction in enforcement costs	1,640
Reduction in housing deterioration	164
	$11,060
Contagion factor (1.25)	2,765
Total per addiction year	$13,825

Nature of the Industry

The drug industry was highly marketing oriented, with an intricate distribution system, and extremely large markups (between 2000% and 8000%). Organized crime controlled all the more lucrative parts of the system, thus accounting for the highly concentrated nature of the industry (despite the low capital and technological barriers to entry). Exhibit 3 describes one model of the distribution system. The typical "nickel bag" bought by the ultimate consumer contained about 3% pure heroin. The lack of quality control and the tremendous inconsistency of the product (from 0% to 75% pure heroin) was the major cause of overdoses and death. One of the best advertisements for a street pusher was to have a buyer die of an overdose, thereby attesting to the quality of his product. The demand curve for heroin was relatively inelastic except at very high and very low prices where it probably became quite elastic. (No one knew at what price these transitions occurred.)

Characteristics of Addiction

Although there were many theories, very little was known about the physiological, psychological, sociological, or epidemiological aspects of addiction. It was difficult, if not impossible, to pinpoint the reasons that led someone to choose a life of addiction. An individual's inability to "cope" with his environment, the environment itself, boredom, the excitement of hustling, and a myriad of other reasons had been suggested. In the early stages of heroin use, it was the euphoric "rush" that provided the strongest motivation for continuing, not the apathetic and somnolent periods that followed. It was not clear whether the primary motivation for continued use over long periods of time remained the "rush" or shifted to the avoidance of withdrawal pains. Most addicts were introduced to heroin by their "friends" rather than by pushers. Once the addict population in a given neighborhood reached a threshold level, heroin use spread in epidemic proportions, that is, geometrically up to a plateau.

Despite the lack of precise knowledge, it was evident that heroin use and the economic and social conditions that are characteristic of urban ghettos were positively correlated. Patterns in New York pointed this out. As Exhibit 4 shows, areas with high usage rates were all characterized by poverty, substantial unemployment, poor housing, and large minority populations. Over seventeen per cent of the city's addicts could be found in Central Harlem alone. Exhibit 5 presents further data on the addict population.

When they were viewed individually, it was difficult to draw a single, suitable picture of the "typical" heroin addict. One city hospital, in an effort to dispel any prototype image, studied addicts in treatment as to their criminality and conventionality. "Criminality" was assessed on the basis of arrest and conviction records while "conventionality" was a function of family and employment records. The results showed a wide divergence of addict behavior with only 30% fitting the "typical" addict description - that is, someone living on the periphery of society and supporting his habit through crime. In fact, almost a quarter of the sample seemed to live normal, non-criminal, working lives. (See below.)

ADDICT PROFILE*

		CONVENTIONALITY	
		High	Low
CRIMINALITY	Low	23% (working addict)	21% (unmasked addict)
	High	25% (two worlders)	30% (hustlers)

*The figures were based on a rather small and select group of addicts and may not be representative of the real situation.

Further addict categorizations were possible. The profile shown in Exhibit 2 was based on the size of the addicts' habits. Another approach was to break down the addict population into different stages of what is known as the "addict life cycle." One such theory suggested that an addict progresses through various "stages" and may ultimately outgrow his need for the drug.[1] The life cycle includes: initiation, experimentation, adaptation, addiction, tolerance (for a life of addiction), potential abstinence (including experimentation, adaptation, and supported drug-free stages), and unsupported abstinence. The desire to kick the habit as a result of age, self-disgust, apathy, or other external stimuli was evidenced by the fact that an increasingly large number of addicts were voluntarily seeking help for their problem.

Alternative Approaches to the Problem

Numerous approaches to the narcotics problem had been proposed. They varied dramatically in their cost, effectiveness, goals, and usefulness. The major programs included:

1) Methadone Maintenance
2) Detoxification
3) Heroin Maintenance
4) Narcotic Antagonists
5) Heroin Legalization
6) Improved Enforcement
7) Voluntary Abstinence
8) Involuntary Abstinence and/or Incarceration
9) Preventive Education

Methadone Maintenance: Methadone was an addictive drug which blocked the euphoric action of heroin for 24 hours. Administered orally it had no side effects, was mildly tranquilizing, extremely inexpensive, exhibited no tolerance behavior, and induced withdrawal symptoms when withheld. Its two disadvantages were: the euphoric effect produced when administered intravenously (thereby creating some abuse potential) and the suspicion that by reducing anxiety and preventing extremes of depression or elation the emotional growth and maturation of the patient might be seriously retarded. In addition, the addictive property of methadone made it a very prolonged treatment.

Pioneered in 1964 by Drs. Dole and Nyswander of Rockefeller University, the experimental methadone program of Beth Israel Hospital had achieved notable results: of several thousand admissions to the program more than 80% were still under treatment after one year. The group's annual arrest record dropped from 18% to 3% and their employment rate increased from 30% initially to 68% after 1 year, 72% after 3 years, and 78% after

---

[1] The existence of a "maturation" phenomenon whereby part of the addict population outgrows its need for heroin was widely disputed. Opponents thought that adherents failed to account for premature addict deaths and differences between generations in addiction rates and characteristics. Advocates believed that maturation could be explained by such factors as improvement with age in perceived employment opportunities, increased penalties for criminal repeaters, and greater probability of apprehension as the addict became better known. Hudson Institute estimated an average period of addiction of ten years.

4 years with an additional 3% to 5% in school. There was a corresponding decrease in the number on welfare. In 1970, there were enough facilities in the city to maintain 5,000 addicts on methadone. The average cost of these methadone programs was close to $1,300 per patient per year including the drug and its administration and a variety of social, vocational, and psychiatric counseling services.

Because of its addictive nature, methadone was not considered desirable for very young addicts or those who were strongly motivated. Moreover, methadone was not attractive to (1) young addicts who believed they could hustle without becoming addicted or (2) addicts who simply refused to give up the pleasure of a heroin rush. Dr. Dole estimated, therefore, that methadone was an appropriate treatment for 50% of the addict population. If the maturation phenomenon was accepted, the average number of heroin addiction years remaining for methadone patients was about seven. (Until recently, the experimental programs had not accepted anyone under 21. In 1970, the age limit was 18.)

Severe criticism of methadone had come from several quarters. Many argued that maintenance was only a sophisticated medical fix for a social problem and that regardless of its "success" it did not get to the heart of the matter. Some Black groups and many of the addicts claimed that methadone maintenance was nothing more than a device to impose state control over them.

Detoxification Programs: Three different methadone detoxification programs had been tried: inpatient detoxification, ambulatory detoxification, and crisis intervention.[1] Detoxification permitted some addicts to discard their addiction habits "permanently," allowed others to decrease the size of their habit temporarily (thus reducing criminal activity and the probability of overdose), provided a referral mechanism into other treatment programs, and provided others with relief from withdrawal symptoms. Very little quantitative information was available on the effectiveness of these different detoxification approaches but the following estimates had been made on the basis of what little information was available.

Inpatient detoxification involving 7-14 days of residential care at an average per diem cost of $75 (which included psychiatric, social, and vocational counseling services) was directed primarily at generating long-term cures. Extended involuntary inpatient detoxification programs in California and the Lexington (Kentucky) Addiction Center had found that the number of long-term successes (patients who remained virtually heroin free after two years) was on the order of 5-10% of those detoxified. Most long-term successes were among the newly addicted or those with strong wills and substantial motivation to give up heroin.

"Best" estimates of various parameters for local inpatient programs were felt to be a 5% to 10% success rate, ten years average addiction remaining and an average period of one month before "failures" became fully readdicted. Presumably, the addict did not engage in criminal activity during that month.

---

[1]In each detoxification approach, methadone was administered only until the addict's system was free of heroin; then the methadone was discontinued.

Ambulatory detoxification could be given in outpatient wards, in storefront facilities strategically located in high addiction areas, or in mobile units. The program took from 7 to 14 days and cost between $36 and $52 per patient. Success rates were very low (2% to 4%) for long-term abstinence. Those who reverted to heroin use did so in about two weeks. It was believed that about 5% of all detoxification patients were referred to inpatient facilities and the rest to ambulatory programs.

Crisis intervention was a one-shot oral dose of methadone given to anyone coming off the street requesting care. The hope was that by treating such an individual, one could reduce his discomfort, persuade him to enter a treatment program, or at the least, reduce the probability that he would commit a crime. In actuality, therefore, crisis intervention was ambulatory detoxification with an expected early program dropout. No information was available regarding its effectiveness.

<u>Heroin Maintenance</u>: Heroin maintenance had been advocated in light of the British experience with this treatment and the possible benefits that might result. It was believed that many addicts, who would not respond to other programs, might be attracted to heroin maintenance. Once in a regulated environment, they could be persuaded to enter one of the other programs. During maintenance, the health hazards normally associated with heroin use would be eliminated as would the need for criminal activity. Some productive employment might result, and the illegal heroin market would be crippled. It was even possible that the number of addicts would decrease since pushers would not have to find new markets to support their own habits. The cost of a heroin maintenance program was estimated to be about $2,000 per addict per year.

There were, of course, a wide range of legal, political, and ethical arguments against this approach. By making an addict's life easier, it was feared that more people might be encouraged to become addicts. Unless the program were instituted nationwide, addicts might swarm to those states or cities that did use the treatment. The danger of abuse was great. Addicts might use their legal dose to supplement other sources. Whatever motivation many addicts already had to give up the drug - particularly addicts enrolled in other programs - could be lost. As with methadone, many in the Black community viewed heroin maintenance as a ploy to make them dependent on the state and the White man.

<u>Narcotic Antagonists</u>: Antagonists were a relatively new method of treatment. Administered orally, an antagonist blocked the euphoric effects of heroin but, unlike methadone, did not satiate the addict's craving for heroin; he just could not get high on it. There were virtually no side effects from these drugs nor did the user develop a tolerance for them over time. They were not addictive, thus eliminating many of the ethical questions about methadone as well as the potential for abuse. Antagonist treatments took between 2 to 3 years before the craving for heroin was gone. Because of their non-addictive nature, antagonists were considered appropriate for young addicts who might not be completely addicted to heroin. (Hence, the average remaining years of addiction for people entering an antagonist program could be as high as fourteen.) Antagonists also had potential as a preventive mechanism in neighborhoods where drug addiction was approaching, or already had reached, epidemic proportions.

Information on and results of antagonist treatments were sketchy and there were still some technological hurdles that had to be solved. The major one was that the blocking effects of the drugs lasted for relatively short periods of time. Cyclazocine was effective for about one day and Naloxone for 4 to 8 hours. Because the drugs were non-addictive, it was difficult to keep an addict coming for his treatment or to prevent him from "chipping" (occasionally using heroin). For this reason, only highly motivated addicts were successful in an antagonist program. (Researchers estimated that long-acting – one week to one year - antagonists would not be feasible for several years. Moreover, in 1970, there was relatively little research being done and those companies who had active programs were quite secretive about their findings.) Probably only 30% of heroin addicts were suitable for treatment by antagonists. The cost per addict per year for Cyclazocine was $2,000. Naloxone was more expensive, costing about $4,000 per addict per year. The success rate for addicts using antagonists was believed to be 50%.

Heroin Legalization: Some observers felt that if the government legalized heroin and controlled it in the same way that it does alchohol, tobacco, or other drugs, many of the problems of drug addiction might be alleviated at little dollar cost. By controlling the quality and consistency of the drug, many health dangers could be avoided. By eliminating the stigma associated with addiction, the psychological and social pressures that an addict faced would be reduced. And, by changing the market structure of the industry, prices might be greatly reduced and with them the need for criminal activity. (A habit might be supported on as little as $2,500 per year.) Controlling the channels of distribution could deal a severe blow to organized crime. The financial costs of legalization would be minimal.

Many people did not believe in or approve of the anti-social life that an addict leads. Inasmuch as legalization would have to be approved on a federal basis to keep any one state from being overrun with heroin addicts, the re-education of the American public would have to be tremendous in order to make such a plan politically feasible. Some believed that the public nuisance created through increased visibility of heroin use and the potentially large number of new addicts would adversely affect the morals and morale of society. Moreover, since the pressures to give up heroin, once a person was addicted, would be greatly reduced, the average period of addiction would probably increase, perhaps to fifteen years.

Improved Enforcement: At the other end of the spectrum from heroin legalization was an improvement in the enforcement of existing drug legislation. This would be directed at the middle and top levels of the heroin distribution system, in order to cut off the major supply lines to the user and the street pusher. The goal would be to inflate the price of heroin to a point where a habit would be financially impossible and the addict forced to enter some form of "voluntary" treatment or to commit crimes for which he would be readily apprehendable. Pushers would also be driven out of business.

The program would put the industry on the defensive, curb the spread of heroin use, and slowly reduce the addict population. While this approach had not been very successful in the past, it was argued that a large-scale, well-funded effort, with adequate governmental and public support, could be successful in the future. Costs and benefits of an enforcement program were almost impossible to assess, but an expenditure of $1,000 per addict did not seem unreasonable, if any real impact on the distribution system is expected.

Such a policy would not be easy to implement, however. Existing laws were cumbersome. Other issues, such as French reluctance to co-operate in shutting down supply houses in Marseilles, were difficult to surmount. A large increase in crime, resulting from the inflated prices of heroin, presented a short-term problem until heroin was completely off the market, a goal that might be unattainable. Moreover, when "panics" or acute shortages of heroin had occurred in the past, there was no large migration to rehabilitation programs nor in the long run, any noticeable reduction in heroin use.

Voluntary Abstinence: There was a wide variety of voluntary abstinence programs. They usually took the form of encounter groups and residential therapeutic communities or of storefront operations where the group convened daily to discuss its problems and to reinforce each others' abstinence. In general, they were controlled by the members and relied on group support, imposing strict behavioral discipline on those involved. (Even cigarette smoking was not allowed in some of them.) This characteristic made them suitable only for older, highly motivated addicts, (the average age was twenty-seven). Thus, the treatment method was probably appropriate for no more than 30% of the addict population and the years of addiction remaining with this group was less than average. Another drawback of the programs was the large number of ex-addicts who did not re-enter society, but continued to work in the communities. Two of the larger programs were Therapy Houses and Citizen Houses.[1]

Therapy Houses were residential communities staffed primarily by ex-addicts. The length of treatment averaged two and a half years at a total cost of $17,250 per addict. ASA reported that 35% of those completing treatment remained off heroin. The drop-out rate was about 70%.

Citizen Houses were similar to Therapy Houses but had even stricter entrance requirements, based on family and employment histories, dress, and attitude. This accounted for the 80% success ratio for those completing the program. As with Therapy Houses, the attrition rate was high with only 30% of those enrolling in the program completing it. The treatment was in three stages covering induction, intensive treatment, and gradual re-entry into society. Its cost was about $12,000.

Involuntary Incarceration and Abstinence Programs: A program designed to "get the addict off the streets" through the enforcement of

---

[1]Names disguised.

existing laws would differ from an effort to cut off the supply lines; it would be aimed, instead, at reducing the number of consumers and thus lowering demand. It would rest on the concept that heroin addiction is a communicable disease and that the state has the right to protect its citizens from contagion by quarantining those who are infected. One program that had been suggested called for rounding up as many suspected users as possible, subjecting them to urinalysis, and, if the test was positive, giving them a choice of treatments. Those who chose a voluntary treatment program would be required to prove continued attendance through regular urinalysis. Those who failed to continue in one of the voluntary programs or whose urinalysis was positive would be picked up again and sent either to prison, a work camp, a special school, or some other involuntary treatment program. They would stay there until cured of their habit or released on parole and returned to a voluntary program.

The annual costs of incarcerating or retaining a prisoner ranged from $5,000 to $8,000. The estimated costs of running special schools for the younger users was between $1,000 and $2,000 per year more than normal schools. Work camps, depending on the security involved, could cost from $3,800 to $5,000 per year.

Involuntary incarceration presented many problems from a civil liberties point of view. To round up suspected addicts and subject them to urinalysis and incarceration could set a precendent for dealing with other problems that society faces.

Involuntary abstinence programs were different in that the addict would be committed to them either through a civil or a criminal court, depending on how he was identified. He might also commit himself to an involuntary program. The programs could be residential communities relying on encounter group techniques or detoxification programs like those at the federal hospitals at Lexington, Kentucky or Fort Worth, Texas. The cost of these treatments was $8,000 to $12,000 per year with a success rate for long-term abstinence of about 10% to 15% and an average stay of about three to five years.

Preventive Education: Although it was difficult to quantify and measure the effects of the various forms of preventive education, many believed that this form of "treatment" did have some effect in averting or retarding the spread of heroin use. Others argued, however, that such programs did nothing but arouse curiosity and educate young people in the ways and means of addiction, thus aggravating the situation. The increase in the growth of heroin use, particularly among the young, was cited to prove the ineffectiveness of this expenditure of resources.

Response to the Problem

As of June 1970, the city's response to the addiction problem consisted of many different programs, funded and administered by a variety of organizations and relying on several of the treatment approaches discussed above. Little or no active coordination existed between them. In early 1970, the Department of Social Services undertook a survey of addiction programs in response to the growing number of addicts who were claiming eligibility for public assistance by virtue of being an active participant in some program or a bona fide registrant on its waiting list (see Exhibit 6). The difficulty encountered by DSS in obtaining and updating its data was a cause of much concern not only to DSS but to others as well. A statement by the Criminal Justice Coordinating Council asserted:

> Treatment programs until now have been equally unsuccessful. No more than 11,000 people are in any kind of treatment today, and the success rate of most modes of treatment, as far as can be measured, is very low. Moreover, the treatment field is torn with controversy. Various programs not only compete but sometimes try to undercut each other, with effectiveness the chief victim.

Three agencies were most influential in shaping the city's addiction programs: the Addictión Services Agency (ASA), the Criminal Justice Coordinating Council (CJCC), and the State's Narcotic Addiction Control Commission (NACC).

ASA's treatment facilities included 17 residential centers and 30 day care centers for treatment on an ambulatory basis. ASA also acted as a channel through which state and federal funds flowed to several private agencies. The major thrust of ASA' work, however, was education and prevention. Operations had been established in every borough to provide advice and counseling to addicts, relatives, and concerned community people. Typical of these activities were the RARE (Rehab of Addicts by Relatives and Employers) and AWARE (Addiction Workers Alerted to Rehab and Education) groups, which usually met weekly. Some thirty-five teacher training programs served 6,750 public school teachers.

CJCC was a mayoral committee designed to solicit funds from the Federal Government under the Safe Streets Act for the city's police, corrections, and judicial systems. Its role in the narcotics field was to create links between the criminal process and addiction treatment activity. In fiscal year 1970-1971, it planned to spend about $750,000.

By far the largest single organization involved in the city's narcotics treatment activity was the New York State NACC. NACC was a committee made up of public officials and private citizens (primarily in the medical profession) who were responsible for distributing state-authorized funds to those groups they believed were deserving. NACC was the source for over 50% of the funds that would be channeled into New York City for narcotics control. The commission supported a wide range of programs, from encounter group treatments and educational programs to detoxification centers and the methadone maintenance clinics being run in several hospitals.

The Health Services Administration had played a somewhat lesser role in the city's drug programs. It was responsible for the Narcotics Register and the Bureau of Laboratories, which performed urinalyses for other treatment programs.

The money for the various programs in the city came from a variety of sources as shown in Exhibit 7. Their breakdown was roughly:

State	55%
City	20%
Federal	15%
Private	10%

In terms of treatment methods, the money was channelled into the various types of programs as follows:

Education/Prevention	56%
Methadone Maintenance	19%
State Narcotics Centers	12%
Detoxification	6%
Citizen Houses	4%
Therapy Houses	3%

One staff member in HSA estimated that the budget level would grow by significant amounts in the future as narcotics addiction began to receive top priority from both the government and the community. He also noted that funds were sometimes available, but not accessible because the city could not always meet the 50% matching requirement that accompanies some state money. He concluded that, in the absence of an emergency program, an annual growth rate of approximately 25% for the total narcotic control budget appeared reasonable over the next five years. This would bring the FY1975-1976 budget to around a quarter of a billion dollars.

When asked what the key constraints to the development and implementation of a major narcotics control program might be in addition to the fiscal ones, a spokesman for NCC noted that one of the most difficult would be the setting of goals for the program. The many directions that such a program could go often led those involved to an impasse in getting the program on the road. He also noted that at the present time there were no adequate criteria for what constituted success in reducing drug abuse.

Another impediment to the expansion of narcotics programs was the need for skilled personnel. For example, a program that distributed methadone or heroin would have to have a physician in attendance for medical screening and prescriptions. If the best size for a methadone maintenance, detoxification, or antagonist clinic was, say, 125 patients, it was not difficult to determine how many doctors would be needed to treat 50% of the city's addicts. It is questionable whether this many would find the work either interesting or rewarding. Furthermore, if each clinic needed a minimum of two nurses, one professional counselor, and one other paramedical assistant, the constraint became even more dramatic.

Most treatment programs also required some form of physical space, a commodity that was rarer in New York than elswhere. Hospitals were already overcrowded; residential facilities and dormitories, work camps, and prisons were all in short supply. To provide the facilities for an additional 50,000 to 100,000 patients in terms of the medical facilities that these treatments required would be difficult. This would be further aggravated by the need to locate them in such a way that they would directly service the communities that needed them most. Indeed, the establishment of neighborhood clinics might face substantial community resistance even if space was available.

A final problem would be that of selling narcotics programs to the addicts themselves. Addict recruitment would become more difficult as the population became more "hard core," yet, successful recruitment would be an essential ingredient to dealing with addiction.

Exhibit 1

ADDICTION CONTROL IN NEW YORK CITY

Organization Chart Showing Drug-Related Activities for the City of New York

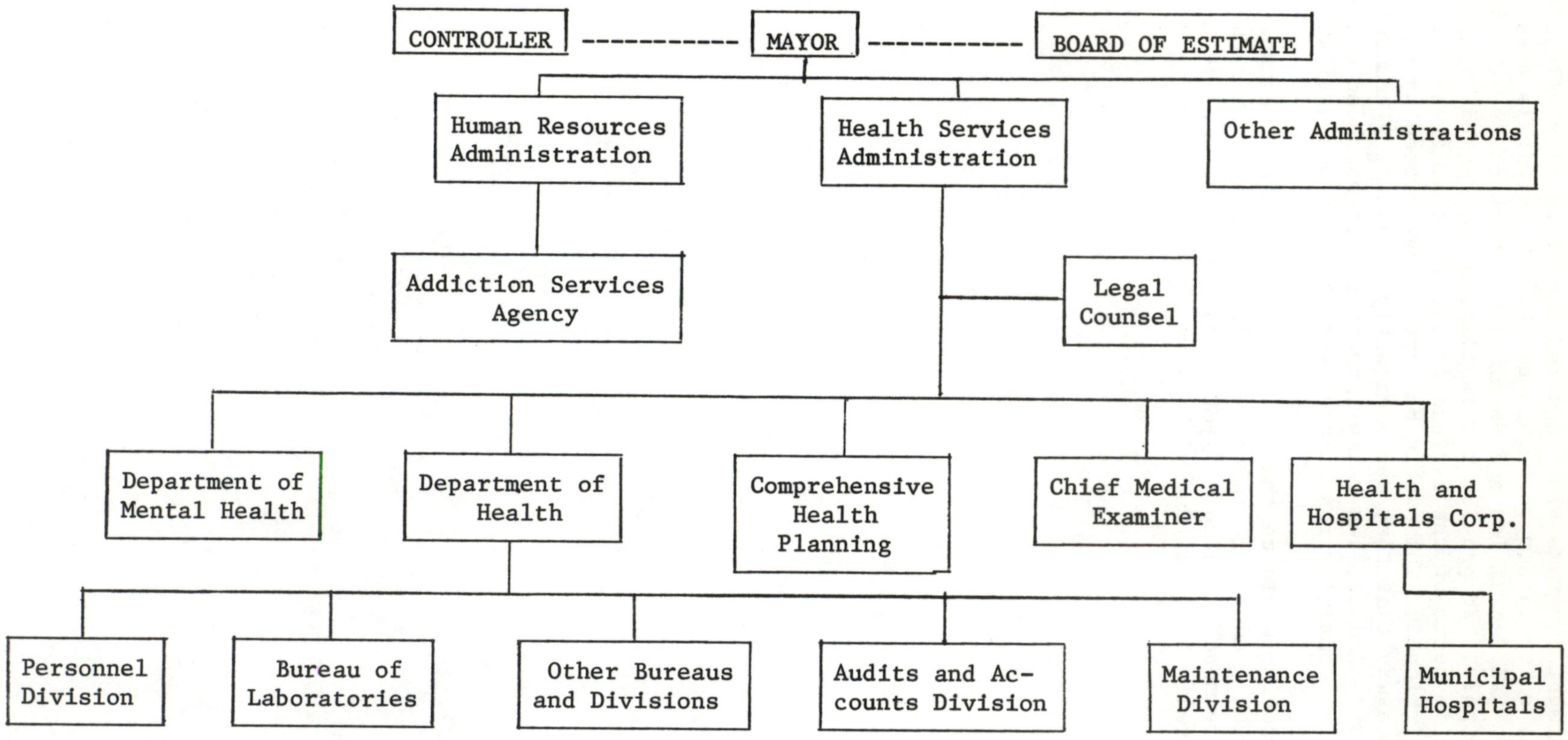

Exhibit 2

ADDICTION CONTROL IN NEW YORK CITY (A)

Sources of Addict Income by Addict Class

ADDICT CLASS*	Shoplifting	Breaking and Entering	Pickpocket	Stealing	Armed Robbery	Con Games	Pushing, Lending, etc.	Prostitution	Welfare	Legal Sources
Joy Poppers	5%									95%
Small Habit Dependents	5%						95%			
Small Habit Apprentices	40%	32%					3%	10%	5%	10%
Medium Habit Hustlers	22%	22%	2%	21%	1%		6%	20%	6%	
Large Habit Hustlers	15%	20%	15%		10%	15%	10%	15%		
Large Habit Dealers							100%			
Women	12%						12%	75%	1%	
Weighted Total**	29%	19%	2%	6%	1%	2%	29%	19%	1%	1%

*See next page for descriptions of addict classifications.

**Represents total % heroin consumption financed by that source with contribution of crime activities evaluated as cost to society.

Source: Policy Concerning Drug Abuse in New York State, Hudson Institute Report, June 15, 1970.

Exhibit 2 (continued)

Estimated Distribution of Types of Heroin Users

Class of Addicts	Characteristics	Percent of Total Pool	Bags/day*
"Joy Poppers"	Intermittent users; may or may not advance to larger habits	10	.4
"Small Habit Apprentices"	Young people getting more involved with drugs; small habit because of low tolerance and few skills in hustling and obtaining drugs	20	2
"Medium Habit Hustlers"	Younger or recently "cleaned-up" hustlers; the young are more skilled and getting larger tolerances; the older are getting started again	23	5
"Large Habit Hustlers"	Older, experienced hustlers; have large tolerances and well-developed earning skills	12	9
"Large Habit Dealers"	Large tolerances; ready supply of inexpensive heroin; "dealers' habits"	11	18
"Small Habit Dependents"	Old and passive hustlers; earning capacity limited by age, laziness, and vulnerability to arrest	9	2
Women	Able to support large habits because they have good "hustlers"; escalate fast because it is easy, given that they get most of it through their male friends and do not have to commit as much crime other than prostitution	15	5

*The results of combining the last two columns are an average consumption rate per addict of 5.6 bags per day.

ADDICTION CONTROL IN NEW YORK CITY (A)

One Model of the Heroin Distribution System*

IMPORTERS	Buy	10 - 100 kg	(80-95% pure)	once every 4 to 20 months
KILO CONNECTIONS (AND "TRADERS")	Buy	1 - 10 kg	(80-95% pure)	2 - 8 times per month
	Sell	1/2 - 4 kg	(40-45% pure)	2 - 4 times per week
CONNECTIONS	Buy	1/2 - 4 kg	(40-45% pure)	3 - 6 times per month
	Sell	2 - 15 ounce	(20-22% pure)	10 - 20 times per week
WEIGHT DEALERS	Buy	2 - 15 ounce	(20-22% pure)	1 - 2 times per week
	Sell	one bundle (1/7 oz) to one ounce	(10-11% pure)	2 - 4 times per day
STREET DEALERS	Buy	one bundle to one ounce		
	Sell	5 - 75 bags	(6 - 8% pure)	3 - 8 times per day
JUGGLERS	Buy	15 - 75 bags	(6 - 8% pure)	3 - 7 times per week
	Sell	1 - 10 bags	(6 - 8% pure)	3 - 15 times per day
USERS	Buy	1 - 10 bags from Street Dealers or Jugglers		1 - 3 times per day

*This chart presents a simplified picture of how heroin is distributed. The actual situation, of course, presents many variations.

Source: Policy Concerning Drug Abuse in New York State, Hudson Institute Report, June 15, 1970.

Exhibit 4

ADDICTION CONTROL IN NEW YORK CITY (A)

Rate of Opiate Use in New York City*

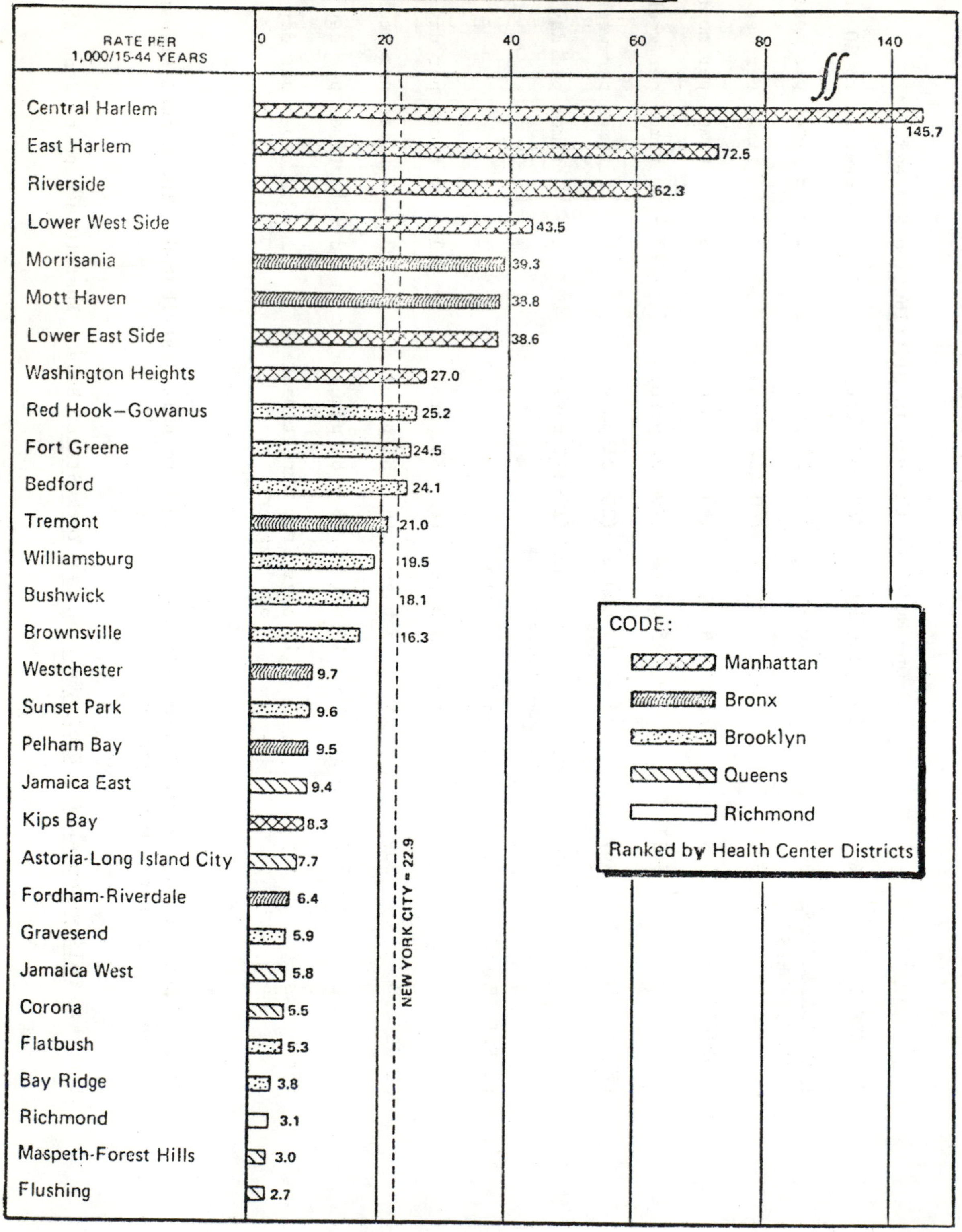

*This exhibit is taken from Opiate Use in New York City, N.Y. State Addiction Control Commission.

Exhibit 5

ADDICTION CONTROL IN NEW YORK CITY (A)

A Profile of Addict Characteristics in New York City*

1. Date of Birth

Date of Birth	%
1901-1910	.1
1911-1920	.3
1921-1930	5.1
1931-1940	18.4
1941-1950	59.3
1951-1960	16.3
Invalid Data	.5

2. Racial Group Association

Racial Group Association	%
Caucasian	59.4
Negro	36.7
Asian (Oriental)	.8
American Indian	.3
Other	2.2
Invalid Data	.6

3. Education

Education	%
Grades 1-8	10.2
9th	14.9
10th	21.2
11th	24.0
12th	23.2
Some College	6.4
Invalid Data	.1

4. Longest Uninterrupted Period of Time at One Job

Longest Uninterrupted Period of Time at One Job	%
0 Months	8.7
1-12 Months	54.4
13-24 Months	17.5
More than 24 Months	18.8
Invalid Data	.6

5. Sex

Sex	%
Male	85.3
Female	14.6
Invalid Data	.1

6. Ethnic Association

Ethnic Association	%
Do not consider being part of an ethnic group	44.4
Mexican	.4
Puerto Rican	29.4
Cuban	.4
Italian	10.9
Other	14.0
Invalid Data	.5

7. Military Service

Military Service	%
Never Served	84.9
Honorable Discharge	9.1
Other Discharge	5.5
Not Discharged	.2
Invalid Data	.3

*Items 1-15 are from a study conducted by the RAND Corporation of 1,166 addicts entering ASA-sponsored treatment programs. Item 16 is based on data from the Narcotics Register.

Exhibit 5 (continued)

8. Primary Job When Working

	%
Higher Executive/ Major Professional	.3
Business Manager/Medium Business Owner	.8
Administrative Personnel/ Small Business Owner	5.0
Clerical/Sales Personnel	26.2
Skilled Manual Worker	16.6
Machine Operator/ Semi-skilled Worker	18.5
Unskilled Worker	23.0
Illegal Activities	.8
Housewife	.2
Student	8.0
Invalid Data	.6

9. Times Treated for Drug Addiction

	%
Never	43.7
Once	20.5
Twice	8.9
3-5 Times	13.5
More than 5 Times	11.3
Invalid Data	1.3

10. Reason for Starting on Drugs

	%
Curiosity	64.7
Kicks	23.6
Medical Problems	1.1
Psychological Problems	6.6
Other	2.4
Invalid Data	1.6

11. Times Arrested

	%
Never	19.8
Once	18.8
Twice	15.6
3-5 Times	21.6
More than 5 Times	23.9
Invalid Data	.3

12. Age at First Arrest

	%
Never or Age Unknown	21.1
Age 7-10	1.2
Age 11-15	19.0
Age 16-18	34.1
Age 19-21	14.2
Over 21	10.1
Invalid Data	.3

13. Longest Period of Being Off Drugs Since Becoming a Regular User

	%
0 Months	24.9
1 Month	15.0
2 Months	7.2
3 Months	6.4
4-6 Months	10.4
More than 6 Months	34.6

14. Status of Parents During First 10 Years of Life

	%
Living Together	64.2
Separated	19.6
Divorced	5.6
Deceased - Mother	2.1
Deceased - Father	3.4
Deceased - Both	1.7
Invalid Data	1.4

Exhibit 5 (continued)

15. Use of Other Drugs

Present Use	Amphetamines	Barbiturates	Marijuana	Inhalants	Psychedelics
Not at All	88.6%	82.9%	65.0%	96.4%	94.6%
Occasionally	7.5	10.7	20.4	2.2	3.1
Often	1.7	1.9	7.3	.6	1.4
Daily	2.0	4.3	7.1	.7	.8
Invalid Data	.2	.2	.2	.1	.1

16. Percentage Distribution of Newly Reported Heroin Abusers, 1964 through 1968, by Age

AGES	1964		1965		1966		1967		1968	
	NUMBER	%	NUMBER	%	NUMBER	%	NUMBER	%	NUMBER	%
TOTALS	5,788	100.0	7,432	100.0	9,582	100.0	8,992	100.0	12,732	100.0
Under 20	471	7.3	760	10.3	976	10.8	1,327	14.7	3,013	23.6
20 - 24	2,220	29.4	2,316	28.3	2,959	31.9	3,063	33.2	4,189	32.9
25 - 29	2,016	22.7	2,169	22.1	2,474	22.6	2,169	22.1	2,236	17.6
30 - 34	1,833	18.2	1,831	17.0	1,919	16.3	1,389	13.4	1,197	9.4
35 - 39	1,077	10.6	1,183	10.7	1,177	9.7	916	8.7	748	5.9
40 and over	815	7.8	854	7.7	905	6.8	632	5.8	558	4.4
Unknown Age	226	4.0	183	3.9	161	1.9	197	2.1	791	6.2

Exhibit 6

ADDICTION CONTROL IN NEW YORK CITY (A)

Results of the DSS Survey of Narcotics Treatment Centers in New York City as of June 1970

Treatment Centers Contacted	Manhattan	Brooklyn	Richmond	Bronx	Queens	Total
Refused to Cooperate	12	1	1	1	2	17
Addressee Unknown	9	6				15
Prevention/Education/ or Guidance Only	4	3		2	1	10
Referrals Only	4			4		8
Induction for Another Center	3	1		1		5
Out-patient Department at Beth-Israel Hospital	9					9
Same as Another Facility	4			1	2	7
Closed	3	1				4
Not a Treatment Center	3	1		3		7
No Program at Present	1			1		2
	52	13	1	13	5	84
Answered	37	23	1	16	7	84
Total	89	36	2	29	12	168

Types of Treatment Facilities	Manhattan	Brooklyn	Richmond	Bronx	Queens	Total
Hospital	10	2	0	4	2	18
Residence House	11	2	1	5	2	21
Residence House with Non-Residents	8	4	0	2	0	14
Storefront	8	15	0	5	3	31
Total	37	23	1	16	7	84

	Hospital	Res. House	Res. House with Non-Residents	Storefront	Total
Length of Time the Programs Have Been in Operation					
Time Open as of 4/15/70 (Years)	4.2	2.3	2.8	1.9	2.6
Centers Reporting	17	20	14	31	82
Capacity of the Treatment Facilities					
Addicts in Treatment	4,010	2,645	1,970	1,530	10,155
Centers Reporting	16	21	14	26	77
Average	250.6	125.9	140.7	58.8	131.9

Exhibit 6 (continued)

	Hosp.	Res. House	Res. House with Non-Residents	Storefront	Total
Number of Addicts on Waiting Lists					
Number on Waiting Lists	7,895	1744	280	323	10,242
Centers Reporting	10	7	4	4	25
Average	789.5	249.1	70.0	80.4	409.7
Number of Centers Reporting No Waiting List	8	12	9	26	55
Number of Full-Time Staff Members					
Number of Staff Members	147	669	418	264	1,498
Centers Reporting	12	20	13	31	76
Average	12.3	33.5	32.2	8.5	19.7
Backgrounds of the Staff Members (Percentage of Facilities)					
Psychologists/ Psychiatrists	44.4	28.6	57.1	12.9	30.9
Social Workers	33.3	14.3	35.7	19.4	23.8
Doctors	44.4	28.6	7.1	3.2	19.0
Nurses	66.7	47.6	14.3	12.9	33.3
Ministers	.0	4.8	.0	3.2	2.4
Ex-Addicts	27.8	76.2	85.7	64.5	63.1
Volunteers	.0	.0	21.4	22.6	11.9
Other	.0	19.0	28.6	32.3	21.4
Types of Treatment Methods (Percent of Facilities)					
Group Therapy	50.0	90.5	92.8	74.2	76.7
Individual Psychotherapy	50.0	42.8	57.1	29.0	41.6
Social Work Counseling	16.7	19.0	21.4	16.1	17,8
Pharmacology, Other than Methadone	38.9	4.8	.0	3.2	10.7
Methadone	55.6	4.8	7.1	6.5	16.7
Encounter Therapy	5.6	19.0	14.3	25.8	19.0
Other	22.3	19.0	35.7	6.5	17.8

Exhibit 6 (continued)

	Hosp.	Res. House	Res. House with Non-Residents	Storefront	Total
Additional Programs Offered at the Treatment Agencies (Percent of Facilities)					
Educational	16.7	52.4	57.1	32.3	38.1
Job Counseling	22.2	14.3	14.3	16.1	16.7
Vocational Training	11.1	14.3	35.7	9.7	15.5
Family Counseling	27	14.3	7.1	29.0	21.4
Physical Education or Recreation		9.5	7.1	3.2	4.8
Referrals	33.3	33.3	28.6	45.2	36.9
Average Length of Time of Treatment Programs					
Months	NA	18.7	22.4	11.0	17.5
Agencies Reporting	NA	18	8	9	35
Number of Addicts between 16 and 18					
Number of Addicts 16-18	299	460	186	229	1,174
Centers Reporting	7	18	11	23	59
Average	42.7	25.6	16.9	9.9	19.9
Centers with 16-18 but Number Unknown	3	2	2	6	13
Centers Which Will Not Accept 16-18	8	1	1	2	12
Number of Addicts under 16					
Number of Addicts	124	133	25	186	468
Number of Centers Reporting	6	8	4	21	39
Average	20.7	16.6	6.3	8.8	12.0
Centers with under 16, but Number Unknown	3	4	4	8	19
Centers Which Will Not Accept under 16	9	9	6	2	26

Exhibit 7

ADDICTION CONTROL IN NEW YORK CITY (A)

Forecast of Sources and Uses of Funds in New York City Narcotics Programs for Fiscal Year 1970-1971

Program	Total	Tax Levy	Tax Levy in Kind	State NACC	Private	Model Cities	OEO*	NIMH*	OCP*	CJCC*
1. ASA Central Staff	$ 1.3	$ 1.3								
2. Therapy Foundation (ASA)	1.7	1.7								
3. Therapy-Hart Island (ASA)	3.2			$ 3.2						
4. After-care Centers (ASA)	1.8	.4						$1.4		
5. Other Community Treatment Programs (ASA)	2.7	.2					$2.2			$.30
6. Prevention and Education (ASA)	42.0	3.4	$6.4	21.0	$8.0	$2.6	.6			
7. Lab for Addictive Drugs (Health Department)	.4	.24		.06				.10		
8. Beth Israel Detox (Priv.)	4.7	2.35		2.35						
9. Addition Rehabilitation and Treatment Corp.(ARTC)(Priv.)	2.65	.70						1.10	$ .40	.45
10. Narcotics Register (Health Department)	.1	.05		.05						
11. Model Cities (Fed.)	.9					.9				
12. NACC Meth. Maint. Program (Private)	9.7			9.7						
13. NACC Demonstration Grants (State/City)	5.9			5.9						
14. NIMH Direct Grants for Pilot Programs (Priv.)	.5							.50		
15. Organization for Community Planning (Fed.)	1.3	.01			.10				1.1	
TOTALS	$78.85	$10.44	$6.4	$42.26	$8.10	$3.5	$2.8	$3.1	$1.5	$.75

*Office of Economic Opportunity, National Institute of Mental Health, Organization for Community Planning, Criminal Justice Coordinating Committee.

APPENDIX A

Benefits from Averting One Man-Year of Heroin Addiction

Individual Monetary Benefits

1. Increased employment earnings. If the median U.S. income levels for various occupations was applied to the addict employment profile (Exhibit 5, Item 8), the average income for the composite profile was \$5,660 per year. To make it more representative of the addict population, this figure was adjusted, first, to reflect the fact that addicts entering treatment programs were employed an average of three months in the preceding year and, second, to take into account three assumptions: (a) wages in New York City were 10% higher than for the country as a whole; (b) the potential earnings for the total addict pool were 20% lower than for the group entering treatment programs; and (c) the post-addiction unemployment rate would be about 10% - twice the national average. The benefit from increased employment earnings, then, was \$3,260 per man-year of addiction averted, calculated as follows:

\$5,660 + 10%(\$5,660) - 20%(\$5,660) - 10%(\$5,660)
- 1/4[\$5,660 + 10%(\$5,660) - 20%(\$5,660] = \$3,260.

2. Reduction in premature deaths. This benefit, brought about by a reduction in premature mortality, was also expressed in terms of additional employment earnings. Unlike the benefit discussed above (which referred to increases in employment during what would otherwise be years of addiction), this benefit applied to increased years of employment beyond this period. Unfortunately, mortality statistics for addicts disaggregated by race, sex, age, and so forth, were unavailable, but actuarial estimates placed the productive lifetime of an addict at one-third that of a normal individual. Placing a value on this decrease was also difficult for while real income of the professional, administrative, and skilled workers was expected to increase over time, the opposite was true with the lower end of the scale. Assuming that these trends cancel each other out, the benefit derived was 1/3[\$5,660 + 10%(\$5,660) - 20%(\$5,660) - 10%(\$5,660)] = 1/3(\$4,530) = \$1,510.

3. Reduction in morbidity. The final benefit expressed in terms of increased employment was a reduction in morbidity attributable to heroin addiction. Based on an annual hepatitis incidence of 3%, a hepatitis treatment cost of approximately \$1,500, a productivity loss of 10% for addict employment (3 months per year with an annual wage of \$4,530), and an increase in employment lifetime of 5%, the net benefit was 3%(\$1,500) + 1/4[10%(\$4,530)] + 5%(\$4,530) = \$384.

4. Reduction in crime. The most visible benefit of averting an additional man-year of heroin addiction was reduction in the amount of crime committed by an addict to support his habit. Although the figures on the cost of an average habit varied dramatically, combining the consumption rates shown in Exhibit 2 with an average price per bag of \$5.00 was felt to be a reasonable approach to the question and yielded a cost per year for heroin of approximately \$10,000 (\$5 per bag x 365 days x 5.6 bags per day). When adjusted for living expenses of \$3,500, the total average support cost was

Appendix A (continued)

$13,500 per year. This figure may have been high given an addict population that spent 30% of its time in jail or treatment programs. Assuming that this segment included a disproportionately larger number of medium and large habit hustlers, then the actual crime figure was probably closer to 60% of $13,500 or $8,100 per addict. Moreover, it was probably naive to assume that once a person was no longer an addict he no longer engaged in criminal activity. A Riker's Island study had shown that in 58% of the cases, criminal activity preceded the heroin addiction. Thus, a more reasonable estimate of this benefit was 1/2 ($8,100) or $4,100.

5. Reduction in enforcement costs. A large reduction in the criminal activities of addicts would also result in a large reduction in costs of police investigation and prosecution, court proceedings, and correctional facilities allocated to heroin addicts. In 1970, the Narcotics Office of the Police Department had a budget of $6.6 million. It was possible, however, to attribute $540 million of the total police budget to crime-related activities; and, with addicts committing an estimated 1/3 to 1/2 of all crimes, from $180 million to $270 million of this larger police budget was allocable to addiction. Using the lower of these two figures and assuming that 50% of all ex-addicts would continue to commit crimes and that there were 100,000 addicts, the savings in police costs would be $900 per addict year of addiction avoided.

Court costs were proportional to the number of arrests, the type of crime, and the disposition of the case. Most addict arrests were for shoplifiting, burglary, robbery, and narcotics offenses (selling and possession). Determination of the cost per addict arrest required assessing the probability that the case would terminate at a particular stage in the judicial process and multiplying that probability times the marginal cost of that stage and all the previous stages. The costs of the latter were rather vague, but $600 per arrest gave a crude basis to work from. If 30% was the probability of being arrested, then 30% ($600) or $180 per man-year of addiction was the court cost. Of this, only half would be saved if the man-year of addiction were avoided.

The final enforcement cost was the cost of incarceration. This varied between $5,000 and $8,000 per year depending on the jail. If addicts spent 20% of their time in jail, the cost was 20% ($6,500) or $1,300, of which one-half, as before, could be attributed to addiction.

The total enforcement cost, then, was $900 + $90 + $650 = $1,640.

6. Reduction in housing deterioration. A great deal of building abandonment in ghetto areas was traceable to addicts who inhabited a vacant apartment, started a fire, and caused the destruction of that apartment. As individual apartments were destroyed, the building became vacant and deteriorated. Vacant buildings were abandoned at a rate of 3,000 each year with an average demolition cost of $5,000. If each dwelling averaged six living units, each with a rental value of $100 per month, then the loss to the city's housing stock (using rental value as a measure) was $1,200 x 18,000 = $21.6 million plus a demolition cost of $5,000 x 3,000 = $15 million for a total

Appendix A (continued)

cost of $36.6 million. This figure was somewhat conservative based on the contagion effect of one vacant building. RAND Corporation estimated that 1/3 of all building abandonments were a result of addict activity. This came to $12.2 million or $122 per addict per year. By adding on marginal costs of $42 for the extra fire equipment needed in these areas, abandonment costs came to $164 per addict year.

Summary of Monetary Benefits

Increased Employment Earnings	$ 3,260
Reduction in Premature Deaths	1,510
Reduction in Morbidity	386
Reduction in Crime	4,100
Reduction in Enforcement Costs	1,640
Reduction in Housing Deterioration	164
	$11,060
Contagion Factor[1] (1.25)	2,765
Total per addiction year	$13,825

Other Benefits

1. Welfare costs. Recently, a growing percentage of recognized heroin addicts had been receiving welfare support ranging from $1,900 to $3,000 per year. No benefit from reducing this amount, however, was computed since it was considered an income redistribution effect.

2. Migration. There was also a cost that reflected the migration of residents out of the city and their replacement by immigrants with lower income levels and greater need for municipal assistance. This cost might also be reflected in lower property values, decreased retail sales, and a smaller municipal tax base. The costs of increased crime had already been calculated, but in this case it was the fear of crime that was the real cost to the city.

3. Impact on addicts and addict victims. Also excluded from the calculation of monetary benefits was the cost of physical and psychological damage to the victims of addict crime. These could include hospitalization or other medical costs as well as loss of wages. Another benefit excluded was the change in the quality of life experienced by an addict when he is cured.

[1]An important effect of preventing an additional man-year of heroin addiction was reduction in the contagion aspect of addiction as the disease spread through a neighborhood. Little quantitative information was known about the epidemiology of addiction which was expected to vary non-linearly by neighborhood, by addict age, and by absolute and relative number of addicts in the neighborhood. In the absence of such information, it was conservatively estimated that elimination of four man-years of addiction resulted in the eradication of one additional potential man-year of addiction. Thus a contagion factor of 1.25 was applied to total benefits from averting one man-year of addiction.

ADDICTION CONTROL IN NEW YORK CITY (B)

By the late 1960s, heroin addiction was one of the most pressing problems facing the city of New York. Its magnitude and costs were increasing each year in almost epidemic proportions; yet the resources allocated to combat heroin had not expanded accordingly. In December 1970, the Department of Social Services had estimated that only 10% to 15% of the city's addict population was receiving some form of treatment. The methods being used ran the gamut from involuntary incarceration to carefully managed encounter groups and were sponsored and operated by a wide variety of public and private organizations [see Addiction Control in New York City (A)]. One of the largest, most successful and widely publicized modalities was methadone maintenance, a treatment developed by Dr. Vincent Dole and Dr. Marie Nyswander, research physicians at Rockefeller University, under a grant from the city's Health Research Council in 1964. Over the years, this program had expanded through contracts between the Department of Hospitals and the Beth-Israel Medical Center (which was the first and largest program) and Bronx State Hospital where a smaller effort was undertaken. Additional funds were provided by the New York State Narcotics Addiction Control Commision (NACC). By September 1970, there were approximately 2,900 patients receiving methadone through one of the five in-patient treatment centers or 22 ambulatory and out-patient facilities involved in the program.

Methadone was an addictive drug that blocked the euphoric action of heroin for approximately 24 hours. This property allowed an addict's craving for heroin to be controlled on a continuing basis through regular, carefully managed, oral dosages of methadone. Properly administered, the drug had no major side effects, although it induced withdrawal symptoms when withheld. There were two characteristics of methadone maintenance to which some people objected: first, methadone, like heroin, was addictive; second, methadone could be abused. (Taken intravenously or in improper dosages orally, it could produce its own euphoric high.) In addition, methadone (while inexpensive) was a very prolonged treatment; not only because the drug was addictive, but because a patient's heroin craving was likely to reoccur if the methadone was stopped even after several years of maintenance. The Dole-Nyswander method consisted of three treatment phases:

<u>Phase I</u>: The addict was started on methadone, and the dosage gradually increased until the maintenance level was reached. About 80% of the patients went through Phase I on an ambulatory

(outpatient) basis. This phase took approximately four to six weeks, during which the patient reported in once or twice a day. Advice and support were given by a counselor and by a "research assistant" who was also a methadone patient.

Phase II: The patient reported to a clinic five days a week, received his medication, provided a urine specimen, and met with counselors and others for any required assistance. With the consent of the staff, the patient could arrange to report to the clinic less often. Phase II lasted for approximately 12 months.

Phase III: The patient reported only once a week, received his medication for the week and provided a urine sample. The services of a counselor were still available to him if needed.

Both the Beth-Israel and Bronx State programs were considered experimental and were the subject of rigorous evaluation. At Dr. Dole's request, an independent research committee, with Dr. Henry Brill of Columbia University as chairman and Dr. Frances Gearing of the University's School of Public Health and Administrative Medicine as director, had been established at the inception of the methadone programs. To measure success, the committee relied on four indicators:

1. Freedom from heroin "hunger" as measured by repeated, periodic "clean" urine specimens.

2. Decrease in antisocial behavior as measured by arrest and/or incarceration frequency.

3. Increase in social productivity as measured by employment or schooling or vocational training.

4. Recognition of, and willingness to accept help for excessive use of alcohol, other drugs, or other psychiatric problems.

In a report to the NACC on March 31, 1970, Dr. Gearing and her evaluation group drew the following conclusions:

> None of the (80% of) patients who have remained in the program have reverted to regular heroin use, and the majority have become self-supporting. Their pattern of arrests has decreased remarkably. This is in sharp contrast to the patients' previous records, and also in comparison with a group...who have left the program. A small proportion of patients (8%) present continued problems with abuse of amphetamines or barbiturates, and another six per cent demonstrate problems with chronic alcohol abuse...(A)ny treatment

> program using methadone maintenance must be prepared to provide a variety of supportive services and should be equipped to deal with problems of mixed drug abuse, chronic alcoholism, psychiatric problems, and a host of other social problems.
>
> Many questions...remain unanswered with reference to the role of methadone maintenance in the attack on the problem of heroin addiction; nevertheless, the methadone maintenance program continues to demonstrate that among heroin addicts who meet the program criteria [18 years old or older and a minimum of two years of heroin addiction], it has been successful, and should be continued and expanded.

In February, a month before the Gearing report was submitted, strong support for methadone maintenance had come from another quarter: The New York State Medical Society had passed a resolution endorsing the Dole-Nyswander treatment and urging the expansion of methadone facilities in the city. Based on these favorable reactions, the NACC decided to increase its support of methadone maintenance programs (MMPs) and research activities to $15 million during the fiscal year beginning April 1, 1970. This amount was more than double the expenditures for the current fiscal year.

By early 1970, the city government's own experience and involvement with methadone was quite limited. The Addiction Services Agency (ASA), created in 1967 as the co-ordinating and planning agency for all the city's drug rehabilitation and treatment programs, was concentrating primarily on educational efforts and non-drug treatment modalities. Overall, the city's narcotics control program was piecemeal and unorganized. Testifying before a Senate Sub-Committee on narcotics addiction, Mayor Lindsay pointed out:

> Today, the federal effort, such as it is, is hopelessly fragmented. No fewer than four separate agencies fund programs in my own city, each with a different viewpoint, a different set of standards and priorities, and a different manual of procedures. Lacking coordination at the federal level, there is an appalling waste of time and energy as local officials attempt to weave these contributions into a focused program.

This pattern was repeated at the state and local levels. The city's Criminal Justice Coordinating Committee, Health Services Administration, Addiction Services Agency, Police Department, and Narcotics Control Council as well as the State Narcotic Addiction Control Commission and several private groups all had a hand in formulating policy and/or directing programs [See Addiction Control in New York City (A)].

A City Methadone Program

When Mayor Lindsay began his second term in January 1970, he appointed Gordon Chase as the new Administrator for the Health Services Administration (HSA). Chase had formerly been Deputy Administrator for Management in the City's Human Resources Administration (HRA)[1] where he had earned a reputation for management competence. He brought with him to HSA a number of his staff including Chip Raymond, a proven trouble-shooter, who had successfully and quickly straightened out the finances of HRA's Neighborhood Youth Corps after several million dollars of government funds had been "misplaced." At HSA, Raymond became involved in one of Chase's top priority tasks - rapid expansion of the city's response to its narcotics problem. Because of the support that the Dole-Nyswander program had been receiving and the favorable disposition of the Mayor's Narcotics Control Council toward methadone maintenance, Chase focused his attention on ways to achieve a dramatic citywide increase in MMP capacity. At first, he and Raymond explored the idea of forming a New York City Methadone Commission that would bring together those people in the city with the most experience and expertise with methadone and would (i) set up a central staff to coordinate all methadone programs in the city and (ii) oversee an expansion effort that built on existing MMP facilities and organization. In early March, this concept was rejected as administratively cumbersome. With speed the overriding consideration, Chase recommended implementation of a massive, city-managed methadone program designed to accommodate 20% of the addict population (now estimated to total more than 100,000). This would require 200 methadone clinics, each serving 100 patients. Funds would be sought from NACC.

By the end of March 1970, Chase's staff had developed a first cut of HSA's proposal for the city's MMP. Almost $25 million would be spent over the course of three years to establish facilities for 20,000 addicts.

In April Chase convened an interagency committee to work out a final proposal for MMP. The group included Chip Raymond, Andy Kerr from the Project Management Staff (PMS),[2] and representatives of the Bureau of the Budget, the Mayor's Office, and the Addiction Services Agency. In the days that followed, two factors forced the group to reduce substantially the size of the MMP program outlined in the draft proposal. First, the NACC

---

[1]HRA was responsible for managing public assistance, manpower, community development and youth programs. The Addiction Services Agency (ASA) was also part of HRA.

[2]PMS was a group of professional project managers, attached to the Mayor's Office and reporting to the Deputy Mayor, the Mayor, and the Director of the Budget Bureau. They worked with and assisted city agencies in the development, planning, and implementation of high priority projects and programs. Most projects assigned to the Project Management Staff were large, complex, had severe time constraints, and required the coordination of activities of more than one city agency. The group's responsibility included design, planning, development, and implementation of projects; design of the monitoring and control systems; and the regular reporting to the Mayor and other top city officials of the plans and status of projects. Chase had requested that PMS help plan, schedule, and monitor the methadone project. Prime responsibility for project management, however, would remain with Chase's staff at HSA.

announced awards of $2.7 million and $1.0 million for expansion of methadone activities at Beth-Israel and Bronx State Hospital, respectively. This meant less NACC money would be available to fund the HSA proposal and also that Chase's goal of 20,000 addicts in treatment would be met, at least partially, by expansion of the two existing programs. The second factor was PMS' estimates of the time it would take to open a series of clinics. These estimates left no doubt that the pace of openings required by a program to accommodate 20,000 patients in three years was simply not feasible. Given the number of agencies involved, the amount of space and renovations that would be required, and other matters that would have to be tended to, the best that HSA could do would be to open 6 clinics within 26 weeks of proposal submission and 42 clinics by the end of the program year (the program year beginning with the approval of the grant by NACC). Accordingly, a proposal was drafted and submitted to NACC (on June 5) calling for establishment of 50 out-patient clinics, each with a capacity of 100, and six in-patient facilities and requesting $7.6 million during the first fiscal year. Even this smaller program proved more than NACC wished to support. The city was asked to reduce the size of its project and submit a revised proposal. This was done, and in July, NACC agreed to fund a program that would cost $4.5 million during its initial year of operation (Exhibit 2) and $4.3 million annually in succeeding years. Key goals of the program were to:

- Establish a Bureau of Methadone Maintenance in the Department of Health with key staff hired by September 1970.

- Establish 20 out-patient clinics by February 1971, as follows:

Clinics	1-2	in October
"	3-6	in November
"	7-9	in December
"	10-15	in January
"	16-20	in February

- Open an intake unit on Riker's Island by October 1970 for the purpose of counseling prisoners about the maintenance program and screening and processing applicants for admission.

- Establish one in-patient treatment unit by October 1970.

- Create a mobile intake unit to screen and process applicants by November 1970.

- Establish a fully operational urinalysis program by November 1970.

- Achieve a patient capacity of 2,500 by February 1971.

- Have 1,400 patients in treatment by March 31, 1971.

Staffing requirements for the program are shown in Exhibit 3.

Plans to create a Bureau of Methadone Maintenance (BMM) had been laid in May following a mayoral decision to give administrative responsibility for the city's methadone program to HSA rather than the Addiction Services Agency. ASA would still be the channel through which funds flowed from NACC to HSA and the new bureau. Dr. Robert Newman had been selected to head the BMM and took an active role in developing the proposal and negotiating final terms with the NACC. Chip Raymond was appointed Administrative Assistant to the Director. Newman had just finished directing the National Nutrition Survey in New York and, previously, had served as City Health Officer in two of the most addiction-prone areas in the city. One HSA spokesmen described him as a "fiery young doctor" and give him high marks for his management of the nutrition survey.

The basic form of the program that Newman would head was as follows: Each clinic would be operated by one of the city's voluntary (private) or municipal hospitals under a contract with the Department of Health. Some clinics would be ambulatory units in the hospital itself, some would be located in district health centers run by the Department of Health, and others would be located in rented space. Location of the facility would be subject to negotiation with each hospital but initial expectations were that ten to fourteen rented spaces would be needed. Patients for each clinic would be supplied by the program's two intake units - clinics would not be allowed to accept any patients on their own. In addition, to ease the problems of a tight schedule for clinic openings, the city's program would take only a few Phase I (of the Dole-Nyswander treatment) patients on its own until February 1971. Beth-Israel, which was currently inducting about 120 addicts per month, had agreed to supply the city's needs for Phase II patients (see Exhibit 4).

The Central Staff of the Bureau of Methadone Maintenance would have three broad responsibilities: directing the set-up phase of the entire program; managing the two intake units on a continuing basis; and long-term monitoring and control of overall program performance. The specific tasks required to meet these responsibilities are outlined in Exhibit 5. Hospitals that agreed to operate a methadone clinic would be expected to recruit and hire clinic personnel, provide "direction" to the clinic, and make available essential back-up medical and pharmacy services including drug storage. The clinics, themselves, under the direction of a physician would be charged with (i) regulating patients on methadone in accordance with the procedures and standards developed at Beth-Israel, (ii) providing patients with needed counseling services, (iii) collecting urine samples from patients at prescribed frequencies, and (iv) maintaining records and reporting to the data collection and evaluation units.

Other organizations also had important roles in the city's MMP. Rockefeller University and the Columbia University School of Public Health and Administrative Medicine had agreed to serve as the data collection and evaluation units, respectively. The city's Department of Real Estate would have to negotiate the leases and renovation contracts for all rented space. A large urinalysis capability was to be developed by the Bureau of Laboratories. Finally, many city and state agencies would have to provide approvals of one kind or another and the process of obtaining these approvals would have to be repeated for each clinic.

PMS found it useful to describe the MMP effort in two phases. The first covered the opening of clinics 1-6 and included the initial set up of BMM, itself (see Exhibit 6); the second was the iterative process that would be necessary to open each additional clinic after the start up effort was complete (see Exhibit 7). Setting up each clinic required completion of a number of key tasks:

- Negotiating a contract with the hospital.
- Obtaining contract approvals from the
  - (i) Bureau of the Budget
  - (ii) Board of Estimate
  - (iii) Corporation Counsel
- Identifying private space, if necessary.
- Obtaining lease approval.
- Renovating the space.
- Hiring clinic personnel
  - (i) Medical Directors
  - (ii) Unit Supervisors
- Training clinic personnel.

PMS' first project plan, issued in August, indicated several potential problem areas that might impede progress as scheduled; among them were community resistance, the availability of qualified personnel, and difficulties in locating space.

Opening the First Four Clinics

Even before the final contract with NACC had been signed or the project plan formulated and issued, work had begun to implement the city's MMP. In April, Newman and Raymond had sent letters to over 80 hospitals, explaining the program and asking if they would be interested in sponsoring one or more methadone clinics. The response was disappointingly light, and, during the summer, the two men made personal visits to the hospitals to explain the city's program and ask for help. The returns improved, and each time that a hospital agreed to operate a clinic, Newman and Raymond were joined by Alan Gibbs, an assistant administrator from HSA, who took charge of contract negotiations. The contracts set forth the hospital's responsibilities (as outlined above) and specified a time schedule for opening the clinic and taking patients. The usual intake rate was 20 per month until 100 were in treatment. Also included in the contract was the date (one month before clinic opening) when the clinic's staff should be hired. The hospital could cancel the contract whenever it wanted to. Because Newman and Raymond were trying hard to convince as many hospitals as possible to locate their own clinic space, contract negotiations frequently took longer than anticipated.

During these early months, June Fields (who had been assigned to the project by PMS) and Bruce Gantt were also active on the MMP project. Gantt had joined the BMM to take responsibility for setting up the intake units and the training programs. Chip Raymond described the group's activities as follows:

> My role, essentially, was jack-of-all-trades. I got involved in pretty much every aspect of the program from setting up the pharmacy system to working on urinalysis, to being responsible for setting up the central office, negotiating contracts--a whole series of little petty things--being responsible for getting all the personnel through the Department of Personnel. Newman's basic responsibility was going out and selling the program, negotiating contracts, and recruiting doctors which was a very big problem, initially. Gibbs was pretty much involved in setting up the contract with NACC and negotiating all the contracts with the hospitals and handling everything with the different city agencies to get the contracts approved. June Fields helped us in just kind of overseeing the program and feeding out reports and kind of checking up on everybody to see where they were. She helped us get things through the Board of Estimate and the Bureau of the Budget and helped us set up the central office--pushing equipment through and things like that. Bruce Gantt worked on setting up the intake unit and was responsible for training.

By mid-September, when the first project status report was issued, these efforts had produced significant progress. Contracts had been negotiated with 7 hospitals for 11 outpatient clinics. Most personnel for the first two clinics had been recruited. In the central office a number of key positions had been filled, although neither a deputy director nor a coordinator of community relations had been found. PMS concluded that all 20 outpatient clinics would be open, as scheduled, by February 5, 1971.

Despite this progress, there had been slippages. All were slight and a variety of causes could be identified. Delays in ordering equipment and planning laboratory renovations were affecting the urinalysis program. Nothing at all had been done to start the inpatient clinic, largely because no one at BMM had had time, but also because Dr. Newman was no longer sure that one was needed. Because of the slowdown in the rate of contract negotiations, clinics five through eight would not be opened as originally scheduled. Finally, the first four clinics all had been affected by community sentiment. Delafield Hospital - which was sponsoring three of the first four units - decided, unilaterally, to set back the opening date from mid-October to October 31. This would coincide with the opening of a community-sponsored detoxification unit that the hospital was also going to operate. Delafield's administration feared adverse reaction if the city's clinics were opened first. The fourth clinic, at Jamaica Hospital, met with more specific hostility. As Raymond described it:

> The problem was that the hospital was trying to do some blockbusting out there and we got in the middle of it. They owned a building on a residential street that was partially occupied as a residence. They were going to move the clinic into the other half of that building without ever consulting the community at all; so the community heard about it and really raised hell at a very large meeting. Newman went out and spoke to them and agreed with the decision of the community that the clinic should not go there. The hospital found a very adequate two-story building right behind their hospital that they owned. It borders on the same street but the entrance is around the corner and now the community's perfectly happy.

PMS rescheduled major milestones as shown below:

	Original Plan	Revised	Number of Weeks' Slippage
Central Staff Hired	October 2	-	0
Clinics 1-4 Opened	October 16	October 30	2*
Inpatient Treatment Unit Opened	October 23	December 4	6
Riker's Island Intake Unit Operational	October 30	-	0
Clinics 5-8 Opened	November 6	November 27	3

	Original Plan	Revised	Number of Weeks' Slippage
Central Intake Unit Operational	November 20	-	0
Urinalysis Program Fully Operational	November 27	December 11	2
Clinics 9-14 Opened	January 15, 1971	January 1, 1971	-2
Clinics 16-20 Opened	February 5, 1971	-	0

*Note: Although there was two weeks' slippage in the scheduled opening date, the number of clinics to open in October increased from two to four.

In the weeks that followed, effort focused on negotiating contracts for the remaining nine clinics and on completing the steps necessary to open the first four units. Raymond recalls that "we were [very] concerned about getting those first four open." By mid-October, contracts for all twenty units had been signed (see Exhibit 8). Private space, supplied by the city, would be required at only six locations instead of the ten to fourteen expected. Two of the first four clinics (Group I in Exhibit 8) would be located in hospital-owned space and two in city-operated health centers. Most clinic personnel for the four Group I units had been hired and were ready to begin training.

Training for the medical staff of each clinic was to be carried out on a part-time basis at Beth-Israel over a four-week period. This would permit the staff to work simultaneously setting up the clinics and learning the Dole-Nyswander treatment. Raymond commented on the training arrangements:

> There was a verbal contract. We spoke to Harvey Gollance [Hospital Administrator at Beth-Israel] in August and he said that they'd be delighted to do the training and so we set it up with their head of social services and told them we'd be sending so many people. We talked about something in the range of $60,000 that we were going to give to Beth-Israel to do our training, and Harvey Gollance said "Oh, no! We don't need any money." So we knocked the money out of the contract [with NACC].

Dr. Newman described what happened as follows:

> Beth-Israel, with an extensive network of treatment units of the same type that we were implementing, had a huge resource in terms of staff and facilities which we thought would allow us to give newly recruited staff members exposure to exactly what this system is; to learn first hand from nurses what the nursing procedures are; to learn first hand from the doctors how the orders are written and what medication problems they run into.

> The first problem was that Beth-Israel grossly underestimated our ability to open new units. They kept telling us no matter how many staff people we wanted trained, they would train them; and all of a sudden the day came that we said, "We have fifteen people we'd like trained. Where do you want them to go?" And Beth-Israel said, "Impossible! Maybe two or three we might be able to handle."
>
> So we arranged to have the first group spend a little time in the Beth-Israel clinics, some time in the Bronx State clinics, and a lot of time in the central office talking to us about paper work, procedures, and what we wanted done and how we wanted to do it.
>
> Then, within a couple of weeks after it turned out that Beth-Israel was not going to be able to handle our training, we made an arrangement with Bronx State. They have a very well-organized, tightly controlled training program which is a two-week, intensive nine-to-five, five-days-a-week operation. They agreed to take our people but they had to make a commitment to be in the training session the full time. So we had a handful of people go through the Bronx State program but their rigidity, in terms of attendance, was impossible for us because at the same time that we were training people, we also had them opening up units and starting to treat patients.
>
> This is why the next logical step was to run our own two-week training program. . . . We still do it that way.

Fearing that Beth-Israel's inability to meet the city's requirements would be repeated when it came time to supply large numbers of Phase II patients, BMM abandoned its plan not to accept Phase I patients. This placed further demands on the Bureau's training program, for Phase I patients were expected to be more difficult to manage and would require clinic physicians to be familiar with procedures for bringing them up to maintenance dosage levels. Nevertheless, on November 4, BMM's central intake unit was opened and began inducting addicts (directly from the street) for treatment at Group I clinics; and on November 17 and 18, despite training delays, the Group I units began operation - four and a half weeks behind the schedule outlined in the PMS project plan.

Opening the Remaining Clinics

Besides the opening of the first four clinics, two other significant events took place in November: the Riker's Island intake unit was activated and plans for an inpatient unit were abandoned. NACC agreed to let funds earmarked for the inpatient clinic be used, instead, for two additional outpatient units, bringing the total to twenty-two. Despite these accomplishments, when the project group turned its attention to the remaining clinics, it was clear that further slippage had taken place. The status report issued on November 20 indicated that the hiring of key central staff was now seven weeks late. As before, the cause was failure to find either a deputy director for BMM or a community relations representative. The urinalysis program, too, had continued to slip since the last report. While the Bureau of Laboratories was successfully handling the current load of urinalyses, no renovation plans had been made or equipment orders placed preparatory to handling the much larger requirements that would have to be met in the future. The two agencies involved, HSA and the Department of Public Works had yet to agree on the amount of new capacity that would be needed. Finally, all clinics in Groups II through V were even further behind their initial schedules (see Exhibit 9).

By January 1971, contracts had been negotiated for the two new outpatient clinics; but the accomplishment of other major milestones had slipped further behind. Central staff hiring was now fifteen weeks delinquent; the urinalysis unit eleven weeks late; and clinics in Groups II through V further in arrears (see Exhibit 9). The reasons for slippage in central staff hiring and the urinalysis program remained unchanged. For the eighteen clinics (as had been the case with the first four clinics), continued delinquency was attributable to several causes, the most important being the availability of space, the pace at which hospitals were recruiting personnel, and continued community resistance.

Space Availability. For those clinics where private space was to be rented by the city, the Department of Real Estate was responsible for locating suitable quarters, negotiating leases, providing the Board of Estimate with information necessary to approve each lease, and carrying out all the other paper work that was required. PMS pointed out in its Project Plan that:

> The speed at which space for facilities is found and leases negotiated will most likely be the determining factor in setting the level of the program. The grant. . .provides for 20 clinics, but additional money has been reserved by the (NACC) and will be given to the City if the program progresses according to the planned time frame.

The Municipal Services Administration, of which the Department of Real Estate was a part, was described by a member of the Project Management Staff as "one of the most important and least efficient administrations in the city. The departments in MSA are old-line, paper-pushing agencies where only long-time bureaucrats, who know their way around every dusty desk, can get anything done. The complexity of the paper traveling through and the nature of the services performed give it great potential for losing something in the shuffle." The Department of Real Estate, under the direction of Ira Duchan, was an agency where verbal negotiations and personal contacts built up over long periods of time were believed to be the most important aspects of getting anything done. Duchan joined the DRE in 1946, worked his way up through the civil service ladder without ever leaving the department, and was appointed its commissioner by Mayor Lindsay.

In October, when the requirements for rented space were firmed up, Alan Gibbs sent a letter to Duchan requesting that DRE begin locating facilities for eight clinics. The letter indicated where the spaces should be, the physical properties called for, and included a schedule showing when the space would be needed to meet program deadlines. It also requested that someone in the department be assigned to the methadone project on a full-time basis, a method frequently used for large projects. The letter was followed by a meeting between June Fields and the Commissioner to discuss DRE's participation in the project. She described her experiences with DRE as follows:

> They were not very cooperative. We had to have a meeting with them and say, "Look, this is a Mayoral priority," before they would assign anyone. We did get someone assigned, but that person had a lot of other responsibilities, too, and he really didn't spend much time on the methadone program. We've never had the Mayor's office talk directly to the Commissioner [of Real Estate]; I arranged the meeting and I've talked to the Commissioner several times. There were also several letters that tried to say that we certainly appreciated the work they were doing but that it wasn't quite enough.
>
> An agency like that can throw a lot of monkey wrenches just by being unwilling to be hurried. It may not even be a question of whether or not they've found the space; there are other steps that they are responsible for like negotiating and preparing the lease, preparing a resolution for the Board of Estimate, carrying it to the Board, and defending it. So you have to really be on good terms with them. If the space has been negotiated on a Tuesday and you want to get it on the Wednesday Board of Estimate calendar, someone has to work very hard to get a resolution ready, and he's not going to do it if you're always dumping on him.
>
> They were asked in October to find eight spaces; ultimately, one space actually turned into a city lease. As a result, other agencies had to be deeply involved in looking for space. We suggested maybe forty to fifty different sites for the real estate department to look at, most of which were obviously unsuitable.[1] What we were doing in suggesting sites was trying to get the DRE people, who were professionals, to say how lousy Fields was at doing this and begin to do it themselves. But they didn't. This is not to say that they didn't work, but it was very haphazard and only done under pressure with someone else taking substantial parts of the initiative.

---

[1]Fields began her own facilities search in January.

> It's hard for me to think of how it could have been done differently. The man who was the representative of Real Estate apparently understood that methadone was very high priority and talked about it as being high priority, but he had a lot of other things to do. A call from the Mayor's office might have helped but it may just be that DRE's whole sense of priorities is not budged by outsiders. If they're used to taking things as they come, and someone inserts something and says it's an "expedite," it may just jar them so much that they won't even talk about it.

The January 15 status report identified as the project's key problem the failure to find space for seven clinics. Already, the scheduled opening of three clinics had been delayed for lack of space. Several hospitals, at HSA's urging, agreed to open their units in temporary space but, without exception, these facilities would be inadequate in the long run and permanent space would still have to be found. In addition to looking for space herself, June Fields requested help from several community groups, and the DRE placed ads in the newspapers.

Recruiting. Each hospital was responsible for recruiting and hiring all personnel for its clinic(s). Physicians, unit supervisers, and research assistants had to be approved by Dr. Newman. (Research assistants, all of whom were Phase III patients, were interviewed by a member of the central staff who was also a patient.) In fact, Dr. Newman rarely disapproved of anyone that a hospital said it wished to hire, and, throughout the project, he and Raymond made substantial efforts to help the hospitals recruit their staffs. They gathered resumes for various positions, placed ads in the newspapers, and [Dr. Newman] made frequent appearances before medical groups and societies. Still, very few hospitals met the contractually specified deadlines for staff hiring. In some instances, this occurred because the hospital refused to put anyone on its payroll until clinic facilities had been located. In others, the only cause seemed to be the absence of any sense of urgency regarding clinic opening dates.

June Fields attributed this problem to the large number of hospitals involved and the fact that each one had its own way of doing things. Even though the contracts were very specific, she believed that:

> The effort to get people to live up to the contract was relatively soft because lots of people thought the hospitals were doing the city a favor.

Commenting on the same topic, Dr. Newman said:

> The main problem we have is avoiding the hospitals' and unit staffs' impression that we're just a funding agency; because on paper that's what it looks like. It looks as though we're like OEO; that we give a hospital a contract to run a methadone clinic and that at the end of six months or a year, we might come in and look around and see how they're doing and decide whether or not to refund them. That's exactly the opposite of what we really are.

By mid-January, all the staff for Group II clinics were hired, but accomplishment of this milestone had been delinquent, and their training consequently was seven weeks in arrears. Recruiting and hiring of Group III staff had also slipped a total of seven weeks.

Community Resistance. The desirability of community support for the city's MMP was something of which HSA had been keenly aware from the beginning. In late May 1970, Dr. James Haughton, First Deputy Administrator at HSA, met with representatives of the Addiction Services Agency to discuss the problem. He reported to Chase:

> We had hoped that it might be possible to build upon the city's existing community groups involved in the addiction problem, but it quickly became apparent that since these groups were developed by ASA and committed to the Therapy House[1] rehabilitation approach, it would not be possible to involve them in the methadone program.
>
> The representative of ASA regretfully informed us that the staff of that agency are so committed to abstinence programs that they have instilled in their community groups an absolute and complete resistance to any kind of substitution program. He felt therefore that an attempt to use these groups would only increase the general community's resistance to the methadone program.

In June, HSA's proposal to NACC described the agency's plans for a public information and community participation program of its own as follows:

> To generate the broadest possible public understanding of the methadone maintenance treatment program, a major community-based public information effort, directed by the central unit, will be undertaken. Community education workshops and seminars will be established to provide citizens with information about the methadone program. Community relations representatives will work with community groups to involve them in this educational effort. Mass media will also be utilized to extend the outreach of the program and inform the public as to its goals and procedures. The unit will also dispense general information regarding methadone programs, including criteria for admission and locations of facilities.

As the MMP program got under way, however, very little was done to meet the community relations aspects of these plans. Instead, it was left up to the hospitals to establish and maintain good rapport with area residents and to pave the way for the new clinics. Some expended considerable effort doing

---

[1]Disguised name. Therapy House treatment is based on helping heroin addicts abstain from taking any drugs whatsoever.

this - working either through the appropriate neighborhood health councils[1] or the hospitals' own community liaison apparatus. Some, on the other hand, simply disregarded community reaction altogether.

One example of a hospital that did not consult the community - Jamaica (Group I) - has already been described. Another was Bronx Lebanon, which had agreed to open two Group III clinics. Operating almost completely without help from the central office, the hospital located one space on its own premises and one in a building in the South Bronx already leased to the city for other purposes. (The Department of Health planned to take over the lease.) "Things were going along fine with this space, internally," said June Fields, "when suddenly there began to be a whole network of calls from South Bronx residents to Bob Newman and Chip Raymond, all dumping on the Department of Health." The reason for the opposition was not any objection to methadone. It was based, instead, on the pending opening, some two blocks away, of a methadone clinic sponsored by Bronx State Hospital. Bronx State had worked closely with various neighborhood groups for over six months and it was these same groups that resented the city's failure to consult them about its program. Their resentment was sufficient to force Bronx Lebanon to abandon the South Bronx unit and open both its clinics as a combined unit in the remaining space. This meant inadequate facilities for both clinics as well as the absence of a city-sponsored clinic in an area where one was badly needed.

In contrast to Jamaica and Bronx Lebanon, Long Island College Hospital in South Brooklyn was highly sensitive to local feelings. According to June Fields:

> There are a lot of groups in the South Brooklyn area because it covers a lot of little communities--Red Hook, Brooklyn Heights, Cobble Hill, and others. When they first began with the methadone program, the hospital asked the ghetto medicine involvement committee to suggest locations for three clinics and the committee recommended one in Red Hook, one in Gowanus and one in Cobble Hill.
>
> We moved along on the first clinic [in Cobble Hill] in space that had been found by a member of the committee, but when it came time to open, there was a lot of controversy because it was right across the street from a Catholic elementary school.

Chip Raymond elaborated:

> There was a tremendous meeting and Newman went out and spoke and pretty much quelled most of the fears about putting it in there. Their greatest concern was bringing addicts in

[1] Neighborhood health councils usually had representatives from local community development corporations, poverty programs, health and medical facilities, and so forth.

> from outside the community; but we had about ninety applications and seventy-five of them were from people living within five blocks of the clinic location. That killed most of the objections, but about two weeks later, someone threw a couple of ash cans through the clinic windows. That was a little disturbing and we had to have a couple more meetings about it.

Trouble also developed with the second Long Island College clinic planned for the Red Hook area. Again, June Fields commented:

> There were a lot of community contacts and continuing discussions with people like the doctors who headed the Red Hook Neighborhood Health Council. Chip talked to the Health Council and the Tenants' Association and I negotiated with a sort of neighborhood council that had representatives from a number of local agencies.
>
> The hospital wanted to open this clinic in the hospital, itself, but the Neighborhood Health Council wanted it in the local health center. The Council won and then they thought that local people should be hired to staff it. They advertised locally but found out that most of the people who showed up were not acceptable for clinic jobs. So they had to get the resumes that the hospital had gathered and do the job over again. It all took time.

In Fields' view, the delays caused by these community troubles were hard to assess but she thought they ranged from a few weeks, in the case of Bronx Lebanon, to well over a month for the first Long Island College unit. Dr. Newman recalled the Long Island College problem as follows:

> The hospital made sure that they met and that we met with every single community group they could think of. So we had a tremendous amount of prior contact. We sought these groups out. After meeting with "eighteen" different community groups, three days before the clinic was to open there was another group that either was created specifically for this purpose or that came out of nowhere and said, "Listen, nobody asked us and we don't want it!"
>
> The complaints were always the same: "Do anything you want with these junkies, just don't do it in our neighborhood!"
>
> The need for community relations people is not as clearcut as you might think from reading the project plan. June wrote the plan and she felt that there was a tremendous need for community relations. I had mixed feelings about it, initially; during the first months of the program, I became even

even more ambivalent about it. First, you have to assume that it's possible to anticipate community problems; second you have to assume that it's feasible for a community relations person to handle those problems; third, you have to be confident that your community man won't create problems where there wouldn't have been any. Whenever I go to a community meeting, I always ask myself if we could have avoided this with a community relations person or if that person could have replaced me at this meeting.

We're not telling the community that this is the solution to their drug problems, because it's not. It probably has virtually no impact on their drug problems. This is not a community-oriented program; methadone is a means of treating individual patients. So it has a clinical rather than a public health orientation, and as long as this is true, why should a community group any more than a professional group decide what's best for the patient.

* * * * *

The influence of space availability, recruiting, and community resistance continued to be felt in the months that followed. On March 26, the PMS project status report showed that the urinalysis unit was operating at the capacity needed,[1] but that clinics in Groups III through V were now 10 1/2, 9, and 14 1/2 weeks behind schedule, respectively (see Exhibit 9). Community problems were affecting both the Mary Immaculate unit and the second clinic at Long Island Jewish. (A comparison of the planned and actual rates of patient intake since the beginning of the program is set forth in Exhibit 12.)

Evaluation and Control

The evaluation and control function for the city MMP was to include both an external and an internal component. The first would examine the outcome of the MMP in relation to society; the second would assess the effectiveness and efficiency with which the program was managed. A description of the two components as outlined in BMM's June proposal to NACC is shown in Exhibit 10. According to Bureau procedures, patient control began at the time an addict made his initial application for admission to the methadone program. Application blanks were available at any of the MMP treatment units, all district health centers, and several prisons. Completed forms were sent to the central intake unit where they were reviewed to ensure that all criteria for admission were met (age, addiction history, and residence) and that an application had not been filed previously. If an applicant was not acceptable, he was notified by the central intake unit by mail. If acceptable,

---

[1]The first serious efforts to determine what the Bureau of Laboratories needed in the way of new equipment and renovation were undertaken by HSA and the Department of Public Works in January. It was found that much less would be required than had been estimated, initially. In February, moreover, a computerized record system was installed which greatly increased the lab's capacity to process urine samples quickly.

his name was sent to the unit nearest his home that had openings available. The unit then interviewed the applicant, gathered the data shown in Exhibit 12, and made a final decision to accept or reject him. Interview data was sent to the central office which also sent copies to the Rockefeller Institute for storage in the central data bank.

While the patient was in treatment, a monthly report was submitted by the clinic to the central office describing his reaction to methadone, if any, and updating the interview information. (This data was also forwarded to Rockefeller Institute.) In addition, the hospital was required to keep, on its own, a detailed, written medical record on each patient that expanded on basic interview data and included medication histories, nurse's notes on patient appearance and behavior, referrals to other outpatient clinics, and so forth. A similar record was kept by the patient's counselor, giving a history of clinic efforts to assist the patient to reaclimate himself to society and of the patient's response. Both the medical and counselor's files were required by state and federal regulation. Patients could be transferred to another unit for treatment or terminated altogether only after formal application to and approval by the central intake office. In addition to the monthly report on individual patients, each clinic submitted a weekly summary report to the central office listing all its patients and their status for the week (regular attendance, missed appointments, in jail, in a hospital, transferred, or discharged).

Dr. Newman commented on the effectiveness of the control and evaluation procedures:

> We have a lot of data coming in from the units that is helpful in gaining an impression of how effective they are. The two most obvious criteria are how many patients they're accepting and how many they're terminating. It's a numbers game, but it can be a pretty good tip-off if something's wrong at a clinic. It's a question of deciding what the components of a "good" clinic are. Some people would say that mandatory, in-depth counseling sessions with every patient are crucial; others would say that's a disaster. One of the reasonably objective measures of effectiveness is how many patients stay with it. After all, the main goal is to serve individual patients.
>
> [One way we exert control] is admissions. Patients cannot be accepted into the program except through the central office. The actual acceptance of a patient occurs when a unit number is issued through the central office. Without a number, they can't get into the computer system; this means they won't get medication labels and the pharmacist won't make up any medication. Finally, the physicians are all operating under my federal IND number, so if they give medication to patients that aren't registered in the program, it's their legal neck.[1]

---

[1]Doctors must obtain an IND number before administering drugs that are still classified "experimental" as methadone was.

What about the internal record system? We don't have a formal way of ensuring compliance with that. But when a patient is terminated, I get not only a summary of the patient's book but the entire patient folder. Before I sign the termination, I look through the record from A to Z. This gives us a pretty good ongoing look at records, at least for the problem cases. About five per cent of the admissions have been terminated.

Also someone from the central office has been visiting each of the clinics at least once a week.

Chip Raymond did not agree with all of Newman's observations.

No one will follow procedures! You can lay them out step-by-step and people don't do it. We have a procedure for admissions with a very clearcut paper flow, a very specific description of who's supposed to do what, but nobody takes the time to do it properly. One of the problems is that we can't hire adequate staff. Turnover has been high. Bob and I have just been super-clerks - Bob, especially.

We have liaison people who go out to the clinics and sit down and talk with the counselors, the supervisors, and the patients. But methadone hasn't really established any set level of ancillary services that should go along with medication, so it's hard to evaluate.

The Rockefeller [evaluation] program really doesn't tell you if you are successful. All they're doing is pushing papers around and tabulating statistics. We have weekly reports and monthly reports, but all they tell us is "X" number of patients got jobs, "X" number of patients are on welfare, "X" number of patients have been arrested. Those kinds of things don't really tell me anything. I'd rather find out if the clinics are open on time, if they're open late enough at night, are the counselors being utilized, are they offering the services they should be offering, are the patients responding to the services offered. A successful clinic to me is one that is giving the patients the services we promised them. I went up to one of our clinics and there was one nurse there; all the other staff was out to lunch. That kind of stuff is intolerable!

The statistics from Gearing's report are a complete waste of time. They're great for people who look at them and say "wow, methadone's just fantastic! It's got an 80% retention rate." I could have an 80% retention rate just by giving people medication and nothing else. The medication is just a device to grab the guy by his ears and hook him on something other than heroin so you can do something for him. I don't want to change his personality or his life style if he doesn't want us to, but I want the services available to him if he does want to change.

> One place we run into great difficulties is in controlling who is actually the administrator of a clinic. The doctor is the Unit Director in title, but the Unit Supervisor is really the guy that we want running the day-to-day operation. The doctor is there to handle the medical aspects of the program.

Further Expansion

As Raymond reviewed the March status report, he wondered what changes he should suggest to Bob Newman with regard to their management of the MMP start-up. The question was particularly important because plans were already under way for a vastly expanded treatment program. The goal was to be 15,000 patients in treatment at BMM facilities by March 31, 1973. Patient care would be carried out by three components:

1. Forty treatment units with a capacity of 200 patients each.

2. Thirteen Phase III units with a capacity of 500 patients each. Patients would be transferred to these units after at least six months in one of the treatment units.

3. Private physicians who would care for patients that had been in the program at least six months and whose need for supportive services was relatively small.

As he looked back over the preceding months, Raymond was aware that Newman, Fields, and he had not always agreed on how the initial program should be managed, but he was not sure what modifications would be necessary to handle the expanded effort.

Exhibit 1

ADDICTION CONTROL IN NEW YORK CITY (B)

Organization Chart Showing Drug-Related Activities for the City of New York

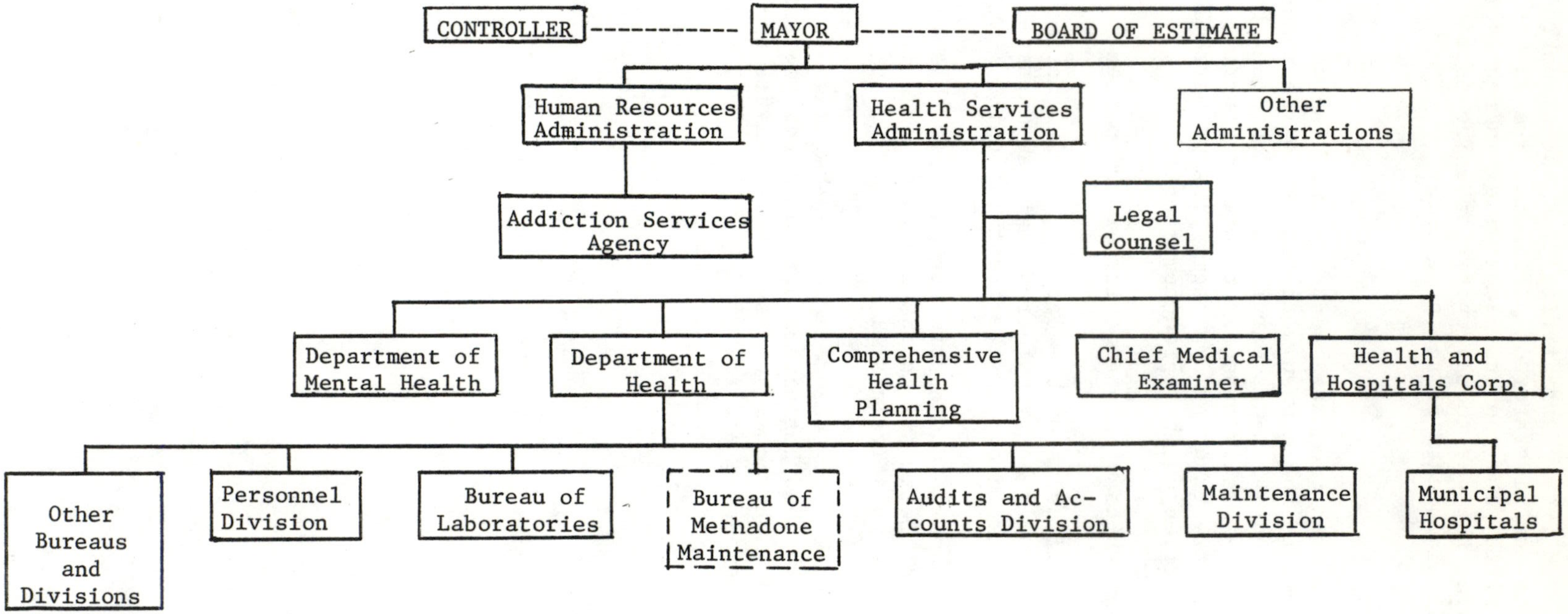

Exhibit 2

ADDICTION CONTROL IN NEW YORK CITY (B)

Methadone Maintenance Treatment Program
Annualized Budget Summary

CENTRAL STAFF			
PERSONNEL		$385,374	
CONSULTING FEES:			
Legal Services	$ 30,000		
Facility Planning (For Intake and Out-Patient Units)	35,000		
Total Consulting Fees		$ 65,000	
OTPS (OTHER THAN PERSONAL SERVICES)			
Space Costs, 4,000 sq. ft. @ $10.00	$ 40,000		
Consumable Supplies	3,500		
Equipment	26,382		
Communications, Utilities	5,800		
Travel (2 persons to A.P.H.A. in Texas)	750		
Miscellaneous	10,000		
Total OTPS		$ 86,432	
TOTAL CENTRAL STAFF COSTS			$536,806
INTAKE UNIT			
PERSONNEL		$107,836	
OTPS			
Space Costs, 1,000 sq. ft. @ $10.00	$ 10,000		
Consumable Supplies	1,000		
Equipment	11,220		
Communications, Utilities	1,052		
Total OTPS		$ 23,272	
TOTAL INTAKE UNIT COSTS			$131,108

Exhibit 2 (continued)

Methadone Maintenance Treatment Program
Annualized Budget Summary

RIKER'S ISLAND INTAKE UNIT					
PERSONNEL		$78,560			
OTPS					
Consumable Supplies	$700				
Equipment	690				
Communications	300				
Total OTPS		$ 1,690			
TOTAL R. I. INTAKE UNIT COSTS				$80,250	
INPATIENT TREATMENT UNIT					
PERSONNEL		$152,173			
OTPS					
Equipment, Medication, Facilities, Maintenance, Supplies, Other Service Costs		$100,000			
TOTAL INPATIENT TREATMENT UNIT COSTS				$252,173	
TYPICAL OUTPATIENT TREATMENT UNIT					
PERSONNEL		$118,122			
OTPS					
Space Costs, 1,200 sq. ft. @ $10.00	$12,000				
Consumable Supplies	7,300				
Equipment	4,857				
Communications	1,150				
Miscellaneous, Including Maintenance	6,600				
Total OTPS		$31,907			
TOTAL OUTPATIENT TREATMENT UNIT PERSONNEL COSTS				($150,029)	
20 OUTPATIENT CLINICS				$3,000,580	
LABORATORY					
PERSONNEL			$338,508		
OTPS			$161,492		
TOTAL LABORATORY EXPANSION COSTS					$500,000
GRAND TOTAL					$4,500,917

Exhibit 3

ADDICTION CONTROL IN NEW YORK CITY (B)

Methadone Maintenance Treatment Program
Personnel Requirements

POSITION TITLES	NUMBER
CENTRAL STAFF	
Director	1
Secretary to the Director	1
Administrative Assistant to the Director	1
Deputy Director	1
Co-ordinator, Evaluation & Control Services	1
Program Analyst	2
Co-ordinator of Counselling Services	1
Vocational Counselor	3
Co-ordinator, Community Relations	1
Community Relations Representative	1
Co-ordinator, Fiscal Affairs	1
Accountant	2
Senior Steno	6
Clerk Typist	1
Motor Vehicle Operator	2
INTAKE UNIT	
Intake Director	1
Intake Counselor	3
Research Assistant	1
Intake Secretary	5
RIKER'S ISLAND INTAKE UNIT	
Intake Director	1
Intake Counselor	2
Research Assistant	2
Intake Secretary	2
INPATIENT TREATMENT UNIT	
Physician, half-time	½
Head Nurse	1
Staff Nurse	5
Counselor	2
Research Assistant	2
Secretary	1

Exhibit 3 (continued)

Methadone Maintenance Treatment Program
Personnel Requirements

OUTPATIENT TREATMENT UNIT	
Physician, half-time[1]	½
Unit Supervisor[2]	1
Head Nurse	1
Staff Nurse	1
Counselor	3
Research Assistant[3]	1
Secretary	1
LABORATORY	
Senior Research Scientist (Biological)	1
Senior Chemist	1
Junior Chemist	5
Laboratory Technician	20
Laboratory Helper	6
Clerk	3
Administrative Assistant	1
Total Supervisory	62
Total Other	209
Grand Total	271

[1]The physician is responsible for the overall operation of the clinic and for the initial medical examination of each patient as well as on-going medical evaluation and treatment as necessary.

[2]Unit supervisors are responsible for supervision of the clinic staff subject to direction by the physician in charge.

[3]Research Assistants are selected from Phase III methadone patients.

EXHIBIT 4

ADDICTION CONTROL IN NEW YORK CITY (B)

Planned Schedule of Patient Induction

	1970 Nov. 1	Dec. 1	1971 Jan. 1	Feb. 1	Mar. 1	Apr. 1	May 1	Jun. 1	Jul. 1	Aug. 1	Sep. 1
PHASE I											
No. of Patients from Last Month	0	0	10	50	115	195	295	365	350	285	205
Total New Patients	0	10	40	75	120	175	190	160	125	80	25
No. Transferred to Phase II	0	0	0	10	40	75	120	175	190	160	125
Total Patients in Phase I	0	10	50	115	195	295	365	350	285	205	205
PHASE II											
No. of Patients from Last Month	0	40	150	290	525	845	1,145	1,445	1,760	2,060	2,270
New Patients Transferred From											
City Clinics - Phase I	0	0	0	10	40	75	120	175	190	160	125
Transferred from Other Source - Phase I	40	110	142	229	288	239	199	164	139	84	37
Total New Patients	40	110	142	239	328	314	319	339	329	244	162
Number Discharged	0	0	2	4	8	14	19	24	29	34	37
Total Patients in Phase II	40	150	290	525	845	1,145	1,445	1,760	2,060	2,270	2,395
Total Patients in Phase I and Phase II	40	160	340	640	1,040	1,440	1,810	2,110	2,345	2,475	2,500

NOTE: Discharge rates are based on the Beth-Israel experience.

Exhibit 5

ADDICTION CONTROL IN NEW YORK CITY (B)

List of Task Responsibilities
for the Bureau of Methadone Maintenance

- Negotiating with hospitals and arranging for their participation
- Overseeing the establishment of clinics and monitoring clinic operations
- Approving clinic medical directors and unit supervisors
- Mounting an out-reach program to reach more of the addict population
- Creating a community liaison program to explain the use of methadone
- Assisting hospitals in recruitment
- Establishing and staffing two intake units
- Providing vocational support services and working with business and industry to develop jobs for patients
- Providing legal assistance to patients in the Program as required
- Arranging for training of clinic personnel by the Beth-Israel Medical Center
- Developing and supervising a City-orientation program
- Arranging for data processing and evaluation
- Developing adequate systems for record-keeping and reporting

Exhibit 6

ADDICTION CONTROL IN NEW YORK CITY (B)

Network Analysis for Opening of First Six Clinics

Methadone Maintenance Treatment Program

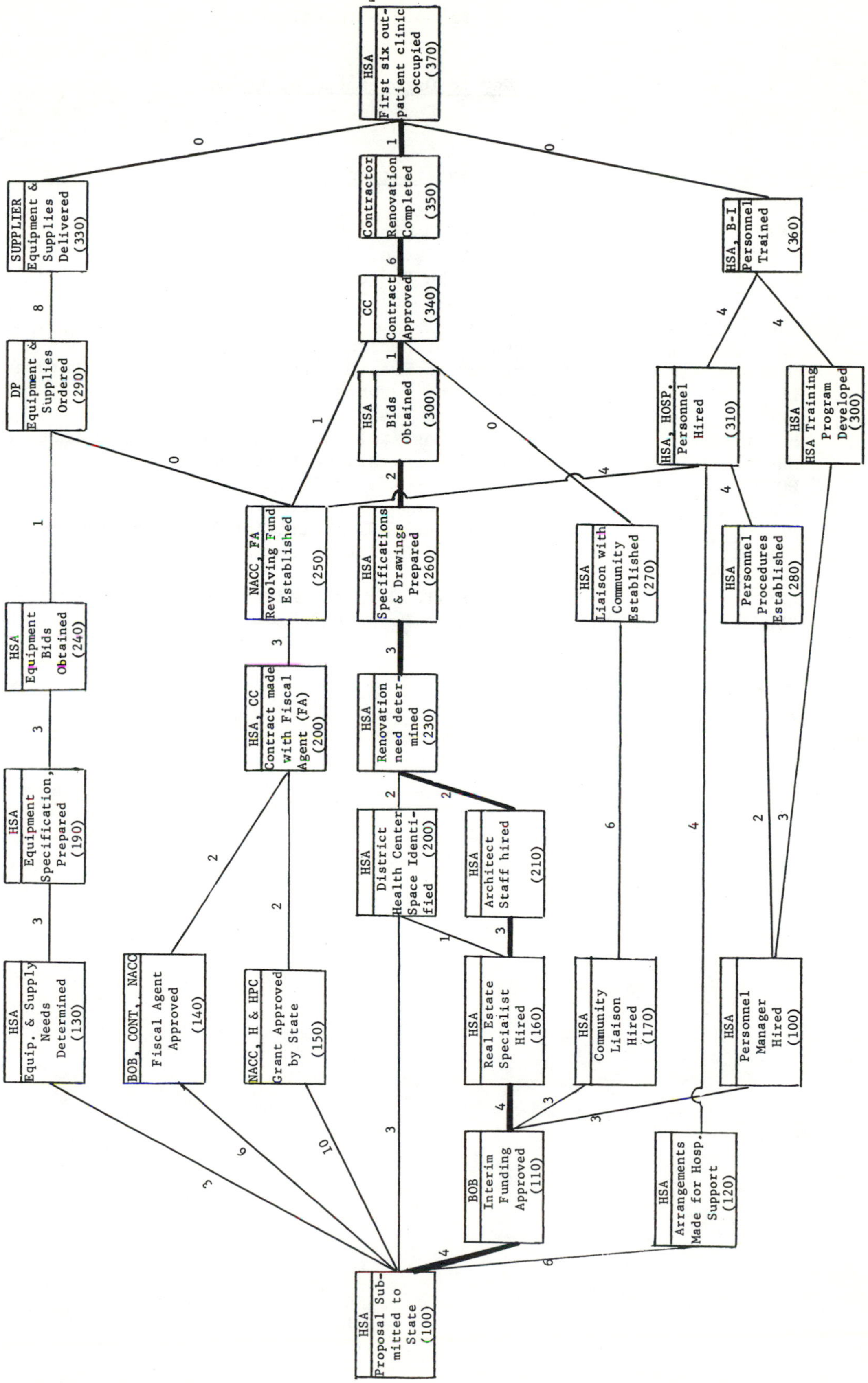

Exhibit 6 (continued)

Key to Organizational Codes

Organizational Code	Organization
B-I	Beth-Israel Medical Center
BDEST	Board of Estimate
BOB	Bureau of the Budget
CC	Corporation Counsel
CONT	Controller
DH	Department of Health
DHBMM	Department of Health Bureau of Methadone Maintenance Treatment
DP	Department of Purchase
DRE	Department of Real Estate
H&HPC	Health and Hospital Planning Council of Southern New York, Inc.
HHC	Health and Hospitals Corporation
HOSP	Hospitals
HSA	Health Services Administration
HSLEG	Health Services Administration Legal Counsel
LAB	Department of Health Bureau of Laboratories
LAND	Landlords
NACC	New York State Narcotic Addiction Control Commission
PERS	Department of Personnel

Exhibit 7

ADDICTION CONTROL IN NEW YORK CITY (B)

Standard Network for the Establishment of Clinic

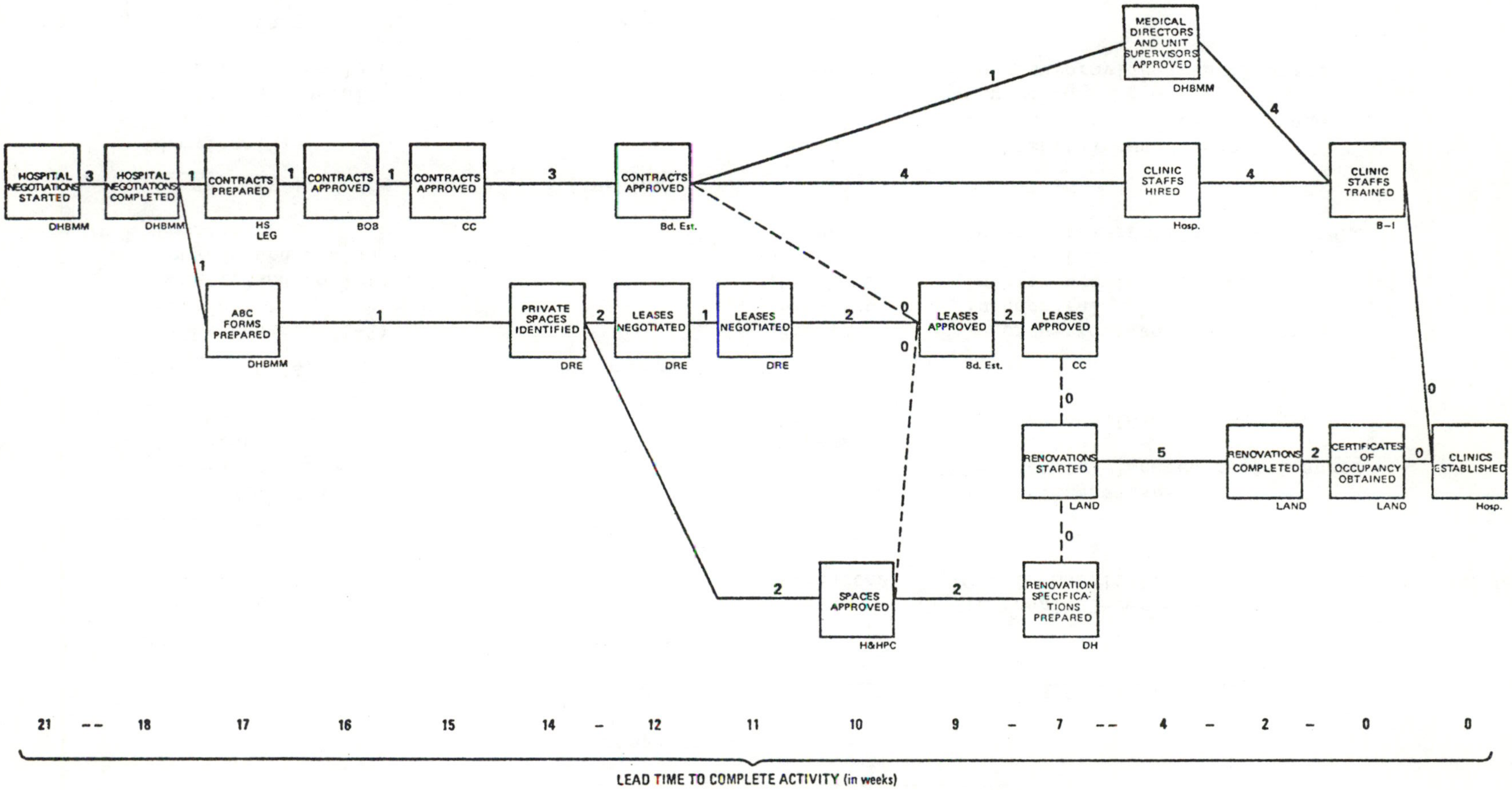

Exhibit 8

ADDICTION CONTROL IN NEW YORK CITY (B)

Clinic Locations

	Scheduled Opening Month	Location	Space Requirements
GROUP I (1-4)	November		
Jamaica (1)		Queens	In hospital-owned space
Delafield (1-3)		Manhattan	One in hospital, two in a city health center
GROUP II (5-8)	December		
Lower East Side		Manhattan	In city-owned space
Beekman-Downtown		Manhattan	In hospital-located rental space
Elmhurst (1)		Queens	In hospital
St. Mary's		Brooklyn	In city-provided rental space
GROUP III (9-14)	January		
Bronx Lebanon (1-2)		Bronx	In city-provided rental space
Greenpoint		Brooklyn	In hospital
Long Island College (1)		Brooklyn	In city-provided rental space
Long Island Jewish (1)		Queens	In hospital
Roosevelt		Manhattan	In hospital-provided rental space
GROUP IV (15-17)	February		
Jamaica (2)		Queens	In hospital-owned space
Mary Immaculate		Queens	In city-provided rental space
Peninsula General*		Queens	Cancelled
Long Island College (2)		Queens	In city-provided rental space
GROUP V (18-22)	March		
Elmhurst (2)		Queens	In city-health center
St. Mary's (Charles Drew)		Brooklyn	In city-provided rental space
Long Island College (3)**		Brooklyn	In hospital-provided rental space
Long Island Jewish (2)*		Queens	In city-provided rental space
Richmond Memorial**		Richmond	In hospital

*Peninsula General cancelled its contract with the city in January and was replaced by a second clinic at Long Island Jewish.

**Added as clinics 21 and 22 when the in-patient unit was abandoned.

Exhibit 9

ADDICTION CONTROL IN NEW YORK CITY (B)

Original and Revised Target Dates for Major Milestones

	Original	Revised 9/16		Revised 11/20***		Revised 1/15		Revised 3/26	
	Completion Date	Completion Date	Weeks Slippage	Completion Date	Weeks Slippage	Completion Date	Weeks Slippage	Completion Date	Weeks Slippage
Key Central Staff Hired	10/2	-	0	None Set	7	2/19	15	4/16	25
Group I Clinics Open (1-4)	10/16	10/30	2	X**	4 1/2	X	X	X	X
Inpatient Treatment Unit Open	10/23	12/4	6	Abandoned	-	-	-	-	-
Riker's Island Intake Unit Operational	10/30	-	0	X	2 1/2	X	X	X	X
Group II Clinics Open (5-8)	11/6	11/27	3	1/15	9	1/29	11	X	12
Central Intake Unit Operational	11/20	-	0	X	-2	X	X	X	X
Urinalysis Program Fully Operational	11/27	12/11	2	2/12	11	2/11	11	X	11
Group III Clinics Open (9-14)	1/15	1/1	-2	2/12	4	3/26	10	3/31	10 1/2
Group IV Clinics Open (15-17)	2/5	2/5	0	3/5	4	4/2	8	4/12	9
Group V Clinics Open (18-20)*	2/5	2/5	0	3/5	4	4/2	8	6/7	14 1/2

*Increased to 22 clinics total in November.

**X = Completed.

***Schedule revisions were made monthly by PMS. Only bi-monthly revisions are shown in the exhibit.

Exhibit 10

ADDICTION CONTROL IN NEW YORK CITY (B)

MMP Maintaining and Control Procedure as Proposed to the State Narcotic Addiction Control Commission

Evaluation will be carried out on an ongoing basis from a medical care administrative perspective. For the Methadone Maintenance Program this will be in two main areas, external and internal.

1. External Evaluation - This will be evaluation of the outcome of Methadone Maintenance in relation to society. Pre-methadone behavior of addicts will be compared with the behavior of addicts after they join the treatment program.

   For instance, the arrest and prison records of addicts prior to treatment will be compared with their records after treatment. The ability of an addict to support himself prior to entrance into the program will be compared with his work record after going on methadone. Meaningful indexes of social stability relative to spouses and the individual's community will be developed and comparisons before and after treatment will be made. Close cooperation with the Rockefeller data bank and its Director, Dr. Alan Warner, will be developed so that both retrospective and prospective studies can be carried out. Hypotheses in the area of the impact of methadone on society will be formulated and tested so as to evaluate the program from a cost to society and human wastage basis.

2. Internal Evaluation - This will be evaluation of the Methadone Maintenance Program from an effectiveness and efficiency approach. Procedures will be instituted so that there are constant checks on the ongoing program. For instance, a system will be instituted so that any drug reactions that occur are immediately referred to Central Office. Records will be constantly updated so that it is always known which patients received methadone from each drug batch.

   Differences in dropout rates between units will be carried out by the Central Office so that it is understood why these different rates occur. Since there will be differing ratios of counsellors and other personnel per addict in the units, the effect of these differences, if any, will be noted. Studies of these differences will be done and performance standards developed. Because of the complete biographical data obtained and stored in the Rockefeller data bank it will be possible to measure the outcome statistics for matched groups of patients in the various units. This will give precise measurements relative to the efficiency and effectiveness of the units operating in the program. The findings in regard to efficiency and effectiveness in the beginning stages of the program will lead to the most economical and beneficial units being developed while the program is expanded.

Exhibit 11

ADDICTION CONTROL IN NEW YORK CITY (B)

NEW YORK CITY METHADONE MAINTENANCE TREATMENT PROGRAM

BASIC DATA INTERVIEW FORM

Where Screened: ____________ On Waiting List for: ____________

Mother's First Name: ____________ Social Security No.: ____________

____________ Interview Date | 1-6) ______

Patient's Name: ____________ Last First Middle | 7-28) ______

Address: ____________ Street No. Borough Zip

Sex: 1. Male 2. Female | 29) ______

Birth Date: ____________ | 30-35) ______

Classification: 1. White 2. Black 3. Puerto Rican 4. Other ______ | 36) ______

Marital Status: 1. Single 2. Married 3. Separated 4. Divorced 5. Widowed 6. Common-law (now) | 37) ______

Education: (last grade completed) 1. Elem. grades 1-4 2. Elem. grades 5-7 3. Elem. grade 8 4. Some H.S. 5. H.S. Grad. 6. Some Coll. 7. Coll. Grad. 8. Other (Specify) ______ | 38) ______

Vocation: 1. Laborer 2. Semi-skilled 3. Skilled 4. Clerical 5. Professional 6. Sales 7. ______ 8. None | 39) ______

Work History: 1. Never worked 2. Working now 3. Worked in past | 40) ______
If worked or working, longest job (months) ______ | 41-43) ______
If worked but not now, months since last job ______ | 44-46) ______

Welfare: 1. On now 2. On previously 3. Never on | 47) ______

Addiction: Age when started using heroin daily: ______ Year ______ | 48-49) ______

Legal: Number of previous convictions: ______ | 50-51) ______

Treatment: Times in treatment for addiction: ______ | 52-53) ______

Medical Complications: 1. No 2. Yes (Specify) ______ | 54) ______

Alcohol: 1. No problem 2. Had problem 3. Has problem | 55) ______

Other Drugs: (Addict. or heavy use) 1. No problem 2. Barbiturates 3. Amphetamines 4. Other (Specify) ______ | 56) ______

Referral: 1. Voluntary 2. Involuntary | 57) ______

Disposition: 1. Accepted, immediate treatment 2. Accepted, waiting list 3. Not accepted: (Reason) ______ 4. Accepted (No dècision for immediate or waiting list) | 58) ______

Date Admitted: ______ .... | 59-64) ______

Patient's Program Number: (I.D.) ______ .... | 67-71) ______

Initial Census Group: ______ .... | 72-74) ______
Zip | 75-79) ______

Exhibit 12

ADDICTION CONTROL IN NEW YORK CITY (B)

Patient Intake Record as of March 26, 1971

	Planned					Actual				
	Nov.	Dec.	Jan.	Feb.	Mar.	Nov.	Dec.	Jan.	Feb.	Mar.
Patients enrolled at beginning of month	0	80	240	420	700	0	39	103	266	461
New admissions	80	161	183	285	369	39	64	164	197	325
Discharged	0	1	3	5	9	0	0	1	2	11
Patients enrolled at end of month	80	240	420	700	1060	39	103	266	461	775

PUBLIC ASSISTANCE

PUBLIC ASSISTANCE (A)

Nearly one-third of all families living in New York City are eligible for some kind of public assistance. Of these, nearly 65% were receiving financial aid in some form by the summer of 1971. This meant a case load of over 475,000 families (1,200,000 persons), an increase of almost 300,000 families since 1966. During this same period (1966 to 1971), the amount distributed to recipients annually grew from $382 million to $1.2 billion. Responsibility for the management of this large and growing program rested with the city's Bureau of Public Assistance (BPA).

The Bureau of Public Assistance

BPA, in 1971, was one of six bureaus included in the Department of Social Services (DSS), itself an arm of one of the city's superagencies, the Human Resources Administration (HRA). (Exhibit 1 shows the HRA organization.) Of all the organizational units within HRA, BPA was by far the largest. Its annual budget of $1.3 billion for fiscal year 1970-1971 was 69% of the DSS total. It employed over 16,000 of the 25,000 people working for DSS. Six basic categories of public assistance were under its jurisdiction:

(1) Aid to Dependent Children (ADC) and Aid to Dependent Children of Unemployed Parents (ADC-U): ADC served minors deprived of parental support or care by death, incapacity, or absence of one or both parents. Grants were provided so the minor could be cared for in the home of his parent(s) or other relatives. ADC-U provided similar assistance where there was an employable but unemployed parent, provided the parent was registered with the New York State Employment Service and had not refused (without good cause) an offer of employment or training.

(2) Aid to the Blind (AB): Provided grants to persons who were legally blind and in financial need.

(3) Aid to the Disabled (AD): Provided assistance to persons in need who were permanently and totally disabled. The category included those who were mentally ill, alcoholic, or addicted to narcotics.

(4) Home Relief (HR): State and locally supported assistance for persons who were in their own homes and who were unable to provide for themselves or to secure help from any other source including other public assistance categories.

(5) Old Age Assistance (OAA): Assisted persons who were 65 or older who could not support themselves and were not in a hospital, public home, or state institution.

(6) Veterans Assistance (VA): State and city aid supplied to needy veterans who did not qualify for federal programs.

The monthly grants under these programs averaged $200 per month per family but varied according to program and family size as shown in the table below.

Monthly Allowance as of April 1971

Number in Family	AB, AD, OAA	HR, VA, ADC, ADC-U
1	$ 84	$ 76
2	134	121
3	179	161
4	231	208
5	284	256
6	329	296
Each additional person	45	41

The amounts shown in the table are exclusive of additional amounts given for shelter, fuel, and several other items for which special allowances were available. In the case of shelter and heating fuel, these were based on the type and quality of housing as well as family size and ranged in amount from $100 to $300 per month. Information on the case load and growth rates for the six assistance categories are set forth in Exhibit 2. In July 1971, the growth rate in total case load was about 5,000 per month.

For all grants except Home Relief and Veterans Assistance, the Federal Government reimbursed the city for 50% of the grant while the state paid 25%. For Home Relief and Veterans Assistance, the city and state each paid 50%. When these sharing formulas are applied across the six assistance categories in 1970-1971, the city's share of the $1.2 billion paid was 28.5% ($340 million).

The Welfare Center

The delivery of both financial assistance and social services was carried out by BPA's 44 welfare centers - 12 in Manhattan, 17 in Brooklyn, 12 in the Bronx, 2 in Queens, and 1 in Richmond. In the late 1960s, as the number of public assistance cases increased so did the number of welfare centers (from 26 in 1966 to 44 in 1970) and the number of people who staff these centers. In 1971, 12,000 of BPA's 16,000 employees worked in the centers while the remaining 4,000 were at the bureau's central office. The total cost to run BPA's operations exceeded $100 million per year.

Experience showed that a new center had to be opened for each additional 10,000 cases. An "average" center had a case load as shown below. (Individual centers varied substantially from this norm.)

Category[1]	Number of Cases	
HR	1,500	
ADC	5,000	
ADC-U	200	6,700[2]
OAA	1,650	
AB	50	
AD (Nonnarcotic addict)	1,200	
AD (Narcotic addict)	400	3,300
		10,000

The services provided by the welfare centers could be divided into two categories - income maintenance and social. The former included determining an applicant's eligibility for financial aid, establishing the size of regular and supplementary grants to which a recipient was entitled, and assuring that payments were actually made. The latter included a number of other services designed to help the recipient and his family in matters not directly related to income maintenance. Some of these social services were mandated by law and had to be accepted by anyone wishing to receive financial support. These required services were job counseling for those judged able to work, protective services for children where there was evidence of either neglect or abuse, access to family planning information, and a periodic assessment of the family's total social service needs. Voluntary services included help with housing, advice on housekeeping and budgeting, and others. A few social services were provided by referring clients to public or private agencies

---

[1] Veterans Assistance was handled by a single, specialized center.

[2] HR, ADC, and ADC-U cases combined were known as "family" cases.

outside the welfare center. Most were given by the general caseworkers at the center or by the center's specialist group. Specialist groups were composed of:

- A Homemaker/Housekeeper to secure homemaking and housekeeping services for qualified recipients.

- A Home Economist to assist clients in learning to run a household and to help establish budget levels for recipients.

- A DAB[1] Worker who specialized in helping clients in the AD, OAA, and AB categories.

- A Housing Adviser to help recipients locate housing, handle relocation problems, and solicit vacancies from real estate contacts.

- An Employment Specialist to help clients find jobs.

Until 1969, the effective delivery of both income maintenance and social services depended heavily on a close relationship between the recipient of public assistance and a person designated as "his caseworker." The first floor of a typical center consisted of an intake area, a waiting room, and conference rooms. Caseworkers' offices were on the second floor. A new client or reapplicant was interviewed, in the intake area, by a caseworker who filled out the necessary application forms. During the next few days, another caseworker verified the statements made on the application to determine whether or not the client was, indeed, eligible under one of the public assistance programs. If the applicant was eligible, his case was permanently assigned to a single caseworker who filled out additional forms and determined the size of the new client's monthly grant. From that point on, whenever the recipient returned to the center with a problem, question, or change of status, the intake caseworker would notify the client's caseworker who would come downstairs and talk to the client in one of the conference rooms. If some specialized service was needed - such as housing assistance - the caseworker would consult a center specialist and pass the information on to the recipient. Clients also contacted their caseworkers frequently by mail and telephone.

The caseworker was required to make periodic field trips to a recipient's home to see for himself the conditions under which the client and his family were living. After the first six months, and yearly thereafter, each client's eligibility was reviewed by his caseworker to ensure that any change in status was properly reflected in the amount of the recurring grant.

---

[1] OAA, AB, and AD cases combined were called "DAB" cases (Disabled, Aged, and Blind).

The intent of this arrangement between caseworker and client was to develop a close and continuing relationship that would be of maximum benefit to those receiving public assistance. On the one hand, each client would have a single, familiar person to contact and consult at the center, thus increasing his willingness and ability to seek advice and counsel. On the other hand, the caseworker's ability to provide the services needed by a particular family would be enhanced because of his familiarity with its problems and progress over an extended period of time. Moreover, by involving the caseworker in the delivery of financial assistance as well as social services, there was assurance that every transaction between caseworker and client regarding income maintenance would provide an opportunity to reassess the need for services other than financial. Studies showed that most caseworkers spent between 75% and 90% of their time dealing with income maintenance matters. These included not only the determination of initial grants but also changes in grant levels as recipients' circumstances changed, processing special grants, following up complaints that checks were not delivered, and making clerical changes.

To be eligible for a job as caseworker, an applicant was required to have a college degree, although the field of study was not considered critical. Thus, while many caseworkers held majors in sociology and psychology, many others had academic backgrounds in fields like political science and home economics. Few below the rank of supervisor had an advanced degree. In addition, during the past several years, the profile of the typical caseworker had been changing. There were still a number of the traditional "mother hen" type who had been caseworkers for many years but, more and more, the increasing demand for caseworkers had been filled by young people directly out of undergraduate school. Turnover, particularly among the new workers, was extremely high (over 100 per month).

The caseworkers were represented by the Social Service Employees Union (SSEU). This union had fought a bitter battle in the early 1960s to wrest control and bargaining rights from Local 371 of the American Federation of State, County, and Municipal Employees, AFL-CIO. Following its certification, the SSEU took a militant, hard-line approach to its dealings with the city regarding both wages and working conditions. In early 1968, a 28-day strike (the longest for public employees in the city's history) brought the caseworkers substantial pay raises and the right to make the number of cases assigned to each worker a bargainable issue. The new contract set this number at 60 per worker. The supervisory ratio, also part of the contract, was set at one-to-five through four levels of supervision; that is, one unit supervisor for five caseworkers, one case supervisor for five unit supervisors, and so forth.

In 1969, the number of cases per worker was increased to 67 in return for an across-the-board pay raise of $740 per year. In 1970, it was increased again, to 75, for a raise of $380. (By the middle of 1970, a number of factors - including the rapid growth of case load - had brought the apparent number of cases per worker to 93. There was evidence that some caseworkers were "dumping" everything over their quota of 75.)

Exhibit 3 shows the total staffing for a 10,000-case center based on the case load quota of 75, the five-to-one supervisory ratio, and a rule of thumb that one clerical person was required to support each two caseworkers. Information is also shown on salary levels and total direct labor costs.

The Separated Center

During the late 1960s, some of the assumptions underlying the operation of public assistance programs began to change. In particular, many people concluded that financial assistance should be considered more a right than a privilege and that eligibility should be established on the basis of the applicant's word rather than an elaborate verification procedure. Second, they believed, now, that the need for monetary assistance did not necessarily imply a need for social services. Based on these conclusions, the city began in 1968, to restructure BPA and its 44 welfare centers so that income maintenance services would be (i) provided on the basis of a simple declaration of need by the applicant and (ii) separated organizationally from the delivery of social services. One DSS manager referred to this "separation" program as "the most significant change in public welfare administration in the last three decades."

In 1969, the first step in the over-all separation process was completed; income maintenance and social services delivery for DAB cases were separated in all welfare centers. Clerks[1] were hired to do the income maintenance work and the social workers thus freed were transferred to other centers and/or other duties in the system. In 1970, the separation effort was expanded to include the remaining public assistance categories - ADC, ADC-U, and HR. By March, three centers were completely separated. At each one, approximately 60 income maintenance clerks were hired and 65 caseworkers transferred to other centers. By February 1971, three more centers had been fully separated.

During the spring of 1971, the city's program to separate the remaining centers took on new urgency. Officials in Washington announced that on July 1, 1971 the formula for reimbursing the administrative cost of public assistance services would be changed. The Federal Government would reimburse only 50% of the costs of operating nonseparated systems.[2] For separated systems, it would continue, as in the past, to pay for 75% of the cost of social services and 50% of the cost of income maintenance

---

[1] These clerks were called "Income Maintenance Specialists" and were paid at the level of a supervisory clerk - $8,800 per year.

[2] This referred to the operating cost of the centers, not to the grants provided welfare recipients.

services. The difference could mean almost $460,000 per month to the city. In order to minimize this loss of income, a crash program was undertaken to ensure the completion of separation by October in accordance with an interim plan. Under this plan, caseworkers would be used temporarily to fill income maintenance specialist and eligibility investigator positions.

A separated center operated as follows: Eligibility for monetary assistance was determined solely on the basis of a client's declaration of need. If his statement indicated that he met federal and state eligibility requirements (and a simple check showed that he had not defrauded the system in the past), he received aid without further investigation. Only the applications of addicts and a few other special categories were subject to complete verification by the center's staff of approximately 18 eligibility investigators. (A staff of special investigators, located at the DSS Central Office, performed a monthly quality control audit of a random sample of 1/2 of 1% of all ADC and DAB cases. The audit verified eligibility and checked for errors in payment amounts.) With regard to social services, all (except those mandated by law) were completely voluntary; that is, the welfare client was made aware of the selection of social services that were available but it was up to him to request whatever services he wished. This was based on the premise that the client was the best judge of his own needs. In addition to making services voluntary, all (including the mandated ones) were delivered in what was termed a "goal-oriented/time-limited" fashion. In other words, before a service was given, the caseworker and client had to establish a specific goal toward which the service was directed and a date by which the goal was to be accomplished. This date could not be more than 90 days after delivery of the service started.

Income maintenance (IM) services were provided by IM specialists working in groups of five with one supervisor and the direct support of two clerks. Five IM groups were under the supervision of an assistant office manager. IM specialists were supported by a number of ancillary services including eligibility investigation, disbursements and collections, and a number of other routine office services. The groups were divided alphabetically within a center; when a client needed assistance regarding an IM problem, he was helped by any specialist available within his alphabetical group.

The staffing pattern for the delivery of social services was somewhat more complicated. Caseworkers were assigned to one of four new organizational groupings or to the specialist corps (now called the "Special Service Section") that existed in the nonseparated centers. The four new groups were Assessment, Counter, General, and Protective.

<u>The Assessment Section</u>: This section developed with the recipient of ADC or HR a plan for social services encompassing voluntary and mandated services. It served as the entry for newly accepted applicants of family cases to the social services system.

The assessment fulfilled the federal and state mandate that "a plan and program of service" be developed for each family and child who was accepted for public assistance and who required services.

The assessment was carried out through interviews with families and individuals and included the following activities:

(1) Gathering facts about the current situation of the family or individual which bore on needs for social services.

(2) Identifying problem areas and assessing needs for services to help solve the problems.

(3) Formulating a social service plan with the family or individual.

The Counter Section: The Counter Section included all those services, largely of a concrete and environmental nature, that could be delivered with promptness and that did not require a sustained relationship with the deliverer of services. They included those services that could be delivered by a generalist as distinguished from the more specialized services.

Services given at the counter were:

Information-Giving: Listening to the request made by the potential user of a service, clarifying the request, and providing options from among which the user might choose.

Referral: Deciding which agency, division or section was appropriate to meet the request and explaining the intake procedure of the system to the potential user. The goal of referral was making the connection between the user and the resource's service.

Intercession: Reviewing the request of the user for assistance in negotiating with DSS or other agencies and honoring those requests with which DSS was capable of dealing for the purpose of obtaining delivery of requested services.

The General Service Section: This section had two broad objectives:

(1) To provide a link to needed services for persons who, because of lack of knowledge, inexperience, fear, illness, or incapacity, were unable to find and use service facilities without active assistance and support. Examples might be young high school dropouts.

(2) To provide sustaining services to families and individuals to help them improve or maintain current levels of functioning, or to prevent further breakdown.

General Service units acted as a backup and supplement to all other service sections, including Assessment, Counter, Protective, Special, and other social services.

Need for General Service might arise from many aspects of a person's life - general family functioning, problems of child rearing, home or money management, unmarried parenthood and so forth.

Those served included:

(1) Youths 16 to 21 who had dropped out of school and/or lacked marketable skills and needed counseling around preparation for employment, training, or education.

(2) Pregnant adolescents needing assistance in planning for themselves and their babies.

(3) Families with members who had physical, mental or emotional disorders and needed sustained assistance in coping with the problems that resulted from the disorder or illness (e.g., mentally retarded children or adults, child-caring persons suffering from incapacitating illnesses, and so forth).

(4) Families experiencing problems in child rearing and supervision, marriage, and so forth, who requested help in identifying and working on these problems.

Protective Service for Children Section:[1] Protective Service was a specialized and distinctive service especially designed to protect the child whether the need for that protection manifested itself on the basis of neglect or abuse. The service was mandated. Referrals came from the Assessment Section or other sections or individuals within DSS who had reason to believe a child was neglected or abused. Also, there was prompt investigation of all community complaints of child abuse or neglect. The case-load delivery system was utilized in this section. There was intensive effort to strengthen the role of the parent to assume his responsibilities, but at all times the protection of the child received first consideration.

The Special Service Section:[2] The Special Service Section, in addition to providing consultant services to staff, provided direct

---

[1]Protective Services might be given to families not receiving public assistance as well as to those who were.

[2]The Special Service Section corresponded to the specialist group in a non-separated center.

services to recipients and took a more active role with community groups in relation to their specialty.

The Special Service Section was staffed by personnel who had developed expertise in their particular specialty. The work of the specialist was focused on services that required a high degree of competence and expertise in particular fields.

As in all other sections, services were goal-oriented and time-limited. In contrast to past practice, the specialist worked directly with recipients either individually or in groups.

The specialist identified those areas of his specialty which lent themselves to direct service delivery both through the individual and group methods. One-to-one contact with the recipient was limited to those situations which were highly complex and made individual interpretation necessary.[1]

The benefits that DSS management expected from the separation of income maintenance and social services were substantial. In a speech before the New York Public Welfare Association, DSS Commissioner Winifred Lally commented:

> The restructuring process is an attempt to streamline and modernize the administration of Public Welfare so that those eligible for money payments receive assistance as a matter of right and that those eligible receive this assistance promptly and in an atmosphere that enhances their dignity and self-respect. On the other end, social services are being viewed on the basis of their own intrinsic value for those who need and desire services rather than as a prerequisite to financial assistance. Under the new system the effectiveness and validity of both programs can be considered, delivered, and evaluated on their own terms as they could not be in the past when they were considered and operationalized as interdependent.

The Operations Improvement Study

As the separation effort got underway, DSS management decided to undertake a broad scale operations analysis of center operations to determine whether or not significant productivity improvements could be made as part of the separation process. Accordingly, arrangements were made to have the city's Project Management Staff carry out an operations improvement study in the spring and summer of 1971. During that time, a nine-man team gathered data by conducting personal interviews at 14 centers and making a detailed six-week study of one center that had been separated.

---

[1] The description of Social Service Sections has been adapted from the Summer, 1970, issue of Welfarer, the DSS house organ.

The group focused on the measurement of direct labor work loads, the analysis of forms and procedures, center organization, the handling of narcotics addicts on public assistance, evaluating parts of the DSS EDP system, and analyzing total system capacity. The results of their studies in four of these areas are summarized below.

Check Issuance

Over 600,000 checks were issued by DSS every two weeks to satisfy the recurring and special needs of public assistance clients. Most checks were issued centrally by the EDP Bureau but some were prepared at the welfare centers. Several different payment "rolls" were used to meet a variety of regular and special needs: The Regular Roll, A-Roll, B-Roll, Daily Special Roll, and Emergency Roll.

Most active public assistance cases received a biweekly grant under the Regular Roll covering rent, food, and other recurring expenses. Over 450,000 of these checks were issued automatically by EDP on the first and sixteenth of the month based on authorizations issued by IM groups at the centers. A reauthorization was required every 12 months or whenever a change in financial status required that a client's normal budget be amended. These amendments could be made up to 13 days before the date of check issuance. After that, the Regular Roll was closed and the rebudget could not be picked up until the following check cycle.

The A-Roll was used to process budget changes that could not be submitted prior to the 13-day closing deadline for the Regular Roll. To provide for proper cash assistance during the skipped cycle a special grant was processed under the A-Roll and issued concurrent with the Regular Roll checks. On the next and succeeding cycle, the A-Roll special grant was automatically made part of the client's Regular Roll check. About 20,000 A-Roll checks were issued each cycle. The A-Roll was active for a six-day period beginning when the Regular Roll closed. A-Roll checks were issued for both up and downbudgets and as the initial grant for new cases. For downbudgets, an A-Roll check was written for the full amount of the recipient's budget and the Regular Roll check was cancelled. For an upbudget, the A-Roll check could be issued either for the full budget amount or a supplementary amount.

The B-Roll was used for two purposes: To provide grants covering certain nonrecurring expenses (such as moving costs, day-care fees, and employment program expenses) and to cover budget changes that occurred after the A-Roll had closed. Approximately 18,500 B-Roll checks were issued biweekly for nonrecurring expenses and 6,500 for rebudgets. Rebudgets under the B-Roll could be handled up to three or four days before the date for issuance of Regular Roll checks. (A breakdown of the reasons for issuing A- and B-Roll checks is set forth in Exhibit 4.)

The Daily Special Roll was used to cover nonrecurring expenses that required more immediate assistance than was possible with the two-week interval of the B-Roll. Checks processed by EDP as part of the Daily Special Roll reached the client within two or three days following his request. Some of the reasons for issuing checks under the Daily Roll were large upbudgets, lost check replacements, and family disasters. Approximately 50,000 of these daily checks were written every two weeks.

The Emergency Roll was made up of those checks issued directly by the disbursement activities at the individual welfare centers. These grants, as their name implies, were made when a client's need was so immediate that he could not wait the two or three days that were required to process and deliver a check under the Daily Special Roll. Each day, 5,500 of these checks were issued by the 44 centers.

All checks printed by EDP were sent to the Check Release Section at the DSS central office. Here, they were prepared for mailing and mailed on the proper date. Whenever a client's budget was reduced or his case closed, the IM specialist working on the case would send a notice to the Release section who would pull the client's check before mailing and return it to EDP for cancellation.

The pulling operation required the full-time attention of five clerks, one senior clerk, and one supervising clerk. An additional staff of nine people during the day shift and eight at night worked part time on check pulling. Altogether, they pulled approximately 385,000 checks per year at a cost of $73,500 or 19¢ per check. This cost, together with others incurred in processing checks under the A-, B-, or Special Daily Rolls, is shown in Exhibit 5. Data regarding the dollar amounts of both rebudgets and special grants is shown in Exhibit 6.

Staffing for Social Services

Before separation, the number of employees in each center was determined on the basis of only two considerations: First, the quota of cases that could be assigned to a caseworker; second, the number of supervisory and clerical personnel needed to support each caseworker. Both considerations were subject to contract provisions. As soon as the number of cases was known for a center, the size of the required staff to meet contractual obligations could be determined. No performance standards existed beyond the quota of 75 cases per worker, nor had any data been collected regarding the time that a worker spent servicing a welfare case.

To make staffing decisions for a separated center required considerably more information than the old quota per caseworker. First, it was necessary to have some understanding of the time it took to service clients in each of the social service sections (Counter, General, Special, and so forth). Second, it was important to know what the demand would be now that clients had the option of accepting only those services that they wanted. When the separation effort began in 1969, Larry Perlman and Al Pinchoff, two experienced social work supervisors now assigned to the DSS Office of Program Development (OPD), were asked to make reasonable estimates of both these quantities. Advised by the DSS labor relations specialist, that the SSEU would not allow "time studies" in any form to be taken, Perlman and Pinchoff made their estimates solely on the basis of their own experience in the social service system. They described the process as follows:

> With regard to Counter Services, we decided that giving information or making a referral should take about twenty minutes. That figure was simply an estimate. We recognized that some referrals might take only a minute while others might require the better part of a day to make seven or eight phone calls and write a letter or two. The twenty minute estimate also assumed that the counter would have access to good, well-catalogued information about the kinds of social services that were available and where they were located.
>
> On the demand side, we looked at client inflow in nonseparated centers and concluded that twenty per cent of it was for social services and the rest for income maintenance. We assumed that it would remain about the same in volume under separation and that the total demand for Counter Services, including telephone calls and mail inquiries would be about four times as great as the demand from clients who came in to the center.
>
> General was real guesswork. We figured that no more than five per cent of the case load would require General Services and that some portion of that five per cent would be referred outside the center. We then estimated that two-thirds of the cases would be handled through group work and the other one-third on an individual basis. We also concluded that about one-half of the cases would have a second family member that required services.
>
> Then we estimated that an average group would contain fifteen people, that group sessions would last for one hour, and that each one would require an hour's set-up time by a caseworker. Cases being treated on an individual basis would require an average of one hour per week of direct contact and one and a half hours per week of other activity. A factor was also added to allow for the time to do field work with those cases that were handled one-to-one.

Similar estimating procedures were applied to the activities of the other social service sections to develop estimates of demand and standard times to perform typical services. These were combined and summarized into the following quotas:

Section	Services per Worker per Period	Quota
Counter	88/week	1 Caseworker/1,000 total cases
Assessment	68/month	1 " /750 family cases
General	8/week	1 " /500 family cases
Protective	5/month	1 " /800 family cases
DAB	N/A	1 " /800 DAB cases
Special	N/A	N/A

(A quota of one IM specialist per 150 cases was also established.) Staffing for the first six centers to be separated was based on these standards and is summarized in Exhibit 7.

One of the tasks set for the operations improvement team was to check the operation and validity of these standards to see whether they were appropriate for the thirty-eight additional centers currently undergoing separation. To do this, the team reviewed weekly reports submitted by caseworkers over a 47-week period (April 1970 to March 1971) at three of the separated centers - East End, Clinton, and Franklin. The results of this data gathering are shown in Exhibit 8. In addition to collecting the material shown in the exhibit, the analysts also examined the size of the backlog of uncompleted Protective and General Services cases in the three centers with the following results:

Center	Number of Active Cases	
Protective Services	April 1970	March 1971
East End	69	52
Franklin	58	45
Clinton	220	173
General Services		
East End	1,346	816
Franklin	274	302
Clinton	2,755	615

In the process of gathering this basic information, the operations improvement team made several other observations. First, they concluded that, for the most part, the original standards for the number of social services completed per worker per time period, as developed by Perlman and Pinchoff, were a reasonably accurate reflection of actual operations in the separated centers. Nevertheless, caseworkers at all three centers seemed to be idle a great deal of the time. The team thought that efficiency might be improved substantially if, for administrative purposes, the functions performed by Counter and Assessment were absorbed into the General section and General's quota modified to one caseworker per 445 family cases. The team also observed that the 90-day limit for the duration of Protective and General cases was frequently being circumvented. In the case of General Services, this was done by closing the case and then reopening it, ostensibly for another problem, but actually for treatment of the old one. In Protective, caseworkers were seeking frequent extensions of time, sometimes because court proceedings and/or child placement took longer than the 90-day limit, sometimes because they were reluctant to turn their cases over to the General section which they considered less skilled and less conscientious about handling cases of child neglect and abuse. Finally, it was noted, with some concern, that the typical narcotic case handled by the DAB section took six times as much of the caseworkers' time as the blind, aged or other disabled.

Income Maintenance Staffing

The study of income maintenance staffing, as performed by the operations improvement group, had two purposes: To develop time standards for each element of an IM specialist's job and to measure the demand for these elements that was originated by recipients in each category of public assistance. The study was conducted with the cooperation of the Deputy Director of DSS for Income Maintenance, the clerical workers' union, and the office managers of the six centers already separated. Four IM groups at each center, selected randomly, participated in the data-gathering phase between April 12 and May 7, 1971. The specialist's job was broken down into 13 work categories[1] and the potential clientele into seven groups.[2] Each specialist kept a running record of the kind of work he was doing, when he started the job, when he finished it, and the type of public assistance client being served.

From this data, time standards were developed for each work category by averaging the reported times to perform that kind of service. In addition, a record was developed of the rate at which each type of public assistance recipient would require each kind of IM service. The results of this analysis are shown in Exhibits 9 and 10. (In both exhibits, the data have been condensed substantially.) For purposes of applying the time standards, the group knew that IM specialists worked a 35-hour week of which 2.5 hours was scheduled for coffee breaks. Of the remaining time, it was believed that 20% would be nonproductive. (Twenty per cent is a relatively standard figure for clerical work.) The group also noted that the demand for various kinds of service by different clientele groups showed a marked change between "normal" days of the check cycle and "peak" days (the two or three days immediately following issuance of checks). Exhibit 10 shows the demand characteristics normalized to a one-week period - for both the normal and peak demand times.

---

[1]The 13 work categories were: Budget change, reclassification, address change, change in case composition, application, closing, suspension, transfer in, transfer out, emergency grants, ID cards, information and referral, and miscellaneous.

[2]The seven-clientele groups were: Home Relief, Old Age Assistance, Aid to the Blind, ADC, ADC-U, Aid to the Disabled (nonnarcotic addicts), and Aid to the Disabled (narcotic addicts).

Processing Narcotics Addicts

In November 1969, DSS instituted a procedure for granting public assistance to narcotic addicts under the federal category of Aid to the Disabled. (This meant that the city's share of financial support would be 25% compared to 50% if the Home Relief category had been used.) By the late spring of 1971, the number of addicts receiving assistance had reached 23,000 and was growing at the rate of over 1,200 per month. Grants were running at more than $68.4 million annually. Both the growth rate and the addict population as a whole were very unevenly distributed throughout the city and, therefore, among welfare centers. The Queens center, with an addict population of 2,459, was adding about 200 per month, while Euclid, with 101 addicts was adding only 3 per month. The distribution of addicts in the centers is shown below.

Number of Addict Clients	Number of Centers
< 200	7
200-500	23
501-1,000	10
1,001-2,000	3
> 2,000	1
	44

To be eligible for public assistance, an addict had to meet two requirements: First, he had to provide medical verification of his addiction; second, he had to be a participant in an addiction treatment program or be on the waiting list for one. Only a few addicts were already receiving treatment when they applied for assistance. Most were not and, in a separated center, it was the DAB worker's job to enroll him in a program of his choosing or place him on the waiting list. The addict could remain on a waiting list for one month and still receive assistance. If no opening was available after this time, however, he had to begin treatment in any program where there was a vacancy. If he refused to enroll, assistance was terminated.

BPA attempted, with difficulty, to maintain an up-to-date catalogue of reputable programs throughout the city. No standards existed for evaluating programs; most were small and frequently transient. Of over 180 programs listed by BPA in early 1971, only 23 had capacity for more than 100 addicts, and only 35 had 50 or more public assistance recipients enrolled. Nearly all (particularly those using methadone maintenance) had substantial waiting lists.

Once placed in a program, an addict had to attend regularly or his assistance was stopped. For the first few weeks of treatment and during the time that he was on a waiting list, he picked up his check at the welfare center. Once his attendance in the program was regular, the check was usually sent by mail. This process continued as long as his attendance, which was verified monthly by the DAB service worker, continued. If he dropped out of the program, assistance stopped.

Several centers departed from the basic procedures outlined above. One, for example, when it placed an addict on a recurring grant, had the check mailed to him at the center rather than his home. This was especially true when the addict or the program in which he was enrolled was considered unreliable. Other centers tended to keep addicts on a single issue, emergency roll grant even after they were officially enrolled in a treatment program. In either case, the frequency with which addicts returned to the centers was greater than the standard procedure would have required. Indeed, the operations improvement team's survey of the six reorganized centers showed that over one-half of the addict population returned to the centers to receive weekly special grant checks.

All of these procedures, both standard and nonstandard, reflected the need to control addict cases more carefully than others. Of all clients, addicts were most likely to attempt in some way to defraud the system, often through multiple registration, under different names at different centers. In addition, it was extremely difficult to monitor attendance at treatment programs effectively and accurately. If a program closed (which was not unusual) or an addict stopped attending, it was frequently a month or two before the center was able to verify the addict's change in status and discontinue assistance.

On the other hand, attempts to exert stronger control by increasing the number of times that addicts visited the centers posed other problems. To begin with, addicts were a security risk. With the advent of separation, clients (including addicts), had to move about the centers to transact their business. Reports indicated that "business," as far as addicts were concerned, often included theft, vandalism, and harassment of both staff and clients. Addicts had been known to make purchases of drugs on the premises and shoot-up in the rest rooms. There was evidence that pushers were accompanying addicts to the centers or waiting for them just outside. In fact, some staff members believed that pushers were notifying their customers of the availability of public assistance and "managing" their applications to be sure they were properly filled out.

Another consequence of the growing number of addicts visiting the centers was a deterioration of service to other DAB clients. DAB workers at the six separated centers were observed to spend three or four hours per day placing addicts in programs, checking attendance at these programs and authorizing special grant checks. The time left for servicing other disabled and the blind and aged was extremely limited. At the East End center, for example, where there were 580 narcotic and 2,420 other DAB cases, less than a third of the nonaddicts received any social services whatsoever during 1970, although there was a backlog of demand.

Several suggestions had been made for dealing with the addict problem at the centers. Two, that represented opposite points of view, were to (i) create special welfare centers that would handle only addicts and (ii) outstation income maintenance specialists at selected narcotic treatment programs.

The first called for creation of four centers (one in each borough - except Staten Island) each handling 5,000 to 6,000 addicts and each capable of expansion to accommodate 10,000. The centers would be located in nonresidential fringe areas such as docks or industrial sites. They would be staffed much like a normal welfare center with a director, administrative staff, and income maintenance and social service personnel. The social workers would be responsible for maintaining close liaison with and placing addicts in the various narcotic treatment programs. Other social services, such as housing and employment, would be handled by specialists who would visit the addict centers periodically.

The second alternative involved distributing checks at the treatment program sites thereby increasing the probability that addicts, once enrolled, would continue to attend the programs regularly. An income maintenance specialist would be assigned to distribute special issue checks at those programs where the number of addicts receiving treatment was large enough to justify the time spent by the specialist and the administrative costs necessary to operate the system. The specialist would visit a few programs each day and return to each program semimonthly. If an addict missed the specialist, he could go to the welfare center to pick up his check. The centers would continue to be responsible for addict intake, eligibility determination, program placement, and other services.

A number of criteria seemed to the operations improvement group to be important in evaluating these two, or any other, alternative means of providing assistance to the addict population. They included: capacity to service a rapidly growing case load; start-up and operating costs; level of service to both addicts and other DAB clients; control of treatment program attendance and check issuance; security at the regular welfare centers; and probable community reaction. In addition to these considerations, there was some chance that pending federal legislation would remove DAB clients from the welfare system and place them under Social Security. Since federal officials believed that addicts would not qualify as "disabled" under this new legislation, it seemed important to prepare for a shift of addicts to the Home Relief category if the federal legislation were passed and the city decided to continue supporting its addicts despite the increased cost.

Exhibit 1

PUBLIC ASSISTANCE (A)

Organization of the Human Resources Administration*

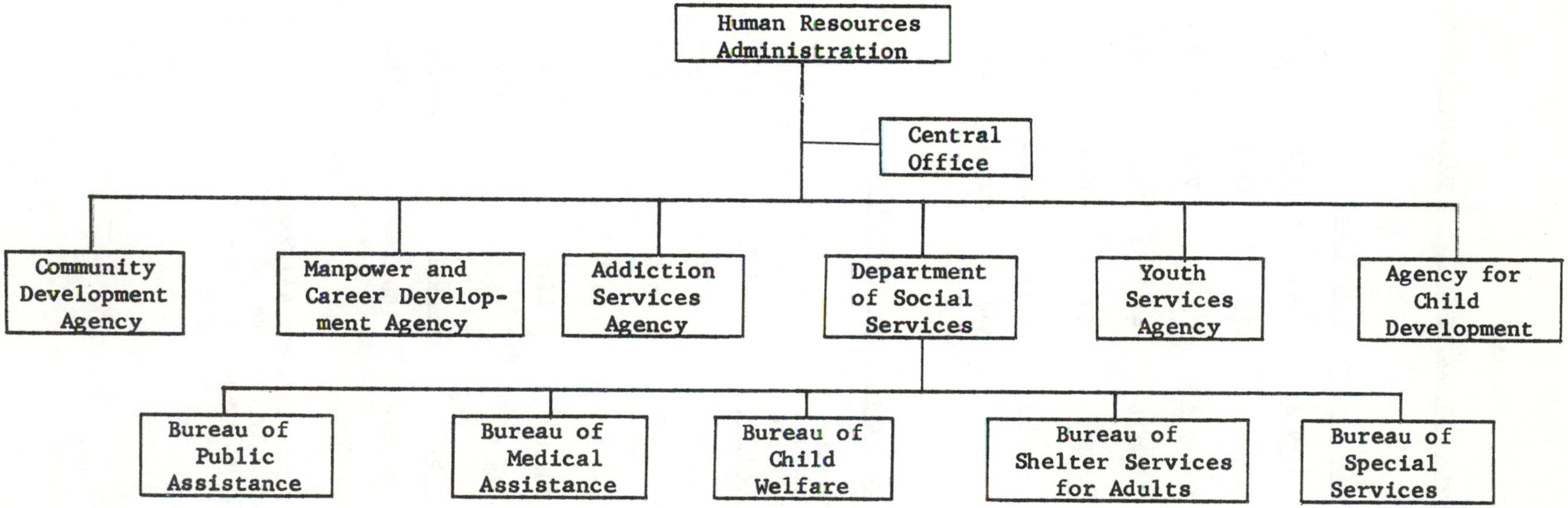

Exhibit 2

PUBLIC ASSISTANCE (A)

Case Load Growth and Mix by Public Assistance Category

Case Load as of April (000)

Category	1966	1967	1968	1969	1970	1971
ADC & ADC-U	96.5	121.6	156.9	195.6	208.3	239.8
AB	2.1	2.0	2.2	2.4	2.4	2.6
AD	21.4	23.9	26.8	41.1	55.7	76.1
HR	35.2	48.6	72.2	80.4	69.7	73.7
OAA	33.5	43.1	49.4	57.1	65.2	75.2
Total	188.7	239.2	307.5	376.6	401.3	467.4

Data for Fiscal Year 1970-1971

Category	Average Number of Cases (000)	Average Number of People (000)	Per Cent of Total Cases	Funding (000,000)	Per Cent of Funding
ADC & ADC-U	215.8	818.9	50.8 %	$ 755.4	69.0%
AB	2.4	2.4	0.6	4.1	0.4
AD	68.3	68.3	16.1	109.9	10.0
HR	66.0	138.8	15.5	117.9	10.8
OAA	69.1	69.1	16.2	101.3	9.2
VA	3.3	8.7	0.8	6.1	.6
	424.9*	1,106.2**	100.0	$1,094.7***	100.0

* Total number of cases as of July 1971 was 475,000
** Total number of people as of July 1971 was 1,200,000
*** Yearly grant rate as of July 1971 was $1.2 billion

Exhibit 3

PUBLIC ASSISTANCE (A)

Pre-1969 Staffing for a Typical 10,000-Case-Welfare Center

Title	Number of Employees	Average Annual Salary	Annual Direct Labor Cost (000)
Professional Staff			
Caseworkers (1/75 cases)	134	$ 9,800	$ 1,310
Specialists (5/ center)	5	9,800	49
Supervisor I (1/5 caseworkers)	27	10,800	292
Supervisor II (1/5 supervisor I)	6	12,400	74
Supervisor III (1/5 supervisor II)	2	14,500	29
Assistant Director (1/ center)	1	16,300	16
Total	175		$ 1,770
Clerical Staff			
Clerks (1/2 caseworkers)	67	6,800	455
Supervisory Clerks (1/5 clerks)	14	8,800	123
Administrative Assistants (1/5 supervisory clerks)	3	10,300	31
Senior Administrative Assistant (1/ center)	1	12,200	12
Total	85		$ 621
Total for Center	260		$ 2,391

Exhibit 4

PUBLIC ASSISTANCE (A)

Comparison of A and B Rolls by Reason for Check Issuance

Reason for Check Issuance	A Roll Checks: Number Issued per Cycle	A Roll Checks: Per Cent of Total	B Roll Checks: Number Issued per Cycle	B Roll Checks: Per Cent of Total
Downbudget - Full amount	5,000	25	1,240	5
Upbudget - Full amount	1,540	8	380	2
Upbudget - Supplement	7,660	38	1,880	7
Initial Grant - New Cases	4,900	25	2,860	11
Transfers and Errors in Regular Grant	900	4	220	1
Special Grants - Recurring and Nonrecurring	0	0	18,420	74
Total	20,000	100	25,000	100

Exhibit 5

PUBLIC ASSISTANCE (A)

Estimated Cost to Process an A-or B-Roll Check

Welfare Center Staff	Man Minutes per Check	Labor Cost per check
I.M. Specialist	40	$ 3.20
I.M. Supervisor & Other Supervisors	10	.96
Clerks	30	2.08
	80	6.24
E.D.P.		
Processing Cost		.31
Check Release		
Check Stopping	5	.33
Check Pulling	*	.19
		.53
Total Cost		$ 7.07

*Cost based on average number of full- and part-time staff

Exhibit 6

PUBLIC ASSISTANCE (A)

Distribution of Dollar Amounts of Rebudgets and Special Grants per Check Cycle

Number of Rebudget Transactions

	Net Dollar Change*				
	$1 to $5	$6 to $10	$11 to $20	>$20	Total
Upbudget	3,850	1,930	2,640	15,640	24,060
Downbudget	2,750	915	1,570	7,865	13,100
Total	6,600	2,845	4,210	23,505	34,100

Number of Special Grant Transactions

	Dollar Value of Grant**				
	$1 to $5	$6 to $10	$11 to $20	> $20	Total
B-Roll	555	370	1,110	15,965	18,000
Daily Special Roll	2,500	2,500	5,500	39,500	50,000
Total	3,055	2,870	6,610	55,465	68,000

*The average upbudget is $43; the average downbudget, $29

**The average B-Roll special grant is $63; the average Daily Special Roll grant, $59

Exhibit 7

PUBLIC ASSISTANCE (A)

Staffing Pattern for the First Six Separated Centers

(Assuming 10,000 Cases/Center)

Title	Nominal Employee Requirements	Number of Five-Man Groups Required	Actual Employees on Staff
Social Services Staff			
Counter (10,000/1,000)*	10.0	2	10
Assessment (6,700/750)*	8.9	2	10
General (6,700/500)*	13.4	3	15
Protective (6,700/800)*	8.4	2	10
DAB (3,300/800)*	4.1	1	5
Special (5 workers per center)	5.0	1	5
Total		11	55
Supervisor I (1/ Service unit)	-	-	11
Supervisor II (1/5 Supervisor I)	-	-	2
Supervisor III (1/5 Supervisor II)	-	-	1
Assistant Director (1 per center)	-	-	1
Total			15
Income Maintenance Staff			
IM Specialists (10,000/150)**	67.0	14	70
Eligibility Investigators (18 per center)	18.0	-	18
Total			88
Administrative Assistants (1 per IM group)	-	-	14
Clerical Staff			
Clerks (40 per center plus 1 per IM group plus 1 per social services group)	-	-	62
Supervisory Clerks (1/5 clerks)	-	-	13
Administrative Assistants (1/5 supervisory clerks)	-	-	3
Senior Administrative Assistant (1 per center)	-	-	1
			79
Total for Center			251

*Based on the number of cases for a typical center.
**IM specialists were paid at the same rate as supervisory clerks.

Exhibit 8

PUBLIC ASSISTANCE (A)

Data on the Delivery of Social Services at Three Separated Centers

Assess	Case Load (Family)	OPD[1] Standard Quota Cases/ Caseworker	Mean Number of Caseworkers on Duty	Mean Number of Actions Per Worker	OPD Standard Number of Actions per Worker per period
East End	5,400	750	8.5	44/mo.	68/mo.
Franklin	3,400	"	7.6	22	"
Clinton	5,800	"	15.3	31	"
Counter	(All Cases)				
East End	7,800	1,000	3.5	34/wk.	88/wk.
Franklin	4,300	"	3.1	32	"
Clinton	9,000	"	8.7	24	"
General	(Family)				
East End	5,400	500	16.2	5/wk.	8/wk.
Franklin	3,400	"	9.5	4	"
Clinton	5,800	"	16.8	6	"
Protective	(Family)				
East End	5,400	1,000	6.3	2.4/mo.	5/mo.
Franklin	3,400	"	3.0	3.3	"
Clinton	5,800	"	11.0	1.9	"

[1]Office of Program Development.

Exhibit 9

PUBLIC ASSISTANCE (A)

Time Standards for Processing Income Maintenance Transactions

Transactions	Mean Time (Minutes)
Rebudget	34.7
Emergency Grant	30.9
Information and Referral	25.5
Application	56.1
I.D. Card	13.8
Other*	31.4

* Includes reclassification, address change, change in case composition, closing, suspension, transfer in, transfer out, and miscellaneous.

Exhibit 10

PUBLIC ASSISTANCE (A)

Number of Income Maintenance Transactions Demanded Weekly for Each 1,000 Clients in Each Client Category

	Client Category			
Transaction Type	HR	DAB (Nonaddict)	DAB (Addict)	ADC ADC-U
Normal Week				
Rebudget	29	21	24	38
Emergency Grant	46	23	271	38
Information and Referral	59	33	84	69
Application	18	8	30	12
I.D. Card	20	16	33	20
Other*	54	31	96	51
Total	226	132	538	228
Peak Period				
Rebudget	54	28	19	53
Emergency Grant	70	30	299	57
Information and Referral	67	41	55	70
Application	13	7	24	17
I.D. Card	31	26	39	30
Other*	56	40	88	70
Total	291	172	524	297

*Includes reclassification, address change, change in case composition, closing, suspension, transfer in, transfer out, and miscellaneous.

PUBLIC ASSISTANCE (B)

By July 1971, over 1,200,000 people (475,000 cases) in New York City were receiving some form of public assistance.[1] Grants were running at an annual rate of $1.2 billion. Delivery of these income maintenance services, as well as a broad range of social services, was the responsiblity of 44 welfare centers located throughout the city. Organizationally, these centers were part of the Bureau of Public Assistance (BPA) which, in turn, was part of the Department of Social Services (DSS). DSS, with an operating budget of more than $100 million per year, was the largest agency within the Human Resources Administration (HRA). The administrator of HRA, Jule Sugarman, together with the administrators of the city's other superagencies, reported directly to the mayor. (Sugarman was also the director of DSS).

Beginning in 1969, basic changes were implemented in the way in which the welfare centers were organized to provide income maintenance and social services. Previously, a single social worker acted as the focus for delivery of both kinds of service to each public assistance family. In essence, the family was assigned "its" social worker and that worker was responsible for determining the family's financial needs and entitlements and for assessing its requirements for nonfinancial assistance. Under the new, or "separated" system, the provision of income maintenance and social services was divided between separate groups of workers at the centers. In order to free clients from the stigma of dependence on a single social worker (and to cut the administrative costs of public assistance), clients now dealt with any of several income maintenance specialists on questions of

---

1 The average caseload during fiscal year 1970-1971 was divided among assistance categories as follows:

Category	Persons (000)	Cases (000)
Aid to Dependent Children (ADC & ADC-U)	819	216
Aid to the Blind (AB)	2	2
Aid to the Disabled (AD)	68	68
Old Age Assistance (OAA)	69	69
Home Relief (HR)	139	66
Veterans Assistance (VA)	9	3

financial assistance. As to social services, clients were free to ask for them if they wished, but no social service worker was given direct responsibility for bringing these services to the client and his family. (Public Assistance (A) provides a more complete description of the center operations before and after separation.) At the same time that separation was going on, there was a change instituted in the procedure for determining an applicant's eligibility for public assistance. Instead of an extensive field investigation of his financial and family status, a simple declaration of need by the applicant was now sufficient to allow income maintenance payments to begin.

Separation had been carried out in response to a Congressional directive that threatened to reduce the amount of federal support for any state or local welfare system that was not separated after July 1, 1971. New York City already had been experimenting with separation on its own before the directive was issued and had carefully and slowly reorganized six centers in the period between January 1970 and March 1971. In June 1971, in order to minimize the potential loss of federal funds, a crash program was initiated to separate the remaining centers. A team composed of experienced project managers from the mayor's office, together with several people from BPA, was formed and succeeded in accomplishing the entire separation task by October 1971. So quickly was the job completed that it became known as "instant" separation.

During the separation project, a detailed operations management study was undertaken to determine how center operations could be improved at the same time that reorganization was taking place (see Public Assistance (A)). One of the strongest recommendations made by the study team was that DSS management capabilities be substantially re-enforced with the addition of new, qualified personnel at the agency's top level. In September 1971, in response to this recommendation, Mayor Lindsay appointed Arthur Spiegel, age 32, to be Executive Director of DSS. Spiegel, a graduate of the Harvard Business School, had been Director of Plans and Programs in the city's Housing and Development Administration and responsible for implementing the new rent control program. He had left the city government after this position and, until his appointment at DSS, had been selling second home real estate developments in Pennsylvania's Pocono Mountains. Spiegel reported directly to Jule Sugarman. Sugarman had been named to head HRA in 1970 after a 20-year civil service career which included the successful implementation of the Head Start program.

A short time after his appointment, Spiegel was quoted in _The New York Times_ as saying:

> In any large organization, you're bound to get some slop but what you have here is a walking disaster. The problem is that for years the Department was run by social workers instead of administrators and its gotten so out of control that no one can get on top of it. You've got a three billion dollar budget - you've got 30,000 people in the Department and it's a mess which means that it's wide open. It's exciting in another respect which is that welfare politics are up for grabs today. There are no truths so in very broad terms, it's a good time to be in welfare.

Spiegel's first project was to recruit a support staff for himself - a group which could design and implement some of the policy and operational changes that he felt would be necessary. He obtained a $3 million authorization for 200 new administrative posts. His top three appointments were Kenneth Brody, a 41 year-old Assistant Vice President of the American Stock Exchange, to run the EDP operation; Kenneth Harris, 29 years old, who had headed the operations improvement team that had studied DSS, was put in charge of a project management group; and John Alexander, the 44 year-old Director of Corporate Development at Allied Chemical, was selected to recruit and direct a management engineering department.

Harris was enthusiastic about the possibilities of his new job:

> I really knew the workings of DSS after spending nine months there. It was a once-in-a-lifetime opportunity to have the authority and responsibility for implementing a consulting study. Professionally, it was an opportunity to see if I could really manage something large. I wanted to see how good I really was.

Alexander, after surveying the operations of DSS, remarked:

> I visualize the Department as a big paper factory. You put a client on the conveyor belt at the beginning and she gets off at the other end with a check or some other service. That's what is supposed to happen but too often she gets sidelined and this sideline becomes a second conveyor.

These men placed advertisements in the financial section of The New York Times addressed to "results-oriented MBAs and Engineers" which read: "We've been charged with turning around a $3-billion government agency and have two years to do it." Harris sent recruiting brochures to business schools with a lead statement as follows: "This is not a career opportunity. It is a once-in-a-lifetime chance to get in on the ground floor of a massive undertaking and experience the thrill of having your abilities and personality as the major constraints on achieving results. This is an opportunity to find out how good you really are."

Spiegel next moved to fill the post of Director of BPA. (Mrs. Hilda Hollyer, an experienced social service worker who held the post of deputy director had been serving as acting director for almost a year.) It took time to find an appropriate person, but in April 1972, Charles Morris, age 32, was named to head the Bureau. (In the interim, BPA's name had been changed to the Bureau of Income Maintenance (BIM).) Morris an Assistant Director of the city's Bureau of the Budget (BOB) and formerly Director of the New Jersey Office of Economic Opportunity, was the first person to head BPA without holding a Master's degree in Social Work. At BOB, he had been in charge of designing a budget reform system that decentralized decision-making authority by allowing individual agencies to make spending and personnel hiring decisions. His work at BOB proved Morris to be not only a creative planner but also a skilled negotiator and administrator. He earned the reputation of being someone who was as likely to illustrate a point by quoting a line of poetry as by citing a statistic.

BPA Organization

Before separation BPA's top level organization consisted of a director and three deputy directors (Exhibit 1). Two of the deputies had responsibility for social service activities and had 11 field directors reporting to them. Each field director, in turn, supervised four center directors and was concerned with the demand for social services, the initiation of new service activities, and the referral and progress of clients who used these services. The field directors, who visited each of their centers about twice a month, periodically prepared and submitted studies and surveys on these activities to their supervising deputy directors. The two deputy directors and all 11 field directors had graduate degrees in social work and had come up through the social service ranks: from case worker, to senior case worker, to senior case supervisor, to center director.

The third deputy director was in charge of clerical operations. He had responsibility for processing the paper work required to provide financial assistance, for developing statistical reports, and for ensuring that there was a large enough staff to perform other clerical support activities at the centers. He had ten field office supervisors reporting to him who acted as technical consultants to the office managers at the centers. The office managers were responsible to their center directors for clerical and administrative activities. The field office supervisors had about the same frequency of contact with office managers as field directors had with center directors but lacked any direct authority over center personnel. Field office supervisors had moved up through the clerical ranks of DSS having held positions as clerks, section heads, assistant office managers, and office managers in the centers.

Center directors supervised 300 to 350 people and were responsible for the entire operations of their centers. Their main tasks involved designing the implementation of policy changes dictated by the BPA central office; dealing with local representatives of the Social Services Employees Union (SSEU) and the Clerical Workers Union (CWU); deploying staff to meet increases in case load and changes in the composition of the case load; reviewing the productivity of different units; and keeping track of absenteeism and lateness through the center's timekeeper. Center directors had to contact the BPA central office for decisions on a number of matters concerning questions of client eligibility and extra allowances for such expenses as housing and educational expense for dependents. If a director simply needed advice, he could consult either his field director or one of several special units set up at BPA headquarters to answer questions about housing, DAB[1], employment, and so forth. Some center directors communicated with the BPA staff frequently, while others did so rarely, preferring to keep all decision-making at the center, even to the point of making decisions which supposedly required BPA approval. A center director's relationship with his field director depended primarily on the personalities of the two individuals, with certain field directors visiting some of their centers constantly and actually taking part in the direction of daily operations.

---

[1]OAA, AB, and AD cases combined were known as DAB cases (Disabled, Aged, or Blind).

Center directors, most of whom had at least 25 years service with DSS, were reluctant, by and large, to discuss very many of their problems with BPA staff. There was a strong feeling that the central office would not understand the particular conditions at the center which contributed to the problem. Center directors also believed that exposing problems could be taken as a sign of ineffective management by high level DSS officials and were unsure of the amount of protection and support they would receive from their field supervisors. Although, under civil service regulations, dismissal or demotion could come only as a result of gross incompetence or criminal activity, there were cases of center directors being transferred to obscure staff positions at BPA headquarters.

Reporting to each center director was a senior case supervisor and an office manager who were responsible for social service and clerical activities, respectively. Center directors relied heavily upon the senior case supervisors, who also had graduate degrees in social work. About half the office managers had college degrees and all had more than 20 years of experience in DSS. The relationship between the office manager and his field office supervisor depended, to a great extent, on how the center director managed his center. In centers where the director avoided contact with the central office, office managers were inclined to communicate less with their field office supervisors. In other centers where there was greater interchange between the director and BPA management, there was likely to be frequent contact between office managers and field office supervisors.

Although separation required a great deal of organizational realignment at the centers (see Public Assistance (A)), only one significant change took place at levels above the center director: BPA's deputy director of clerical operations was put in charge of all income maintenance activities at the headquarters. (At the centers, these activities were now supervised by the office managers.) This was consistent with one of the basic reasons for separation - to make income maintenance into a relatively simple, straightforward clerical operation. It was anticipated that the change would compel both center directors and their office managers to work much more closely with the clerical field office supervisors than they had in the past.

In addition to this organizational change, BPA management also instituted new, separate reporting systems for income maintenance and social service activities. All actions that required a change in the type or amount of income maintenance authorized by a center were compiled by the center's statistical unit for inclusion in a Daily Report of Action Taken (DRAT). Multiple copies of the DRAT were distributed each day to various offices at the center and to a central DSS statistical unit which used the information to develop a monthly book of statistics. This book became available approximately five months after the referenced month and was the agency's primary information document.

At the centers, the statistical units tabulated various categories of actions on the DRAT (case openings, closing, transfers in or out of center, change in the number of dependent children and so forth) into two weekly reports which were sent to a statistical group attached to the deputy director of BPA for IM operations. Here the data was condensed into the IM Activity

Report (Exhibit 2) and the IM Specialist Report (Exhibit 3). Both were available the week after the data was submitted by the individual centers. These reports were utilized by BPA management to spot center-specific or city-wide operational problems and trends. The centers also submitted a weekly personnel status report to BPA which compared the actual number of employees in various categories with the number authorized. This was used to analyze general staffing patterns and spot unfilled positions.

The different social service units at the center submitted reports on the number and type of services given such as placements in educational and vocational training programs and health care assistance rendered. This data was condensed and forwarded on a weekly basis to the two deputy directors in charge of social service activities.

At the time separation was taking place, Mrs. Hollyer and several other top level BPA managers had been skeptical about the ultimate benefits of reorganization and concerned about the pace at which change was taking place. She commented:

> There was a great deal of ambivalance among the operations people about the reorganization of public assistance. But when you're part of a bureaucracy - outside of writing a few memos - it is difficult to take too strong a position because if whatever you do fails it is believed that it failed because of your lack of enthusiasm.

Conditions Postseparation

The basic unit in the separated center was the income maintenance group of five specialists, two clerks and a supervisor. The number of IM groups assigned to each center was determined using a formula developed by the operations improvement team during its study. The formula was based on empirical observations of (i) the average number of each different kind of income maintenance transaction required each week by clients in different categories of public assistance (ADC, OAA, and so forth) and (ii) the mean time required to perform each kind of IM transaction. These two figures could be used to determine how many man-hours per week were required to process all the transactions for a recipient of, say OAA or ADC and this standard, in turn, could be applied to the actual client mix at a center to determine the total number of specialists needed. (For a center with a typical case load, this process resulted in a quota of about 1,000 cases per IM group.)

Social service staffing patterns for the newly separated centers duplicated the staffing arrangements at the centers that had been separated earlier. These were arrived at by estimating client demand for social services - as separate from IM assistance - and calculating the amount of time a social service worker would need to provide these services. (For further information see Public Assistance(A).)

BPA obtained IM Specialists in two ways. Since the job was defined as "clerical," people were hired who could pass a third level civil service clerk examination. These were mainly city employees who were high school graduates. The salary for an IM specialist ranged from $8,000 to $11,000 a year. New specialists were scheduled to have six weeks formal training with special emphasis on face-to-face interviewing but because of the pressing need for IM personnel immediately following separation, this formal training was cut to two weeks with the remainder scheduled to be given on-the-job.

DSS had also made a contractual arrangement with the SSEU to allow many of the 4,500 case workers, whose jobs were done away with by separation, to perform IM specialist roles until social service jobs were available. (Before separation, approximately 7,000 of BPA's 13,500 employees were social workers assigned, in the traditional way, to handle both the income maintenance and social service needs of individual public assistance cases.) Case workers with the lowest seniority were put into their own IM groups and ended up doing IM work in 34 of the 44 centers. Despite the fact that a number of social service workers transferred out of BPA or quit their jobs while separation was taking place, 75% of the 3,800 IM specialist jobs were filled initially by former case workers who earned from $9,500 to $14,000 annually. By April, when Morris entered office, 50% of the IM slots were still held by social workers.

During the months following separation, two trends became clearly evident at the centers. First, the amount of social services delivered to public assistance clients dropped to less than half the preseparation level. Now that most of these services were voluntary, clients simply were not asking for them. Second, the number of welfare recipients visiting the centers for one reason or another was growing dramatically. Part of this increase in traffic could be attributed to growth in the welfare population. The number of public assistance cases continued to rise at a rate of approximately 5,000 per month of which 1,900 were narcotics addicts. (As of the end of October, approximately 30,000 of all DAB cases were addicts.) Addicts were required to report to the centers either to pick up their checks or for mandatory interviews with social service workers regarding their enrollment and attendance in treatment programs. After separation, more and more of them could be found at the centers each week.

Changes in regulations regarding employable home relief (HR) recipients were also responsible for some of the increased traffic. A state law that went into effect on July 1, 1971, required these clients to pick up their checks at a New York State Employment Services (NYSES) office and to accept employment if a suitable job was available. The law also stipulated that if HR employables could not be placed in jobs by NYSES within 30 days, then DSS had to place them in city created public works projects where they could work off their welfare grants at $2 to $4 an hour depending on their skills and experience. In order to make the necessary determination of employability for the 60,000 HR cases and to process referrals to NYSES and public works projects the employment sections at the centers had been increased to between seven and ten specialists. (The IM sections were responsible for the actual transference of checks to NYSES, the closing or suspension of assistance due to no compliance, and the reclassification of HRs to the DAB roles in the event that medical unemployability was proven.)

Even these identifiable causes could not explain all of the increase in clients visiting the centers. Many were ADC mothers who seemed to be present in unprecedented numbers. They could often be found, accompanied by their families, wandering through the center searching for the correct person to answer a question or solve a problem. During the three-day period following the biweekly issuance of checks, it became routine to find as many as 500 persons waiting in line, before a center opened, to pick up a check or lodge a complaint about the amount of payment.

Physically the centers were ill-equipped to handle the increased work load. Many were former warehouses and it was not unusual to find falling plaster, cockroaches and empty beer bottles in the hallways. Steve Rosa, an industrial engineer who had been assigned to work with BPA commented:

> Most of the buildings were not designed as welfare centers. The Department of Real Estate got space anywhere because it was hard to find landlords who were willing to rent their buildings for use as welfare centers. The buildings were not prepared to hold the case load levels. There were dark hallways, crevices, addicts shooting up in the bathrooms, muggings on the stairwells. The centers had just about the most atrocious combination of factors which in some instances put them in violation of fire and building ordinances.

By the end of 1971, conditions had deteriorated seriously. Some centers were seeing as many as 900 persons a day. Violence was erupting with increasing frequency and SSEU was responding by calling two and three work stoppages per week. Following an incident, IM specialists and social service workers were staying off the job as long as three or four days. Those who took part in the stoppages lost their pay for the time they were absent, but this did not prevent the absences from aggravating the traffic situation and interrupting the completion of routine work.

In early 1972, the incidents continued. During January, 75 workers at two Bronx centers walked off the job demanding more security, after a staff member was assaulted by an irate applicant. At the time the incident occurred, three patrolmen and several unarmed guards in civilian clothes were in the center. The SSEU, which did not sanction this particular walkout, reported 45 instances of violence at centers from January to April with a number of major incidents taking place in March. On March 6, several hundred workers left two centers when lye was thrown in a supervisor's face by a client. In another center, 600 clients occupied the building when they did not receive their scheduled checks.

Two weeks later in a Queens center servicing 30,000 clients, 300 workers locked themselves in when a drug addict drew a gun and threatened to shoot workers unless he received a check. The following week, 500 staff members walked out when a Home Relief recipient in the employable category allegedly struck a supervisor when he could not find his check at the state employment office or at the welfare center. A BPA staff member remarked that these were only the overt instances of violence: "You don't read about the number of clients who sit down at the IM specialist's desk and pull out a knife, nail file, or letter opener which they put on the desk before they ask to go on welfare."

Patrolmen at the centers had job actions of their own in which they refused to patrol singly and demanded that they be assigned in pairs. An SSEU official was quoted as saying, "It has reached a point where workers, to protect their own health and safety, may have to discontinue reporting to centers."

In April, during a campaign to elect new union officers, a group challenging the incumbent SSEU leadership distributed a platform statement to all union members which included the following section:

> INCOME MAINTENANCE has become the most unpopular assignment ever given to our members. In their rush toward "instant reorganization" the Department created this understaffed, chaotic and even dangerous mess and [the incumbent leadership] must bear the blame for allowing it to happen and for tolerating its continued existence. Perhaps the Department does not care when workers and clients are verbally and physically assaulted, but this union must respond. Despite the directive adopted at the Delegate Assembly in January, workers remain in IM, the physical plant remains unchanged, and workers still must lose pay for refusing to work in unsafe conditions. In short, [the incumbent] has produced nothing. Are we going to wait for someone to get killed before anything is done? [Our] slate will force the city to bring in enough staff to meet the needs of the clients; we will make them provide a physical setup conducive to the comfort and safety of both workers and clients. Most importantly, we will get our workers out of IM now on a large scale basis before the federalization threat becomes a reality.

In addition to the problems of violence and disruption at the centers, a growing backlog of unprocessed work began to develop. By January 1972 this had risen to over 160,000 actions including 10,000 case closings and suspensions, 5,000 suspected fraud actions and 22,000 budget adjustments. Management Engineering was asked to initiate a plan for dealing with the situation. One ME staff member remarked:

> The average biweekly check was $100. Considering the number of unprocessed case closings we had a potential loss of $25 million a year from that alone. We went to the centers and found that there was no system for categorizing backlog. In one center there was a large wicker basket filled with unprocessed cases. The supervisor didn't know it was there much less how to handle it. You would see one IM group very busy while the next group was twiddling their thumbs doing nothing.

The ME plan, implemented by BPA management, called for the use of 52,000 hours of paid overtime, costing $335,000, at the 17 centers with the worst backlog problems. Two major features of the plan were the systematic separation of new input from backlog and the establishment of case closings and suspensions as priority actions to be taken.

Another problem area in the newly separated centers was the workings of the declaration system for determining client eligibility. Prior to separation each center had an intake section made up of case workers who interviewed all incoming applicants. Each applicant had to supply documents such as birth certificates, rent receipts, and certificates of unemployability in order to establish his need for public assistance. The concept of the declaration system was that eligibility should be based on the applicant's word rather than on corroborating evidence. After separation, therefore, a new application form and an interview by an IM specialist were used to determine eligibility. The specialist was responsible for questioning the applicant on each of the major areas of the form (financial, housing, identifying information, and case composition) and insuring that the applicant's answers had the internal consistency that a prudent person would demand. If the specialist concluded that the applicant's answers were acceptable, income maintenance assistance began immediately. Applicants were not asked to present any documented proof of need.

Mrs. Hollyer explained what took place after the introduction of the declaration procedure:

> The client was supposed to come in and give a story and we were supposed to believe it, much like an income tax return, and issue assistance on the spot. But it was really different than the income tax return. With income tax you have employee records, bank statements and so forth but you didn't have any of that here.

Preseparation the city-wide reject rate on new applications had been in the area of 30%. In the months following separation this rate dropped to less than half of what it had been formerly and at one center it remained in the neighborhood of 1% for a period of months. This phenomenom was not totally unexpected since the rejection rates at the six centers that had been separated earlier had declined dramatically after separation but then climbed back steadily to their original levels. (See Exhibit 4.)

The magnitude of the traffic, the unprocessed case action backlog, and rejection rate problems led both Management Engineering and the DSS Project Management Staff to begin a thorough examination of the operations at several centers. In one they found an average of 40% of the IM specialists absent daily. In another 31 of 49 IM specialists were late eight times or more during a 90-day period; most reported to work after 9 a.m.; and all IM supervisors and specialists took lunch from noon to 2 p.m. Conditions were by no means uniform across all centers, however. One center, typical of about one-third of the total, had, from separation until April, continual incidents of violence, a growing backlog problem, numerous grievances registered by the unions, high absenteeism among all workers and a reject rate that had leveled off at about half of what it was before separation. Another center, representative of a much smaller group, had avoided disturbances by clients, cleaned up its backlog quickly, had good relations with the unions, pushed its reject rate up to preseparation levels and was beginning to show productivity gains under the new system. No center, however, was able to escape all of the problems following separation.

Pressure from the State

One of the persistent questions regarding public assistance in New York City was the number of people receiving welfare who were actually ineligible. Many BPA people believed that the nature of the problem was systemic and this position was articulated by Mrs. Hollyer:

> It must be remembered that people who come for income maintenance come at a time of crisis in their lives and in most cases they are not able to explain themselves very well. The income maintenance specialist must know how to ask, how to listen - to hear what is being said. Can you imagine what it means to say "no" to a person coming in for public assistance? It's possible to say "no" - but to say it in such a way that you show empathy. You can make other referrals that are necessary. You can say "no" on a reasonable, human basis so that you don't degrade the other fellow. To say "no" without being God is a tremendously difficult thing to do. It brings out the worst in people and they say "no" when they shouldn't or it brings out the fear in people and they say "yes" when they shouldn't.

One SSEU member, doing income maintenance work, was quoted in The New York Post as saying:

> Client misrepresentation is a necessity because poor families will do anything not to go under. The welfare grant level is under the federal poverty level. If a family claims an extra child to increase their grant, it's reported as welfare cheating but such claims would be generally accepted by society if people knew the facts.

In August 1971, Governor Nelson Rockefeller named George Berlinger, a retired businessman, to the newly created post of Welfare Inspector General with the broad mandate to examine all phases of public assistance to insure proper expenditure of funds. Berlinger had the authority to issue subpeonas and conduct investigations in any manner that he saw fit. He made it clear that his major function would be "to restore public confidence in the welfare system."

Soon after his appointment Berlinger began investigations of new applications and recertifications of clients at individual New York City centers to determine ineligibility rates. In December, he announced to the press that ineligibility among new applicants accepted and clients recertified ranged from 16% to more than 30% in three centers that his staff had investigated. On the basis of these findings, Berlinger claimed that 6% of all families on public assistance were actually ineligible; 20% were overpaid; and 10% underpaid. He was quoted as saying that the basic reason for these errors was "loose administration at HRA and the absence of proper controls."

Berlinger's pronouncements on ineligibility contrasted sharply with DSS claims that total ineligibility among the city welfare population was about 3%. The DSS findings were derived from quarterly quality control investigations mandated by the Federal Government and from validation studies carried out by the state comptroller. The quality control reports were compiled by 200 civil service inspectors who reviewed a random sample of 0.5% of the city's ADC and DAB cases each quarter to assess both eligibility and payment errors. Federal guidelines set a 3% tolerance level on ineligibility and 5% on payment errors, which if not met could result in a discontinuance of federal funds. A summary of data from the quality control reports for the last three calendar quarters of 1971 is shown in Exhibit 5. The state validation covered both the ADC and HR categories. Based on samples of about 3,000 of these cases in nine centers in September 1971 and 3,000 cases in ten different centers in December, the state had concluded that 1.2% of the ADC cases and 5.2% of the HR cases were financially ineligible. (Cases in state's sample that were indeterminate were excluded from the results. An "indeterminate" case was one that the inspectors were unable to locate (UTL) or who failed to cooperate (FTC) with the inspectors.)

Jule Sugarman, the HRA Administrator, stated that Berlinger had grossly misrepresented the facts and commented:

> I think it is recognized that we are trying to do the best job that we can here. It is one thing to have the luxury of Mr. Berlinger to take pot shots but it is quite another to make the system work.

Berlinger responded with another study that involved the investigation of 45 cases at random out of 450 acceptances in one month at one center. At a second press conference he announced an ineligibility rate of 17% to 26% based on the sample and claimed ineligibility in the city was conservatively 10% to 15% with a potential loss of $120 million a year. Sugarman accused Berlinger of being "recklessly irresponsible" for basing his findings on 45 cases out of a city-wide total of 500,000. He was quoted as saying that such a sample was subject to a probability error of better than 99.9%.

In an effort to resolve these conflicting views on the amount of ineligibility, Harris' DSS Project Management Staff undertook a thorough analysis of the issue early in 1972.[1] Harris assigned a team to look at 800 cases drawn from three centers. A major effort of the investigation was to track down those cases that the quality control and state validation reports excluded because the recipient would not cooperate with eligibility investigators or could not be located. Berlinger always cited two numbers in giving his estimates of ineligibility - one based on the assumption that all these eligibility indeterminates were in fact eligible and another based on the opposite premise. The quality control reports that DSS relied upon did not take these cases into account at all.

---

[1] Harris' group now consisted of almost fifty MBAs, industrial engineers, and systems analysts plus a few young BPA staff members.

The PMS team was able to gather information on 93% of a sample group of 72 cases listed as FTC and located 96% of 101 cases which were in the UTL category. They concluded that 43% of the FTC group and 30% of the UTL group were ineligible. When added to the previously known ineligibles, this meant that 5.5% of the total case load was ineligible at a cost of $37.4 million per year. As to over- and underpayment of those who were eligible, PMS determined that 28.7% of the total case load was incorrectly paid at a net loss of $31.5 million per year. In addition, 2.2% of all cases were misclassified. Thus, there were errors of some kind in 36.4% of the case load at a minimum annual cost of $68.9 million. (Misclassifications, when corrected, would not mean a change in payment amount but only a move, say, from the ADC to the HR rolls.) PMS also studied the source of these errors and concluded that 61% ($42.0 million per year) were the fault of the BPA system while the remainder were the result of client fraud. About one-third of the BPA errors occurred at the point of initial client entry into the system and the remainder after a client was on the rolls. Exhibits 6 and 7 are a condensation of the PMS error analysis.

Harris and his staff believed that several causes underlay the size of the ineligibility problem. These included 1,000 fewer center employees than specified by PMS standards, the impact of "instant" separation, the limited experience and training of center personnel, poor working conditions, the rapid growth of the addict population on welfare, increased client traffic at the centers, and the absence of a good management control system. By April, they had developed a nine-part corrective action plan. The plan emphasized the following programs:

New Application Process: A pilot study of applicants recently certified as eligible for public assistance at three welfare centers showed that 5.3% were ineligible based on the information that appeared on their applications; 5.3% were found to be ineligible when asked to supply corroborating documentation such as birth certificates or rent receipts; and 16.9% would not cooperate when asked to document the information submitted in their applications. PMS suggested that the "simple declaration of need" now used by the IM specialists to determine eligibility be modified to require a reasonable amount of client documentation and that a supervisory review be made of the specialists' actions before financial assistance could begin. Further, they recommended that field investigation units be re-established in each center for the purpose of gathering data on specific questions about selected applicants (not for making full field investigations as was done before separation). And they suggested that one IM unit in each center should be responsible for all eligibility determinations. It was expected that these new procedures would increase the average rejection rate from its present level of 23% to over 30%, thereby saving about $30 million per year.

Face-to-Face Recertification: Under existing regulations, each client's eligibility had to be reconfirmed every six months. This was done by mailing recipients a questionnaire on which they could explain the nature of any change in status. If the client indicated there was no change, he was automatically recertified and assistance was continued at the previous level. Clients who did indicate a change were called in for interviews to redetermine their eligibility and the correct amount of support. During its three-center study of BPA operations, PMS had pilot tested a different approach to recertification - one in which everyone would be called in for an interview rather than sent a questionnaire. Of those called during the test, PMS found that 14.8% were being overpaid, 6.5% underpaid, 3.6% were totally ineligible, and 9.8% failed to report. PMS proposed, therefore, that a program be undertaken to provide at least a one-time face-to-face recertification of all public assistance clients in order to purge the roles of ineligibles and eliminate existing payment errors. These face-to-face interviews would include documentation checks (birth certificates for children, rent receipts, income statements, and social security cards); collateral verifications with employers, landlords, banks, and other sources; and referral, as appropriate, to employment, social service units, or law enforcement officials. PMS anticipated that net overpayments of $30 million per year could be eliminated during this one-time recertification and another $30 million per year saved through case closings. It was also recommended that the initial face-to-face recertification be followed by a continuing program of regular recertification interviews with the period between interviews and the depth of questioning tailored to the characteristics of different client groups. For example, addicts would be recertified by interview more frequently than recipients of Old Age Assistance.

An Error Accountability Program: At present, no regular assessment was made of the error rate at individual centers. PMS proposed that it examine a sample of cases from each center each month and rank the centers by type, rate, and cost of eligibility, payment, and classification errors. The BPA central office would publish a monthly ranking report and an intensive review would be undertaken by PMS of cases in the five centers with the lowest ratings. This review would place responsibility for errors with individual IM groups and recommend, as well as implement, corrective action.

The New Management Control System

While the Project Management Staff had been conducting its analyses of the eligibility problem, John Alexander and his staff of 55 at Management Engineering had been busy designing a new control system for BPA.[1] Their goal was a system that would lead eventually to the following innovations: work load forecasting; work standards; scheduling techniques; assignment procedures; work schedule control; and individual productivity measures.

One engineer who worked on the project stated:

> In the new system the first-level supervisors will hand out all work and will pick up incomplete work at the end of the day. They will check on group productivity and question why differences exist among groups. Each management level will review the preceding level and the center director will be held responsible for differences in output between IM groups.

[1] Most of the group were industrial engineers and systems analysts with at least ten years experience in business.

The proposed management control package, which was ready for Morris when he arrived in April had four integrated procedures:

- A backlog control form to be filled out daily by each IM specialist. This would enable individual center directors and BPA managers to monitor progress on the reduction of backlogs. The form would show the beginning work load and daily production for each specialist and would indicate the hours so that individual productivity could be calculated.

- A Daily Record of Activity that would supersede the present weekly reports (Exhibits 2 and 3) and contain the same basic information.

- A Director's Action Report that center directors would complete on a weekly basis. It would list major problems, corrective action planned, and follow-up action required. This would create a regular channel of communication between the directors and the central office and would allow BPA management to become more closely involved in center operations.

- A Weekly Personnel Report that would give management an accurate picture of staff availability. The report would provide a count of center staff that could be matched against client demand. This would allow BPA management to evaluate long- and short-term staffing requirements and review measures of productivity.

BPA Raction

BPA personnel, from Mrs. Hollyer (now the deputy director) on down were not very enthusiastic about the recommendations made either by PMS or by Management Engineering. They were particularly distressed when PMS suggested, in February, that the increased demands for income maintenance services created by steadily expanding rolls be met by hiring personnel in accordance with the formula of 1,000 cases per IM group. The resulting city-wide quota of 524 groups they felt, was much too low, and could only hamper efforts to tighten eligibility procedures and reduce the backlog of unprocessed actions. Most center directors believed a more reasonable standard would be 750 cases per group and 600 to 700 groups in the system. In an effort to prove BPA's point, Mrs. Hollyer asked Steve Rosa, the industrial engineer, to re-examine the PMS standard. After interviewing several field office supervisors and center directors and observing the operations at a number of centers, Rosa concluded that most of the centers did, in fact, have to cope with one or more "special" conditions that required an upward adjustment in the number of IM specialists as determined by the PMS quota.

> We did things like calling in the Field Office Supervisors to find out if particular centers were the kind of neighborhood building where people just like to hang out. If they were, it meant more traffic for the specialists and more specialists needed to handle the same size case load. It also turned out

to be important to know how many stories the building had because more stories meant more time in traveling from office to office to process a case. Alcoholics had to be figured in and were as bad a problem as addicts. Some centers had large transient case loads with people disappearing all the time. We devised 16 criteria [Exhibit 8] for adjusting the PMS quota. When we applied these adjustments systemwide, we came up with 686 groups - about 750 cases per group.

Also in February, BPA management had asked each center director to comment in writing on his major problems. The responses tended to confirm the differences of opinion regarding staffing levels and suggested, moreover, that there were a number of other issues on which BPA managers and Spiegel's staff at DSS did not share the same priorities (see Exhibits 9 and 10). Said one official at BPA:

> We welcomed assistance in correcting operational problems and devising new systems. They jumped right in, but this was not a factory for bottling beer. Here, people handle people - alcoholics, broken homes, addicts. Our feeling was that in order to be able to understand these problems you have to have daily contact with the people. Business education, graphs, and numbers aren't the same thing. We told center people how these new people would be helpful, how they could improve center operations and assist us. We said, "Give them a chance." But the centers only saw useless studies and instant experts.

Exhibit 1

PUBLIC ASSISTANCE (B)

Bureau of Public Assistance

(BPA) Organization (Preseparation)

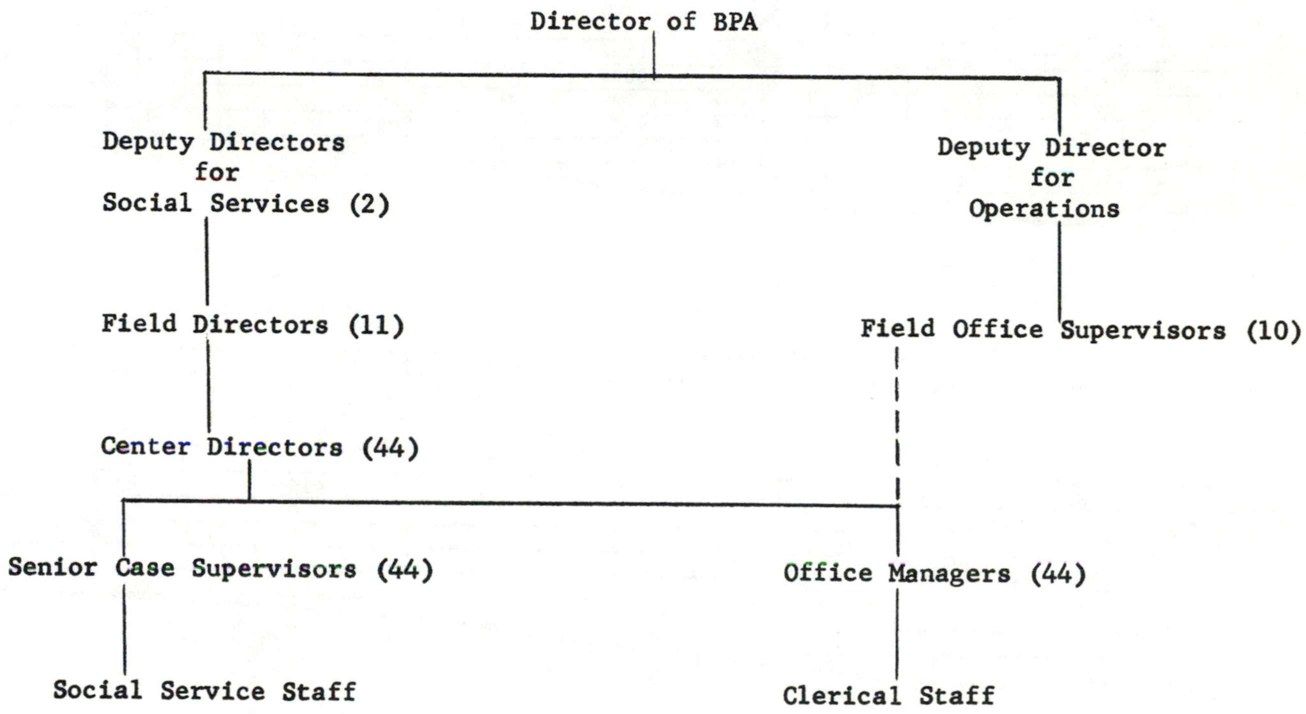

Exhibit 2

PUBLIC ASSISTANCE (B)

INCOME MAINTENANCE OPERATIONS

ACTIVITY REPORT

Page 1

Includes 3556 Cases in Transit

Week Ending 6/16/72

CENTERS	Accept	NA'D	Closed	Total Under Care Incl. Chelsea	Old Age Homes	Income Maint.	Family Cases	A.S.C. CASES
Total This Week	6993	253	6545	# 527233	9787	213074	#295801	1967
Total Last Week	5930	220	6107	# 526845	9605	213562	295016	1911
11- Low. Manhattan	244	0	280	11307	202	4559	6748	24
13- Waverly	249	0	301	10099	164	5634	4465	35
15- Gramercy	164	0	187	11099	0	3748	7351	2
19- Yorkville	114	0	104	8684	297	8684	-	102
23- East End	111	0	92	7059	0	7059		
24- Amsterdam	161	5	145	8474	[illegible]			
25- Franklin	69	0	57					

Page 2

Week Ending 6/16/72

CENTERS	PENDING ACTIVITY: BALANCE PREV. WEEK	BALANCE THIS WEEK	INT. + PTI - PTO	CREATED
Total This Week	1873	1919	575	2912
Total Last Week	1841	1861	419	2292
11- Lower Manhattan	0	0	0	156
13- Waverly	0	0	0	144
15- Gramercy	0	0	0	79
19- Yorkville	0	0	0	3
23- East End	0	0	[illegible]	
24- Amsterdam	16			
25- Franklin				

Abbreviations:
- NA'D - Not Accepted
- A.S.C. - Approved State Charges (for recipients whose support is fully paid by the state)
- INT - Intake
- PTI - Pending Transfers In
- PTO - Pending Transfers Out

Exhibit 3

PUBLIC ASSISTANCE (B)

WEEKLY RECORD OF ACTIVITY OF INCOME MAINTENANCE SPECIALISTS

Week Ending:

	Intake	Mail	Tele-phone	Appl.	Under-care	Total Actions	Man Days Worked	Av. No. Actions Per Day Per Spec.	Group Back-log
Low. Man.									
Waverly									
Gramercy									
Yorkville									
East End									
Amsterdam									
Franklin									
St. Nicholas									

Exhibit 4

PUBLIC ASSISTANCE (B)

Average Rejection Rates for Three Welfare Centers Separated in 1970*

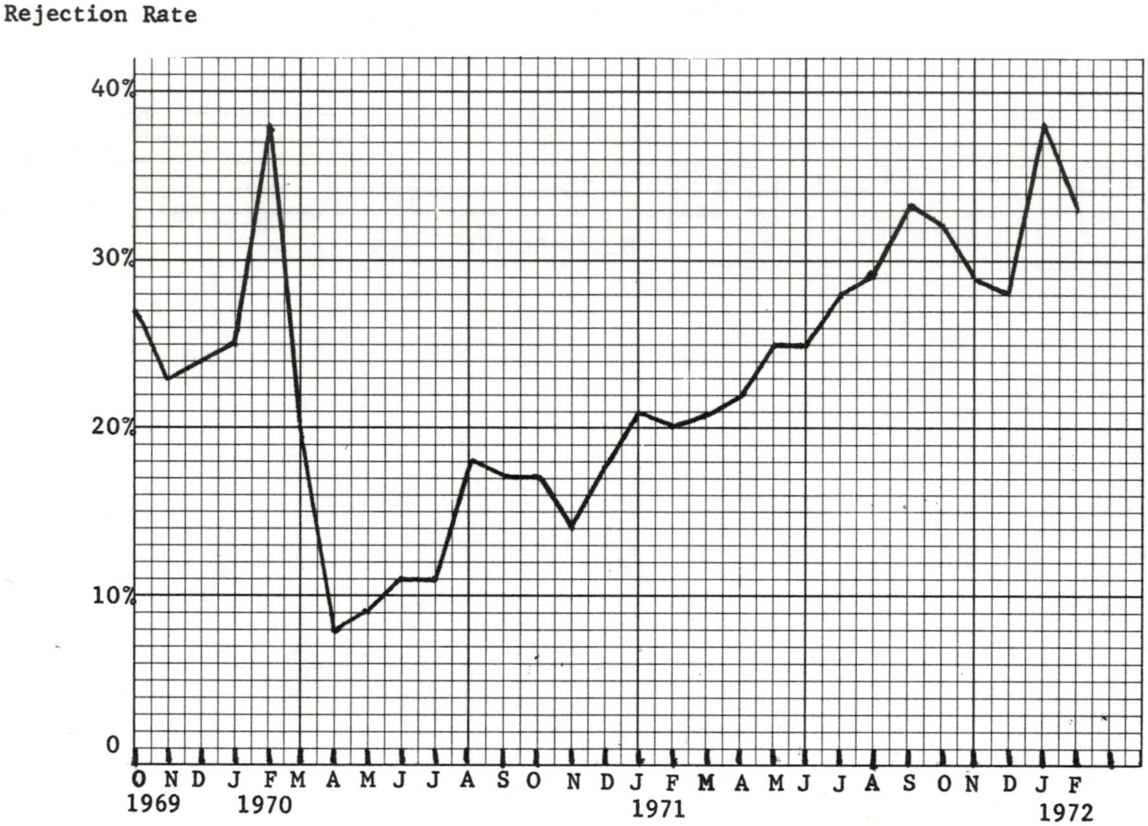

* The three centers were East End, Franklin, and Clinton.

Exhibit 5

PUBLIC ASSISTANCE (B)

Summary of Federal Quality Control Reports

for Last Three Quarters of Calendar Year 1971

	Federal Government Tolerance	National Average		Three-Quarter Average, NYC		
		AFDC	DAB	AFDC	DAB	Combined
Not eligible for assistance	3.0%	5.6%	4.9%	5.3%	1.2%	3.7%
Incorrect Payments	5.0	-	-	27.1	30.2	28.7
Overpayment	5.0	14.6	7.9	18.1	22.4	-
Underpayment	5.0	9.7	4.9	9.0	7.8	-
Failed to cooperate	-	-	-	-	-	2.0
Could not be located	-	-	-	-	-	3.3
Miscellaneous	-	-	-	-	-	3.1
Total						40.8%

Exhibit 6

PUBLIC ASSISTANCE (B)

Responsibility for Identified Eligibility Errors

		Annual Cost of Errors (millions)			
		Agency Errors		Client Errors	
Client Category	Total	Failure to Act	Incorrect Action	Unintentional*	Fraud
Totally Ineligible	$ 23.7	$ 4.7	$ 4.6	$ 4.4	$ 10.0
Underpayment/overpayment	31.5	12.7	6.6	7.6	4.6
Unable to locate	7.0	-	1.4	-	5.6
Failed to cooperate	6.7	-	-	-	6.7
Total	$ 68.9	$ 17.4	$ 12.6	$ 12.0	$ 26.9

* PMS believed most unintentional client errors might really be due to agency neglect. The amount of $12.0 million, therefore, was added to agency error in the PMS summary statistic.

Exhibit 7

PUBLIC ASSISTANCE (B)

Distribution of the Cost of Agency and Client Errors

	Percentage of Total Cost
Agency Errors (Total Cost = $42.0 million)	
Failure to Act	
1. Failure to rebudget for known change	32.6%
2. Failure to act on Social Security	15.9%
3. Failure to act on return of spouse	15.2%
Other Agency Error	
4. Incorrect policy application	14.1%
5. Misbudgeting	11.1%
6. Incorrect budget computation	4.9%
7. Other	6.2%
Total	100.0%
Client Errors (Total Cost = $26.9 million)	
1. Failure to acknowledge income/benefits/support	45.5%
2. Failure to report change in earning/income/benefits (Social Security)	22.8%
3. Failure to notify of returned employed spouse	21.2%
4. Dependent children leave home	4.8%
5. Payment for person not in home	5.4%
6. Other	0.3%
	100.0%

Exhibit 8

PUBLIC ASSISTANCE (B)

Criteria Developed by Steve Rosa
for Adjusting a Center's Quota of Income Maintenance Specialists

	Criterion	Additional IM Specialists
1.	Abnormally high rate of new applications.	
	450 - 550 applications per month	1 additional IM specialist
	550 - 650 " " "	2 " " specialists
	650 - 800 " " "	3 " " "
	800 and up " " "	4 " " "
2.	Number of stories in building over three.	1 specialist per additional story
3.	Abnormally high traffic because center is conveniently located in the neighborhood it serves.	2 specialists
4.	Responsibility for special State or Federal Programs.	1 IM specialist group
5.	Employment (adjust for every 10% of case load over 50% family cases).	1 specialist
6.	No on-line computer facilities for calculating clients' budgets.	3 specialists
7.	Known disruptive client groups.	2 specialists
8.	Known disruptive staff union groups.	2 specialists
9.	Serious language problems (Spanish, Chinese, and others).	½ specialist per 2,000 clients
10.	Known excessive client mobility (transfers to and from other centers).	½ specialist per 2,000 clients
11.	Known areas of excessive housing costs.	½ specialist per 2,000 clients
12.	Known unpopular center location (security problems created for center employees).	1 specialist for each 2,000 cases over 7,000
13.	Centers with large hotel populations.	1 specialist
14.	Known high number of hospital discharges.	½ specialist per 2,000 clients
15.	Absence of instructors for training specialists.	2 specialists
16.	Special problems such as large numbers of alcoholics.	To be determined individually

Exhibit 9

PUBLIC ASSISTANCE (B)

Form W-4-600M-501132(69)
Rev. 7/1/67 346

MEMORANDUM

THE CITY OF NEW YORK
DEPARTMENT OF SOCIAL SERVICES

DATE: 2/9/72

TO: Mr. John Stackhouse, Field Office Supervisor
Bureau of Public Assistance

FROM: Mr. William Johnson, Director, Willis Center (49)
Mrs. Constance Benson, Office Manager

SUBJECT: NEEDS OF WILLIS CENTER

STAFFING: Since Reorganization our caseload has increased to 10,000 cases. Our quota is ten I.M. Groups. Each group has an average of 900 cases. As a result staff has not been able to handle the current work, nor attack the accumulated backlog, except through overtime work.

Willis at the current time does not have a person available to take the position of Homemaker-Housekeeper. Our D & C[1] staff is inadequately staffed to handle the normal flow of work and in addition, the installation of the plastic I.D. cards has created the need for at least two additional clerks.

Our Timekeeping Section is also in need of an additional clerk due to the tremendous volume of work. The assistant office managers, whose span of supervision is too great, is in need of additional supportive staff.

The Control Unit is also considered under-staffed due to the need to designate a person as the Duplications Control Clerk and also to handle the increased number of financial transactions which the enlarged caseload has brought about.

The staffing situation is especially crucial since there is no reserve to offset the increased absenteeism that we are experiencing.

The General Service staff cannot perform its mandated services due to their insufficient number. The Center is also handicapped by the inability to use staff selectively because of contractual agreements. It was not possible at the point of separation to utilize staff in the most effective manner because of the requirements of seniority and juniority provisions.

It is our considered opinion that we would require, on the basis of our current caseload, at least 4 additional groups. This lack of adequate staff to provide service to the client has aroused community resentment.

MORALE: The staffing condition as described above has led to a deterioration in staff morale. The inability to provide services has created hostility between the income maintenance specialists and the clients. This in turn has led to confrontations and a demand for greater security. Until recently Willis did not have adequate security

Exhibit 9 (continued)

- 2 -

MORALE contd.

patrolmen assigned to this Center. We feel that we need at least six patrolmen assigned to Willis alone, pending more suitable physical arrangements.

PHYSICAL STRUCTURE AND WORKING CONDITIONS

The physical structure of Willis Social Service Center has certain difficulties. We share the building with the Bergen Social Service Center. The three elevators are not sufficient to handle the traffic, particularly in the morning rush. Due to the increased caseload and the inability of clients to reach their caseworkers, the traffic in Willis has greatly increased, leading to overcrowding in every section of the office. There is an urgent need for additional chairs in our primary reception area. The D & C Unit must be either removed from its present location or physically rearranged in such a manner as to prevent them being overwhelmed by clients reaching for their checks. In addition Group 1, which services some 150 people on a check day (primarily narcotic users), must be relocated to a more protected area or there must be again some type of physical barriers erected. Without adequate security patrolmen it is impossible to attempt to handle the flow of clients. Willis normally serves on check days, 450 to 500 people. In addition we have had adverse experiences with clients seeking to use our telephones. We feel that there should be installed in this Center public telephones.

For six months the toilet facilities on our 4th floor has been out of order despite efforts made by our custodial staff to have the landlord make the necessary repairs. There is no valid reason why this condition should exist.

OTHER PROBLEMS

Willis is an ABC^2 Center and is dependent upon the machines in our office as well as the Central EDP to process financial actions and reduce the flow of clients into our office. We reported on several occasions the fact that one of our machines is in a state of constant disrepair and the other in a state of almost constant breakdown. Central EDP with its failure to deliver checks to the proper place at the proper time, creates almost insurmountable problems in terms of handling the irate client and disgruntled staff who must duplicate their work.

In summary, the needs of Willis Social Service Center can be summarized as follows: 1) inadequate staff; 2) inadequate physical facilities and layout; 3) poor working conditions.

One of our immediate and pressing needs is the erection of a partition to enclose Group 1 located on the first floor. This group services narcotics users and always have a large number of clients and applicants waiting to be seen. Because the group is located on the open floor clients have access to records, supplies, etc. They constantly harrass the staff of this group to a point where the original group clerk would have to leave her desk at the

Exhibit 9 (continued)

- 3 -

OTHER PROBLEMS contd.

point of tears and has since been replaced. The caseload for this group is rapidly increasing and we do not expect any improvement if the physical set-up remains as is. This situation is critical and demands immediate attention.

WJ/dg

---

[1] Disbursing and Collecting (D&C).

[2] ABC was an on-line computer system that IMSs could use to determine the level of income maintenance to which a client was entitled. Not all centers were equipped with ABC.

Exhibit 10
PUBLIC ASSISTANCE (B)

Form W-4-700M-425110(68)
Rev. 7/1/67 346

MEMORANDUM

THE CITY OF NEW YORK
DEPARTMENT OF SOCIAL SERVICES

DATE: Feb. 22, 1972

TO: Mr. Irving Novin, Field Office Manager
9th Floor
C.O.

FROM: Isidore Gosian, Director
Greenwood Center

SUBJECT:

We are requesting additional I.M. groups inasmuch as the growth of the caseload in this center, and various concomittant problems are making it rapidly impossible for us to function any further.

Our family I.M. groups range from 808 cases to 859 cases. Our narcotics groups have 651 cases, our DAB I.M. group from 1495 to 1705. It should also be born in mind that these figures are after our ATO cases have gone out and before our ATI cases have come in.

Since 10/1/71 we have 260 cases more in DAB, 538 cases more in the family groups; there appears to be no prospect whatsoever that the increase will not continue at the same or even a higher rate.

The various groups in this building are scattered over five floors. We have only t o small elevators which are constantly crowded, making communication between floors very difficult. It is necessary to go to the first floor for emergency checks. It is necessary to go to the 4th floor to see the consultants. There is a great deal of leg work required because of this. In addition, although we have 16 groups, we have only 3 file clerks. This has put an extra burden on our group clerks to the extent that a number of them have requested to be transferred.

Further, our telephone situation has augmented the work to be done. For instance, we have 3 groups which have no telephone in the groups whatsoever; and several others which have only a single phone.

Inasmuch as our experience has indicated that a family group cannot adequately handle more than 700 to 750 clients, we are requesting the addition of two family groups.

Although the increase in the DAB groups has not been as high, a problem has arisen in the handling of na cotics cases, increasing numbers of which (as they become reclassified from PAD[1] to AD) are being transferred from the drug unit to the various DAB units. For example, most of these become AD group 2 so that continuing work is necessary on them. In additioh they present greater difficulty in handling by the DAB I.M. workers who, being all clerical, have had no experience in handling such persons. Some of the experiences that this clerical force has had with the narcotic cases have been so frightening that several of the I.M. workers are requesting demotions.

This rise in the caseload (which in this office is now nearly 17,000 cases) in addition necessitates an increase in both the Control and Statistics quota. Much additional work has been added to the Control Section such as the 325H's, checking on number of duplications, more 2 party checks for rent due to duplic tion. Due to vacations and heavy absences a realistic quota for this section can mean no less

Exhibit 10 (continued)

Mr. I. Novin -2- 2/22/72

than 12 persons. Obviously in handling follow up 661's or special checks which do not go out ontime, many extra hours are needed to undo and redo these checks for a later date or to process what would have been an unnecessary emergency check.

As for Statistics, our office, which in the last 3 months has reclassified PAD cases to the extent of 485 cases, in addition to all of the extra work occasioned by the caseload increase cannot manage without at least one additional person added to the quota of that section.

There can be no question that the great backlog of control and movement of the I.M. work in both family groups and DAB falls on the shoulders of the Asst. Office Managers. Not only to facilitate their work, but to enable them to do it at all, there must be at least ohe administrative assistant for each two Assistant Office Managers, as well as a secretary. The time of the Asst. Office Managers is being wasted on leg work and the handling of controls which should be handled by such administrative assistant and/or secretary.

Further, the great backlog of work concentrated with the office manager requires a second administrative assistant to her. It should be noted that this same work (with a lesser caseload) when it was assigned to two senior case supervisors, had a quota of four administrative assistants to the two senior case supervisors.

It should additiohally be recalled that the quotas for I.M. groups were set not at the point of separation but some time prior to that when our caseload was even less so that the increase of 800 cases, as shown above, does not dearly present the increase as allied to the number of I.M. groups.

The gravity of this situation has now reached a point where we will soon not be able to guarantee an adequate control of whatever backlog is currently being accumulated, despite the fact that due to the heroic efforts of these staff members the old backlog (for which paid oevertime has been made available) has been completed.

I am requesting immediate consideration of this problem and a very early reply as to what will be done about it.

IG:JB

---

[1] Provisionally accepted on the AD roles (PAD).

ENVIRONMENTAL PROTECTION

SANITATION (A)

An Overview of the System

New York City is the world's largest final market. It receives an incredible variety of products from the Americas as well as from abroad: Cars from Germany, cameras from Japan, fruit from the Caribbean--a greater total quantity of products than any other city. At the end of their useful lives, these products become inputs to the city's solid waste management system. The 22,000 tons per day handled by the New York system in 1968 made it by far the largest in the world. Responsibility for collecting and processing most of this waste lay with the city's Department of Sanitation (DS), an arm of the Environmental Protection Administration (EPA).

EPA had been created in March 1968. It was the third of nine superagencies proposed to the City Council in the mayor's reorganization plan for city government. In addition to the Department of Sanitation, it also included the Department of Air Pollution Control, the Bureau of Water Supply, and the Bureau of Water Pollution Control.[1] EPA was the first comprehensive "environmental" agency in the country.

The Department of Sanitation was organized primarily by function, with each major task the responsibility of a separate bureau. An organization chart is shown in Exhibit 1. The first task was refuse collection. This was done for commercial locations (12,000 tons per day) by private cartmen licensed and regulated by the Department of Consumer Affairs (not a part of the EPA). For noncommercial locations (10,000 tons per day from private residences and certain tax-exempt and governmental buildings), the responsibility belonged to DS and was discharged by the Bureau of Cleaning and Collection (BCC). BCC was also responsible for street cleaning and snow removal. (The refuse load on various days of the week is shown in Exhibit 2.) Over the years, the amount of refuse had grown

---

1 The latter three agencies were later consolidated into the Department of Air Resources and the Department of Water Resources.

persistently. Exhibit 2 shows this growth from 1965 to 1969 for household refuse only. Although this was the major work load, Exhibit 2 underestimates the rate of increase in total waste load since its other components were growing even faster. For example, over the ten-year period from 1959 to 1969, while household refuse grew 40%, bulk refuse grew 110% and the abandonment rate for cars by 1700% (to 150 per day).

After collection, about one-third of the refuse was burned in municipal incinerators and the remainder, including the ashes from incineration, was transported (by truck or barge) for ultimate disposal in one of the city's land fills. These tasks were the responsibility of the Bureau of Waste Disposal. Supporting the major collection and disposal operations, a force of mechanics (Bureau of Vehicle Maintenance) and maintenance crews (Bureau of Plant Maintenance) kept the equipment fleet and capital plant in operation. The Bureau of Administration and Field Inspection combined two tasks: the administrative group processed the fiscal and personnel actions of the department, and the field inspection group had primary responsibility for enforcing laws specifying appropriate private sector behavior (i.e., alternate-side-of-the-street parking regulations that enabled mechanical sweepers to reach the curbs, regulations regarding proper containerization of refuse, and prohibitions against illegal dumping by private carters). Engineers (Bureau of Engineering) were responsible for the specification of new plant and equipment (garages, trucks, barges). Finally, the commissioner's office provided coordination and control and over-all policy direction.

Refuse Collection and Street Cleaning

The tasks of refuse collection and street cleaning consumed most of the Department of Sanitation's resources. Most collection was done manually by crews of three men (two loaders, one driver) with a collection truck. The annual cost for the men was $12,000 each (including 12½% in fringe benefits) and for the truck, $8,400 ($15,000 purchase price amortized over five years plus annual maintenance costs of about $5,400).

The crews generally covered assigned areas called routes. With exceptions for a few large locations like hospitals, all the noncommercial stops within a given area would be on a single route and would receive the same collection frequency. Collection frequencies were higher than anywhere else in the nation; 60% of the noncommercial locations received daily collections (six times weekly), another 30% received thrice weekly collections, and the remainder received two, four, or five collections weekly. There were no regular collections on Sundays. The frequency was determined, in principle, by the availability of space for refuse storage within the premises and at curbside. Areas receiving daily collections, for example, were primarily multiple dwelling and ghetto areas, while those receiving thrice weekly collections were one- and two-family residential areas. Since the collection work force was at work six days a week while an individual man worked only five days, some men were required to work Saturdays and were given days off on other days of the week. The system for assigning days off put each sanitationman into one of six groups called "charts." Each chart group would be off Monday one week, Tuesday the next, Wednesday the next, and so on. This meant that five-sixths of the force was on duty each of the six workdays of the week. (On the average, 14% of the total force were sick or on vacation.) Those on duty who were not needed for refuse collection were assigned to other activities. These included street cleaning and the collection of bulk material both of which had a lower priority than refuse collection because the refuse was putrescible. (Bulk materials were items unable to fit in the hopper of many of the collection trucks--old mattresses, sofas, refrigerators and so forth. Special collections using open bed dump trucks were usually made for these items.) Men working in the same geographic area and on the same chart developed strong and enduring friendships and frequently were members of elaborate car-pool arrangements.

The collection routine, itself, consisted of lifting cans, carrying them to the truck, dumping the cans into the hopper of the truck, returning the empty cans to curbside, and walking on to the next stop. Routes averaged 1.6 miles in length with 250 stops and 600 cans. Roughly one-third of the total weight lifted and carried was due to the cans themselves. Once the truck was filled, the driver would take it alone to the dump site; the loaders were responsible for taking brooms off the truck and sweeping the streets until the truck returned. A truck typically required two trips to the dump site per shift at an average time of 40 minutes for each round trip.

Of the six hours per shift the loaders spent on the route, about 60% went to loading cans, 15% to walking between stops, and 25% to waiting for the dump cycle to be completed. The remining 1½ hours of the shift were spent at roll call, driving to and from the route, eating lunch, or taking coffee breaks. The average tons loaded per truck shift were 8.0, which was the most important productivity figure of the bureau. In 1968 the tons per shift had remained virtually unchanged for three years and had risen at less than 2% per year for the preceding decade.

The other major activities subsumed under cleaning and collection were mechanical street sweeping, manual street sweeping, litter basket collection, and bulk collection.

Mechanical sweeping was the major street cleaning program. Power brooms were driven by one man and, under appropriate conditions, swept cleaner than most manual sweepers. They were usually used on predesignated routes where alternate-side parking regulations were designed to provide access to curbs. About 50% of the city's curb miles were scheduled for regular sweeping either one, two, three, or six times per week. The remainder was swept intermittently on an "as-needed" basis. The greatest obstacle to mechanical sweeping was illegally parked cars. One parked car would prevent access to three car lengths of curb and cause the broom to leave a pile of material at each point where it turned in passing. Another problem for the power brooms was finding nearby dump sites since the hoppers on the brooms were small and the speeds were slow in traveling to the dump.

Manual sweeping was the most costly street cleaning program, claiming some $5 million per year. Manual sweepers used a broom, a shovel, and a pushcart and dumped the material they collected into a garbage truck or in piles for a passing power broom. Sometimes the manual sweepers flushed the curbs with hydrant water. Although manual sweepers had some flexibility in negotiating parked cars, they covered only one-ninth as much street area in a shift as did a man in a power broom. It would have cost $90 million per year to sweep each street manually each day. Despite these inherent inefficiences, 530 men were assigned to full-time manual sweeping duties in 1968 (i.e., in addition to those sweeping part-time during refuse collection duties), compared to 340 men on power brooms. Some of the full-time manual sweepers were required in high use areas like Times Square, and as many as 320 were more or less permanently assigned to light sweeping duties because of medical disabilities.

The final street cleaning program was litter basket collection. Some 17,000 wire mesh litter baskets were on the streets in 1968. They were used most heavily in commercial areas and were often collected by regular three-man collection crews known as motorized litter patrols (MLP).

Bulk collections were made with an open dump truck and crew of two. In some areas, residents could schedule individual pick-ups, while in other areas crews would patrol the streets on specific days of the week. Bulk service, which was not required by the city charter, had been started experimentally in 1955 and, by 1968, had grown to take 7.5% of the total collection manpower.

The Bureau of Cleaning and Collection

The Bureau of Cleaning and Collection (Exhibit 3) was by far the largest subdivision of DS, with approximately 6,000 men on the streets and 4,000 in overhead and supervisory support as of late 1968. Its yearly budget was $115 million (70% of the DS total of $162 million). Organizationally, it was a many-levelled, rigid hierarchy.

Across the city, groups of four to six collection routes were organized into 254 sections, each headed by a section foreman (see Exhibit

4). An average section serviced a population of 31,000 and encompassed about 130 blocks. Included in the area were a section foreman's office and a locker room for the crew. The foreman managed the activities of 20 men and 5 trucks. His duties included assigning loaders to trucks and trucks to routes; supervising crew performance; authorizing collection trucks to proceed to disposal points; issuing sanitation summonses (for violation of alternate-side parking, other DS rules and regulations, or the city's health code); and keeping section personnel and performance records. He had discretion over such matters as how often to send the trucks to a disposal site (once, twice, or three times a day), which streets to clean, and--when all collections could not be made on time--which areas to leave uncollected. Although a large part of the section foreman's time was spent in the field, he was in contact with (or in sight of) each crew for only a short period of time (Exhibit 5). One observer summed up the job as "a lot of walking."

The next organizational aggregation were the 58 sanitation districts each consisting of three to five sections, each covering about 600 blocks, and headed by a district superintendent. Each district had an office with several clerks and operated a district garage (which sometimes was located outside the district's boundaries) where all the district's equipment was housed and where routine maintenance was performed. Garages were staffed with two to four mechanics from the Bureau of Vehicle Maintenance and headed by a garage foreman. District supers, in addition to supervising section activities, were directly responsible for scheduling and overseeing bulk collections, power-broom street cleaning, and mechanized street flushing. (A typical district had five power brooms assigned.) District supers also scheduled and managed the motorized litter patrol (MLP) and were responsible for developing and adjusting the collection routes followed by the sections. To assist them in performing these duties, district supers had a radio-equipped car and driver at their disposal but, even so, they saw only about 20% of their streets daily.[1] An assistant district superintendent directed all second-shift activities.

The district was an important level in the DS management hierarchy for several reasons. First, it was the lowest level at which performance data was collated and published. Second, because of its size (in both area and manpower assigned) it was the usual focal point for the expression of grievances when they arose. Sometimes these originated with the sanitationmen's union and concerned working conditions. Sometimes they came from citizen groups that were dissatisfied with the level of service they were receiving.

Above the districts were the borough commands--eleven of them

---

[1] Individual crews did not have radios.

in total, each one covering four to six districts and headed by a borough superintendent. Boroughs covered approximately 3,000 blocks, and had roughly 1,000 men and 150 trucks assigned. Both borough headquarters, where several clerks were assigned, and the superintendent's car were radio-equipped. All radio communications with the mechanized equipment were carried on through the borough command; bulk trucks, snow-removal vehicles, and some cleaning equipment were dispatched from the borough. Three of the boroughs had broom depots where their power brooms were housed and maintained. (Power brooms in other boroughs were housed in the district garages.) The borough super not only supervised the normal operations of the districts, he also had immediate responsibility for scheduling vacant lot cleanups, managing snow-removal operations, and overseeing the removal of abandoned autos. He was aided by an assistant (or night) superintendent and a snow superintendent.

As far as possible, the work loads of the trucks, sections, districts and boroughs were equalized so that everyone had the same degree of responsibility and authority.

The central headquarters of the Bureau of Cleaning and Collection was located at 125 Worth Street in Manhattan as were the headquarters of most other bureaus of the Department of Sanitation. There was an assistant chief of staff for operations, and four functional assistant chiefs of staff--street cleaning, refuse collection, snow operations, and bulk collection. Each assistant chief of staff (ACS) had two deputy assistant chiefs of staff reporting to him. The ACSs reported to the chief of staff for BCC who was the top ranking uniformed officer in BCC and reported directly to the commissioner of sanitation. The BCC headquarters staff consisted of 125 clerks and uniformed men on deputation. Similar, though smaller, organizational structures existed for the Bureaus of Waste Disposal, Vehicle Maintenance, and Inspection.

The primary function of the BCC headquarters staff was to keep abreast of day-to-day operations. Long-range planning was done only in anticipation of snow season and this activity went on continuously. Detailed plans were made for the deployment of men and snow-removal equipment so that as soon as snow fell, it could be removed rapidly and efficiently. But, by and large, the primary work of the staff was to determine on Monday what the cleaning and collection situation was on Monday so that it would know where the trucks and men ought to go on Tuesday. The information had been collected in much the same way for years. It was a massive manual and telephone system directed by the assistant chief of staff for operations. The basic record at the section and district level was the daily performance collection trip ticket on which were recorded the activities of one truck and one crew collecting one load. It included information on:

- Individuals on the crew
- Time of
    - Disposal point weigh-in
    - Route arrival and departure
    - Garage departure and arrival
    - Relay arrival and departure
- Truck mileage
- Load information (number and weight)
- Type of collection (refuse, bulk, and so forth)
- Collection route identification
- Work shift

The form was filled out by the truck driver and turned in to the section foreman.[1] The foreman telephoned the information in to district headquarters where it was compiled as part of the District Collection Summary. The district super telephoned the summary in to borough headquarters once a day. The borough compiled the information from all its districts and then telephoned the information in to BCC headquarters where it was compiled once more.

When the district superintendent sent his report to the borough, he also sent a tentative assignment list for his trucks for the next day, based on the information collected. He also added a request for additional personnel if he felt they were needed. His recommendations were evaluated by the borough which then drew up a borough assignment chart that frequently recommended temporary transfer of personnel and equipment between districts within the borough. Detachments came from districts that had completed their assignments early and attachments went to districts which had lagged behind. In addition, the borough super sometimes requested that more personnel and equipment be assigned to the borough if it had fallen behind.

At headquarters, the ACS for operations and the appropriate functional ACS evaluated all the recommendations from the boroughs and made final decisions on assignments and on detachments and attachments between boroughs, districts, and even sections. Thus, although the basic assignments were made at the district level, they could be, and often were, overruled at the borough and BCC central level. Ultimate authority rested at BCC central, which decided how often that authority would be exercised. For the past several years, BCC central had intervened with growing frequency because of a continuous sense of crisis in the bureau. Work loads had been increasing but the growth in BCC resources had not kept pace. The result was a greater tendency for borough commanders to override district superintendents' wishes and recommendations, and for BCC central to take a more active role in daily operating decisions. Friction between levels was not unusual. District superintendents looked

---

[1] Similar tickets were filled out by manual sweepers and power-broom operators.

on the central officers as meddlers. For their part, the central officers thought that the district men were inefficient greenhorns who weren't doing half as well as the central officers had done when they had run the districts.

The BCC Environment - Internal and External

Internal relationships in BCC (and in the entire department) were dominated by the formal hierarchy of authority. BCC was a paramilitary organization. Command status was emphasized by uniforms and by the bearing of the participants in work interactions. Discipline was a key focus of training programs, and disrespect or disobedience of the orders of a superior was punishable by suspension without pay or, in flagrant cases, by dismissal.

At no time did the bureau seem more in character, for example, than during snow emergencies. The chiefs of staff manned central headquarters around the clock, where there were beds kept available for cat naps along with coffee and showers to keep alert. Huge maps lined the walls with conditions throughout the city posted and continually updated. Contact was maintained with field commanders via two-way radios and officers were driven to the field to survey battle progress and the condition of the troops. The commissioner of DS and the chief of staff of BCC sent orders via teletype to the borough and district headquarters. The bureau was entirely mobilized and obviously important, and the men were usually serious and excited about their work.

Coexisting with the authoritarian rigidity of the formal structure were many informal relationships. These grew from the backgrounds and outlooks of the men at work. To begin with, six or seven of every ten sanitationmen were Italian. Germans and Irish were the next dominant groups and less than one in ten were either Black or Puerto Rican. As the officers were chosen from the ranks, middle and top management levels were also strongly Italian and working class. Most of the men were sensitive to their low public status as "garbage men" and sought recognition as professionals on a par with policemen or firemen. As a group, they were coherently, and self-consciously, ethnic.

A typical, individual sanitationman or officer might be the second generation of his family with the bureau. More than likely, however, he would not have joined until he had tried something else and given it up. He would not have completed high school or, if he were older, probably not have completed elementary school. He would consider his job good money, but, except for some of the officers, he would consider it a poor career. He would likely have an outside job and intend, if he were younger, to retire on half-pay on reaching the 20-year mark and start something new.

A common value in BCC was respect for the power of the chain of command combined with disrespect for many of the formal rules associated with it. BCC and DS were full of rules; the "book" of standard operating procedures was bureaucratically elaborate.[1] Developed historically to constrain personal abuses of the hierarchical powers of the system, the rules covered almost everything: Some required specific uniforms at specific times; others prohibited taking out trucks with defective windshield wipers, taillights, or heaters; others prevented walking across private property or riding outside the truck on the running board; and yet other rules prevented certain job assignments on other than a seniority basis. In toto, the "book" was generally perceived as a "Catch 22" situation: You were subject to punishment if you did not do your job or if you did break the rules, but you could not do your job and not break the rules. The lack of legitimacy given to the formal rules was crucial for daily operations. Rules were broken continually in getting the work done, and there was broad acceptance of the differences between "the book" and reality.

Outside of DS and BCC, the single most powerful force was the unions. All of the men in DS, with the exception of a few who reported directly to the commissioner, were "uniformed" and all uniformed personnel belonged to one of two unions--the Uniformed Sanitationmen's Association (U.S.A.) or, if they were officers, the Officer's Union. The powers of the U.S.A., in particular, were formidable. To field officers and middle management, its presence was pervasive and constant in the form of its business agents and shop stewards. These men, supported by departmental salaries while on special assignment to the union, were day-in and day-out ombudsmen for the rights of union members. In some areas of the city the shop steward was considered more powerful than the district superintendent.

Much union power was exercised through the grievance procedure, particularly at higher levels, where written testimony and evidence was subject to cross examination in front of a departmental hearings officer. In these hearings, union members were always represented by a lawyer, and departmental officers were rightly concerned about being made to appear foolish.

Most significantly, union demands were backed by an extremely credible strike threat. In February 1968, a ten-day walkout had made New Yorkers miserable and won a large settlement for the union. Even if an all-out strike was not called, the union could threaten to bring the system to a standstill through a work-rules slowdown or through a hidden

---

[1]The "book" referred to the combined record of teletyped general orders sent out by the chief of staff and the commissioner.

strike with shifting pockets of mischief. Either one would be politically embarrassing to City Hall and difficult to pin on the union.

The results of union power were effective for the interests of the men, if not always for the department and the commissioner. By 1968, the average sanitationman's take-home pay was over $10,000, probably the highest real income for such work anywhere in the world. Further, there were attractive overtime, health, and pension packages that were the envy of the other uniformed services. After 20 years' service, for example, BCC employees could retire at one-half their pay for the preceding year (including overtime). A basic indicator of the union's success was the waiting line of those wanting to become sanitationmen; when the Civil Service exam was given for 500 positions later in 1969, some 20,000 people took the test.

The citizens of New York were another important influence on BCC. By 1968, their cooperation with the bureau and their opinion of it had eroded seriously from previous levels. In many of the city's communities, street conditions had deteriorated markedly and the Department of Sanitation had become a focus of demands for community control. The department's response had been to create a series of small "Self-Help" offices to act as a buffer group between ghetto community groups and the department. These units were often manned by Black or Puerto Rican sanitationmen and officers who volunteered for the service and reported directly to the commissioner's office. They helped organize clean-up drives and coordinated the supply of trucks and other support from local district officers. Although they met with some success, they were clearly outside the normal chain of command.

A final important factor, external to DS and BCC, was the mayor himself. Sanitation was one of John Lindsay's top priorities. He had been known to leave his car to pick up litter and give it back to the offender with an admonishment not to do it again. Several times a week--day and night--he would call the commissioner to report areas that he wanted cleaned up. He put the pressure on all the time. He was not sure the department was doing all it could to keep the city clean and he said so publicly.

The Clean City Task Force

For a combination of reasons, the Lindsay administration considered solid waste problems the priority environmental concern in 1968. Sanitation services and street conditions had deteriorated noticeably since the mayor had taken office in 1966. In middle-class communities in the city, people were carrying their cans to the curb in the morning and finding them still uncollected at night. This was a new, irritating, widespread, and growing phenomenon. In some sections, where the wait for collection of bulk items had earlier been several days, it had grown to several months. The carcasses of as many as 2,000 abandoned cars were strewn about the city. Litter surveys showed the streets were dirtier than prior to the 1965 election, and street cleaning manpower was down nearly 40%. Thirty-five per cent of the collection trucks were not operable on an average day. In February, the "garbage strike" had focussed public attention on sanitation and complaints about it had risen dramatically. In Black poverty areas, ever-present garbage was a visible grievance around which disturbances were organized, and a symbol of continued neglect on the part of the city. In White neighborhoods, on the other hand, recently reduced services were blamed on the mayor's "favoritism" toward the Blacks. Nineteen sixty-nine would be an election year. Thus, in late 1968, when Deputy Budget Director Cantwell Bain proposed a change in normal budget procedures that would focus attention on sanitation, the mayor was receptive.

In the usual budget process, departments submitted their requests to the Budget Bureau during the fall. Then, from January through March, the mayor attended a series of "retreat" meetings with the budget director and budget staff to which the departmental staffs were not invited. The decisions made at these meetings were communicated to the departments primarily through publication of the budget itself, and also through associated policy messages and memos. In theory, the initial decisions from the budget retreat meetings were followed by a "reclama" period, or series of further meetings where departmental staff could select several issues and present final arguments to the mayor before the mayor's budget was sent to the city council. In fact, however, the "reclama" was often cut short in the hectic period immediately prior to the budget deadline.

Bain proposed that a Clean City Task Force (CCTF) be formed that would supplant the usual "retreat" format with a series of carefully prepared meetings in which officers from the Department of Sanitation (assisted by EPA's small analytic staff) could make their own proposals for improving service directly to the mayor. The task force would consist of representatives from the Budget Bureau, and the mayor's personal staff as well as EPA and DS. Between February and May, the CCTF held six formal meetings with the mayor and between these sessions there was substantial activity among the working members of the task force. It was agreed, for example, that a dress rehearsal would be held for all presentations that were to be made to the mayor and this procedure was closely followed for most of the meetings. The rehearsals were expected not only to sharpen the presentations but also to bring to the surface (and hopefully resolve), outside the mayor's office, conflicts between the Budget Bureau and the Department of Sanitation.

At the initial task force meeting with the mayor, the Commissioner of Sanitation gave a carefully prepared overview of the options and possibilities from his department's perspective. Thereafter, the focus shifted to specific proposals and, in subsequent meetings, the sanitation officer (usually an assistant chief of staff) with primary responsibility for implementing the program under discussion presented the analytic material directly to the mayor using slides and other visual materials. The officer worked in tandem with one of EPA's analysts to prepare the presentation and develop the visual aids. Then at the meeting, the analyst would run the projector, while the officer did most of the talking. For most of the officers, it was the first time they had been face-to-face with the mayor and, for all of them, it was the first time they had ever stood in front of a critical audience using a set of viewgraphs to outline and defend a new program or a change in an on-going one.

During the meetings, a number of innovative proposals were discussed and several approved by the mayor for implementation. Four of them are discussed below.

Detachable Containers: One means of decreasing the number of missed trash collections would be to increase the productivity of the sanitation force by improvements in technology. One possible improvement was the use of large detachable containers that held much more than standard trash cans and that could be unloaded mechanically into a collection vehicle. Three alternatives were investigated by the task force: large containers (8-10 cubic yards); small containers (1-3 cubic yards); and very large roll-on/roll-off containers. The first of these options would involve replacement of existing "Dempster dumpster" containers with larger ones that could be dumped on-site by a hoist-fitted collection truck. (Dempster dumpsters must be picked up by a special truck and transported one at a time to the dump site.) All three detachable container programs would serve to cut both the frequency of collection required at each site and the time to make each collection.

Following presentation of data on all three options, the mayor decided to provide $800,000 for the purchase of 12 trucks and 500 large containers. These would replace Dempster dumpsters at 250 locations and add 250 more locations throughout the city. He also decided to experiment with a limited number of small containers to test their acceptance in several neighborhoods and to determine how the sanitation force would react to them. Finally, a single roll-on/roll-off truck was slated for use experimentally for bulk collections and "self-help" dumps in the city's poverty areas rather than for routine trash collections.

Disposable Bags: Health and housing codes in the city required that trash left for the Sanitation Department be stored in closed metal containers. When these conventional trash cans were used, approximately 70% of a sanitationman's time was used at the point of pickup to handle the can and dump the trash. The potential increase in productivity from a shift to disposable bags, therefore, was very large; for the loader would have only to pick up the bag and toss it into the truck. Additional potential benefits would be reductions in noise, litter, and unpleasant odors. Despite these apparent advantages, a number of uncertainties remained about the efficacy of bags. These included the possible impact of vandalism and rodents and the willingness of householders to absorb the slightly higher costs. The task force recommended (and the mayor approved) an experimental utilization of the bags that would serve to answer these questions and to determine whether or not changes should be requested in existing codes. The program would last eight weeks and involve about half-a-dozen locations with different population densities and economic characteristics.

Abandoned Automobiles: By 1969, the rate at which cars were being abandoned on New York City's streets was approaching 50,000 per year. Current procedures required that the Police Department identify these cars and authorize towing them away. If the owner could be identified (as was the case with one of every three abandoned vehicles), towing was done by the police. If the owner could not be identified, the Department of Sanitation did the towing. (Except in South Manhattan, the actual towing for DS was done by private contractors.) These procedures had succeeded in reducing the average number of derelict cars on the streets from over 2,000 in July 1968 to about 1,500 in early 1969, but the task force believed that this number was still excessive and that a goal of 500 should be set. Because of the irreducible delay between abandonment, authorization to tow, and actual removal, this goal could not be met under current policies. Acting on suggestions by the task force, therefore, the mayor decided on a series of changes that would:

- Transfer to DS the responsibility for reporting, authorizing removal, and actually removing all derelict autos (five of six on the streets). The police would continue to be responsible for abandoned autos that were not derelict. This included stolen cars and those that had been in serious accidents.

- Establish and publicize a free towing service including a telephone number that any citizen could call if he wished to have his car taken away.

- Begin drafting legislative changes that would increase the penalty for abandonment.

Missed and Night Collections: Perhaps the two most critical issues with which the task force dealt were missed collections and night collections. Since 1965, the amount of refuse to be collected had grown more than 12% while the productivity of the collection crews had increased only 3%. By 1968, moreover, the sanitation force had decreased (through attrition and budget pressures) by 450 men and, since mid-1968 when a city-wide hiring freeze went into effect, by another 335 men. In combination, these factors had brought about a fivefold increase in the percentage of scheduled collections that were being missed--from less than 1% in

1965 to over 5% during the summer of 1968. The problem had abated somewhat during the fall and winter as the men returned from vacation, but in March 1969, EPA analysts estimated that about 100 truck shifts worth of uncollected refuse was being left on the streets each Monday. This meant 400,000 citizens had not been serviced as scheduled.

In developing a recommended course of action, DS had projected both the demand for service and the probable availability of collection manpower (if the hiring freeze remained in effect) through the summer of 1969. Both projections were highly uncertain. With regard to crew availability, normal attrition rates were expected to grow for two reasons: First, a large number of men hired just after World War II were beginning to reach retirement age; second, because pension levels were determined by the amount of pay received during the last year of employment and because there had been a great deal of overtime worked during the snowstorms in early 1969, those eligible to do so in 1969 would be more likely to opt for retirement rather than continued active service. DS thought that the net effect of the increased retirement rates and of more men on vacation during the summer would be to reduce the number of crews available each day by about 160 between March and August 1969.

During the same period, demand for collection services would continue to increase because of the normal growth of the refuse load. Added to (or subtracted from) this increase would be the impact of the city's on-going program to reduce air pollution caused by incinerators. Some incinerators were to be improved thereby lowering the amount of residue that would have to be picked up. Others were to be shut down, thus increasing the amount of unburned refuse that would have to be collected. It was extremely difficult to say which effect would be dominant in the short run. A final factor that made the prediction of demand difficult was the introduction of new, larger collection trucks and the change in crew productivity that would result. Purchase of the new trucks had begun in 1968 and, by March 1969, they numbered 650 of the total fleet of 1,600. By mid-1969, when the new truck orders were complete, there would be 800 on hand. Productivity improvements from the trucks were expected because fewer trips to disposal points would be required; but these improvements could be realized only if collection routes were lengthened appropriately. Devising new routes took time and no one was sure how fast the Department of Sanitation could make the adjustments. Because of these uncertainties, DS presented three estimates of the probable change in demand for crews on Mondays during the coming summer: "Optimistic" (136 fewer crews); "Best" (80 fewer crews); "Pessimistic" (84 more crews).

Based on these estimates of the probable demand for and supply of crews, DS recommended that its field force be expanded immediately by 100 crews (450 men). The new men would be available for work during June and July. At that time, their performance could be evaluated (in light of greater certainty about actual attrition and refuse generation rates) and more men could be hired or a further cutback begun by means of attrition.

If a cutback was ordered, the entire cost of the hiring program would be $1.7 to $2.7 million depending on how fast the 100 additional crews were eliminated by attrition. If the additional men were retained, the annual cost would be about $5 million.

Night collections (from 4 p.m. to midnight) were considered undesirable for several reasons. They produced more complaints than daytime collections (largely because more people were at home to be bothered by the noise); they were less efficient (because supervision was not as good and the cans were more likely to be blocked by parked cars); and they resulted in more property damage and accidents.

The number of night collections needed was the difference between the number of crews available (and needed) for collections and the number of trucks available--in other words, it was equivalent to the number of trucks that had to be double shifted. Since the summer of 1968, both the number of trucks in the fleet and the number of crews available had grown slightly. About 1,000 trucks were now up and running on an average day. Because of attrition and vacations, however, the number of mechanics in the Bureau of Vehicle Maintenance was expected to decrease from 920 in November to 630 in August 1969. The impact would be to reduce the number of trucks available to about 900 each day. DS proposed that steps be taken to increase the number of maintenance hours available through a program of Saturday overtime. If 300 repairmen worked Saturdays until July, approximately 250 to 300 additional trucks could be kept in operation. The cost of the overtime (through July) would be $3.6 million.

In April, the mayor decided to accept the DS recommendation for hiring additional sanitationmen. In fact, on the basis of additional analysis of attrition rates, the number was increased from 450 new hires to 850, an amount equal to the total number of budget-line vacancies. (Although this was decided before the state legislature had authorized its funding support levels for the city for the coming year, it was not announced publicly in order not to contradict the city's bargaining posture.) Although the mayor agreed to authorize small amounts of overtime for vehicle maintenance, he declined to allow as much as the task force had recommended. Instead, he gave the go-ahead for a major study of the entire vehicle maintenance operation (see Sanitation (B)).

The Primaries

In May, shortly after the last meeting of the Clean City Task Force, the mayor was defeated in the Republican primary and began his campaign for reelection as an Independent.

Exhibit 1

SANITATION (A)

Department of Sanitation

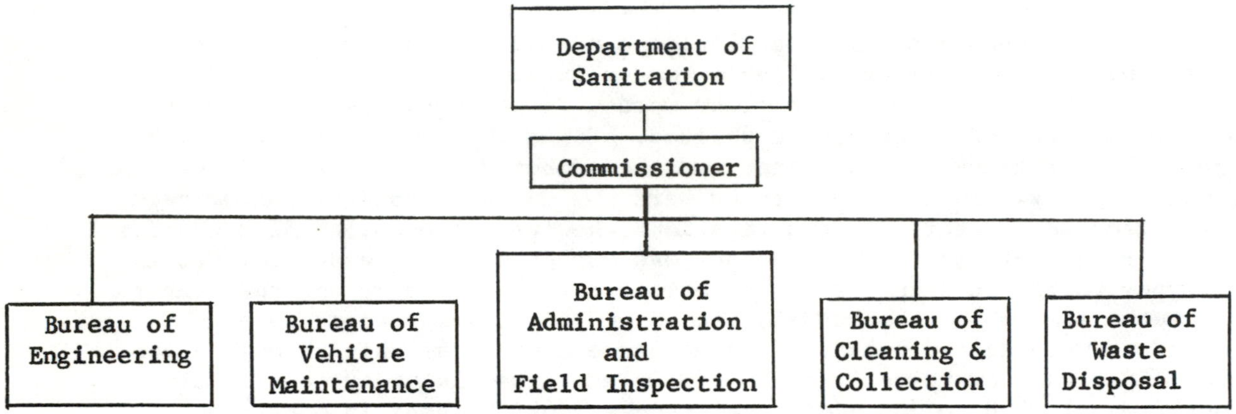

Exhibit 2

SANITATION (A)

Data on Household Refuse

Yearly Growth

Year	Weekly Load (Tons)
1965	51,000
1966	52,500
1967	54,500
1968	56,200
1969	57,000

Daily Load (1969)

Day	Tons to be Collected
Monday	12,200
Tuesday	10,600
Wednesday	8,500
Thursday	8,100
Friday	8,300
Saturday	8,400
Sunday	1,000
	57,100

Exhibit 3

SANITATION (A)

Bureau of Cleaning and Collection

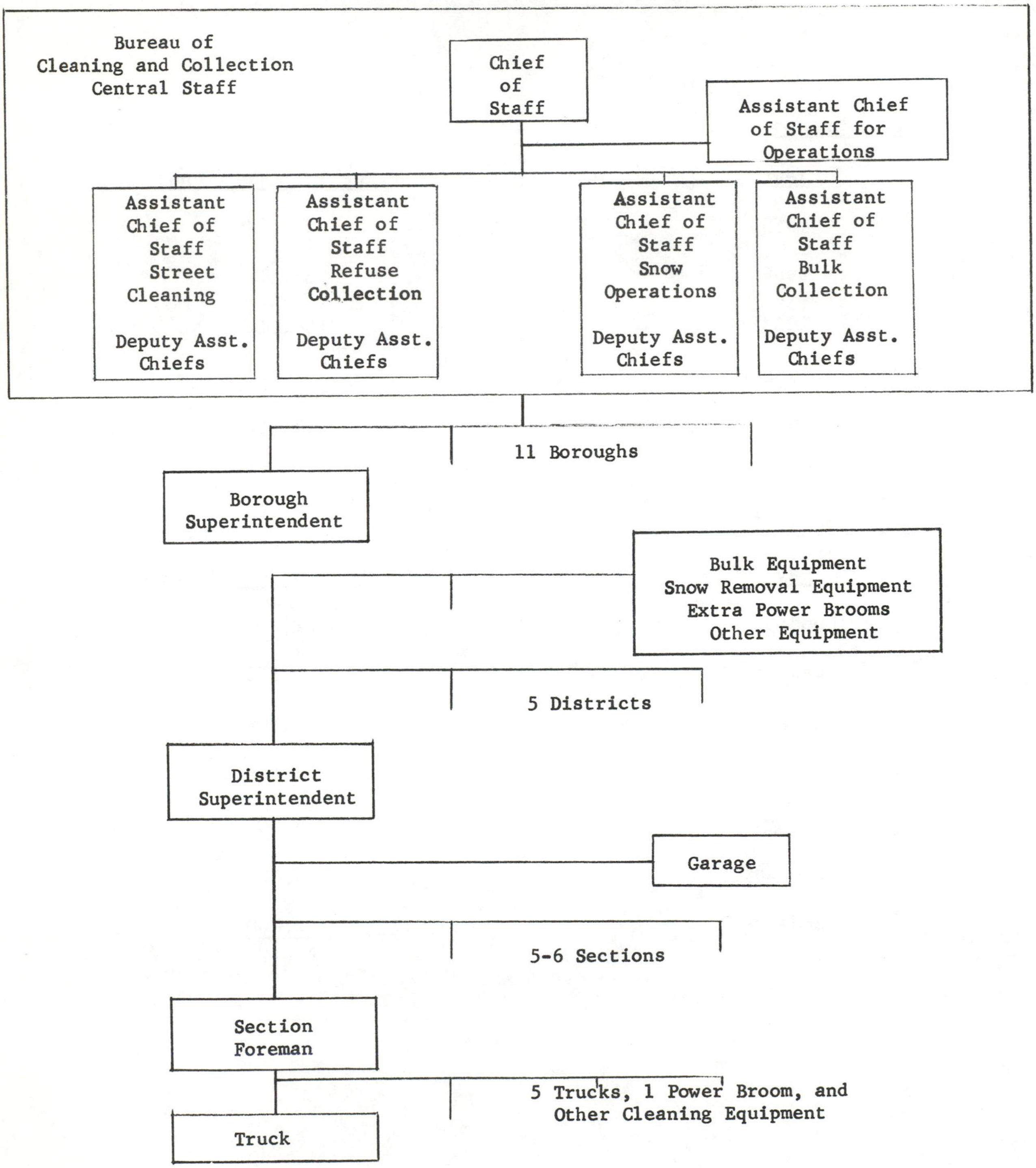

Exhibit 4

SANITATION (A)

Map of Typical Sanitation Section

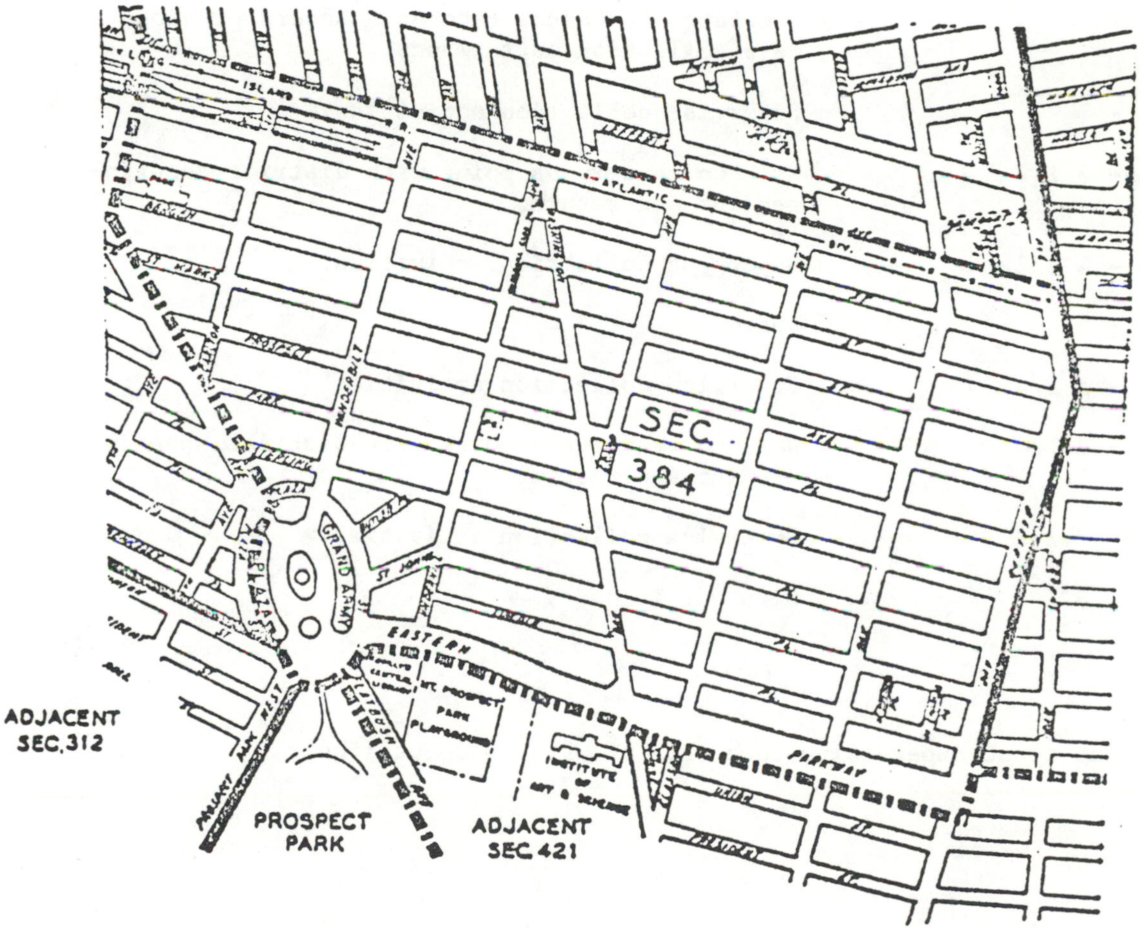

Exhibit 5

SANITATION (A)

Typical Section Foreman's Day

Shift Hour	Activity
0 - 1/2	Assign loaders to routes and dispatch trucks.
1/2 - 1	Complete attendance records. Record previous day's collection performance.
1 - 3	Supervise collection activities.
3 - 3 1/2	Walk to rendezvous point with district superintendent and return.
3 1/2 - 4 1/2	Supervise collection activities.
4 1/2 - 5	Lunch
5 - 5 3/4	Supervise collection activities.
5 3/4 - 6 1/4	Walk to rendezvous point with district superintendent and return.
6 1/4 - 7 1/2	Supervise collection activities.*
7 1/2 - 8	Sign out loaders.

*Total time spent supervising each crew at work is about 1 hour.

SANITATION (B)

Maintenance Operations

In early 1969, representatives of New York City's Department of Sanitation (DS) recommended to the mayor that substantial amounts of maintenance overtime be used to improve the condition of the city's fleet of refuse collection vehicles (see Sanitation (A)). The mayor, at the urging of the Budget Director, had deferred any decision on this recommendation until a full-scale investigation of current maintenance practices had been made. During the summer and fall, a group of industrial engineers attached to the city's Project Management Staff (and supervised by Andrew Kerr and John Thomas) carried out the study with the cooperation of the policy analysis staff of the Environmental Protection Administration (EPA) and the Director of the Bureau of Motor Equipment (BME).[1] The remainder of this case summarizes some of their findings as they were reported toward the end of 1969.

Overview

The Environmental Protection Administration operated a fleet of 4,900 vehicles of which the major portion were used on repetitive trash collection and disposal, street cleaning and snow removal, land fill, and other sanitation responsibilities. Of the total fleet, 82% were assigned to the Department of Sanitation, 17% to the Department of Water Resources, and 1% to the Department of Air Resources. The characteristics of the total fleet are shown below:

Type of Equipment	Quantity	Per Cent	Approximate Replacement Value
Collection trucks	1,600	33	$ 24,000,000
Street sweepers	380	8	3,500,000
Salt spreaders	240	5	5,500,000
Flushers	110	2	2,200,000
Other trucks[2]	1,250	25	8,800,000
Mobile equipment[2]	810	16	12,000,000
Passenger vehicles	530	11	1,300,000
	4,920	100%	$ 57,000,000

1 Previously called the Bureau of Vehicle Maintenance.

2 Vehicles classed as "other trucks" and "mobile equipment" (41% of the total) included a variety of large items with complex maintenance requirements such as 87 crawler tractors, 488 other tractors with loaders or plows attached, 125 wreckers and assorted cranes, graders, concrete mixers, and plows.

This fleet was maintained by the Bureau of Motor Equipment, part of the Department of Sanitation, at an annual direct cost of approximately $14 million. The maintenance function was strongly oriented toward the requirements of the cleaning and collection forces who operated their major equipment at least one and sometimes two shifts per day and consequently, required the greatest portion of maintenance effort. Fifty-five per cent or more of the maintenance work load was created by collection trucks. Thus, on the average, the direct maintenance cost per year for the entire fleet of 1,600 collection trucks was $5,100 to $5,700 per truck. This amounted to some 35% of the purchase price of $15,000 for a new truck. In the past, acquisition of new vehicles had varied widely from year to year. For instance, in 1969 the city's 1,600 collection trucks consisted of 800 acquired in 1968, and the remaining 800 purchased sporadically over the 10 years prior to 1966. No trucks were purchased in 1966 or 1967. The average age of the 800 older trucks was about seven years. Despite the recent effort to modernize the fleet, the percentage of trucks out of service had remained unchanged.

Eight hundred seventy-five people worked in the Bureau of Motor Equipment. Most were members of a mechanics' union, an organization that had neither the militancy nor the colorful leadership of the sanitationmen's union. The job categories and work locations of the men are shown in Exhibit 1. The bureau was organized into four line divisions:

- Field Maintenance which performed preventive maintenance and minor repairs in 67 district garages, two tractor repair shops, and a borough shop in Richmond.[1]

- Central Vehicle Repair which did major on-chassis repair work at the large central repair shop in Queens on all vehicles sent in from the field maintenance unit (except Richmond) and a tractor repair shop at the same location.

- Central Unit Repair which did off-vehicle repair and overhaul of engines and other components and operated a machine shop. It was also located at the central repair shop in Queens.

- Water Resources Vehicle Repair which included five borough shops that repaired Water Resources equipment.

The average daily volume of collection trucks repaired by BME was 150.[2] Two-thirds of these vehicles needed only minor repairs; that is, repairs that could be completed in one or two days unless delayed for parts. An analysis showing the length of time collection trucks were out

---

[1]The district garages were the same ones in which the DS housed its equipment and from which crews were assigned and dispatched each day.

[2]This did not include so-called "running" repairs where the driver stopped by the garage to have a mirror adjusted, a door handle tightened, or some other small item attended to before starting or resuming his route.

of service is shown in Exhibit 2. The bulk of the repairs were usually performed in the local garages in the field. Normally, about 900 vehicles were out of service at any given time and over 60% of these were collection trucks. (The average number of out-of-service collection trucks decreased by 35 between 6:00 a.m. and 9:00 a.m.) The results of a special analysis of the status of out-of-service collection trucks are shown below.

Field Repairs	Number of Vehicles	Per Cent
In-process	146	35
Waiting for parts	90	21
Waiting for labor	119	28
Central Shop and Richmond Borough		
Central Shop	42	10
Richmond Shop	7	2
Warranty Repairs	18	4
	422	100

Field Maintenance

The field maintenance organization performed preventive maintenance, initial problem diagnosis, and minor and semimajor repairs. Vehicles needing repairs that could not be done by field maintenance were taken to the central repair shop. Field operations were decentralized throughout the city in 67 garages and 8 repair shops. The Bureau of Cleaning and Collection was the primary tenant of the 67 garages, but maintenance was usually allotted space (about 2,000 square feet) for one or two vehicles to be worked on. The eight repair shops included one large installation (that performed all levels of maintenance and serviced all of the Borough of Richmond), two tractor repair shops, and five smaller garages (one in each borough) that serviced Water Resources vehicles. For the most part, personnel assignments and work schedules were developed independently for each of the field activities. Over one eight-week period, the average backlog of out-of-service collection trucks varied from a high of eighteen at one district garage to a low of three in another. During the same period, 31% of the collection trucks were out of service city-wide (although only 19% were out of service in Richmond).

Organizationally, the field maintenance activity paralleled the Bureau of Cleaning and Collection; that is, district garages served sanitation districts and, for administrative purposes, district garages were grouped into "borough" units that coincided roughly with the borough commands in BCC. Borough foremen in BME supervised the activities of from four to ten district garages. They were responsible for setting priorities, scheduling the sequence of work, and expediting the delivery of spare parts. A typical foreman spent about four hours per day supervising the work at his garages, one hour doing administrative chores and expediting work at the central repair shop, and the remainder traveling between garages. All maintenance foremen in BME had been promoted through the ranks.

Some of the scheduled preventive maintenance (PM) tasks on BCC vehicles were performed, at the district garages, by 540 BCC employees temporarily assigned to garage duty each day. At a typical garage, two BCC men worked from midnight to eight in the morning, four during the day shift, and three worked from four in the afternoon until midnight. They were expected to carry out such routine tasks as changing oil and tires, greasing packer mechanisms and chassis, replacing minor parts, and steam cleaning engines. Truck drivers were responsible for checking water, oil, air pressure, and truck body condition at the beginning of each shift. A more comprehensive preventive maintenance schedule was supposed to be carried out by BME mechanics every 45 days on new collection trucks only. (BME personnel worked only during the day shift.) Frequently, however, BCC refused to release the trucks for this comprehensive PM because they were needed to meet collection schedules. And, even when the trucks were available, the mechanics were often too busy to do the PM. A record of preventive maintenance work was kept on master vehicle cards that were filed at the garages.

<u>Repair</u> work at the district garages was carried out by BME mechanics. Most of the district garages were not equipped to handle any repairs except those requiring hand tools. Only half had any lifting capability other than hand jacks and most did not have welding equipment. Nevertheless, many of the mechanics took this as a challenge; wheels weighing 200 pounds were often lifted and moved manually and front ends were raised by rigging chains to lift truck hoists. This kind of ingenuity permitted the district garages to do difficult jobs like spring and gasket replacements that normally would be done at the central repair facility. The mechanics were paid on a par with "civilian" mechanics of similar skills and grade. Time standards for various repair jobs, while long in use in industrial repair shops were not applied in BME, however.

The Central Repair Shop

About 10% of the out-of-service vehicles could not be repaired by the field maintenance organization. They were taken to BME's central repair shop in Queens where there was space to work on 120 vehicles simultaneously and where there was usually a backlog of about one week's work. The shop had fifteen work centers, six on-vehicle and nine off-vehicle, or "unit," centers. The on-vehicle shops were specialized by vehicle type (collection trucks, sweepers, automobiles, and so forth) while the unit shops were organized by craft skill (electricians, sheet-metal workers, machinists, and so forth). Unit shops did overhaul work on items that had been removed from vehicles by the on-vehicle repair shops or the district garages. When the overhaul was completed, the item was returned to the activity that sent it and it was reinstalled in the waiting vehicle. Typical jobs performed in the unit shops were:[1]

- Electric Shop (26 men): Alternators, starters, voltage regulators, and other electrical components.

- Radiator Shop (10 men): Radiators, other light sheet-metal work.

- Upholstery Shop (14 men): Primary seat repair.

- Unit Repair Shop (40 men): Clutches, transmissions, springs and other mechanical components.

- Machine Shop (7 men): Manufacturing and remachining of parts for other unit shops, central on-vehicle shops and district garages.

- Motor Room (39 men): Engine overhaul, unit repair of fuel system components.

- Broom Shop (23 men): Refilling of sweeper brooms, snow chain salvage and manufacture.

- Forge Shop (13 men): Forging and welding of snow plows and other heavy components.

- Tire Shop (31 men): Dismounting, tube repair and remounting. (Tire repairs were contracted out.)

The over-all distribution of work effort in the total shop was as follows:

Function	Number of People	% of Total
On-vehicle repair	162	31
Off-vehicle repair	209	41
Machining	25	5
General floor labor	55	11
Crib attendants, clerks, etc.	43	8
Supervision	23	4
	517	100%

In early December 1969, a work sampling study was taken covering the entire production force at the central repair shop. The results are shown in Exhibit 3. The engineers who made the study reported frequent instances of late starts, early quits, and group gatherings. They also

[1] In addition to the work done in the unit shops, 34 men assigned to the on-vehicle shops actually did off-vehicle work.

believed that work was being pegged. A second study, performed by the same engineers, compared the in-house costs of high volume unit repair work with estimates of contracting the work to an outside source. Exhibit 4 lists these comparisons for selected items.

Spare Parts

In theory, there were no spare parts stocked at the district garages although each one had accumulated a few items that its mechanics thought were particularly important. Normally, when a part was needed by a district mechanic, he notified the borough foreman who picked it up at the central repair shop the next time he stopped there. This usually took two or three days. (To prevent pilferage, the old part had to be turned in before a new one was issued.) Ten of the shops at central repair had controlled parts stocking and requisitioning. These stockrooms were staffed by 21 clerks who sometimes did minor salvage work in addition to their normal stockroom duties. The five shops that did not have stockrooms kept some parts, raw materials, and salvage items on the floor. These were low value or bulky items not subject to pilferage. Decisions with regard to proper stock levels, reorder quantities, and so forth were made by the shop foremen.

When a part was needed but not in stock at the central repair shop, it had to be ordered from a vendor by the Department of Purchase. (The Department of Purchase was not part of EPA.) This could mean a substantial delay because of bidding requirements and the fact that low bidders were often unable to make delivery on time. When these delays occurred, the central repair shop often rebuilt the original part rather than scrapping or, in some cases, fabricated the item itself.

Exhibit 1

SANITATION (B)

Present Staffing by Function and Job Category

Job Category	Manager and Staff	Adminis- tration	Engi- neer- ing	Field Mainte- nance	Central Vehicle Repair	Central Unit Repair	Water Re- sources	Total
Supervision								
General Supervision	3	4	1	1	1	-	1	11
Foremen	-	-	-	11	11	6	4	32
Assistant Foremen	-	-	-	2	1	-	-	3
Staff								
Technical	-	-	2	-	-	-	-	2
Secretarial/Typist	2	-	-	-	-	-	-	2
Clerical	-	18	-	-	3	-	-	21
Maintenance Operations								
Mechanics and Machinists	-	-	-	194	109	107	10	420
Machinist Helpers	-	-	-	15	22	9	1	47
Welders	-	-	-	9	32	2	-	43
Blacksmiths	-	-	-	10	50	-	-	60
Blacksmith Helpers	-	-	-	9	24	2	-	35
Electricians	-	-	-	6	5	9	-	20
Carpenters	-	-	-	2	4	-	-	6
Glaziers	-	-	-	-	1	-	-	1
Sheet-Metal Workers	-	-	-	-	-	10	-	10
Upholsterers	-	-	-	-	-	9	-	9
Motor Vehicle Operators	-	-	-	7	4	1	-	12
Sanitation Men	-	-	-	12	13	5	-	30
Maintenance Men	-	-	-	-	-	1	-	1
Laborers	-	-	-	7	57	16	8	88
Elevator Operators	-	-	-	-	3	-	-	3
Rubber Tire Repairers	-	-	-	-	19	-	-	19
	5	22	2	285	359	177	24	875

Exhibit 2

SANITATION (B)

Aging Distribution of Collection Trucks Out-of-Service

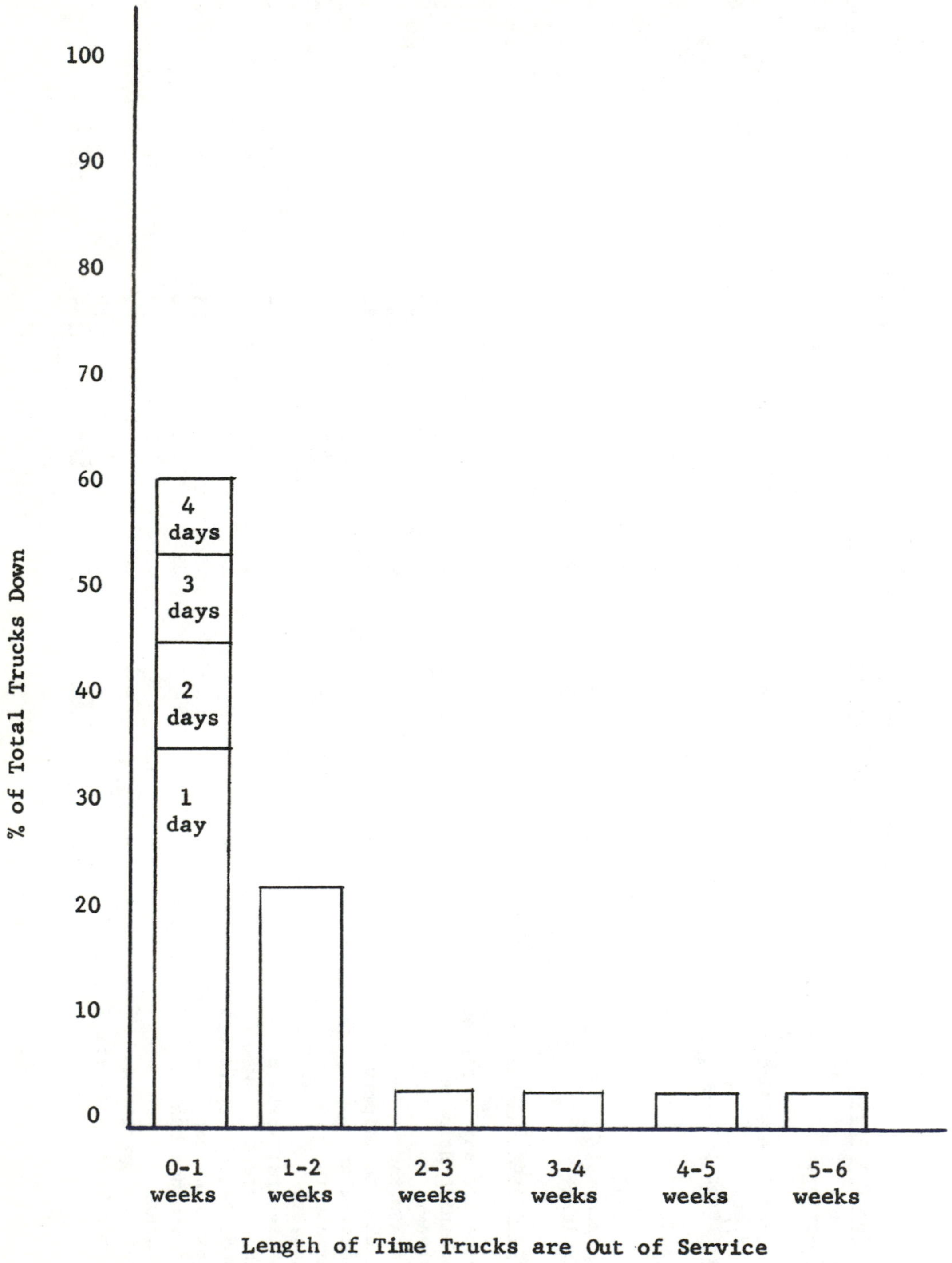

Exhibit 3

SANITATION (B)

Work Sampling Findings by Work Center

Department	Work Obs.	Work %	Related Effort Obs.	Related Effort %	Nonwork Obs.	Nonwork %	Total Obs.	Total %
South Chassis	73	36	33	16	99	48	205	100
North Chassis	111	45	59	24	75	31	245	100
Power Sweeper	121	44	45	16	112	40	278	100
Body Shop	141	41	20	6	183	53	344	100
Passenger Car	23	23	22	22	53	55	98	100
Subtotal	469	40	179	15	522	45	1,170	100
Electric Shop	86	52	19	11	62	37	167	100
Radiation Shop	36	62	2	3	20	35	58	100
Upholstery	23	50	3	7	20	43	46	100
Unit Repair	120	59	26	13	56	28	202	100
Subtotal	265	57	50	10	158	33	473	100
Machine Shop	128	60	22	10	62	29	212	100
Engine Overhaul	84	45	38	20	65	35	187	100
Subtotal	212	53	60	15	127	32	399	100
Tire Shop	67	33	5	2	134	65	206	100
Broom Repair	45	62	2	3	26	35	73	100
Tractor and Forge	52	43	7	6	61	51	120	100
Subtotal	164	41	14	4	221	55	399	100
Grand Total	1,110	45	303	12	1,028	43	2,441	100

Observations and Per Cent of Total*

*These observations were taken at random during the last week of November and the first week of December, 1969.

Exhibit 4

SANITATION (B)

Summary of In-House and Contractor Overhaul Costs for Selected Items

Item and Model	Purchase Price	Contract Overhaul Estimate	In-House Overhaul Cost: Direct	In-House Overhaul Cost: With Overhead
Motor I.H. 501	$1,370.00	$700.00	$1,100.00*	$1,650.00*
Tire** Michelin 1200 x 20	176.30	6.00	9.60	14.40
Starter Leece Neville 93002	182.50	97.00	36.00	46.45
Alternator Leece Neville 2078A	215.62	150.00	62.00	83.00
Volt Regulator Leece Neville 3511	23.00	-	15.75	23.65
Distributor Delco-Remy 1111868	23.31	20.50	19.25	27.15
Front Brake Timken	***	16.60	33.60	50.40
Rear Brake Timken	***	31.08	33.60	50.40
Hydraulic Pump Heil A-219	269.78	147.10	105.10	127.65

*Excludes parts for comparison.

**The work involved in the tire shop to mount and dismount tires, inspect, repair and replace tubes. Tire recapping is contracted out and not included in this comparison.

***These items are not purchased as complete assemblies.

SANITATION (C)[1]

Cleaning and Collection Productivity

The search for ways to improve the operation of New York's Bureau of Cleaning and Collection (BCC) did not end with the mayor's Clean City Task Force, or with the study of maintenance operations carried out by the Bureau of the Budget (see Sanitation (A) and Sanitation (B)), or with Mayor Lindsay's reelection as an Independent in the fall 1969. In mid-1970, at the urging of the Bureau of the Budget and the central staff at the Environmental Protection Administration (EPA), a team of consultants from McKinsey & Company, Inc., was retained to begin a thorough analysis of the cleaning and collection operations and to recommend productivity improving changes. This case summarizes some of the team's findings.[2]

Collection Operations

> These guys work like hell! A three-man team picks up about ten tons of garbage a day--plus the cans--and walks an awful lot of miles.
>
> Harvey Cole, McKinsey & Company, Inc.

One of the first things that the McKinsey team did was to identify two of the stronger sanitation districts (one in the South Bronx and one in Brooklyn) and then spend over a month in these districts riding the trucks, talking to the men, the section foremen, and the district supers, all in an effort to learn what was "really going on out there." The overall impressions of one of the team members, Harvey Cole, are summarized above. Another, Jack Irwin, gave his views as follows:

---

1 Some of the names in this case have been disguised.

2 McKinsey was retained to help the new administrator of EPA--who later became acting commissioner of sanitation--make an early impact on the cleanliness of the city. Improving cleaning and collection operations was one of several projects undertaken.

One thing that strikes you early on is the dedication of those guys, especially the officers. One of the toughest jobs out there is section foreman, particularly in ghetto areas like the South Bronx. It's difficult to get the men to work well because they don't like being in those areas. The foremen all speak of being under tremendous pressure from the communities although I didn't see any specific instances when I was there. They believe they're doing all they can to collect the garbage on time and I believe they really do try. But it's a frustrating job and many of them have tried for years without success to keep the place clean and so have given up. In their view, the community doesn't understand and doesn't appreciate their efforts. Keeping the place clean, they think, is a cooperative venture between the sanitation department and the residents. But there are some young foremen out there who are really trying--who really want to make the place clean.

The section foremen also feel that the union and, therefore, the men are more powerful than the officer corps. I didn't see any friction between the officers and the men, but I sensed in my conversations with the foremen that they were concerned and that they never made demands on the men that might be refused because they didn't want to get into a confrontation over work conditions or whatever.

The men had routes established which they did every day and, if there was more garbage out on the route than usual, they tended to give a little extra to clean it up. But the section foremen thought it would be difficult to ask the men to work harder on their route so they could help someone else who had more than he could handle. Another example was sweeping when the truck went to the disposal point. I've seen section foremen in the afternoon--maybe two hours before the shift was over--standing on a street corner talking with two or three sanitationmen and the catch basins were still dirty. Of course, these men had already done a full day's worth of collection work.

Generally speaking, though, the section foremen did a good job. They felt that they were poorly trained; that they were taught how to complete the forms, but never told how to lead men or how to relate to the community. They got promoted to district superintendent on the basis of a written test; and some of them went to school at night to help themselves pass the test.

Different district superintendents carved out different roles for themselves. Some were like generals leading an army. Others were passive; they just established the routes, assigned the trucks, and then drove around being pleasant to the section foremen. One district super felt his job was to keep track of the mechanical brooms so that if one broke down he could reassign the others.

But for all of them, the basic job was to match the number of men they had assigned to their districts against the demand that they knew would be out there because it was Monday, or because it had been a long weekend, or because they hadn't been able to clean one day last week. They knew how to cut a man here and there from cleaning (don't man a power broom or a flusher today) so that the collection task got done. They decided all this the night before, based on the number of men that were supposed to be on duty the next day. In the morning, when the districts knew who had actually showed up, they telephoned all the assignment information to borough headquarters. Borough headquarters then made adjustments between districts. The criteria for these adjustments were to get as many trucks on the streets as possible, not to leave garbage out in very bad areas, and to equalize the number of missed collections from district to district. At noon, the section foremen called in to report progress and the district super made decisions regarding whether or not to begin cleaning and if so where.

One important thing for a district super was to know what was going on so he could answer questions asked by borough headquarters. What were the morning weights? How many trucks have you got in district 51? Are you going to clean today? The borough people were always asking things like that so they would know how to deploy the night trucks.

Expanding on his initial comments ("ten tons" and "an awful lot of miles"), Harvey Cole had this to say about his observations in the districts:

In the so-called "bad" districts, one of the major problems was that most of the buildings had no superintendents. No one brings the cans out when they're supposed to. They bring them out after the truck has gone by, and there aren't enough, and they don't take them back in after the truck has gone. I've watched the trucks going down the street, picking up everything that was there, and five minutes later some guy comes out and sets his cans out on the curb. Without the cooperation of conscientious building superintendents and, for that matter, of small store owners, you have no hope of making a dent in the problem.

The basic thing that district supers had to manage against was a manning table in the borough and district offices that says, "We know by experience that on Monday in this district, in this section, we need two trucks and it might fluctuate a little bit, but that's all right because the guys will work a little harder, if necessary, to clean the route up." These tables were set up by the district supers, mostly by experience, and they shifted the resources a little bit when it was necessary. Within his own pool of men and equipment, the district super could do anything he wanted including changing the truck routes.

One guy in Brooklyn used to deploy his trucks and hold back about five. Then he'd throw the five into the breach wherever he had a problem. He was like a sheep dog among his trucks, charging down the street and moving his guys around here and there. Apparently he was an unbelievably charismatic supervisor who could really lead men. And apparently he was relatively successful in turning around a poor district.

In addition to observing operations in the South Bronx and Brooklyn, McKinsey also compiled productivity data for all of the city's 58 sanitation districts. Some of this data is shown in Exhibits 1, 2 and 3. Cole commented on its probable reliability:

One of the problems we had with sanitation is that there's no hard evidence for anything. Reliable data does not exist. There's a lot of data generated, but it's not necessarily meaningful and it's probably biased one way or another. You hear lots of anecdotes although we never got any concrete evidence. The guy will tell you how he always stopped by the firehouse and got them to squirt the truck full of water to make the load heavier. There's no question the scales are out of order a lot. Still, tons per truck shift, as reported by the department, is a pretty good index number. It may be biased but, if it shows trends, they're probably real ones.

Several "environmental" factors tended to influence the number of tons collected per truck shift. Relative to areas where one- and two-family houses were predominant, more densely populated districts had more cans per stop and the cans were more completely filled. This meant more tons collected per truck shift. The physical layout at individual stops was also important. Some locations and areas presented easy access for the trucks and men while others had heavy traffic or rows of small fences and gatework which interfered with getting to the cans. In some areas the refuse was always neatly containerized, while in others the material was piled haphazardly in small sacks or even "air mailed" out tenement windows and strewn about the general area.

Truck characteristics were a further influence on loading rates. Because the hoppers were higher on some models than on others, the cans had to be lifted farther. The older escalator trucks had a kick plate on the tailgate and a hopper floor that sloped sharply down and away from the kick plate; this allowed cans to be dumped down into the hopper and made it easy to jar material loose on cold or wet days. The newer batch compactor trucks, on the other hand, had a larger loading area which held items that would not fit in the escalator truck, but it had a high, level hopper floor with no kick plate. This meant that material had to be shaken out by rolling the cans back and forth. (The different truck models were randomly distributed throughout the city. The new compactor trucks, as they came into the fleet, were used to replace the oldest escalator models.)

The new compactor trucks also affected productivity because their greater carrying capacity made it possible to reduce the number of trips per shift to the disposal site and thereby increase the amount of on-route collection time.[1] Loads of 5.0 to 5.5 tons could be carried by the compactors compared to only 3.2 to 3.5 tons for the escalators. Current practice, in areas where the garbage was fairly dense, was to make three trips to the dump site with the escalator trucks and two with the compactors. One factor that tended to decrease the advantage of the compactors' larger capacity, however, was the time required for the compacting mechanism to complete its cycle. The mechanism was actuated after each five or six cans and took from 15 to 25 seconds to complete. During the cycle, the truck had to remain stationary and this meant a total waiting time of between 42 and 55 minutes per shift.

All of the items discussed above influenced manual collection productivity. But the biggest determinant of over-all collection productivity was whether or not the loading action itself was mechanized. While 95% of the refuse collected by DS was loaded manually, 5% was collected with hoist-fitted-chassis (HFC) trucks. Many locations that generated large quantities of refuse (such as hospitals) were equipped with metal bins of from 8 to 12 cubic yards. These bins were lifted by a winch to the bed of an HFC truck, driven to the dump site, and returned empty. A single sanitationman was required, and the yearly costs per ton were only 40% of those for manual collection. Although the department had initiated HFC service in the 1950s with containers supplied free as part of the service, later budget reviews had adopted the policy of requiring the user to purchase the containers (about $800). At least partly as a result of this action, the expansion of HFC service had slowed and was virtually stagnant in 1968.

Cleaning Operations

Several methods were used to keep the city's streets clean. Motorized litter patrols, consisting of a truck and several men equipped with brooms picked up and emptied city-owned and maintained litter baskets, swept catch basins and corner areas, and did other spot cleaning work. Approximately 200 flusher trucks, with water tanks and spray nozzles, were used to suppress dust and to move dirt and debris from the center of the street to curbside. Once at curbside, the material was swept up either by manual sweepers or power brooms. Manual sweepers used hand brooms and

[1] On-route collection time was also affected by the round-trip time to the dump.

pushcarts and were assigned full time to sweeping either because they were not needed for collection work or because they were limited duty men--that is, physically unable to do hard manual work. Part-time manual sweeping was also done by the collection truck loaders when the trucks went to the dump site to deposit a load. Of all the street cleaning methods, however, power brooms were the most important. In most boroughs, the number of man days spent on manual cleaning was greater than the number spent driving power brooms, but the amount of dirt picked up and the number of curb miles swept was much greater for the power brooms.

In 1970, following a concerted effort to modernize and expand the fleet, there were about 450 power brooms on hand as shown in Exhibit 4. Except in Manhattan East, Manhattan West, and Richmond, brooms (like collection trucks) were housed and given routine maintenance and minor repairs in the district garages. Major repair work was done at the central repair facility in Queens (see Sanitation (B)). In Manhattan East and West, brooms were housed and maintained in two special broom depots and in Richmond they were serviced at the borough repair shop. The average number of brooms up and running is also shown in Exhibit 4.

Both long- and short-term allocations of cleaning resources (men and equipment) were made without any formal procedures or explicit criteria. Brooms were assigned to borough commands by the assistant chief of staff for street cleaning at BCC Headquarters largely on the basis of experience and intuition. Headquarters personnel felt that the varying difficulty of the cleaning job in different parts of the city (amounts of dirt, traffic conditions, distances to routes and dump sites), varying rates of broom down time, and both internal and external political pressures made any other approach to allocation impossible. Borough commands also relied heavily on intuition and experience when allocating brooms to districts. Once assigned to a borough, brooms were seldom reassigned to another borough; but borough superintendents frequently adjusted the allocation of brooms to districts when one district fell behind in its cleaning work because of an extra heavy load, an abnormally high rate of broom down time, or some other reason. On a day-to-day basis, district superintendents allocated the men in accordance with the following list of priorities:[1]

- Meet collection schedules.
- Fill requirements for clerks, district garage help, and motorized litter patrol.
- Meet power broom sweeping schedules or man all available power brooms, whichever requires fewer men.
- Assign manual sweepers to areas needing sweeping and not accessible to or scheduled for power broom sweeping.
- Man flushers.

---

[1]Limited duty men were always assigned to light work.

For the purpose of determining power broom sweeping schedules, the city's streets were classified as A, B, or C. Category A streets were those in heavily parked residential areas. They were posted for alternate side of the street parking (ASP) and were swept during the day. In addition to being classified A, they were further subdivided into streets that were to be swept, one, two, or three times a week. Thus, for an A(2) street, parking might be prohibited on Tuesday and Friday mornings. Class B streets were located in the central business areas. They were scheduled for power sweeping six nights a week and for attention from motorized litter patrols during the day. Class C streets were in outlying residential areas and were machine cleaned either day or night without special traffic regulations. They were supposed to be swept an average of 1.5 times per week but it was up to the district foreman to determine the actual frequency based on his assessment of cleanliness and the other demands on his men and equipment.

The number of curb miles in each of the three classifications for the eleven sanitation boroughs is shown in Exhibit 5. Also shown are the number of miles scheduled for sweeping in the morning and afternoon of that day in the week with the greatest total mileage of class A streets scheduled for sweeping. (Usually, this peak demand occurred on Mondays.) Exhibit 6 shows the class A morning and afternoon schedules on peak days in some of the districts.

Once ASP regulations had been set for the class A streets in a district and the "No Parking" signs posted, it was difficult and expensive to change the arrangement. All changes suggested by the Department of Sanitation had to be approved by the Traffic Department and, once the changes were made, there was a period of adjustment for residents during which compliance was worse than usual. (Even "usual" compliance was bad--less than 40% throughout the city and, in Manhattan, where a substantial number of the cars parked at curbside during the day were from out of state, the rate was even worse.) One ball park estimate of the cost simply to repost a single sanitation district was about $60,000. Enforcement of ASP regulations was the responsibility of the Police Department and the Department of Sanitation. (Section foremen and officers of higher rank could issue summonses.) The actual number of summonses given out, in relation to the number of blocks scheduled for sweeping in May 1970, is shown in Exhibit 7.

One of the unresolved problems about cleaning operations was how to measure output. DS collected data about cleaning in essentially the same form as it did for collection--that is, records were kept manually of the number of broom shifts worked, the hopper loads collected, and the curb miles swept. The data was collected and collated for each district and for the three street classifications within districts. Once a month, it was published in the form shown in Exhibit 8. The information was subject to the same doubts about its accuracy that surrounded other items of input to the department's information system: Were the reported hopper loads full or partial? Was the number of curb miles swept a real or "gun-decked" figure?

Even if the numbers were relatively accurate, they gave little indication of the actual cleanliness of the streets and "cleanliness," of course, was the ultimate output of the cleaning operation. Several alternative measures were proposed. One was to make regular surveys of the streets and rank them according to a cleanliness scale. There had been some experimentation in other cities, for example, with a scale that used photographs (see Exhibit 9). The system would require that sanitation supervisors or special inspectors do the rating. A second proposal was to use existing data but to process it one step further. An index could be created by dividing hopper loads collected (HL) by curb miles swept (CMS). This index (HL/CMS) would give a clear indication of how dirty the streets were when the sweepers went by. Districts with consistently low indices could be said to have cleaner streets than those where the HL/CMS ratio was higher. Critics of this concept acknowledged its simplicity, but were concerned that it did not take into account the question of how many people were exposed to the dirt. It was more important, they believed, to keep the HL/CMS low in areas of high population density than to do so in less densely populated areas.

Exhibit 1

SANITATION (C)

Data on Collection Operations:

Average Monday Performance by Sanitation District

Borough	District	Off-Route Miles*	Average Tons Collected	Average Tons Left Uncollected	Average** Truck Shifts	Tons Collected/ Truck Shift	Curb Miles Scheduled	Tons/ Curb Mile
Manhattan West	1	4.0	175	11	17.50	10.0	99.8	1.86
	3	5.0	129	9	14.00	9.2	92.0	1.50
	5	3.0	286	72	26.25	10.9	84.2	4.25
	7	8.0	238	71	22.50	10.6	81.8	3.78
	9	9.5	263	17	24.50	10.7	71.2	3.93
Manhattan East	2	6.5	242	47	23.50	10.3	98.8	2.93
	4	6.0	195	28	21.00	9.3	110.8	2.01
	6	4.0	294	67	26.75	11.0	100.6	2.59
	8	7.5	272	65	26.50	10.3	70.2	4.80
	10	6.0	252	51	24.50	10.3	66.4	4.56
Bronx West	21	12.0	229	43	21.25	10.8	104.8	2.60
	23	13.0	194	46	19.50	9.9	90.5	2.65
	25	12.5	191	45	19.50	9.8	98.0	2.41
	27	10.5	185	46	19.50	9.5	121.2	1.91
	29	17.5	193	10	19.25	9.9	148.0	1.37
Bronx East	20	8.0	281	34	25.00	11.2	144.9	2.17
	22	12.5	228	34	22.25	10.2	122.2	2.14
	24	8.0	208	26	17.00	12.2	174.3	1.34
	26	10.0	219	27	19.00	11.5	147.4	1.67
	28	15.5	204	27	17.00	12.0	150.0	1.54

* Includes distance to and from district garages and dump sites.
** Fractional shifts result from overtime.

Exhibit 1 (continued)

Borough	District	Off-Route Miles*	Average Tons Collected	Average Tons Left Uncollected	Average** Truck Shifts	Tons Collected/ Truck Shift	Curb Miles Scheduled	Tons/ Curb Mile
Brooklyn West	30	6.0	187	87	22.50	8.3	68.8	3.98
	31	4.0	217	35	20.75	10.5	68.8	3.66
	32	8.0	223	36	22.00	10.1	92.7	2.79
	33	6.0	215	39	21.50	10.0	71.5	3.55
	34	7.5	223	44	21.50	10.4	89.3	2.99
	35	6.0	231	60	23.00	10.0	206.0	1.41
Brooklyn North	36	7.0	201	60	21.75	9.2	141.8	1.84
	37	8.0	222	32	22.50	9.9	82.1	3.09
	38	10.0	181	12	21.00	8.6	64.0	3.02
	39	3.0	273	121	24.00	11.4	100.6	3.92
	40	16.0	214	133	25.00	8.6	116.6	2.98
	41	7.5	208	22	24.25	8.6	84.7	2.71
Brooklyn East	42	9.5	230	13	22.50	10.2	87.4	2.78
	43	11.0	243	33	25.25	9.6	144.2	1.91
	44	6.0	157	35	17.50	9.0	129.7	1.48
	45	9.0	224	19	26.25	8.5	104.6	2.32
	46	12.5	192	18	23.00	8.3	100.7	2.09
	47	13.5	204	20	21.50	9.5	114.4	1.96

* Includes distance to and from district garages and dump sites.
** Fractional shifts result from overtime.

Exhibit 1 (continued)

Borough	District	Off-Route Miles*	Average Tons Collected	Average Tons Left Uncollected	Average** Truck Shifts	Tons Collected/ Truck Shift	Curb Miles Scheduled	Tons/ Curb Mile
Queens West	50	13.0	208	60	23.25	8.9	129.6	2.06
	51	11.0	250	39	23.75	10.5	109.8	2.63
	52	6.5	169	36	17.50	9.7	155.3	1.32
	53	8.0	254	24	24.75	10.3	130.7	2.13
	54	7.0	194	33	24.00	8.1	108.7	2.09
	55	13.5	243	21	26.50	9.2	101.7	2.40
Queens North	60	5.5	239	43	24.00	10.0	153.8	1.83
	61	16.0	190	40	32.75	5.8	121.8	1.89
	62	10.5	214	39	24.25	8.8	131.2	1.93
	63	6.5	174	25	31.75	5.5	140.0	1.42
	64	20.5	212	42	22.75	9.3	145.8	1.74
Queens South	65	23.0	226	53	24.75	9.1	144.2	1.93
	66	13.5	209	72	22.00	9.5	138.0	2.04
	67	8.0	147	50	19.25	7.6	139.9	1.41
	68	20.5	136	43	16.75	8.1	120.1	1.49
	69	12.0	219	97	25.25	8.7	171.4	1.84
Richmond	70	15.0	159	11	15.25	10.4	73.1	2.33
	71	13.5	149	-	13.75	10.8	118.7	2.03
	72	14.0	177	40	18.00	9.8	142.4	1.83
	73	10.0	133	28	14.00	9.5	201.9	0.79

* Includes distance to and from district garages and dump sites.
** Fractional shifts result from overtime.

Exhibit 2

SANITATION (C)

Regression Analysis of Data on Collection Operations[1]

Variables:

X_1 = Tons collected per truck shift

X_2 = Tons of refuse per curb mile

X_3 = Off-route miles

Regression Data:

a) $X_1 = 9.26 + 0.30\ X_2 - .03\ X_3$

$R^2 = 0.05$

Probability that the coefficient shown is not zero and has the sign indicated:

Coefficient of X_2: 0.943
Coefficient of X_3: 0.807

b) $X_1 = 8.80 + .36\ X_2$

$R^2 = 0.05$

Probability that the coefficient of X_2 is not zero and has the sign indicated: 0.976

c) $X_1 = 10.19 - .05\ X_3$

$R^2 = 0.02$

Probability that the coefficient of X_3 is not zero and has the sign indicated: 0.928

---

[1] The regression analysis was not carried out as part of the McKinsey work. It is set forth here as an aid to case analysis.

Exhibit 3

SANITATION (C)

Record of Weekly Average of Tons

per Truck Shift in District 39 (Brooklyn North)

		Tons/Truck Shift	
Week of	District 39	Highest District in Borough**	Lowest District in Borough
8/24/69	7.5	7.8	7.3
9/28/69	7.5*	7.8	7.3
11/2/69	8.3	8.3	7.6
12/7/69	10.4	8.7	7.3
1/11/70	8.5	8.0	5.6
2/15/70	9.3	7.7	7.3
3/22/70	8.9	8.2	7.1
4/26/70	9.0	8.5	7.2
5/31/70	10.6	8.4	7.4

* A new superintendent took charge of District 39 in September.
** Other than District 39.

Exhibit 4

SANITATION (C)

Data on Power Brooms (Mid-1970)

Borough		Brooms Assigned by Year of Acquisition 1970	1969	1968	Pre1968	Total	Average Brooms Up and Running Number	Per Cent
Manhattan	West	4	5	11	18	38	21	55%
	East	20	3	7	11	41	23	56
Bronx	West	20	5	12	14	51	26	51
	East	15	5	12	10	42	24	57
Brooklyn	West	20	7	8	23	58	28	48
	North	14	6	14	23	57	28	49
	East	16	7	13	15	51	25	49
Queens	West	15	7	12	9	43	29	67
	North	15	6	3	4	28	9	32
	South	7	4	4	5	20	10*	50*
Richmond		4	4	4	5	17	8*	50*
Total		150	59	100	137	446	231	
Per cent		34%	13%	22%	31%	100%	52%	

*Estimated.

Exhibit 5

SANITATION (C)

Data on Curb Mileage

Borough		Curb Miles in Borough: Class A 1*	Class A 2*	Class A 3*	Class A Total	Class B	Class C	Peak Class A Miles A.M.	Peak Class A Miles P.M.	Average CMS/ Shift**
Manhattan	West	-	133	201	334	208	13	90	75	13.7
	East	-	179	274	453	106	-	110	115	16.6
Bronx	West	-	339	180	519	-	103	125	133	11.4
	East	114	246	44	404	-	305	78	95	13.6
Brooklyn	West	271	746	-	1017	47	59	213	224	13.0
	North	-	550	228	788	-	46	208	180	12.6
	East	120	525	74	719	16	342	152	178	10.9
Queens	West	276	368	-	644	-	1141	140	100	14.7
	North	231	22	-	253	-	1341	57	60	11.7
	South	-	-	-	-	-	1150	0	0	13.3
Richmond		-	-	-	-	8	1018	0	0	13.5

*Sweeping frequency per week.
**CMS = Curb miles swept.

Exhibit 6

SANITATION (C)

Data on Peak Class A Mileage for Selected Sanitation Districts

Borough	District	Peak Day Class A Miles A.M.	Peak Day Class A Miles P.M.	Borough	District	Peak Day Class A Miles A.M.	Peak Day Class A Miles P.M.
Manhattan West	1	13	4	Brooklyn West	30	29	33
	3	1	7		31	37	43
	5	22	21		32	49	37
	7	20	21		33	16	20
	9	32	23		34	29	17
					35	29	57
Manhattan East	2	37	10	Brooklyn North	36	37	40
	4	9	27		37	32	34
	6	22	25		38	33	28
	8	22	32		39	27	23
	10	17	16		40	29	27
					41	52	28
Bronx East	20	10	33	Brooklyn East	42	40	38
	22	28	29		43	34	44
	24	5	23		44	2	37
	26	27	19		45	49	40
					46	11	8
					47	12	17

Exhibit 7

SANITATION (C)

ASP Summonses Issued per 100 Blocks Scheduled for Sweeping

(May 1970)

Borough		Summonses per 100 Blocks Scheduled
Manhattan	West	10
	East	4
Bronx	West	4
	East	2
Brooklyn	West	3
	North	2
	East	1
Queens	West	3

Exhibit 8

SANITATION (C)

Sample of Monthly Report on Power Sweeping Operations

S T R E E T   C L E A N I N G : P O W E R   S W E E P I N G
By Borough and District

	Curb Miles in Area				POWER SWEEPING: Curb Miles Swept				Hopper Loads				Broom Shifts				Curb Miles per Broom Shift — TOTAL
Dist.	A	B	C	TOTAL	A	B	C	TOTAL	A	B	C	TOTAL	A	B	C	TOTAL	Current Month
30	123.8	47.2	28.7	199.7	1,304	804	546	2,654	188	113	70	371	93	53	33	179	14.8
31	160.3	-	19.6	179.9	1,211	-	1,270	2,481	150	-	157	307	82	-	80	162	15.3
32	172.8	-	18.0	190.8	1,613	-	-	1,613	223	-	-	223	145	-	-	145	11.1
33	192.4	-	26.9	219.3	1,428	-	634	2,062	198	-	53	251	113	-	46	159	13.0
34	179.5	-	12.5	192.0	930	-	378	1,308	161	-	48	209	93	-	41	134	9.8
35	191.9	-	38.5	230.4	900	-	683	1,583	178	-	138	316	91	-	68	159	10.0
TOTAL	1,020.7	47.2	144.2	1,212.1	7,386	804	3,511	11,701	1,098	113	466	1,677	617	53	268	938	12.5
36	153.7		35.3	189.0	1,309	-	1,243	2,552	182	-	185	367	90	-	94	184	13.9
37	127.2		8.4	135.6	1,183	-	669	1,852	186	-	89	275	98	-	61	159	11.6
38	123.8		4.2	128.0	1,902	-	171	2,073	319	-	26	345	160	-	18	178	11.6
39	101.6		-	101.6	1,293	-	-	1,293	339	-	-	339	171	-	-	171	7.6
40	112.5		4.8	117.3	2,083	-	-	2,083	191	-	-	191	161	-	-	161	12.9
41	158.8		5.8	164.6	2,055	-	1,327	3,382	241	-	163	404	137	-	91	228	14.8
TOTAL	777.6	-	58.5	836.1	9,825	-	3,410	13,235	1,458	-	463	1,921	817	-	264	1,081	12.2

Exhibit 9

SANITATION (C)

RANKINGS FOR DETERMINING CLEANLINESS
OF STREETS, GUTTERS, SIDEWALKS

1 Few paper items, smaller than paper cups.
(cigarette butts or gum wrappers)
Very few larger items of any type.
No dirt.
Area basically free of litter and gives
"clean, washed" appearance.

2 Moderate amounts of litter, smaller than paper cups.
Few items larger.
Some dirt.
Area somewhat littered, does not present
wholly clean appearance.

3 Moderate (scattered) amounts of average-sized paper items. (cigarette packs, wads of paper, paper cups, candy wrappers)
and/or
Large amounts of small items (cigarette butts, gum wrappers)
and/or
Moderate amounts of dirt, dog droppings.

4 Same as #3, plus:
Moderate amounts of miscellaneous items
(metal, glass, rocks, cans, blocks of wood, etc.).

5 Moderate amounts of large paper items
(newspapers, large bags, paper containers, aggregations of smaller paper items)
Little garbage spillage
and/or
Heavy accumulation of average-sized items
(cigarette packs, wads of paper, cups)

6 Moderate amounts of garbage spillage
Large amounts of large paper items (newspapers, large bags, paper containers, large aggregations of smaller items)
or
Large amounts of miscellaneous items
(metal, glass, rocks, cans, blocks of wood, etc.)

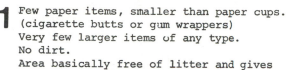

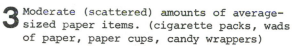

7 Piles of rubble, mattresses
Piles of cans and bottles
Stripped abandoned cars
Dump outs, street piles, accumulations
of dirt, trash overturned

SANITATION (D)

A New Commissioner

One concern was that the department might be kill- itself with the "Peter Principle."

Jerry Mechling, EPA staff

I was the youngest commissioner ever. I had two-and-a-half years. My main problem was to get them to pay attention, to do something, to see that it really made a difference what they did.

Herbert Elish, Commissioner of Sanitation

Management Changes at EPA and DS

The period from September 1969 to March 1971 saw the completion of two major analytic efforts in New York's Department of Sanitation (DS): The Bureau of the Budget's study of maintenance operations (see Sanitation (B)) and McKinsey & Company's review of cleaning and collection activities (see Sanitation (C)). It also saw important revisions in the top management roster at the Environmental Protection Administration (EPA) and at DS.

During 1968 and 1969, there had been a steady erosion in the relationship between Mayor Lindsay and Merle Eisenbud, the administrator of EPA. In the mayor's view, neither Eisenbud nor Griswold Moeller, the commissioner of sanitation had responded effectively to the complaints of the mayor and the citizens about poor sanitation services. A particular sore point was the slow pace of snow removal following a blizzard in February 1969. Some streets had remained impassable far longer than usual and the mayor's press--with a spring primary imminent--had suffered badly. It was not surprising, therefore, that in January 1970, following the mayor's successful campaign for reelection, Eisenbud's resignation was tendered and accepted. His replacement was Jerry Kretchmer, Manhattan

West's reform Democratic assemblyman to the state legislature.

Kretchmer and Eisenbud were a study in contrasts. Eisenbud was a scientist-administrator who had come from academia and planned to return to it. He believed in order and deliberation and these beliefs were reflected in his administrative style. Kretchmer on the other hand was unabashedly political. Mayoral aspirations were a reason for his taking the job as administrator and he made no bones about it. He spent much of his time and energy taking himself and the problems of EPA to the people. Always available for press and TV interviews, he also made frequent appearances before civic and community groups. By April, when the first Earth Day was scheduled, he had successfully lobbied for shutting down parts of 14th Street and 5th Avenue so that street fairs could be held to raise the public's consciousness of environmental issues. Nor were his efforts confined to the public. He visited all of the sanitation boroughs and many of the districts where he talked to the superintendents, getting their ideas and telling them his. At the district garages, he attended roll call, swapped pleasantries with the men, and posed for photographs. No administrator or commissioner had ever paid the men that much attention before and his actions drew their praise, the suspicion of union leadership, and a cover picture on the New York Times Sunday magazine section appropriately titled, "Running for Mayor on a Garbage Truck." Through it all, however, Kretchmer knew there was more to the job of administrator than being flamboyant and staying in the headlines. This was the first time that he had ever managed a large organization and, if he did it poorly, the publicity could ruin rather than further his future career. Besides, he was a native New Yorker and, like John Lindsay, genuinely interested in the city's cleanliness.

Kretchmer's style and his decisions brought him into increasing conflict with Griswold Moeller. Moeller was a retired Navy captain and the sixth commissioner of sanitation to hold office since the Lindsay administration had begun in 1966. His sympathies had come to rest increasingly with the department in its debates with the mayor and the public over who was responsible for dirty streets and uncollected garbage. Like most of his officers, he saw the greatest need for change and improvement, not in the department, but in the attitudes and habits of the citizens. While Kretchmer viewed the McKinsey contract as an opportunity to gain the immediate services of some bright and eager minds, Moeller opposed it as unnecessary and threatening. In the summer of 1970, he resigned and was replaced by Kretchmer himself who decided, with the mayor's concurrence, to occupy the positions of administrator and commissioner until a suitable replacement for Moeller could be found.

This arrangement continued until April 1971, when Herbert Elish was appointed to be commissioner. Elish, like Kretchmer, was in his thirties, Jewish, a lawyer, a native of New York City, and without previous experience managing a large organization. He had graduated from Williams College and Harvard Law School and, before coming to EPA and DS, had been in Washington directing the legal staff of the Civil Aeronautics Board. If he had political aspirations, they were not yet clear; certainly, he was less flamboyant than Kretchmer. Elish had been with EPA as a deputy administrator since June 1970 and had become both a friend and confidant of Kretchmer's. During his stint as deputy administrator, moreover, he had had ample time to observe the operations of DS and to form his own opinions.[1] He had also had a unique opportunity to develop an understanding of the union leadership at the Bureau of Cleaning and Collection (BCC). Because of the city's policy of negotiating with all uniformed unions (fire, police, and sanitation) at the same time and the small size of the city's negotiating team, the representatives of the Uniformed Sanitationmen's Association (USA) had been left alone in their hotel suite in October 1970 while negotiations went on with the Police Department. Elish and Kretchmer spent days with the union leader, John DeLury; his long-standing economic consultant, Jack Bigel; and the other union representatives, getting to know them in an increasingly relaxed environment where they learned more and more about what were and were not sensitive issues for the union.

For Elish, getting to know DeLury had the potential of being a great "leg up" on the commissioner's job. All of the men in the Bureau of Cleaning and Collection were "uniformed" and all were members of either the USA or, if they were officers, of the Officers' Union. The two unions worked together and were, without question, the greatest single force in EPA (see Sanitation (A)). Whether the unions exercised their power or not and how they chose to exercise it were matters largely determined by John DeLury. He had both founded the USA and become its president in the late 1940s. Since then he had accomplished extraordinary improvements in the wages, fringe benefits, and working conditions of the men. To quote him: "There's no job in New York City, with all our benefits and wages, to compare with a sanitationman's." He was also on record with, "I don't care who's commissioner. He's only a figurehead for the mayor, anyway." Indeed, DeLury frequently asserted that the management at DS was poor and that it was only he, DeLury, who had any real control. Most commissioners who preceded Elish promoted men to officer ranks and officers to higher rank only after checking with DeLury and receiving his concurrence. Despite his unwavering support of the sanitationmen when there was conflict with the mayor, the management of EPA or DS, or with New York's citizens, DeLury thought of himself as a "liberal." While no date had been set, he was getting to the age when he had to begin thinking about his retirement from active direction of the union.

As deputy administrator at EPA, Elish had been involved in several efforts to enhance productivity in the Department of Sanitation. During the McKinsey study (see Sanitation (C)), he had been the prime point of contact between the consultants and EPA. He had also served as EPA's liaison with

---

[1]It was, in fact, difficult to say exactly when Elish had really become commissioner. With Kretchmer's concurrence, he had simply assumed more and more of the commissioner's responsibilities and duties while retaining the title of deputy administrator.

the Project Management Staff (PMS) when PMS began implementing its recommendations for improving vehicle maintenance operations (see Sanitation (B)). PMS had suggested a major deemphasis of the 67 repair shops and of the central repair facility in Queens. The bulk of the repair and overhaul work would be shifted to five, well-equipped "area" garages (of which the old central repair shop would be one). These new shops would be modern facilities, adequately stocked with spare parts, and with much more direct supervision than had been possible with the many district shops. The district shops would remain open, but would be staffed with only one mechanic and one auto serviceman. They would work on the day shift and be strictly limited to minor repair and overhaul and routine preventive maintenance work.

PMS, working with Elish and a newly appointed director of motor equipment--hired from the private sector--had managed the opening of the first area garage near the Brooklyn-Queens border in November 1970. Within two months, the average number of collection vehicles out of service in the nine sanitation districts served by the new facility had dropped from about 35% to approximately 25%.[1] Two more area garages were scheduled for opening during 1971.

Another productivity issue in which Elish had been deeply involved was chart days (see Sanitation (A)). He had worked with a group of faculty and students from the State University of New York's Stony Brook campus to develop an alternative to the old six chart system. He had then worked hard to convince the mayor and John DeLury that adoption of the new system was both important and feasible and that it should be included as a key item on the agenda during the contract negotiations that had begun in the fall of 1970 between the city and the Uniformed Sanitationmen's Association. Now, with those negotiations drawing to a close, it looked as though the new system would become part of the contract. Henceforth, sanitationmen would

---

[1]Most of the improvement noted by early 1971 was achieved by reducing the time an out-of-service vehicle spent in the maintenance system from the time it arrived for repairs to the time it was back on the job. This reduction, in turn, stemmed largely from the existence of more repair facilities and more rapid access to spare parts. The time that individual mechanics spent repairing a truck, once they started working on it, remained almost exactly what it had always been--just about twice the standard times set forth in the industry flat-rate manual. (The manual established standards for a large number of well-defined repair and overhaul jobs and was the basis on which most mechanics in the private sector were paid.) Of particular interest, was the fact that these were not average figures--the times for all jobs were approximately twice those specified in the manual. The maintenance union had always insisted upon a pay scale equal to the private sector but felt that civil servants could not be expected to achieve the same level of output as the private sector. They asserted, moreover, that the quality of work done by the union was substantially higher as a result of the more measured pace. Contract negotiations with the union were just beginning when Elish took the reins as commissioner.

be divided evenly into 30 chart groups instead of 6. Every man would still receive one chart day a week (in addition to Sunday), but now between two and seven chart groups would be off on any particular day. The 30 chart system, which varied manpower on duty to match the cleaning and collection work load (see Exhibits 1-3) can be compared to the old one through the table shown below. As yet no plans had been made for implementing the revised chart system.

Number of Charts and Per Cent of Total Force Not Working by Day of Week

Day of Week	6 Chart System		30 Chart System	
	# of Charts	% Force	# of Charts	% Force
Monday	1	31%	2	21%
Tuesday	1	31	3	24
Wednesday	1	31	5	31
Thursday	1	31	7	37
Friday	1	31	7	37
Saturday	1	31	6	34

Note: (1) 14% of work force is sick or on vacation on any given day.

(2) Average percentage of force not working on any given day is the same under both chart systems (roughly 31%); the averages do not appear the same in the table above due to rounding.

BCC Central

Organization charts of the Department of Sanitation are shown in Exhibits 1 and 3 of Sanitation (A). The functions of the various bureaus in DS were also described in Sanitation (A). Of the five bureaus, the Bureau of Cleaning and Collection was by far the largest and to a great extent, the other four existed to support BCC's operations. Thus, for any commissioner, management of the Department of Sanitation essentially meant management of BCC, and this, in turn, meant developing a successful relationship with the Central Staff at BCC headquarters. This group consisted of a chief of staff, five assistant chiefs of staff (ACS), their ten deputy assistant chiefs of staff, and 125 clerks and uniformed sanitationmen on deputation.

All of the ACSs and their deputies and the chief of staff were "senior managers," uniformed sanitationmen who had been promoted up through the ranks of the department. Advancement to the level of senior manager was based strictly on achievement in civil service examinations. Once a man entered the department's pool of senior managers, however, he could be assigned, at the commissioner's discretion, to any of several jobs. These included borough superintendent, deputy assistant chief of staff, or any of the more senior positions at BCC central. He could also be demoted and/or transferred from one senior manager job to another. Almost invariably, senior managers had finished the 20 years of duty required for retirement with full pension benefits--that is, at half pay. Perhaps for this reason, it was the "ethic" at BCC central that when the commissioner asked for an officer's "retirement," he got it without a fuss. It also meant that lower level officers were sometimes reluctant to accept a senior manager's position and thus forfeit their immunity from being "fired." This tended to be particularly evident when a change in administration was about to take place.

When Elish took the commissioner's job, his two seconds in command were Harry Scharaga, first deputy commissioner for operations, and Jim Scully, chief of staff at BCC. Relationships between the two men were neither cordial nor well-defined.

Scharaga had been promoted to the newly created post of first deputy commissioner by Jerry Kretchmer during the previous fall. Before that, he had been chief of staff, a position he had reached through the unique process of promotion directly from borough superintendent (of Manhattan East). This promotion (over about 15 men with greater seniority and rank) was done at the mayor's insistence. Scharaga had come to the mayor's attention in 1968 during the period when middle-class communities throughout the city were complaining about the sanitation department and holding community meetings to state their grievances. At these meetings, Scharaga had proved himself an able spokesman for the administration. What was more, he was viewed as one of the few officers who did not pass the blame for poor service on to the mayor. He had a reputation for enormous energy and devotion to his job. Once appointed to chief of staff, he was known during a snow emergency to arrive at headquarters in the middle of the night and stay for days without going home. On several occasions, when it was evident that the mayor wanted a change made in the department's operations, Scharaga had worked hard to bring it about. On the other hand, he had tended to remain aloof from his subordinates and to do many things himself that the chief of staff normally delegated to the ACSs. He had a long-standing friendship with John DeLury; the two men ate dinner together once or twice every week. As a result, when anyone wanted to be really unpleasant about Scharaga, he would claim that the mayor had promoted him in order to ensure peaceful relations with the union. Neither Scharaga, himself, nor the other officers at BCC central were quite sure what authority and responsibility went with the new first deputy's job.

Scully, who had been promoted from a borough command shortly after Scharaga became chief of staff, was viewed as one of the brightest men at BCC central. He had served as the assistant chief of staff for operations--

the top ACS position--running the phalanx of clerks and sanitationmen who composed BCC's operations department. His promotion to chief of staff had followed Scharaga's move to first deputy commissioner. Shortly thereafter, he had been stricken with TB and was returning to work (after several months convalescence) at about the time Elish became commissioner. Scully was close to and well liked by the ACSs. Indeed, Scully's loyalties lay down the line to the men and the unions. And, while he was exceedingly conscientious about his job, he tended to think of doing it "the same way only better" rather than a different way.

Exhibit 1

SANITATION (D)

Effects of the Six and Thirty Chart Systems on
Bureau of Cleaning and Collection Work Force

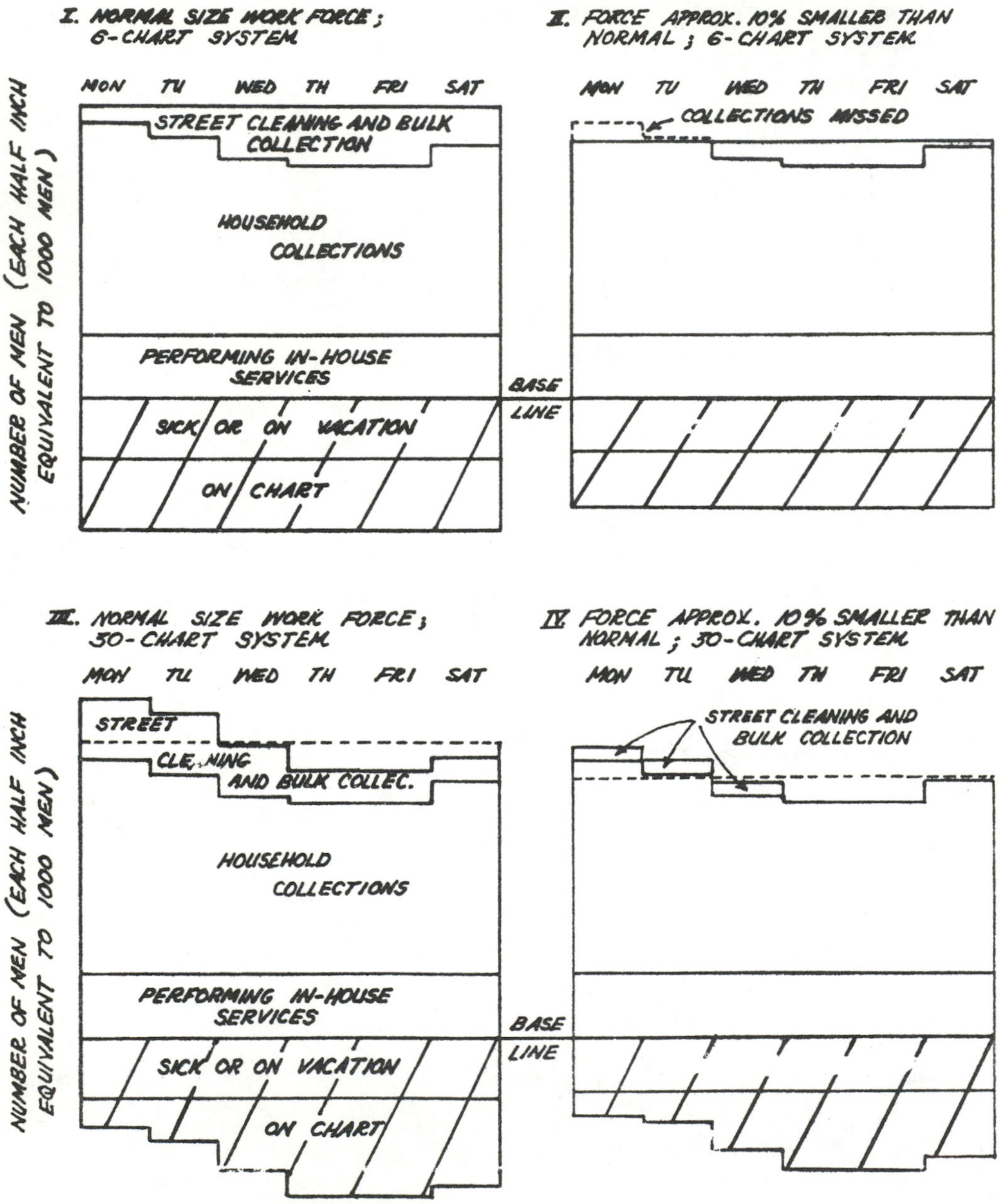

NOTE: DOTTED LINE IN GRAPH III. REPRESENTS NORMAL SIZE WORK FORCE UNDER 6-CHART SYSTEM. DOTTED LINE IN GRAPH IV. REPRESENTS 10%-SMALLER-THAN-NORMAL WORK FORCE UNDER 6-CHART SYSTEM.

Exhibit 2

SANITATION (D)

Chart Day Schedule under the Present 6 Chart System

day of the week

weeks	M	T	W	Th	F	Sa	Su
1	x						x
2		x					x
3			x				x
4				x			x
5					x		x
6						x	x
7	x						x
8		x					x
9			x				x
10				x			x
11					x		x
12						x	x
13	x						x
14		x					x
15			x				x
16				x			x
17					x		x
18						x	x
19	x						x
20		x					x
21			x				x
22				x			x
23					x		x
24						x	x
25	x						x
26		x					x
27			x				x
28				x			x
29					x		x
30						x	x
Total	5	5	5	5	5	5	30

x indicates the man or the group has the day off

Exhibit 3

SANITATION (D)

Chart Day Schedule under the New 30 Chart System

weeks	M	T	W	Th	F	Sa	Su
1	x						x
2			x				x
3				x			x
4					x		x
5						x	x
6		x					x
7				x			x
8					x		x
9						x	x
10			x				x
11				x			x
12					x		x
13						x	x
14		x					x
15					x		x
16	x						x
17			x				x
18				x			x
19					x		x
20						x	x
21		x					x
22				x			x
23					x		x
24						x	x
25			x				x
26				x			x
27					x		x
28						x	x
29			x				x
30				x			x
total	2	3	5	7	7	6	30

x indicates the man or the group has the day off

MODEL CITIES SANITATION PROJECT (C)[1]

Mr. Steven Rank of the New York City Project Management Staff (PMS) had just reread Miguel Herrera's memo of July 7, 1970. Copies of the memo, Exhibit 1, had gone to a long list of recipients including Mayor John Lindsay. Herrera was Neighborhood Director of the Bronx Model Cities Program and, as such was responsible for the Bronx Model Cities Sanitation Project (BMCSP). A Project Plan for the BMCSP (the cover letter for this Project Plan is presented as Exhibit 2), had recently been distributed by Rank and it was this event that triggered Herrera's memo. In the memo Mr. Herrera expressed astonishment at the procedures used by Rank and accused him of being inaccurate, discourteous and unprofessional. Rank wondered if the PMS response to Herrera was adequate and how to avoid a reoccurrence of this type of embarrassing situation in the future.

The Project Management Staff (PMS)

The PMS had been in operation since early 1968. Over 25 staff members were engaged in various types of management activities. A current recruiting description of the PMS included the following comments:

> The Project Management Staff is a high level group of experienced project managers and professional management consultants attached to the Mayor's Office and reporting, through the staff director, to the Deputy Mayor and the Mayor. The main function of the Project Management Staff is to work with and assist the various City agencies in the development, planning, and implementation of high priority projects and programs. Most projects assigned to the Project Management Staff are large, complex, have severe time constraints, and require the coordination of activities of more than one City agency.
>
> Projects are under way covering such areas as: Model Cities, air pollution abatement, drug addiction, hospital renovations, economic development, day care and other pre-school programs, experimental sanitation programs, parks maintenance and operations, housing, lead poisoning control, neighborhood government and stabilization programs, municipal services, and police.

---

[1] Some of the names in this case have been disguised.

A second function of the staff is to engage in assignments to upgrade the operation and management of City administrations and agencies. Assignments and the roles of staff members are similar to that of the traditional management consultant. Typical projects include: Planning the expansion of facilities, installing and designing computer systems, designing and implementing operating control systems, planning organizational changes, planning and establishing new City agencies, installing maintenance management systems, improving budget and payment.

A third function of the Project Management Staff is to perform special research and staff work in response to requests by the Mayor, the Deputy Mayor, or the Director or Deputy Director of the Budget.

Finally, the Project Management Staff provides a training ground and a source of management talent for the City agencies.

The position of the PMS in the municipal organization (see Exhibit 3) was formally that of a staff group reporting to the director of the Bureau of the Budget and acting as the implementation arm of the Programming Planning and Budgeting Staff who were responsible for the identification of issues requiring concentrated and rigorous attention by the administration. In practice, however, the staff director reported to the mayor and the deputy mayor whose influence was often called upon to lubricate the bureaucratic machinery.

The Bronx Model Cities Sanitation Program (BMCSP)

The Bronx Model Cities Sanitation Program fell under the aegis of the Federal Model Cities Act of 1966. This act provided federal and city funds for comprehensive area-centered projects in housing, physical redevelopment, welfare, education, manpower, health, sanitation and other areas of social concern. NYC had designated three areas of the city as Model Cities areas. This case involves the Bronx area program.

Originally, the organization for Model Cities included a central administrative and decision-making body known as the Model Cities policy committee composed of the administrators of the city planning agency, the Human Resources Administration, the Housing and Development Authority, the Bureau of the Budget and the Housing Authority. This body had responsibility for coordinating and integrating city services in each of the Model Cities areas as well as for allocating funds, approving program plans and filing for state and federal grants. The Model Cities administration was established in early 1970 to replace the Model Cities policy committee. Planning in each of the areas was done under the authority of a local Model Cities policy committee elected by residents of the area. Planning and implementation were designed to involve widespread citizen participation. The city received a one year, $65 million federal grant for the Model Cities Program in July 1969. City administrators hoped to obtain another, larger grant upon completion of the first.

In addition, each area had a neighborhood director appointed by the Model Cities administration from a list of candidates supplied by community leaders and representatives. The neighborhood director had responsibility for assuring full and effective participation by neighborhood groups and assisting the local Model Cities policy committee in planning, coordinating and integrating the area's city services.

The Bronx Model Cities area consisted of 300 residential blocks comprising about 6% of the borough's land area, one-third of which was devoted to streets and highways. The area, with 450 people to the residential acre was characterized by high density; a growing and rapidly changing population estimated at 320,000 in 1970; and poverty. Many of the Bronx families were receiving welfare assistance and unemployment was a critical problem.

Physical deterioration, obsolescence, poorly maintained housing and accumulated wastes were features of the Bronx Model Cities neighborhood. The rapidly growing population, in an almost unchanging physical infrastructure, had placed severe strains on public services. Many tenement buildings lacked superintendents and an adequate number of garbage cans. Bulk refuse, litter and garbage had accumulated in many vacant lots, backyards and alleyways. An active street life by residents, partially stimulated by the lack of adequate public play space, had created serious problems of street litter.

Since regular sanitation collections at curbside were not adequate to meet the neighborhood sanitation needs, the BMSCP was initiated. The stated over-all goals were: (1) to reduce and eventually eliminate unsanitary conditions which existed in the Bronx Model Cities neighborhood, (2) to improve the results of continuing services in the area, (3) to decentralize program operations and involve residents in planning for and delivering sanitation services.

Mr. Tom Yost, a 29-year-old MBA, was the PMS member assigned as project manager for BMCSP. Yost's job was to work with and assist a number of agencies in planning and implementing BMCSP. Typically, once a project was operational, PMS people were no longer involved. Yost worked with the Model Cities Administration, Environmental Protection Administration, Bronx Model Cities neighborhood office, Model Cities central office, and Department of Sanitation.

Yost also had responsibility for developing and distributing the "Project Plan," a 50-page document. Contents included background and introduction to the program, definition and objectives, the organization and approach, resource requirements, and implementation activities and schedule. A modified PERT-CPM network diagramming the education and initial cleanup element (Exhibit 4), was also included. In addition, milestone charts indicating those events which the PMS had designated as milestones and the responsible agency were contained in the "Project Plan," (Exhibit 5).

The project was divided into three program elements with objectives stated for each as indicated by the following excerpts from the "Project Plan":

> The education and cleanup campaign element aims at removing accumulated wastes and informing residents about means to maintain a clean environment.
>
> Specific objectives were:
>
> - To begin removing refuse from vacant lots and backyards by July 1970.
> - To initiate an educational program using four education instructors by July 1970.
> - To hire 60 community residents as community aides by July 1970.
>
> The sidewalk sweeping and alternate side compliance element called for sweeping sidewalks and enforcing alternate side parking regulations.
>
> Specific objectives were:
>
> - To initiate sweeping sidewalks by community aides on a regular basis by August 1970.
> - To assure that street curbs are free of vehicles when they are scheduled for sweeping by enforcing alternate side parking regulations by August 1970.
>
> The full vacant lot and backyard cleanup program element was designed to clean vacant lots and backyards through the efforts of community aides and with the use of heavy equipment.
>
> Specific objectives were:
>
> - To intensify the vacant lot and backyard cleanup program with the use of heavy equipment by November 1970.
> - To set up decentralized program operations in three field office sites by November 1970.
>
> Exhibit 6 contains additional material from the plan.

Miguel Herrera, who was 29 and a graduate of a well-known law school, had been appointed Bronx neighborhood director in early March 1970 after the Bronx committee had worked for a year developing the plan and program submitted for funding in 1969.

Herrera commented on the sanitation project situation he confronted upon his appointment:

All the agency approvals had been obtained and it was just a question of coordination. But there are certain steps which take a long time--such as equipment deliveries which, in the case of the trucks, takes up to nine months. Therefore, when I took over we had to check back to make sure all of the paper work essential to expediting deliveries had been completed. I found out that even this had not been done and took immediate steps to submit the necessary purchase orders and provide for temporary rentals where necessary. It was also necessary to recruit, hire, and train the men who were to do the actual cleanup and perform sundry other tasks elemental to the program.

Herrera commented on Yost's entry into the project:

In late April or early May the fellow assigned to work on the project came in and said that someone downtown (I don't know who or why) had decided BMCSP needed project management and he was going to be working on it.

It wasn't a matter of someone being assigned formally with an introductory explanation. Yost merely presented himself saying he had been assigned to the project by the project management team. I heard nothing officially until about a month later.

(Casewriter's note: Herrera had encountered the PMS previously from his former position in the mayor's office.)

Herrera continued:

I said fine so long as I was kept informed of their activities and had an input into what they produced. About a month later I learned from an informal source that a meeting had been set up to include the Department of Sanitation and the Model Cities central staff to discuss the BMCSP "Project Plan" studies. And while it's only hearsay, the same source told me it had been suggested that a representative from the Bronx attend but that the PMS response was, "No, we don't want to get the neighborhood director involved yet." As it turned out I understand the meeting was never held.

Mr. Gregor Malloya, Deputy Director and Counsel for the Bronx Model Cities area commented:

Not having representatives from the neighborhood put the central staff in a bind as they didn't know much about the program as it stood in a specific neighborhood. The PMS had called in the central staff technical assistant to the Bronx to represent our neighborhood and he quite understandably did not know enough to be a reliable information source.

Herrera continued:

Even at the time I was somewhat disturbed that these meetings were being held and the project being developed during an entire month without anyone letting us see what they were doing or coming to me to talk about it. It wasn't until a week prior to the distribution of the "Project Plan" that Yost told me he had completed a first draft and was going to forward it to me for review. When the report arrived I was not only disturbed that this massive document had been prepared without my once having been consulted to check figures, statistics, policy statements and accuracy, but I was even more disturbed that the plan neglected to include a number of things which had been done and contained several misleading statements. It gave a false impression of where the project stood simply because they weren't able to know of the things which had happened without talking to me. They may have talked to the people on the staff but one of what may be described as my managerial failings is that I'm not always able to keep my staff up-to-date.

From reading the "Project Plan" first-hand one would get the impression that the BMCSP had not really started and that the start-up date was June 26, 1970--the date of the "Project Plan" submission. For at least two months before that a whole lot of things had happened. We had already hired the supervisory staff. We had ordered all the equipment and we had hired and were in the process of training all the sanitation aides. None of this was recorded in the "Project Plan."

If you sit down carefully enough, and are smart enough and have the understanding of those flow charts and plans and whatnot, you are able to get a little better understanding--but who is! Besides, even in those diagrams, all of the completed activities were not recorded.

The day after I sent that letter, which was quite a missile, Tom called me for the first time. Even so simple a thing as asking me if the network was an accurate picture of what had happened would have prevented this problem. I told Tom of my complaints and he agreed that it was a mistake not to let me approve the first draft before circulating it to everyone, including the mayor, all of whom saw it before I did.

We can't have managers not touching base with the people they're doing the management for and doing it in some ivory tower far removed from where things are really happening.

Some people see PMS representatives as young upstarts, who want to be controversial, producing status reports incriminating to administrators without giving them so much as a glance at the first draft. They seem to think this is what project management is all about.

It may be effective but only in getting people to mend their fences and guard their rears...but to start thinking creatively... no. It doesn't spur long-range planning which is the long-term objective of management. Other administrators say, "Why should I work with a guy who's supposed to be providing a service but instead is producing reports damaging to me?"

Tom Yost commented on the BMCSP, and Miguel Herrera's memo:

May 15 was the original Project Plan deadline. That original deadline slipped because the job was bigger than we anticipated. Also, we were working on the Central Brooklyn program and we had to balance the priorities. Developing the plan was time-consuming... it involved a lot of reconnaissance work...meeting and talking with people--estimating, writing, working out sensitive issues, and so on. People would go on vacation and we'd have to wait for them.

Most things have to be done through existing agencies. The problem has been getting the bureaucracy to move, so most of our time has been spent with them rather than the community groups.

We had been fearing a garbage incident of some kind. The first incident came in late May in the Central Brooklyn area. This is an area where the program had been operational for some time.[1] We had to get the program moving and I knew the Project Plan was the most effective tool I had for monitoring. Without established deadlines the only way to control is informally. In the absence of a Project Plan what we did do was to isolate long lead-time items and get them moving.

We were under tremendous time pressure...anxious to get the Project Plan out so we could start pushing through the bureaucracies. I did review the plan with the central Model Cities office and the Department of Sanitation. In the interest of saving time I did not review it carefully with the Bronx. I felt we had a pretty good grasp of the program, but they were upset. It was important that neighborhood thinking be reflected in the plan. I made a big mistake by not making sure it was...besides I didn't do a good enough stroking job. Even though all the facts were right, it nevertheless wasn't enough.

What Herrera said in the "nasty gram" wasn't really true because we did consult with him. I met with Miguel once, and again several times with his people. The program is so simple you don't have to wrestle with the concepts. The problem is pushing it through the bureaucracies. It takes a good deal of human effort to get people to work for you.

---

[1]There had been a public demonstration over garbage conditions in the Brooklyn area in May.

Originally I intended to send the Project Plan to Herrera and ask him to review it. We decided at the last minute to send it to the mayor and ask the agencies for comment. I feel this was a mistake. We should have stuck to the initial plan. We made the decision in about one minute at the very last because we wanted to get the plan out as quickly as we could.

It's not unusual for Herrera to send that kind of memo, but it is unusual for PMS to receive one. He is probably admired now by many neighborhood directors. You just can't afford to bypass people...you need to have their support.

According to Steven Rank:

We were running behind on this one, the program was highly visible, and I was feeling pressure to let the mayor know we were making progress on it. In June, the City had spent $32 million of the first grant. I asked Yost if he had reviewed the "Project Plan" with everyone concerned and he said yes. Being assured those bases were covered, I decided to change our distribution plans at the last minute. One of the hardest things about this business is getting our project managers to keep everyone involved.

On August 13, 1970, in response to Herrera's objections, a revised "Project Plan" was issued. The revised plan was accompanied by the covering letter included as Exhibit 7, a modified network diagram for the "Education and Initial Cleanup Program" (Exhibit 8) and a revised set of "Milestone Charts" (not shown). The covering letter also noted that the first monthly status report (dated July 26) was being issued concurrently with the revised Project Plan. Milestone charts from that report (for the educational and initial cleanup program) are shown in Exhibit 9.

Exhibit 1

MODEL CITIES SANITATION PROJECT (C)

M E M O R A N D U M

TO: Mr. Steven O. Rank DATE: July 7, 1970

FROM: Miguel Herrera RE: Bronx Model Cities Sanitation Program

---

I received the copy of your Project Plan for the Bronx Model Cities Sanitation Program.

It astonished me that you would put together such a report without having once touched base with my office.

The report contains several critical omissions which give a completely misleading impression of where the program stands in the Bronx.

To name one, your Plan calls for June 26, 1970 (coincidentally the date of your Report) as the start-up date for implementation of the Program, thus leaving the impression that nothing has happened prior to your Day One. In fact, however, implementation of our Program began more than two months ago. Since then, and prior to June 26, we achieved the following:

--Hired and trained all Project Directors and supervisory staff

--Hired and trained staff for the educational component

--Completed a comprehensive survey of every vacant lot in the Hunts Point section of Model Cities from which priorities will be determined

--Recruited all Sanitation Aides (who are now undergoing training)

--Arranged for temporary space in all three areas of the Model Neighborhood

Exhibit 1 (continued)

--Requisitioned permanent space

--Requisitioned supplies and equipment

--Pushed through the purchase order for our trucks and loaders

--Made temporary arrangements for trucks and heavy equipment until permanent trucks arrive

--Arranged some community meetings as part of the educational program

These are all steps that were arranged by and occurred in the Bronx Neighborhood while your report was being prepared downtown. The report could have presented a complete and accurate picture if your staff had bothered to touch base with us. We deserve at least that much, if only as a matter of courtesy, or as the most elementary step of professionalism.

cc: Report distribution

Exhibit 2
MODEL CITIES SANITATION PROJECT (C)

To: Honorable John V. Lindsay
Honorable Richard R. Aurelio
Honorable Timothy W. Costello
Honorable Frederick O'R. Hayes
Honorable Donald H. Elliott
Honorable Joseph Williams
Honorable Jerome Kretchmer

cc: Griswold Moeller
Hugh Marius
Miguel Herrera
Jay Kriegel
David Grossman
James Cavanaugh
Ronnie Eldridge
Steven Isenberg
Michael Ainsley
Horace Morancie
Wittie McNeil
Steven Lambert
Leonard Mancusi
Joseph Magucha
Biaggio Leggio

From: Steven O. Rank SOR.

Date: June 26, 1970

Subject: Project Plan for the Bronx Model Cities Sanitation Program

Attached is the Project Plan for the Bronx Model Cities Sanitation Program. This plan is based on the program narrative, developed by the Bronx Neighborhood Office. It outlines the background, objectives, responsibilities, resource requirements and time schedules for implementation of the Bronx Model Cities Sanitation Program.

As discussed in the attached plan, the Education and Initial Cleanup element of the program calls for hiring sixty Community Aides by July 31. These aides will begin initial cleanup activities by placing refuse in plastic bags for weekly pickups with rented trucks.

The Sidewalk Sweeping aspect will commence on August 28. A Full Vacant Lot and Backyard Cleanup Program will begin on November 13, when twelve purchased trucks become available.

We request that all concerned parties review this Project Plan. Should you have any comments or suggestions, would you kindly provide them by July 8. Otherwise we will assume you are in agreement with this Plan and committed to accomplishment of each task and its scheduled date.

Attach.
/fe

Exhibit 3

MODEL CITIES SANITATION PROJECT (C)

THE GOVERNMENT OF THE CITY OF NEW YORK

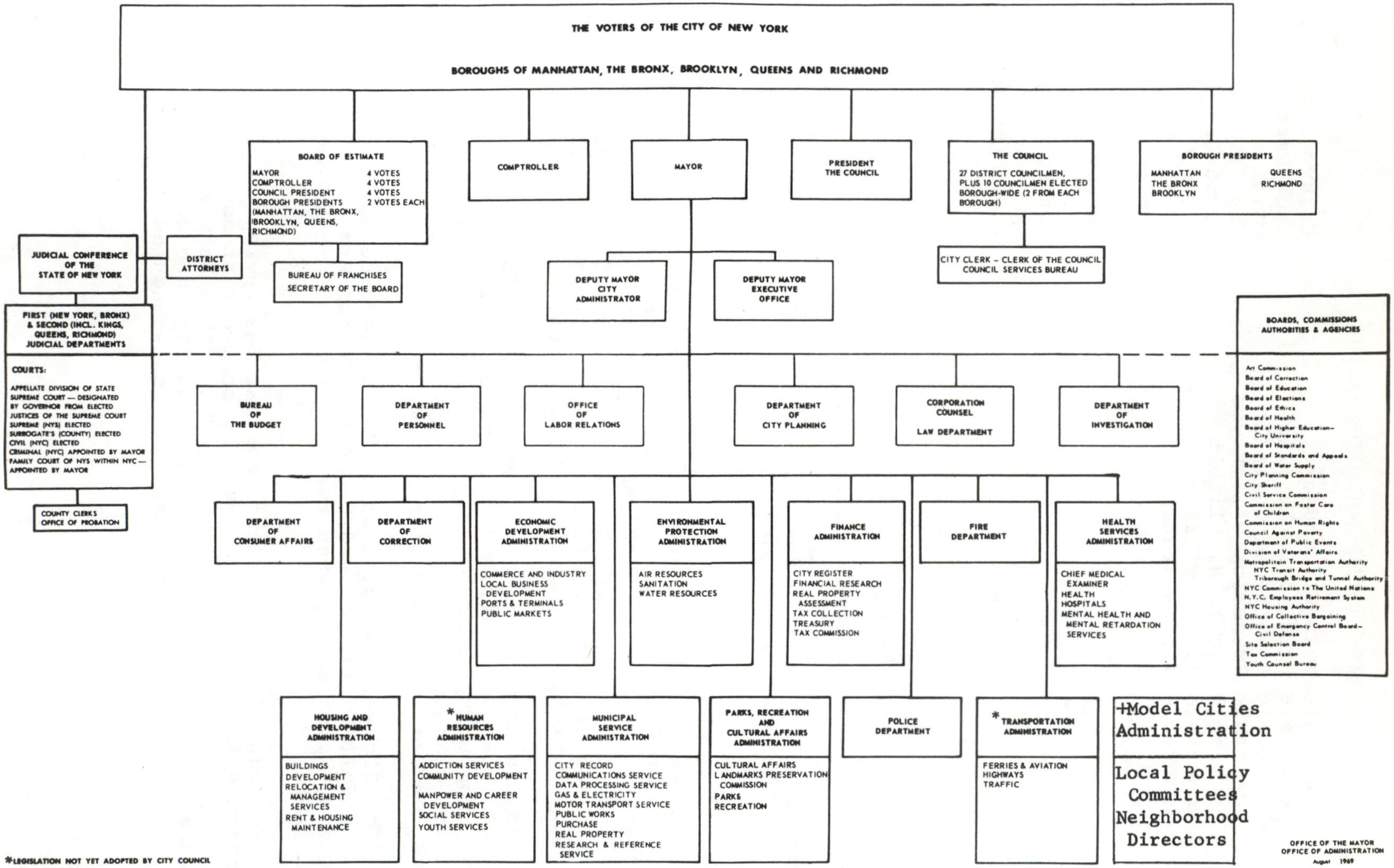

*LEGISLATION NOT YET ADOPTED BY CITY COUNCIL

+Established early 1970.

Exhibit 4

MODEL CITIES SANITATION PROJECT (C)

Network in Original Project Plan

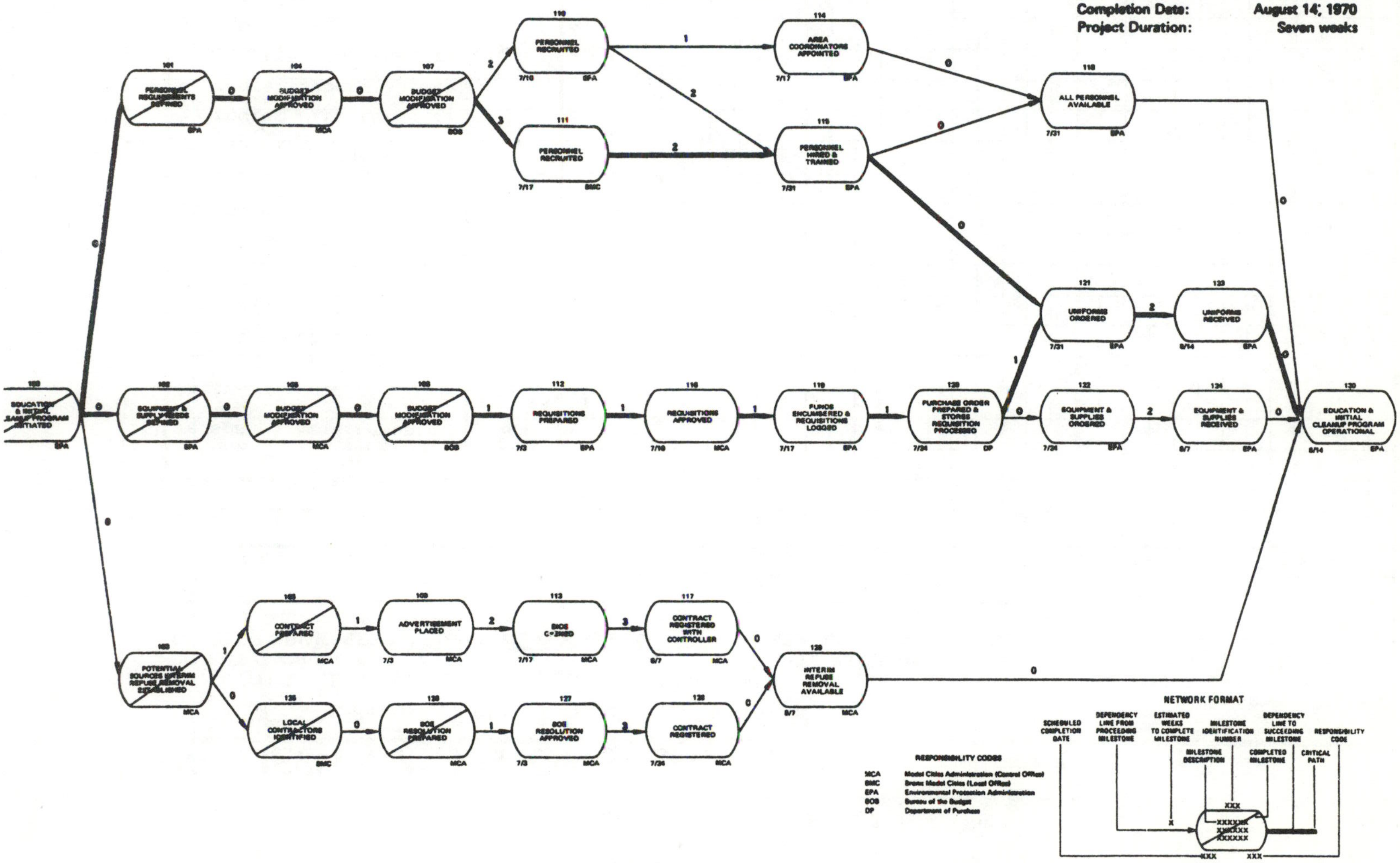

Exhibit 5
MODEL CITIES SANITATION PROJECT (C)

Milestone Chart Original Project Plan

PROJECT MILESTONE CHART

Bronx Model Cities Sanitation Program

PROJECT TITLE: Education and Initial Cleanup Program
PROJECT COORDINATOR: Tom Yost
OFFICE OF PRIME RESPONSIBILITY: EPA,MCA

DATE PREPARED: June 26, 1970
STATUS AS OF: June 26, 1970

KEY:
TARGET DATE: o
COMPLETION DATE: ø

NO.	MILESTONES	RESP.	Ju	July					Aug.				Sept.				Oct.					Nov.				Dec.				Jan.				
			26	3	10	17	24	31	7	14	21	28	4	11	18	25	2	9	16	23	30	6	13	20	27	4	11	18	25	1	8	15	22	29
100	Education & Initial Cleanup Program Initiated	EPA	ø																															
101	Personnel Requirements Defined	EPA	ø																															
104	Budget Modification Approved	MCA	ø																															
107	Budget Modification Approved	BoB	ø																															
111	Personnel Recruited	BMC																																
	- Program Directors (3)		ø																															
	- Program Supervisors (6)			o																														
	- Education Instructors (4)			o																														
	- Crew Chiefs (6)		ø																															
	- Community Aides																																	
	. First 20			o																														
	. Second 20				o																													
	. Third 20					o																												
	- Secretary-Typists (6)				o																													

Exhibit 5 (continued)

NO.	MILESTONES	RESP.	Ju	July					Aug.				Sept.				Oct.					Nov.				Dec.				Jan.				
			26	3	10	17	24	31	7	14	21	28	4	11	18	25	2	9	16	23	30	6	13	20	27	4	11	18	25	1	8	15	22	29
110	Personnel Recruited	EPA																																
	- Office Machine Opr.(3)				o																													
	- Area Coordinators(3)				o																													
114	Area Coordinators	EPA																																
	Appointed (3)					o																												
115	Personnel Hired & Trained	EPA																																
	- Program Directors (3)		ø																															
	- Program Supervisors(6)					o																												
	- Education Instructors (4)					o																												
	- Secretary-Typists (6)						o																											
	- Office Machine Opr.(3)						o																											
	- Crew Chiefs (6)		ø																															
	- Community Aides																																	
	. First 20																																	
	Hired				o																													
	Trained					o																												
	. Second 20																																	
	Hired					o																												
	Trained						o																											
	. Third 20																																	
	Hired						o																											
	Trained							o																										
118	All Personnel Available	EPA						o																										

Exhibit 5 (continued)

NO.	MILESTONES	RESP.	JU 26	July 3	10	17	24	31	Aug. 7	14	21	28	Sept. 4	11	18	25	Oct. 2	9	16	23	30	Nov. 6	13	20	27	Dec. 4	11	18	25	Jan 1	8	15	22	29
102	Equipment & Supply	EPA																																
	Needs Defined																																	
	- Uniforms		ø																															
	- Plastic Bags		ø																															
	- Small Tools		ø																															
105	Budget Modification	MCA																																
	Approved																																	
	- Uniforms		ø																															
	- Plastic Bags		ø																															
	- Small Tools		ø																															
108	Budget Modification	BoB																																
	Approved																																	
	- Uniforms		ø																															
	- Plastic Bags		ø																															
	- Small Tools		ø																															
112	Requisitions Prepared	EPA																																
	- Specs Determined																																	
	. Uniforms		ø																															
	. Plastic Bags		ø																															
	. Small Tools		ø																															
	- Forms Completed																																	
	. Uniforms			o																														
	. Plastic Bags		ø																															
	. Small Tools			o																														

Exhibit 5 (continued)

NO.	MILESTONES	RESP.	Ju	July					Aug				Sept.				Oct.					Nov.				Dec.				Jan.				
			26	3	10	17	24	31	7	14	21	28	4	11	18	25	2	9	16	23	30	6	13	20	27	4	11	18	25	1	8	15	22	29
116	Requisitions Approved	MCA																																
	- Uniforms				o																													
	- Plastic Bags		ø																															
	- Small Tools				o																													
119	Funds Encumbered and	EPA																																
	Requisitions Logged																																	
	- Funds Encumbered																																	
	. Uniforms					o																												
	. Plastic Bags		ø																															
	. Small Tools					o																												
	- Requisitions Logged																																	
	. Uniforms					o																												
	. Plastic Bags		ø																															
	. Small Tools					o																												
120	Purchase Order Prepared	DP																																
	and Stores Requisition																																	
	Processed																																	
	- Uniforms																																	
	. Bids Obtained						o																											
	. Order Prepared						o																											
	- Plastic Bags																																	
	. Bids Obtained		ø																															
	. Order Prepared		ø																															
	- Small Tools																																	
	. Stores Order Processed						o																											

Exhibit 5 (continued)

NO.	MILESTONES	RESP.	Ju 26	July 3	10	17	24	31	Aug. 7	14	21	28	Sept. 4	11	18	25	Oct. 2	9	16	23	30	Nov. 6	13	20	27	Dec. 4	11	18	25	Jan. 1	8	15	22	29
121	Uniforms Ordered	EPA						o																										
123	Uniforms Received	EPA								o																								
122	Equipment and Supplies																																	
	Ordered	EPA																																
	- Plastic Bags		ø																															
	- Small Tools							o																										
124	Equipment & Supplies																																	
	Received	EPA							o																									
103	Potential Sources of	MCA																																
	Interim Refuse Removal																																	
	Established																																	
	- Source Identified		ø																															
	- Cost Determined		ø																															
	. Equipment																																	
	. Personnel																																	
106	Contract Prepared	MCA	ø																															
109	Advertisement Placed	MCA		o																														
113	Bids Opened	MCA				o																												
117	Contract Registered	MCA							o																									
	With Controller																																	

Exhibit 5 (continued)

NO.	MILESTONES	RESP.	Ju	July					Aug				Sept.				Oct.					Nov.				Dec.				Jan.				
			26	3	10	17	24	31	7	14	21	28	4	11	18	25	2	9	16	23	30	6	13	20	27	4	11	18	25	1	8	15	22	29
125	Local Contractor Identified	BMC	ø																															
126	BoE Resolution Prepared	MCA	ø																															
127	BoE Resolution Approved	MCA		o																														
128	Contract Registered	MCA					o																											
129	Interim Refuse Removal Available	MCA							o																									
130	Education & Initial Cleanup Program Operational	EPA								o																								

Exhibit 6

MODEL CITIES SANITATION PROJECT (C)

Selected Text Original Project Plan

V. IMPLEMENTATION ACTIVITIES AND SCHEDULE

1. GENERAL IMPLEMENTATION ACTIVITIES

(1) Implementation of the overall program will occur over the next five months.

The target completion dates for each phase of the program are as follows:

- Education and cleanup program - August, 1970
- Sidewalk sweeping and alternate side compliance program - August, 1970
- Fully implemented vacant lot and backyard cleaning program - November, 1970

When the Program is fully implemented, its operation will include all the elements described in this Project Plan: cleanup activities, sidewalk sweeping, education and enforcement of sanitation codes and alternate side parking regulations.

The schedule calls for hiring all Community Aides during the initial cleanup phase of the Program. Their work assignments will depend on the availability of equipment.

(2) The major implementation activities for the establishment of the Education and Cleanup Program falls into four areas.

The major activities to set up the education and cleanup portion of the Program are:

- Arranging for trucks and drivers on a temporary basis.
- Obtaining equipment, including:
  . Uniforms
  . Plastic bags
  . Small tools
- Obtaining temporary office space.
- Recruiting and assigning three area coordinators.
- Hiring and training other personnel, including:
  . 3 program directors
  . 6 program supervisors
  . 6 crew chiefs
  . 60 community aides
  . 6 secretary-typists
  . 3 office machine operators
  . 4 education instructors

Exhibit 6 (continued)

(3) Implementation of the Sidewalk Cleaning and Alternate Side Compliance Program consists of obtaining equipment and supplies, and hiring personnel.

The major activities of the sidewalk cleaning and alternate side compliance portion of the program are:

- Arranging for transportation of vacuum sweepers on an interim basis.
- Obtaining equipment, including:
  . Sidewalk vacuum sweepers, additional bags
  . Motor scooters
- Assigning 3 sanitation inspectors
- Hiring personnel, including:
  . 1 maintenance man
  . 2 maintenance helpers
  . 3 watchmen

(4) Implementation of the Full Vacant Lot and Backyard Cleanup Program requires obtaining heavy equipment, garage and storage space, permanent office space, and hiring personnel.

The major activities required to fully implement the Vacant Lot and Backyard Cleanup Program are:

- Obtaining equipment, including:
  . 12 dump trucks
  . 2 front end loaders
  . Office furnishings
  . Office equipment
  . Maintenance supplies and equipment
- Obtaining garage space
- Obtaining 3 offices
- Assigning 1 Department of Sanitation garage foreman
- Hiring personnel, including:
  . 4 sanitation officers
  . 40 sanitationmen
  . 1 maintenance man
  . 2 maintenance helpers

2. DETAILED IMPLEMENTATION SCHEDULE

Attachments A, B, C at the end of this report present a network plan for the Education and Cleanup Program, the Sidewalk Sweeping Program, and the Full Vacant Lot and Backyard Cleanup Program respectively.

Attachments D, E, F are milestone charts for the same three phases of the Program. These charts indicate the agency responsible and target completion date for each significant task required to complete the project.

* * * * * * *

The milestone charts show the tasks required for the completion of the project: the target date for completion of each task is indicated by a zero (o) and slippage is indicated by (o....o). When the task is completed, this is indicated by a zero and a slash (ø).

Exhibit 7

MODEL CITIES SANITATION PROJECT (C)

To: Honorable John V. Lindsay
Honorable Richard R. Aurelio
Honorable Timothy W. Costello
Honorable Frederick O'R. Hayes
Honorable Donald H. Elliott
Honorable Joseph Williams
Honorable Jerome Kretchmer

cc: Herb Elish
Hugh Marius
Miguel Herrera
Jay Kriegel
David Grossman
James Cavanagh
Ronnie Eldridge
Steven Isenberg
Horace Morancie
Wittie McNeal
John Forrer
William Ling
Steven Lambert
Leonard Mancusi
Bob Aten
Joseph Magucha

From: Steven O. Rank

Date: August 13, 1970

Subject: Revised Project Plan for the Bronx Model Cities Sanitation Program

Attached is a revised project plan for the Bronx Model Cities Sanitation Program. The primary purpose for issuing this revised plan is to meet the objections raised by the Bronx Model Cities Office. They felt that the original project plan gave the impression that nothing had been done prior to the issuance of the plan on June 26, 1970. Objections were also raised because the Bronx Office did not have an opportunity to review the plan before it was issued.

While we did discuss the Bronx Sanitation Program at length with representatives of the Bronx Model Cities Office, we neglected to provide them with an opportunity to review the final written document before it was issued. This was an error on our part for which we apologize.

Section V of the plan has been amended to recognize activities completed prior to June 26, 1970. By including completed activities in the text of the plan, emphasis is given to those activities which were indicated as completed in the milestone charts in Appendices D, E, and F of the original plan.

The Department of Sanitation comments are also noted, recognizing their inability to store equipment at Sanitation locations until Model Cities is able to provide storage space. The project plan was revised to reflect this. Other comments were discussed with the Department of Sanitation, but required no change in the project plan.

The effective date of this revised project plan is the same as the original plan, June 26, 1970. The first status report, dated July 24, is also attached. Status reports will be issued monthly until the program is fully implemented.

Attach.
/fe

Exhibit 8

MODEL CITIES SANITATION PROJECT (C)

Network in Revised Project Plan

ATTACHMENT A

EDUCATION AND INITIAL CLEANUP PROGRAM

Network Start Date:	June 26, 1970
Completion Date:	August 14, 1970
Project Duration:	Seven weeks

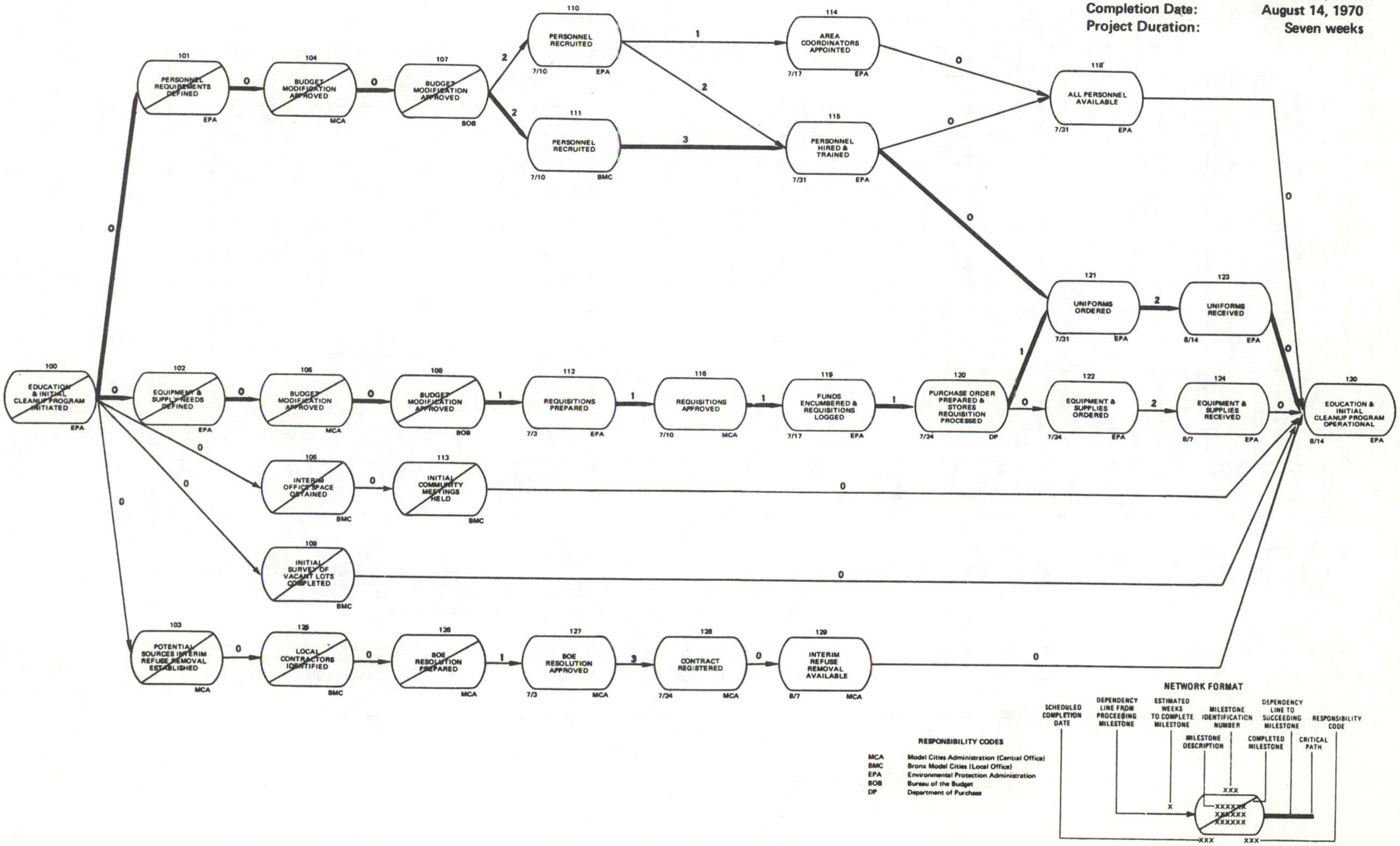

Exhibit 9

MODEL CITIES SANITATION PROJECT (C)

Project Status Report

PROJECT MILESTONE CHART

PROJECT TITLE: Bronx Model Cities Sanitation Program Education and Initial Cleanup Program
PROJECT COORDINATOR: Tom Yost
OFFICE OF PRIME RESPONSIBILITY: EPA, MCA

DATE PREPARED: June 26, 1970
STATUS AS OF: July 24, 1970

KEY:
TARGET DATE: o
COMPLETION DATE: ø

NO.	MILESTONES	RESP.	Ju. 26	July 3	10	17	24	31	Aug. 7	14	21	28	Sept. 4	11	18	25	Oct. 2	9	16	23	30	Nov. 6	13	20	27	Dec. 4	11	18	25	Jan. 1	8	15	22	29
100	Education & Initial Cleanup Program Initiated	EPA	ø																															
101	Personnel Requirements Defined	EPA	ø																															
104	Budget Modification Approved	MCA	ø																															
107	Budget Modification Approved	BOB	ø																															
111	Personnel Recruited	BMC																																
	- Program Directors (3)		ø																															
	- Program Supervisors (6)			o	.	.	.	.	o																									
	- Education Instructors (4)			o	.	.	.	.	o																									
	- Crew Chiefs (6)		ø																															
	- Community Aides		ø																															
	- Secretary Typists (6)				o	.	.	.	o																									

Exhibit 9 (continued)

NO.	MILESTONES	RESP.	Ju	July					Aug.				Sept.				Oct.					Nov.				Dec.				Jan.				
			26	3	10	17	24	31	7	14	21	28	4	11	18	25	2	9	16	23	30	6	13	20	27	4	11	18	25	1	8	15	22	29
110	Personnel Recruited	EPA																																
	- Office Machine Opr.(3)				o	.	.	.	o																									
	- Area Coordinators(3)				ø																													
114	Area Coordinators	EPA																																
	Appointed (3)					o																												
115	Personnel Hired & Trained	EPA																																
	- Program Directors (3)		ø																															
	- Program Supervisors(6)					o	.	.	.	o																								
	- Education Instructors (4)					o	.	.	.	o																								
	- Secretary-Typists (6)						o	.	.	o																								
	- Office Machine Opr.(3)						o	.	.	o																								
	- Crew Chiefs (6)		ø																															
	- Community Aides																																	
	. First 20																																	
	Hired				ø																													
	Trained					ø																												
	. Second 20																																	
	Hired				ø .	o																												
	Trained				ø	.	o																											
	. Third 20																																	
	Hired				ø	.	o																											
	Trained				ø	.	.	o																										
18	All Personnel Available	EPA						o	.	o																								

Exhibit 9 (continued)

NO.	MILESTONES	RESP.	JU	July					Aug.				Sept.				Oct.					Nov.				Dec.				Jan.				
			26	3	10	17	24	31	7	14	21	28	4	11	18	25	2	9	16	23	30	6	13	20	27	4	11	18	25	1	8	15	22	29
102	Equipment & Supply	EPA																																
	Needs Defined																																	
	- Uniforms		ø																															
	- Plastic Bags		ø																															
	- Small Tools		ø																															
105	Budget Modification	MCA																																
	Approved																																	
	- Uniforms		ø																															
	- Plastic Bags		ø																															
	- Small Tools		ø																															
108	Budget Modification	BoB																																
	Approved																																	
	- Uniforms		ø																															
	- Plastic Bags		ø																															
	- Small Tools		ø																															
112	Requisitions Prepared	EPA																																
	- Specs Determined																																	
	. Uniforms		ø																															
	. Plastic Bags		ø																															
	. Small Tools		ø																															
	- Forms Completed																																	
	. Uniforms			ø																														
	. Plastic Bags		ø																															
	. Small Tools			ø																														

Exhibit 9 (continued)

NO.	MILESTONES	RESP.	Ju	July					Aug				Sept.				Oct.					Nov.				Dec.				Jan.				
			26	3	10	17	24	31	7	14	21	28	4	11	18	25	2	9	16	23	30	6	13	20	27	4	11	18	25	1	8	15	22	29
116	Requisitions Approved	MCA																																
	- Uniforms				Ø																													
	- Plastic Bags		Ø																															
	- Small Tools				Ø																													
119	Funds Encumbered and Requisitions Logged	EPA																																
	- Funds Encumbered																																	
	. Uniforms					Ø																												
	. Plastic Bags		Ø																															
	. Small Tools					Ø																												
	- Requisitions Logged																																	
	. Uniforms					Ø																												
	. Plastic Bags		Ø																															
	. Small Tools					Ø																												
120	Purchase Order Prepared and Stores Requisition Processed	DP																																
	- Uniforms																																	
	. Bids Obtained						Ø																											
	. Order Prepared						O..C																											
	- Plastic Bags																																	
	. Bids Obtained		Ø																															
	. Order Prepared		Ø																															
	- Small Tools																																	
	. Stores Order Processed						Ø																											

Exhibit 9 (continued)

NO.	MILESTONES	RESP.	Ju.	July					Aug.				Sept.				Oct.					Nov.				Dec.				Jan.				
			26	3	10	17	24	31	7	14	21	28	4	11	18	25	2	9	16	23	30	6	13	20	27	4	11	18	25	1	8	15	22	29
121	Uniforms Ordered	EPA						o																										
123	Uniforms Received	EPA								o																								
122	Equipment and Supplies Ordered	EPA																																
	- Plastic Bags		ø																															
	- Small Tools						ø	o																										
124	Equipment and Supplies	EPA					ø	....	o																									
106	Interim Office Space	BMC	ø																															
113	Initial Community Meetings Held	BMC	ø																															
109	Initial Survey of Vacant Lots	BMC	ø																															
103	Potential Sources of Interim Refuse Removal Established	MCA																																
	- Source Identified		ø																															
	- Cost Determined		ø																															
	. Equipment																																	
	. Personnel																																	

Exhibit 9 (continued)

NO.	MILESTONES	RESP.	Ju	July					Aug.				Sept.				Oct.					Nov.				Dec.				Jan.				
			26	3	10	17	24	31	7	14	21	28	4	11	18	25	2	9	16	23	30	6	13	20	27	4	11	18	25	1	8	15	22	29
125	Local Contractor Identified	BMC	ø																															
126	BOE Resolution Prepared	MCA	ø																															
127	BOE Resolution Approved	MCA		ø																														
128	Contract Registered	MCA					o	o																										
130	Education & Initial Cleanup Program Operational	EPA								o																								

INCINERATION AND LOCAL LAW 14 (A)

The problem of air pollution is not a new one; the first smoke abatement law was passed in England in 1273, during the reign of Edward I, in response to a popular belief that food cooked over burning coals could cause illness and even death. In 1306, a royal proclamation prohibited the burning of coal in London; and, shortly thereafter, a manufacturer who failed to comply was tried, found guilty, and beheaded. Since then, the problem of air pollution has grown both more acute and more lethal. Between October 27th and 31st, 1948, 17 people died from air pollution poisoning in Donora, Pennsylvania. Between December 5th and 9th, 1952, a dense fog that covered parts of the British Isles including London killed 4,000. By the mid-1960s, nearly every city of any size had an air pollution problem and public awareness and concern had increased substantially. Studies found air pollution to be a major contributing factor in cardio-respiratory problems, chronic bronchitis, emphysema, acute repiratory diseases, asthma, and lung cancer.

New York City was a striking example of the extent of air pollution. In 1965, it poured 730 pounds of filth and poisons into the sky for every man, woman, and child who lived there. Breathing its air was said by some to be the equivalent of smoking nine cigarettes a day. Others put the number as high as forty a day. Yearly, emission levels for the five major air pollutants were:

(1) 230,000 tons of particulate matter (soot, fly ash, and so forth)

(2) 597,000 tons of sulphur dioxide (SO_2). In combination with oxygen and the moisture in the air, SO_2 produces sulphuric acid which corrodes the lungs as well as buildings, statuary, paintings, and other items.

(3) 298,000 tons of the oxides of nitrogen. Nitrogen dioxide is the major cause of smog.

(4) 567,000 tons of polynuclear hydrocarbons, the most potent of which, benzopyrene, has been shown to cause cancer in experimental animals.

(5) 1,536,000 tons of carbon monoxide which impairs the oxygen carrying capacity of hemoglobin in blood.

Once in the atmosphere, some of these contaminants combined with other elements to produce secondary pollutants such as ozone, formaldehyde, and organic hydroperoxides.

That New York had not suffered a disaster such as the one that struck London was due entirely to the nature of the topography and meteorology of the area. In 1966, a mayoral task force reported:

> New York City pumps more poisons per square mile into its air than any other major city in the United States. The main reason this condition has not produced widespread disaster in the past is that New York has open topographic surroundings and therefore enjoys the cleansing effects of the prevailing winds.
>
> Given the same topography as Los Angeles, New York City would be uninhabitable.[1]

The causes of the pollution were as varied as the pollutants themselves. Five were major: power generation, space heating, industry, waste incineration (both apartment house and municipal),[2] and transportation (automobiles, trucks, buses, aircraft and ships). The percentage breakdown of pollutants by cause for Manhattan in 1965 is shown below.

Source	Particulates	Hydrocarbons	Carbon Monoxide	Oxides of Nitrogen	Sulfur Dioxide
Municipal Incinerators	19.6%	0.4%	0.1%	0.8%	--
On-site Incinerators[4]	19.9	7.5	--	--	--
Space Heating	26.7	2.3	2.2	39.3	50% (approx.)[3]
Power Generation	25.9	0.6	0.1	47.3	50 (approx.)[3]
Industry	0.6	41.5	--	0.9	--
Transportation	7.3	47.7	97.6	11.7	--

[1] Freedom to Breathe: Report of the Mayor's Task Force on Air Pollution in the City of New York, June 20, 1966, p. 10.

[2] Municipal incinerators were the very large installations where the Department of Sanitation burned a substantial part of the raw refuse collected from households and businesses.

[3] The proportions changed substantially with different seasons. Power generation accounted for about 25% of the SO_2 during the winter months, but over 99% in the summer.

[4] Includes apartments, hospitals, schools, commercial and office buildings, and public housing projects.

Under mounting pressure (from the U.S. Department of Health Education and Welfare and Citizens for Clean Air) to do something about air pollution, the New York City Council began to react. In June, 1965, a special committee on air pollution, chaired by Councilman Robert Low, released a comprehensive report on air conditions. It concluded that the level of particulates in the air was higher than any major U.S. city as were the average and maximum sulphur dioxide levels. The annual city-wide dust fall was 60 tons per square mile per month, while for Manhattan, it was 80 tons per square mile per month.

Following release of its report, the council held a series of public hearings. Then, in early 1966, shortly after the inauguration of Mayor John Lindsay, Councilman Low introduced an air pollution control bill to deal with three of the five major sources of pollutants (incineration, space heating, and power generation). The bill, which became known as Local Law 14, was passed unanimously by the Democratically-controlled council on May 3, 1966 and signed by the new, Republican mayor on May 20. Its provisions covered the reduction of sulphur dioxide emissions from the burning of fuel oil for heat or power generation, the gradual elimination of bituminous (soft or high sulphur content) coal for power generation, the upgrading of municipal and apartment house incinerators, and the banning of refuse incineration in new buildings.

Local Law 14 divided refuse incineration into two distinct types - apartment house (or "on-site") incineration and municipal incineration. With regard to on-site incineration, the law specified that no incinerators could be installed in buildings built after May 20, 1968. Instead, any new apartment building of four stories or more and occupied by twelve or more families would be required to install compacting equipment that would reduce the volume of refuse by two-thirds before it was hauled away by the Department of Sanitation (DS). New buildings would be permitted, (for the first time) to install garbage grinders that would grind solid kitchen waste and release it in fluid form into the sewer system. As for buildings already constructed, the incinerators would have to be upgraded or shut down. Continued use of incinerators in multifamily dwellings of more than six stories after May 20, 1967, or in multifamily dwellings of six stories or less after May 20, 1968, would require a certificate of operation issued by the Department of Air Pollution Control (DAPC). Any incinerator that continued in operation without a certificate after the prescribed date could be sealed and the owner or lessee of the equipment fined $25 a day for as long as it remained sealed. In addition, the penalty for operating an incinerator without a certificate was a fine of not less than $25 and not more than $200 and/or imprisonment of up to 60 days for each day of violation. The Department of Sanitation was authorized to charge for refuse pickups from locations where incinerators had been sealed. In the case of municipal incinerators, the deadline for upgrading was May 20, 1969.

The provisions of Local Law 14 concentrated on the means of controlling pollution rather than on defining allowable levels for emissions. That was left for the Commissioner of DAPC to decide. Municipal incinerators were required to install "control apparatus which incorporates the most effective advances in the art of air pollution control as determined by the Commissioner."[1] For on-site incinerators it specified:

> An operating certificate as required by this section for refuse burning equipment shall not be issued unless the applicant's equipment includes the installation and use of an auxiliary gas burner regulated by automatic firing clocks, an over-fire air fan and nozzle system and control apparatus such as a scrubber or such equivalent or additional control apparatus as may be determined by the commissioner.[2]

There had been no input into Local Law 14 from either Mayor Lindsay or the commissioner of the DAPC whose duty it would be to enforce the law. The legislative hearings that gave birth to the bill were held before the mayor was elected; and, when the bill was being considered, he had not yet appointed a commissioner. As a result, Local Law 14 was the responsibility primarily of the City Council and Councilman Robert Low. The mayor supported its intent and most of its provisions, but objected to specifying the kind of equipment to be installed and opposed garbage grinders because they would add to the water pollution problem. Soon after his inauguration, he appointed his own task force, chaired by Norman Cousins, to report on air pollution. The Cousins' report, released in mid-June, 1966, supported Local Law 14.

On-Site Incineration

The new Commissioner of Air Pollution Control, Austin Heller, took office in July, 1966. He found that the detailed design specifications that had been developed to fulfill the requirements of Local Law 14 with regard to on-site incinerators--specifications that had been drawn by DAPC engineers prior to his arrival--would reduce particulate emissions by only 65%. Over Councilman Low's criticism that the commissioner was "foot-dragging," Heller convinced the Board of Air Pollution Control[3] to reject these design standards and vote to consider a new set that would result in a 90% reduction in particulate emissions. At a hearing on the proposed change, Heller was strongly supported by citizens groups and equally strongly opposed by real estate interests who wanted the city either to ease the requirements or delay enforcement of the law. They argued that the formulation of detailed requirements

---

[1] Local Laws of the City of New York for the year 1966, No. 14.

[2] Ibid.

[3] The Board of Air Pollution Control consisted of the Commissioners of Air Pollution Control, Health, and Buildings and two other members appointed by the mayor. Within the framework of its enabling legislation, the board had broad powers to establish air pollution control policies and regulations.

for upgrading had been so long delayed as to make compliance impossible; there simply were not enough manufacturers to supply the equipment in time. Donald Reed of the Incinerator Institute of America, which claimed to represent 70% of the companies in the business, said, "Even if we used every employee in all of our firms we couldn't do the job in 10 years." Representatives of the Department of Air Pollution Control argued that an extension would be just an excuse for doing nothing. They noted that several manufacturers tried to sell their products on the spot at the hearing and that other pollution control equipment, such as that used in industry, was adaptable to on-site incinerators. The more stringent design regulations were adopted by the board in January 1967.

Shortly thereafter, a committee (consisting of members of DAPC, the Housing Authority, the Rent and Rehabilitation Administration, and the Mayor's Office of Administration),was convened to study the economics of implementing Local Law 14. They found that the average cost of upgrading on-site incinerators could vary from $6,500 to $8,200 (gas burner, time clocks, over-fire air system, $1,500; enlarged grate and hearths, $0 - $700; scrubber and installation, $5,000; structural support for scrubber, $0 - $1,000). Exhibit 1 shows the changes necessary to upgrade an incinerator. The annual increase in operating costs including a 10-year depreciation schedule was estimated to range from $1,375 to $2,480. The committee concluded:

> The need for owners of thousands of buildings to upgrade their incinerators by May 1967 and many other owners by May 1968 constitutes a crash program of such magnitude as to defeat the intent of the legislation. Not only will necessary equipment, instruments and parts be difficult or even impossible to obtain, but the great demand on suppliers and contractors will boom prices way above the costs given herein....[1]

The committee also warned that there would inevitably be many inadequate and faulty installations as a result of the rush. Further, the report warned that smaller buildings might be forced to close or raise rents substantially to pay for the upgrading.

In early 1967, the city's corporation counsel stated his opinion that some 4,000 of the 9,000 on-site incinerators due to be upgraded could not be forced to do so. These incinerators had been installed in apartment buildings prior to 1951, the year the building code had been changed to require incinerators in all new multifamily dwellings. Counsel believed that since the 4,000 units had been installed voluntarily, their owners could not be forced to upgrade them involuntarily, but must be given the opportunity to close down and have the raw refuse hauled free of charge by the Department of Sanitation.

---

[1] Quoted in Decision-Making in Air Pollution Control, George H. Hagevik (New York: Praeger Special Studies, 1970) p. 135.

For its part, the Department of Air Pollution control supported counsel's ruling, contending that it would be the oldest and, therefore, the least efficient incinerators that would be shut down. But those landlords who would still be required to upgrade reacted to counsel's ruling with anger and a charge that the law was discriminatory. The Department of Sanitation also expressed concern, stating that it was already underequipped and understaffed and that it would be unable to handle the extra influx of refuse if a large number of incinerators were shut down or sealed. If it did manage to haul the extra refuse, DS would have to dispose of it in the city's limited remaining landfill area since no additional municipal incineration capacity would be available. Moreover, since no buildings built after 1968 could have incinerators, the refuse generated by those buildings would also have to be sent to landfill. By 1974, these post-'68 buildings would be generating 650,000 tons of refuse annually, and that figure would increase as time went by.

By April 25, 1967, only half the city's landlords had indicated their intent to comply with the law by the deadline. Commissioner Heller announced that he would seal noncomplying incinerators within five days after the May 20 deadline had passed and impose the $25 a day fine and the charge for refuse removal. On May 6, the city mailed postcards to 32,000 real estate owners reminding them that they were required to have operating certificates by May 20. On May 12, just eight days before the deadline, the 3,400-member New York City Real Estate Board voted to take legal action to block enforcement of Local Law 14. The Board claimed that 99% of all on-site incinerators would be in violation on May 20. A week before the deadline, Commissioner Heller relaxed his position and agreed to accept a signed contract between a landlord and an incinerator manufacturer as evidence of good faith and a sincere attempt at compliance with the law. He said he was also considering a plan to let landlords put up a cash deposit signifying their intentions to comply.

The day before the deadline, more than 100 landlords of "voluntary" buildings--buildings built prior to 1951--informed the Department of Sanitation that they intended to shut down their incinerators on the following day and requested refuse pickup. In response, they received telegrams from Commissioner Samuel Kearing of the Department of Sanitation directing them to continue incineration until the department could arrange for refuse collection. Soon after, a slightly reworded message was sent over the signatures of both Kearing and Heller. The voluntary buildings were given extensions of 10-24 days before having to discontinue incineration. The stated reason for the extension was that DS did not know how much refuse there would be and needed time to phase the new buildings into existing truck routes.

On the first day of enforcement of the law, DAPC made 300 inspections and found 200 violations. Councilman Low accused the Lindsay Administration of bungling. He pointed out that no supplementary request had been sent to the Bureau of the Budget to ask for an increase in the sanitation budget so it could handle the added load. Within a matter of days, the Real Estate Board filed its suit contesting the constitutionality of the law on the grounds that it was arbitrary and capricious and that it did not apply equally to all polluters of the air. On June 1, DAPC sealed three incinerators, only to have them reopened as a result of pressure exerted by the Department of Sanitation. Despite these events, by the end of June, 75% of all building owners had submitted for approval either (i) their proposed design specifications for upgrading, (ii) their contracts for upgrading, or (iii) in the case of some voluntary buildings, their applications to shut down. Although only two incinerators had actually been upgraded, DAPC concluded that the compliance program, while delinquent, was proceeding satisfactorily.

Unfortunately, its conclusion was premature. During the early weeks of July, DAPC and DS continued to work at cross purposes. Every time someone submitted an application to discontinue incineration, he was sent a telegram signed by the Commissioners of Sanitation and Air Pollution Control telling him to continue incineration until DS changed its schedules and could pick up the refuse. Commissioner Heller had signed this notice with the understanding that DS would complete its arrangements within ten days but this seldom happened. Landlords, sensing that DAPC would be unable to enforce either upgrading or shutdown, began to delay.

Then, in mid-July, enforcement was brought to a complete standstill when the City Council passed, and the mayor signed, a new building code. Among other things, the revised code rescinded the 1951 requirement that new multifamily dwellings have incinerators. After reviewing the code, Corporate Counsel ruled that <u>all</u> on-site incinerators must now be considered "voluntary" and could not, therefore, be forced to upgrade. It was apparent, at this point, that changes in Local Law 14 would have to be made if pollution from on-site incinerators was to be dealt with effectively.

In an effort to develop options for these changes, Carter Bales of McKinsey & Company, Inc., (working with the mayor's ad hoc Operations Research Council) undertook an analysis of the on-site incineration issue. Ignoring, for the moment, the existing provisions of Local Law 14, Bales identified four courses of action that landlords might take to reduce, or eliminate, the air pollution caused by on-site incinerator(s). The four were:

1. Upgrade with a scrubber.
2. Upgrade without a scrubber[1].
3. Shut down the incinerator and install a compactor.
4. Shut down the incinerator and have raw refuse hauled.

[1]Bales felt that the marginal effectiveness of scrubbers might not justify the large expense of installing them.

For purposes of examining the costs and effectivenesses of these alternatives, Bales divided the city's incinerator-equipped apartments into three groups: large, medium, and small as described below.

Category	Apartment Units/Building	Number of Buildings	Total Refuse/Day (Tons)	Total Particulates/ Day (Tons)
Large	50-100	6,775	1,771	29.7
Medium	13-49	2,644	263	4.4
Small	3-12	110	3.9	.07

Then, with the help of a computer model, the impact of each option for each apartment house category was assessed using the following criteria:

i) The annual reduction in particulate emissions. (For those options involving shutdown, these emissions were eliminated.) For upgrading, estimates were made on two bases: either that the incinerators were operated at their "rated" efficiencies or at a somewhat lower, more likely efficiency labelled "probable."

ii) The additional landfill (measured in tons per year) that would be needed for raw refuse, compacted refuse, or incinerator residue.

iii) The additional number of sanitation trucks that would be required.

iv) The incremental cost to the landlord. This cost included capital expenditures for incinerator improvements, and compactors and annual expenses for operation and maintenance of equipment and for the expense of hauling refuse to the curb. Data were taken from existing engineering studies and from actual observations of trash handling procedures at various apartment buildings.

v) The incremental cost to the city.

The results of this work are shown in Exhibit 2.

Municipal Incineration

Local Law 14 also required that municipal incinerators be upgraded (by May 20, 1969). The Department of Sanitation operated 11 such incinerators, with a total of 46 furnaces, and burned over 2.1 million tons of refuse each year. The four oldest incinerators had been built before World War II; the two newest ones had come on line in 1961. None of the 11 met recommended federal and state standards for particulate emission levels and none was equipped with up-to-date devices to control these emissions. Moreover, there was considerable disagreement over the exact operating characteristics of the units. One set of data (which DS believed overstated emission levels) was as follows:

Incinerator	Actual Capacity Tons/Year	Per Cent of Total	Emissions Tons/Year	Per Cent of Total	Emission Rate Pounds/Ton
Prewar Incinerators	517,000	24%	5,565	31%	22
Flushing	86,000	4%	909	5%	21
Zerega Avenue	127,000	6%	1,449	8%	23
215th Street	154,000	7%	1,629	9%	21
W. 56th Street	150,000	7%	1,578	9%	21
Postwar Incinerators	1,617,000	76%	11,658	69%	14
73rd Street	184,000	9%	1,239	7%	13
Hamilton Avenue	221,000	10%	1,875	11%	17
S. Shore	234,000	11%	1,638	10%	14
Gansevoort	244,000	11%	1,686	10%	14
Betts Avenue	206,000	10%	1,542	9%	15
S.W. Brooklyn	264,000	12%	1,839	11%	14
Greenpoint	264,000	12%	1,839	11%	14

The higher rate of emissions for the prewar incinerators was not merely due to their greater age, but also to their design. They were manually stoked and batch fed while the newer incinerators were stoked continuously by mechanical means. This made it easier to maintain furnace temperatures at the 1,800^{o} F. level necessary for efficient burning. The design also affected operating costs. Manually stoked plants cost $10.73 per ton; mechanically stoked units, $6.67. Future incinerators were expected to cost even less; probably between $1,500 and $6,000 in capital expense per ton of 24-hour rated burning capacity and $5.50 per ton in operating costs. Plans were already underway to construct a modern incinerator in the South Bronx that would handle 3,200 tons per day when it came on line in mid-1975.

To comply with Local Law 14, the Department of Sanitation had available the same two options as did the owners of on-site apartment house incinerators; they could upgrade or shut down.[1]

There was general agreement that the 19 furnaces in the four pre-World War II units should be closed. The expense of an upgrading program for this obsolete equipment would be extremely high and its effectiveness, in all probability, quite low. The decision with regard to the 27 newer furnaces was not so clear-cut. New municipal incinerators, of comparable size, that incorporated emission control equipment had been built and were

[1]As an interim measure, DS could install 500 foot stacks at a cost of approximately $1.5 million per incinerator. These would not reduce the amount of particulate matter emitted, but would increase the efficiency with which it was dispersed by the prevailing winds.

operating in a few locations in the United States. But there was no experience, whatsoever, in upgrading units as large as New York's seven post-World War II installations. A number of control technologies were available, but their costs and their success in controlling emissions were extremely uncertain.

Because of this technological uncertainty and because the cost of any program to upgrade would probably exceed $20 million, DS managers wanted to pursue a plan that would accomplish two objectives. First, they wanted to test four control technologies before committing themselves to any one of them. Second, when the tests were complete and the best control method had been selected, they wanted time to have several manufacturers submit design proposals and competitive bids for the upgrading job. This second objective, they believed, would help to minimize the final cost to the city. The four air pollution control (APC) methods that DS wanted to examine were baffles, cyclones, venturi scrubbers, and electrostatic precipitators. DS engineers had made rough estimates of the various operating characteristics for the four technologies as shown below. Appendix A describes their principles of operation.

Device	Probable Effectiveness	Capital Cost per 250 Tons per Day	Operating Cost per Ton	Engineering and Construction Lead Time
Baffles	50%	$180,000	$0.75	9 months
Cyclones	75%	120,000	0.81	12 "
Venturi scrubber	95%	294,000	1.51	12 "
Electrostatic precipitator	95%	420,000	0.65	15 "

The department recommended to the Policy Planning Council the following schedule for completing the test and installation program:[1]

January 1968:	Install pilot models of control equipment at selected furnaces.
July 1968:	Shut down the W. 56th Street incinerator.
December 1968:	Begin evaluation of pilot models.
March 1969:	Complete evaluation of pilot models and select technology.
March 1970:	Finish design specifications and issue requests for proposal to contractors.
March 1971:	Award contracts.
April 1971:	Begin installation of APC equipment.
January 1973:	Complete installation

[1]The Policy Planning Council, whose purpose was to advise the mayor on important issues, was chaired by the mayor and included the deputy mayor, the deputy mayor-city administrator, the chairman of the City Planning Commission, and the budget director.

June	1973:	Shut down second prewar unit.
January	1974:	Shut down third prewar unit.
June	1974:	Shut down fourth prewar unit.

With heightened public consciousness of pollution, mayoral primaries in the spring of 1969, and an election that fall, some of the mayor's advisors felt that the DS plan was too slow and cautious. Accordingly, they developed three additional alternatives. Alternative 2 was almost the same as the DS approach, except that the last three prewar incinerators (Flushing, Zerega Avenue, and 215th Street) would all be closed in May 1969 instead of during the 12-month period from June 1973 to June 1974.

Alternatives 3 and 4 were substantially different and were labelled "crash" programs. Both involved an initial commitment to electrostatic precipitators as the major means of emission control. Pilot installations of the other technologies would be made at three furnaces as a means of checking (after the fact) that the precipitators were, indeed, the most effective APC device. Contracts would be negotiated without a formal public bidding procedure. The schedule for Alternative 3 was:

January	1968:	Begin installation of pilot APC devices at three furnaces.
April	1968:	Negotiate turnkey contracts covering the design and installation of electrostatic precipitators at the remaining 24 furnaces.
July	1968:	Shut down the W. 56th Street incinerator.
May	1969:	Shut down the remaining prewar units.
June	1969:	Begin installation of precipitators at 24 furnaces.
June	1971:	Complete installation of precipitators at 24 furnaces.

Alternative 4 was only slightly different from alternative 3. Wet baffles would be installed at the Zerega Avenue incinerator by October 1968 so as to cut back immediately on its emissions. Only the two prewar incinerators without baffles would be closed down in May 1969. (W. 56th Street would have been shut down in July 1968.) Zerega Avenue might be shut down at a later date, or might even be upgraded.

The cost of the upgrading program would vary depending on the alternative chosen. The estimated ten-year capital and expense budget costs for each option are shown in Exhibit 3.

Selection of an alternative, the mayor's aides felt, rested on consideration of many factors. Among them were cost, the amount and timing of emission reduction, and the effect on the remaining life of the city's landfill areas. In addition, there were important political ramifications with regard not only to the 1969 elections but also to the city's ability to enforce the provisions of Local Law 14 that applied to industrial and residential sources of air pollution. In the case of the crash programs, moreover, it was quite possible that the expected schedule could slip by as much as six months to a year unless everything went exactly as planned. Finally, there was the problem that a successful program--one that eliminated most of the particulate emissions from municipal incinerators--would probably go unnoticed by the average citizen. The amount of soot deposited on his window sill would have decreased an imperceptible 25%. Haze reductions, too, would probably go unobserved. Visible progress would take a long time and, in the interim, the public would have only the mayor's word to convince it that things were getting better. And, so far, the administration had nothing in its record that showed more than good intentions about reducing air pollution.

Impact on Landfill[1]

Most of the refuse collected by the Department of Sanitation in New York was disposed of in two major landfill areas--Fresh Kills on Staten Island and Pelham Bay Park in the Bronx. In 1967, the department picked up 6.3 million tons of refuse. Some had already been burned in on-site incinerators and was in the form of residue. Of the remainder, an additional 2.3 million tons was burned in municipal incinerators where it produced 0.6 million tons more residue. About 20% of the refuse collected was considered nonburnable and had to be taken directly to the landfill areas.

The city was using up available landfill area very rapidly. In 1967 it was estimated that Fresh Kills (1,200 acres) and Pelham Bay Park (100 acres) could absorb about 27 million cubic yards of additional refuse. This capacity would be exhausted between January 1973 and January 1975 depending on the rate of increase in refuse generation (currently running between 2% and 3% annually). The most likely date was mid-1974. Local Law 14 would also effect these estimates of remaining lifetime if any substantial changes were made in the amount of raw refuse sent, unincinerated, to the landfills. A ton of raw, burnable refuse used about 1.16 cubic yards of landfill. The same ton of refuse, if incinerated, would weigh about 500 pounds and, because the residue was very dense, use only 0.07 cubic yards of landfill.

As yet, the city had made no decision about what to do when

[1]Sanitary landfill is refuse deposited in an organized manner in specially prepared areas (usually swampland). Each day, the refuse is covered with a layer of dirt so it does not attract rodents or cause unpleasant odors. Landfill operations usually raise low lying swampy areas to the level of surrounding ground. They can then be made into parks or developed in other ways. (Part of Kennedy International Airport is built on filled land).

present landfill sites were exhausted. Preliminary analyses were underway of a number of basic alternatives as well as various combinations of these alternatives. The basic alternatives were:

(1) Prepare and open several small new landfill areas. The preparation time varied from two months to two years depending on the site. If all potential sites were used, enough additional landfill would be available to last four or five years.

(2) Open an additional, large landfill area in Jamaica Bay (2,400 acres) or Lower Bay between Brooklyn and Staten Island (3,000 acres). Either site would last between six and seven years even if all incinerators were shut down Preparation would take two to three years.

(3) Negotiate the use of a 2,000-acre site in the New Jersey meadows. Preparation time: about four years.

(4) Raise the height of Fresh Kills above the surrounding area in Staten Island. Preparation time: two months.

(5) Have the Reading Railroad haul the refuse to some remote location (such as the Pennsylvania strip mines) for dumping. Preparation time: eight months after a contract was signed with the railroad.

(6) Build one, two, or three 5,000-ton per day incinerators. Preparation time: 5½ to 8½ years per installation.

The most expensive alternatives would be those that relied heavily on incineration. The least expensive would be those that made maximum use of nearby landfill areas.

Exhibit 1

INCINERATION AND LOCAL LAW (A)
Upgrading Process for On-Site Incinerators

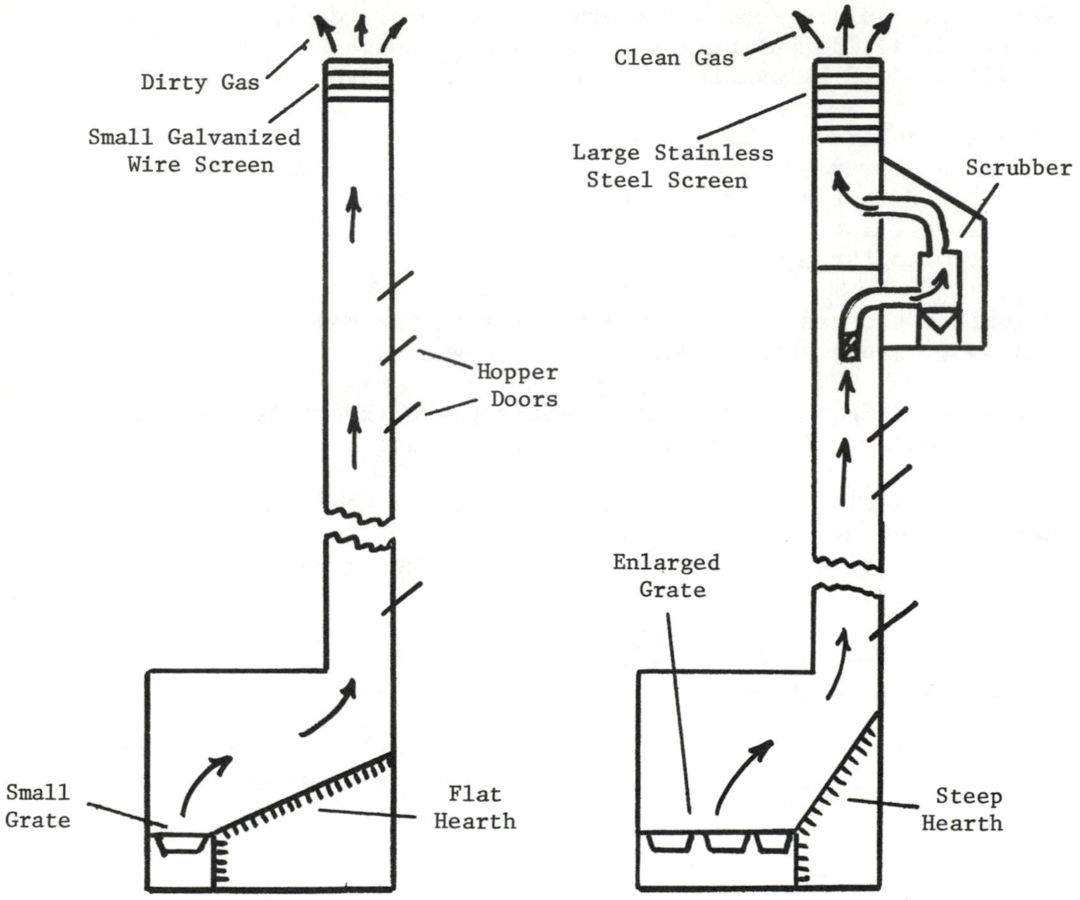

Before After

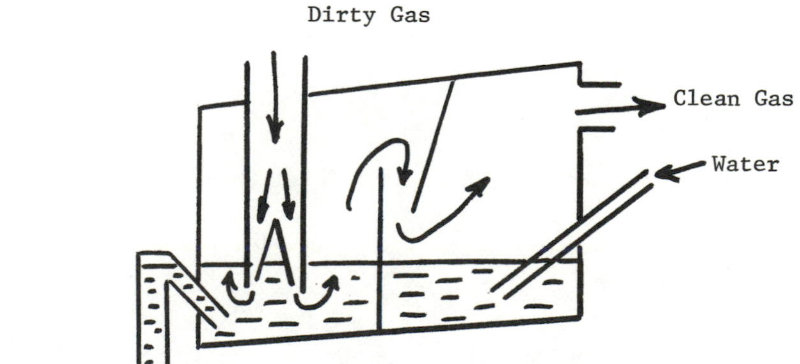

Doyle Scrubber

(Simplest and cheapest
scrubber design)

Exhibit 2

INCINERATION AND LOCAL LAW 14 (A)

Data on On-Site Incinerators

	Effectiveness: Reduction in Particulates (tons/year)		Impact		Cost to Landlords			Cost to City
	Rated	Probable	Additional Sanitation Trucks Required	Additional Landfill Requirements (tons/year)	Capital Costs: Per Building ($ 000's)	Capital Costs: Total ($ Millions)	Yearly Operating Cost per Building ($)	Expense + Amortized Capital ($ Millions)
Large Buildings (50-100 units per building) 6,775 Incinerators								
1. Upgrade including scrubber	9,421	7,084	-	-	9	61	310	-
2. Upgrade without scrubber	6,708	5,038	-	-	3	20	300	-
3. Haul compacted refuse	10,840	10,840	210	648,605	6	40	960	97
4. Haul raw refuse	10,840	10,840	314	648,605	4.5	30	2,800	127
Medium Buildings (13-49 units) 2,644 Incinerators								
1. Upgrade including scrubber	1,405	1,151	-	-	9	24	310	-
2. Upgrade without scrubber	995	749	-	-	3	8	300	-
3. Haul compacted refuse	1,606	1,606	31	95,995	5.5	15	510	14
4. Haul raw refuse	1,606	1,606	47	95,995	2.0	5	990	19
Small Buildings (3-12 units) 110 Incinerators								
1. Upgrade including scrubber	22.5	17.4	-	-	9	1	310	-
2. Upgrade without scrubber	14.6	12.9	-	-	2.5	0.3	350	-
3. Haul compacted refuse	25.6	25.6	0.5	1,424	5.5	0.6	360	0.1
4. Haul raw refuse	25.6	25.6	0.7	1,424	1.5	0.2	400	0.1

Exhibit 3

INCINERATION AND LOCAL LAW 14 (A)

Cost of Upgrading Municipal Incinerators ($000's)

	Year	1968	1969	1970	1971	1972	1973	1974	1975	1976	1977	Total
Alternative 1	Capital	220	99	99	99	411	412	653	653	653	653	3,953
	Expense	26	(163)	(163)	(163)	295	751	751	1,131	1,131	1,131	5,109
												9,063
Alternative 2	Capital	346	604	604	604	604	916	917	653	653	653	6,605
	Expense	26	419	835	835	1,292	1,749	1,131	1,131	1,131	1,131	9,683
												16,495
Alternative 3	Capital	346	1,372	1,372	1,372	1,372	1,032	768	768	768	768	8,838
	Expense	608	881	1,178	1,475	1,771	1,771	1,153	1,153	1,153	1,153	11,098
												21,036
Alternative 4	Capital	375	1,084	1,271	1,271	1,271	939	923	936	936	936	9,893
	Expense	37	(110)	425	425	425	425	1,153	1,153	1,153	1,153	6,101
												16,214

APPENDIX A

INCINERATION AND LOCAL LAW 14 (A)

Air Pollution Technology in Municipal Incineration[1]

The Department of Sanitation planned to test four major types of air pollution control (APC) equipment before seelcting one for use on all its incinerator furnaces. The four were baffles, cyclones, venturi scrubbers, and electrostatic precipitators. A fifth device--fabric, or baghouse, filters--might also be tested. All five devices are described below.

Baffles

Baffles are also known as gravitational settling chambers. They consist of a chamber in which the velocity of the carrier gas is reduced so that the particulates settle out by the force of gravity. The settling chamber may be a simple balloon duct (Figure 1), an expansion chamber with dust hopper (Figure 2), or a dust settling chamber (Figure 3). The velocity of the incoming gas stream is kept as low as possible--normally one to ten feet per second.

Cyclones

Cyclones are also called centrifugal collectors. The most common type is the tangential inlet-axial outlet cyclone (Figure 4). Dust laden gas enters a cone tangentially and flows downward in a vortex. Dust particles are forced to the sides of the cone and drop down through the dust outlet. At the base of the cone, the vortex reverses itself and begins to flow upwards in the opposite direction. More dust is forced against the wall and drops out. Clean gas flows out of the axial outlet at the top of the cone.

Venturi Scrubber

Scrubbers, or wet collectors, use a liquid, usually water, in the separation process either to remove particulate matter directly or to cause particles to stick together and make collection easier. Obtaining high collection efficiency of fine particles requires a small diameter for the obstacle (in this case water drops) so that there is less space between obstacles, and high relative velocity of the particle. In a venturi scrubber, this effect is obtained by introducing the scrubbing liquid at right angles to a high velocity gas flow (up to 600 feet per second) in the throat of the venturi (Figure 5). In addition to the particles directly trapped by the water, particles condense on the sides of the throat due to

---

[1] Technical information on devices drawn from U.S. Department of Health, Education and Welfare, Control Techniques for Particulate Air Pollutants (Washington, D.C., 1970).

Appendix A (continued)

supersaturation of the throat. Condensation is increased if the gas is hot, due to the cooling effect of the water.

Electrostatic Precipitators

The high voltage electrostatic precipitator is used at more large installations than any other type of high efficiency particulate matter collector. It is normally used when most of the particulate matter to be collected is smaller than 20 microns in mean diameter. When particles are large, cyclones are sometimes used as precleaners since they have a high efficiency when particles larger than 15 microns are involved. Separation of suspended particulate matter from a gas stream by high voltage electrostatic precipitation requires three steps:

(1) Electrical charging of suspended matter.
(2) Collection of the charged particulate matter on a grounded surface.
(3) Removal of the particulate matter.

The charge is applied by passing the suspended particulates through a high voltage, direct-current corona. The corona is established between an electrode maintained at a high voltage and a grounded collecting surface. Particulate matter passing through the corona is subjected to an intense bombardment of negative ions that flow from the electrode to the collecting surface. They become highly charged within a fraction of a second and migrate toward the collecting surfaces.

Two major configurations are used--the flat type (Figure 6) and the tubular type (Figure 7). In the first, particles are collected on flat parallel collecting surfaces 6 to 12 inches apart with wire or rod discharge electrodes equidistant between the surfaces. In the tube configuration, the grounded collecting surfaces are cylindrical and the electrode is centered along the longitudinal axis. Several such configurations make up an electrostatic precipitator. The particulate matter is periodically dislodged from the collecting surfaces by means of pneumatic or electromagnetic vibrators ("rappers") or is flushed with liquids. The collected material falls into a hopper from which it is removed.

Baghouse Filters

One of the oldest methods of removing solid particulates from a gas stream is by fabric filtration. The filter can provide a high collection efficiency for particles as small as 0.5 microns and will remove a large quantity of particles as small as 0.01 microns. The dust bearing gas is passed through a fabric in such a manner that dust particles are retained on the upstream or dirty gas side of the fabric while the gas passes through to the downstream or clean gas side. The fabric filters are usually tubular or flat and the structure in which they hang is called a baghouse. The number of bags may vary from one to several thousand and baghouses may have

Appendix A (continued)

more than one compartment so that one unit may be cleaned while others continue in operation. Figure 8 illustrates one type of baghouse filter.

The particulate matter is removed from the gas by impinging, or adhering, to the fibers of the fabric. The fibers are loosely woven so that there are sometimes spaces of 100 microns or larger. Obviously, therefore, direct collision between particle and fiber is only one way of trapping particles. Others are inertial impaction (large particles are unable to follow the air stream as it goes through holes in the fabric and inertia carries them into the fabric); diffusion (particles are so small that they collide with gas molecules, resulting in random motion); and gravitational settling. Once a mat or cake of dust accumulates, further collection is facilitated by sieving the air stream through the mat.

INCINERATION AND LOCAL LAW 14 (A)

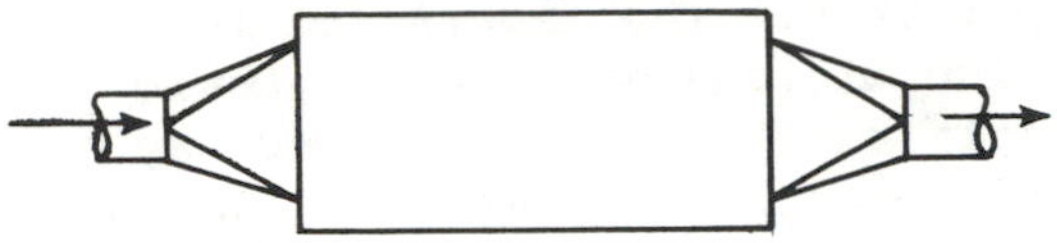

FIGURE 1 Balloon duct baffle

(Courtesy of Buell Engineering Company, Inc.)

FIGURE 2 Baffled expansion chamber with dust hopper

INCINERATION AND LOCAL LAW 14 (A)

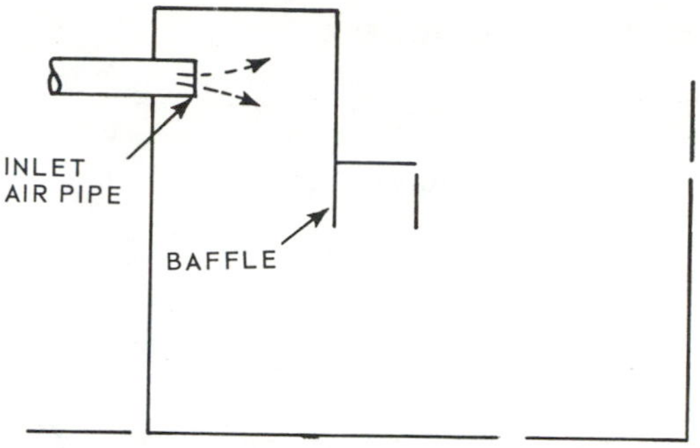

FIGURE 3 Dust settling chamber

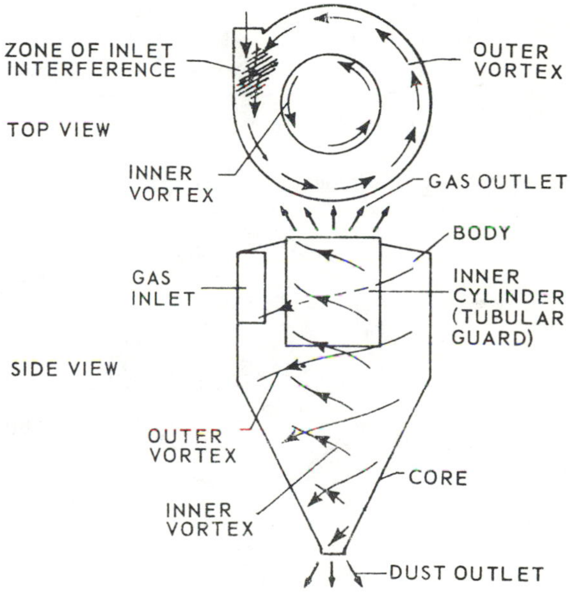

FIGURE 4 Conventional reverse-flow cyclone

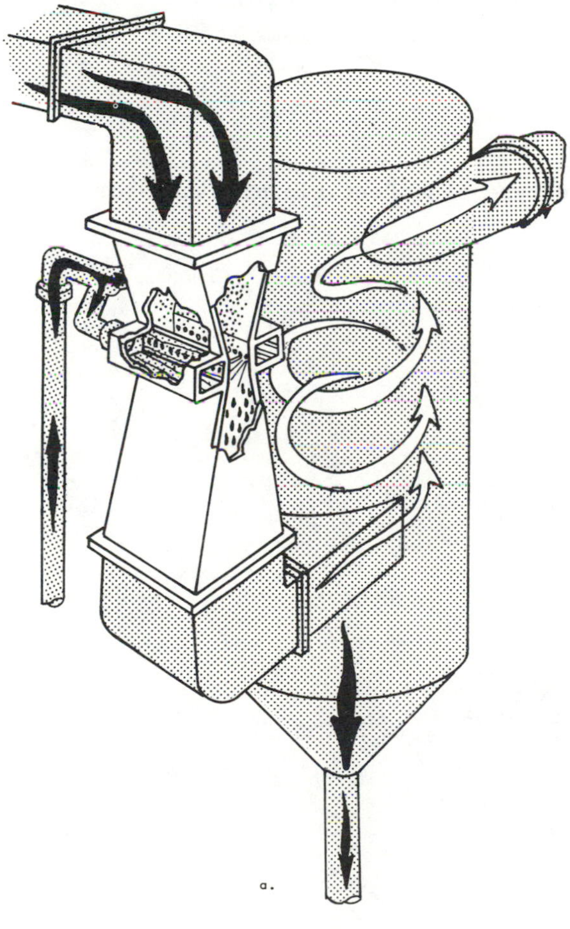

FIGURE 5 Venturi scrubber (liquid fed through jets)

INCINERATION AND LOCAL LAW 14 (A)

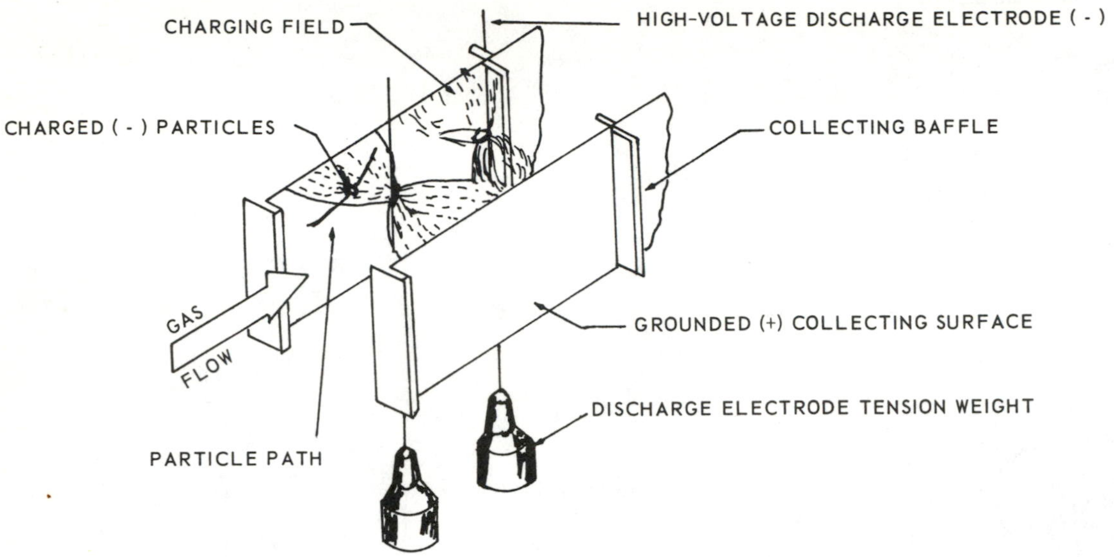

FIGURE 6 Schematic view of a flat surface-type electrostatic precipitator

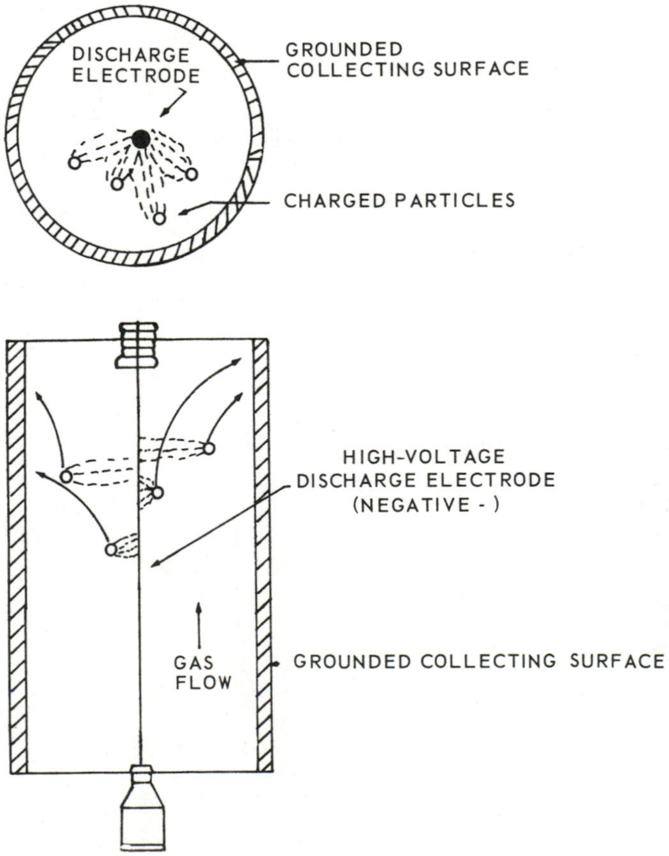

FIGURE 7 Schematic view of tubular surface-type electrostatic precipitator

INCINERATION AND LOCAL LAW 14 (A)

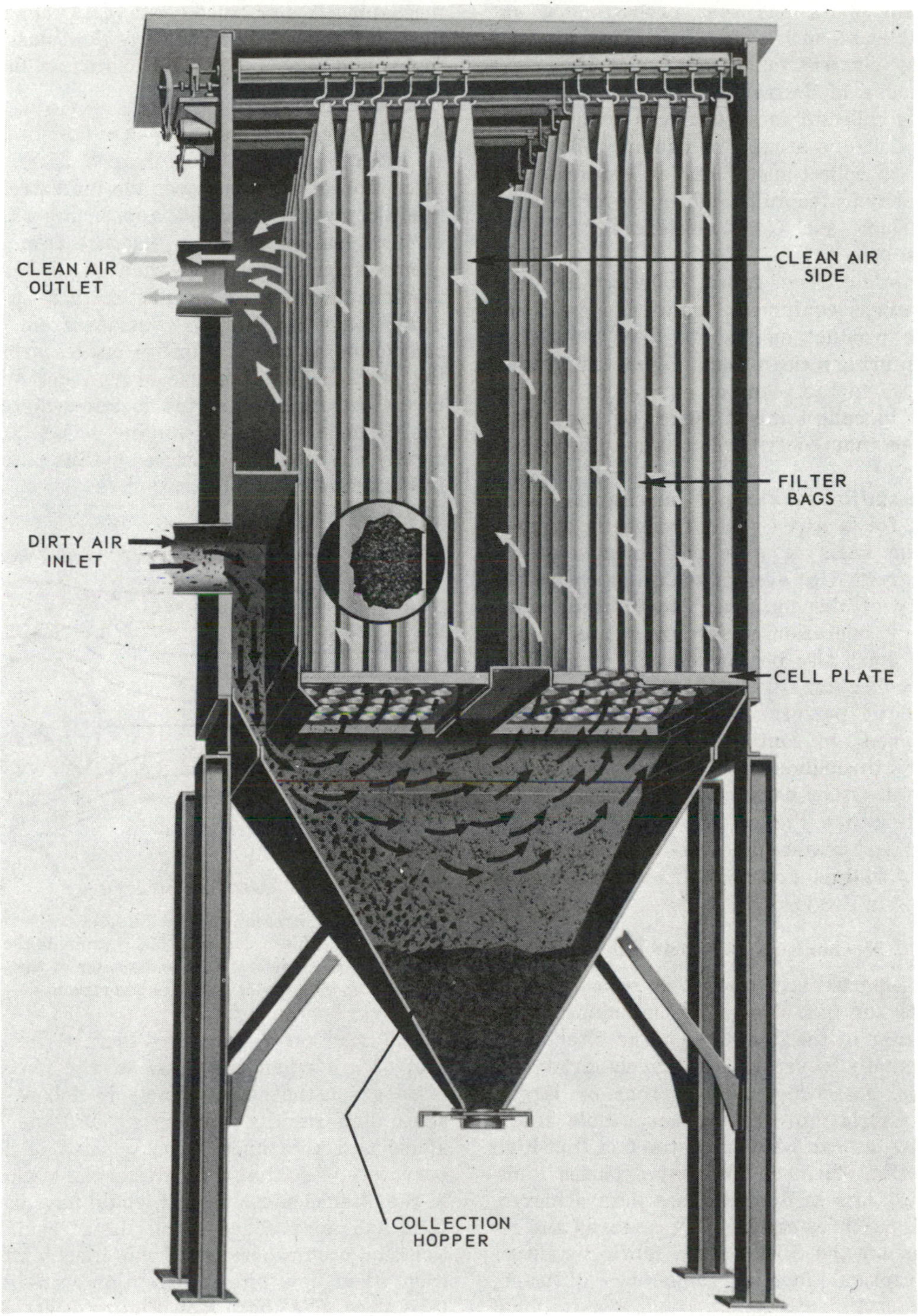

FIGURE 8 Typical simple fabric filter baghouse design

NEW YORK CITY HOUSING AUTHORITY INCINERATOR AIR POLLUTION ABATEMENT PROJECT

The New York City Housing Authority (NYCHA) incinerator project consisted of upgrading 2,656 on-site incinerators at 150 locations throughout the city. The incinerators represented some 75% of the total number of public sector incinerators and about 17% of the city-wide total (see Exhibit 1). This project was part of the over-all New York City Air Pollution Abatement Program which involved both the public and private sectors.[1]

In the fall of 1970, project management responsibility for the NYCHA incinerator project was carried by Chuck Masella, a Project Coordinator on the Project Management Staff. Masella reported to Andy Kerr who had helped conceive and develop the PMS operation.

According to Kerr:

> This (incinerator) program has slipped badly in the past, but I think we are in pretty good shape now. Masella is doing a good job. He's very results-oriented and has the ability to focus on what's important. He's been able to get people to understand their roles, and to get them to move. He keeps people informed and gets them working together. I think they see him as representing the mayor's interest in results...not blame. I've been wondering though whether to move him to another project and put a less experienced man in his place. We need people on important new projects coming up and Masella is the only experienced man available.

Project Management Staff

In 1966, through executive order, Mayor Lindsay created the Policy Planning Council (PPC), consisting of the Mayor, the Budget Director, the two Deputy Mayors, and the Chairman of the City Planning Commission. The PPC which acted as a high level policy making body, established two staff groups: one to conduct analysis of issues and the other to implement high priority programs. The implementation function was served by the Project Management Staff (PMS). Under the leadership of Andrew Kerr, a

---

[1] See Appendix A for a discussion of air pollution in New York City.

1964 business school graduate, the group in 1968 was staffed with seven (there were 40 in mid-1970) professionals of various backgrounds and experience attached to the Mayor's office and reporting to the Deputy Mayor, the Mayor, and the Director of the Budget Bureau. PMS worked with and assisted city agencies in the development, planning, and implementation of high priority projects and programs. Most projects assigned to the Project Management Staff were large, complex, had severe time constraints, and required the coordination of activities of more than one city agency. The group's responsibility included design, planning, development, and implementation of projects; design of the monitoring and control systems; and the regular reporting to the Mayor and other top city officials of the plans and status of projects.

A second function of the staff was to engage in assignments to upgrade the operation and management of city administrations and agencies. A third function was to perform special research and staff work in response to requests by the Mayor, or the Director or Deputy Director of the Budget. Finally, PMS provided a training ground for management talent for other city agencies.

Kerr had been retained in late July 1968 as management consultant responsible for the creation and development of a staff of professional project managers. PMS, and more especially Kerr, had been introduced to the operating agency commissioners and directors at one of the Mayor's regularly scheduled super-cabinet meetings. Lindsay described the staff to his super-cabinet (the administrator of each super-agency sat on the cabinet) as a group that would be coordinating the activities of all agencies involved in high priority projects requiring inter-agency cooperation. He did not specify the precise position of PMS in the municipal hierarchy.

The organization of the Project Management Staff was relatively unstructured. Assignments were distributed and all projects monitored in summary form by Kerr. Each project was managed by a project coordinator who had overall responsibility for its progress and who reported directly to Kerr. Depending upon the scope of the project, project coordinators sometimes were assigned assistants to whom they delegated whatever tasks and/or authority they wished. It was not uncommon to find an individual performing the function of a project coordinator while at the same time acting as an assistant to another project coordinator. The project coordinators' responsibilities are outlined in Exhibit 2. A written project plan was developed for each project (see Exhibit 3).

New York City Housing Authority

The public sector air pollution abatement project was typical of PMS projects which involved a number of city agencies. The Department of Air Resources of the Environmental Protection Agency was the "enforcing agency" for the program. Others involved included: New York City Housing Authority, Hospital Administration, Board of Education, Department of Sanitation, Bureau of the Budget, and the Office of the Mayor. An organization chart of the New York City government is included as Exhibit 4.

The New York City Housing Authority, employing close to 12,000 was one of the City's several operating agencies. The Authority provided approximately 160,000 low rent apartments for selected low income tenants; and was a quasi-public corporation established by the state legislature and funded by its own privately issued debt. The members of its governing board, only three of whom were salaried, served five-year terms with the exception of the Chairman who served at the pleasure of the Mayor. The position of Vice-Chairman rotated annually between the two members serving five-year terms. In 1968, Albert Walsh was Chairman of the NYCHA. The position of Director of Management and Deputy Director of Management were held by Irving Wise and Sidney Schackman, respectively. The Management Department was responsible for janitorial and maintenance services in public housing projects.

Department of Air Resources

The Department of Air Resources (DAR) was a sub-agency of a super-agency known as the Environmental Protection Agency. The Department was responsible primarily for the setting and enforcement of air quality control standards. The department employed approximately 325 people. Austin Heller was Commissioner of the DAR in 1968.

Local Law 14

Public concern with air pollution had risen dramatically in the past few years and government response had taken shape in legislation to develop air quality standards and plans for implementing them. In New York City this legislation was Local Law #14.

Local Law #14 (as enacted in 1966), required upgrading within specified periods of incinerators in multiple dwellings and in buildings other than multiple dwellings as well as the upgrading of municipal incinerators. The upgrading was to be accomplished by improving combustion and/or treating effluents by the installation of scrubbers or electrostatic precipitators to reduce the particulate emissions allowed to escape into the air. The total number of incinerators and fuel oil burners subject to compliance with Local Law #14 exceeded 47,000.

To aid in managing so large a program, it was broken down into two major categories - public and private sector. Within each sector, projects were further distinguished as to whether incinerators or fuel oil burners were being upgraded. Then, for the public sector, a separate action plan was written for each of the following agencies directly responsible for the operation of furnaces or incinerators:

- New York City Housing Authority (NYCHA), incinerators
- New York City Housing Authority, fuel oil burners
- Board of Education (BOE), incinerators
- Board of Education, fuel oil burners
- Municipal Hospitals, incinerators
- Municipal Hospitals, fuel oil burners
- Pre-W.W.II municipal incinerators
- Post-W.W.II municipal incinerators

Project plans were not undertaken for the private sector. Exhibit 1 illustrates the project breakdown structure for the New York City Air Pollution Abatement Program as managed by the Project Management Staff commencing 1968.

Amendments to Local Law #14, effective March 12, 1968, specified that compliance date requirements for upgrading NYCHA incinerators be broken down into phases and categories according to the number of dwelling units serviced per incinerator as follows:

Category*	Units per Incinerator	Number of Incinerators	Program Phase	Compliance Dates
I	20 and under	565	I	December 20, 1968
II	101 and over	548		
III	61 to 100	186	II	October 20, 1969
IV	21 to 60	1,357	III	May 20, 1970
TOTAL		2,656		

*Category refers to the number of dwelling units serviced by each incinerator.

The amendments provided for the DAR Commissioner to seal refuse burning equipment not in compliance with the law by the required dates and provided for fines of not less than $25 and not more than $200 for each day of violation.

Local Law #14 provided alternative methods to achieve compliance. These were:

- upgrade incinerators by installing emission control devices such as scrubbers.[1]
- install compactors and discontinue incineration.[2]
- discontinue incineration without installing compactors.[3]

The total cost of the upgrading program for NYCHA was estimated to be about $32 million broken down by funding source as follows:

Federal	-	$16.0 million
State	-	8.5 million
City	-	7.5 million

These estimates, prepared in 1968, assumed that compactors would not be used. They reflected the fact that, although NYCHA owned all of its housing developments, Federal and State agencies provided funds to finance capital expenditures on sites which their monies had originally constructed. Of the 2656 incinerators operated by NYCHA, 2148 were located on sites whose development had originally been financed by state or federal agencies. The specific breakdown of the number of incinerators by project funding source was as follows:

Category	Units Per Incinerator	Federally Aided	State Aided	City	TOTAL
I	20 and under	463	27	75	565
II	101 and over	264	217	67	548
III	61 to 100	70	57	59	186
IV	21 to 60	636	414	307	1,357
		1,433	715	508	2,656

Events up to March 1970

In late November 1968, Tom Terry of the PMS was assigned responsibility for the NYCHA project. He faced a tense situation. Little progress had been made toward meeting the December 20 deadlines for

[1] Scrubbers were devices designed to cleanse and purify the smoke emissions issued by incinerators. Smoke was forced through a cascade of water which trapped the particulate matter present in the smoke (i.e., "scrubbed" the smoke). The remaining vapor was then dried and released. The water was in turn recycled leaving only the particulate matter as a deposit to be disposed of.

[2] A compactor was a device which automatically compressed raw refuse discharged by tenants into incinerator chutes and sealed it in polyethylene bags ready for transport, without burning, to municipal dumping or incineration depots.

[3] This option was open to Category I incinerators only.

Category I and II incinerators. And, just before Terry's arrival, the DAR had threatened to cite the NYCHA for violation of the law if the deadline was missed. To break this embarrassing confrontation of two city agencies, Terry scheduled a meeting with chairman Walsh of the NYCHA and Commissioner Heller of DAR. After some persuasion from Terry, DAR agreed to extend the deadline for Category II since compliance was dependent upon funds from the federal and state level that had not been received. The extension was contingent upon NYCHA receiving sufficient funds by September 20, 1969 from federal and state agencies to allow for the design drawings of incinerator modifications to be prepared. With regard to Category I, the Housing Authority agreed to discontinue using all 565 units.

Shutting down so many incinerators meant that a large amount of additional refuse would have to be picked up. On December 3, 1968, Terry met with Chief Lane of the Department of Sanitation (DOS) to discuss plans for handling the increase in demand. They agreed that collection frequency could not be increased; merely keeping the frequency of pick-up the same after December 20 as before that date would necessitate the assignment of additional men and equipment. There just wasn't enough equipment or personnel to increase the collection frequency, too. In addition, neither of the men wanted to create a situation where tenants in adjacent areas might demand that collection frequencies in their areas also be increased.

Later in the day Terry met with Irving Wise, the Director of Management of NYCHA and the man responsible for the janitorial and maintenance work in NYCHA-owned buildings. The meeting was held to discuss strategy for implementing the decision to close down the Category I incinerators. It was decided that Wise would issue a directive to all tenants in affected buildings advising them of the decision and instructing them to carry their garbarge out to containers on the sidewalks in front of their buildings. It was felt that this procedure would deal with the objection of the sanitation men's union to carrying raw refuse from buildings to sidewalks.

To minimize the unsightly accumulation of refuse cans in front of each building and the attendant rats and vermin, the Housing Authority agreed to draw up plans to have the refuse cans transported by Housing Authority personnel to a remote location, central to the housing unit, acceptable to the Department of Sanitation.

In a memo to Kerr, also on December 3, 1968, Terry noted that "this approach would allow for full transition incorporating the problems of tenant resistance, Sanitation Department constraints and Housing Authority needs."

Wise's directive (Exhibit 5) went out on January 6, 1969 and the incinerators were shut down shortly thereafter.

Tenant reaction was swift and vocal. They viewed the shutdown as unfair, inconvenient, and (in the case of the elderly) a genuine physical burden. They complained that the sidewalk refuse cans were unsightly, unsafe, and an attraction for rats, roaches, dogs, and other animals. Many took to "air expressing" their garbage from kitchen to sidewalk.

The Housing Authority, too, was dissatisfied. It complained of lacking the men and equipment to move the increased volume of refuse or to store it between DOS pick ups. They demanded more frequent collection. Sidney Schackman, NYCHA's Deputy Director of Management, commented:

> We notified the tenants of our intention to discontinue and they complained, quite reasonably, about the smell and about the fact that Sanitation did not pick up often enough and simply that after having moved from slum areas, where they were required to carry down their own garbage, to a more modern facility, they were now being asked to return to earlier practices. Many went to their legislative representatives and pressure kept building up. We wanted to implement the whole incinerator program gradually, but Heller insisted on going ahead full steam.

On February 3, 1969 a meeting was held in Chairman Walsh's office at the Housing Authority to discuss the rising crescendo of tenant complaints. The following people were present:

Chairman, NYCHA (Walsh)
Director of Management NYCHA (Wise)
Counsel, NYCHA
Chief of Technical Services NYCHA
Deputy Commissioner, DAR
Project Coordinator, PMS (Terry)

The options listed earlier - scrubbers, compactors, and discontinuance of incineration - were reviewed and it was agreed that only discontinuance would allow for an immediate legal and feasible solution for Category I units. It was decided that tenants would simply have to comply. Terry recommended to Kerr that the Mayor's Office write a letter to Walsh stating that a return to incineration was not acceptable.

On February 5, the situation became even more confused. On that day, the State Supreme Court handed down a decision on a case brought by the New York City Real Estate Board against New York City, testing the validity of Local Law 14. While the Court ruled that the law was constitutional, it questioned whether enough time had been given to comply with the law. As a result, DAR's right to levy fines was in doubt. The Mayor decided to refrain from issuing summonses until the constitutionality of the compliance schedule could also be tested.

A few days later, the City was struck by a snow storm of blizzard proportions. Refuse collections were delayed and tempers flared among tenants residing in developments where the incinerators had been sealed. In the face of this new crisis, the Housing Authority gave up. By March 7, 521 of the 565 Category I incinerators were back in operation. Schackman later recalled that "the snow storm gave us an excuse to open up all but a few small developments where we maintained raw garbage collection."

During the latter half of March 1969, Bob Reid joined PMS and took over prime responsibility for the Air Pollution Abatement Project from Terry. Reid felt that the compliance deadlines had become meaningless and so a new project plan (see Exhibit 3) was prepared and discussed in detail with NYCHA and the DAR. The new plan called for deadlines as follows:

Category	Original Target Completion Date	Revised Target Completion Date
I 20 and under	12/20/68	3/71
II 101 and over	12/20/68	4/71
III 61-100	10/20/69	9/70
IV 21-60	5/20/70	1/72

It was agreed that the information in the plan was a correct appraisal of the project's current situation and that the new targets were acceptable. The revised project plan of April 4, 1969 summarized the situation to date. It showed that of the 565 Category I incinerators, 44 had been shut down; the rest were back in operation. Only 145, 34, and 6 incinerators in Categories II, III and IV, respectively, had progressed toward upgrading at all; and most of these were in the design stage. Indeed, difficulties in getting an incinerator through the design phase was a prime cause of overall project delay. NYCHA did not have the in-house capability to do the design work and so had to go outside. Outside engineering consulting firms, in turn, were approaching the limit of their capacity and a backlog of in-process designs was building up.

Once a design was finished, moreover, the Housing Authority needed DAR's approval of the plans before work would proceed. (Without prior design approval, DAR might refuse a certificate of operation when the upgrading was finished.) The DAR had been extremely slow in approving designs for the 521 Category I incinerators which were to be upgraded. Another cause of delay was NYCHA's failure to request funding from state and federal agencies for the upgrading work. Finally, there were delays on deliveries of equipment and when equipment arrived on installation because of the lack of enough installers.

On September 15, 1969, Mr. Joseph Christian, General Manager of the NYCHA, wrote to state authorities requesting funding approval to let contracts for the final working drawings on specifications for scrubbers at state funded locations. On September 17 he received a reply from William F. Meyers, Assistant Commissioner of the New York State Division of Housing and Community Renewal (an agency similar in function to HUD). The letter advised Christian that it was now the policy of the division that compactors were to be used to replace incinerators that required a capital investment to comply with air pollution regulations. Design work on incinerators at state funded locations was halted.

Exhibit 6 shows planned and actual project progress up to January 30, 1970. Of 240 incinerators that should have been upgraded and back in operation, only 40 were ready. Project management's status report laid equal blame on NYCHA and DAR. The former, it said, had given the project a low priority, assigning it neither adequate manpower nor funds. DAR was accused of setting arbitrary and ambigious inspection criteria for design approvals and the issuance of certificates of operation. This resulted in high rejection rates even for second and third reviews of design drawings, and high disapproval rates for final inspection of completed incinerators. In addition, engineering consultants and construction contractors were not meeting their schedules. And, finally, both the state and federal authorities were now favoring compactors and refusing to fund scrubber installations.

A New Cast of Characters

In March 1970, two months following the Mayor's re-election to office for another four-year term, a new chairman, Simon Golar, was appointed to the NYCHA; a new commissioner, Robert Rickles, was appointed for DAR; and "Chuck" Masella replaced Reid as project coordinator for the Air Pollution Abatement Program.

Masella described his initial approach to the project:

> My introduction to the Air Pollution Program was a surprise as the whole thing was turned over to us completely. We had to establish personal contact with administrators who really didn't give a ... that we were from the Mayor's Office. The first administrators that I met said "How many of you guys do you think I see in a day from the Mayor's Office." It was left to the project manager to display competence and most of all persistence to exert influence.
>
> The first thing I did was meet the cast of characters, to discover the work and decision centers. We are all aware that there are groups of individuals within agencies who account for a disproportionately large share of activity. Our first meetings were not only for pleasantries but to find out about what was wrong. There had been significant slippage in the project and I tried to discover why. I tried to discuss the reasons I

saw for the slippage. Some they liked, some not; nobody likes criticism. But it was preferable to saving only what they wanted to hear and I told them what my analyses revealed. I discovered that being a nice guy doesn't get the job done. But persistence - going back again and again does. Reid (Masella's predecessor) introduced me to all the participants in order to assure that the formal transition of coordinators was done in a professional manner. I was curious to note that a great many of the participants didn't know Reid.

I had two predecessors, the first (Terry) was greatly liked by everyone - but the project died. The second (Reid) was a highly qualified senior management consultant from an outside firm who as far as I could tell knew all of the relevant management consultant techniques but this wasn't enough. He wrote all the plans and knew what had to be done but nothing was accomplished.

I realized that I wasn't going to do it with a winning personality or merely on a qualification basis. I needed continual follow-up on routine implementation not only to identify the bottlenecks but also to get to the guys who can eliminate them. Of course, I had the help of the Mayor's Office and the staff image which had been enhanced by Andy's performance. I tried to get involved in day-to-day operations with these guys with a sort of "stafferations" approach - that is, by acting both a staff and line role - which by the way presented some of the traditional line and staff conflicts.

As a matter of fact another function I serve is to get people talking to each other. When I first started, nobody was expressing their discontent over lack of progress. People were too involved in the protocol of who calls who; we opened lines of communication.

I had little contact with Walsh (former NYCHA chairman) as Reid had established a relationship with Schackman (Deputy Director of Management). I talk to Schackman about three or four times a day now.

Schackman contrasted Reid and Masella, and commented generally on the PMS:

I first became aware of the PMS three years ago when they were introduced as people assigned to coordinate activities for air pollution control. At the beginning I felt they were doing little other than designing pretty charts. After a while a different relationship developed. They became a valuable tool because they developed a liaison with all the other agencies involved in the program and they stepped out of the chart-keeping role into a more active role.

Reid was an engineer who worked with our engineers on getting up milestone schedules. Chuck (Masella) is more of a generalist, and sees things from a practical point of view. Perhaps we get along so well because I am a generalist; it is a generalist speaking to a generalist and our liaison is more than just the technical aspects. To duscuss the technical aspects and monitor the progress in the field Chuck talks frequently to Joe Loughlin, (NYCHA Director of Engineering, responsible for monitoring on-site progress). I don't know how often he sees him but it may be every day and I don't mind that at all. Although Chuck is not really a liaison with the funding authorities, he is continually prodding us to contact them and expedite their approvals.

I talk to Chuck about twice a week; I suspect he talks to Joe Loughlin even more often that that. Parenthetically, his last report (June 5, 1970) bothered me bacause where he had previously praised us, this report criticized us. Air pollution is a small item on my calendar although unfortunately I have recently been spending 25% of my time in this area.

I find myself having more contact with Rickles (current Commissioner of the Department of Air Resources) than with the former commissioner, perhaps once a week on the phone. We also hold policy meetings occasionally which are not initiated by the PMS. Our first meeting with the new Commissioner of the Department of Air Resources was set up by Kerr and Masella.

Bob Rickles (Commissioner of DAR) commented on his relationship with Masella and the PMS:

Ten days before I took the job it was suggested to me that the first thing I do is go and see Andy (Kerr) because he was close to the Mayor and also because of the important role Andy's group plays. Chuck (Masella) has effectively become a member of our staff - at least we treat him as such. This is not to say that any attempt has been made to split Chuck between PMS and ourselves; it's just that I regard Chuck as part of our team. He does a fine job in keeping track of progress and telling me where we stand and telling me where pressure has to be put.

Masella commented further on the program and Rickles' involvement:

In the case of air pollution everybody shot like a bolt during the first two years; then everything died down and we came to the second crisis period which ran from January through April 1970. During this period, we were gearing up the system and making contacts; trying again to make various agencies recognize the seriousness of the administration's desire to comply with Local Law 14. A culmination of the process was the successful appointment of Rickles.

We introduced Rickles to all of the participants. He came up here when he was first appointed to review the status of the program first with Andy and then with me. We set up all the meetings and acted as his calling card. He didn't have to spend an excessive amount of time becoming oriented. Now we have daily contact with him because he is the key. I communicate best with him in person about three times a week and on the phone about five times a week. I find the most effective means of communication is personal interviews rather than the telephone, so that words can be matched to expressions and people's sensory facilities can be utilized. I look at Rickles as a boss as well as a commissioner for whom I am consulting. I think for all commissioners, information is the key, especially outside information which is something I provide for Schackman and Rickles.

Although we have done analyses of the problems and obstacles we could not have done a thing without Rickles who reorganized the priorities and the organization of the Department of Air Resources. Prior management had frustrated the implementing agencies. Contractors were having designs rejected two or three times. These agencies have now developed the spirit required to achieve their objectives and it is our job to stimulate and sustain this spirit.

Rickles' greatest attribute is not only his technical competence but his aggressiveness and capacity to work with the agencies within the framework of their operating procedures. When reforms are necessary, he pursues their adoption and he is candid and straightforward and most people know where they stand with him. He is also easy to talk to and to criticize. I feel free to tell him if I don't agree and the converse is also true. Obviously from the way I'm talking he is the kind of guy I like to work for - not afraid to try new techniques and approaches. Another side of the coin is that Andy is relatively open. I can walk in any time and say I've got a problem or I don't know how to handle a guy, and he is always available to talk and there is no such thing as 9 to 5.

Rickles elaborated further on his management style and the operations of DAR:

I don't review correspondence that goes out from other people. A lot goes out under my name because sometimes it is prescribed by policy. For example, requisitions for municipal supplies must go out over the Commissioner's name. I believe strongly that each section must have recognized goals and responsibilities. The Commissioner cannot on a day-to-day basis be involved in everything that is going on. We have a weekly report from each bureau on major successes and disruptions. We have a comprehensive management reporting system. Every two weeks we have a staff meeting with each bureau at which they are required to report on their plans. We also review the progress made to date on previously presented plans. Seventy-five per cent of our work is highly routinized as our major job is really effective manpower utilization.

The former Commissioner must have had staff meetings as well and in my view they're productive. We have conflicts over both information and viewpoints at these meetings, but they are resolved through discussion.

The executive staff mixes socially to a reasonable degree. As a matter of fact, the engineers play softball on Thursday evening. (Rickles played second base.) However, there isn't much inter-bureau contact as they are different types of people. Our bureaus are made up of engineers, scientists and inspectors.

Feedback from the Mayor is very infrequent as most of my contact is with EPA. The Mayor has so many problems that it is not difficult to understand why this program doesn't occupy all his time. Perhaps this program doesn't deserve to be so far down on his list of priorities but I would be insensitive to his problems if I said that he should devote substantially more time to this issue than he does. I talk to Steve Issenberg several times a week. (Issenberg was the mayoral assistant responsible for liaison between city hall and EPA.) In these conversations we both report our progress and ask him for favors and I would say the latter is more often true.

Lines of communication are really me to Kretchmer (Commissioner of EPA) and Kretchmer to the Mayor, although there is frequent direct communication at our weekly cabinet meetings. Kretchmer is responsible for communicating with the Mayor largely on a problem basis. Andy is really the communication link between the Mayor's office and ourselves. We generally bring to the Mayor's attention only those matters where we feel his unique position might be of advantage to us, such as his leverage over other city agency administrators.

I talk to the Housing Authority only infrequently as Chuck handles the liaison function. We do talk in occasional meetings when problems arise. Chuck sets up these meetings. I think it important that you realize that the city incinerators are only a part of the problem on which I spend only 5% to 10% of my time. Relative to the share of pollutants contributed by the Housing Authority incinerators, this is perhaps a disproportionately large amount of time but there are the credibility and clean hands problems to be considered as well. (Rickles was referring to the difficulty of enforcing compliance on the private sector if the public sector remained in violation of municipal standards.)

Masella commented in August of 1970:

> I have only recently begun to establish a relationship with Golar by reviewing the status reports with him, which seems imperative to solidifying the relationship. Golar has become very much involved in the program. More so, I think, than his predecessor Walsh. Walsh was being restrained by his technical people who were doubtful about the relative effectiveness of compactors and scrubbers. Nevertheless, it was his job to resolve those doubts.

Events After March 1970

One of Masella's most critical initial problems was to find a way to overcome the state and federal resistance to funding the installation of scrubbers. Kerr suggested to Golar that the PMS do a brief comparative cost study of scrubbers versus compactors. The major finding of this initial analysis was that the total operating cost for the Department of Sanitation and New York City Housing Authority in the aggregate would increase by approximately $5 million per annum if compactors were chosen rather than scrubbers. The final paragraph summarizing key findings of this report noted "factors other than cost should also be taken into consideration in making the final decision. These factors might include the relative efficiency of scrubbers and compactors in their primary task of eliminating pollution, the prospects for further legislation which might eliminate all forms of burning, and therefore scrubbers, and the status of labor management relations regarding the operation of compactors, which is the chief source of the cost differential." This study was performed on April 17, 1970 and is summarized below:

Costs to Modify 663 Incinerators
(000,000)

	Scrubbers	Compactors
Initial Installation[1]	$7.9	$6.6
Yearly Operating Cost (NYCHA)	.4	.5
Additional Cost to DOS/Year	Unchanged	4.9

[1] Based on an average capital cost of $11,000 and $10,000 for scrubbers and compactors, respectively.

The PMS analysis also compared the cost of scrubbers with the recently introduced "Gator" compactor for NYCHA developments with incinerators serving 20 or fewer dwelling units. Cost estimates for initial installation of a Gator unit ranged between $2,000 and $4,500. Operating costs were also uncertain; they might be anywhere between $666,000 and $875,000 per year depending on the number of men required to run the compactors at the 559 locations where they could be installed. (Estimates of these manpower needs were from 50 to 80 men.) The cost of operating standard scrubbers in the 559 small buildings would be only about $347,000 per year. In addition, if the Gators were installed in all eligible buildings, DOS would need to spend $380,000 more per year to remove the compacted waste. The study went on to say :

> ...it should be apparent that no strong economic case can be made for either compactors or scrubbers without the benefit of some substantial operating experience. Immediate action is, however, a necessity. Because the initial cost for "gator" compactors is substantially less than for scrubbers and because compactors did not appear to demand major construction, the recommendation can be made to install a substantial number of compactors (perhaps 50 to 100) as soon as possible if the installation price is satisfactory. The cost of operating these compactors should quickly become apparent. The investment will not be substantial and the policy changed if facts warrant. If, however, as expected, costs for the compactors will be less in total than the scrubber, the Housing Authority can proceed with the program on an accelerated basis.
>
> It should be stressed that any pilot program should be large enough so that a true picture of operating costs will emerge. Critical variables are the additional personnel needed to operate compactors and the impact on the Department of Sanitation and these cannot be learned in a test tube.

Masella commented on the PMS decision to recommend scrubbers wherever possible on incinerators serving more than 20 units:

For the New York City Housing Authority the best solution is scrubbers because of the sanitation problem. The city can't handle the increased demands on its incinerators and men. The gap between the capacity of the city to dispose of garbage and the garbage being generated is widening every year. If compactors were used that problem would only be compounded. Scrubbers, moreover, are a proven device which when properly maintained are an effective means for achieving compliance in meeting air pollution standards. Dependability, of course, is contingent upon preventative maintenance and the proper training and instruction of operators. Given the cost studies and the city sanitation problems, scrubbers would appear to be the best solution. Although scrubbers are preferable the city will probably go to compactors for the smaller buildings where only one shift is required to operate them.

Schackman added:

The problem with either raw garbage or compacted garbage is that they require more pickups by Sanitation than incinerated garbage. It is estimated that incineration reduces garbage by a ratio of 10 to 1 where as compaction reduces garbage on a ratio of 4 to 1 which means that 2 1/2 times more garbage must be picked up weekly by the Department of Sanitation. They simply haven't the personnel or equipment to do it.

Scrubbers in my opinion are technically able to comply with the law and we are currently hiring consultants to do the technical tests to support this view.[1]

Compactors have been installed for the last two years and they can work in the smaller buildings. Part of the problem is that there is a general feeling on the part of some people that incineration will ultimately be outlawed. As a matter of fact incineration has been outlawed on all buildings constructed after 1968. The private sector has been going to compactors on a ratio of about 3 to 1 because the scrubber is difficult to maintain and its performance is difficult to scrutinize. Part of the problem is that the city requires a 4 to 1 compaction ratio to facilitate burning on their grates even though compaction can be done on a ratio of 15 to 1. However, the Sanitation Department

---

[1]Generally speaking, while scrubbers had been demonstrated on a laboratory scale as an effective means of purifying incinerator omissions to reduce pollution to the standard required by law, field tests to date in an operating environment had proven unsatisfactory. Notwithstanding the field tests, each of which was reported to have been conducted under a typical circumstance, the City of New York vigorously supported their installation as a means for upgrading pre-1968 incinerators.

claims they are unable to burn such a dense charge. Though I would personally lean toward compactors, scrubbers is a political decision because the city can't pick up more garbage.

Following completion of the PMS study, negotiations were held between NYCHA and the state and federal funding agencies. The federal agencies agreed to fund scrubber installations at sites serving more than 20 units. The state acquiesced to funding scrubbers only when 61 or more units were served. Other incinerators would be replaced by compactors. Except for this breakthrough, the Project Status Report for June 5, 1970 reported that "during the first four months of this reporting, little significant progress was achieved." Progress had been so poor that even the revised targets had become useless. Newly revised completion dates were developed by PMS as follows:

Category	Original Target Completion Dates	Revised Completion Dates (4/69)	Revised Completion Dates (6/70)
I 20 and under	12/20/68	3/71	9/71
II 100 and over	12/20/68	4/71	5/71
III 61-100	10/20/69	9/70	5/71
IV 21-60	5/20/70	1/72	5/72

The report noted that the delays were due to the same causes outlined earlier but added that the NYCHA was to blame for not pushing harder to keep things on schedule and for not having taken significant action on city owned incinerators that required no outside lending agency approval. The report went on to note that action had been taken to remove obstacles in several agencies:

<u>In the Department of Air Resources</u>:

- A separate section to handle public agency jobs solely.

- Firming up of DAR criteria which had previously been difficult to interpret.

- Establishment of an Appeal Board to which contractors may appeal if they do not agree with objections or violations cited by DAR examiners.

- Creation of teams consisting of an engineer and inspector who will follow a job from the initial filing to inspection of the completed installation.

- Creation of a provisional approval for design drawings with minor objections with the condition that they be corrected within 30 days and a provisional notification sent to the DAR.

- Establishment of a provisional certificate of operations given for 60 days where minor violations are observed during DAR inspection.

- Arrangement for testing four scrubbers by state officials with federal representatives present.

- Arrangement of meeting with federal representatives on 6/28/70 to discuss the 1160 federally aided incinerators for which approval to install pollution control devices has not been obtained.

In the Housing Authority:

- Designation of Mr. Joseph Loughlin as Air Pollution Coordinator to achieve better management and tighter control of the project.

- Award of a contract to Burns and Roe to design scrubbers for 306 city-funded incinerators in the 21-60 category.

- Preliminary assignment to Burns and Roe for the contract to perform design work for compactors to replace 67 city-funded incinerators in the 20-or-fewer category. With this contract all 501 city-funded incinerators will be moving toward compliance.

- Arrangement for a meeting between the director of the state funding agency and the chairman of the Housing Authority to discuss the 663 incinerators for which approval has not been obtained.

- Commitment from the authorities to double the rate of construction contract awards to 150 per month.

- Commitment to take immediate action to move federal and state incinerators toward compliance as soon as federal and state approvals have been received.

The August 1970 status report indicated progress to date:

Category	Total Incinerators	Dis-continued	Upgrading requested or Awaiting Funding	Funding Approved or Upgrading in Progress or Completed
I (20 or less)	565	44	438	83
II (101 or more)	548		0	548
III (61-100)	186		41	145
IV (21-60)	1,357		627	730

In replying to the case writer's question as to why the program had seemingly accelerated since he took office, Rickles commented:

> It's difficult to pass judgment but it could be because of the importance the Mayor has placed on the problem in the press and also because the agencies involved are more aware of the problem. Perhaps also the prior administrators were unwilling to take risks, as regards the technological decision. In my view the essence of government is the willingness to take risks. The basic fault in Civil Service today is the unwillingness to take risk and responsibility. I take these risks frequently as on design drawing approvals.

Andy Kerr commented on the improved progress of the Air Pollution Abatement Program:

> There is no one reason responsible for the progress being made currently. Among the reasons are the new and increased public concern over air pollution, "Earth-Day" which was a significant factor in bringing pressure to bear on the city authorities, and the appointment of new administrators in NYCHA and DAR. Golar, the new chairman of the housing authority was impressed that air pollution was a mayoral priority. Before his appointment the common cry of the Housing Authority was that they had no money and couldn't proceed, when the real truth was that they didn't want to commit themselves to either compactors or scrubbers. Now the commitment has been made and progress is being made accordingly.
>
> Also Rickles seems to be a very effective administrator.

Masella commented on the use of "status reports" and schedule display boards:

> There is a certain degree of strategy in the tone of the status reports. During the last reporting period we hit them hard but now I recognize that they have made a sincere effort and have toned down the report accordingly. If there has been an effort to resolve problems, I try to note them. We no longer use display boards as the schedules were unrealistic and people stopped looking to them for information. The agencies don't review the status reports before they go to the Mayor although the data is reviewed before the report is drawn up. Never, however, the tone or format. As a matter of fact, DAR probably would have preferred the status report of June 5, 1970 written slightly differently as it was mildly critical of them.

Schackman commented on the PMS monthly status reports and in general on the incentives provided him to complete the project:

> I receive pressure directly from the Director of Management and from the Mayor's Office who upon receiving monthly status reports can easily see the progress made. Besides there is a certain personal satisfaction in that we are a quasi public authority and we should get things done more quickly than the other agencies. We hold weekly meetings with the Authority members which are in essence operating reviews at which time we discuss such items as construction currently in progress. The first item reviewed is always progress on the incinerator modification program. The original project plan was discussed with me before final drafting. At that time I seriously objected to the established milestones which were somewhat but not totally modified to satisfy my objections. Afterwards I began to take a more active role when I discovered I would be held accountable for the progress on the project even though I could only devote a portion of my time to concentrating on the Air Pollution Abatement time-table.

Masella on communication with the Department of Sanitation (DOS):

> We talked with the DOS perhaps twice a month and actually had very little contact with them regarding this project. When we first got involved in the project, we had a PMS liaison with the DOS; and when I needed him, I found he had resigned to work on Goldberg's campaign. I guess I was lax in not finding a replacement for him. When I do talk to them, I talk to their Director of Engineering - in fact, I have dealt mostly with people on an operational level rather than on a policy level at DOS. We had made our decisions in this program with a predetermined parameter dictating that all efforts should be made to relieve their load, so contact with them was not really that important. I have, however, been doing work with Steve Issenberg from Lindsay's office who is his liaison with the DOS and is very much up-to-date on the issues. The DOS is not on the distribution list (status report mailing list) and doesn't receive copies of the status reports, but Issenberg does. While the compactor decision is indeed relevant to the DOS, it was only made last January. I guess upon reflection that they should get the status reports although I feel their interests are constantly represented by PMS. Andy set the original parameter seeking a minimal load for sanitation and we originally decided compactors were not a feasible solution.

By October 5, 1970, a summary report prepared for the Mayor showed that the project had slipped 20 weeks behind the new schedule and that the target completion date was now September 30, 1972 (Exhibit 7). Exhibits 8 and 9 contain information from the status report of October 16, 1970.

After briefly reviewing the history of the project, Andy Kerr was a bit unsettled.

> The mayor looks to us to get these jobs done. There have obviously been some problems on this one. I wonder what the key sources of delay were and what PMS could have done about them. I'd hate to make the same mistakes again.

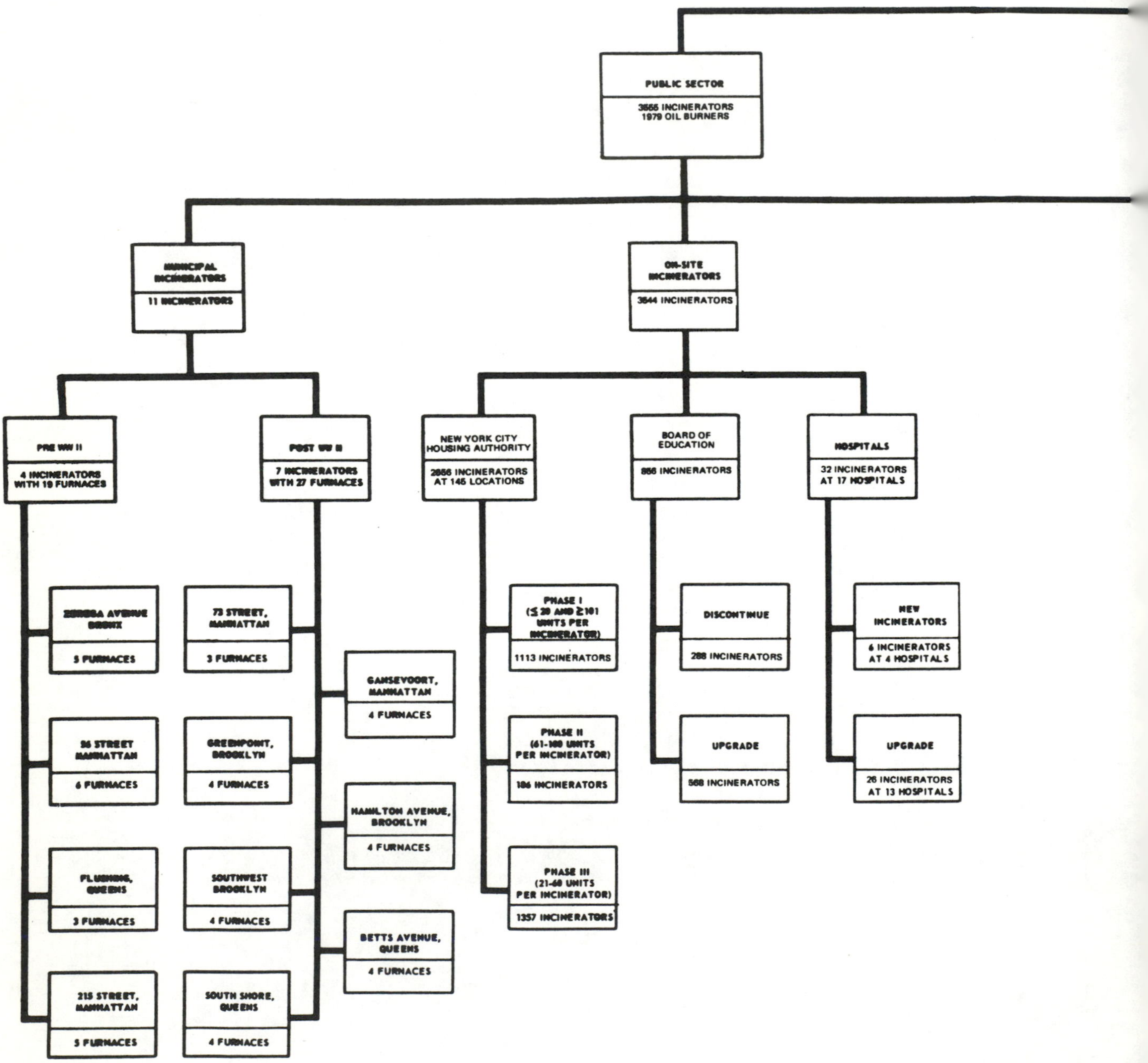
PUBLIC SECTOR
3655 INCINERATORS
1979 OIL BURNERS
MUNICIPAL INCINERATORS
11 INCINERATORS
ON-SITE INCINERATORS
3644 INCINERATORS
PRE WW II
4 INCINERATORS WITH 19 FURNACES
POST WW II
7 INCINERATORS WITH 27 FURNACES
NEW YORK CITY HOUSING AUTHORITY
2656 INCINERATORS AT 145 LOCATIONS
BOARD OF EDUCATION
856 INCINERATORS
HOSPITALS
32 INCINERATORS AT 17 HOSPITALS
AVENUE
5 FURNACES
56 STREET MANHATTAN
6 FURNACES
FLUSHING, QUEENS
3 FURNACES
215 STREET, MANHATTAN
5 FURNACES
73 STREET, MANHATTAN
3 FURNACES
GREENPOINT, BROOKLYN
4 FURNACES
SOUTHWEST BROOKLYN
4 FURNACES
SOUTH SHORE, QUEENS
4 FURNACES
GANSEVOORT, MANHATTAN
4 FURNACES
HAMILTON AVENUE, BROOKLYN
4 FURNACES
BETTS AVENUE, QUEENS
4 FURNACES
PHASE I (≤ 20 AND ≥ 101 UNITS PER INCINERATOR)
1113 INCINERATORS
PHASE II (61-100 UNITS PER INCINERATOR)
186 INCINERATORS
PHASE III (21-60 UNITS PER INCINERATOR)
1357 INCINERATORS
DISCONTINUE
288 INCINERATORS
UPGRADE
568 INCINERATORS
NEW INCINERATORS
6 INCINERATORS AT 4 HOSPITALS
UPGRADE
26 INCINERATORS AT 13 HOSPITALS

Exhibit 1

NYCHA INCINERATOR AIR POLLUTION ABATEMENT PROJECT

Project Breakdown Structure

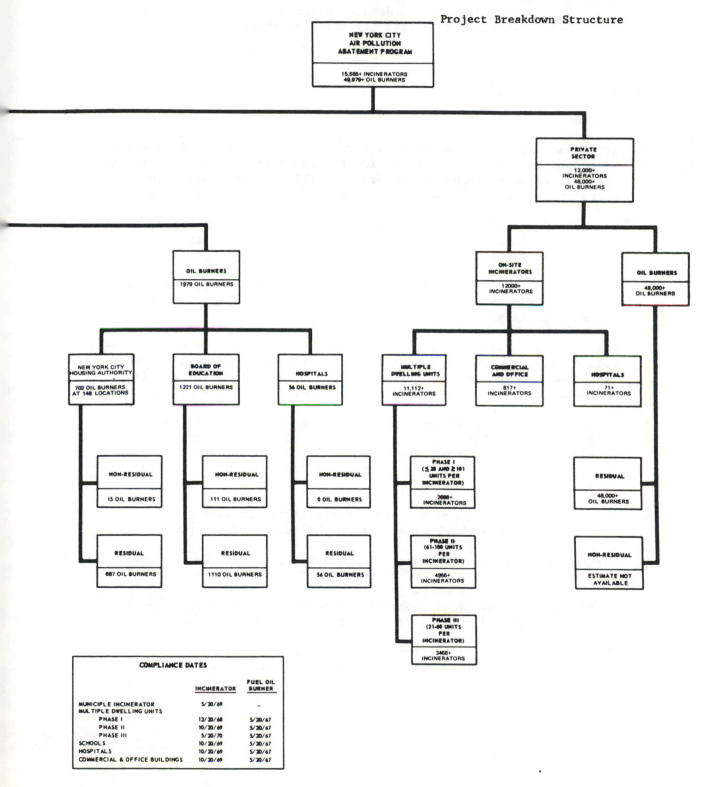

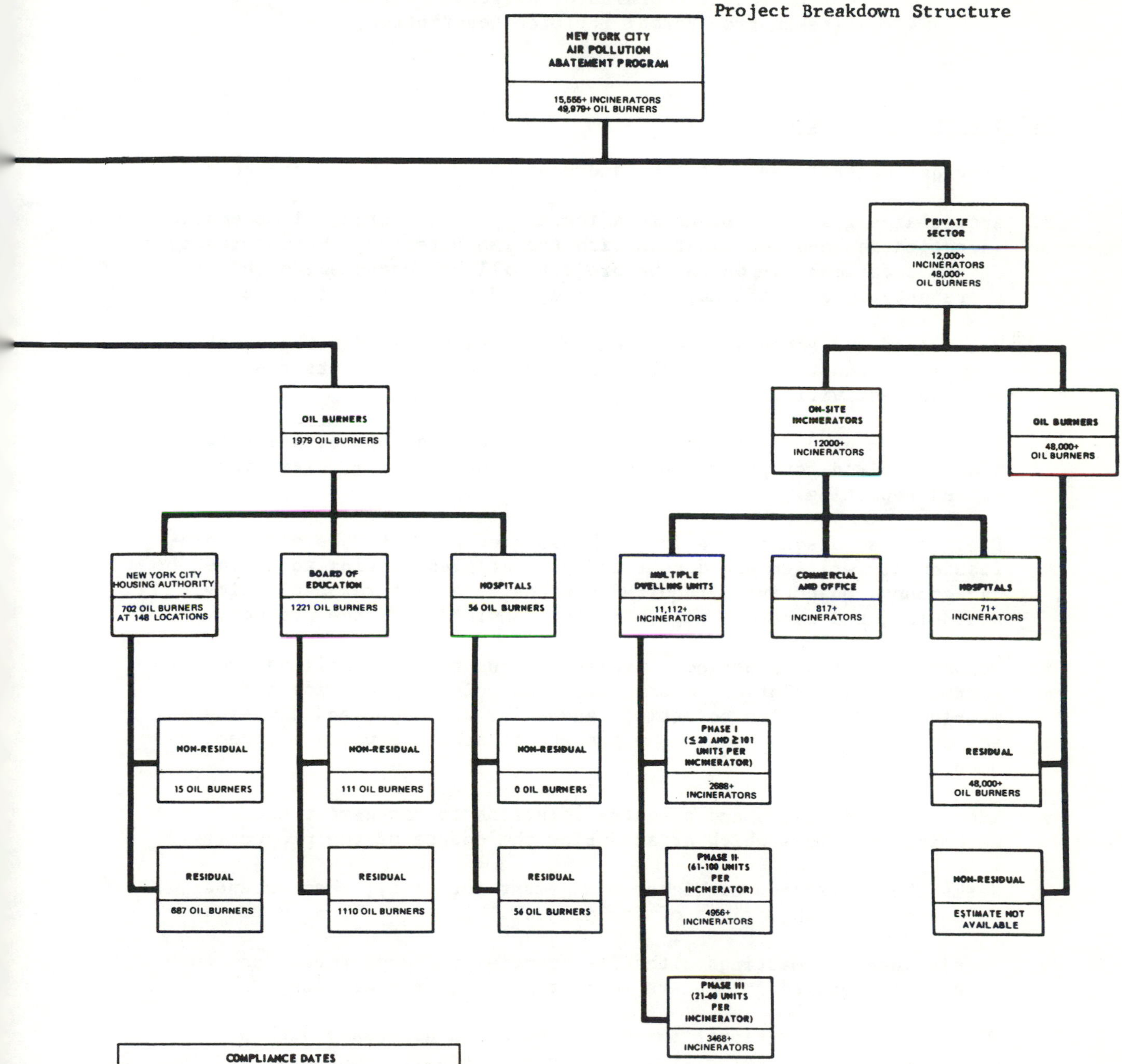

COMPLIANCE DATES

	INCINERATOR	FUEL OIL BURNER
MUNICIPLE INCINERATOR	5/20/69	–
MULTIPLE DWELLING UNITS		
PHASE I	12/20/68	5/20/67
PHASE II	10/20/69	5/20/67
PHASE III	5/20/70	5/20/67
SCHOOLS	10/20/69	5/20/67
HOSPITALS	10/20/69	5/20/67
COMMERCIAL & OFFICE BUILDINGS	10/20/69	5/20/67

Exhibit 2

NYCHA INCINERATOR AIR POLLUTION ABATEMENT PROJECT

Senior Project Coordinator Responsibilities
(taken from Formal Position Description)

Major Responsibilities:

1. Provides centralized direction and control over assigned projects.

2. Articulates goals and objectives for the project through independent investigation and coordination with the PMS Director, the commissioner of the department in which the project will be conducted, other representatives of the Mayor's office, and the Bureau of the Budget.

3. Determines and schedules detailed activities required for project completion and the individuals, agencies, and departments responsible for such activities.

4. Establishes project implementation schedules and appropriate network plans required for project planning and understanding, direction, and status reporting.

5. Prepares and disseminates for each assigned project a detailed, professionally written and documented project plan setting forth the background, objectives, required actions, specific responsibility, schedules, and controls necessary for completion of the project.

6. Prepares and issues periodic project status reports, delineating current status in relation to schedules, anticipating and identifying problems, identifying potential causes for slippage, and devising actions required to return the project to schedule where slippage has occurred.

7. Identifies, devises, and executes solutions to management and technical problems which arise during the course of the project.

8. Seeks the assistance of higher management authority, when necessary to achieve the objectives of the project.

9. Participates in meetings with City agencies and departments and such others as required in matters related to project operations.

10. Takes whatever additional initiative he deems necessary within organizational and authority guidelines to assure successful completion of his projects.

Exhibit 2 (continued)

NYCHA INCINERATOR AIR POLLUTION ABATEMENT PROJECT

11. Keeps the PMS Director informed regarding accomplishments, problems, and slippages, or whenever unusual actions may be required in order to accomplish the project objectives. Coordinates with the Director all meetings with Bureau of the Budget personnel and other Mayor's Office personnel.

12. Directs the work of and delegates responsibility to Project Coordinators, and Assistant Project Coordinators assigned to his supervision.

13. Participates in the education and training of Project Coordinators, Assistant Project Coordinators, and management personnel in City agencies in the use of project management techniques.

14. Monitors and reviews periodically with them the performance of Project Coordinators and Assistant Project Coordinators assigned to his supervision.

Principal Working Relationships:

1. Work with commissioners, assistant commissioners, other responsible personnel in City agencies, and Mayoral assistants to obtain cooperation in defining and implementing project goals and keeping City officials informed of project status.

2. Works with and under the supervision of the PMS Director to assure that his actions are consistent with the over-all goals and the assigned responsibilities and role of the staff, to obtain his assistance in the conduct and management of projects and in exerting appropriate additional pressure when required to assure implementation of project goals, and to enable the Director to function effectively in his role on the Mayoral staff.

3. Works with Project Coordinators and Assistant Project Coordinators assigned to his supervision to move effectively in his role on the Mayoral staff.

4. May work with others outside the City government in special circumstances, as required, or other members of the project Management Staff in order to accomplish project goals.

Exhibit 3

NYCHA INCINERATOR AIR POLLUTION ABATEMENT PROJECT

Description of Project Status Report and Project Plan

Project "Status Reports" were approximately 10-page documents in large highly readable type prepared monthly by the PMS and distributed to all parties involved in the active project including the Mayor. The report included a summarized background of the project consisting of a brief description, statement of objectives and intended completion date. It was as simple and quantitative as possible and was intended as a means of impressing the reader with the goals and most important aspects of the project.

The introduction was followed by a summary of project progress consisting of a statement about the portion of the project completed, based on the number of milestones concluded compared to the number required for the completion of the project. For projects with many components, the subsequent sections were used to briefly review the progress of each program component.

Another section on project progress and current status described the activities completed by each responsibility center during the reporting period. Usually a one-sentence comment for each milestone accomplished was sufficient. The following sections detailed milestones for the period that were not completed as well as the reason for the slippage, the person or agencies responsible, the expected completion date, and the required action to be taken. These sections were followed by a similar section dealing with milestones which were scheduled for past periods and still not completed. Milestones which had been rescheduled were included in the following section.

The progress anticipated by the end of the next reporting period was then presented including the agency responsible for completing each milestone and the scheduled completion date. This was intended to clearly identify responsibility for tasks leading to completion of the program. The final section briefly described the major activities and major obstacles affecting the on-time completion of the project. Actions planned to overcome these obstacles were always indicated. Attached to the end of each report was a milestone chart showing the task required for completion of the project.

Exhibit 3 (continued)

<u>The "Project Plan"</u> was similar in format to the project status report, but was typically prepared only once during the development stage of the project. It presented in detailed form the background of the project, the objectives which were to be fulfilled, the actions or tasks necessary to achieve completion, and the responsibility centers which were to be held accountable for the completion of designated milestones. Also included was a detailed milestone chart depicting events by scheduled completion date and responsibility center. This plan was reviewed and discussed with all interested parties and it was understood that their agreement to a scheduled completion date or milestone constituted commitment.

Exhibit 4

THE GOVERNMENT OF THE CITY OF NEW YORK

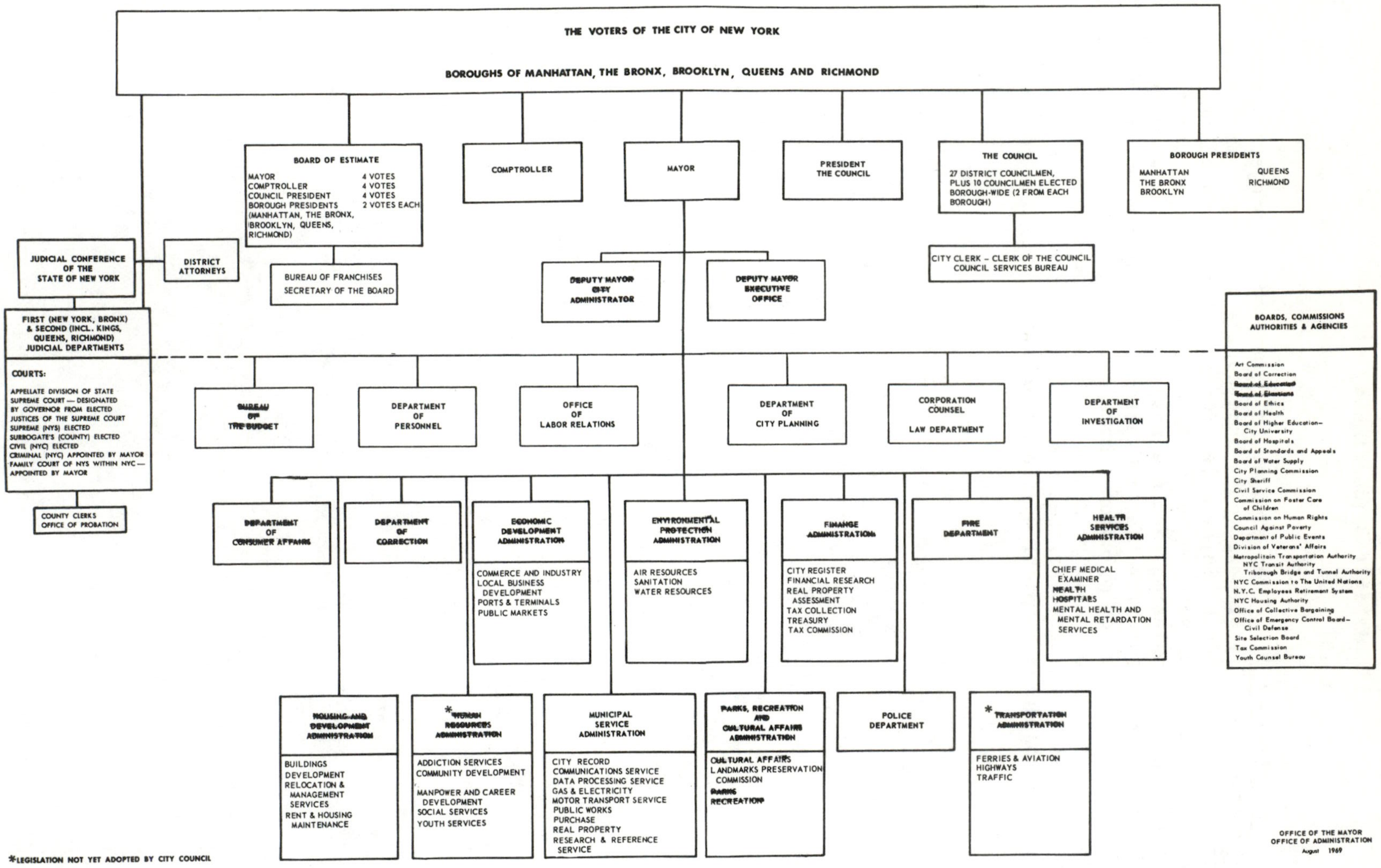

Exhibit 5

LETTER FROM NYCHA TO TENANTS ADVISING OF INCINCERATOR DISCONTINUANCES

NEW YORK CITY HOUSING AUTHORITY
250 Broadway · New York, N.Y. 10007

January 6, 1969

Dear Tenant:

Air pollution is a very serious problem in this City as well as in other major cities. The emission of various irritants and pollutants into the air from automobiles, heating fuels, incinerators, and other sources, according to the experts, adversely affects the health of all people.

To reduce the contamination of the air in this City, an Air Pollution Control Law was recently passed. This Law regulates the burning of heating fuels and the operation of incinerators, and applies to both private and public buildings. The Authority has already fulfilled some of its obligations under the Law by installing special boiler controls, by burning a low sulphur fuel oil, and by installing special smoke control devices in the incinerators of the very large buildings.

Unfortunately, with regard to the very small buildings, it is not practical to install smoke control devices in the incinerators. We, therefore, have been experimenting extensively with garbage compaction machines. As of this time, these compactors have not been adequately developed for immediate installation in these small buildings. Because we must comply immediately with the Law, we have no other choice at this time but to shut-down these incinerators and collect garbage in the simplest possible manner. We anticipate that this shut-down will be for a temporary period until there are developed practical mechanical devices, which will meet the requirements of the Law.

We sincerely hope that you will understand our position in this matter, and cooperate fully with the staff of your development in implementing the new procedure, as described below, in a safe and sanitary manner:

1. Effective on______________, the incinerator hopper on each floor will be locked.

2. Tenants are requested to place their garbage and refuse in bags or otherwise wrapped securely, and deposit them in special heavy duty refuse cans, which will be located near the entrance to each building.

3. Tenants are requested to be careful not to spill any refuse on the floor or ground, and to replace the cover on the can after depositing their refuse.

4. Tenants are requested to place bulk refuse and debris, such as furniture, at the usual locations designated by the Management Office.

We regret any inconvenience that this change may cause you. We have been promised the full cooperation of the Department of Sanitation for increased pick-ups, and we do assure you that every effort will be made to maintain the most sanitary conditions.

Thank you for your cooperation.

Very truly yours,

(s) Irving Wise

Director of Management

Exhibit 6

NYCHA INCINERATOR AIR POLLUTION ABATEMENT PROJECT

Project Status Report, January 30, 1970

Cumulative Status to Date

Phase	Category: Units per Incinerator	Number of Incinerators	Design Starts		Design Completions		Construction Starts		Construction Completion		Certificates of Operation	
			Planned	Actual	Planned	Actual	Planned	Actual	Planned	Actual	Planned	Actual
I	20 and under	565	343	54*	214	54*	44	44*	44	44*	44	44*
	101 and over	548	548	548	548	380	426	144	227	114	196	36
II	61 to 100	186	186	186	186	89	162	39	38	31	38	3
III	21 to 60	1,357	5	6	5	6	5	6	5	5	5	1
Totals (Cumulative for entire program)		2,656	1,082	794	953	529	637	233	314	194	283	84

Current Status (January 30, 1970)

Phase	Category: Units per Incinerator	Number of Incinerators	Under Design	Design Completed Awaiting Construction Approval by DAR	Under Construction	Construction Completed Under Inspection by DAR	Issued Certificate of Operation
I	20 and under	565	0	10	0	0	44*
	101 and over	548	168	236	30	78	36
II	61 to 100	186	97	50	8	28	3
III	21 to 60	1,357	0	0	1	4	1
Totals (Currently in each category)		2,656	265	296	39	110	84

*44 of these Category I incinerators have been shut down. They are included here for convenience.

Exhibit 7

PROJECT STATUS REPORT: IMPLEMENTATION PHASE

NYCHA ON-SITE INCINERATOR AIR POLLUTION ABATEMENT PROGRAM

Date of this report 10/5/70 Reporting period: 8/31/70 to 10/2/70
Report issued: Weekly ___ Biweekly ___ Monthly xx Bimonthly ___ Report number:
Project leader C. Masella Other PMS assigned: Denise Lawrence
Office of prime responsibility: NYCHA Date project started: 2/69
Date project plan issued: 4/4/69 Target project completion date: 5/72

Brief description of project and statement of objectives:

The NYCHA operates 2,656 incinerators. Local Law 14 specifies the following compliance deadlines: Phase I (less than 21 and greater than 100) 12/20/68; Phase II (61-100) 10/20/69; Phase III (21-60) 5/20/70. Funding is to be provided for the 2,656 incinerators as follows: City, 501; State, 725; and Federal, 1,430. The object of this project is to bring all incinerators into full compliance as soon as possible.

Summary of project status: This project is ahead ___, on ___. Behind X, schedule. If behind, estimated number of weeks: 20 Current estimated project completion date: 9/72

DWELLING UNITS PER INCINERATOR

	Total		Less than 21		More than 100		21-60		60-100	
	#	%	#	%	#	%	#	%	#	%
Total No. of Incinerators	2656	100%	565	100%	548	100%	1357	100%	136	100%
	668	25%	0	0%	0	0%	627	46%	41	22%
No Decision/No Action	617	23%	0	0%	0	0%	617	45%	0	0%
Funding Approval Obtained	1988	75%	565	100%	585	100%	730	54%	145	78%
Awaiting Design	847	32%	438	76%	0	0%	409	30%	0	0
Under Design	240	9%	67	12%	0	0%	163	12%	0	0
Awaiting Construction	691	26%	10	2%	391	71%	143	11%	147	79%
Under Construction	0	0%	0	0%	0	0%	0	0%	0	0%
Under DAR Inspection	145	5%	6	1%	104	19%	5	61%	33	18%
In FULL COMPLIANCE	116	4%	44	8%	53	10%	10	1%	9	5%

REMARKS: Funding approval has been obtained and equip. options selected for the 501 incinerators to be funded by the City, 762 incinerators to be funded by the Fed's and 725 incinerators to be funded by the State. Funding remains to be obtained for a total of 668 Federally aided incinerators.

Major obstacles affecting the on-time completion of the project:

- Federal lending agency requires additional testing of newly upgraded incinerators in the 101 or greater category before acting upon Authority request to install 668 scrubbers in the 21 to 100 categories.
- A testing procedure has not been determined by Federal and City regulated agencies.
- The contractors have been slow to commence construction on jobs where design drawings have been approved by DAR.

Exhibit 8

NYCHA INCINERATOR AIR POLLUTION ABATEMENT PROJECT

Status Report October 16, 1970

Number of Incinerators

Funding Source	Category	Total Number of Incinerators	No Action	Under Design	Awaiting Construction	Under Construction	Under Inspection	In Full Compliance
City	20 or fewer	75	0	67	0	0	0	8*
	21 - 60	307	0	163	143	0	0	1
	61 - 100	53	0	0	52	0	0	1
	101 or greater	66	0	0	57	0	6	3
	TOTAL	501	0	230	252	0	6	13
State	20 or fewer	27	19	0	0	0	0	8*
	21 - 60	418	409	0	0	0	0	9
	60 - 100	59	0	0	52	0	0	7
	101 or greater	221	0	0	179	0	32	10
	TOTAL	725	428	0	231	0	32	34
Federal	20 or fewer	463	419	0	10	0	6	28*
	21 - 60	632	617	10	0	0	5	0
	61 - 100	74	0	0	43	0	30	1
	101 or greater	261	0	0	155	0	66	40
	TOTAL	1,430	1,036	10	208	0	107	69
TOTALS		2,656	1,464	240	691	0	143	116
City		501	0	230	252	0	6	13
State		725	428	0	231	0	32	34
Federal		1,430	1,036	10	208	0	107	69
Per cent of the Total		100%	55.1%	9.0%	26.0%	0.0%	5.5%	4.4%

Exhibit 9

NYCHA INCINERATOR AIR POLLUTION ABATEMENT PROJECT

Status Report October 16, 1970

Funding Sources	Total Number of Incinerators	Dwelling Units per Incinerator				Funding Approvals	
		< 21	> 100	21-60	61-100	Obtained	Not Obtained
City	501	75 Comp	66 Scrub	307 Scrub	53 Scrub	501	----
State	725	27 Comp	221 Scrub	413 Comp 5 Scrub	59 Scrub	725	----
Federal	1,430	0 ND	0 ND	627 ND	41 ND	---	668
		6 Scrub 457 Compact	261 Scrub	5 Scrub	33 Scrub	762	----
TOTAL	2,656	565	548	1,357	186	1,988	668

Key: ND - No Decision
Comp - Compactor
Scrub - Scrubber

Appendix A

NYCHA INCINERATOR AIR POLLUTION ABATEMENT PROJECT

Perspectives on Air Pollution

Five major pollutants are: hydrocarbons, carbon monoxide, sulphur oxides, nitrogen oxides, and particulate matter. Not only has the total quantity of pollutants discharged to the atmosphere increased greatly in recent years, but the relative scale of the problems posed by different pollutants has changed. Prior to 1968 the most prominent problem was the emission of particulate matter, mostly solid but sometimes liquid - smoke, dust, fumes and mists.

According to the Long-Range Planning Service of the Stanford Research Institute the major concern is shifting to gaseous pollutants. These far exceed particulate pollutants in total quantity and they are generally much more active chemically.

In the following tables provided by the U.S. Public Health Service, the pollutant emissions in 1966 were broken down by type and source.

Whereas Table 1 breaks down emissions on a national scale, Table 2 below gives a similar breakdown for the island of Manhattan which, according to a 1967 consultant's study, has the worst air pollution in the state and is also the location in which 51% of the complaints registered in New York City arose. Most of these complaints were submitted by citizens reacting to visible emissions.

Table 1

U.S. POLLUTION SOURCES
(millions of tons)

Types of Pollution	Motor Vehicles	Industry	Power Generation	Space Heating	Refuse Disposal	Totals
Hydro carbons	12	4	less than 1	1	1	19
Carbon monoxide	66	2	1	2	1	72
Sulphur oxides	1	9	12	3	less than 1	26
Nitrogen oxides	6	2	3	1	less than 1	13
Particulate matter	1	6	3	1	1	12
Totals	86	23	20	8	5	142

Source: U.S. Public Health Service 1966

Appendix A (continued)

Table 2

MANHATTAN POLLUTION SOURCES
(by percentage contributed)

Types of Pollution	Motor Vehicles	Industry	Power Generation	Space Heating	Refuse Disposal	Totals (in tons)
Hydro carbons	47.7%	41.5%	.6%	2.3%	7.9%	90,222
Carbon monoxide	97.6	-	.1	2.2	.1	344,673
Sulphur oxides	4.0	1.0	44.4	50.3	.2	225,286
Nitrogen oxides	11.7	.9	47.3	39.3	.8	71,688
Particulate matter	7.3	.6	45.9	26.7	39.5	48,000

Source: U.S. Public Health Service 1967

Whereas the information in Table 2 deals only with the Island of Manhattan for the period 1966-1967 an interdepartmental memorandum dated July 7, 1970, from the Department of Air Resources to the Project Management Staff set the total particulate emissions for the City of New York as 68,270 tons and went on to break down the emission sources by city agencies between incinerators and fuel burners as follows:

Table 3

PARTICULATE EMISSION SOURCES - ISLAND OF MANHATTAN
(tons)

Agency	Incinerator	Fuel Burners	Total
New York City Housing Authority	450	340	790
Municipal Hospitals	300	1,350	1,650
Department of Sanitation (Post W.W. II)	10,560	na	10,560
Board of Education	300	1,410	1,710
		Total Public Sector	14,710
		Total Private Sector	53,560

Source: Department of Air Resources, N.Y.C. 1970

DECENTRALIZATION

COMMAND DECENTRALIZATION (A)

New York is one of the hardest cities in the world to manage. It is hard for one man to govern and even harder for one average citizen to change. Two of Mayor John V. Lindsay's objectives for New York were to make it more manageable for its administration and more responsive to its citizens.

The Superagencies

Mayor Lindsay's effort to make New York City more manageable began shortly after his inauguration in January 1966. Looking at the city administration, the mayor and his advisors saw a chaotic array of some 50 independent agencies, all responsible directly to him. Although many performed similar functions, few coordinated their efforts with any of the others. For example, the Department of Health operated well-baby clinics; the Department of Hospitals operated sick-baby clinics; and the Bureau of School Health of the Department of Health maintained school clinics. Thus, one child might be attended by three different agencies depending on its state of health and whether or not it was in school. None of the agencies would have a complete medical history of the child and it was entirely possible for a mother to have her child diagnosed as ill by a well-baby clinic and then have to take it to a sick-baby clinic for treatment. In Morrisania, the two clinics were side-by-side. The well-baby clinic was underutilized while the sick-baby clinic was overcrowded; yet sick children were not permitted to go next door to the well-baby clinic. Street paving provided a second example of the problem; three city agencies and one authority had some jurisdiction. As a result, Cross Bay Boulevard in Queens was paved by the Highway Department until it reached North Channel Bridge. The Department of Public Works paved the bridge. The Highway Department paved the road again until the Cross Bay Parkway Bridge which was maintained by the Triborough Bridge and Tunnel Authority. Thereafter, the road became the Shorefront Parkway and was maintained by the Department of Parks. The distance covered was less than ten miles.

Convinced that some consolidation was necessary, the mayor appointed a Task Force on Reorganization of New York City Government under the chairmanship of Louis A. Craco and asked it to recommend ways that the city's administrative structure could be improved. In December 1966, the Craco Commission proposed a series of local laws that would group together all but two of the line operating functions of the executive branch of city government into ten new Administrations (or "superagencies" as they came to be called). The ten were: Correctional; Economic Development; Environmental Protection; Financial Management (now Finance); General Services (now Municipal Services); Health Services; Housing and Development; Human Resources; Recreation and Cultural Affairs (now Parks, Recreation, and Cultural Affairs); and Transportation. Both the Police and Fire Departments would remain independent.

The proposed reorganization was intended to do several things. First, it would combine the multitude of agencies and departments into a sufficiently limited number of administrative units to permit more effective control and supervision by the mayor. Instead of 50 commissioners, only the administrator of each superagency would report to the mayor. Second, bringing together groups of related functions would enable duplicative efforts to be reduced and better resource allocation decisions made. Third, a simpler organization would permit more effective use of new approaches to planning, budgeting, and control.

The administrator of a superagency would be given considerable authority. In addition to direct control over the commissioners in his agency, he would be responsible for developing and managing the agency's budget. He would also have the power to reorganize the agency internally provided the organizations that were changed had not been established by law. The mayor, moreover, would be able to detach parts of certain agencies and integrate them into others. For example, the program of the Department of Hospitals for training paraprofessional technicians and aides could be taken out of the Health Services Administration and made part of the manpower training activities of the Human Resources Administration.

With two exceptions, the Craco reorganization plan was enacted by the City Council in January 1967, essentially as proposed. The exceptions were the laws creating the Correctional Administration and the Human Resources Administration (HRA),[1] respectively. The first was withdrawn before the council voted; the second was still pending as of June 1971. (HRA existed only by executive order of the mayor which meant that the commissioners retained all their old powers and reported

---

[1]A glossary of case abbreviations is provided in Appendix A.

directly to the mayor. The administrator could seek coordination and cooperation between HRA's subagencies, but could not enforce it legally.) The city's new organization is shown in Exhibit 1. Appendix B describes, briefly, the eight chartered superagencies and HRA.

The reorganization did nothing to change the basic structure of city government at the top. Power remained balanced between the mayor, the Board of Estimate, and the City Council. The city's charter had created a strong central government focusing on the mayor who had both legislative and executive prerogatives. Of these, the most significant was the power to spend--that is, to allocate the city's yearly expenditures for both capital and expense items. The Board of Estimate also had substantial power in the areas of financial and personnel matters, local assessments, capital projects, and contract awards. It also had the authority to approve or disapprove the mayor's proposed expense and capital budgets. The board consisted entirely of elected officials: the mayor (4 votes), the borough presidents (2 votes each), the comptroller (4 votes), and the president of the City Council (4 votes). The City Council included one member from each of twenty-seven districts plus two at-large members from each borough who had to be of different political parties. Although it had the power to approve the mayor's budgets and to initiate legislation, the council was the weakest of the three power centers, being severely constrained by the actions of state and federal legislatures and by the authority of the Board of Estimate.

Citizen Input

As he endeavored to make the city more manageable by reorganizing it, Mayor Lindsay also tried to make it more responsive and more accountable to its people. Creation of the superagencies had rationalized city government for the mayor and brought similar functions under the jurisdiction of the same organizational unit. But at the local level, where the agencies came face-to-face with the citizens, there remained roughly the same number of smaller organizational units, each responsible for a small piece of an over-all function. Thus, the Bureau of Child Welfare and the Agency for Child Development both dealt exclusively with children. They were different programs but they dealt with parts of the same problem. At the top, they were both part of HRA, but at the bottom they were still separate activities. The Department of Water Resources (DWR) and the Department of Sanitation (DS) were both part of the Environmental Protection Administration (EPA). Again, coordination was possible at the top level, but at the local level, the two were independent agencies. If a street catch basin clogged, it was the responsibility of DWR to unclog it and keep it unclogged. However, the catch basin may have clogged because DS had failed to clean the streets adequately. Since DS was not responsible for cleaning the catch basin and DWR was not to blame, no one was accountable. DWR could clean the basin but it could not prevent it from clogging again. For a troubled citizen, trying to deal with situations like this was - as one mayoral staff member put it - "similar to making the stations of the cross."

The mayor's initial answer to the problem was to create a number of programs that would give individual citizens and neighborhood groups a more effective way of being heard at the top. Three of these programs were: Little City Halls, Urban Action Task Forces, and Mobile City Halls.

Little City Halls: In 1966, a Ford Foundation grant was used to set up six Little City Halls. They were store-front operations staffed by a mayoral liaison man who tried to deal with local problems on a local level. In many ways, they were walk-in complaint bureaus. Often the liaison men had to use mayoral influence on commissioners to get anything changed because local line officials of the superagencies were unable to make changes on their own. Instructions had to come from above and it was usually faster for the liaison men to work from the top than to wait for a request to drift up through the chain of command. In 1967 the City Council refused to fund an expanded program on the grounds that it established political clubhouses for the mayor at city expense.

Urban Action Task Forces (UATF): Thirteen such forces were set up in the spring and summer of 1966 when other cities were experiencing riots. The UATF was intended to communicate with the low income areas of the city and to locate potentially flammable situations before they ignited. The task forces, too, were store-front operations and complaint bureaus staffed by a secretary. Each local task force was composed of a group of neighborhood citizens chaired by a commissioner of one of the agencies or an administrator of a superagency. To keep from tying up senior city officials with task force business, there was a coordinator at the mayor's office for every three task forces. What the store-front personnel could not deal with, was passed on to the coordinators, who were also responsible for new ideas and new programs. Only if there was a necessity for contact with top ranking officials were task force chairmen brought in. Thus a chairman had no involvement with the day-to-day activities of his task force. The only regular contact he had was chairing meetings. The coordinators at the mayor's office and the presence of a senior official as chairman, however, gave credibility to the task forces when they promised change. The program was considered a success (although it was not responsible for any major structural change in the system) and, in 1969, the task forces were expanded to cover middle income areas. The number jumped from 13 to 47. In addition, a special unit was formed that would take over operation of a task force when there was a crisis in its area.

Mobile City Halls: These were similar to Little City Halls but were located in trucks that travelled around the city. They, too, were outreach operations with people from the mayor's office taking complaints and trying to make changes at the local level when possible and at the top when necessary.

Unfortunately, as time went by, the results produced by these, and other "neighborhood" programs proved more and more disappointing. The first six months after a Little City Hall was opened the response was enthusiastic but thereafter interest waned as people realized that while a few minor problems were solved or alleviated, the major, basic problems remained. No fundamental change took place in the way a superagency delivered its services to the public. Indeed, the existence of the neighborhood programs may have ensured that no such change would ever occur. As Lew Feldstein, the Mayor's Executive Assistant for Neighborhood Government, put it:

> All of the systems we had set up were essentially communications devices by which citizens in a community could make their complaints known to the city at a somewhat higher than local official level; that is, they could talk to somebody who ostensibly had some kind of direct line to the mayor. And that person's leverage on dealing with the problem was generally a central mechanism. He could not deal too effectively on the local level either. He had to go up to the commissioner of the affected agency and say, "Look, I'm hearing these complaints. What can we do about it?" What that did was two things, both very destructive. First of all it forced all decision making, even on the smallest local crisis, up to the top of the administration, so that we had administrators of superagencies dealing with the pothole problem - not the most effective way to use a $40,000 a year man. Second, it confirmed the present practices of the agencies. It was as if the system was a $9 billion machine trundling down the road - that was the city as a whole - and it was spewing out behind it all these screw-ups. And running along as fast as they could behind it were our various offices, task forces, and city halls, catching these things as quickly as they could before they hit the ground and broke and caused a riot or a problem. No mayor ever used his office to get alongside the machine and tinker with the mechanism. So we caught everything before it blew up and the effect was that the agencies could afford to keep creating screw-ups because there was someone there to catch the worst of those screw-ups before they made a major blowup which would force the city - like Newark or Detroit - to sit back and say, "Hey, we're doing something very wrong here. Let's stop and look at the whole system." We never had to because there was this fail-safe mechanism catching all the real hot ones.

There came gradually the realization that, to date, the city's programs had done little to make its agencies more responsive to their constituents; that they simply did not include the necessary ingredients to change the underlying system. In the neighborhoods, things were much as they had always been. Perhaps the only change of note was an increase in the public's cynicism as it watched one more approach fail to measure up to its promises.

The Concept of Neighborhood

For many, the answer to making city government more responsive lay in creating mechanisms that went beyond communication and provided the city's neighborhoods with more control over the management of urban services. In 1969, for example, Norman Mailer campaigned for mayor of New York under the slogan, "power to the neighborhoods." Proposals for transferring power in some form to neighborhoods had been many and varied. But, because there was no body of experience with neighborhood government in urban America, all were relatively speculative. In fact, the concept of "neighborhood," itself, had no single accepted standard.

To many city planners, an ideal neighborhood was an introverted unit of about 7,000 - sufficient to support an elementary school and a shopping and community center. Jane Jacobs saw this ideal as silly, and even harmful.[1] In a town of 7,000, people might be expected to know each other from work, school, church, and so forth. But a neighborhood of 7,000 persons in a city would not have that characteristic. Its inhabitants might go to private or parochial schools, work on the other side of the city, or make their friends elsewhere. And, said Mrs. Jacobs, if the planners did succeed in making these "neighborhoods" into the introverted ideal, they would have destroyed the city by turning it into a collection of small towns.

Mrs. Jacobs saw three levels of neighborhood. The first, often overlooked, was the city as a whole. This was the source of all public money, whether federal, state, or city. This was where administrative and policy decisions were made. And this was where city-wide special interest and pressure groups met. It was in this neighborhood, for example, that the people interested in art and music congregated. By and large, Mrs. Jacobs said, most big cities had done fairly well at creating effective city-wide neighborhoods. People with similar and supplementing interests had been able to find each other fairly well.

At the other end of the scale was the city's streets, the second level of neighborhood. Street neighborhoods could be quite small or fairly large. Typically they were interlocking and overlapped as one passed from

---

[1] Jane Jacobs, The Death and Life of Great American Cities (New York: Random House, 1961) pp. 112 ff.

neighborhood to neighborhood. They tended to be physically, socially, and economically homogeneous. These neighborhoods dealt with the common local interests of the members of the community. Their other function was to draw effectively on help when they could not handle a problem. American cities had been reasonably successful with this kind of neighborhood as well.

In between the city and the street was the third kind of neighborhood - the district. Mrs. Jacobs felt that this was where most cities failed. According to her, the chief function of a successful district was to mediate between the indispensable but inherently powerless street neighborhoods and the inherently powerful city as a whole. Most big cities were much too large and complex to be comprehended from any one vantage point, even the top. The result was ignorance and well-meaning decisions that were disastrous when implemented. Districts must bridge the ignorance and help bring the resources of the city down to the street. In terms of district size, they must be small enough so that individual streets don't get lost, yet large enough to fight City Hall if necessary. This latter fact meant that the size of the district would vary depending upon the size of the city; for the population had to represent enough votes to give the decision maker pause before he overrode the district's wishes. In terms of geographic size, Mrs. Jacobs recommended no absolute size but suggested that physical barriers should form boundaries rather than cut through the middle of districts and that there should be some community of interests among its citizens.

New York's Community Planning Districts

In 1961, a revision to the New York City Charter required that the five boroughs be divided into a number of Community Planning Districts (CPDs) by early 1968. The charter amendment stated:

> Such districts shall coincide, so far as feasible with the historic communities from which the city has developed and shall be suitable as districts to be used for the planning of community life within the city.[1]

During the process of setting CPD boundaries, the City Planning Commission developed and used criteria in addition to those set forth in the charter. First, the Commission decided that although it might be useful if all districts had roughly equal populations, such a division would be arbitrary and artificial. The Commission, therefore, agreed on a minimum population of 125,000 and a maximum of 300,000. Second, they decided that physical features that separate communities should become CPD boundaries and that districts should not have unusual contours or isolated areas. Using these standards, the Commission delineated 62 Community Plan-

---

[1] New York City Planning Commission, CPD-Community Planning Districts, (New York, March 1968) p. 2.

ning Districts effective as of March 1, 1968. Whether intentional, or not, the CPDs embodied many of the characteristics of Jane Jacobs' middle-level neighborhood, "the district." Exhibit 2 is a map showing the CPDs; Appendix C gives brief descriptions of five of them.

The charter amendment calling for creation of the CPDs also required that a Community Planning Board be established in each one. The boards would consist of the councilmen-at-large from the borough in which the community district was located, the councilman from the district, and between five and nine members who were residents of the district, appointed by the borough president. The duties of the board were to advise the borough president about any matter dealing with the development or welfare of the CPD and to advise the City Planning Commission on any matter pertaining to physical planning within the area. In July 1969 the residency requirement was repealed and the number of the borough president's appointees increased to 50. Each board elected one of its members to be chairman.

Although the Community Planning Boards had an advisory role, they had very little real power. Since the members were all appointed by the borough president, rather than elected, they could not be called representative of their districts. If a board was strongly opposed to something, it could sometimes hold it up or stop it. But anyone who could swing more power could prevail upon the borough president or the City Council to overrule the board. In 1971, for example, the Williamsburg Board unanimously vetoed a proposed day care center. Williamsburg was a largely Italian and Jewish community but the center would have served mostly Blacks and Puerto Ricans. The local politicians supported the board and the community was overwhelmingly opposed to the center. The City-Wide Coalition for Day Care, a powerful interracial group was for it, however, and the Board of Estimate overruled the community board.

Thus, while the size and demography of the CPDs seemed to make them highly suitable for the mediating role between street neighborhoods and the city-wide neighborhood that Mrs. Jacobs suggested, they simply did not have the political power to play that role effectively. Nevertheless, it was to the CPD concept and structure that the Lindsay administration turned next in its attempts to increase the responsiveness of the superagencies to the demands of the citizens. In June 1970, it announced the Plan for Neighborhood Government (PNG).

<u>The Plan for Neighborhood Government</u>

In essence, PNG was a proposal to expand dramatically the powers of the Community Planning Boards in the CPDs. The boards would be enlarged and, instead of being chosen by the borough presidents, would now be appointed by a complicated system that would involve the mayor and several other elected officials.[1] The new Community Boards would carry out all the functions of the old Community (Planning) Boards, the Urban Action Task Forces, the Little City Halls, and several other neighborhood agencies. A community director for each CPD would be appointed by the mayor from a list of five names provided by the board. Once selected, a board was supposed to be responsive to the neighborhood that it served rather than the politicians who appointed it.

The Community Board was to meet regularly with line officers of the various superagencies to discuss problems of mutual concern. Furthermore, the community director would be given information on service levels in the district so he could set priorities, evaluate city services, and recommend future actions. Reports on agency performance in each CPD would be sent regularly to the mayor, the Board of Estimate, and the City Council. The Community Board would also hold hearings on capital budget projects affecting the community and make recommendations. Finally, the city would attempt to identify and publicize the allocation of agency expense budgets to neighborhoods. Together, these changes were expected to increase substantially a CPD's capability to state its case to a superagency and get action.

PNG also proposed to remedy a second problem of the existing CPD set-up; namely, the fact that no city agency organized its services along CPD boundary lines. Instead, the geographic divisions to which each agency delivered its services were the historic product of that agency's unique kind of service and particular clientele. Sanitation districts had been drawn primarily to equalize the tonnage of waste material that had to be removed; the location of welfare centers and the areas they covered reflected the concentrations of those receiving public assistance; school districts were drawn to equalize the number of pupils in each one and to take into account the location of junior and senior high school facilities. To the agencies, these various divisions were administratively logical. To a CPD, they could be an almost indecipherable tangle. Crown Heights (Brooklyn CPD #8), for example, encompassed two complete police precincts and parts of two others; was part of four different sanitation districts; and, although it was covered almost entirely by one school district, included small pieces of three others. (See Exhibit 3.) Consequently, for a CPD to elicit a response from one city agency might require that it deal with three or four geographic subdivisions of that agency. To elicit a coordinated response from two or three agencies could mean the involve-

---

[1]The mayor, the borough president, and the councilmen for the district, together with the councilmen-at-large, would each appoint seven members; the community school board(s) covering the district would appoint three members; any community corporation boards or model city advisory committees included within the boundaries of the CPD would appoint up to three members, in proportion to the total population of the district which they served.

ment of six or more such subdivisions. The Plan for Neighborhood Government recommended that all agency district lines be redrawn to conform as closely as possible to CPD boundaries.

To manage the development and implementation of PNG, the mayor established the Office of Neighborhood Government (ONG) and made Lew Feldstein its director. (Feldstein had been a mayoral assistant since the beginning of the Lindsay administration. He was a favorite of the mayor's, saw him frequently, and commanded his respect and support.) From the beginning, ONG tried to make it clear that the Plan for Neighborhood Government was only a proposal designed to provide a basis for discussion. The powers of the community boards, for example, had been left undefined deliberately. During the months that followed the announcement of PNG, ONG researchers interviewed hundreds of local groups and organizations to get their thoughts on neighborhood government. They found great support for the idea among the citizens but opinions on how it was to be achieved, how the boards were to be chosen, and what powers they should have were quite divided. There was also some skepticism about the probability that the Plan for Neighborhood Government would be any more successful than previous attempts at giving citizens a say in decision making. It had become clear that there was a cost in pushing for neighborhood government programs that failed to achieve real change or solve major problems. People whose hopes had been raised were embittered. And each attempt to give citizens a voice in decision making made City Hall more suspect to the unions and the civil service.

Another growing realization was that the problems that PNG was intended to solve went beyond questions of political power. At the bottom was the fact that few city agencies were organized in a way that would permit them easily and naturally to respond to the demands or wishes of a constituency defined by CPD boundaries. And this would be as true under PNG as it had always been. On one hand, PNG did propose that agency service boundaries be made coterminous with CPD lines and this would help; but it would be extremely difficult to implement if for no other reason than the existence of enormous amounts of capital facilities that were located to accommodate current agency districts. On the other hand, PNG planned to leave most other important aspects of agency operations unchanged.

This might be a workable approach for such agencies as police, fire, and sanitation where there were strong line organizations coming together at the top. But what about others, such as the Human Resources Administration, which were more like federations of semi-independent organizations, whose constituents were not geographically based, and whose internal structure simply did not reflect a neighborhood perspective for the delivery of their services? Continuing with HRA as an example, a typical welfare mother might come in regular or intermittent contact with several of that superagency's many branches. (See Exhibit 4.) She might be unaware that the services she was receiving were all part of HRA, and HRA, because of its structure, would not be coordinating delivery of the services nor consolidating their physical location. The woman would receive financial support through the efforts of the Income Maintenance activity at the nearest of the city's 44 welfare centers. Social services would originate with another group at the same center. One or more of her children might be attending a day care center operated by the agency's Child Development Staff. If an older child developed troubles in school or became a truant, both the mother and the child might deal with a caseworker from the Bureau of Child Welfare of the Children's Services Staff. Another Bureau of Child Welfare worker might be dealing with her in connection with her 15-year-old daughter who had run away from home and was now being cared for in a shelter. And then there was the 17-year-old son. A third Bureau of Child Welfare worker might be trying to coax him back to school because he had dropped out. But he may have decided to get a job and registered with the Regional Manpower Center Staff. An RMCS worker might be trying to get him into a training program and, later, a job. While he was waiting to get into the program, the boy might use one of the Youth Service Centers maintained by the Youth Services Staff, to work out, swim, play pool, and so forth; still another contact with an HRA agency. In total, this one family would be dealing with eight different branches of HRA, all in different locations, and all unaware that any of the others was involved. For each one, the lines of authority could be traced upwards from the caseworker until they reached the commissioner for that function. Not until the administrator's level did the pieces come together and, because HRA had not been given charter status by the City Council, he could only ask that his commissioners show some willingness to coordinate the activities of their agencies.

Another aspect of agency operations that PNG left unchanged was the highly centralized pattern of command. Most decisions affecting one agency's operations or its relationship with another agency had to go to the top of the chain of command, negotiations were carried out at the top, and the decisions came back down the chain. Thus, before an agency line officer at the CPD-level committed himself to a course of action, he had to clear it with his superiors downtown. If, for instance, the community wanted a park cleaned more often, but PRCA trucks could not haul away the rubbish more than once a week, a simple solution might be for the rubbish to be bagged and put outside the park to be picked up by a regular sanitation truck on its route. But before either the PRCA or the DS officer could agree to such a course of action, they each would have to consult with their respective superiors. Negotiations between the two organizations would take place downtown, the decision would be made downtown and would then wend its way down the chain of command to the line officers in the CPD.

Under these circumstances it was easy to understand why these line officers concentrated on pleasing their superiors rather than their neighborhoods or why their approach to other agencies was to avoid conflict rather than promote cooperative solutions to neighborhood problems. Besides, there were often substantial cultural differences between personnel in different agencies and between agency personnel and neighborhood residents. Feldstein described the kind of reaction that earlier neighborhood groups had faced when they succeeded in getting local line officers together and then suggested a common approach to the problems of service delivery:

> The chairman goes around and says, "Let's put on the table all the problems we have here and then let's try and figure out which problems we want to address." Well, after two minutes they've gone around the table. There were no problems in Brownsville. Every guy is covering up and is not about to air his own dirty linen in public and say, "I've got a problem with this." Nor is he going to point the finger at another agency and say, "You're screwing up," because they might come right back at him! So everyone says, "No problem," "No problem," "No problem." So two minutes later, here's this guy in Brownsville[1] and all the agency guys say, "We've got everything in hand!" It's just not the way the world operates. Somehow you've got to give them enough confidence so they're willing to start talking to one another. Right now, these guys can't even commit themselves to tie their shoes, let alone deal with a community problem.

This same centralized control of each agency's day-to-day operations was reflected in the process by which the city allocated its resources. Budgets for each agency were compiled at agency headquarters and allocations to the neighborhoods were controlled at the same level. There was no authority below the Bureau of the Budget and the mayor's office to shift resources from one superagency to another in the process of developing the city's annual budget. And even BoB and the mayor were constrained in their ability to do this by the fact that so much of the city's funds came from the federal and state governments and were earmarked for particular programs. Thus, current city procedures made it extremely difficult for tradeoffs to be made at the neighborhood level as between, say, greater expenditures for park maintenance, or increasing the number of weekly garbage collections. Nothing in the PNG proposal would change this impediment to CPD-decision making.

Feldstein summed up ONG's conclusions:

> Too often - in every instance - when the city has created a politically decentralized structure, we have not accompanied it with the necessary, detailed, tedious, very complex and very exact

---

[1] Brownsville is one of New York City's worst slum areas.

> staff work that allowed the city to change its own structure of delivery of services to be able to respond at the local level to this new political body we created out there. The result has always been a lot of frustration and bitterness and cynicism on the part of people who find themselves nominally on a board with certain responsibilities but no power to meet them, and they rail against the city as you expect them to.

Command Decentralization

During the spring of 1971, Lew Feldstein and the Office of Neighborhood Government came to the opinion that effective agency response at the CPD level would not be possible unless many of the decisions that affected and were affected by local conditions were made at the local level by the officers responsible for serving the community. The first step towards meaningful political decentralization (as envisaged by PNG) would have to be administrative or "command decentralization" - that is, an internal decentralization in each of the agencies and superagencies that would bring decision making down to the CPD level. This could be done by an in-house reorganization of the way line authorities functioned. Power would not have to shift out of the Department of Sanitation, for example, just vertically down from the top to the district line officers.

There were two good reasons for turning to command decentralization other than the fact that political decentralization could not work unless it was preceded by command decentralization. First, its implementation required no one's permission although union support would be a necessary prerequisite. Command decentralization was purely a management change. Since the mayor would relinquish none of his powers, no legislation or special referendum would be needed. In fact, Feldstein thought that people might criticize command decentralization because it did not delegate any power to the people. Effectively, all that would be done was to shift power from one hand to the other; from the commissioners to the district personnel.

The second reason why an emphasis on command decentralization made sense was that several of the superagencies themselves had concluded that they needed to decentralize in order to function more effectively. Police Commissioner Murphy had already given his precinct captains significant new decision-making powers. Each one was responsible, now, for discipline, assigning patrolmen to shifts and to plainclothes duty, and making a number of other operating decisions that had always been made at higher levels of command. Perhaps by coincidence, these changes had been made at a time when pressure for greater community control over the police was severe. Their success had relieved the pressure and suggested that command decentralization could accomplish some of the things the communities wanted and be far more palatable to the police than civilian control. In fact, most agency personnel believed that the delivery of better services to the communities was a much more important issue than local control.

Several other agencies were also considering, or actually undertaking, changes in the way they delivered their services. HRA was considering the creation of district offices headed by a district director. The Health Services Administration had begun to develop Comprehensive Health Planning Boards in each of its Health Planning Districts. The boards would be composed of members of the community (with a district manager appointed by HSA) and would be responsible for comprehensive health planning for the district. The actual command structure of HSA, however, was to remain unchanged. Finally, the Parks Recreation and Cultural Administration had appointed PRCA general foremen who would have increased decision-making powers and responsibilities which had not yet been defined.

The existence of these efforts meant that, if ONG decided to pursue a program of command decentralization, it would not be proposing something that was radically new. All that Feldstein and his staff would be asking of the superagencies would be that they orchestrate their activities - that is, concentrate on the same areas and use similar timetables. They could argue that it would maximize the effect and minimize the conflict if all the superagencies decentralized at once to the same level and in the same geographic area so that service integration could be truly accomplished.

The Command Decentralization Project

Early in 1971, ONG decided to ask the Department of Health, Education, and Welfare (HEW) for a renewable one-year grant of $350,000 to set up a series of pilot projects to test the feasibility of command decentralization. In his presentation, Feldstein noted the mayor's commitment to decentralization and referred to a number of the mechanisms whereby this commitment had been put into practice - Little City Halls, etc. Feldstein also noted, however, that these mechanisms had failed to address a number of significant problems - the inadequate impact of new programs on the operation of established service agencies, the centralized structure of the line agencies, the lack of coordination of services at the local level and the tendency to create mechanisms that could articulate community demands before creating effective administrative mechanisms to respond to those demands. The solution to these problems, Feldstein said, was to decentralize administratively first and only then to involve the citizens by means of a single, unified community board with formal policy, budgetary, and planning powers. But the first step was to decentralize the command structure of the agencies.

ONG's proposal stated that a number of city agencies - the Human Resources Administration (HRA), the Health Services Administration (HSA), the Housing and Development Administration (HDA), the Police Department, and the Department of Sanitation (DS) - were already involved in some form of decentralization of their own. But these efforts were being undertaken in isolation. To be effective, ONG thought, these efforts must be integrated at the local level since the problems that faced a community were interrelated. The proposal cited the example of the welfare recipient in need of housing, the drug addict facing the police, and the refuse in the streets that became a health hazard.

ONG proposed a pilot project, to be directed by the Office of Neighborhood Government, that would try to implement command decentralization in New York City. The project would encompass a limited number of districts but would create a model that was applicable city-wide. The basic unit for decentralization would be the CPDs. In order not to spread the effort too thin, the number of superagencies participating in the project would be limited to those offering the most critical services.

Not only would the number of districts and the number of agencies be limited, so would the changes. The impact of each step would be carefully controlled to ease the transition. There would be no attempt to accomplish full decentralization all at once. ONG was interested in transferring to the CPD level some authority over normal operating matters, special projects, community relations, planning and budgeting, performance measurement, personnel management, and interagency liaison. Although the extent of the delegations would be left to the administrators of the superagencies, and the delegations might be unofficial, explicit commitments would be made to ONG at the outset so there would be no misunderstandings about the extent of the delegations.

The local organization, Feldstein told HEW, would consist of a neighborhood manager presiding over a community cabinet composed of the senior district officers of each of the agencies to be decentralized. The manager would give full-time support to the cabinet and serve as an integrator who would focus attention on priority problems. He would also supervise a small, local staff from the city's overhead agencies - Bureau of the Budget, City Planning Commission and Corporation Counsel. These people would provide technical expertise for the cabinet and the neighborhood manager.

As with the Plan for Neighborhood Government, the command decentralization project envisaged redrawing service district lines to achieve co-terminality with CPD boundaries. While redrawing the lines would be difficult, ONG thought, if the project was to succeed, it had to be done.

The neighborhood manager and the community cabinet would be given all available information on resources assigned and actually available in the district, expense and capital budget breakouts for the district, service complaint analyses, and the status of on-going local projects with completion dates and milestones. This would mean developing, in association with the agencies and superagencies, a common information system that would bring together both the needs and the resources identified by each agency and superagency.

Lastly, the command decentralization project proposed that in the 1972-1973 budget cycle, the cabinets would make recommendations on what they felt to be the highest priority items in their districts. The budget, ONG believed, was a key policy making tool in city government, and as such must eventually be subject to citizen input. This input would take time to establish but giving local agency officials a voice was a logical first step. (At the present time, the city prepared a capital budget identifying the projects proposed or underway for each CPD. However, it did not identify any CPD's share of the expense budget or of large lump sum capital items such as park maintenance or highway strip paving. In the future, it was hoped that a budget could be assembled that identified the dollar value of all services going into a CPD. Because very few agencies gathered their data on a CPD basis, and because the dollar value of the overhead services used by a CPD were difficult to measure, this, too, would take time.)

The final step, after the value of command decentralization had been proved and it had been implemented in all 62 CPDs would be to take the program one step further and create the Community Boards proposed by the Plan for Neighborhood Government. This would permit citizens to exercise control over their neighborhood manager and the operation of his cabinet. The powers of the board would be defined at a later date.

The project, therefore, consisted of eight stages, some to be undertaken sequentially, others in parallel:

1. District selection
2. Redistricting
3. Delegation of powers
4. Appointment of neighborhood managers and community cabinets
5. Assignment of overhead staff
6. Compilation of information
7. Preparation of neighborhood budgets
8. Creation of representative Community Boards of local citizens

In February 1971, ONG sent copies of the HEW proposal to the superagencies and asked for their comments. Between February and April, Feldstein and other members of the ONG staff gave a series of briefings to commissioners and administrators to explain what command decentralization meant. Reaction was either skeptical or apathetic. Feldstein said:

> That was probably indicative of the fact that no one really took us that seriously. And also because people in this city have lived through so much talk about decentralization that this was just one more plan. "Here comes Feldstein from the mayor's office again with another one of those plans of theirs. Sure, we'll be very polite to them, Lew's a good guy. Let's talk it out with him. But nothing's going to happen with this. It's too difficult, or if someone is _really_ serious about this, I'll get a call from the mayor or the deputy mayor telling me to _do_ it."

Most of the officials agreed to participate, however, and, in April, ONG submitted its proposal to Washington.

As transmitted to HEW, the proposal left many questions unanswered, many issues unresolved. There was, first, the question of boundary lines. If service integration was to succeed and if information was to be useful to the neighborhood manager, the service districts would have to be redrawn so that they at least approximated CPD lines. At first glance this seemed fairly easy since the service districts were either approximately the same size or twice the size of CPDs. There were 78 police precincts, 58 sanitation districts, 60 parks districts, 31 school districts and 31 health planning districts. However, as pointed out earlier, redrawing lines would create considerable problems for the agencies and superagencies. ONG had to find a way to make the changes as painless as possible and find a way to persuade the reluctant commissioners, administrators, and other key people to go along.

Second, ONG had to decide how many CPDs and how many agencies and superagencies to involve in the pilot project. There ought to be few enough of both to make the project viable and yet enough to make it valid. A decision also had to be made as to the kinds of CPDs to choose. Rich or poor? Black or White?

Third, there was the question of the neighborhood managers and the community cabinet. What sort of people ought the neighborhood managers to be? What kind of experience should they have? How old should they be? What powers should or could they be given? What criteria should or could be used to select the officers from the agencies to serve on community cabinets? Should they receive special training for their new roles or learn on the job? How could they be made responsive to the neighborhood manager?

Fourth, there was the issue of citizen involvement. While it might be best if local residents were not consulted until there was enough decision making power at the local level to make the cabinet responsive, it might be difficult to avoid citizen involvement once it became clear what was happening. That being the case, would it be better to prepare for involvement? How much involvement should be allowed and how should it be managed?

Fifth, how was ONG to persuade everyone to adopt a common information system? And even after one was developed, how would it measure the input and output of services to the neighborhoods? Who should have access to the information?

Sixth, there was the question of getting the cooperation of the superagencies. How was ONG to persuade the commissioners and administrators that participation was to their advantage? What arguments could he use to convince them to follow his lead on command decentralization rather than do it alone or not do it at all? So far, Feldstein had emphasized that he was asking them to cooperate rather than telling them. As a senior member of the mayor's office, however, he could involve the mayor and have the mayor or deputy mayor do the talking. Should he? And if so, when?

Finally, there was the problem of funding the effort on a continuing basis. If the pilot project was successful, could it be expanded city-wide without continued federal support? Or could ONG expect that the city, itself, would be willing to carry on the initial effort with its own funds once sufficient momentum had been built?

These were all questions that were running through Feldstein's mind. If he received HEW funding, most of them were questions that he would have to answer before the pilot project could get underway and the rest would come up and have to be dealt with during the course of the project. How he dealt with them would have much to do with the success or failure of the program for command decentralization.

Exhibit 1

COMMAND DECENTRALIZATION (A)

THE GOVERNMENT OF THE CITY OF NEW YORK

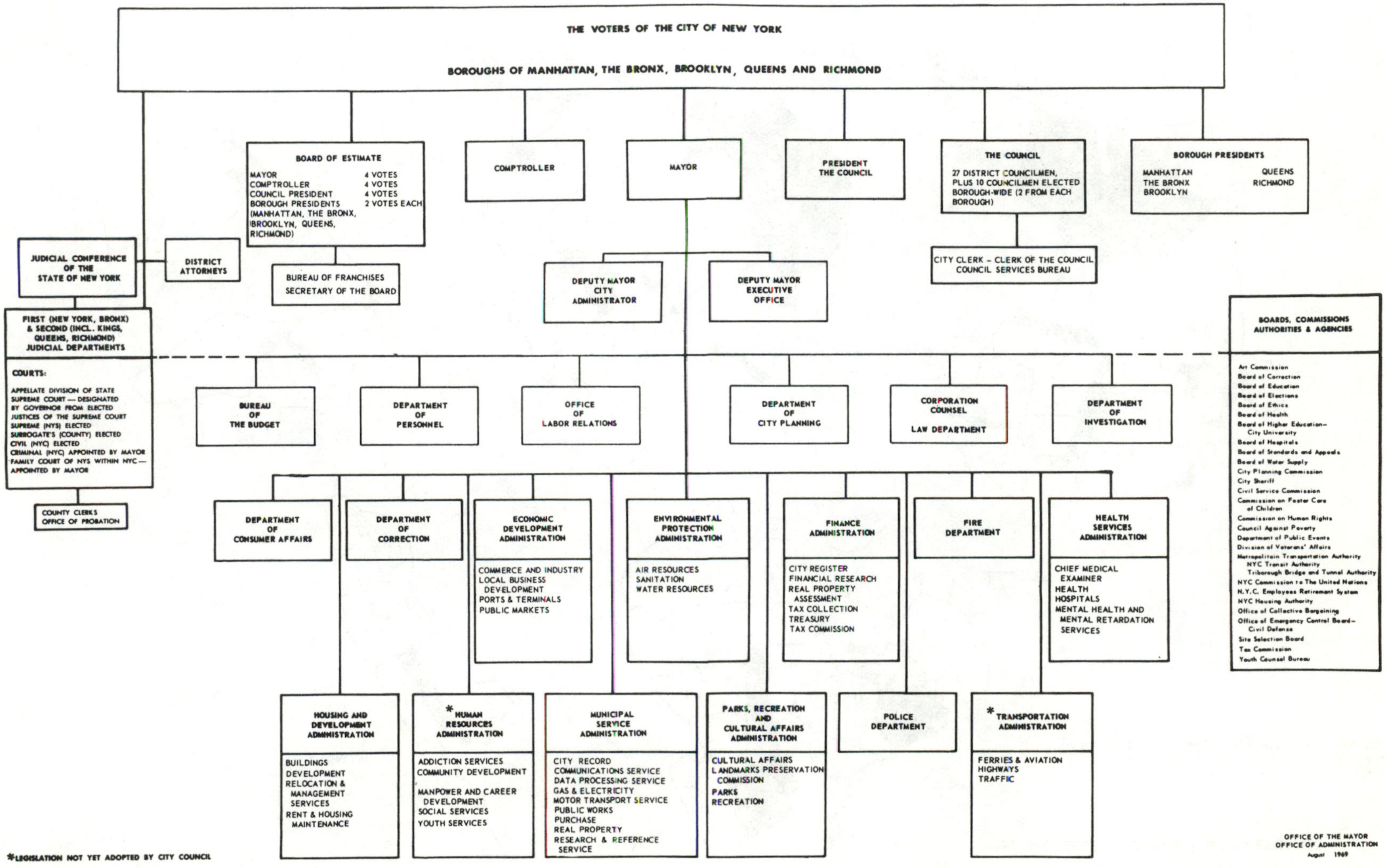

Exhibit 2

COMMAND DECENTRALIZATION (A)

New York City's Community Planning Districts

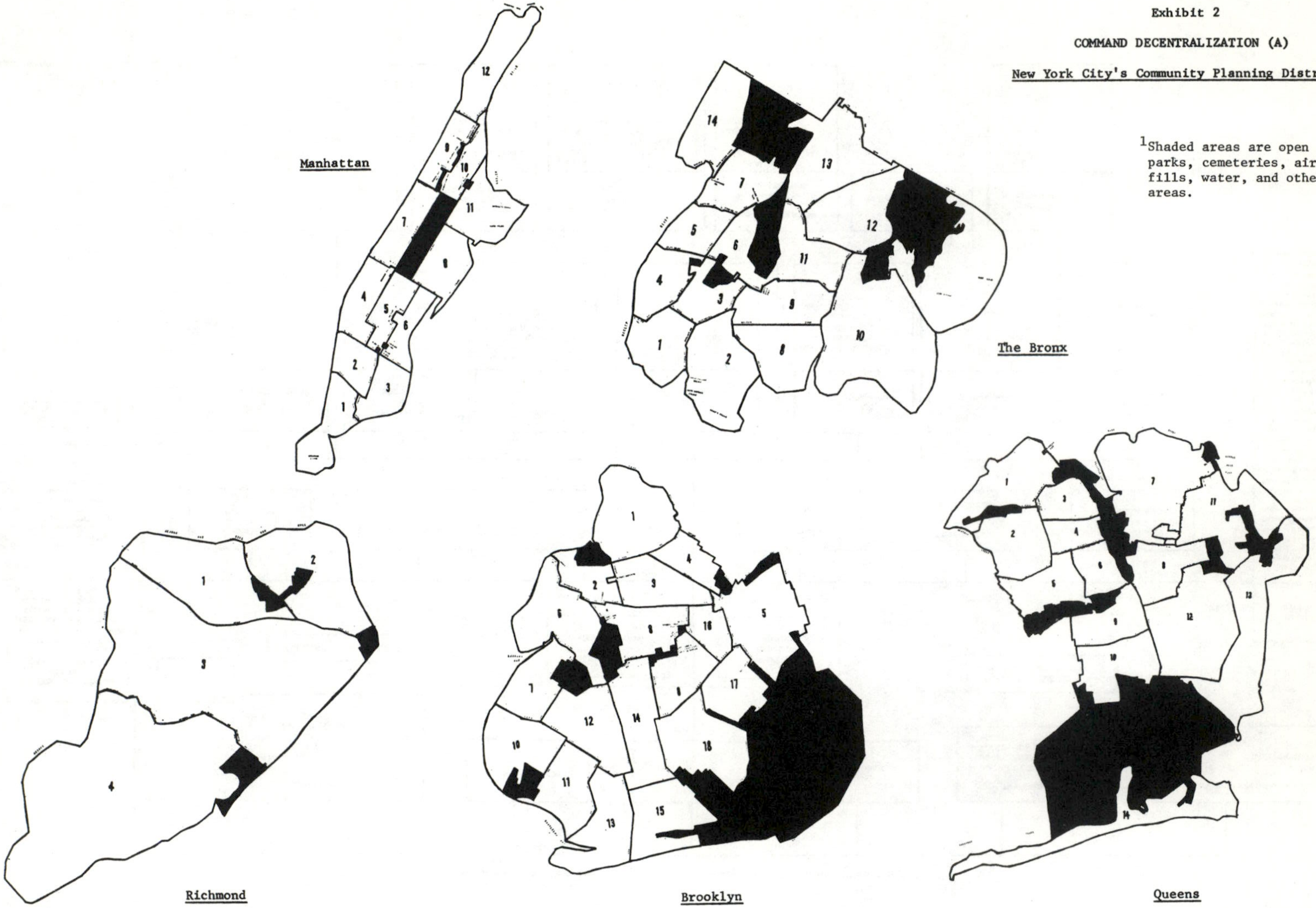

[1]Shaded areas are open spaces such as parks, cemeteries, air fields, land fills, water, and other uninhabited areas.

Exhibit 3

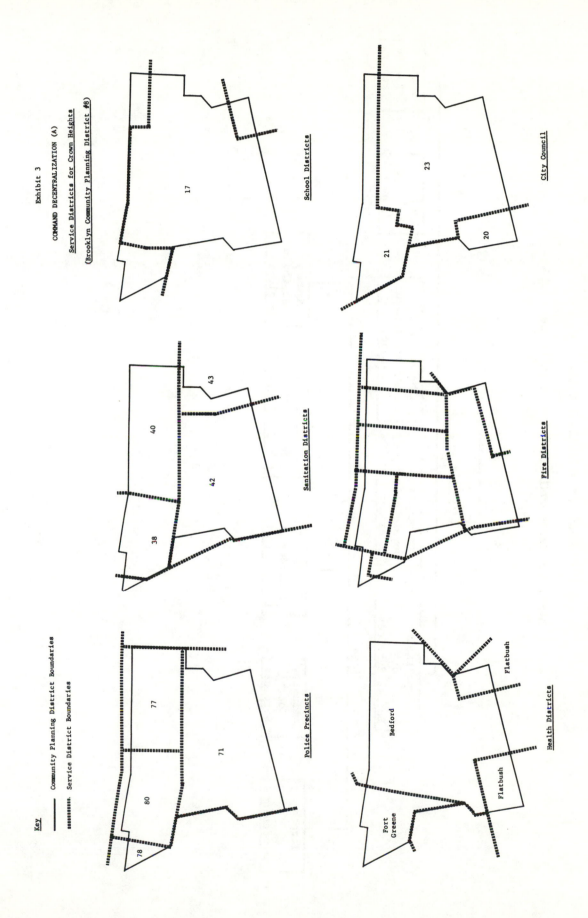

COMMAND DECENTRALIZATION (A)

Service Districts for Crown Heights

(Brooklyn Community Planning District #8)

Key

———— Community Planning District Boundaries

▪▪▪▪▪▪▪▪▪ Service District Boundaries

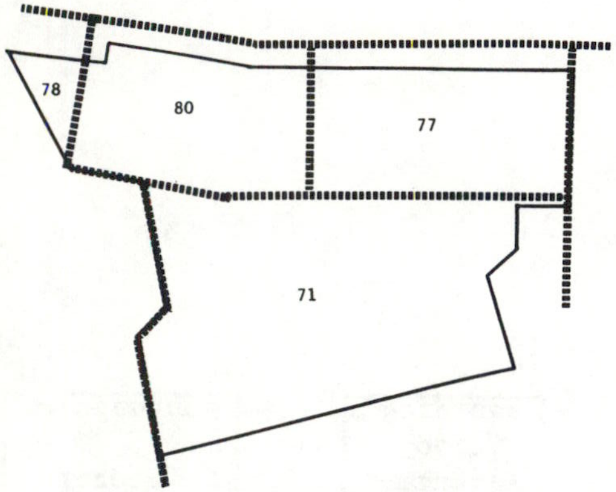

Police Precincts

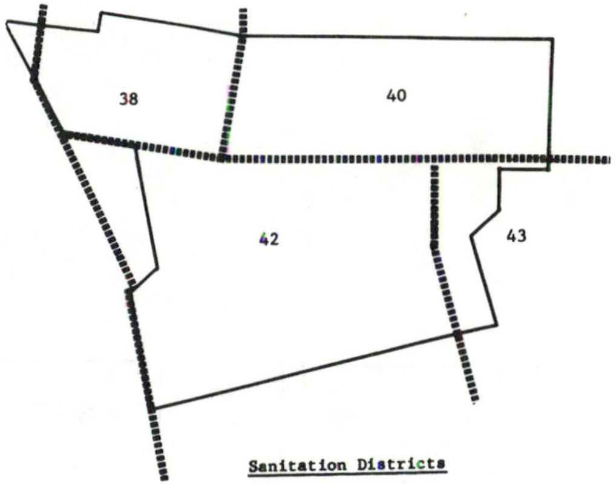

Sanitation Districts

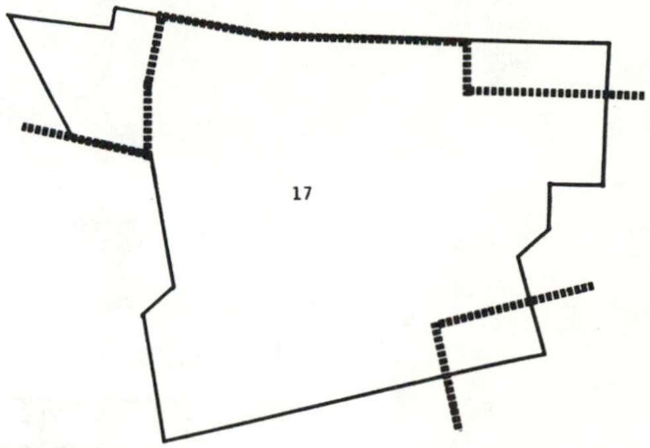

School Districts

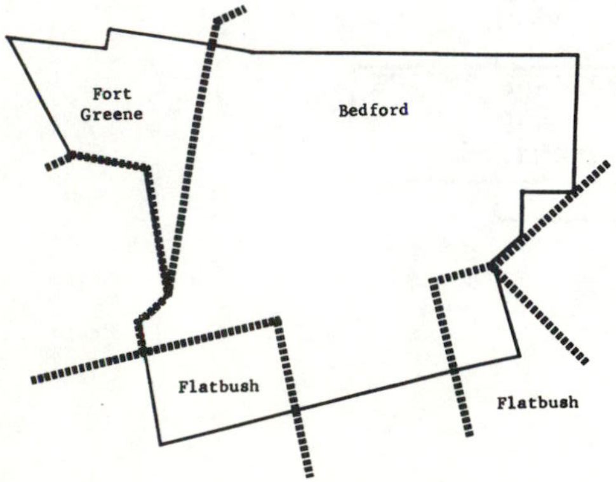

Health Districts

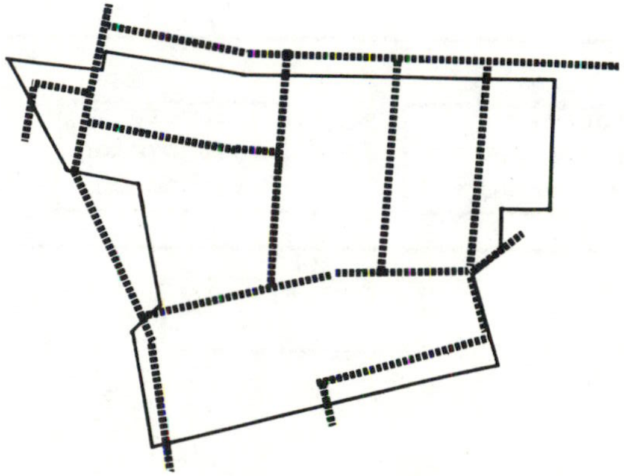

Fire Districts

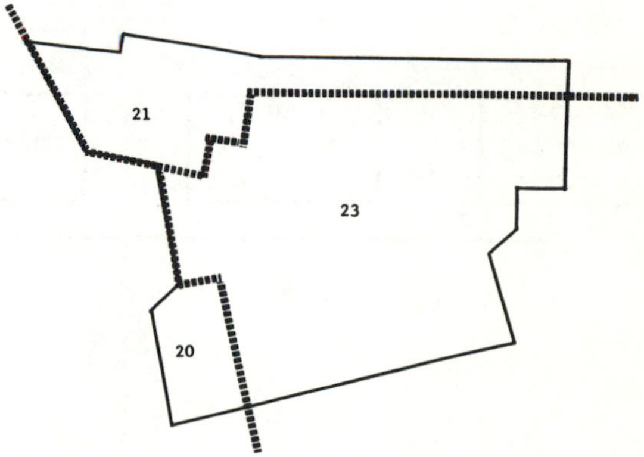

City Council

Exhibit 4

COMMAND DECENTRALIZATION (A)

HUMAN RESOURCES ADMINISTRATION ORGANIZATION

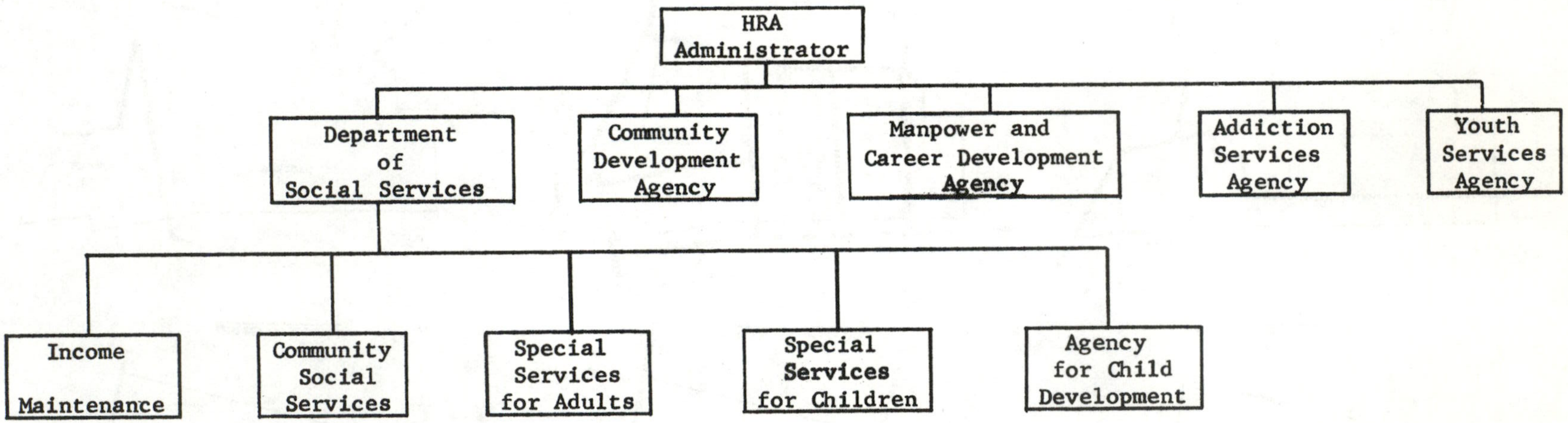

Appendix A

COMMAND DECENTRALIZATION (A)

A Guide to Acronyms used in the Case

ACD	Agency for Child Development, part of HRA
ASA	Addiction Services Agency, part of HRA
BCC	Bureau of Cleaning and Collection, a part of the Department of Sanitation and therefore of EPA
BOB	Bureau of the Budget
CDA	Community Development Agency, part of HRA
CPD	Community Planning District
CSS	Community Social Services, part of HRA (not yet operative)
DAR	Department of Air Resources, part of EPA
DS	Department of Sanitation, part of EPA
DSS	Department of Social Services, the largest part of HRA
DWR	Department of Water Resources, part of EPA
EPA	Environmental Protection Administration
HDA	Housing and Development Administration
HEW	Department of Health Education and Welfare, U.S. Government
HHC	Health and Hospitals Corporation
HRA	Human Resources Administration
HSA	Health Services Administration
IM	Income Maintenance, part of HRA
MCDA	Manpower and Career Development Agency, part of HRA
OEO	Office of Economic Opportunity
ONG	Office of Neighborhood Government
PNG	Plan for Neighborhood Government

Appendix A (continued)

PRCA	Parks, Recreation, and Cultural Affairs Administration
SSA	Special Services for Adults, part of HRA
SSC	Special Services for Children, part of HRA
YSA	Youth Services Agency, part of HRA

Appendix B

COMMAND DECENTRALIZATION (A)

Brief Description of Nine Superagencies and the Human Resources Administration*

Economic Development Administration - Performs all those functions relating to

(a) promotion and study of the city's economic development;

(b) studies of labor conditions and voluntary settlements of private labor/management disputes;

(c) construction, operation and maintenance of city-owned wharves and waterfront property and regulation of other waterfront property;

(d) development and regulation of public markets; and

(e) protection of consumers including enforcement of weights and measures laws and issuance and cancellation of licenses.

Environmental Protection Administration (EPA) - Draws together all functions relating to sanitation, sewage disposal, air and water pollution, and water supply. It is organized into the Department of Sanitation (DS), the Department of Air Resources (DAR) and the Department of Water Resources (DWR).

Finance Administration - Performs all the functions dealing with collection, receipt, handling and disbursement of city monies and administration and collection of taxes.

Municipal Services Administration (MSA) - Responsible for all the housekeeping functions of other superagencies. It combines Public Buildings Service, Real Estate and Property Management Service, Supply Service, Motor Equipment Services, Data Processing Service, Records Management Service, Communications Service, Engineering Services and Gas and Electric Utilities. These functions are drawn from a large number of old agencies.

Health Services Administration (HSA) - Consolidates the old Departments of Health and Hospitals, the Community Mental Health Board and the Office of Chief Medical Examiner. The Department of Hospitals became the Health and Hospitals Corporation in 1969.

Housing and Development Administration (HDA) - Carries out all the activities previously performed by the Housing and Redevelopment Board, the Department of Relocation, the Rent and Rehabilitation Administration and those functions of the Department of Real Estate which relate to property acquired or to be used for development purposes. This superagency is responsible for urban renewal and the development of adequate housing in New York.

---

*See case Exhibit 1.

Parks, Recreation, and Cultural Affairs Administration (PRCA) - As the title suggests, PRCA is responsible for the recreational activities of the city. This includes parks, libraries, museums and other cultural institutions owned and operated by the city as well as playgrounds and other recreational facilities. It also includes the Landmark Preservation Commission.

Transportation Administration (TA) - This superagency is responsible for:

(a) traffic regulation and enforcement;

(b) construction and maintenance of the city's streets, highways, parkways, bridges and tunnels, previously split up between the departments of Highways, Parks and Public Works;

(c) construction, operation and maintenance of the city's ferryboats, ferry-houses, and related property, previously in the Department of Marine and Aviation; and

(d) construction, operation, and maintenance of city-owned airports and heliports and regulation of such privately-owned facilities.

Not included are the functions of a number of state authorities; the Long Island Railroad (operated by the Metropolitan Commuter Transportation Authority); P.A.T.H. and the Hudson River vehicular crossings (operated by the Port of the New York Authority); all but four of the other major vehicular crossings in the city (operated by the Triborough Bridge and Tunnel Authority); and the city's public transportation system (operated by the Metropolitan Transportation Authority.)

Human Resources Administration (HRA) - This Administration exists only by Executive Order. As an unchartered Administration the HRA has no real coordinating power. The Administrator has no authority in his role as Administrator but he draws power from his second role, that of Commissioner of the Department of Social Services (DSS) which constitutes some 70% of HRA. All Commissioners report directly to the Mayor.

HRA is responsible for all those functions of the city relating to elimination of poverty and creation of economic and job opportunities, providing social services, public assistance, and youth counseling, and the development of related educational opportunities.

HRA is organized into nine line departments and a number of staff departments. (An HRA organization chart is shown in Exhibit 4.) Income Maintenance handles all matters regarding the delivery of financial support to public assistance recipients. Community Social Services (CSS) (not yet operative as of the summer 1971) is designed to provide a contact point in the neighborhoods where those in need can seek out various social services such as homemaking assistance, family counseling, and so forth. In some cases, CSS will provide the service; in others it will refer the client to another agency. Special Services for Adults (SSA) is the department responsible for senior citizens, and shelters for adults and alcoholics. Special Services for Children (SSC) is primarily the

Bureau of Child Welfare which is responsible for children having trouble in school, dropouts, truants, adopted children, foster children, and runaways. It also manages orphanages and homes for runaways. The Agency for Child Development (ACD) is responsible for the Headstart and Day Care programs. ACD contracts these programs to private agencies. The five line departments described so far constitute the Department of Social Services (DSS). The other HRA agencies are:

Community Development Agency (CDA): The CDA, together with the Council Against Poverty (CAP), was responsible for administering the city's antipoverty programs, most of which were funded through HEW-OEO. CAP was a 51-member council appointed by the mayor to set policy for the administration, coordination, and funding of community action programs. Its members were composed of a representative from each of the city's 26 designated poverty areas, nine from the private sector, and eleven public officials. CDA carried out the policies of CAP in coordinating existing community action programs; it also developed and administered its own community programs independent of CAP.

Outside of CDA, the functional units for administering programs in the community were the community corporations which served CAP, CDA, and the community by analyzing community needs, evaluating existing and proposed programs, and presenting new programs to CAP. Under contract to MCDA, each corporation operated a neighborhood manpower service center to provide recruitment, referrals, training, and job placement. Community corporations also fund a large number of independent agencies in the communities to implement approved programs.

Manpower and Career Development Agency (MCDA): The primary concern of the Manpower and Career Development Agency was to develop the job capabilities of New York City residents who were without skills or underemployed. Through its field operating unit, the Regional Manpower System and contracts with outside vendors, MCDA provided job training, education, work experience, and job placement for an estimated 25,000 people annually. In the past MCDA programs have been oriented toward increasing the employability of females. In fiscal year 1971, however, MCDA programs were being expanded to encompass a target population of males in the 17-35 age range, especially fathers of children on welfare.

Addiction Services Agency (ASA): ASA was responsible for channeling funds from both public and private sources to the various drug treatment programs in the city. It was also in charge of a major educational program designed to curtail the spread of addiction and to help neighborhoods deal with their addiction problems. Finally, it operated a small number of experimental drug treatment programs.

Youth Services Agency (YSA): The Youth Services Agency was the official agency concerned with youth and their development in New York City. It was placed under the jurisdiction of the HRA in August 1966, becoming a full-fledged HRA agency a little over a year later. YSA's target population was young people between the ages of 11 and 21. For these young people YSA provided a variety of services: On-the-job training and employment placement, counselling, family case work, college preparation, and recreation. In 1970 YSA worked with over 250,000 youth.

Agency for Child Development (ACD): The Agency for Child Development was formed in January 1971. By July 1971, it was expected to carry out the administration, funding and coordination for all day care and Head Start programs previously under the jurisdiction of the Department of Social Services and the Community Development Agency. In addition, ACD was to assume the licensing function for all public and private day care services in the city; and to work with a city-wide policy commission to help community groups lay the groundwork for permanent child-care facilities.

Appendix C

COMMAND DECENTRALIZATION (A)

Descriptions of Five Community Planning Districts

Wakefield Edenweld (Bronx CPD #13)

First settled in 1673, Wakefield Edenweld is one of the oldest parts of the Bronx. Parts of it figured prominently in the Revolutionary War. For two months, in 1797 a house in the district was the nation's executive mansion when John Adams moved there to escape a yellow fever epidemic in Philadelphia. Today, it is chiefly a middle income area (the 1960 median income was about $6,000) of middle density. It became primarily residential with the heavy influx of immigrants around the turn of the century. The Irish and the Jews, the first groups to settle in large groups have been replaced by Italian-Americans except in one area where Jewish families are still numerous. In the last 20 years, many Black and Puerto Rican families have moved there. By 1960, they constituted about 14% of the population of 113,361. By 1969, these figures had increased to 27% and 123,000 respectively.

Housing ranges from one-family houses on tree-lined streets to large apartment complexes. Two-thirds of the 35,400 housing units in 1960 were owner occupied and 4,500 were public owned or assisted. Most one-family homes have backyards and most of the housing in the district is sound. One area has been designated a preventive renewal area. The city is considering rezoning an area along a now unused highway for residential and local commercial development. Before the New England Thruway opened, the Boston Road (the district's eastern boundary) was the city's major truck and auto route to New England. Commercial development along the road is dominated by gas stations which are now marginal. There is little other industry in the district.

The district's public schools are among the finest in the Bronx. Most primary schools have unused space, although several lack auditoriums, gyms and cafeterias. Parks and playgrounds are scattered throughout the CPD and facilities are good. Outstanding facilities are available in three nearby parks. Shopping and transportation are adequate and health facilities, while sparse within the district itself, are easily available since there are a number of large hospitals located nearby.

Washington Heights (Manhattan CPD #12)

This CPD includes almost all of Manhattan north of 155th Street as well as a small piece of the Bronx on the North Shore of the Harlem river. Surrounded by water on three sides, it is ringed by hundreds of acres of some of the most beautiful parkland in the city. Much of this green-belt is, however, inaccessible to the community, cut off as it is by railroad tracks and highways.

The district's name reflects both its history and its topography. George Washington established several forts in the area and for a brief time during the Revolution, a mansion in the area served as his headquarters. Throughout the 18th and 19th centuries, Washington Heights was the country preserve of the rich, and it was 1906 before any regular settlement of the area began. The housing in the district reflects the fact that residential development took place in waves moving from south to north. Early New Law tenements sprang up in the southeastern part of the CPD and attracted many Irish families. A second building boom took place in the 1920s when large walk-ups and elevator buildings were built on the southwestern part of the CPD. The rest of the CPD was built up after 1932. Most of the one-family homes in the CPD were built during this period. Although the housing is generally sound and there are many attractive apartments to be found, a general shabbiness has crept over the area and in some places the deterioration is severe. The whole district has been designated a preventive renewal area. Of the 73,391 occupied housing units in 1960, 71,990 were rented (2,849 were publicly owned). Of the 1,401 owner-occupied housing units, 205 were publicly assisted.

Washington Heights has always attracted moderate income families (median 1960 income was about $5,000), usually families moving up the ladder from poorer parts of the city. In the years before World War I, the more successful married offspring of Eastern European and Irish parents moved in from lower Manhattan. Post-war settlers were second generation Eastern European Jews. They were followed in the 1930s and 1940s by large numbers of Jews from Germany and Western Europe. The total population has declined since World II and Blacks and Puerto Ricans have moved in as the Whites moved out. Today Puerto Ricans are the fastest growing single group among the newcomers. Between 1950 and 1960, the population declined from 206,859 to 199,357. The estimated 1969 population was 190,000. In 1960 the population was 82.9% White, 10.9% Black and 6.2% Puerto Rican. In 1969 the ethnic composition was estimated at 74.5% White, 10% Black and 15.5% Spanish-speaking.

School facilities in the CPD are adequate. In 1960, 9,400 students one-third of the total school enrollment, were attending parochial schools. The financial problems of these institutions along with the increase in the school population might worsen the school situation drastically. At present, the elementary schools are slightly underutilized, the middle schools are slightly overcrowded, and the one high school is very overcrowded. The health facilities of the district are excellent since Washington Heights is where the huge Columbia-Presbyterian Medical Center is located. Shopping facilities, transportation, libraries and museums are more than adequate and, although there could be more, there are 530 acres of accessible parks. This includes four major parks, one of which, Fort Tryon Park, is the site of the Cloisters which houses the priceless medieval art collection of the Metropolitan Museum.

Buskwick (Brooklyn CPD #4)

As recently as the 1940s, Bushwick was an attractive middle income suburb. It is now deteriorating rapidly and could soon become a slum. Settled by the Dutch in 1660, Bushwick was originally an agricultural community whose farms and tobacco plantations produced for the New York market. It was heavily wooded; in fact, its name is derived from the Dutch word, "Boswijk," meaning "Town of Woods." Bushwick was incorporated into Brooklyn only two years before Brooklyn was incoroprated into New York.

The original Dutch settlers were followed by German and Austrian immigrants who arrived in the middle of the 19th century when the area was being developed. Eventually, the German population was joined by a few English, Irish, Russian and Polish settlers, some of them Jewish. In the decade following the depression, large numbers of Italians, generally lower middle income workers, moved in and many middle income Germans moved out. By 1950 Bushwick was the second largest Italian-American community in Brooklyn. Over the last 20 years the ethnic composition of Bushwick has changed from almost entirely White to predominantly Black and Puerto Rican. There has been very little interchange between the two groups. The Whites live in the northern part of the CPD, the Blacks and Puerto Ricans live in the southern part. With the sudden influx of low income groups, the median income has dropped drastically so that in 1966 the area was designated a poverty area, and in 1967 more than half the population had an income below $4,000 and more than 20% were on welfare.

Bushwick's population has increased dramatically over the past ten years. In 1960, it was 124,800. A survey made by the Bushwick Neighborhood Community Council in 1967 showed a rise of at least two-thirds. Although the children of many of the old Italian families have moved out, they have been more than replaced by young Italian and Yugoslav immigrants.

Additional problems are created by friction between Blacks, Puerto Ricans and Italians, the three largest ethnic groups; pronounced language barriers; and an unemployment rate, estimated to be as high as 35%. Industry in the CPD is minimal with the exception of several breweries in the western section.

The housing in Bushwick is old, crowded and rundown. Of the 40,778 occupied units in 1960, 33,339 were rented and 7,439 were owner-occupied. There was no public housing although some is planned. Forty-five per cent of the homes were built before 1900 and 95% before 1920. Except for a few in the northwest corner the newest homes are almost 50 years old. At least one-fourth of the CPD's housing is deteriorated or dilapidated and the deterioration continues steadily. The majority of the buildings are frame structures particularly in the southern half. In the northern half, where the Whites live, masonry structures predominate, most of the homes are owner-occupied and are well maintained. The most common residence in the CPD is a three-story or four-story walk-up. Frequent fires are a problem; in 1968 there were 2,200, of which 932 caused structural damage. They add to the impression of general decay because absentee landlords, lacking the resources to rebuild, leave the burned-out and debris-filled lots untouched.

Health services are inadequate because of the rapid growth in the population and the closing of several hospitals in the last 15 years. Public school enrollment is predominantly Black and Puerto Rican because most White residents send their children to parochial schools. The schools are extremely overcrowded, with average enrollment more than 25% above capacity. The one high school is 66% overutilized. About 400 high school students drop out each year.

Recreation opportunities are poor for both children and adults. In the southern part of the CPD there are almost no parks. Throughout the area, parks lack modern equipment and supervised activities. Most organized social life is sponsored by the Catholic churches. Shopping facilities are limited to several small stores. There is no major shopping district in the CPD. A 1967 survey indicated that 80% of the residents did their shopping, except for food, outside the district. Fortunately, public transportation is generally good, although the elevated subway lines are eyesores that discourage the development and maintenance of adjoining property.

Crown Heights (Brooklyn CPD #8)

This district lies between the ghetto areas of Bedford Stuyvesant and Brownsville and the White middle class sections of Flatbush. Crown Heights was a wooded section once and, between 1820 and 1870, it was the home of the first free Black community in Central Brooklyn. The community, known as Weeksville, was a relatively prosperous one. As the surrounding area developed towards the turn of the 19th century, Whites moved into the neighborhood and Weeksville lost its identity. Most of the Blacks left. A large number of doctors settled in the district because of its proximity to the Kings County-Brooklyn State Hospital complex. The CPD's development in the early part of this century was largely the work of its Jewish population. A move to Crown Heights was a substantial step upward for the Jews. Smaller numbers of Italian, Irish, German and Scandinavian families also moved into the neighborhood and by 1916 the area boasted some of Brooklyn's finest homes. In 1912, the Brooklyn Dodgers moved to Crown Heights where Ebbett's Field had been build. The Dodgers moved to Los Angeles in 1956 and today an immense high rise building stands on the site of the baseball diamond. After 1920, Crown Heights' fortunes gradually declined until the 1950s when it was described as a lower middle income area.

After World War II, middle income Blacks seeking to move upward moved into the northeast corner of the CPD, known as Children's Museum (so named because of the location there of the world's first natural science museum especially for children). Among the first to arrive were Blacks of West Indian origin. Between 1950 and 1960 the Black population in the Children's Museum area increased from one-third to two-thirds of the population.

During this period, there was trouble in the form of gang fights, racial tensions and growing blight. The remainder of the CPD was largely White.

The population shift has continued. In 1960, the population of 214,000 was about two-thirds White and one-third Black with approximately 2% Puerto Rican. A 1969 estimate listed three-fifths of the population of 225,000 as Black with about 4% Puerto Rican and the remainder White. The shift has created tensions. As Whites moved out and Blacks moved in, rents went up and maintenance was neglected. The crime rate increased and in 1964 a group of Hasidic rabbis and other White residents banded together to form an unarmed vigilante group called the Maccabees, to supplement and later to aid the police. Initially, this group created even greater racial tension because the Blacks believed the organization was aimed at them. The misconception was later rectified and the group ultimately took in Blacks. The Maccabees remained active until 1966 when conditions improved and it was disbanded.

Housing in the CPD ranges from single-family dwellings to high-rise apartments. Apart from some Old Law tenements and old frame buildings, the housing is basically sound although in need of rehabilitation. The whole district is designated a preventive renewal area. Of the 72,022 occupied housing units in 1960, 63,379 were rented (2,299 were public housing units). Of 9,634 owner-occupied units, 448 were publicly assisted. By 1970, the number of public housing units had increased to 2,713 and 1,463 more families were renting apartments with public aid.

Educational facilities in the CPD are adequate though somewhat overcrowded at the elementary and intermediate levels. The Health facilities are excellent with eight private hospitals and several nursing homes serving the area and the large complex of Kings County Hospital, Brooklyn State Hospital and the Downstate Medical Center located on the southern boundary. Industry is generally limited to the northern boundary. The public transportation system is good and shopping areas are more than adequate. Sufficient recreational and cultural facilities are available although neighborhood park space is scarce around the Children's Museum.

<u>College Point, Whitestone, Flushing (Queens CPD #7)</u>

This CPD is composed of three rather definite communities, two of which have subareas of their own that operate as communities. College Point is the only major area with a sense of community in historic and civic terms. It is the smallest of the three constituent areas with a 1960 population of 16,000, 9% of the population of the CPD. It is almost 100% White. Whitestone, with a population in 1960 of 59,000 (33% of the CPD) has a splintered community identity. The area has seven smaller enclaves each with a relatively common community identification. It is 99.5% White, the rest being Black. Flushing has a population of 105,000, 58% of the 1960 population of 180,000. It, too, has a splintered community identity with many smaller enclaves, some with a common identification and some without. It is 97% White but there are pockets where the Black population is much higher. The Mitchell-Linden area is 7% Black and the Flushing-James Bland Housing Project is 36% Black. In 1960, there were 2,700 Blacks in the CPD.

The district appears to be a major settling place for Whites. While New York City as a whole was expected to lose 1.1 million Whites between 1960 and 1970, Queens County was expected to gain 34,000 Whites of whom 32,000 would settle in CPD 7. As a result, the population was estimated to be 210,000 in 1970 and the newcomers were overwhelmingly White. The non-White population was expected to rise 77% between 1960 and 1970 to 8,500 or 4% of the total population of the CPD.

CPD 7 has the highest median income of any CPD in the city. The 1960 median income in College Point was $7,785; Whitestone's was $7,782, and Flushing's was $6,628. There are pockets of poverty where the non-White population lives. The 1960 median family income of Mitchell-Linden was $3,414 and the Flushing-James Island Project median income was $3,093. Approximately 1% of the CPD was on welfare compared to 9% city-wide.

Perhaps because of the relative affluence of the area, the rate of new housing construction is high as is the proportion of owner-occupied dwellings. The number of units increased 15,245 or 28% from 56,228 in 1960 to an estimated 71,473 in 1968. In 1960, approximately 30,000 dwellings (53%) were owner-occupied and 26,000 (47%) were rented. By comparison, the percentage of owner-occupied dwellings is 41% in Queens and 22% city-wide. Of the owner-occupied homes 29,600 (99%) were owned by Whites.

The CPD is much less densely populated than the average for New York. There are 35.2 persons per acre in CPD 7 as compared to 54.9 persons city-wide. The CPD has 41 different recreation areas of all types and 2,091 acres of open area.

COMMAND DECENTRALIZATION (B)

In October 1971, Lew Feldstein, Director of New York City's Office of Neighborhood Government (ONG), was trying to decide how next to proceed with the command decentralization project. As described in Command Decentralization (A), ONG had sent a proposal (in April 1971) to the U.S. Department of Health, Education, and Welfare (HEW) requesting funds to set up a pilot project to test the feasibility of command decentralization. The proposal noted that previous attempts at decentralizing the city's operations had aimed at giving local political organizations a larger voice in decision making, but that they had fallen short because authority within the operating agencies was too centralized to permit effective response to local demands. The new proposal, while it would keep decision-making power inside each superagency, would decentralize that power to the local level. Local service officers would be given the authority to make decisions that affected local conditions instead of being forced to ask permission from higher levels. It was hoped that this decentralization of command authority would greatly increase the efficiency of service delivery and enable city government to address multiservice problems at the local level where they most affected the people. In June, ONG received a renewable, one-year grant for $350,000 to conduct the experiment.

Some Initial Questions

With funds in hand, ONG had to become far more specific about the experiment. Command Decentralization (A) noted some of the issues left unresolved in the HEW proposal. Now, if the experiment was to be successful, these issues had to be resolved.

First of all, ONG had to decide on the number of Community Planning Districts (CPDs) to be involved in the experiment. Initially, Feldstein had intended to include between six and eight. However, with an average population of over 130,000, CPDs were very large. To attempt to improve service delivery in so many districts ran the risk of spreading the effort too thin and not improving services at all. Nevertheless, not having a wide enough cross section of districts ran the risk of invalidating the experiment. Eventually, ONG chose four CPDs: Wakefield Edenwald, Bronx CPD #13 (a blue collar area); Washington Heights, Manhattan CPD #12 (a middle-class area); Crown Heights, Brooklyn CPD #8 (a transition district - that is, a largely black middle-class area turning into a poverty area); and Bushwick, Brooklyn CPD #4 (a poverty area).[1]

The same principle of not spreading the effort too thin applied to the number of agencies and superagencies to be involved in the experiment. Accordingly, four superagencies - the Human Resources Administration (HRA), the Health Services Administration (HSA), the Housing and Development Administration (HDA) and the Parks, Recreation, and Cultural Administration (PRCA) - were chosen to take part in the experiment along with the Police Department and the Department of Sanitation (DS). DS was part of the Environmental Protection Administration (EPA).[2]

The third problem that ONG had to deal with was coterminality of service district lines. Since a neighborhood manager (NM) was expected to help the various agencies work together in a CPD, and since all the local service chiefs were expected to sit in a service cabinet to discuss common problems, it made sense to have everyone talking about, and responsible for, the same geographic area. The experiment would become far more difficult and unwieldy if there were three district sanitation superintendents responsible for different parts of one CPD or if the neighborhood manager, in order to find out about sanitation services in his CPD, had to delve through information on parts of three adjoining CPDs as well. Nevertheless, there were severe obstacles to redistricting [see Command Decentralization (A)] that had to be dealt with. ONG decided to confront the issue of redistricting on an agency-by-agency basis and to remain flexible in what it asked of each agency.

Next came the question of the selection of neighborhood managers. ONG concluded that all the agencies involved in the project should have a hand in choosing, or at least approving, the choice of neighborhood managers. Feldstein described the first man to be hired to the post, a senior project coordinator from the city's Project Management Staff named John Sanderson:

> He looks as little like a Lindsay guy as you can look. We didn't want any young flashers out there, people who look like B-school wizards. We wanted guys who looked clearly like they were technicians, they were managers, they were pros, and this guy was perfect. He's a guy who's head of his parish council, a guy in his midforties, cigar-smoking, bald-headed - a real pro. He has just finished running the major reorganization of the parks maintenance operation. He's done work in corrections - he knows agencies.

---

[1] Descriptions of the four districts can be found in Command Decentralization (A).

[2] The Addiction Services Agency (ASA) and the traffic and highways departments of the Transportation Administration also became involved early in the project.

As to the amount of power that a neighborhood manager should have, ONG realized from the beginning that the cost of fighting for line authority could well sink the project. The neighborhood managers might better be coordinators between agencies. It would be their task to look at whole patterns of service delivery and multiservice problems. They would have to persuade line chiefs that by changing certain things, service delivery could be improved at minimal cost. The neighborhood managers were to be unobtrusive. Their prime constituency was the line officers at the local level. They would have no obligation to the community and little contact with it. Thus, any credit for improved services would accrue to the line officers rather than ONG.

In defining a role for the neighborhood managers, ONG found it useful to begin by defining what they were not. They were neither politicians, nor ombudsmen, nor public relations men for the mayor or the superagencies. They would simply be coordinators of services. In order to help them do this, they would be empowered by the mayor to call the local service officers to meetings and to ask for information on local problems. Through the Office of Neighborhood Government, they could raise policy issues to the top level of city government. It was expected that the NM would be consulted before an agency made any significant changes in its local operations; for example, development of new social service programs, cancellation of social or health service contract operations, shifts in sanitation collection schedules, introduction of neighborhood sector police patrols, or marked shifts of local police manpower allocation from uniformed to plain-clothes efforts. ONG was careful to emphasize that the NMs would have no control over these policy or personnel changes; they were simply to be thoroughly briefed before implementation and well in time to make their views known to the mayor's office.

After the funds had been received from HEW, Feldstein returned to each of the superagencies that were to be involved in the project. When he had talked with them before sending the proposal to HEW, he had merely asked for their comments on ONG's plan. Now, he needed commitment to its implementation and that meant negotiating with great care exactly what each agency was going to do and when it was going to be done. Feldstein commented:

> We recognized from the front that this was a project that we could not carry out alone through this office; that if we were to be at all successful, the agencies would have to pick up the ball entirely and run with it. If you could describe this program solely as a mayor's office operation, then the program would probably be a failure, because it would mean that we had not gotten the agencies to go along nor convinced them that it was in their interest to go along. After all, ONG is 50 professionals spread out all over the city dealing with agencies of thousands of people. And in the end I can't tell one of those agency guys what to do.

The remainder of this case deals with ONG's negotiations with just one city agency - the Department of Sanitation.

The Department of Sanitation

The Department of Sanitation (DS) was one of three departments that were combined to form the Environmental Protection Administration. The others were the Department of Air Resources (DAR) and the Department of Water Resources (DWR) (see Exhibit 1). DS was by far the largest, employing some 15,000 people. DWR employed 8,000, and DAR had 400. The department had five bureaus - Cleaning and Collection (BCC) with 10,700 sanitation men and 1,000 officers; Vehicle Maintenance with 900 men; Administration and Inspection with 250; Waste Disposal with 650; and Engineering with 60.

The Bureau of Cleaning and Collection had five organizational layers (see Exhibit 2) and provided 10 major services; routine refuse collection, incinerator residue collection, bulk collection, containerized refuse collection, power street sweeping, street flushing, manual street sweeping, litter basket collection, litter patrol service, and vacant lot cleaning. Of these, routine refuse collection was the most important, accounting for 73% of BCC's manpower resources. The bureau also contracted with private firms for the removal of abandoned autos (see Exhibit 3).

At the bottom of the BCC hierarchy were the individual collection trucks - 1,400 of them, each with its own route. Each truck had three men and collected about nine tons of refuse per day. A section consisted of five refuse trucks, a power broom that swept approximately 12 miles of curb a day, additional cleaning equipment, and about 30 men. It was supervised by a foreman and an assistant foreman and had a geographical territory of about 130 blocks. The foremen directed refuse collection crews, manual sweepers, and power brooms. They also enforced alternate side parking regulations and kept payroll and operations records.

Four or five sections comprised a district. A district consisted of some 30 trucks, five brooms, some other cleaning equipment, an office, and a garage. (Garages and offices were not always located within district boundaries.) It covered an area of about 600 blocks. Each district had a superintendent, and an assistant superintendent who was in charge at night. District headquarters also had a number of clerks. In total, there were 160 men in a district. Different districts required different mixes of BCC's 10 services, and, within a district, the requirements for these services changed from day to day and from season to season.

A "borough" consisted of four to six districts. Each of the 11 borough commands covered an area of some 3,000 blocks with a force of 1,000 men, 150 refuse trucks, 40 power brooms, bulk trucks, and other equipment. All radio communications with the mechanized equipment was carried on through the borough command; bulk trucks, snow removal vehicles, and some cleaning equipment were dispatched from the borough. The borough headquarters staff was very similar to that of the district, consisting of a borough super, an assistant (or night) super, and a number of clerks. There was also a snow superintendent. The borough command's primary concern was supervising operations in the districts, although it was also responsible for vacant lot clean-up services and overseeing the removal of abandoned autos.

As far as possible, the work loads of the trucks, sections, districts and boroughs were equalized so that everyone had the same degree of responsibility and authority.

The central headquarters of the Bureau of Cleaning and Collection was located at 125 Worth Street in Manhattan as were the headquarters of most other bureaus of the Department of Sanitation. There were assistant chiefs of staff for street cleaning, refuse collection, snow operations, and bulk collection each of whom had two deputy assistant chiefs of staff reporting to him. The assistant chiefs reported to the chief of staff for BCC who was the top ranking uniformed officer in BCC and reported directly to the commissioner of sanitation. The BCC headquarters staff consisted of 125 clerks and uniformed men on deputation. Similar, though smaller, organizational structures existed for the Bureaus of Waste Disposal[1], Vehicle Maintenance, and Inspection.

The primary function of the BCC headquarters staff was to keep abreast of day-to-day operations. Long-range planning was done only in anticipation of snow season and this activity went on continuously. Detailed plans were made for the deployment of men and snow removal equipment so that as soon as snow fell, it could be removed rapidly and efficiently. But, by and large, the primary work of the staff was to determine on Monday what the cleaning and collection situation was on Monday so that it would know where to send the trucks on Tuesday. The information had been collected in much the same way for years. It was a massive manual and telephone system. The basic record at the section and district level was the daily performance collection trip ticket on which were recorded the activities of one truck and one crew collecting one load. It included information on:

- Individuals on the crew
- Time of
  - Disposal point weigh-in
  - Route arrival and departure
  - Garage departure and arrival
  - Relay arrival and departure
- Truck mileage

---

[1]The Bureau of Waste Disposal operated municipal incinerators, sanitary landfills, and transfer (from truck to barge) facilities.

- Load information (number and weight)

- Type of collection (refuse, bulk, and so forth)

- Collection route identification

- Work shift

The form was filled out by the truck driver and turned in to the section foreman.[1] The foreman telephoned the information in to district headquarters where it was compiled as part of the District Collection Summary. The district super telephoned the summary in to borough headquarters once a day. The borough compiled the information from all its districts and then telephoned the information in to BCC headquarters where it was compiled once more.

When the district superintendent sent his report to the borough, he also sent a tentative assignment list for his trucks for the next day, based on the information collected. He also added a request for additional personnel if he felt they were needed. His recommendations were evaluated by the borough which then drew up a borough assignment chart that frequently recommended temporary transfer of personnel and equipment between districts within the borough. Detachments came from districts that had completed their assignments early and attachments went to districts which had lagged behind. In addition, the borough super sometimes requested that more personnel and equipment be assigned to the borough if it had fallen behind.

The headquarters staff at BCC evaluated all the recommendations from the boroughs and made final decisions on assignments and on detachments and attachments between boroughs, districts and even sections. Thus, although the basic assignments were made at the district level, they could be, and often were, overruled at the borough and BCC central level. Ultimate authority rested at BCC central, which decided how often that authority would be exercised. For the past several years, BCC central had intervened with growing frequency because of a continuous sense of crisis in the bureau. Work loads had been increasing but the growth in BCC resources had not kept pace. The result was a greater tendency for borough commanders to override district superintendents' wishes and recommendations, and for BCC central to take a more active role in daily operating decisions. Friction between levels was not unusual. District superintendents looked on the central officers as meddlers. For their part, the central officers thought that the district men were inefficient greenhorns who weren't doing half as well as the central officers had done when they had run the districts.

---

[1] Similar tickets were filled out by manual sweepers and power broom operators.

Jerry Mechling, formerly Assistant Administrator for Program Analysis and Development at EPA, said of the organizational layers at BCC:

> The basic job is where do you put those trucks and three men, and there's a lot of overhead that's helping make that particular decision. It's done on a day-to-day basis. Those at the top know that they have more people doing that job than most other collection operations in the country, even though they don't think about it very often. They also know that without any planning capacity in there, they're not changing the system very much.

The written reporting system used by DS relied on the same collection trip tickets that were used in the telephone system. Each day, at the district level, a daily functional report (Exhibit 4) and a daily report of personnel (Exhibit 5) were compiled. These were summarized at the borough level and at BCC central and, once a month, the department used the data in its monthly summary of operations (The Green Book). On a fairly irregular basis, varying from biweekly to bimonthly, summary city-wide performance reports were sent to the mayor and deputy mayors. (A sample report is shown in Exhibit 6.)

Budgeting for the Department of Sanitation was the responsibility of the top echelon of DS and EPA. There was some input from the district, borough, and bureau levels but the decisions were made at the top. The budget was broadly divided into two parts - the expense budget and the capital budget (summary requests for the 1970-1971 budget cycle are shown in Exhibits 7 and 8). There was, however, another budget request known colloquially as the "wish list." While the official budget submitted to the mayor and the budget director requested funds to maintain current operations and make small additions to the service, the "wish list" consisted mostly of items the department believed had been removed from its budget unfairly in the past. For example, although DS had been making bulk collections free of charge as a matter of policy for some years, it had never hired additional men to make the pickups. The men had been reassigned from street cleaning with a resultant loss of efficiency in that sector. For several years, the wish list had included $5 million to hire "bulk collection" men who would actually be used to build the street cleaning force back up to strength.

The McKinsey Study

In December of 1970, consultants from McKinsey & Company, Inc., completed a study of the Department of Sanitation and recommended hiring 120 technical experts to be organized into a Bureau of Industrial Engineering (BIE). The new bureau would include not only industrial engineers, but also statisticians, methods analysts, and quality control engineers. BIE would:

1. Provide the technical and analytical support needed to resolve BCC and BVM operating problems.

2. Help design a new management information system and management control system.

3. Assist in the preparation of the capital budget, especially for BCC equipment.

4. Maintain and operate the quality measurement system (a system that measured such things as hopper loads per curb mile picked up by the power brooms and statistics on missed collections and curb miles not swept).

5. Assist in developing a new training program for BCC officers.

There would be very little overlap between BIE and the old Bureau of Engineering since the latter did not attempt to provide regular staff support to BCC. It worked, instead, on activities such as containerization pilot projects, new capital facilities specifications, and apartment house compactor design approvals.

The consultants also recommended the creation of an Office of Project Management to help implement major DS projects. Finally, they expressed concern over the growing role that BCC central was playing in the management of day-to-day operations. In their view, the central office was too remote and the organization too large for operational control to be exercised effectively from "downtown." At the same time, the consultants were convinced that the present management information system in the Department of Sanitation (short as it was of adequate measures of output and suspect as some of the input data seemed to be) would not support significant shifts of command authority as far down the line as the district level. It seemed apparent, moreover, that borough commanders would be reluctant to give up significant amounts of the authority they already had and that district managers did not have the management support that would permit them to accept and exercise much more authority. The consultants suggested, therefore, that DS emphasize the borough's role in managing operational performance while stressing BCC central's responsibility for monitoring the level of that performance and ensuring that it improved.

This emphasis on the borough command would be compatible, as well, with conclusions that some of McKinsey's staff had reached regarding economies of scale in the department. It seemed clear that various industrial engineering tasks such as truck and power broom routing could be done more effectively at the borough level (where there were 150 trucks and 40 power brooms) than at the district. The same thinking applied to truck and broom maintenance; the borough was the smallest division where the expense of major repair and overhaul facilities was justified.

The Commissioner of Sanitation, Herbert Elish, who had worked closely with the McKinsey team accepted their recommendations and decided to follow through on them. By October 1971, some 30 industrial engineers had been hired and the Bureau of Industrial Engineering had been organized with Marvin Karp as Chief Industrial Engineer. When Lew Feldstein asked the department to join ONG's experiment, the move to strengthen the borough commands had already begun.

Three Key Decision Makers

As Feldstein looked at the Department of Sanitation, he concluded that any significant change in the department's operations could take place only with the consent and cooperation of three men - John de Lury, President of the Uniformed Sanitationmen's Association; Jerry Kretchmer, Administrator of EPA; and Herb Elish, Commissioner of Sanitation.

John de Lury: All of the men in the Department of Sanitation, with the exception of a few who reported only to the commissioner, were "uniformed." They were all members of either the Uniformed Sanitationmen's Association or, if they were officers, the Officer's Union. Each man had begun his career by "tossing lettuce" and promotion was through the ranks, from sanitationman to the chief of staff. Usually, the two unions worked together, following the lead of John de Lury, President of the Uniformed Sanitationmen's Association. Because de Lury was politically astute and his union tightly organized and because sanitation was such a political issue in New York, the unions had tremendous power. Any slowdown resulted in a mountain of garbage in city streets and outraged calls to the mayor and the sanitation commissioner. De Lury credited the sanitation strike of 1968 with shutting down the city more effectively than any other work stoppage in New York's history. As a result of their power, the unions were the greatest single force in EPA. Any administrator or commissioner knew that he must get along with the unions in order to function effectively. In practical terms that meant that they must get along with one man - John de Lury.

Since he founded the union and became its president, de Lury had strengthened the power of his organization considerably. He did away with the three separate classifications of sanitationmen with their separate pay scales and replaced them with one category.[1] In pay, pension benefits, work hours, and so forth, de Lury had improved the lot of his members considerably. Contract negotiations in 1971 brought the sanitationmen's base salary to $12,888 for a 40-hour week (five days between Monday and Saturday). There was a 10% premium for night work and the first two hours of Saturday were

---

[1]Until 1951, the three sanitationmen assigned to a truck were classified as: "A", the dump man who received the least pay; "B", the loader; and "C", the driver, who received the most pay. After 1951, all three men were classified the same and pay differentials were based on seniority alone.

paid at time-and-one-half; Sundays and holidays were double time. Lunch time was included in the basic 40-hour week. According to de Lury, all this might bring a sanitationman's gross salary and benefits to $15,000 or $16,000. Snowstorms could mean even more. Said de Lury, "There's no job in New York City, with all our benefits and wages, to compare with a sanitationman's." He also liked to point out that it was a tough job with an injury rate second only to logging.

De Lury's right hand man was an economic and pension consultant named Jack Bigel who had been one of the brains behind the union for over 20 years. He and de Lury did all the negotiating. Said one observer:

> Between them, Bigel and de Lury are a real team - a Punch and Judy show. One of them will pound on you for an hour and then the other one will lift you up just a little bit. Then the first guy will come back in and play the tough guy again. They play off each other very effectively. You feel very happy that you're allowed to walk out of the room alive.

There were a number of reasons to suspect that de Lury and Bigel would be skeptical about the merits of command decentralization. To begin with, both men were highly suspicious of anything that smacked of community control over the Department of Sanitation. Although command decentralization was not supposed to involve this kind of control, the neighborhood, they thought, would inevitably be looking on. And this meant that sooner or later someone in the community would demand authority over the operations and the right to hire and fire. Second, since de Lury had rid the union of the three tier classification system for sanitationmen, it had become an easy and manageable system for him. There was little reason for him to want to change it. Finally, de Lury felt that sanitationmen were not trained for the kinds of problems that might result from a close interface with the community. His men believed that certain areas of the city were dirty because people who lived in them were dirty, not because the garbage wasn't picked up. He realized that no love was lost between sanitationmen and residents of those communities. He felt, therefore, that to put an officer into a situation where he had to face the hostility of these people without any training in how to handle it, would result not in a dialogue but in a fight. And de Lury felt that if that sort of situation developed, his men would refuse to go into certain neighborhoods and that he would back them in their refusal. He did not want to be put into that position. He thought of himself as a liberal and was worried that he might be made into a reactionary villain by the force of circumstances. One EPA staff member says of de Lury:

> He's about ready to retire. He'd like to go out with a good name as a liberal labor leader and he's a little bit worried that in politics there's a villain sooner or later, that people get moved on issues that aren't abstract; and that they get very personal. The environmental issue in New York City is a garbage issue, and if there is a guy who's going to look bad on the garbage issue it *might* be John de Lury, because his guys get accused of nasty things.

Jerry Kretchmer: When Jerry Kretchmer was appointed EPA administrator in January 1970, there was considerable sensitivity on the union's part to his nomination. Kretchmer had made his reputation on the school decentralization issue. As the West Side's reform democratic assemblyman in the State Legislature, he had pushed very hard for community control of school districts. Bigel assumed, therefore, that Kretchmer had been appointed to implement, in EPA, the mayor's ideas regarding neighborhood government. And when Kretchmer assumed the position of sanitation commissioner (following Griswold Moeller's resignation from the post in July 1970) as well as that of administrator, Bigel and de Lury came to him and accused him of trying to break up the Department of Sanitation. Kretchmer disavowed any such intention and said that, while everyone knew he had favored school decentralization in the past, he had taken no position on decentralizing DS. He had been appointed as sanitation commissioner and EPA administrator and intended to do his best at those jobs. Very shortly after that meeting, on a Friday, Kretchmer was shown a copy of the mayor's Plan for Neighborhood Government [see Command Decentralization (A)]. Feeling that release of the plan would undermine his personal credibility with de Lury and Bigel, and run into tremendous union opposition, Kretchmer protested. But the plan was released the following Monday.

Mayoral aspirations were a part of Kretchmer's taking the job as EPA administrator. He realized that if he was to help his political career he would have to do an excellent job as administrator and that in order to do that, the union and John de Lury were going to be very important to him. He attended garage roll calls at least once a week and sometimes rode on sanitation trucks as they went on their routes. Because he was a political and colorful personality, he got a lot of publicity. The union leadership was suspicious of his contact with the rank-and-file since it might enable him to bypass union channels, but he was very popular with the men. No other sanitation commissioner had paid them so much attention.

Kretchmer also spent a lot of time with the union leaders. Because of the city's policy of negotiating with all uniformed unions at the same time and the small size of the city's negotiating team, the Sanitationmen's Union was left alone in its hotel suite in October 1970 while negotiations went on with the Police Department. Kretchmer and his then deputy administrator of EPA, Herbert Elish, spent days with de Lury, Bigel, and the other leaders of the union finding out what were and were not sensitive issues for the union.

Herb Elish: Jerry Kretchmer had been sanitation commissioner only until a new one could be found; and, in March 1971, Herb Elish was sworn in as the seventh occupant of the position since the Lindsay administration began in January 1966. He was well aware of the implications that this high turnover would have for his ability to exercise power. Said de Lury, "I don't care who's commissioner; he's just a figurehead for the mayor, anyway." Nevertheless, Elish had his own plan for changing the department.

He had accepted and, as deputy administrator of EPA, already begun to implement McKinsey's recommendations. He honestly believed that the proposal to introduce industrial engineering and project management, and to move command authority away from BCC central toward the borough level made sense; more sense, at any rate, than ONG's command decentralization program. Shortly after his appointment as commissioner, Elish took steps to decentralize authority to the boroughs. During the summer, he informed the borough commanders that they would be free to schedule their own men and equipment provided they did not request more resources to do the job. They would continue to provide BCC central with the same kinds of data as before and BCC central, from time to time, might ask for additional information about borough operations. The boroughs were to assume, however, that this was, in fact, for purposes of information and not control.

Within a matter of two months, departmental reports began to show deterioration in some of the major productivity indicators, in particular, the tonnage of refuse collected per truck per shift and the number of curb miles swept per shift by the power brooms.

Elish took immediate steps to return control to BCC central. He felt he had learned a lesson; BCC was indeed much like a military organization. It was accustomed to working through a strict chain of command to which orders flowed from one level to the next and were carried out without question. Borough commanders who were told to do the same job this month with 142 trucks, instead of 143, generally were able to do it. Also, like the military, word got around about who was giving the orders and the response at the bottom might be different depending on whether the originator was at BCC central, the borough, or the district.

It seemed clear to Elish that effective management of routine departmental operations required strong central control. And, if he wanted to change and improve those operations, centralized control would be even more critical. He was concerned, therefore, that ONG, since it was an outside group that came in at the top, would neither understand his conclusions nor have as great an incentive as he did to move carefully.

Like de Lury, Elish was also concerned that command decentralization would lead inevitably to demands for community control and that he and the union leadership would be left to deal with the unpleasant confrontations that might erupt.

Negotiations with the Department of Sanitation

When the HEW proposal was first circulated to the agencies for comment, Jerry Kretchmer was Commissioner of Sanitation. His reaction was generally one of support, but he wanted very much to know specifically what Feldstein wanted DS to do. Robert House, ONG's coordinator for the Department of Sanitation, said:

That put us in the position of telling him what specific powers he should give to his district sanitation supers. We felt that was not a good way to start; instead, we should limit ourselves to defining the general intention of the program - shifting significant new powers to the districts - and Kretchmer should have to decide on specifics because he was the guy running the agency.

When the proposal had been funded and ONG came to work out details with DS in the summer of 1971, Kretchmer still wanted ONG to take the initiative. Feldstein finally agreed to provide a rough idea of what they had in mind. Kretchmer and Elish were told that the district superintendents should have some significant control over six things:

1. Ticketing alternate side of the street violations and health code violations - e.g., store owners who litter. (This control was now at the borough level.)

2. Street cleaning schedules and frequency (also at the borough level).

3. Refuse collection schedules and routes (currently controlled at central headquarters).

4. Allocation and disposition of his own men and equipment so that he could control the mix of services. (Now controlled at the borough level with ultimate authority at BCC central.)

5. Abandoned car removal including how much work was contracted, to whom, and what service could be expected (controlled now at the borough level).

6. Capital expansion in the district. (The total available to BCC was controlled by EPA. Allocations were made at BCC central.)

Furthermore, Feldstein wanted all complaints about service passed to the affected district superintendent. The super would be held responsible for the number of complaints and his disposition of them.

With regard to a new information system, ONG had two things it wanted. The first was a common geographical area for the base-line data. That meant that the boundary lines of the experimental sanitation districts would have to be redrawn to conform as closely as possible to the experimental CPDs. Second, ONG wanted the district superintendents and the neighborhood managers to receive several items of information not presently generated by the DS reporting system (see Exhibit 8).

For their part, Kretchmer and Elish were concerned about three key issues. (As Elish became increasingly familiar with his job as commissioner, he took more and more responsibility for the negotiations with ONG, and the key issues became the issues that bothered Elish rather than Kretchmer.) The most important of these was the question of authority over his men. Elish was very insistent on wanting to know exactly what powers the neighborhood manager would have. As noted earlier, he was unwilling to let the NM have any line authority. He was also concerned because ONG had failed, in his view, to define carefully a role for the community.

The second major issue was that of boundaries. DS thought sanitation district lines should not be changed; rather, other agency district lines should be redrawn to conform to the sanitation districts. If DS did change its boundaries, there would be a substantial delay in the experiment because of the ripple effect. DS was obligated to equalize work loads between districts. If it began to reassign sections from one district to another in order to create four districts that matched the four experimental CPDs, it would be forced, eventually, to redistrict most of the city. Simply changing alternate-side-of-the-street parking signs in one experimental district (so that broom routes could be changed) might cost over $60,000. With no change in districts, DS said it could be ready to take part in the experiment by the beginning of April 1972. If a few whole sections were reassigned to different districts, DS wanted the starting date slipped to September 1972. If sections were going to be broken up, the department wanted the first community cabinet meeting postponed until April 1973. The situation regarding district boundaries in the four CPDs was:

Bushwick: Three-quarters of the CPD was in district 37 and one-quarter in district 41. The CPD was exactly coterminous with two sections of district 37 and one of district 41.

Crown Heights: One-half of the CPD was in district 42, one-third in district 40, one-fifth in district 38, and a small fraction in district 43. Three district garages were located in the CPD.

Wakefield Edenwald: Sanitation district 28 covered all of the CPD except for a small portion covered by district 26. Part of one section of district 28 also extended out of the CPD.

Washington Heights: The CPD lines were exactly coterminous with district 9.

Implicit in the department's objection to redistricting was an opportunity cost. DS provided a highly visible service. Any disruption was obvious immediately because of piled up garbage or snow or filthy streets. Major boundary changes might cause such a disruption. Monte Wasch, EPA's project officer and negotiator for command decentralization, noted that the last physical redistricting had been done in 1967 but that reverberations in terms of productivity were still being felt. In 1971, DS had reduced its cost per ton by 7% of refuse removed and increased its manpower efficiency by 10%, figures of which Commissioner Elish was very proud since they could be attributed to changes in the department that he had brought about - industrial engineers, new equipment, new management techniques, and others. Wasch felt that Elish would resist a plan that would reduce productivity again because of hasty redistricting. Feldstein was sympathetic:

> God forbid, if the result of this thing ever meant that our ability to pick up the garbage or remove the snow is significantly diminished in one of these areas during the transistion - disaster! We'd never recover!

In addition to the potential for service deterioration, there was also the problem of diverting the attention of DS managers away from improving the old system and toward efforts to make ONG's plans operative. DS, like most city agencies, was not overloaded with management talent, and Elish thought it made more sense to use what talent there was to do things better rather than just differently.

Feldstein acknowledged that Elish had been very open and honest with the Office of Neighborhood Government about his reactions to the plan. Unlike some others, Feldstein said Elish had deceived neither ONG nor himself about his desire to carry out the project or the ease with which the project could be carried out. He was not anxious to get involved with ONG's plan and said so. He believed his own plan was better and was afraid that pushing too hard or trying to move too fast might prevent anything from happening at all. Said Feldstein:

> He's got a very clear sense in his own mind as to what his priorities are and how he's going to go after them. He's not easily sidetracked into lots of flashy ideas and seemingly attractive things. He's out to do a job and he's going to do it. And he never minces words with us in saying that.

Feldstein pointed to the Police Department as an example that command decentralization <u>could</u> work, and tried to get Elish excited by the idea of several agencies working together towards the same end. Elish was unconvinced, pointing out that middle management in the Police Department had been much better trained and prepared for decentralization than were their counterparts in DS.

Feldstein believed that had Kretchmer remained as Sanitation Commissioner, the project would have moved much faster but that Kretchmer would not overrule Elish on this issue:

> Kretchmer has been trying to make it clear that he is overall committed to this but that Herb is the Commissioner and has the major responsibility to make the decision on it.

Feldstein also concluded that there were two major reasons for his inability to move DS faster. First, at the time that ONG got its funds and was ready to move, Elish had just taken over as commissioner. He wanted to get to know his department and establish his own relationships and was unwilling to be rushed into hasty action, especially since those who wanted him to act quickly did not have to stay to repair any broken fences. The second reason was Elish's own reluctance to subscribe to the plan, a reluctance that probably existed throughout the department:

> His has been the toughest department to move, quite apart from his own objections. It's probably because he speaks so accurately for the difficulties of the men he has to manage.

Exhibit 1

COMMAND DECENTRALIZATION (B)

Environmental Protection Administration

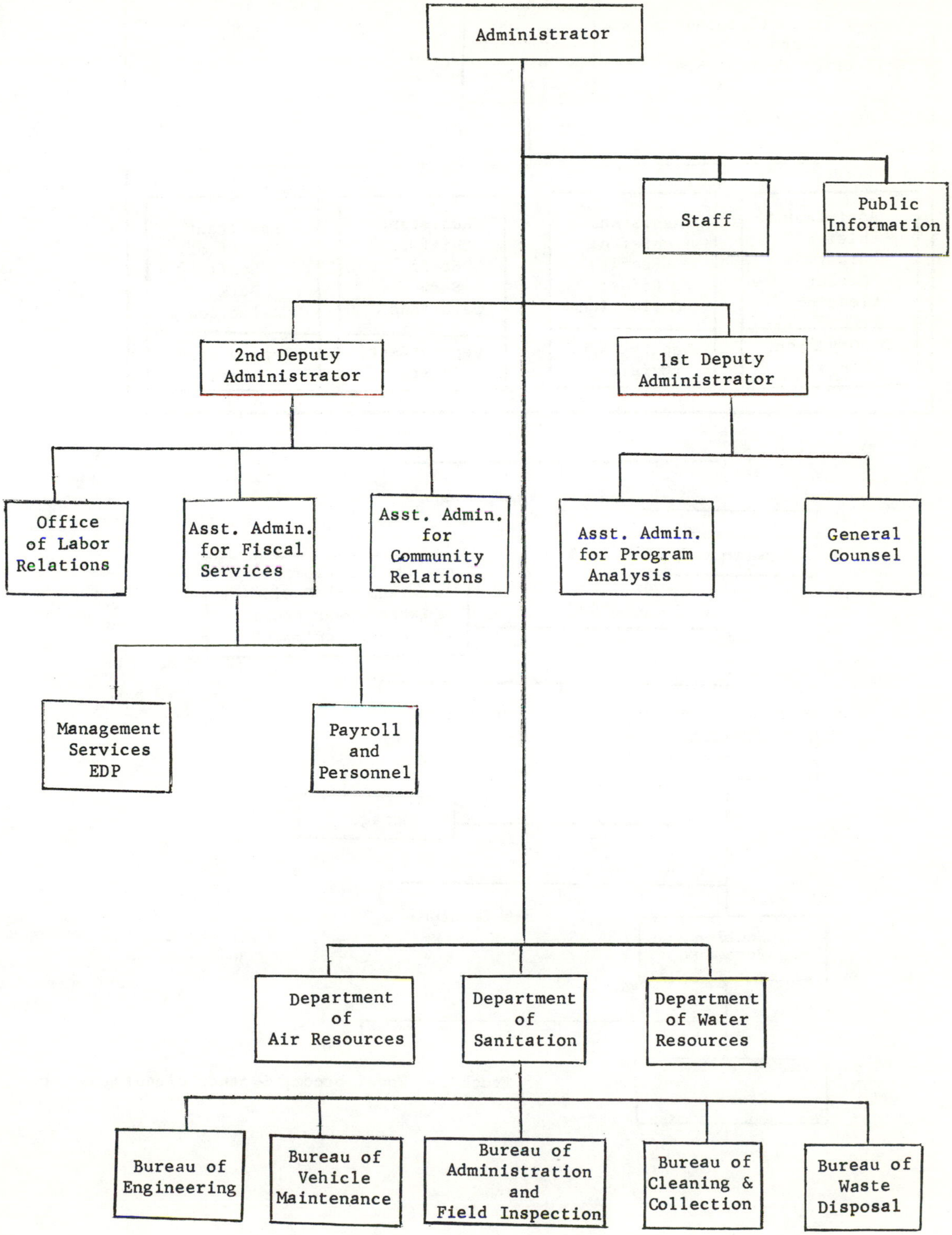

Exhibit 2
COMMAND DECENTRALIZATION (B)
Bureau of Cleaning and Collection

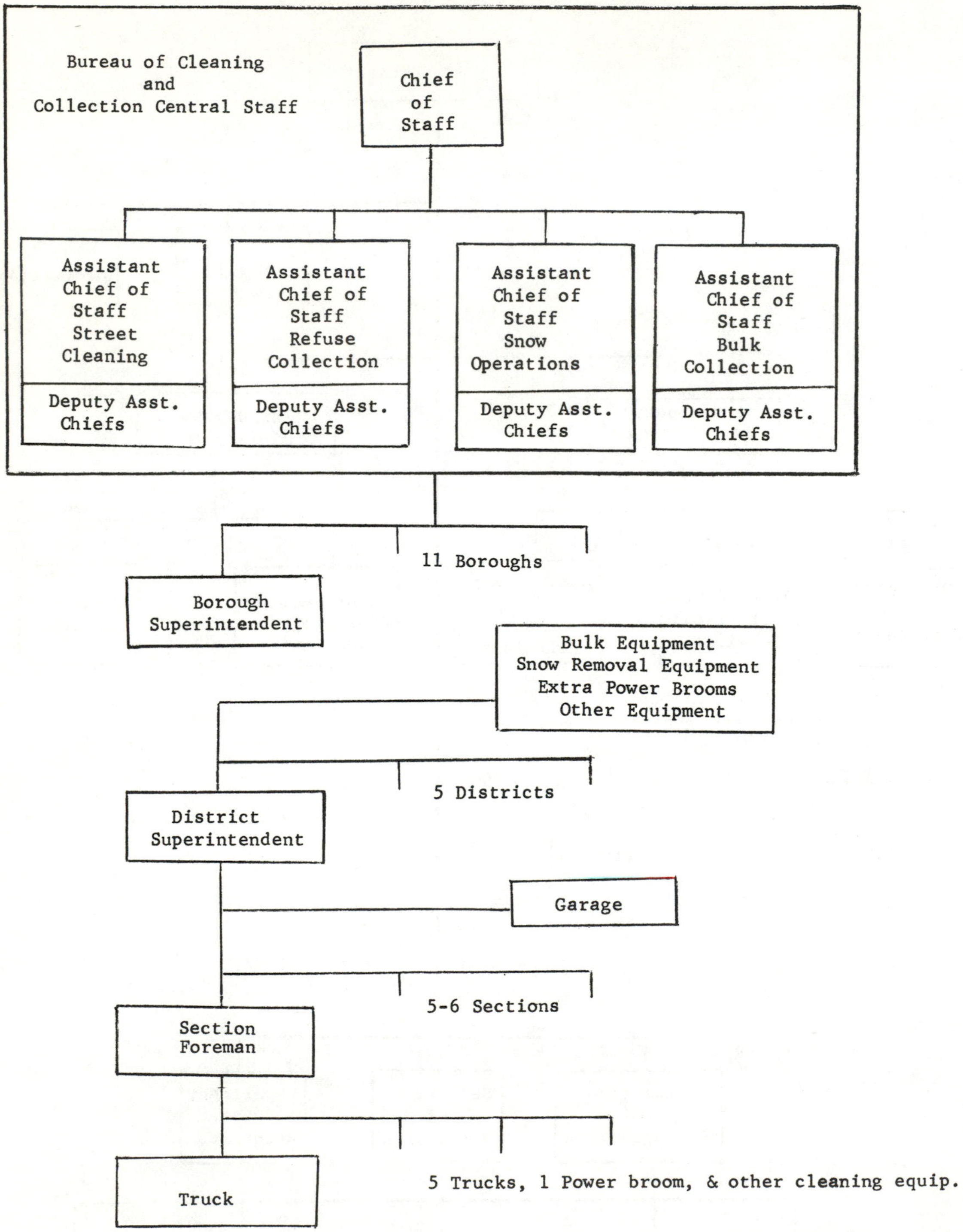

Exhibit 3
COMMAND DECENTRALIZATION (B)

EXHIBIT II

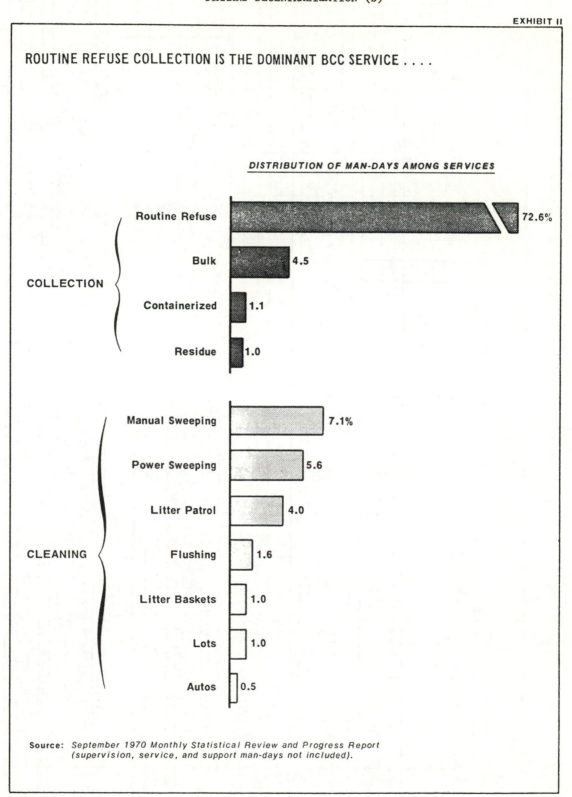

ROUTINE REFUSE COLLECTION IS THE DOMINANT BCC SERVICE . . . .

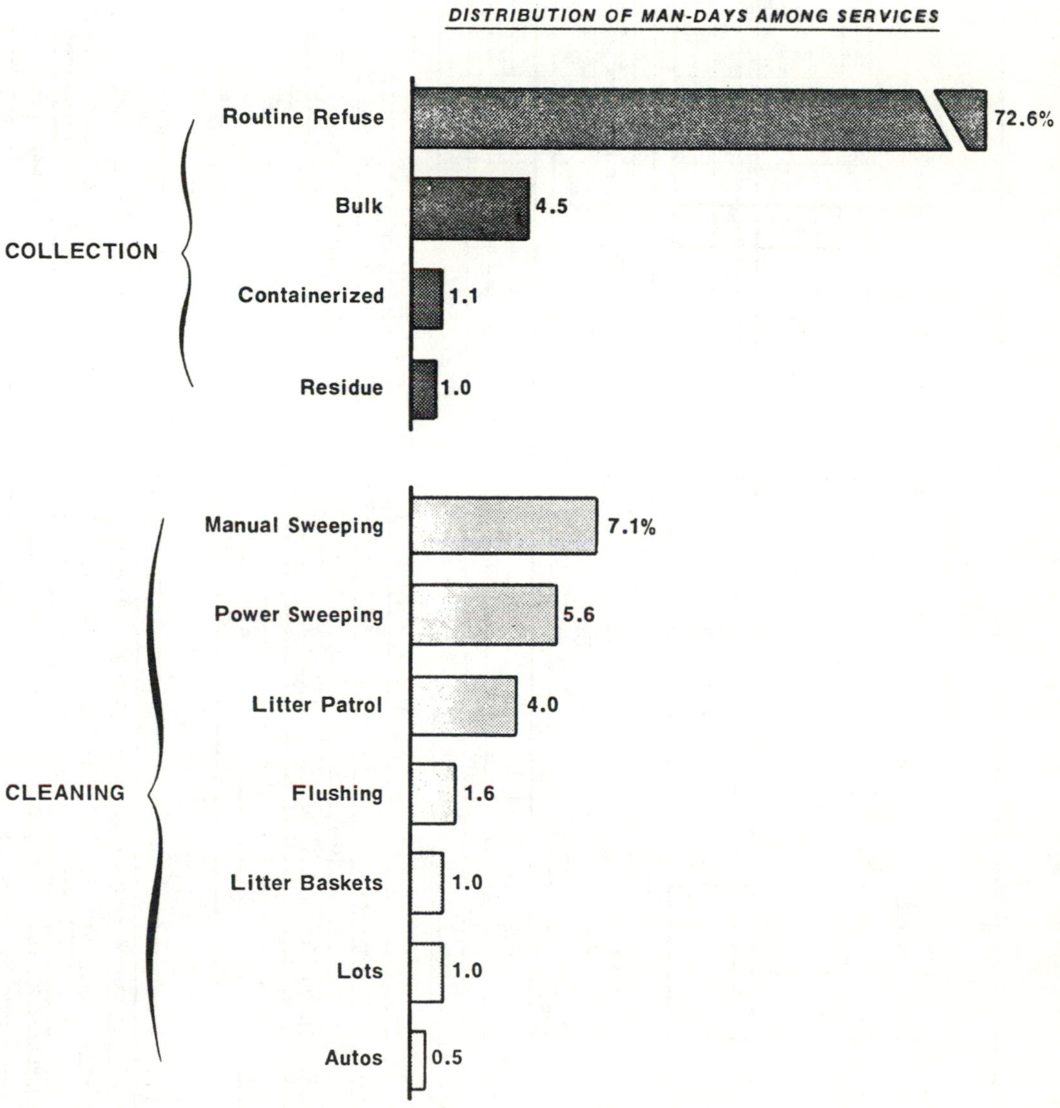

Source: *September 1970 Monthly Statistical Review and Progress Report (supervision, service, and support man-days not included).*

Exhibit 4

COMMAND DECENTRALIZATION (B)

D.S. #363 REV 7/63

THE CITY OF NEW YORK
DEPARTMENT OF SANITATION
BUREAU OF CLEANING AND COLLECTION

DAILY FUNCTIONAL REPORT

PREPARED BY ____________ TITLE ________

APPROVED BY ____________ TITLE ________

REPORT OF DISTRICT # ____________

DAY ________ MONTH ________ DATE ________ 19 ____

ACTUAL SIZE OF FORM 19'' x 12''

	RECAPITULATION OF PERSONNEL AT WORK: TOTAL PRESENT FOR DUTY	SERVICE PERSONNEL	COLLECTION OPTNS	STREET CLEANING	SNOW OPTNS			OVERTIME HOURS		
1	2	3	4	5	6	7	8	9	10	11
1 DAY										
2 NIGHT										
3 TOTAL										

	SERVICE PERSONNEL: SUPERVISION	CLERICAL	OPER PASS CAR	GARAGE DUTY: IN QUOTA ASSIGN	GARAGE DUTY: OTHER	BASKET SERVICE	SERVICE TRUCKS	BUILDING MAINTENANCE: WATCH PORTER ELEV OPR ETC	BUILDING MAINTENANCE: ATTEND 3 HRS 5 HRS	ON JOB TRAINING				TOTAL SERVICE PERS
1	12	13	14	15	16	17	18	19	20	21	22	23	24	25
1 DAY														
2 NIGHT														
3 TOTAL														

	SERVICE TRUCK SHIFTS		OVERTIME HOURS: ADMINISTRATION	GARAGE	REFUSE COLLECTION	STREET CLEANING	SPREAD TRANS OR HANDLING SALT & ABRAS	PLOWING	CLEARING CROSS WALKS	SEWERING	SCATTERING FLUSHING	PILING LOADING HAULING	TOTAL OVERTIME HOURS
1	26	27	28	29	30	31	32	33	34	35	36	37	38
1 DAY													
2 NIGHT													
3 TOTAL													

COLLECTION OPERATIONS

	HOUSEHOLD COLLECTION OF MIXED MATERIAL: PERS	TRUCK SHIFTS	LOADS	TONS	PUBLIC BUILDINGS COMPACTOR COLLECTION: PERS	TRUCK SHIFTS	LOADS	TONS	HOUSEHOLD RESIDUE: PERS	TRUCK SHIFTS	LOADS	TONS	ASHES: PERS	TRUCK SHIFTS	LOADS	TONS
39	40	41	42	43	44	45	46	47	48	49	50	51	52	53	54	55
1 DAY																
2 NIGHT																
3 TOTAL																

	BASKET COLLECTION AND LITTER PATROL: PERS	TRUCK SHIFTS	LOADS	TONS	HOIST FITTED CHASSIS COLLECTION: PERS	HOIST SHIFTS	LOADS	TONS	BULK COLLECTION: PERS	TRUCK SHIFTS	LOADS	TONS	OTHERS: LEAVES, BRUSH, STREET PILES, ETC.: PERS	TRUCK SHIFTS	LOADS	TONS	RELAY LOADS	TOTAL: PERS	TRUCK SHIFTS	LOADS	TONS
39	56	57	58	59	60	61	62	63	64	65	66	67	68	69	70	71	72	73	74	75	76
1 DAY																					
2 NIGHT																					
3 TOTAL																					
PRIVATELY OWNED LOT CLEANING																					

Loads of material OUT - DAY ________ NIGHT ________

STREET CLEANING

	POWER BROOM OPERATIONS: CLASS A: PERS	CURB MILES	HOPPERS	CLASS B: PERS	CURB MILES	HOPPERS	CLASS C: PERS	CURB MILES	HOPPERS	BROOM SHIFTS	FLUSHER OPERATIONS: CLASS A: PERS	CURB MILES	TANKS	CLASS B: PERS	CURB MILES	TANKS	CLASS C: PERS	CURB MILES	TANKS	FLUSHER SHIFTS
77	78	79	80	81	82	83	84	85	86	87	88	89	90	91	92	93	94	95	96	97
1 DAY																				
2 NIGHT																				
3 TOTAL																				

	MANUAL CLEANING: CLASS A	CLASS B	CLASS C	TOTAL	MOTORIZED MANUAL CLEANING: PERS	TRUCK SHIFTS	CANS / LOADS	TOWING OPERATIONS: PERS	TRUCK SHIFTS	ENCUMBRANCE TOWED	Misc Operations: LEAVES-STORM DEBRIS LOTS & OTHERS: PERSONNEL: MANUAL	EQUIP OPER	EQUIPMENT SHIFTS: F.E.L.	CROSS WALK	POWER BROOMS	FLUSHERS	OTHER	TOTAL: PERSONNEL	EQUIPMENT SHIFTS
77	98	99	100	101	102	103	104	105	105A	105B	106	107	108	109	110	111	112	113	114
1 DAY																			
2 NIGHT																			
3 TOTAL																			
PRIVATELY OWNED LOT CLEANING																			

SNOW OPERATIONS

	SERVICE PERSONNEL: ADMINISTRATION: SUPERVISION	CLERICAL	SPECIAL	GARAGE: CHAINS PLOWS	OTHER	SPREADING, TRANSFER or HANDLING of SALT or ABRASIVES: PERSONNEL	EQUIPMENT SHIFTS: SPREADERS	TRUCKS	OTHER	SALT SPREAD: LOADS	TONS	ABRA. SPREAD: LOADS	TONS	LINEAR MILES SPREAD	STRAIGHT PLOWING: PERSONNEL	EQUIP SHIFTS	LINEAR MILES PLOWED
115	116	117	118	119	120	121	122	123	124	125	126	127	128	129	130	131	132
1 DAY																	
2 NIGHT																	
3 TOTAL																	

	CLEARING OPERATIONS: PERSONNEL	EQUIP SHIFTS: CROSS WALK PLOWS	OTHER	X WALKS HYDRANT CLEARED BUS STOPS	SEWERING: PERSONNEL	EQUIP SHIFTS	FLUSH-SCATT: PERSONNEL	EQUIP SHIFTS	PILING - - HAULING (D. S. & CONTRACT): PERSONNEL	D.S. EQUIP: TRUCKS	OTHER	OTHER CITY DPT & HIRED EQUIP: TRUCKS	OTHER	D. S. AND OTHER HAULING: LOADS	CUBIC YARDS	CONTRACT HAULING: LOADS	CUBIC YARDS		TOTAL: PERSONNEL	EQUIP SHIFTS
115	133	134	135	136	137	138	139	140	141	142	143	144	145	146	147	148	149	150	151	152
1 DAY																				
2 NIGHT																				
3 TOTAL																				

Exhibit 5

COMMAND DECENTRALIZATION (B)

D.S. #365 REV 9/58.

THE CITY OF NEW YORK
DEPARTMENT OF SANITATION
BUREAU OF CLEANING AND COLLECTION

DISTRICT DAILY REPORT OF PERSONNEL

PREPARED BY ____________ TITLE ____________

APPROVED BY ____________ TITLE ____________

REPORT OF DISTRICT # ____________

DAY ______ MONTH ______ DATE ______ 19___

TITLE	PAYROLL	PAYROLL CHANGE PENDING		ATTACHED			DETACHED						RECAP. OF		NET AVAILABLE	ABSENT W.O.P.		ABSENT WITH PAY						SICK AND COMPENSATION	TOTAL ABSENCE	TOTAL PRESENT	PAID CHART & HOLIDAY
	ASSIGNED	IN	OUT	WITHIN ZONE	WITHIN BUREAU	FROM OTHER BUREAUS	WITHIN ZONE	WITHIN BUREAU	TO OTHER BUREAUS	TO OTHER CITY DEPTS.	TRAINING	OTHER	ATT. +	DET. —		CHART	SUNDAY SUSPENDED AND OTHER	VACATION ANNUAL LEAVE	COMPENSATORY TIME	MILITARY & JURY	TERMINAL LEAVE	CAREER AND SALARY CHART & SUNDAY	OTHER ABSENCE WITH PAY				
1	2	3	4	5	6	7	8	9	10	11	12	13	14	15	16	17	18	19	20	21	22	23	24	25	26	27	28
5 DISTRICT SUPT																											
6 FOREMAN																											
7 ASST FOREMAN																											
8 SANITATION MAN																											
9 MOTOR VEH OPER																											
10 ATTENDANT																											
14 SUPERVISING CLERK																											
15 SENIOR CLERK																											
16 CLERK																											
21 ELEVATOR OPER																											
22 COMPT OPERATOR																											
25 SENIOR TEL OPER																											
26 TELEPHONE OPER																											
27 LABORER																											
28 WATCHMAN																											
35 TOTAL																											

ACTUAL SIZE OF FORM 17" x 11"

COL NO.	NO. EMPLOYEES	TITLE	FROM	TO	COL NO.	NO. EMPLOYEES	TITLE	FROM	TO	COL NO.	NO. EMPLOYEES	TITLE	FROM	TO	COL NO.	NO. EMPLOYEES	TITLE	FROM	TO	NAME
1					7					13					19					
2					8					14					20					
3					9					15					21					
4					10					16					22					
5					11					17					23					
6					12					18					24					

OTHER CITY DEPARTMENTS	
EMERGENCY AUTO TRUCK DRIVERS	
EMERGENCY LABORERS	
TOTAL EMERGENCY PERSONNEL	

Exhibit 6

COMMAND DECENTRALIZATION (B)

Sample Performance Report to the Mayor

July 14, 1971

To: Hon. John V. Lindsay
Hon. Richard Aurelio
Hon. Edward Hamilton

From: Herbert Elish

Re: Sanitation Performance for June 28 - July 11

All service functions were adversely affected by the July 4 holiday.

There was a 7.1% rate of missed collections for the two week period. Cleanup following the holiday was completed by Thursday morning. Last year there was an 11.3% rate of missed collections for the comparable period.

Missed power broom routes on alternate side parking streets were 11.5% of the total scheduled, compared with 14.3% missed last year.

The daily average number of men on street cleaning operations on the day shift was 751, compared with 558 last year. This year 204 men were on power brooms, 48 on flushers, 76 on motorized litter patrols, 334 on manual cleaning, and 89 on other cleaning operations.

Calls for bulk removal continued to be serviced within 3 days. Last year bulk callers waited 17 to 19 days for service.

There were 2,729 cars removed during the two weeks, 5% more than last year. The average backlog was 531, about 20% of the total removed, or two days' workload. Last year the backlog averaged 1,427 or about 4 workdays from report to removal.

A total of 36,300 summonses were issued for the two weeks, compared with 6,800 last year.

Collection trucks down increased to 30% of the fleet for the first week of the period, but declined to 2 % in the second week, due to Saturday overtime work by 177 mechanics.

Collection productivity, in tons per truck shift, was 11% above a year ago.

There were 3,300 complaints for the period of June 21 - July 4. This does not reflect the effect of the holiday on complaints. This number is two-thirds below last year's complaint level.

Exhibit 7

COMMAND DECENTRALIZATION (B)

SUMMARY EXPENSE BUDGET PREVIEW ESTIMATES

PROGRAM TOTALS AND ANALYSIS OF CHANGES

(In Tenths of Millions of Dollars)

CODE	PROGRAM	FY 1969-1970 MODIFIED	FY 1970-1971 PROPOSED	NET CHANGE	ANALYSIS OF NET CHANGE: MANDATORY OR INESCAPABLE INCREASES	ANALYSIS OF NET CHANGE: REDUCTIONS IN BASE BUDGET	ANALYSIS OF NET CHANGE: DISCRETIONARY INCREASES
	ENVIRONMENTAL PROTECTION ADMINISTRATION	355.0	384.2	29.2	26.4	4.3	7.1
A	Refuse Collection, Street Clean-ing and Snow Removal	115.1	131.5	16.4	16.0	2.7	3.1
B	Refuse Processing and Disposal	24.3	26.1	1.8	1.5	0.3	0.6
C	Plant and Vehicle Maintenance	17.2	19.8	2.6	2.2	0.7	1.1
D	Executive Management	6.0	8.2	2.2	1.2	0	1.0
E	Community Services and Enforcement	1.5	1.8	0.3	0	0	0.3
F	Air Resources	3.1	4.5	1.4	0.4	0	1.0
G	Water Resources	65.4	67.9	2.5	2.5	0	0
H	Pensions, Debt Service, and Fringe Benefits	122.4	124.4	2.0	2.6	0.6	0
	Total	355.0	384.2				
	Less Payable from Non-EPA Codes	-108.0	-108.0				
	Net EPA Code Total	247.0	276.2				

BUREAU OF THE BUDGET FORM 1

Exhibit 8
COMMAND DECENTRALIZATION (B)
SUMMARY CAPITAL BUDGET PREVIEW ESTIMATES
(In Tenths of Millions of Dollars)

CODE OR PROJECT NUMBERS	PROGRAM GROUPING OF PROJECTS	PROPOSED CAPITAL APPROPRIATION	SOURCES OF FUNDS				
			FEDERAL	STATE	CITY-INSIDE DEBT LIMIT	CITY-OUTSIDE DEBT LIMIT	OTHER
	ENVIRONMENTAL PROTECTION ADMINISTRATION	56.8					
A	Refuse Collection, Street Cleaning and Snow Removal	15.3					
B	Refuse Processing and Disposal	41.5					
C	Plant and Vehicle Maintenance	0					
D	Executive Management	0					
E	Community Services and Enforcement	0					
F	Air Resources	0					

BUREAU OF THE BUDGET FORM 3

Exhibit 9

COMMAND DECENTRALIZATION (B)

Outline of ONG's Proposed Neighborhood Information System for Sanitation

On-going information on services: (i.e., productivity figures, "effort statistics," internal performance measures).

The Neighborhood Manager will be charged with lending technical assistance to the District Superintendent in order to improve productivity and responsivity of the district service delivery system. The Office of Neighborhood Government is well aware th t both productivity and responsivity are extremely difficult to define and measure. However, it is recommended that Office of Neighborhood Government and the Department of Sanitation work together to develop measures of productivity and responsivity that accurately reflect the impact of work done on the street and in the community. Most measures collected today reflect internal work or effort and lack the impact attribute.

In general, what is needed is the development of postcollection and postcleaning inspection parameters. Some work has already been done in the area by McKinsey. What is needed is further development and implementation of these parameters in the experimental neighborhood government districts.

Having stated in general terms, what needs to be developed by Office of Neighborhood Government and Sanitation Department, the following Data Requirements Chart summarizes what data should be made available to the Neighborhood Manager and District Superintendent on an on-going basis:

Refuse Collection

Tonnage per district and service type
Tons per load per district and service type
Missed collections citywide
Days wait for service on call bulk citywide average
Post collection inspection parameter

Street Cleaning - Mechanical

Curb miles swept per A, B and C class[1]
Curb miles flushed per A, B and C class
Per cent of broom and flusher shifts missed citywide
Post street cleaning inspection parameter

[1]Streets were classified A, B, or C depending on the frequency with which they were to be swept.

Exhibit 9 (continued)

Street Cleaning - Manual

Catch basins cleaned per section
Post street cleaning inspection parameter

Abandoned Cars

Number ticketed and towed per month citywide
Days wait from report to removal citywide
Waiting list of cars to be towed per district

Additional Information to be Developed for
Neighborhood Manager and Department of Sanitation use

Complaints: The Neighborhood Manager should receive an analysis of all community expressed complaints regarding Sanitation services in the district. This analysis should be compiled at the district level by having all complaints on the district received by EPA channeled to the District Superintendent. The District Superintendent should use his staff (which we recommend be beefed up with a planner in the experimental districts) to analyze the volume of complaints monthly and send complaint analysis to the Neighborhood Manager and EPA Central.

The complaint analysis should:

(a) Breakdown by service function
(b) Indicate follow-up if any
(c) Indicate adequacy of resources to handle
(d) Take special note of any complaints received by elected officials

Service Assessment Report: The District Superintendent should be given a report format monthly and asked to assess his capacity to deliver services. He should be encouraged to point out weaknesses and service delivery problems. The report should be minimally formatted and open-ended; broken down by:

Service functions - e.g., how well are you able to make your collections?
Auxilliary services - e.g., do you get fast enough turn around on your down trucks in central repair to make collections?